Thomas Jefferson
FAMILY SECRETS

Thomas Jefferson
FAMILY SECRETS

WILLIAM G. HYLAND JR.

PALMETTO
PUBLISHING

Charleston, SC
www.PalmettoPublishing.com

THOMAS JEFFERSON

Copyright © 2021 by William G. Hyland Jr.

All rights reserved.

No portion of this book may be reproduced, stored in a retrieval system, or transmitted in any form by any means—electronic, mechanical, photocopy, recording, or other—except for brief quotations in printed reviews, without prior permission of the author.

First Edition

Hardcover ISBN: 978-1-68515-571-1
Paperback ISBN: 978-1-68515-572-8
eBook ISBN: 978-1-68515-573-5

DEDICATION

*To my "Earthly Trinity," Lourdes, Victoria and William.
And to the Memory of Jefferson Scholar and true Gentleman, Herbert Barger*

TABLE OF CONTENTS

LIST OF IMPORTANT NAMES ix
INTRODUCTION xiii
PROLOGUE xxi

Chapter 1   The President's Daughter 1
Chapter 2   Sins of the Father 22
Chapter 3   Jefferson Randolph: Life at Monticello 39
Chapter 4   Ellen 62
Chapter 5   Love 82
Chapter 6   War and Death 97
Chapter 7   Domestic Violence 118
Chapter 8   Murder: The Jefferson Nephews 136
Chapter 9   The "Family Denial" 155
Chapter 10 "Uncle Randolph": The Unknown Brother 186
Chapter 11 The "Academical" Village 203
Chapter 12 Jefferson's Health 225
Chapter 13 "Is It the Fourth?" 239
Chapter 14 A Troubled Twilight 259
Chapter 15 A Fire Bell in the Night 282
Chapter 16 Boston to London 306
Chapter 17 A Carriage Accident 326
Epilogue   DNA *Redux*: Sally Hemings 345

APPENDIXES 365
BIBLIOGRAPHY 393
ILLUSTRATION CREDITS 423
ABOUT THE AUTHOR 425
ENDNOTES 427
INDEX

LIST OF IMPORTANT NAMES

Edmund Bacon: Jefferson's overseer at Monticello from 1806 to 1823.

Charles Bankhead: Husband of Jefferson's granddaughter Anne Randolph Bankhead.

Anne Cary Randolph Bankhead: Eldest grandchild of Thomas Jefferson; eldest daughter of Martha (Patsy) and Thomas Mann Randolph.

James Callender: Alcoholic, muckraking journalist who first published the allegation in 1802 that Jefferson had fathered Sally's children.

Ellen Randolph Coolidge: Jeff's sister; granddaughter of Thomas Jefferson. Wrote letter to her husband implying that Samuel Carr was the father of Sally's children.

Joseph Coolidge: Boston merchant and husband of Ellen Randolph.

Maria Cosway: Recipient of Jefferson's love letter in Paris, *Dialogue between My Head and My Heart*. It was thought the relationship was flirtatious but not carnal, after the death of Jefferson's wife, Martha.

Dr. Robley Dunglison: Jefferson's twenty-seven-year-old English physician, who treated Jefferson for migraines, rheumatoid arthritis, and intestinal and urinary infections.

Mary Jefferson Eppes (Maria, "Polly") (1778–1804): Second daughter of Thomas and Martha Jefferson to survive to adulthood; married John Wayles Eppes. Mother of Francis and Maria Eppes. Resident of Eppington.

Critta Hemings: Sister of Sally Hemings. Daughter of Elizabeth Hemings ("Betty") and allegedly John Wayles, Jefferson's father-in-law.

Elizabeth (Betty) Hemings: Mother of Sally Hemings, and her role model. Had twelve children.

Eston Hemings (b. 1808): Son of Sally Hemings. Alleged son of Thomas Jefferson based on DNA match, but also matched the DNA of Jefferson's younger brother, Randolph, and twenty other Jefferson males.

Madison Hemings (1805–1877): Son of Sally Hemings. Alleged that Jefferson was his father.

Sally Hemings (1773–1835): Alleged mistress of Jefferson. Youngest daughter of Elizabeth (Betty) Hemings and, allegedly, John Wayles, Jefferson's father-in-law; mother of six children likely fathered by Randolph Jefferson, and Peter and Samuel Carr, Jefferson's nephews. Sally never commented publicly or privately on the father of her children.

Isaac Jefferson: Former slave who worked at Monticello until seven years before Jefferson's death and dictated his recollections.

Martha Wayles Skelton Jefferson, aka "Patty" (1748–1782): Beloved wife of Jefferson. Daughter of John Wayles. Mother of two children who survived to adulthood, Martha ("Patsy") and Mary ("Maria/Polly").

Peter Jefferson (1708–1757): Father of Thomas Jefferson; Jane Randolph's husband.

Randolph Jefferson: Thomas Jefferson's younger brother and most likely the father of one or more of Sally's children.

Isham Lewis: Son of Charles Lilburne Lewis and Thomas Jefferson's sister, Lucy Jefferson Lewis; murderer.

Jane Randolph Jefferson: Mother of Thomas Jefferson, b. 1721, Shadwell, England; d. 1776, Virginia.

Lilburne Lewis: Son of Charles Lilburne Lewis and Thomas Jefferson's sister Lucy Jefferson Lewis; murderer.

Lucy Jefferson Lewis (b. 1752): Thomas Jefferson's younger sister; mother of Isham and Lilburne Lewis.

James Parton: Early biographer of Jefferson. Published *The Life of Thomas Jefferson* in 1874. Recipient of a letter from Henry Stephens Randall alleging that one of Jefferson's nephews, Peter or Samuel Carr, fathered Sally Hemings's children.

Henry Randall: Historian who first recorded the "family denial" of Jeff and his sister, Ellen, implicating the Carr brothers as the true lovers of Sally Hemings.

Cornelia Jefferson Randolph: Daughter of Patsy and Thomas Randolph; never married.

George Wythe Randolph: Jeff Randolph's brother. A former naval officer, George Wythe was one of three Virginia peace commissioners who went to Washington in April 1861 hoping to meet with President Lincoln and avert the Civil War. When this effort failed—the commissioners never got their meeting with Lincoln, and Fort Sumter was fired on before they left Washington. Wythe gave up his law practice to fight for the Confederacy. He organized, financed, and led the Richmond Howitzers and personally oversaw the defense of Yorktown.

Martha Jefferson Randolph ("Patsy"): Eldest daughter of Thomas Jefferson, wife of Thomas Mann Randolph Jr., and mother of twelve children, including Thomas Jefferson Randolph (Jeff) and Ellen Randolph Coolidge.

Sarah Nicholas Randolph: Daughter of Thomas Jefferson Randolph and great-granddaughter of Thomas Jefferson. Author of *The Domestic Life of Thomas Jefferson*.

Thomas Jefferson Randolph ("Jeff"): Oldest grandson of Thomas Jefferson and patriarch of the family after Jefferson's death. Told his grandfather's biographer that Peter Carr, Jefferson's nephew, had admitted to being the father of Sally's children. Told his sister Ellen that he overheard Carr say that "the old gentleman had to bear the blame of his and Sam's (Col. Carr) misdeeds."

Thomas Mann Randolph: Patsy's husband and Jeff and Ellen's erratic and dyspeptic father. Referred to as "Tom" in this book.

Nicholas Trist: Husband of Virginia Randolph, grandson of Thomas Jefferson's friend Eliza House Trist.

Virginia Randolph Trist: Jefferson's granddaughter; sixth child and fourth surviving daughter of Martha Jefferson and Thomas Mann Randolph.

S. F. Wetmore: Political editor of the *Pike County (Ohio) Republican* and abolitionist census taker for Pike County. Recorded, published, and influenced Madison Hemings's memoirs in 1873.

INTRODUCTION

I consider [you] as the greatest of the god-sends which Heaven has granted to me.

—**Thomas Jefferson** to his grandson
Thomas Jefferson Randolph (1826)

On April 13, 1943, President Franklin D. Roosevelt dedicated the Jefferson Memorial on the edge of the Tidal Basin in Washington, DC. World War II had injected the two hundredth anniversary of Thomas Jefferson's birth with special significance. The tide of history had just shifted its course. One of the foremost political figures in American history finally took his place in the ultimate American pantheon, within sight of George Washington's soaring monument and Abraham Lincoln's brooding, seated statue. No American has ever before enjoyed such a transcendent status as Thomas Jefferson. And over the next 250 years of American history, no public figure would ever reach the same historic heights.

This is the triumphant "political" image of Jefferson, yet one far from reality. Jefferson had desired to live in the "tranquil, permanent felicity" that flowed from a secluded home life at his elegant mountain estate, Monticello.[1] But during the last seventeen years of his cloistered family life, his story was infused with high drama in a congealed world of alcoholism, domestic violence, family jealousies, bankruptcy, and a grisly murder. Then came a humiliating series of political wounds, including an alleged sexual affair with a slave, corroding Jefferson's personal and professional reputation.

Thirteen years before he died, Jefferson emphasized to his friend and compatriot John Adams, "I leave others to judge . . . what I have done, and to give me exactly that place which they shall think I have occupied."[2] And for the past two centuries, authors and historians have obliged him. No founder has been so closely judged, studied, psychoanalyzed, and dissected as Thomas Jefferson. This book contends that Jefferson has been subjected to pernicious stereotypes that grossly impede our complete understanding of the man. The relentless focus on his views on slavery or his alleged affair with Sally Hemings has obscured his monumental life.

Jefferson's full image remains unfinished. As a man laden with many secrets and grinding anxieties, he unburdened himself to only a small circle of confidants. My biography is an entirely new and provocative look at the intimate period of Jefferson's turbulent later life, through the eyes of his oldest and most trusted relations—his adult grandchildren, Thomas Jefferson Randolph (Jeff) and Ellen Randolph Coolidge. These important figures in Jefferson's life have been lost to history—until now.

Jeff and Ellen possessed intelligence, wit, and charm. Their glimpse of Jefferson's soft character spots provides a riveting psychological profile, illuminating thematic clues to his twilight years. By reading the family correspondence, one is struck by Jefferson's softer emotions: this man of granite self-control was sensitive and prone to tears at family tragedies. With his intimate family, Jefferson was not the placid figure he presented to the world. His voluminous letters to Jeff and Ellen reveal a phase of his nature that he carefully concealed from others. With Jefferson, trust had to be earned gradually, and he retreated at instant familiarity. He masked his emotions behind his fabled reserve and guarded his privacy like an anchorite. But not from his inner circle of family. It was only his young correspondent, Ellen, who could lead the taciturn president to write this effusive birthday greeting: "On Sunday next . . . receive the kisses I imprint for you on this paper."

The public Thomas Jefferson is a familiar and oft-chronicled figure, but it is time to look at the last chapter of his secluded life through an entirely new prism—not from a slave family's perspective, a sexual scandal, or his political adversaries, but the lens through which his immediate family saw him. They viewed

Jefferson as a sensitive and misunderstood man with a genius mind, a rich supply of penetrating insights, and wry humor. At the same time, they recognized that Jefferson could be utterly naive in business and finance. Over the years, Jefferson had accumulated heavy expenses, saved little, and was beset by financial turmoil. Because his grandfather was brilliant and his own father erratic, Jeff Randolph was anointed to cobble together the pieces of Jefferson's ruined fortune.

Thomas Jefferson's inner delicacy that lay beneath his reserved exterior was never more evident than when surrounded by his immediate family. We know more about Jefferson's physical appearance, health, and daily regimen during his last decade than at any other period of his life, due solely to Jeff and Ellen's candid reminiscences. The patriarchal Jefferson has been little studied. It was during his remaining years—from Jefferson's return to Monticello in 1809, after two terms as president, until his excruciating death in 1826—that his idealism and sense of family unity would be severely tested. In his ideal world, Jefferson would preside over a family who all lived together in harmony. Yet everyday difficulties, scandal, bankruptcy, declining health, and life-changing tragedies stood in the way of Jefferson's dream.

This book pierces Jefferson's private family veil, uncovering the dynamic relationship between Jefferson and his grandchildren, sealing their roles as central figures in his autumn years. Through firsthand accounts of the people closest to him in his final years, I reveal little-known poignant scenes, bringing Jefferson's family out of the shadows into vibrant life. It is my hope that you find this biography a deeply moving portrait of this famous American. Jefferson's loving, complicated relationship with his innermost family, especially Jeff and Ellen, is a narrative that has never been told. I chronicle their time together and Jefferson's lasting life lessons to them, as well as Jefferson's emotionally distressing retirement years, including new details on his health and his relationship with his younger, "unknown" brother, Randolph. It is the story of Jefferson as a family man that readers will find one of the most interesting chapters in his long life.

This is the unique historical backdrop for the appearance of two of the most influential figures in Jefferson's life—Jeff Randolph and his sister, Ellen Coolidge: Jeff was Thomas Jefferson's oldest grandson, "Godsend" of his old age, sole executor of his estate, and the first editor of Jefferson's official papers. Jeff was in a unique position to shape and carve out his grandfather's legacy. He literally grew up at Jefferson's feet at Monticello, where some of Jefferson's most intimate and important papers were available to him. Equally important, Jeff benefited from the stories and intellectual mentoring of Jefferson himself. This book brings the experiences and insights of Jeff Randolph—who experienced the aftermath of the Revolutionary War and served in the bloody Civil War— to the forefront.

Jefferson's favorite granddaughter, Ellen, became equally important in his life, and had a profound influence on him. Ellen delighted in gardening with Jefferson, remembering, "As a child, a girl and woman I loved and honored him above all earthly things."[3] Jefferson dug his garden or read with Ellen, "and for him both kinds of work bore the same name—both he called gardening. 'The spirit is a garden,' he declared."[4] As an adult, Ellen fondly remembered her days at Monticello, commissioning an artist to paint a watercolor of her and Jeff on its lush lawn. She recalled catching a glimpse of the former president astride his favorite horse, Eagle, in the early afternoon, when he rode for two hours through the fields around Monticello. Ellen looked forward to every moment with her grandfather, absorbing all that Jefferson had to offer. "Our Grandfather seemed to read our hearts, to see our invisible wishes."[5]

Though much has been written about Jefferson's famous daughter Martha ("Patsy"), most historians have overlooked or minimized Jeff and Ellen altogether. Yet, both were present for and influenced four of the most pivotal events in his life: the Sally Hemings sexual scandal and its devastating political effects on Jefferson's personal reputation; the insidious domestic violence that infected Jefferson's family; the construction of Jefferson's crowning achievement, the University of Virginia; and Jefferson's slow slide into bankruptcy, which eventually resulted in Jeff Randolph's painful decision to sell Monticello and its slaves to pay creditors. In fact, it was Jeff who single-handedly prevented Jefferson from certain bankruptcy, personal ruin, and foreclosure on Monticello.

Jeff and Ellen's intertwined life with their "Grandpapa" Jefferson is nothing less than an account of abject courage, love, sacrifice, and wisdom. It was from Jefferson's example that these two grandchildren developed their industrious work ethic, their appreciation of nature and the arts, their intellectual curiosity, and their perspectives on civility, family, aging, and forgiveness. Jeff and Ellen remain two of the most important, but unheralded figures in American history, who have left priceless vignettes.

My goal with this biography is to examine afresh, not the "political" Jefferson, but the loving father, grandfather, and conflicted patriarch to an emotionally and financially troubled family. This is a portrait of a private Jefferson, one that will make him tangible and magnetic in the same way he was perceived by his own family.

By gleaning anecdotes from a myriad of new and little-known sources, especially from eyewitness accounts over two decades, I have tried to make Jefferson vivid and immediate, rather than the flawed, slave-owning icon he has recently become for most historians. This is a textured saga of a vulnerable and doting man in retirement, needing Jeff and Ellen's unerring judgment, sterling character, unflagging sense of duty, and civic mindedness. These exemplary virtues sustained both Jefferson and the whole family, emotionally, politically, physically, and fiscally. And, finally, we are privy to intimate moments of Jefferson's final months with his family as he lay dying from a terminal illness.

Many fine biographies of Jefferson have appeared in the last few years. However, the most recent tomes have highlighted his contradictory views on slavery or his purported sexual liaison with his slave, Sally Hemings. What has been critically absent from recent biographies, what even eminent historians have gotten wrong, is Jefferson's final views about the institution of slavery before his death. Sifting through the different layers of Jefferson's beliefs on this tortured topic is inherently complicated. Jefferson was acutely aware of the discrepancy between noble revolutionary words and the harsh reality of slavery, yet his later views on abolition and deep moral revulsion at human bondage have not been fully explored.

In his unpublished *Memoirs,* Jeff writes extensively of Jefferson's evolving views on slavery. The Sage of Monticello left the mantle of his antislavery sentiments to be carried out by his grandson. Jefferson emphasized to Jeff, for the historical record as well as for his own place in the American pantheon, that his moral revulsion to slavery should be known to later generations.

We will examine this and other issues through an exacting account of Jeff and Ellen's time with Jefferson, studying the trials and tribulations they experienced together. I highlight Jeff's and Ellen's little-known, private letters, which offer true historical insight, portraying Jefferson as a distinctly domestic character in the last, troubled years of his life.

By his own admission, Jefferson cherished "tranquillity too much."[6] According to Jefferson's daughter Patsy, he became angry in her presence only twice in her lifetime: the first when a slave disobeyed his order concerning the use of a carriage horse, and the second when two men let a ferry in which he and Patsy were passengers drift into turbulent, whitewater rapids, nearly capsizing the boat.[7] It is ironic that Jefferson so prized tranquility but the last years of his life on his secluded mountain were anything but peaceful.

Ellen and Jeff were deeply devoted to Jefferson and his historical legacy, yet both became accomplished in their own right due to Jefferson's profound influence. Jeff became a remarkable legislator, agile editor, and one of the early rectors of the University of Virginia. He would eventually become the patriarch to the entire household for over fifty years, steering the family through their darkest hours with self-sacrifice, hard work, and good humor. Along with Ellen and his mother, Jeff compiled and edited the first collection of Jefferson's official papers. Ellen also became a central figure in the Sally Hemings sexual and political imbroglio, as well as a devoted wife and mother, and traveled extensively to Europe and China.

This book will also explore the so-called family denial of the Sally Hemings sexual scandal of 1802. Both Jeff and Ellen fervently defended Jefferson's honor in the scandal, concluding that the allegations against Jefferson of having "sexual commerce" with a slave was "a moral impossibility."[8] Perhaps, this is the most explosively persistent myth about Thomas Jefferson. The "sexual" issue, both real and imaginary, so permeated Jefferson's final years that a thoroughgoing account is needed to settle the matter. My original research of Jeff and Ellen's papers, coupled with rumored new DNA results and personal interviews, will lead you to one inevitable conclusion: historians have the wrong Jefferson. These new DNA studies, as well as other supporting material, appear to most likely implicate Jefferson's younger brother, Randolph, and possibly Jefferson's two wayward nephews, Peter and Samuel Carr, as the true candidates for a sexual relationship with Sally. Randolph is a major historical figure in the Hemings scandal one who is completely unknown to the public and has eluded historians. The new research injects new ingredients into the sexual controversy and most likely will monumentally changes the Jefferson-Hemings debate through forensic scruple.

My volume will not bring an end to all arguments about Jefferson, but it should help distance him from the image of modern biographers. In my view, Jefferson has been unfairly excoriated in recent years, with an endless row of verbal and written coffins. The hyperbolic 1998 DNA findings that stoked the possibility of a sexual relationship with his slave has given fresh assault to a depreciated, misleading image of Jefferson. While a decade of enshrining biographies of George Washington, John Adams, and Alexander Hamilton accentuated the virtues of their subjects, Jefferson was depicted in an excessively harsh light. Yet one biographer observed, "Thomas Jefferson, of all our great presidents, was the most orderly and the most acquisitive. He was also the most controlled."[9]

Dumas Malone, author of six peerless volumes on Jefferson, affirmed that Jefferson was a hard man to know intimately. Historian Merrill Peterson wrote that Jefferson "concealed his inner feelings behind an almost impenetrable wall of reserve."[10] Even among his contemporaries, Jefferson was the "least self-revealing and the hardest to sound to the depths of being."[11] This makes Jefferson the most internal of the founders. This veneer was penetrated by a select few family members, those who loved, perhaps even adored Jefferson. He had that effect on those close to him. A young Margaret Bayard Smith, wife of a prominent editor, remembered her first encounter with Jefferson: "There was something in his manner, his countenance, and voice that at once unlocked my heart."[12] Ellen echoed this sentiment. "As a child, girl, and woman I loved and honored him above all earthly beings."[13] Jefferson seemed to have this influence on most women, and he handled this unexpected adulation with perfect aplomb.

We do not need another epic painting of Thomas Jefferson, but rather a fresh incarnation focused tightly on his family and character. I hope to resuscitate the rich flavor of Jefferson's personality long enough to answer certain intimate questions. Through considered reappraisal and new perspectives, the rehabilitation of Thomas Jefferson is long overdue. My goal is the faithful recovery of illuminating moments that will be both authoritative and poignant, enriching our understanding of Jefferson's eclipsed personality. He donned a silent mask for others, but conviviality among family. The upshot, I trust, will be that instead of having a frosty respect for Jefferson (or lack of respect because he was a slave owner and possibly kept a slave-mistress), you will experience a visceral appreciation of the tender family man who scaled the highest peak of political greatness, only to return to his true passions in the last years of his life—"my family, my farm and my books." As one historian has contended, "the way Thomas Jefferson would have wanted his private story to end is with a definition of his humanism."[14]

Although my book places Jeff and Ellen at the center of their own story and lives, Thomas Jefferson is omnipresent in the book through his elegant estate, his physical presence, and copious letters, providing a crisp narrative that flowed in polished sentences. Jefferson was a genius, one of the few people in history who deserve that appellation. He was fluent in Latin, Greek, French, Italian, and taught himself Spanish in nineteen days. Neither Jeff nor Ellen was graced with their grandfather's exalted brilliance. Instead, Jefferson's wisdom cleaved to them. Ellen's acumen was her judgment, not emanating from books or formal education. Jeff willed his way to his own patriarchal genius, avoiding his grandfather's frenetic political thoughts. Jeff's commanding personality derived from his steadfast loyalty and sacrifice to his family. He became the personification of the eighteenth-century man: an imposing physique at six foot five, head of an extended family, mentally enigmatic, and emotionally restrained.

No glittering, multivolume biographies have burnished the fame of either Jeff or Ellen. I contend that they have not received their due from posterity. One of the most brilliant American statesmen who ever lived—Thomas Jefferson—depended almost solely on these two grandchildren in his autumn years. In the end, as he recognized filial intimacy as the one lasting grace in his life, he found it in his grandchildren, Thomas Jefferson Randolph and Ellen Randolph Coolidge. They provided a tremendous tonic to his spirits.

Jeff and Ellen knew that this man of many parts and generosity offered something of interest to everybody. Indeed, not only was Thomas Jefferson "an intensely devoted family man; he was a friend to mankind."[15]

PROLOGUE

I was given a lavishly comfortable spare bedroom, took meals with the family and sipped wine and brandy with Jefferson late into the evening. But in all that time he never said another word to me about what had happened in Kentucky. Indeed . . . Jefferson, in all the years remaining in his life, never wrote or spoke to anyone about his nephews' crimes.

—**Ron Burns,** *Enslaved*

Thomas Jefferson removed his spectacles and rubbed his red-rimmed eyes,[1] then opened the small door leading from his study to an outside terrace, absorbing the April dawn. He gazed down to Mulberry Row, a plantation street on the side of his elegant mansion, Monticello.[2] Shortly after he began building Monticello, Jefferson had planted the mulberry trees that gave the street its name. As he breathed in the morning mountain air, he realized that Monticello was not just a place where he lived; it had been his bucolic anchor in the many storms throughout his life. And now another storm had come to his front porch.[3]

Tall and slender in a blue frock coat, Jefferson stood at the entrance of his Monticello study.[4] His towering height had always caught visitors by surprise. "Mr. Jefferson was six feet two and a half inches high, well proportioned, and straight as a gun barrel," his overseer Edmund Bacon once described him.[5] Potted plants bursting with flowers shaded his siesta chair on the terrace deck, filling the air with a fragrance heavier than perfume. In the breaking dawn, the brick walkways smelled of damp stone. Wild spearmint grew in green clusters between the bricks. As the sun rose over the majestic Blue Ridge Mountains, the light turned the mist pink as cotton candy over Monticello's vast lawn.

Jefferson needed fresh air after reading the *Kentucky Gazette* sent to him by William "Baptist Billy" Woods. Woods, Jefferson's longtime friend and colleague, had left Albemarle County, Virginia, a year before and settled near Salem, Kentucky. Jefferson felt a throbbing in the back of his head, a baleful omen.[6] He rubbed his temples, first shocked, then angry over what he had just read. The article involved a gruesome murder of a slave, allegedly committed by his own two nephews on December 16, 1811. The sons of his younger sister, Lucy Lewis, Lilburne and Isham stood accused of one of the most heinous crimes of the nineteenth century. Jefferson knew Lilburne to be a dyspeptic and worthless individual whose life was a testimony to failure.[7] But Isham's involvement was surprising to Jefferson. A young Isham had visited his uncle and stayed at Monticello several times. For a time, the Lewises had lived at Monteagle plantation near Monticello and had prospered, owning several farms and thousands of acres. Eventually, however, they had lost everything and moved to Kentucky for a fresh start. Soon after, Lucy had died, leaving the boys motherless.[8]

Jefferson pondered the date of the alleged murder as given in the article. On that very date he had noted in his memorandum book that the thunderous rumblings of the massive "New Madrid earthquake" had stopped in Virginia. Except for disturbing the household in its sleep, the earthquake did not prevent life at Monticello from proceeding. However, hundreds of miles to the west, the devastating 8.1-magnitude earthquake "would play an eerie role" in the lives of the Jefferson nephews.[9]

Jefferson returned to his study, then to his bedroom—a suite of rooms no one entered without him being present. It was in these rooms—his library, his study, and his bedroom—that his privacy was most guarded. This sanctum sanctorum, which "even his own daughters never sat in," was closed to all members of the household.[10] As one story goes, an invited guest had been looking forward to browsing Jefferson's vast library, which she had heard was "one of the best private libraries on the continent."[11] But she learned what every guest at Monticello soon discovered—no one but Jefferson had access to his private quarters. Although there were three inside doors to his suite, they were all kept locked. To enter the library, guests had to be personally escorted by their host. One guest wrote that on the day of her visit, she found the library suite "constantly locked, and I have been disappointed much by not being able to get in today."[12] Jefferson's seclusion was sweetly congenial to him after toilsome years of political battle and the frequent lack of privacy at Monticello, enlivened by young grandchildren. He often fled the rambunctious shrieks of frolicking children to the silence of his study.

Jefferson's study—he called it his cabinet—was less formal than either his huge parlor or the dining room. A clutter of papers lay on his writing table next to Jefferson's "polygraph" machine, for copying letters.[13] For Jefferson, keeping up with his correspondence was not simply a matter of putting pen to paper. "He carried with him a portable copying press," making duplicates "of every letter he sent."[14] An inveterate record keeper, the former president kept an index of every letter written and received. His writing table had a revolving top, and the high-backed chair facing it revolved as well. When Jefferson was afflicted by periodic rheumatic arthritis in his back, he added a bench seat, enabling a comfortable chaise lounge in order to read in a reclining position.[15]

To the right of his study was his private bedroom. He always slept facing east on a bed built into an alcove between his working cabinet and a hall anchored by a fireplace. Crimson curtains draped each side of his bed.[16] A 1790 clock rested on a wooden shelf inside the bed. With soft chimes, it marked the hour and the half hour.[17] Supported by two black marble obelisks, the clock "was made for him in Paris from his own design. [Jefferson] rose each morning at daybreak, or . . . as soon as he could see the hands of this clock on the dial."[18] Below the clock hung a sword, the gift of "a long forgotten Arabian prince."[19] Fixated on organization, he had constructed a turntable clothes closet at the foot of his bed, described by one visitor as "a horse with forty-eight projecting hands on which hung his coats and waistcoats and which he could turn with a long stick."[20]

The profound silence of his bedchamber was only interrupted by the soft chirps of Jefferson's mockingbirds, his favorite bird, which he occasionally let fly out of their cages.[21] During his presidency, Jefferson had kept mockingbirds at the "President's House," often allowing them to fly around his room. One visitor reported that one bird "would perch on his shoulders and take food from his lips . . . How he loved this bird!"[22]

When closed, the three solid oak doors connecting Jefferson's inner sanctum formed an impenetrable buttress between the former president and his hectic household of grandchildren, allowing him to enjoy a solid seven hours of sleep a night after reading for an hour before bedtime. Jefferson rose at dawn every morning. His unforgiving mother, Jane, had drilled habits of industry into her ten children, including rising with the sun, a farmer's habit that Jefferson retained for the rest of his life. When he woke at sunrise, his bed was in direct line with the morning light streaming in from the eastern window. Sitting up in his alcove, he would turn and plunge his feet into a bowl of cold water,[23] believing that the frigid water benefited his aging body. "I have for 50 years bathed my feet in cold water every mornin," he wrote, ". . . and having been remarkably exempt from colds (not having had one in every 7 years of my life on an average) I have supposed it might be ascribed to that practice."[24] After his foot bath, Jefferson would then examine his thermometer, as he kept a regular meteorological diary.[25] "My method is to make two observations a day," he wrote, "the one as early as possible in the morning, the other from 3 to 4 o'clock, because I have found 4 o'clock the hottest and daylight the coldest point of the 24. hours."[26]

Jefferson stared at the tray his butler had brought in for a solitary breakfast this morning—coffee, muffins, hot wheat, corn bread, and butter.[27] Usually the former president ate only a moderate breakfast, "hot bread and occasionally some cold ham," unlike at Montpelier, James Madison's home, where Dolley Madison served "a most excellent Virginian breakfast—tea, coffee, hot wheat bread, light cakes, a pone or corn loaf—cold ham, nice hashes, and chicken."[28] At the President's House in Washington, Jefferson had his French chef, Etienne Lemaire, make him what he referred to as "pannequaiques," thick, rising pancakes coated with a layer of powdered sugar. The pancakes were then stacked into a small torte, cut in wedges, and served like a piece of cake. The recipe later became a favorite at Monticello.[29]

This morning, however, Jefferson, had lost his appetite and poured himself a snifter of his legendary Armagnac instead, as he skimmed the newspaper a second time. Although he never drank hard liquor, Jefferson needed the alcohol today—though it was barely seven in the morning.[30] The headline screamed out to the Sage of Monticello in the quiet room, and the gory details went beyond his most horrific imagination, describing the murder and mutilation of a slave by a "high-toned" family.[31] On the night of December 15, 1811, drunk and enraged over the breaking of a family heirloom, Lilburne and Isham bound their seventeen-year-old slave, George, in front of the assembled household slaves. Wielding a sharp ax, Lilburne cut off his head, then dismembered George's entire body into a fire pit. The brothers were indicted for murder and released on bail, later attempting suicide.

The scalding reality of what Jefferson had read jarred him. His arthritic right hand began to spasm. Jefferson squeezed it into a fist to make it stop. He called for his trusted butler, Burwell Colbert, subduing a quaver in his voice.[32] Jefferson had known Burwell for the past twenty years as "a Gentleman in manners and character."[33] Burwell, whom Jefferson had always treated like a friend instead of a slave, entered the inner sanctum. Not a line on Jefferson's face gave any indication of what he must have felt. With atypical brusqueness, he instructed Burwell that he was not to be disturbed for the rest of the morning. Colbert appeared surprised at Jefferson's sharp tone, but he immediately closed and locked all the doors to the former president's private chambers.[34]

Jefferson tried to scrub the graphic vision of the murder from his mind. But it was still there, like a feral presence hiding in his subconscious. How could such a thing happen? He considered the lawlessness of the frontier settlements in Kentucky, the dehumanizing effects of chattel slavery, and the Lewis family's history of mental instability.

Jefferson swayed dizzily from the shock of it all. And a part of him died a little that day. His skin paled, and the youthful light faded from his bright hazel-gray eyes.[35] Along with great fame, Jefferson had already known much tragedy in his life: he had lost his parents and his wife while in the flower of his youth. He had seen a touch of madness, alcoholism, and violence in his own family. He had lost all his children, save one daughter. But what could be worse than what he had just read, that his own sister's sons had committed such a vicious, unspeakable crime?

Jefferson's knees buckled, and he collapsed on his alcove bed with a searing pain in both his head and his heart.

1
THE PRESIDENT'S DAUGHTER

I never saw her at all out of temper . . . As she was attending to her duties about the house, she seemed to be always in a happy mood. She was always busy.

—**A description of "Patsy" Jefferson Randolph**

September 6, 1782, emerged as one of the worst days of Thomas Jefferson's life, for it was on this day that his beloved wife, Martha Wayles Skelton Jefferson, died at age thirty-three from complications following childbirth the previous spring. Shortly before her death, Martha copied some poignant lines from one of Jefferson's favorite books, Lawrence Sterne's *Tristram Shandy*:

> The days and hours of it are flying over our heads like clouds of a windy day never to return . . .

Martha was too weak to complete the lines, so Jefferson wrote them for her:

> —and every time I kiss thy hand to bid adieu, every absence which follows it, are preludes to the eternal separation which we are shortly to make.[1]

Before Martha drew her last breath, she feebly held up three petite fingers to her adoring husband. Jefferson's face was set as he stared into the blue eyes of the woman he affectionately called Patty. She whispered the names of their children and clutched Jefferson's long, slender hand. Martha held his gaze, then asked him for a sacred promise—to never marry again.[2] An edge of almost manic desperation permeated her tone. Her words had an ominous double meaning for both husband and wife. The memory of her own harsh stepmothers colored Martha's protective thoughts of her three young daughters, Patsy,[3] Polly, and Lucy.

Outside, the encroaching dusk cast ominous, jagged shadows over Martha's pale face. Jefferson wiped away a single tear, bent forward, and kissed her on the forehead. In a tender moment of complicity, Jefferson stroked her hair and lovingly agreed to her dying plea—then it was over.[4] Jefferson wrapped a snippet of Martha's hair with a scrap of paper containing a poem and stored the token in his desk. It remained there for the rest of his life, only discovered by his daughter upon his death.[5] He also took one of Martha's blonde locks and sealed it in a locket, which he wore around his neck into his grave.[6]

After ten years of "unchequered happiness," Martha's death devastated Jefferson and his ordered life.[7] She had given him his emotional identity with love, affection, and children. Psychologically, he never fully recovered from this tragedy. The shock of her death was so grave that he found it almost unbearable to speak her name, burning every letter that had passed between them.[8] At thirty-nine, the soft-spoken Virginian was now left widowed with three young children to raise, his political career seemingly dissolved. He lost all interest in Monticello and believed he could never be happy there again. When Congress nominated him as minister to France, he immediately accepted, although his appointment was ultimately postponed. In 1784, an emotionally broken Jefferson left for France with just one critical family member: his beloved twelve-year-old daughter, Martha, whom he called "Patsy."[9] Patsy emerges as one of the most important influences on Jefferson's life, a cherished daughter and doting but firm mother. She had a profound influence on her own children, especially Jeff and Ellen, and molded them into the substantial figures they both became.

To intimately know Thomas Jefferson, then, one must first know Patsy Jefferson—the industrious, accomplished, heroic, and tragic daughter. Her stoic perseverance through severe family stress, death, and economic woes is quite a remarkable, and unknown, story.

Patsy would become well educated for her time, setting her apart from most southern women. These two facts, as one historian points out, demonstrate that "her life was extraordinary."[10] As Jefferson's devoted daughter, Patsy was far-traveled in the circles of presidents and aristocrats, educated on two continents. Yet, as the future head of a large household, she was not spared the same physical and emotional challenges that most plantation women endured. Peachy Gilmer, a family friend, seemed a more objective observer of Patsy than her children. He described Patsy as "decidedly the most accomplished woman I have ever known" and "her person" as "tall, large loosely made . . . An expression of intelligence always animate[d] her countenance," and her "frankness and eloquence [were] far above any other person of her sex." Gilmer believed that Patsy's "exemplary life, her devotion to the instruction of her children and everything in her history," made her "one of the most interesting persons of the age."[11] As one author has eloquently commented:

> The sweet, resolute face under the frilled cap of the tall, middle-aged woman resembled strikingly the serene countenance of the tall, spare old man whose graying sandy hair fell over his old-fashioned white stock; under the same reserve of manner were hidden their ever-young idealism and their tender hearts.[12]

Following her mother's tragic death, Patsy lived in Paris with Jefferson for five years.[13] She later served as hostess at the "President's house" (White House) and at Monticello. Her fitful and unstable husband, Thomas Mann Randolph, straddled between chronic emotional distress and financial woe. Patsy and her eleven children lived mostly at Monticello, greeting famous guests and debating issues with her father, ranging the spectrum from women's education to religious freedom. And later, after her family's financial ruin upon Jefferson's death and bankruptcy, a nearly destitute Patsy became a fixture in Washington during Andrew Jackson's presidency.[14]

Ellen Coolidge, Patsy's devoted daughter, lamented that her mother's virtues and achievements would be lost. "It may be told for a while in the neighborhood of her in her father's home, that a daughter of Thomas Jefferson sleeps by his side in that neglected burying ground at Monticello," Ellen conveyed sorrowfully, "but of who or what she was, otherwise than the daughter of Thomas Jefferson, [the] well known statesman and great political leader, no tradition will after one generation remain."[15] Unlike her friend Dolley Madison, who became a symbol of hospitality and fashion, Patsy never became an American icon, and to the extent that history remembered her at all, it was indeed as an accessory to her famous father.

***

In 1871, Sarah Nicholas Randolph, Patsy's granddaughter, wrote *The Domestic Life of Thomas Jefferson*, describing Patsy's school days and her devotion to her father and her children. While not a formal biography, Sarah's book explained Jefferson's "private character," which had been "foully assailed and wantonly exposed to the public gaze" in his lifetime and after death.[16] Sarah's book is a vibrant portrait of Patsy and her life struggles at Monticello among the inner Jefferson family. Patsy's domestic life "reveals to modern readers the challenges, complexities, and frustrations that dominated the lives of many women of her era, even those who were members of a privileged social elite."[17] In her lovingly written biography, Sarah described Patsy as a "wife and devoted and attentive mother" and "kind of thoughtful mistress" who was Jefferson's closest companion until his death caused "the great agony of her life."[18] Sarah chronicled Patsy's social triumphs in Paris and Washington, but she emphasized that her most important challenges were "hidden from the world" as mistress of a packed and drama-ridden household. Never mentioning in detail the estrangement between an abusive husband and his wife, Sarah recalled curtly that Patsy was "saddened by her husband's death" in 1828.[19]

Patsy was born into revolutionary Virginia on September 27, 1770, nine months after her parents' wedding at her grandfather's estate, the Forest. The Jeffersons named her after her mother, also a Martha, but the little girl would be nicknamed "Patsy" by an adoring Jefferson. As his oldest child, she became one of the three most important people in his adult life. "He discharged her all the tender duties of a mother, took her with him to France and never separated from her as long as he lived."[20] Left motherless at an early age, and eventually a convent student in Paris, the highly educated Patsy would be unusual for a woman of her day, yet prepared her for a role beyond plantation mistress, with a "home as a sanctuary from the amoral public world."[21] For Patsy, however, education, knowledge, and even mundane household chores were conducted under the guiding eye of Thomas Jefferson. He instructed her on the smallest of life's details.[22]

A year after her own mother's tragic death, twelve-year-old Patsy traveled to Philadelphia as her father's companion. There, she took up residence with Mary Johnson Hopkinson, while Jefferson attended Congress. Jefferson installed Mary, an "educated, patriotic, and pious widow," as a surrogate mother.[23] Cousin Eliza Trist also served as a "valuable friend" to nurture and protect Patsy while Jefferson was away.[24] In his first letter to young Patsy on December 11, 1783, her father echoed themes that would resonate with her for years. "The key features of their situation," explained one historian, "were interpreted as opportunities for constructing a future: physical separation, affectionate attachment, distance from kin, imperatives of public duty, and staying connected through the medium of letters."[25] Jefferson urged Patsy to write letters to her family in Virginia, while suggesting detailed, educational lessons for her. For Patsy, Jefferson's deep devotion would forever bond father and daughter, as in later years her own deep devotion would bind Patsy to her children.

The close father-daughter attachment after Martha's death made Patsy's Philadelphia separation "difficult." Jefferson soothed Patsy, telling her that she would be "more improved in the situation" than if she stayed with him amid his political struggles in Annapolis. "Heaven has been pleased to afflict [us with the loss of your mother]," he told her, so Mrs. Hopkinson was to be considered as her "mother" and the "only person to whom [she could] now look up."[26] "[She will] see that you perform all your exercises, and admonish you in all those wanderings from what is right or what is clever."[27] Jefferson reminded Patsy how important to her future life would be the way she employed her "present time."[28] He recommended the following daily regimen:

> from 8. to 10 o'clock practise [sic] music.
> from 10. to 1. dance one day and draw another

from 1. to 2. draw on the day you dance, and write a letter the next day.
from 3. to 4. read French.
from 4. to 5. exercise yourself in music.
from 5. till bedtime read English, write &c.[29]

According to one historian, for Jefferson it "was essential . . . that daughters no less than sons be industrious and exercise integrity."[30] In the spring of 1787, Jefferson advised Patsy, "It is your future happiness which interests me, and nothing can contribute more to it (moral rectitude always excepted) than the contracting habits of industry and activity. Of all the cankers of human happiness none corrodes with so silent, yet so baneful an influence, as indolence."[31] But he also encouraged Patsy to explore the arts and nature. "Music, drawing, books, invention, & exercise will be so many resources to you against ennui."[32] Jefferson emphasized his own fondness of music to his daughter, and later to his grandchildren, encouraging Patsy not to neglect it: "It will be a companion which will sweeten many hours of life to you."[33] One crucial piece of furniture in the parlor at Monticello was Patsy's pianoforte. "Music had been a part of the domestic life of Monticello," according to one author, "ever since Jefferson moved into the first house with his wife. His musical tastes were varied; his large library of music included pieces for voice and instrument by such composers as Vivaldi, Corelli, Haydn, and Mozart. But he also had an extensive collection of popular songs, dances, ballad operas—just about every kind of secular music written. He owned a great many books on musical instrumentation and technique as well."[34]

Jefferson relished activity and continually stressed to Patsy the need for active pursuits, which she would stress to her own children. According to Jefferson, citizens needed to be active and industrious, avoiding idleness and lethargy.[35] Education became paramount in Jefferson's mind when he whisked Patsy away to Paris on a nineteen-day sea voyage, during which he taught himself fluent Spanish.

Jefferson—a grieving widower and single father—and Patsy arrived in France in August 1784, and Patsy promptly entered the prestigious *Abbaye Royale de Panthemont* school, by recommendation of a female friend of the Marquis de

Lafayette. The diversions of Paris were exactly what father and daughter needed to lift them out of their despair over Martha's tragic death. As one scholar has written, "In contrast to his earthier fellow minister, Ben Franklin, who was legendary in the City of Light for wearing a beaver hat and biting the heads off asparagus, Jefferson fit right in."[36] Although Jefferson called himself "a savage of the mountains of America," he immediately took to Paris's cultured, social life, wearing a powdered wig and a topaz ring. His mansion on the Champs-Élysées was decorated with blue "silk damask curtains, crystal decanters, well-stocked wine cellar, and a household staff that included a frotteur, whose sole function was to clean the parquet floors by spinning around with brushes strapped to his feet."[37] Jefferson would soon host dinner parties, serving the best wines of France.

Patsy's experiences in France also expanded both educationally and socially. She continued to study music and drawing, but also "Latin history and natural philosophy" so that she might fully develop her faculties. Patsy quickly learned conversational French, and in later life taught it to her own children, as Jefferson had likely hoped. The Institute of Learning at the Abbaye provided everything Patsy could have expected—education, the arts, strict discipline, and moral values. She excelled in music and acquired a love for literary pursuits, like her father. These cultivated and refined acquirements prepared her for an appreciation of Jefferson's world.[38] Despite her father's disapproval, Patsy became actively interested in politics. "Even when she was at Panthemont," one historian noted, "she passed on political tidbits about the French court in her letters to her father. Jefferson pointedly let them pass without comment."[39] In later years, Jefferson's younger daughter, Polly, "was much less concerned with politics." From some accounts, she was a "reluctant reader" compared to the industrious Patsy.[40]

Within a year of her arrival, Patsy happily described her new life. "I am very happy in the convent and it is with reason," she reported, "there wants nothing but the presence of my friends of America to render my situation worthy to be envied by the happiest."[41] One scholar wrote of Patsy's time in the convent:

> So adept at French had she become by the following year, she began to worry because she was having "really great difficulty" writing in English. Martha may have begun feeling utterly

bereft of friends and footing, but that situation seems to have been remedied fairly quickly. The Abbess allowed her father to visit her every evening for the first few weeks until she got her bearings. Indeed, with no other option in the daily routine of the convent, [Patsy] quickly surpassed him in her mastery of French. She donned the same crimson uniform worn by all the other pensionnaires, no longer noticeable as a newcomer. The students' uniforms were based on the court dress Louis XIV mandated for women one hundred years earlier.[42]

Both Patsy's and Thomas Jefferson's lives continued to be an adventure for the next five years while in Paris. Father and daughter sealed their close emotional bond even more, although Jefferson did take a three-month sojourn by himself, taking only a single trunk with him in the clattering horse drawn carriage,[43] to see the most fabled vineyards in the world. Missing her father terribly, and perhaps knowing him better than anyone, Patsy remarked in a letter to Jefferson after he left, "[I am] inclined to think that your voyage is rather for your pleasure than for your health."[44]

Away from his diplomatic responsibilities and anonymous in the French countryside, Jefferson relaxed. Then, before sailing home to Virginia, he put his new wine knowledge to use, ordering 252 bottles of 1784 Haut-Brion from a local merchant. He shipped 72 of those to his brother-in-law, Francis Eppes. "I cannot deny myself the pleasure of asking you to participate of a small parcel of wine I have been chusing for myself," he wrote to Eppes. "I do it the rather as it will furnish you a specimen of what is the very best Bourdeaux wine."[45]

In Paris, and then back in Virginia, Patsy continued to meet the most interesting people, including eight of the first nine American presidents—she never met George Washington—and many of the most influential women of her era, including among her closest friends the remarkable Dolley Madison. At a time when most southern women were barely literate, Patsy spoke and read four languages, garnered universal praise for her social skills, and was "fitted to grace any court in Europe."[46]

Patsy's relationship with Jefferson greatly influenced her close rapport with her own son and daughter, Jeff and Ellen. In fact, this warm relationship shaped almost every aspect of her domestic life. One writer observed:

> [Patsy] was so extremely sensitive to any criticism of her father's character or conduct in part because they shared such an extraordinarily close relationship but also because she grew to regard her father's fame and reputation as her own and her children's chief inheritance. In addition, from her love of reading and her determination to see her own children appropriately educated, to her struggles as a penurious plantation mistress . . . Martha Randolph's life reflected important facets of her father's ideals and habits . . . even after his death, [he] remained a continual and influential presence in his daughter's life.[47]

Patsy would become admired from near and far. Monticello overseer Edmond Bacon praised her: "I knew Mrs. Randolph as well as I ever knew any person out of my own family. I never saw her equal."[48]

In the Paris chill on their final night, father and daughter sat together reading as a fire crackled in the drawing room. Their house, at the intersection of the Champs-Élysées and the rue de Berri, "had a spare, half-empty look; much of the contents had already been crated for shipment to Monticello, since Jefferson was soon to quit Paris for what he thought would be a six-month leave in America. Two months earlier," one writer noted, "a mob had overrun the Bastille. Paris was in tumult, and Jefferson had requested that guards be posted outside; his house had been robbed three times recently, the candlesticks taken from his dining table, and he had put bars and bells on the windows."[49]

At the end of their stay, Jefferson and Patsy packed up five years' worth of belongings and mementos. Among the eighty-six packing cases that Jefferson would bring back were crates filled with various wines, "including two containers earmarked for John Jay and George Washington."[50] During his five years in France, according to one scholar, "[Jefferson] had engaged in an epic shopping binge that included the purchase of fifty-seven chairs, two sofas, six large mirrors, wallpaper, silver, china, linen, clocks, scientific equipment, a cabriolet, and a phaeton. All of this was in addition to his art collection, books, and wine."[51] According to one account, Jefferson intended to return to Paris, but Gouverneur Morris bet William Short, Jefferson's secretary, "a beaver hat that Jefferson would not . . . Morris won the bet. Jefferson was appointed secretary of state. His majordomo was left to dismantle the Paris household. He sold [Jefferson's] horses, chariot, cabriolet, and paper press, and packed up the rest of his furniture for shipment to Philadelphia, swaddling each box in oilcloth. Each of Jefferson's books he wrapped in paper."[52]

At seventeen, Patsy returned to Monticello from Paris a young woman. She had grown up and matured. "[Patsy] Jefferson was tall like her father," the slave Isaac Jefferson said. Her sister, "Polly [Mary] low like her mother."[53] Both Patsy and Jefferson had missed Monticello and their family terribly. Jefferson complained of Paris's cold and rainy climate, longing for the warm Virginia summers: "Our sky is always clear; that of Europe always cloudy . . . During a residence of between six and seven years in Paris, I never, but once, saw the sun shine through a whole day, without being obscured by a cloud in any part of it."[54]

When Patsy returned to Monticello, she met her future husband, Thomas Mann Randolph. Patsy and Tom, as he was called, who were third cousins, had met at least twice as youngsters. In 1781, when Patsy turned nine and Tom was thirteen, the British had invaded Virginia. Tuckahoe became one of the Jefferson family's stops as they fled Richmond for Albemarle County. Two years later, Patsy and her father went to Tuckahoe as they made their way south from Philadelphia while Jefferson waited to receive his assignment in Paris. During that visit, eleven-year-old Patsy struck up a friendship with Judith Randolph, who was also eleven. "Patsy must have also made an impression on Judith's older brother Tom, who sent his 'compliments to Miss Jefferson'" when he asked for her father's advice about his education in 1786.[55] In fact, Patsy and Tom shared much in common:

> They both had deep roots in Virginia and shared many mutual kin and acquaintances, though each had also experienced life in the wider cosmopolitan world. Both were comparatively well educated and valued learning and those who had it. Tom,

for instance, believed that "an accomplished woman cannot be entirely ignorant" of science, though he also thought that his sisters and other members of the "delicate sex" were overall better suited to the "elegant and agreeable occupations."[56]

Unlike most young men Patsy met in Virginia, Tom Randolph stood out with his European experience, having spent two years studying abroad. Their courtship featured long rides in the Albemarle countryside. Like her father, Patsy had become an expert rider from childhood, taught by Jefferson, and had honed her riding skills while in Paris. In 1885, at age seventeen, Tom had written to her that their "renewal of the correspondence [between them]. . . cannot fail of being very agreeable . . . the many obstacles which hitherto prevented it, being now entirely removed."[57] Once Patsy returned from Paris, Tom, four years her senior, viewed his cousin in a romantic light. A strong attraction drew him to call on her at Monticello.

From the beginning of their relationship, however, Tom foreshadowed mental instability, mercurial behavior, and a volcanic temper. Both father and daughter—wrongly, it turns out—attributed Tom's temperamental personality to mere immaturity; he was only twenty-one. Patsy hoped he would soon grow out of it.[58]

Jefferson had "scrupulously suppressed" his own wishes and allowed Patsy to "indulge her own sentiments freely," agreeing that she could marry.[59] He wrote of his "real and extreme pleasure" from the "intended Union." Tom's "talents, disposition, connections and fortune" were such that he would have been Jefferson's "own first choice."[60] His earlier concerns that she would "draw a blockhead" seemed allayed. Thomas Mann Randolph, by education and family heritage, most certainly was not a "blockhead."[61]

There are no surviving letters to provide rich detail of Patsy's love affair with Tom or any letters from the beginning of their marriage. Yet, on paper, Tom seemed the ideal husband. An accomplished Virginia scion and the son of Jefferson's good friend, it appeared that he was an excellent pick as a future husband. Still, Patsy may have had her own doubts before the wedding. As one historian has aptly written, she probably grasped "the full weight of the financial suicide she was committing, an 18th century prisoner to her husband's finances."[62]

It would not be unusual for an early American bride to express worry on the eve of her wedding. Tom, on the other hand, seemed certain Patsy was his intended wife; he loved her "and only her, with all [his] faculties."[63]

It appears that Patsy had little hesitation about accepting his marriage proposal, even though she had only known the adult Tom Randolph for mere months. Leading up to the wedding ceremony, Jefferson and Tom's father struck a marriage settlement agreement. Jefferson had been cautious in drawing the papers for his eldest daughter. As a wedding gift, the senior Randolph (also named Thomas Mann Randolph) offered the couple a 950-acre plantation with livestock and forty slaves. The plantation, however, turned out to be a suspect "gift." The property held a monumental $2,900 mortgage ($100,000 in today's dollars). Jefferson urged the younger Randolph to reject the plantation for that reason.[64] But there were was another, more important reason to Jefferson why they should refuse the estate. The plantation, called Varina in Richmond, lay a distant ninety miles away from Monticello—too far away, Jefferson thought. He also sensed Patsy was reluctant to leave his secure family orbit. Yet, not even marriage and a distant plantation would be able to break a daughter's deep devotion to her father. Once, when Jefferson told Patsy of his plans to return to Monticello after a long absence, she told him that the news stirred her heart.[65] And Jefferson returned her sentiment, emphasizing that "the bloom of Monticello's chill by myself . . . makes me wish that more than yourself and sister were here to enjoy it."[66]

On Tuesday, February 23, 1790, Patsy Jefferson and Thomas Mann Randolph were married at Monticello. The only documentation of their wedding is a brief written entry by Jefferson: "My daughter Martha is this day married to Thos. Mann Randolph junior."[67] "Jefferson also recorded having paid the local Episcopal minister, the Reverend Matthew Maury, a fee of £4.16 for officiating at his daughter's" ceremony. Per tradition, Jefferson now referred to Patsy as "my daughter Randolph." Tom, however, still called his wife "Patsy," and she referred to him as "Mr. Randolph."[68]

Now married and in a different city, Patsy remained loyal to her father. "She never placed her husband above Jefferson in her affections," wrote one scholar. "Eight months after Maria's marriage, [Patsy], anticipating Jefferson's arrival home, wrote to her 'Dearest and adored Father' with 'raptures and palpitations not to be described. The heart swellings with which I address you when absent and look forward to your return convince me of the folly or want of feeling of those who dare to think that any *new* ties can weaken the first and best of nature."[69]

One touching story perhaps explains Patsy's deep, psychological devotion to Jefferson. When Patsy's mother scolded her once as a child, "she was deeply mortified, her heart swelled, her eyes filled with tears, she turned away, but she heard her father say in a kind tone to her mother, 'My dear, a fault in so young a child once punished should be forgotten.'" Patsy told her own daughter years later that she "could never forget the warm gush of gratitude that filled her childish heart at [her father's] words."[70]

Patsy never forgot her father's loving defense of her.

***

Jefferson's marriage advice to Patsy reveals his eighteenth-century view of women's roles within the family: "Your new condition will call for abundance of little sacrifices, but they will be greatly overpaid by the measure of affection they will secure to you. The happiness of your life depends now on . . . continuing to please a single person. To this all other objects must be secondary, even your love to me."[71] Jefferson expected that Patsy would put her husband and children's happiness ahead of her own.

Within a year, Jefferson delighted in the news of Patsy's first child, Anne Cary Randolph, born on January 23, 1791. "Your last two letters are those which have given me the greatest pleasure of any I ever received from you. The one announced that you will become a notable housewife, the other a mother. The last is undoubtedly the keystone of the arch of matrimonial happiness, as the first is its daily ailment."[72] Jefferson filled his letters to and about his grandchildren with effusive professions of love "from the moment the first was born . . . He bragged to his sister-in-law Elizabeth Eppes about my advancement to the venerable corps of grandfathers" and declared, "I expect from it more felicity than any other advancement ever gave me."[73] Jefferson often referred to Patsy's sons and daughters as "our children."[74]

Motherhood dramatically changed Patsy's world—now, she was not only a devoted daughter but a loving mother who would be consistently pregnant over the next thirteen years.

Jeff, the first grandson, born on September 12, 1792, bloomed early. Thomas Jefferson Randolph—"your little namesake," as Patsy called him in a letter to Jefferson—was not yet two when Jefferson returned to Monticello.[75] Jeff seemed "little inferior to his sister in point of size," Patsy said, but seemed hardier than Anne, "and bids fair to be as lively."[76]

It is unclear whether Patsy's husband was with her when Ellen was born that September, but in January they were together with their infant at their plantation in Richmond, while their two other children remained at Monticello. Jefferson wrote to Patsy that two-year-old Jeff and his sister were well and had not had so much as a "finger ache" since she left. He described Anne as a pleasingly "placid" girl and Jeff as "robust" and prone to "tempests."[77] Jeff resisted wearing shoes and gloves, despite the frigid weather, and he had an intense fear of dogs, but Jefferson cured him by allowing a puppy to live in the mansion, which soon became the boy's favorite.

Patsy enjoyed her role as Jeff and Ellen's first teacher more than she did "any other aspect of motherhood." But as more children were added to her household, she found herself not only a wife, a full-time mother, and an educator, but the manager of Monticello's slaves. Ellen recalled that her mother's "Sundays then were chiefly occupied with receiving colored visitors from all grandpapa's other plantations that were within walking distance. They came sometimes, to ask small favors, or complain of small grievances, to see and talk to Mistress, notice the children, and take a look at the 'great House' and all its surroundings."[78]

Patsy, like her father, appreciated the importance of ordered, domestic harmony. She listened to Jefferson's advice, assuring him that amid other responsibilities, she was a deferential wife too. "I have made it my study to please [Tom] and . . . [consider] all other objects as secondary to that except my love for you."[79] While she had not forgotten her studies, domestic responsibilities were her main priority. "Nothing comes in or goes . . . [out] without my knowledge and I believe there is as little wasted as possible," she wrote.[80]

Patsy possessed, as one historian observed, an "obsessive reliance on her father," so much so that she refused to name her first child, referring to her baby as "the infant," until Jefferson suggested a name.[81] Jefferson chose Anne Cary, the name of Thomas Randolph's mother, from whom she inherited her blue eyes and fair skin. In a letter to Randolph, Jefferson congratulated him: "Happy is the man whose quiver is full of [children]."[82] Eleven more children followed the couple, one dying in infancy. And each subsequent child was named by grandfather Thomas Jefferson.

"To Jefferson," one scholar believes, "the arrival of each grandchild was an excited pleasure and intensified his desire to keep Patsy as near to him as possible. For Thomas Mann Randolph, however, each increase in the family meant extra efforts to see them properly reared and educated. Patsy truly was her father's daughter."[83] Tom, however, dissolved into a disappointing failure in life. Judged by tangible accomplishments, he chronically ignored his wife and children, went bankrupt, alienated most friends and relatives, served fecklessly in Congress, and was considered one of Virginia's worst governors—-all due to his fickle behavior, sullen moods, and temper.

When Jefferson became president in 1800, Patsy often visited him with her son Jeff in tow. Patsy's gracious demeanor and serene temperament on these festive occasions is remarkable in light of the growing financial ruin that was slowly consuming the Jefferson-Randolph household. Mothering four children aged two to ten, and serving as social hostess to numerous, aunts, friends, and visitors, Patsy soon considered her life as a plantation wife nearly overwhelming, "dreary and monotonous."[84]

In the summer of 1801, she was "crouded" [*sic*] once again with visitors and family. Her sister Polly remained at Edgehill, awaiting the birth of her second child. A "Mrs. Bache" and her family stayed at Monticello until Randolph returned.[85] Patsy delayed sending for Thomas Jefferson's sister, Aunt Marks, because the family was too large for Monticello. Given Patsy's domestic obligations, it was "utterly impossible" to visit Monticello upon her father's arrival, which caused her distress, not "unmixed with pain."[86] Her father's presence marked "a return to the world from which I have been so long . . . secluded," Patsy wrote, "and for which my habits render me every way unfit."[87] Seeing her father was a "good" that would "render every other evil light."[88] Indeed, the source of Patsy's happiness tended to be a single person—her devoted father, Thomas Jefferson.

In 1801, when Jefferson was inaugurated, each of his daughters had a baby—it was Patsy's sixth and Polly's second, her first having died after three weeks. Jefferson encouraged both of his daughters to join him in Washington at the White House. This was an opportunity for high society to have its first inspection of the presidential family. After they had been in the capital for a few weeks, Mrs. Samuel Harrison Smith wrote a letter describing the Jefferson daughters, especially Polly's natural beauty:

> Mrs. Eppes [Polly] is beautiful, simplicity and timidity personified when in company, but when alone with you of communicative and winning manners. Mrs. R. [Patsy] is rather homely, a delicate likeness of her father, but still more interesting than Mrs. E. She is really one of the most lovely women I have ever met with, her countenance beaming with intelligence, benevolence and sensibility, and her conversation fulfils all her countenance promises.[89]

We know that Patsy was a dutiful daughter to Thomas Jefferson, but what kind of mother was Patsy to her own children, Jeff and Ellen? In a word: devoted. The type of mother who saw the immediate need for a stout male figure when her own aloof husband became absent. Motherhood now defined Patsy's adult life. She affirmed time and again that her own children's interests were the "first and dearest objects of [her] life."[90] She instilled a love and devotion within her children that carried well into their adult years. Patsy's daughter Virginia spoke passionately of her attachment to her mother. "In a separation of any length from Mama," she wrote her husband, Nicholas Trist, "I can scarcely trust myself to think of her without the tears coming into my eyes."[91]

Patsy's first decade as a mother and plantation wife seemed typical of the problematic experiences of Virginia women of her era. Between 1790 and 1800, she bore five children, another five in the next decade, and then had two more difficult pregnancies in 1814 and 1818. Still, Patsy was fortunate—only one of her children failed to survive.

By all recorded letters, Patsy's primary focus was her children's emotional well-being. With her husband absent, both physically and emotionally, Patsy depended almost solely on her house servants for daily chores, allowing her precious time with her children.

Patsy's health during these years remained generally good, but the children were prone to illness. And her husband's violent mood swings and verbal abuse were a source of emotional distress. She constantly felt the lash of his tongue. In will but Patsy's one searing tragedy during this period was when her daughter, "little" Ellen, died suddenly in Staunton, Virginia. Ellen's tiny body was sent back to Albemarle to be buried at Monticello. A distraught Patsy traveled first to Warm Springs, where Tom mended from his numerous physical and psychological ailments, making "an almost perfect recovery of his health."[92] By October, after losing one child and being away from the others for more than two months, Patsy and Tom returned to the tender succor of Monticello. Reserved, like her father, Patsy privately mourned the agonizing loss of Ellen, not sharing her emotions. She expressed sorrow in only one letter, years later.

Patsy kept a tight rein on her feelings, as Jefferson had taught her. Yet, when her children were sent to Richmond to be vaccinated for smallpox, Patsy lamented, "The idea of exposing my children to such a disease . . . makes me perfectly miserable. I never look at them but my eyes fill with tears to think how soon we shall part and *perhaps* forever."[93]

But her father, who considered himself an amateur physician, was a constant comfort to her. When Patsy gave birth to her first child, Anne, Jefferson sent her a book by the famous Scottish physician John Gregory, who had also written *A Father's Legacy to His Daughters*, an innovative medical guide for women. Dr. Gregory was an early advocate of breastfeeding, which he believed was healthy for both mother and child. The spacing of Patsy's pregnancies suggests that she followed Gregory's medical advice.[94] For her own children, Patsy "approved Gregory's general scheme, which emphasized cleanliness, freedom of movement, a simple diet, and plenty of outdoor activities."[95]

Jefferson encouraged Patsy to have his grandchildren engage in "sports" and outdoor play at Monticello. From a young age, Patsy herself had valued nature and outdoor recreation. Ellen recalled happy childhood days, racing, running, and playing with her mother, sister, and brothers, outside at Monticello. She even hired an artist to memorialize these happy reminiscences for a painting of Monticello, depicting her and Jeff romping on the plush green lawn while her sisters looked on.[96]

While Patsy and Tom shared parental responsibility, the grandchildren's early education was left almost exclusively to Patsy and Jefferson. "[Patsy] was extremely well educated for a Virginia woman of her time," one author has noted.[97] Jefferson had intended Patsy's education to be preparation to teach her own children. Her expensive Paris education at the *Abbaye de Panthemont* turned out to be a wise investment by Jefferson.

In one letter, Patsy proudly informed Jefferson that three-year-old Anne was "busily employed *yiting*" [sic], adding that "a fond Mother never knows where to stop [boasting] where her children is the subject."[98] Perhaps sharing Dr. Gregory's concern that "a too early application to different branches of education" inhibits a child's development, Patsy did not teach Anne to read until she was eight.[99] In January 1801, even amid severe morning sickness in her sixth pregnancy in eleven years and while nursing her youngest child, Cornelia, Patsy continued to devote as much time as she could to rearing her three older children, Anne, Jeff, and Ellen. She worried that Anne and Jeff were only average students and were "uncommonly backward in everything, much more so than were many others who have not had half the pains taken with them." Four-year-old Ellen, however, was "wonderfully apt." Patsy had high hopes for her, but worried to her father that "the two others excite serious anxiety with regard to their intellect." Still, to Patsy, teaching her children was heartwarming, cementing her emotional bond with them. In fact, she commented, "Duties incompatible with it have surplanted all other enjoyments in my breast—the education of my Children to which I have long devoted every moment that I could command."[100]

In early 1802, Jefferson again asked his daughters to visit him at the White House. By May, Patsy planned a long overdue stay in Washington. However, an outbreak of virulent measles near Charlottesville delayed the journey. Heeding her father's medical advice, Patsy unsuccessfully "courted rather than avoided the infection" in hopes that her children would contract the disease and thereby acquire immunity.[101] Finally, on November 17, 1802, the sisters traveled to Washington, accompanied by Jeff and Ellen. The hard journey over rough, dirt roads took five long days, though Jefferson typically made the carriage trip in three. "The president paid for the trip," notes one writer, "and also for wigs and other dresses that Dolley Madison ordered from Philadelphia milliners so his daughters would have the latest attire 'universally worn' by ladies in society."[102]

During Jefferson's time as president, he and Patsy exchanged many letters dotted with family news—the children's mumps, the replastering of walls at Edgehill, visiting family, and the progress of construction at Monticello.[103] Patsy also shared Jefferson's letters with her children, who reported back to their beloved grandpapa. Jefferson encouraged Jeff and Ellen to be his writing companions. As the grandchildren matured, Jefferson's influence in their lives grew. Over the years, they embraced him as their male role model, mentor, and steadfast protector. In fact, he involved himself in almost every detail of his own daughters' lives, acting as both father and mother. Patsy's devotion to her children drew praise from Jefferson. Her relationship with her father evoked not only love but complete respect—their bond had never been closer than at this time. "Never have I known of a union between any two beings so perfect as that which almost identified this father and daughter," one observer wrote.[104]

One of the few bright spots and source of pride resulting from Patsy's marriage was her oldest son, Jeff, who after a stunted academic sojourn, turned out to be a skilled businessman and plantation manager. Indeed, Jeff's work ethic, aptitude, and growing physical abilities convinced Patsy that Jeff had evolved into the reliable man her husband would never become. Over the next few years, with her avid persuasion, Jefferson turned to Jeff, trusting him with the crucial supervision of all of his vast estates, including his cherished Monticello. But Jeff had earned his grandfather's exacting respect, a respect that Tom Randolph could never achieve.

Tom's resentment and acrimony toward his own son turned violent on several occasions. Sometime before 1822, Monticello overseer Edmund Bacon recalled seeing Tom beat Jeff with a cane ("caning"), a battery intended to inflict not only severe injury but humiliation. Out of filial respect and privacy, Jeff later denied the story, but described his father's volatile temper as "more ferocious than a woulf and more fell than a hyena when enraged."[105]

By the end of her marriage, Patsy's husband was a father in name only and had become penniless and estranged from the family. Her daughter described Patsy in these years: "My mother's life from the earliest moment of my recollection was one of painful economy and self-denying frugality. She had none of the luxuries, few of the gratifications which her birth, early life & habits . . . certainly entitled her to."[106] "[Patsy's] poverty was scandalous," one author bluntly concluded. "She became something of a southern martyr."[107]

Perhaps the courtship of Patsy's daughter Virginia offers the most insight into Patsy's family dynamics. When Nicholas Trist wanted to marry Virginia, he wrote to Patsy, not to Tom, to obtain permission: "Hoping that my sentiments may be agreeable to yourself and Mr. Randolph, I address you these lines to request the permission of making them known to miss Virginia."[108] "[Patsy] responded without giving any indication that she had consulted her husband. She gently but firmly declined the offer because, she said, 'You are both too young to be entangled by an engagement which will decide the happiness, or wretchedness of your lives.'"[109]

Patsy's noble influence on her oldest children, Jeff and Ellen in particular, was indelible and remarkable. Even though her later life turned into one of loss, hardship, and financial suffering, the three brightest prospects in her life remained constant: her father, and her two older children, Jeff and Ellen. Patsy imparted to both of these children an enduring work ethic that would sustain them for life, fueled by an abiding love and devotion to family. Her guiding influence helped Jeff achieve a modicum of education, but more importantly, sealed Jeff's future role as patriarch of the family. Patsy molded Jeff into a man like her own father: diligent, ethical, with unfailing loyalty to his family. Jeff not only took care of his mother and his siblings both emotionally and financially, but he provided Patsy with emotional support from a miserable and odd husband. The bond between mother and son grew so strong that not even an unhinged father could break it. And Patsy taught Ellen to be independent, not to indulge in excesses, and to become a self-reliant woman of means and respect. Both children adored their mother and grandfather. Jeff rightly called them his "earthly Trinity," along with his beloved wife, Jane.[110]

From the beginning of Jeff's young life, Patsy looked to her son to be the godsend—the savior—for Thomas Jefferson's family.

2

SINS OF THE FATHER

I am so much afraid of his strange temper.

—**Ellen Coolidge, describing her father**

Thomas Jefferson took great pleasure in his family, yet certain family members were also sources of anxiety. His son-in-law "Thomas Mann Randolph, Jr.,[1] was in chronic financial trouble, appears to have drunk too much, and is said to have been jealous of Jefferson's centrality in the life of the family. He served three terms as Governor of Virginia, but as he grew older Randolph never really found peace."[2]

In the beginning, Thomas Randolph was an impressive figure in person.[3] He was described as darkly handsome and tall, complementing his future wife's own height, inherited from her six-foot-two father, Thomas Jefferson.[4] Physically imposing, Tom was "lean, and swarthy, an excellent athlete and horseman."[5] The only known portrait of him shows a plainly dressed, good-looking young man who nonetheless exudes a look of profound bitterness.

Oral family history held that the Randolphs of Tuckahoe descended from the famed native American Pocahontas. "In Jefferson's papers, there is a 'Genealogy of Pocahontas' compiled by Randolph, starting with Pocahontas and John Rolfe, and descending to the Randolphs, who were supposedly one-thirty-second Indian."[6] The well-educated, aristocratic, studious Randolph was twice elected to the United States House of Representatives, and served in the Virginia House of delegates. In reality, however, Tom Randolph ended up a massive disappointment, personally and professionally. He dissolved into one of the most erratic, abusive, and depressive figures in the Jefferson family, as well as a destructive father figure to his children, especially his son Jeff. The two men became estranged from each other early in life. Tom harbored simmering jealousy and resentment toward Jeff for most of his adult life.[7]

It is ironic that Randolph ended up with a failed career and marriage, because he was born into one of the largest and most influential families in Virginia. He had an outstanding education by tutors at the University of Edinburgh, and he inherited substantial money and property. Tom showed signs of courage in the War of 1812, and ultimately married Thomas Jefferson's oldest daughter, as we have seen. Yet, early on, Tom suffered from severe depression, perhaps bipolar disorder, aggravated by uncontrollable anger that spiraled into negligence as manager of his ruined finances and property. He bitterly complained to Jefferson of his perceived family affronts, hinting at suicide: "I could flee to the grave with determined mind, to escape from such hateful sophistry and such unprincipled conduct and opinion as I have been compelled so long to witness and to hear."[8]

Tom Randolph died practically a pauper. Both his political and military careers were barren of achievements, as was his personal life. He lived out his last years as a bankrupt, bitter old man, estranged from his wife, Thomas Jefferson, and the extended Randolph family.[9] Perhaps it was Tom's tragedy that he lived his life in the monumental shadow of his famous father-in-law. No doubt, he had become intimidated by Jefferson's superior acumen and outshone by his son's character and industry. Tom strived to please Jefferson but rarely succeeded, coming to blame his self-inflicted failures on Patsy and Jeff. His strange behavior—such as riding to Washington to challenge Henry Clay to a duel over a perceived insult—seemed a result of a deep inferiority complex, leading to a broken life.[10]

As his marriage to Patsy deteriorated, Randolph's chronic black moods and verbal abuse finally forced her to tell him she would no longer share a bedroom with him. Although their daughter Ellen recounted no specific instance of physical violence to her mother, Randolph subjected Patsy to constant verbal abuse for heeding her father's counsel over his.

Jeff and his father had never been close, and as grown men they had little in common. Randolph, despite his alleged knowledge of agronomy and farming techniques, flopped both as a plantation owner and a farmer. By contrast, Jeff, a strapping six-foot-four man, was hardworking, a good manager, and laser focused on supporting his growing family and his grandfather. Jeff's solid competence made him a natural choice to manage Jefferson's estates and, later, his father's. While Randolph had been Jefferson's political protégé early in his political career, Jeff now became Jefferson's financial advisor. Keenly self-conscious about his perceived lack of higher education, Jeff later blamed his father's neglect and insolvency for his lack of formal study and exposure to the fine arts. Years later, Jeff remembered his father as distant and "prodigal," a vast understatement of the stark reality.[11]

Perhaps Randolph's bizarre and erratic relationship with his son and wife can be explained by his own acrimonious relationship with his father. This may clarify why he could not have an emotionally close relationship with anyone.

Born at Tuckahoe plantation on the James River on October 1, 1768, Thomas Mann Randolph Jr. was the son of Thomas Mann Randolph Sr. and his wife, Anne Cary Randolph. Little Tom was christened less than a month later by the rector of St. James North Parish and named after his father. By birth and breeding, Thomas Jr. was a member of one of Virginia's most prestigious and influential families.[12]

Like most marriages in the eighteenth century, the marriage between Thomas Jr.'s parents would be a fruitful one. Over twenty-five years, his mother bore thirteen children, ten of whom grew to maturity. Besides his first son and namesake, there were seven other daughters.[13]

The senior Randolph gave able attention to his sons' formal education. Although he had received no formal education himself, he wanted both his sons—Randolph, then sixteen, and his younger brother, William, fourteen—to have the advantage of college he did not have. Both young men had learned all that the family tutor had to impart, prompting their father to send them, not to the nearby College of William and Mary, but to the more prestigious University of Edinburgh in Scotland. This university provided a classical education and had already produced several prominent Virginians, including three signatories of the Declaration of Independence—Benjamin Rush, John Witherspoon, and James Wilson.[14] To finance the boys' education at Edinburgh, the Randolphs mortgaged their Varina plantation.[15] Late in June 1784, Tom and William, accompanied by their tutor and Archie Randolph, their fifteen-year-old cousin, traveled to Richmond and boarded a ship, the *Marlborough*, for the seventeen-day voyage to London.[16]

As a longtime family friend of his father, Thomas Jefferson had corresponded frequently with the young Tom Randolph, encouraging his studies abroad. He repeated his previous advice to Tom to complete his education in Europe. Jefferson further advised the young man to remain in France for at least two years to learn foreign languages and study the classic philosophers in history and politics—Locke, Montesquieu, and Rousseau. Later, according to Jefferson's advice, Tom should visit various provinces in France, where he could "acquire the habit of speaking French," become familiar with the "fine arts," and form "an acquaintance with the individuals and character of a nation."[17] In the spring of 1787, Tom assured Jefferson he would show "gratitude" for his advice by "implicitly following it" while at Edinburgh.[18] Trying to strike a balance between his father's and Jefferson's competing advice, the young student predicted, "As my Father is very impatient for my return, I shall probably spend this winter in Paris, and set out the next summer."[19] This concerned Jefferson. He "ventured to propose . . . another plan" to Tom's father, involving a two-year educational sabbatical in Italy for the prodigal son. The "plan," which included estimated costs and a specific itinerary, encouraged Tom's initial career choice of "Politics as [his] principal pursuit."[20]

After several months in Scotland, an unforeseen obstacle to Jefferson's plan for young Tom cropped up—Tom's own father's insistence that he immediately return to Virginia. Due to poor grades and wasteful spending, William had received a stern letter from his father ordering him home. Randolph Sr. had grown frustrated with William's pitiable academic performance and mounting debt, insisting that his son had squandered a golden opportunity. Homesick and perhaps bored, Tom wanted to go home to Virginia as well.[21]

Despite acknowledging his "good fortune" and "honor" in having Mr. Jefferson "superintend" his education, Randolph left Scotland for Virginia in the summer of 1788, failing to complete his studies or to travel to France or Italy. He told his beloved mother that he had requested from his father "permission to return home next spring."[22] By the end of June, Thomas Randolph had abruptly left his lodgings at St. Patrick's Square in Edinburgh for a Glasco lodging house. He awaited a ship to the United States, then returned to Virginia, having completely abandoned Jefferson's carefully planned educational blueprint.

This would not be the last time that Tom would fail to finish what he had begun.

Soon after his arrival back home, his mother suddenly died at age forty-four. Randolph left no record of his feelings; however, he had felt close enough to her to confide his reasons for leaving Scotland, so no doubt, he faced a deep emotional loss at her untimely death. His profound grief resulted in moodiness and a restless feeling, leading to constant arguments with his father. Under Thomas Sr.'s severe scrutiny, Tom left Tuckahoe for New York, preparing for a political career. There, he lived with Jefferson's nephew, Peter Carr, who described Tom as "extremely intelligent and cleaver [sic]."[23] When Tom returned home in the fall, his volatile relationship with his father prompted further fiery disagreements, and he soon departed again to a relative's plantation in Goochland County, Virginia.[24]

Fortuitously, at about the same time, Thomas Jefferson had just returned to Virginia with his daughter Patsy after five enjoyable but long years as minister to France. Sometime during December 1789 young Tom visited Jefferson at Monticello. While he consulted with Jefferson about his future plans and possible political interests, Patsy captured his eye. The deep attraction flowered into love, although it was the first time they had seen each other since they were children. Tom was smitten with Patsy from the start, and would soon ask her to marry him, unaware that his future wife's "happiness" was "compleat" [sic] only in her father's company.[25]

The rapidity of Patsy and Tom's romantic relationship is striking. Jefferson landed at Norfolk on November 23, 1789, reaching Monticello on December 23. By January 1790, Tom had asked for and secured Patsy's hand in marriage before even informing his own parents. The couple were engaged swiftly, and they were married on February 23, 1790, with fewer than three months of courtship.[26] As Patsy stood in her father's parlor that winter day to marry Thomas Mann Randolph, Jefferson beamed, pleased with her choice. Randolph was the son of his former schoolmate, Thomas Mann Randolph Sr., a man Jefferson thought of as a brother. As the eldest son, he would inherit the Tuckahoe estate, where Jefferson had spent much of his youth and where Patsy would one day be mistress.[27]

The summer before Patsy's wedding, Tom's father, almost fifty now, had surprisingly announced his decision to marry for the second time. His intended bride was a much younger woman, Gabriella Harvie, still in her teens and a granddaughter of John Harvie, who had served as Jefferson's guardian.[28] She and Randolph Sr. also planned for children. Randolph Sr. decided to sell six hundred of Edgehill's acres to Gabriella's father, saving the rest for his future children with Gabriella. In essence, this would prevent Tom's inheritance of the property.[29] Early family tensions and jealousies were soon apparent. Both Tom and Patsy expressed deep resentment about Randolph's impending marriage to a teenage bride in correspondence to Jefferson.

"Col. Randolph's marriage was to be expected," Jefferson gently reminded Patsy. "All his amusements depending on society, he can not live alone."[30] He expressed his hope that the forthcoming match would not "be the cause of any diminution of affection" between Randolph Sr., Tom, and her. "If the lady has anything difficult in her disposition, avoid what is rough, and attach her good qualities to you," he advised Patsy with regard to Miss Harvie. "None of us, no, not one, is perfect; and were we to love none who had imperfections, this world would be a desert for our love . . . Be you, my dear, the link of love, union, and peace for the whole family."[31] Aware of her husband's mood swings and temperament, Jefferson appealed to Patsy as the peacemaker.[32]

From the beginning of the marriage, Randolph tried to defer to his father-in-law, acknowledging Jefferson's wise and worldly experience. Jefferson, in turn, encouraged Tom and set goals for his future son-in-law, predicting that he would perform many future "commissions." Unfortunately, Tom became caught between a distant father focused on his new wife, and a famous father-in-law determined to keep the "bosom of family" at his cherished epicenter, Monticello.[33] Over time, Tom's sullen temperament and growing mental issues would result in frequent clashes with many family members, including his own son, and with Jefferson himself.

"The more fragile the vessel, the greater the ballast of conceit needed to steady it," noted one writer, "and Thomas Mann Randolph's pride now involved him in a number of difficulties."[34] On one occasion, Randolph engaged in harsh and heated words with his cousin John Randolph, nearly prompting a duel. Tom had made a speech in the Virginia legislature declaring that John was "bankrupt forever as a popular statesman," then stalked out of the House chamber.[35] Outraged by the address, John immediately sent a message to his cousin that he expected an apology or a duel. In turn, Tom secured the services of Isaac A. Coles, the president's secretary, and the stage was set for a fatal duel.[36] Intermediaries, however, persuaded Tom that he should "withdraw his words with honor." Tom returned to the floor and speaking in a voice so low as to be almost inaudible, apologized for his "very severe and harsh language."[37]

Tom argued next with Jefferson's other son-in-law, Jack Eppes, a widower and congressman.

Eppes was a man of "fine temper and manners" and became a trusted and valued son-in-law to Jefferson.[38] When Eppes had asked Jefferson's younger daughter, Polly, to marry him, Jefferson said, "She could not have been more so to my wishes, if I had had the whole earth free to have chosen a partner for her."[39] He told Polly that Eppes possessed "every quality necessary to make you happy and to make us all happy."[40] The couple had married at Monticello's parlor, amid the debris of the brickmasons. Jefferson wrote of the union, "[It] has composed for us such a group of good sense, good humor, liberality, and prudent care of our affairs . . . It promises us long years of domestic concord and love."[41] Seeing that his dream of family harmony was finally coming to fruition, Jefferson wrote to Patsy, "I now see our fireside formed into a group, no one member of which has a fibre in their composition which can ever produce any jarring or jealousies among us. No irregular passions, no dangerous bias, which may render problematical."[42] Thomas Randolph, of course, was the exception.

Polly, nineteen when she married, was a beautiful young woman by all reports. Ex-slave Isaac described her as a "pritty lady jist like her mother."[43] Jack Eppes was twenty-five, and Isaac described him as "a handsome man but had a harelip," which may have indicated a cleft palette, yet there is no other mention of this in other letters.[44] But the couple's happiness soon faded when their firstborn infant suddenly died in 1800. Jefferson wrote immediately to Polly, telling her he had no words that would ease her pain, nor would he "attempt consolation" where he knew "time and silence [were] the only medicines."[45] But the sadness of losing a young child moved Jefferson so profoundly that he could not "find expressions for [his] love."[46]

Polly gave birth again, in 1804, to a baby girl. Although the baby was healthy, Polly fell critically ill with fever and died months later at age twenty-nine. Eppes was heartbroken, as was Polly's beloved father, Thomas Jefferson.[47] Interestingly, although Tom Randolph gave no sign that he was affected by Polly's tragic death, Patsy was severely shaken. Distraught, she became ill that spring with cramps, which her husband diagnosed as "hysterics."[48] From then on, the grieving Jefferson clung more tightly to his surviving daughter Patsy, even as the ties between Monticello and Edgehill were drawn closer than ever.[49]

Both Eppes and Tom lived temporarily with Jefferson in the "President's house," but after the argument with Eppes, Tom moved out. He told Jefferson that he was sure the president loved him less than he did the "jollier" son-in-law. Jefferson tried to soothe Tom's bruised ego. "I had for some days," he said, "perceived in you a gloom which gave me uneasiness. I knew there was a difference between Mr. Eppes and yourself, but had no idea it was as deep seated as your letter shews it to be."[50]

He assured Randolph that his "affections" for both him and Eppes "were warm." "What acts of mine can have induced you to suppose that I felt or manifested a preference for him, I cannot conceive."[51] Randolph must have been touched by the letter, because when his friend William Burwell visited him, he found Tom "inspired" when he spoke of Jefferson.[52]

The father-son relationship between Tom and Jeff, however, would remain tumultuous from beginning to end. He held his father responsible for neglecting him and his formal education, describing Tom's disregard for him as a period of "approbation."[53] Jeff recalled that he had often walked barefoot in the snow and ice to school, that he had been accustomed to sleeping in a "'closet' with only a blanket for his bed," and that he had been reared on the plainest food.[54]

In early 1800, a year after their marriage, Tom finally moved Patsy and his family to Edgehill, a working plantation two miles from Monticello, which became their permanent home. The house paled in comparison to the eleven-thousand-square-foot mansion of Monticello. An ad in the *Richmond Enquirer* described Edgehill as a small, frame-covered structure of brick situated "in the healthiest climate of the whole earth, sheltered by the mountains from the westerly winds of winters, and enjoying the cool breezes invariably descending from wooded crests on summer nights." The estate would turn out to be Thomas Mann Randolph's most significant and valuable asset for most of his life.[55]

A daughter, Ellen Wayles, had been born to Patsy and Tom in 1796; another, Cornelia, in 1799. Soon, their family would increase further. Another daughter, Virginia, was born in 1801. Their new home must have felt small for so large a family. Upon first moving in, they had found themselves "in the midst of mud, smoke, and the uncomfortableness of a cold house."[56] However, they soon made the place "livable and comfortable."[57] Even so, at Patsy's suggestion, perhaps insistence, they spent their summers at Monticello with her father. When the president departed for "Washington City," however, Tom demanded they "reside on his own farm."[58]

Tom had a brief period of political success following his election as governor of Virginia in 1819. His mental issues, bad temper, and excessive drinking were hidden so well that he had won consecutive terms by the smallest of margins in 1820 and 1821. But his final term ended in abject failure and ridicule. Instead of providing for his family during his governorship, he wasted money on his siblings and nefarious acquaintances.[59] His daughter Ellen explained that her father "could not say no to importunate pleaders, to distressed gentlemen relatives or neighbors, or old school fellows. He was always crippled by debts not of his own contracting, and lived a life of painful frugality and self-denial only to enable others to keep above water for a short time their foolish heads."[60]

Patsy soon complained that Tom was such a negligent parent that she "had to act in the double capacity of nurse to [her] children and comforter to their father" when Ellen, Cornelia, and Virginia all suffered from whooping cough.[61]

When Tom was forced to publicly retract his more strident and heated political rhetoric as governor, his professional reputation became permanently sullied. By the end of his third term, he was infamous for heated and very public arguments with political foes. Friends and family alike expressed embarrassment at his unpredictable behavior. One colleague, David Campbell, publicly criticized his boorishness. "We view the state as degraded in his conduct." Even the lieutenant governor inferred that Tom was often drunk in public meetings and an alcoholic.[62] Steadfast in public, Patsy put the best light on her husband's wretched conduct, though admitting that he had shown an embarrassing "warmth in the dispute."[63]

Jefferson, it seemed, chose to disregard the more extreme language Randolph had used during his terms as governor,[64] advising his son-in-law to exchange "official troubles and jealousies for family love, peace and comfort."[65] When Randolph ran for and won the governorship a second time, Patsy remained at Monticello, safe and secure with father and family. In Richmond, from various informed reports, Patsy learned that Tom spent many hours intoxicated. When he finally retired from politics, his "spirit descended into cinders."[66]

After Tom's political career disintegrated, Jeff assumed the management of his father's finances. He tried to pay down his father's growing debts, selling the estates at Edgehill and Varina. Broken, in despair and drinking heavily, Tom was a shell of his former self, that young horseman who had captured Patsy's heart. Sadly, Tom had descended into a moody, "bashful[,] timid man" whose eyes blinked hard in the daylight.[67]

Mental and physical disorders troubled Tom during these years. After numerous visits to doctors, with no diagnosis or cure, he turned to natural spring water spas as a potential remedy. After a week or two, he would seem to recover a modicum of health, but could not pursue vigorous physical activity, such as horseback riding or farming. Jefferson begged Tom, ever more distant, isolated, and estranged, to return to the comforts of his family at Monticello for his own well-being. "Restore yourself to the bosom of your family and friends," he wrote, adding:

> They will cherish your happiness as warmly as they ever did, and more so perhaps, as more needing the soothing balm of their affections, with your varied education and resources of books, you can never want employment of mind, and some excitement to bodily exercise may perhaps be found in experiments of

agriculture . . . Relieve the grief of the family with which your absence afflicts them and resume the place in society which is still yours.[68]

Books, farming, and politics piqued Tom's waning interest, as they did Jefferson's own interest, but his depression foreclosed a successful pursuit of any of these endeavors.[69] Finally, after his failed governorship, Tom decided to run for a seat in the Virginia legislature. Jefferson promoted his candidacy, but Tom barely campaigned and lost badly. Jefferson was supremely disappointed by Tom's feeble campaign performance. However, through Jefferson's connections, Randolph secured an appointed seat in Congress, but even there, he was miserable and depressed. His fiery temperament was incompatible with legislating, where compromise was necessary. Where a certain lightness of touch and flexibility were essential, Tom's obstinacy doomed him to failure as a politician. Living temporarily with Jefferson at the White House, Randolph had no inclination for political amity, drowning deeper in depression from his thin-skinned sensitivity to perceived insults and slights.[70]

Randolph's behavior toward Jefferson, according to one account, "vacillated between fawning acceptance of his subordination to ambivalent participation in the family circle and, by the early 1800s, to vaguely masked resistance."[71] Jefferson's approach "was to proffer unequivocal, detailed and sometimes conflicting support and advice . . . and convey veiled censure when it was not done to his liking."[72] One scholar contends that "the subtext of letters during this early period suggested the emotional tensions of divided loyalties Tom already was experiencing and would continue to do so when he attempted to breach the Jefferson family circle."[73] While remaining publicly loyal to Tom within the family, Patsy could not conceal her profound disdain for her husband. She sought solace with her father, telling others that Jefferson's well-being was always "the first and most important object" for her.[74]

Undoubtedly, Tom knew where Patsy's true affections lay.[75]

In the summer of 1804, Tom became involved in another public dispute in the streets of Milton with an English workman known as "Hope."[76] An argument commenced when the workman called Tom a liar "in such round terms" that the latter "flew into a rage," threatening to "pound his skull for him."[77] As the story goes, the workman apologized and the two proceeded inside a tavern to resume their conversation. Once inside, the argument began anew. Knowing that "Hope was not one of those who fight duels," Tom "dared him to come out into the street and fight with his fists." The workman declined, after which, according to Tom, Hope "adopted the usual defense of cowards, the fabrication of malignant lies."[78]

About this same time, Tom assumed some political opponents had libeled him to Thomas Jefferson as a "Federalist," and that Jefferson was ignoring him as a result. So, Tom "let himself be overwhelmed by melancholy, and, without saying a word to anyone, left the President's mansion in mid-February, moving to Frost's and Quinn's boardinghouse at the other end of Pennsylvania Avenue. There he remained, ignoring all of Jefferson's entreaties to return and disregarding his assurances of affection and esteem."[79]

Frost's and Quinn's was a quiet establishment that limited its guests' liquor. While there, Tom became acquainted with one guest, Senator William Plumer, a moderate Federalist from New Hampshire. Plumer found Tom "a pleasant agreeable companion" and "a man of study much devoted to books."[80] However, he was shocked when he noticed that Randolph displayed a pair of pistols and a sword over his mantel.

During his stay at the boardinghouse, Randolph became so sick with a fever that some family members believed he was near death. Concerned, Jefferson suggested he move back to the White House, where he could supervise his medical recovery. Stubbornly, Randolph chose to remain at the boardinghouse. He eventually recovered, but with lingering, severe pain. As soon as he could travel, he returned to Albemarle County and swiftly secluded himself, deciding against reelection.[81]

With an estranged father, for all intents and purposes, Grandpapa Jefferson became the surrogate father to Jeff and his siblings. Patsy took over the household management duties, while Jeff replaced his father as the day-to-day overseer of the various plantations. Tom then continued to spiral into cheerless delusion, seeing himself as an outsider, a "silly bird . . . in the company of Swans" within the "narrow circle of family."[82] He lamented to Patsy that he was "so essentially and widely different from all within it, as to look like something extraneous, fallen in by accident and destroying the homogeneity."[83] Eventually, he totally severed himself from the family and lived an isolated life at the foot of Monticello Mountain.

Still, Tom continued to respect and pay homage to Jefferson. "The sentiment of my mind when it contemplates yourself alone," he declared, "is one of the most lofty elevation and most unmixed delight."[84] He told Jefferson that his heart overflowed with "gratitude and affection when I attempt to estimate the value to the whole human race of the incredibly, inconceivably excellent political system which you created, developed, and, at last I think, permanently established."[85] Nowhere in Randolph's emotional missive did he refer to Patsy or Jeff—a revealing dynamic fracture within his own family.

Randolph continued to visit Monticello when Jefferson was there, but he was not comfortable, having ostracized himself. Apparently, explained one historian, "Jefferson's brilliance crippled his son-in-law, who never could rise above his conviction of his own inadequacy."[86] Tom became so sullen at one point that he refused to speak to Jefferson and Patsy or engage in minimal dinner conversation.[87] To add to his growing despair, due to crushing debt, Randolph was forced to sell his Henrico plantation. Bitter and delusional, he turned his anger against Jeff, imagining that his own son had cheated him out of his property and protesting to the trustees that Jeff was motivated only by "cold-blooded avarice."[88] Then, Tom almost lost another plantation, Varina, by defaulting on the mortgage payments. He was forced to borrow money from George Jefferson, a Richmond cousin, but it was not nearly enough to pay the demanding creditors. Tom turned to Jefferson for a more substantial loan. Jefferson gladly lent him the money, exchanging Randolph's tobacco crop as collateral, unconcerned about his own economic plight. Wisely, Jefferson reimbursed himself later from its sale. Seemingly deeply grateful to Jefferson, Randolph declared that he had learned his lesson.

He had not.[89]

Over the years, Jefferson tried to repair the rift between Tom and his son. Tom would have none of it. He had declared war against Jeff and was unwilling to reconcile, believing that Jeff had been deceitful in selling his plantations. Tom raged to his family, "My ruin is inevitable, but I am the victim of the avarice of one, encouraged by the vengeance of many."[90] Cut off from his family, Tom spent his final lonely days at North Mountain, only coming to Monticello in secret. When he visited, under cover of darkness, he spoke only to Patsy.

One observer feared that Tom would be "turned out to round the world, house less and penniless" and would "rave as wildly as clear."[91] Cousin John Randolph said of "poor TMR I heartily pity him. He has no more self-command than a child."[92]

Jefferson tried again to assuage Randolph's volcanic anger, urging him to "return and become a member of the family 'in spirit as well as in body,'" not "to continue in solitude over misfortunes and encouraging the ravages of mind and body."[93] Randolph rejected the advice and continued his self-destructive spiral, deluding himself that he had been the victim of a family conspiracy that Jeff had concocted "with great rancor as well as the upmost rigor." He found it impossible to "suppress feelings" of betrayal. Tom was not merely angry but suffered from "nervousness" that led to repeated mental breakdowns. Throughout his marriage, this "mysterious" illness had led him to travel for medical treatment. He took a long trip by himself to New York and Boston for medical help, to no avail. In the summer of 1795, he decided to visit hot springs resorts in western Virginia, which seemed to help temporarily.[94]

During these last months, Randolph expelled himself from the family, and they respected his privacy. His daughters Virginia and Mary paid a brief visit every morning to monitor his well-being. His health failed rapidly. He constantly complained of excruciating pain in his stomach and became emaciated, "thinner and more feeble" than anyone had ever seen him.[95] Weak, lonely, and fearing his end was near, Tom admitted to Jefferson that he was "inspired with shame for having left" but that he had "the same love and respect" for Jefferson that he had always had.[96] His mental despair had simply overwhelmed him, and he was "indifferent to live."[97] Jefferson tried to calm him one last time. "I have been guilty of an error for which I take just blame to myself," he explained, "really loving you as I would a son (for I protest I know no difference). I took it too much for granted you were as sensible of it as myself."[98] Jefferson urged him to return to the president's house, but to no avail.

"As my father advanced in life," Ellen recalled, "and his pecuniary difficulties increased, he became more morose, more irritable, more suspicious. My own belief is that nothing but the mingled dignity, forbearance and kindness of my grandfather prevented some outbreak which might forever have alienated two men bound by the strongest ties."[99] Family matters seemed to inflame Tom Randolph's already unbalanced brain. On one occasion, while in Washington, Ellen criticized her father's financial mismanagement when he failed to send her some money he had promised: "I very much wish Papa could be prevailed on to make some little exertion to relieve me."[100] Ellen considered writing a scolding letter to him but confessed to her mother, "I am so much afraid of his strange temper."[101] In fact, Tom had now decayed into frequent "paroxysms of rage" in front of the family. Ellen remembered that "while he treated his daughters with affection he was unjust and ungenerous to his sons, particularly his eldest, Jefferson's namesake, whom Randolph often tried to cane even after the son had become an adult."[102] Thomas Jefferson "adopted the wise plan of seeming ignorance," Ellen explained, "and his unalterable calm, affectionate politeness made it entirely impossible to begin an unpleasant discussion. The angry spirit was subdued . . . Thus my mother was spared the heaviest of misfortunes, a positive disunion between her father and her husband."[103]

After Jefferson's death, Patsy returned from visiting Ellen, who had moved to Boston in early May 1828. Patsy's children dreaded the thought that she would restore their father as patriarch of the family now that Jefferson was dead and gone. Wisely, Patsy declined. Although her final reconciliation with Tom on his deathbed appeared genuine, it was marred by the reality of her impending financial ruin. Despite Jeff's herculean efforts to pay his grandfather's debts, by the spring of 1828 it was inevitable that Monticello would have to be sold. Thomas Mann Randolph faced the prospect that he would have to leave and "go off begging . . . but he was spared that last humiliation."[104] In a denouement to her relationship with her father, in an 1856 letter to biographer Henry Randall, Ellen discussed Tom's "poor . . . weaknesses" (though also professing, "I loved him much"):

If I speak at all I must speak the truth, and under the circumstances, can I refuse to speak? Would not my silence lead to wrong conclusions? You are preparatory to giving to the world, your *Life of Jefferson*, inquiring, as you are bound to do, most minutely and particularly, into all the details of his private life, and in order to understand him, you must understand those by whom he was surrounded.[105]

A few months later, Ellen declared, "I have been very frank, my dear Mr. Randall, in communicating to you family secrets, whenever they were of a nature to throw light upon character, leaving it to your discretion so to dispose of them that while they were of service of Jefferson himself."[106]

Ever the dutiful wife, Patsy was determined "never to abandon [Tom] to poverty, nor as long as my situation can be endured to propose a separation. In that, however, I must be determined by circumstance."[107] In his last days, Randolph had begged his family to forgive him for his abject neglect and unbalanced temperament. He especially sought Jeff's forgiveness at the very end and "bestowed the most fervent blessing" on him.[108]

On June 28, 1828, in his sixtieth year, Thomas Mann Randolph "died in peace and love with all his family and all friends and neighbors."[109]

Tom was buried in the Monticello family cemetery, at the feet of Thomas Jefferson. A few yards away, near her father's headstone, Patsy would be buried eight years later. The inscription on Tom's tombstone bears only his name and the dates of his birth, marriage, and death. The sparse obituary that editor Thomas Ritchie printed in the *Richmond Inquirer* might have served as a fitting epitaph:

> He enjoyed every advantage which education could confer . . . Danger and fear seem to be words unknown in his vocabulary. And had he possessed less irritability of temper and a larger acquaintance with the volume of men and things, he would've stood foremost.[110]

Apparently, out of a sense of filial duty, Jeff drafted an obituary notice. It summed up his father's desolate life:

> A man of science & genius . . . his defects, those of strong excitement . . . He died at peace with the world, after seeking the forgiveness of all within his call, in particular of his son, to whose rigid integrity, in the presence of friends summoned by himself, he did ample justice; and on whom he bestowed, with the most unqualified expression of esteem, the most fervent blessing.[111]

Upon Tom's death, Jeff became the official head of the sprawling Monticello-Edgehill family. At thirty-five, strong, pragmatic, and dutiful, Jeff Randolph had already been responsible for the family's finances for a decade. When he first became aware of both his father's and his grandfather's enormous debts, Jeff was determined to pay them "to the last copper," as he would write in his memoirs. Feeling morally obligated to protect Thomas Jefferson's legacy, he made sure "that a character like [Jefferson's] should not be tainted with having failed to comply with his obligations."[112]

***

One final story, perhaps, epitomizes Thomas Mann Randolph's ruined life. When he was deep in debt and needed money, he asked Monticello overseer Edmund Bacon to lend him $150. As collateral, Tom offered one of the slave children at Edgehill, a little girl named Edy. When Bacon balked, Tom begged the overseer to "prevail upon your mother" to sanction the loan. In May, Tom sold that slave child for $200.[113]

Jeff had long ago turned away from his venal father and toward Thomas Jefferson for solace and moral guidance. Sadly, Thomas Mann Randolph became conscious of the gap that separated these two men. In the end, he experienced ruin and failure in nearly everything he attempted. His last years, isolated in a cramped outbuilding on the outer grounds of Monticello, were a time of bitterness, debt, depression, and the total eclipse of his reputation. For all of his promising talents, Randolph achieved nothing of significance as a politician, farmer, husband or father. His legacy? A life of loneliness and tragedy.[114]

3
JEFFERSON RANDOLPH: LIFE AT MONTICELLO

Upon the twilight of Thomas Jefferson's life a bright glow was cast by his young grandchildren.

—Barbara Mayo, "Twilight at Monticello"

Today, Thomas Jefferson's graceful mountain estate, Monticello, is "a fascinating museum, a shrine to Jefferson's memory."[1] Indeed, it is similar to "the Jefferson image in the American mind"—cerebral, calm, and elegant. "There can never be another Monticello," observed one author, "a building that is ancient and modern, regular and irregular, classical and romantic, formal and informal, efficient and impractical."[2] Yet, "one misses the snorting horses that Jefferson loved, the smell of manure, the clinking of wine glasses, the shouting of children. There are no jealous adoring women, no drunken or surly relatives, no signs of madness or violence."[3]

This was the Monticello of Jeff's and Ellen Randolph's childhoods. In his advancing years, Jefferson once told his daughter Patsy that soon he must bid "a long, long goodnight." And night would soon fall on Monticello too. Yet for a few fleeting years, "under the Persian willows on the lawn, the shrill voices of little boys, the quick footsteps and laughter of young girls in short-waisted, ankle-length dresses, gave warmth and color to the mountaintop."[4] Surrounded by these children of Patsy and Thomas Mann Randolph, the master of Monticello felt like a patriarch of old. There were four young ladies, Ellen, Cornelia, Virginia, and Mary; a little sister, Septimia; and four small brothers, "boys whose names sound like a roll call of American heroes: James Madison, Benjamin Franklin, Meriwether Lewis, and George Wythe. Ellen most resembled her grandfather—she had the fair Jefferson coloring, even temper, and intellectual tastes."[5]

Patsy's children looked forward to every moment with "Grandpapa" Jefferson, absorbing all the delights of life he had to offer at his vast estate. Jefferson Randolph's 1874 *Memoirs* describes his early years at Monticello, as well as his informal education at the foot of an American icon. Jeff remembered these days with fondness, guided by his grandfather and the house "servants." His *Memoirs* provide intimate details about Jefferson, with little-known anecdotes. For example, Jefferson was passionate about a good "salad oil" being served at his dinner table. To him, the olive was "the richest gift of heaven" and "the most interesting plant in existence."[6] While Jefferson wrote that domestic olive oil was unsatisfactory and imported olive oil too expensive, he explored oil extracted from the sesame seed or benne (*Sesamum orientale*).[7]

Jeff told other tales of when the slaves returned from hunting early in the morning. On some occasions, they roused Jeff for coffee, fried meat, eggs, and honey. Then, as the overseer was just beginning his day and the slaves steeled themselves for their harsh field work, bleary-eyed Jeff would be "toted back to the big house."[8] Jeff recalled, "Having no companion of my own age, I associated entirely with the slaves and formed for them early and strong attachments."[9] There, at Jefferson's knee in the "big house," Jeff learned to read and write. Jefferson saw to his grandson's early instruction at home and later in Philadelphia, where he, reluctantly, sent Jeff at the age of fifteen. Jefferson detailed his hesitancy to send his grandson to the big city: "I am not a friend to placing young men in populous cities, because they acquire there habits and partialities which do not contribute to happiness of their after life."[10] Always the "universal man," as biographer Dumas Malone described him, Jefferson insisted that Jeff's studies include botany, natural history, and anatomy. He also advised Jeff to use copious written notes to certify his memory. He hoped to enable Jeff "to be happier and more useful to [himself], to be beloved by [his] friends, and respected and honored by [his] country."[11] When Jeff asked about changing his studies, his grandfather replied that he and Jeff's father had decided "to leave the matter to [Jeff himself] rather than hazard a decision on [their] imperfect information."[12] This advice was repeated in Jefferson's numerous counseling letters to his nephew, Peter Carr. Jefferson "always pitched his elaborate plans as 'advice' that he hoped, but did not demand, Carr would use."[13] By all accounts, Jeff would eventually become a serious student in Philadelphia. In fact, one of his professors reported that the boy showed signs of becoming "incessantly studious."[14]

When Jefferson returned to Monticello from his presidency in 1809, Jeff Randolph was a strapping nineteen-year-old. At six foot four, he was even taller than Jefferson, who towered over most men. It was at this time that Jeff formed an eternal bond with the former president. Eventually, his grandfather turned over all of his farmland business to the steady, dependable young man, who had a particular claim on Jefferson's affections—as Jefferson had on his. Jefferson could not have wished for a more worthy heir.

Thomas Jefferson's major reconstruction of Monticello and his most influential architectural designs happened while Jeff lived there. Jeff was instrumental in assisting his grandfather in constructing and reconstructing Monticello, overseeing building and materials. Jeff literally saw the magnificent Monticello change before his eyes by his grandfather's constant tinkering, tearing down, then rebuilding. He witnessed Jefferson's love affair with the mansion, Jefferson's "architectural essay." Jefferson had begun to design and build Monticello in 1770, before his marriage to Martha. The home was structured in a strict, neoclassical style with double-storied porticos on opposite sides. The ambitious design was derived from the work of Italian Renaissance architect Andrea Palladio. A French visitor to Monticello remarked, "Mr. Jefferson is the first American who had consulted the fine arts to know how he should shelter himself from the weather."[15]

In 1796, Jefferson expanded Monticello from eight to twenty-one rooms. He retained five first-floor bedrooms but widened the footprint and added a second-floor mezzanine to create four floors, including a cellar. When essentially finished in 1809, the eleven-thousand-square-foot, thirty-three-room home was Jefferson's pride and joy. Only in his retirement years did the estate take the exact shape of the mansion he had imagined twenty-five years before. Both Jeff and

Ellen left letters detailing Monticello's interior. For example, we know that "the rooms of Monticello were not overly furnished by the standard of other large houses of the period."[16] Ellen remarked that "there was but little furniture in [the house] and that of no value." A typical bedroom would be furnished with "a table, a 'walnut stand,' two 'old mahogany chairs,' two mirrors, and a candlestick or lamp."[17] However, Ellen's description was accurate only for the upstairs bedrooms. The center of the house, and Monticello life, was where Jefferson lived and studied, on the decorative main floor. "If it had not been called Monticello," one observer wrote in 1816, "I would call it Olympus, and Jove its occupant."[18] Jefferson's family seemed to agree. When Jefferson was in residence, his "cheerfulness and affection were the warm sun in which his family all basked and were invigorated," a granddaughter recalled.[19]

With Jefferson's acute supervision, a young Jeff Randolph occasionally took guests on a short tour along the curved walkway of the lush lawn, pausing at "spots from which the house appeared to most advantage."[20] In one vignette, Jeff recalled that Jefferson took a "Mrs. Smith" for a tour of Monticello. As they walked, Mrs. Smith viewed her host on "the top of this mountain, as a being elevated above the mass of mankind."[21]

When they returned to the house, a dinner party adjourned to the portico, where Jefferson supervised a footrace for Jeff and his other grandchildren. Seated on the grass with the children, the doting grandfather happily "pressed them to his bosom and rewarded them with a kiss."

Mrs. Smith commented with delight, "What an amusement do these creatures afford us."

"Yes," Jefferson replied, "it is only with them that a grave man can play the fool."[22]

***

In the eighteenth century, marauding wolves still roamed the Virginia hills, howling into the night in rural Albemarle County, Virginia. In many respects, the area was still a rugged frontier when Thomas Jefferson Randolph was born at Monticello on September 12, 1792.

The first recorded recognition of Jeff came when his mother, Patsy, notified then Secretary of State Jefferson of his birth—his "little namesake [was] a remarkably fine boy."[23] Jefferson was always the indulgent grandfather, feeling "the same love for the next generation that he had for his own children."[24] Over the next few years, he would become intimately familiar with Jeff and each successive grandchild.

While the Master of Monticello was in residence, Jeff and Ellen were often left in his care. At times, this supervision became taxing for the serene president—for example, when Jeff, then a rambunctious two and a half years old, refused to warm his hands, which were constantly "like lumps of ice."[25] In fact, Jeff had not worn his shoes an hour all winter, he once complained to Patsy, because as soon as they were put on the child, he would throw them off in a tantrum. Jefferson's cleverness solved the problem: he cobbled comfortable "mockasseens . . . of soft leather," which Jeff wore with delight. Still, Jefferson pleaded to Patsy, "Come home as soon as you can."[26]

The situation a year later was much improved. Jefferson cooed that Jeff has become "the finest boy possible. Always in a good humor, always amusing himself, and very orderly."[27] Jeff's "earliest recollection" of his famous grandfather was being "arrested" by Jefferson on a visit to the Rivanna river, then returned home as a "runaway" when he was three. Jeff's childhood memories included his grandfather urging "manly sport for boys," insisting that by "ten years old" a boy "should be given a gun and sent into the forest alone to make them self reliant."[28]

Jeff's experience fit that pattern. At age twelve he "arose at daylight and in a heavy snow storm walked four miles alone to hunt turkeys in a dense pine forest."[29] From this excursion, he arrived home at three o'clock, "not having tasted food that day," and "no remark [was] made on it." Certainly, Jeff was not pampered, perhaps embellishing that he "slept a whole winter in an outer closet, a blanket [his] only bed," denied delicacies and rich food."[30] One visitor to Monticello reported that Jeff was a "fine young lad," but he was surprised when the boy "walked into the Drawing Room without Shoes or stockings." The visitor was informed that this was a "general custom in Virginia," but he was convinced it was but a "whim" of Jeff's grandfather.[31]

As he grew older and matured in manners, Jeff could dine and converse with the adults. He described some of the lavish dinners for dignitaries in the elegant Monticello dining room. His grandfather was basically a vegetarian, preferring the balance of his diet to consist of fresh fruit and vegetables.[32] The French cooking that Jefferson brought back to America with him "was essentially cuisine bourgeoise" that he reserved for special occasions.[33] While in Paris, Jefferson had read extensively about the French philosopher Rousseau, "who had argued for a simple diet of fresh vegetables, salads, eggs, and milk." According to Rousseau, "meat turned men cruel and barbarous."[34] "The effect of Rousseau," one author has explained, "on many of the philosophes of Paris was to lead them to *cuisine à la bourgeoise*, a style of cooking that was simple, intimate, and refined. This was a kind of dining that would predictably attract Jefferson, for it combined moderation with delicacy. What he admired about the French 'pleasures of the table' was that 'with good taste they unite temperance.'"[35] For everyday dinners, Patsy often prepared a meal including her father's favorite vegetable—peas—as well as boiled fish. The peas were sautéed in butter, then simmered in stock along with onion, cloves, and a pinch of sugar. The onions and cloves were then removed, and the stock was thickened with a mixture of flour and eggs into a creamy sauce. Jefferson's French influence apparent, the boiled fish was topped with a rich sauce of butter cream and nutmeg.[36] Jeff recalled another special recipe of his mother's: bread pudding. "The pudding was simple enough—two loaves of crumbled bread, two quarts of milk, and eleven eggs, all well-beaten together. This mixture was boiled for four to five hours in a cloth bag." This dessert was a favorite at Monticello, recorded as Patsy's "famous sunday pudding."[37]

The ornate dining room at Monticello contained long French windows, French mirrors, and Louis XVI chairs. At dinner—under his grandfather and mother's supervision—Jeff observed his grandfather's "discursive manner and love of paradox, with the appearance of sobriety and cool reason"[38] An observer once recalled that Jefferson "converse[d] with ease & vivacity, possessing true politeness, which places his guests perfectly at their ease."[39]

Dinner conversation often turned to Jefferson's books and collectibles, undoubtedly due to his great love of American antiques and rare books.[40] Indeed, his library was "arranged according to the divisions of human learning made by

Lord Bacon. Jefferson particularly relished a collection which he called the *Book of Kings*, documents of royal scandal."[41]

Jeff related his grandfather's meticulous schedule at Monticello:

> At eight o'clock the first bell is rung in the great hall, and at nine the second summons you to the breakfast room, where you find everything ready. . . . After breakfast the children retire to their schoolroom with their mother, Mr. Jefferson rides to his mills on the Rivanna, and returns at about twelve. At half past three the great bell rings, and those who are disposed resort to the drawing room, and the rest go to the dining room at the second call of the bell, which is at four o'clock.[42]

The sumptuous dinners were impressive, but no wine was set on the table until the cloth was removed—Jefferson's edict.[43] "Wine encouraged lively conversation" commented one scholar, "one of [Jefferson's] greatest pleasures. This is . . . why he served it after dinner, to encourage and prolong table talk."[44] Jeff recalled that his grandfather opposed the consumption of all hard liquor and rarely drank it. Jefferson favored reducing tariffs on the importation of wine because high taxes raised the price and forced Americans to drink "the poison of whiskey, which is desolating their houses."[45] Jefferson argued that "no nation is drunken where wine is cheap; and none sober, where the dearness of wine substitutes ardent spirits as the common beverage."[46]

After dinner, the ladies sat until six, then retired, but returned with the tea tray a little before seven and spent the evening with the gentlemen. At about half past ten, guests retired to their bedchambers, where they "found there a fire, candle, and a servant in waiting to receive . . . orders for the morning, and in the morning was waked by his return to build the fire."[47]

As for Jeff's own routine, since Thomas Jefferson always rose with the sun, Jeff's mother hurried him "out of bed every morning at sun-rise and obliged, after a breakfast of bread and milk, to walk 2 miles to school" which "mended [his] appearance, strength & spirits."[48] The toughening process worked so well that at age twelve Jeff "waded a river covered with ice and [walked] seven miles home . . . barefooted through three or four inches of snow, blythe and cheery as in a summer day."[49]

Some of Jeff's most vivid memories were of visits to the president in Washington. On one of these visits Jefferson's coachman took Jeff to the Navy Yard and informed the commandant that the president's grandson was there to tour the grounds. Assuming the president had sent him, the commandant ordered the officer of the day to give the boy an official tour. When Patsy heard of Jeff's canard, she rushed to the president, bemoaning Jeff's "folly." Amused, Jefferson enjoyed a "good laugh" with the commandant over the incident.[50]

On another trip, Jeff was present at the White House when the Tunisian minister dined with Jefferson. "The minister . . . sat on the right of the President, the two attaches to the right of the Secy., Meriwether Lewis at the other end of the table. [Randolph,] between [the attaches] with a large silver goblet on each side . . . ," was told to keep the glasses filled.[51] He was surprised that, despite their religion, "they emptied them repeatedly and seemed to enjoy and fill their wine."[52] It was at this same table that Jeff saw the Dutch minister cause quite a commotion. The minister, "an elderly bald headed man," had spread a "hot, soft pudding" on his plate, then bent down to pick up his napkin. Unfortunately for him, the plate was protruding slightly over the edge of the table, and when he raised up, his forehead bumped the plate, turning its contents over on the top of his head. With tears streaming from his eyes, the minister said, "I vis I vere in Hell."[53]

For the rest of Jeff's childhood—except when he "caught (that filthiest of all disorders) the itch from a little apprentice boy in the family"—Jeff remained healthy and spent his time playing with his sisters on the vast lawn at Monticello.[54] Of the slave children who were often his playmates, he reminisced:

> Reared on a large slave estate and fourteen years older than my oldest brother, having no companions, I associated when out, entirely with the slaves and formed for them the earliest and warmest attachment . . . Negro association in the country was less corrupting than immoral whites . . . They would often invite me, too young to stand the walk, to go on a tramp or coon

hunt...or taking a bee tree in the forest. When they thought I was getting tired [they would] take me on their backs by turns. We were taught to treat them with as much courtesy and kindness as if they had been free. I always looked to them as my protectors and they would run any risk for my protection.[55]

In stark contrast to these warm memories, Jeff resented that his formal education had been "neglected," solely blaming his absentee and erratic father, Thomas Mann Randolph, who sent him "irregularly to inferior schools"[56] that Jeff found deficient. In a letter to his mother, he criticized his teachers:

> We do almost as what we please in school. Geradin does not attend regularly & Doyle the Latin teacher is drunk every night of his life & does little but blab between the teachers & boys. My old teacher Wood for I have little to do with any other is better tempered than most persons, we vex him he scolds & we laugh at him, he does the greater part of the business of the other teachers the consiquence is he is obliged to neglect those immediately und[er] him & we are often obliged to tease him to hear us.[57]

Jeff remembered walking, between the ages of four and ten, up to four miles "to what were called old field schools, located in a cabin or log meeting house, carrying [his], simple breakfast and dinner in baskets."[58] It is telling that Jeff always blamed his father, never his mother or Jefferson, for his scant education. "My father himself educated at Edinburgh was to[o] prodigal to others to retain anything for himself or his family," he wrote. "I was sent . . . to inferior schools but never to college . . . Anxious to make up for early deficiency of education, I commenced a regular course of study, but was soon compelled to throw my books aside and devote myself, mind, body and effects to the care of my grandfather and his fears. My grandfather, my mother, and my wife were my earthly Trinity."[59]

It is ironic, that though Jeff was born into a sophisticated family that relished knowledge and literature, his own education was paltry. As children, he and his sister Anne gave their mother "serious anxiety with regard to their intellect." Anne in particular appeared to her mother to learn "absolutely without profit." Patsy was relieved, however, that Ellen was "wonderfully apt. I shall have no trouble with her," she wrote in a letter to her father.[60]

Ellen, at that time only five, emerged as Jefferson's favorite correspondent. His little "Elleanoroon" was already competing with Cornelia, age two, for her grandfather's favored attention. "Ellen counts the weeks and continues storing up complaints against Cornelia whom she is perpetually threatening with your displeasure," Patsy noted in that same letter. "Long is the list of misdemeanors which is to be communicated to you, amongst which the stealing of 2 potatoes carefully preserved 2 whole days for you but at last stolen by Cornelia forms a weighty article."[61]

Instead of measuring all the children by one standard, Thomas Jefferson valued each grandchild for their particular gifts. He eagerly nurtured them all.[62]

Jefferson thought Anne "apt, intelligent, good humored and of soft and affectionate dispositions," predicting that she would "make a pleasant, amiable, and respectable woman."[63] He tried to reassure Patsy that Jeff had his own particular talents if not as bright and precocious as Ellen. He believed that Jeff had a strong character and personality and could harness that potential in later years. Jefferson was not worried about the boy's intellect at such a young age: "It is not every heavy-seeming boy which makes a man of judgment, but I never yet saw a man of judgment who had not been a heavy seeming boy, nor knew a boy of what are called sprightly parts become a man of judgment," he wrote. He went on to say, "I set much less store by talents than good dispositions; and shall be perfectly happy to see Jefferson a good man, industrious farmer, and kind and beloved among all his neighbors."[64] While Jeff was sent off "to study with tutors," the daughters for whom college was not an option in the eighteenth century, "learned their lessons at home."[65]

During his presidency, Jefferson conducted a rich correspondence with young Jeff, imparting wise lessons that his grandson cherished for the rest of his life. Jefferson's letters ranged over various important topics: from civic lessons to anatomy to life's moral lessons. He instructed Jeff on how to live a fruitful life—how to control one's anger, what was truly important in life, how to love, as well as on the mundane—payments and memorandum books. Although serious study and pursuits were encouraged, Jefferson added this advice: "I have mentioned good humor as one of the preservatives of our peace and tranquility. It is among the most effectual . . . of first rate value."[66]

Though he was overtly affectionate with all of his grandchildren, Jefferson gently informed them that his devotion depended on their conduct: "The more I perceive that you are all advancing in your learning and improving in good dispositions the more I shall love you."[67] And Jefferson often advised them on their personal conduct and behavior. He firmly believed, wrote one historian, "that adults had a duty to smooth the way for responsible children, and leading Virginians undertook this with great diligence and dedication. Meticulously managed childhoods and endless advices to collegians was only the start."[68] Jefferson even developed a detailed list of guidelines. The most extensive, now famous, list he sent to his granddaughter, Cornelia Jefferson Randolph:[69]

A DOZEN CANONS OF CONDUCT IN LIFE:

1. never put off to tomorrow what you can do to-day.

2. never trouble another with what you can do yourself.

3. never spend your money before you have it.

4. never buy a thing you do not want, because it is cheap, it will be dear to you.

5. take care of your cents: Dollars will take care of themselves!

6. pride costs us more than hunger, thirst and cold.

7. we never repent of having eat[en] too little.

8. nothing is troublesome that one does willingly.

9. how much pain have cost us the evils which have never happened.

10. take things always by their smooth handle.

11. think as you please, & so let others, & you will have no disputes.

12. when angry, count 10 before you speak; if very angry, 100.

Jefferson also foisted civic values to the children, regarding this valuable task as his duty to the young republic of the next generation. Although he corresponded more times with Ellen, the tone of Jefferson's letters to Jeff had a distinct future goal in mind: he was grooming his grandson as his heir apparent, especially given Thomas Mann Randolph's absence and unstable behavior. Assuming the role of affectionate father figure, Jefferson even advised Jeff and his siblings on the subject of love:

> It is a charming thing to be loved by every body [*sic*]: and the way to obtain it is, never to quarrel or be angry with any body [*sic*], never to tell a story, do all the kind things you can to your companions, give them every thing rather than to yourself, pity & help every thing you see in distress and learn your books and improve your minds. this will make every body fond of you, and desirous of shewing it to you: go on then my dear children, and, when we meet at Monticello, let me see who has improved most. I kiss this paper for each of you.[70]

Jefferson's advice included how to control arguments with others. One should never "enter into dispute or argument with another. I never yet saw an instance of one of two disputants convincing the other by argument. I have seen many of their getting warm, becoming rude, and shooting one another." He continued:

> It was one of the rules which, above all others, made Doctor [Benjamin] Franklin the most amiable of men in society, never to contradict any body. If he was urged to announce an opinion, he did it rather by asking questions, as if for information, or by suggesting doubts. When I hear another express an opinion which is not mine, I say to myself, He has a right to his opinion, as I to mine; why should I question it? His error does me no injury, and shall I become a Don Quixote, to bring all men by force of argument to one opinion?[71]

Anxious for Jeff to acquire a firm education in "particular branches of science," Jefferson appealed to his friend Casper Wistar, professor of anatomy at the University of Pennsylvania. He asked Wistar's assistance in placing Jeff in a suitable school in Philadelphia.[72] Jefferson, ever the mentor and teacher, even instructed young Jeff on which courses to take and which books to read:

> You should buy a copy of John & Charles Bell's *Anatomy* as soon as you arrive that you may use it while attending the lectures in Anatomy. [I]t is in 4. vols. 8vo. and [M]r Peale will pay for it. [E]nter yourself for the lectures in Anatomy Natural history & Surgery all of which begin in November, & end in March. [M]r[.] Peale will pay for the tickets amounting to 42. Dollars. The Botanical course does not begin till April. then you must buy a Copy of Dr. Barton's botany, new edition.[73]

Jefferson also suggested learning a foreign language. "French [has] now become an indispensable part in modern education," he wrote. "It is the only language in which a man of any country can be understood out of his own."[74] Spanish, he believed, was secondarily crucial:

> Spanish is most important to an American. Our connection with Spain is already important, and will become daily more so. Besides this, the ancient part of American History is written chiefly in Spanish. To a person who would make a point of reading and speaking French and Spanish, I should doubt the utility of learning Italian. These three languages, being all degeneracies from the Latin, resemble one another so much, that I doubt the probability of keeping in the head a distinct know-ledge of them all.

The voracious author Jefferson delivered further instruction to Jeff on writing and taking class notes, complimenting Jeff on his penmanship: "I have to acknowledge the receipt of your letter of the 3d, my dear Jefferson, and to congratulate you on your writing so good a hand."[75] On a different occasion he wrote:

> As the commencement of your lectures is now approaching, I would recommend to you to set out from the beginning with the rule to commit to writing every evening the substance of the lectures of the day. It will be attended with many advantages. It will be much better to you than even a better digest by another hand, because it will better recall to your mind the ideas which you originally entertained and meant to abridge. Then, if once a week, you will, in a letter to me, state a synopsis or summary view of the heads of the lectures of the preceding week, it will give me great satisfaction to attend to your progress.[76]

Jefferson also imparted his philosophy of good temperament to Jeff:

> I have mentioned good-humor as one of the preservatives of our peace and tranquility. It is among the most effectual, and its effect is so well imitated, and aided, artificially, by politeness, that this also becomes an acquisition of first-rate value. In truth, politeness is artificial good-humor; it covers the natural want of

it, and ends by rendering habitual a substitute nearly equivalent to the real virtue.[77]

Jefferson's wise advice seemed never-ending on many subjects, including personal manners and good habits. "Be very select in the society you attach yourself to," he warned. "Avoid taverns, drinkers, smoakers [sic], and idlers and dissipated persons generally; for it is with such that broils and contentions arise, and you will find your path more easy and tranquil. The limits of my paper warn me that it is time for me to close with my affectionate Adieux."[78]

By 1813, Jeff had become immersed "more and more into the breach of his father's and grandfather's affairs."[79] He left a vivid picture of his rugged life during the years in which he acted as Jefferson's agent and informal overseer:

> I breakfasted in winter by candlelight and never came home until dark. The bad days were those which imperiously demanding my presence at each of these farms. I rarely failed, rain or snow was not recognized as an excuse. All our traveling was done on horseback, frequently of business to Richmond, 80 miles, into an estate of my grandfather's in Bedford the same distance. I had a hearty temperament and could sleep anywhere, eating anything and never tiring. If I was 25 miles from home at dark I, regardless of rough weather, always went home, fording or swimming . . . I cannot refrain from a tribute to the memory of my steeds Leghorn and Cortez, who successfully bore me for 15 years of life of toil and exposure, with a courage, fidelity and endurance which never faltered or flagged.[80]

While Thomas Mann Randolph was in the north with his regiment during the War of 1812, Jefferson told him of Jeff's valuable assistance to him. The production of flour was just getting off the ground, and "the want of a visible and responsible head was applied to a certain degree by young Randolph's taking over." His prided grandson, he boasted, would "discharge satisfactorily the trust."[81]

When Jefferson sent Jeff to inspect his other farms, some of this territory remained dangerous wilderness. Jeff later wrote that the Rockfish gap country was "a neighborhood which abounded . . . with whiskey drinkers, robbers and Tories: 'I write this on my hat in the porch of the tavern with my back to the wall to prevent the Rascals from looking over my shoulder.'"[82]

Though Jeff's boyhood had been "like that of most Virginia plantation youths of his time," as a teen he was still immature in worldly ways. Patsy expressed doubts about his ability "to conduct his own affairs in Philadelphia, where he arrived at sixteen to enroll in the University of Pennsylvania."[83] Relating to his grandson events from his own childhood, Jefferson stressed the importance of influential mentors and good company.

When his father died, Jefferson was only fourteen. He told Jeff that he had wished for his father's guidance during this crucial period in his life. He even confessed to having kept bad company in his early days, but fortunately had not acquired their bad habits. Luckily, Jefferson met three superb mentors in Williamsburg—men of character who guided his path: lawyer George Wythe, Dr. William Small, and royal governor Francis Fauquier. It was their influence, he said, that made Williamsburg "the finest school of manners and morals that ever existed in America."[84] Jefferson called on these men frequently to dine with him. In later years, he would liken these dinner parties to "something like Greek colloquia. At them, he '"heard more good sense, more rational and philosophical conversation, than in all [his] life besides."[85]

Obsessive about his own health, Jefferson encouraged Jeff to exercise his body as well as his mind. Though Jefferson suffered most of his life from migraine headaches that could be excruciating at times, he never permitted them or any other ailment to hinder his activities. In fact, when his wrist was broken and negligently set, causing his writing to be limited, he taught himself to write with his left hand.

Jefferson was an outdoorsman throughout his life, strolling around Monticello or mounting a horse to the year he died. He instilled his philosophy on health and exercise in Jeff and his nephews: "Two hours every day should be given to exercise," he said. "A strong body makes the mind strong."[86] "[Walking] is the best exercise, and one should walk a great distance . . . [It] gives boldness, enterprise, and independence to the mind. Games played with the ball, and others of that nature, are too violent for the body, and stamp no character on the mind," he warned,[87] believing that afternoons were the best times for exercise so as not to hamper one's studies. Yet, walking for a short distance early in the morning would get a man off to a good start each day. Most important, one should rise early and go to bed early. "Sitting up late at night is injurious to the health, and not useful to the mind," he insisted.[88]

Jefferson also taught his grandson to appreciate music. When he and his family were all together, he would often take out his violin and play, "his grandchildren dancing around him."[89] There was no way of growing up at Monticello without being aware of music, because at one point Jefferson practiced the violin for three hours a day.[90] He owned the most delicate musical instruments, which he collected well into his last years.

Jefferson delighted in all his grandchildren, but Jeff most of all, perhaps because he was male and considered him the son he never had. He also sensed a bright future for Jeff. And Jefferson filled a cavernous void left by Jeff's sullen and reclusive father. Jeff later described a childhood without much fatherly supervision or guidance—almost a boy in the wilderness. "My mother allowed me to wonder where I pleased," he recollected. "I never wore a hat or shoe winter or summer until I was 10 years old and wore a watch before I wore shoes in the summer."[91] Thus, his grandfather's attention was all the more necessary.

As Jeff matured, he grew emotionally closer to Jefferson, while more estranged from his withdrawn father. Realizing that his mother had assumed the role of both parents to her growing family, Jeff also came to admire her even more. By 1801, Patsy was spending every spare moment tutoring young Jeff and his sisters. However, she feared that they were increasing "in age without making the acquirements which other children do." Her children "excit[ed] serious anxiety with regard to their intellect. Of Jefferson [Randolph] her hopes were so little sanguine that [she] discovered with some surprise that he was quicker than [she] had ever thought possible."[92] Thus, Patsy wanted Jeff in a good school as soon as possible. Nevertheless, 1802 found him still at home, "reading Latin with his Papa," because the school chosen for him was full and its master could not take another student.[93]

Soon Jefferson became involved in Jeff's education, sending him a French grammar book with the expectation that "within three weeks" he should be able to ask, "*Parlez vous Francais,* Monsieur?" A year later the president inquired about him. "How does Jefferson get on with his French?"

"Jefferson is going to a very good Latin school in the neighborhood," he was informed. And Patsy told her father, "We receive the most flattering reports from Jefferson's master, [describing him] as a boy of uncommon industry and application."[94]

Jeff continued his education in Richmond and in Philadelphia, studying science and French. His family, including Jefferson, had high expectations for him. Another of Jefferson's grandsons would be warned that "something above mediocrity" was expected because of his grandfather's "elevated station."[95] Even so, Jeff struggled with his studies and his grades, but not for lack of effort, for he was studying until two or three o'clock in the morning. Mr. and Mrs. Rembrandt Peale, with whom Jeff stayed while in Philadelphia, even became worried about Jeff's lack of sleep. Many nights, Peale found it "necessary to carry him to bed" when Jeff fell asleep studying.[96] Of Jeff's academic progress, Peale reported to Jefferson, "Mr. Randolph is very attentive to his studies, and I have not a doubt that he will be a valuable member of Society by his skill and disposition to alleviate the miseries that our species are liable to. I am happy in being able to say that he is a charming young man, and others that know him entertain [the] same sentiments of his talents and disposition."[97]

Before going to Richmond, then on to Philadelphia, Jeff recalled that his grandfather had examined his wardrobe as his mother would have done, and sent him to Jefferson's own tailor "with a list of articles."[98] Jefferson received a bill for Jeff's tuition, and a final expense statement. Some items Jeff had bought included an "umbreulla," a skeleton, and a textbook, *Bell's Anatomy,* which cost his grandfather twenty-two dollars—forty dollars in total, not a paltry sum in 1809.[99] But as one historian commented, Jeff's most serious distress in Philadelphia was not his spending; he deeply missed his family and Monticello:

> It was a chronic malady with him; he would never be content for long when away from his family and his Albemarle. At this

stage, failure to receive letters from home aroused him to a bitter and sarcastic pitch. He would even take his grandfather to task for not answering his letters promptly, though he ordinarily excused his elders on the ground of their pressing business. However, he insisted that sisters Ann and Ellen might forego "darning stockings" to keep him informed.[100]

The following spring, Jeff returned to Albemarle County, taking a part-time job surveying his brother-in-law Charles Bankhead's lands.[101] Though, as noted earlier, Jeff later blamed his father, as well as the family's distressed finances, for his failure to finish college or become a "professional man,"[102] the stark reality was that Jeff was but a mediocre student. Patsy, worried about the financial burden of a higher education, had perhaps decided Jeff's skills lay elsewhere.[103]

Upon his permanent return from school, his grandfather proposed to Patsy that young Jeff assist him with managing his various plantations. Patsy heartily agreed, knowing her husband was unfit for the task. In 1809, a proud grandfather proclaimed to Jeff's father, "It will not be long before Jefferson can aid us both."[104] Unfortunately, Jeff described the next four years, from age eighteen to twenty-two, as the most "monotonous" of his life.[105] He missed his adventures and the games he had played with Jefferson in Washington.

In March 1809, Jeff put aside his books to visit his grandfather for James Madison's inauguration. Jeff was Thomas Jefferson's only escort as they rode on horseback to the Capitol to turn over the government to the new president.[106] One observer described the historic scene:

> Having politely turned down a request to accompany the president-elect in his carriage, Thomas Jefferson and Jeff Randolph rode their horses down Pennsylvania Avenue to Jenkins Hill. . . .When Jefferson and his grandson reached the Capitol a little before noon, they tied their horses to a fence post, passed through the crowd to take their places inside the House chamber, and waited for Madison's official entry. After Madison was ushered in, Jefferson stood with his successor as Chief Justice

John Marshall administered the oath of office to the new president. Praising his predecessors, Madison offered special words of gratitude to Jefferson. He had earned his "rich reward," Madison said, "in the benedictions of a beloved country, gratefully bestowed for exalted talents zealously devoted through a long career to the advancement of its highest interest and happiness." Madison and the rest of the party exited, the cavalry fired two rounds from its cannons, and the new president reviewed nine militia companies.[107]

That evening, at Long's Hotel, Jefferson attended the nation's first inaugural ball, headed by first lady Dolley Madison, "resplendent in buff-colored velvet and draped in pearls."[108] Socialite Margaret Bayard Smith observed that Jefferson "seemed in high spirits," beaming "with a benevolent joy." One guest approached Jefferson and said, "You look so happy and satisfied[,] Mr. Jefferson, and Mr. Madison looks so serious[,] not to say sad, that a spectator might imagine that you were the one coming in, and he the one going out of office." Jefferson replied, with a sense of relief, "There's a good reason for my happy and his serious looks. I have got the burthen off my shoulders while he has now got it on his."[109]

Now back at Monticello, Jeff spent much of his time running errands for his grandfather or overseeing the farms. He also became a part-time tax collector for Albemarle, Amherst, Fluvanna, and Nelson counties. The job "barely paid expenses," but was considered "the most useful part of his education" since it helped Jeff "early to know the world and all of its phases, by mixing in business transactions with men of all grades and characters."[110] The unadorned Jeff Randolph had nothing stylish about him, leading some refined people to underrate his talents. Yet, in his post as collector of the county revenue, Jeff gained valuable business experience, and then spent the summer of 1814 on active duty with the militia east of Richmond.[111] His early training in "courtesy [and] civility" inured him in his later political career. Raised with impeccable manners, Jeff was soon acquainted with various merchants, farmers, and neighbors, who would later become his voters.[112]

Often, Jeff rode on horseback with Jefferson, both for exercise and to visit friends and family members, particularly if the roads were too rough or muddy for carriages.[113] Jeff, better than most as a farmer, understood the extreme changes in the Virginia weather. He and his sisters frequently accompanied Jefferson as he traveled between Monticello to his retreat at Poplar Forest, in Bedford County, some ninety miles away. Jefferson would wrap the girls in his furs; then they would set off in the cool, early-morning air. He would sing as they traveled in the jolting carriage. Nonetheless, "the three-day trip was tedious and Poplar Forest was dull, for Mr. Jefferson allowed no company there."[114] One of Jefferson's reasons for his journey to Poplar Forest was to escape the crowd of tourists—"the curious and impertinent mob," Virginia called them—"who wandered about the grounds at Monticello for seven or eight months of the year, staring at the author of the Declaration of Independence as if he were a national monument. Once a woman broke a windowpane with her parasol in order to get a better view of him."[115]

During these trips to Bedford County, the weather often turned extreme. Jefferson, ever the optimist, always presumed the weather would be good for his journey. But hours into a trip, conditions could turn from blazing sun to torrential rains, Jeff recalled.[116] One granddaughter told of another harrowing journey traveling with Jeff in a phaeton carriage to Poplar Forest when they hit a sudden rainstorm:

> Reaching a hovel on the roadside just as the large drops were beginning to fall. A sullen old woman received me very unwillingly into her dirty room, while Brother Jeff and his servant were seeking a shelter for the carriage. Our company soon received the addition of a young waggoner, and the master of the house, an old savage who actually frightened me out of the house, and I remained in the little porch until we could again set forward on our journey.[117]

On another trip in unexpected bad weather, Jefferson's expensive coach barely escaped crashing over a cliff with several of his granddaughters aboard. Other narrow escapes included "one very narrow one of being bitten by a snake" when the ladies had gotten out of the carriage "on a bad hill." On one occasion they were delayed by bad roads for so long that Jefferson contemplated "alarming the neighbors" and sending them out "with torches to beat the woods." Virginia was convinced that "these expeditions, unattended by a gentleman or a servant on horseback were hazardous," though she had been making them all her life.[118]

During these trips, as one historian has observed, "Jefferson's command was total, his love enveloping . . . He took care to wrap his family in capes, and, if needed, furs. He sang and conversed the whole way and served picnic lunches of cold meat and wine mixed with water."[119] Jefferson reveled in his role as grandfather, surrogate father, and mentor. He genuinely enjoyed the company of all his grandchildren, particularly Jeff. As Jeff's younger brothers reached their teens, Jefferson persuaded, perhaps demanded, that their father let him assume their further education. The sulky and estranged Thomas Mann Randolph was more than happy to surrender his patriarchal duty.[120]

Family matters, including those connected with his grandfather's estate, now made pressing demands on Jeff's time and financial resources. His sister remarked that he had "more business on his hands than one man 'could possibly accomplish.'"[121] Worse, a significant family feud with his father loomed. Long before this dispute exploded, Thomas Mann Randolph brooded over his troubles, as his many creditors pursued him. He became ever gloomier and more withdrawn from his family. Ironically, he bitterly complained that it was his family who had become "more and more estranged" from him, till there was "scarcely . . . any intercourse at all and 'much less any interchange of thought or social feeling.'"[122] His dress and appearance were "as bad as they could be," and "he took no pleasure in himself or and anyone else."[123] And though he did not specifically name Jeff, Thomas seemed to blame him for his misfortunes.

With his own father missing and often drunk, Jeff greatly benefited from Jefferson's presence in his life through his formative years. Thomas Jefferson was Jeff's guiding father figure and mentor until his death:

> I can not describe the feelings of veneration, admiration, and love that existed in my heart towards him. I looked on him

as a being too great and good for my comprehension; and yet I felt no fear to approach him and be taught by him some of the childish sports that I delighted in. When he walked in the garden and would call the children to go with him, we raced after and before him, and we were made perfectly happy by this permission to accompany him.[124]

In the end, it was not to the gardener Anne, the cerebral Ellen, or even the supremely capable Patsy to whom Thomas Jefferson would turn when he could no longer manage his estate.[125] It was Jeff. "I threw myself more and more into the breach of his affairs," Jeff wrote.[126] Yet, something greater than these affairs, and even weightier than the arguments with his chronically temperamental father, now captured Jeff's attention. Even his grandfather had observed that Jeff had become distracted. Something—or someone—"at Warren . . . drew him there often." It was "the attraction of . . . two bodies mutual in affection."[127]

Indeed, at Warren, Jeff Randolph found the love of his life for the next fifty-six years.

4
ELLEN

Ellen is perhaps one of the best educated girls in America, a perfect Mistress of the French, Italian and Spanish languages.

—**Eliza House Trist, in Burstein**, *Jefferson's Secrets*

Thomas Jefferson Randolph was the son and prodigy that Thomas Jefferson never had. But it was Ellen Randolph Coolidge who was most like Jefferson himself,[1] both physically and emotionally. Their similarity can even be observed in Ellen's portrait: she inherited her grandfather's distinctive high nose.[2]

Ellen was the third child of Jefferson's beloved daughter Patsy, born in 1796, while he was vice president. One author notes that though "Jefferson paid close attention to . . . all the . . . young women of his family . . . Ellen was unquestionably the granddaughter who most naturally came by her poise and intelligence. He, and everyone else, marveled at her personality. As a student, she was the most gifted. As a writer, she charmed. As a judge of men, she was confident and discerning."[3]

Ellen "was the favorite among [Jefferson's] many granddaughters," says another author, "with whom he corresponded more frequently than with any other and of whom he spoke in terms of unique devotion."[4] Jefferson himself referred to Ellen as "my peculiarly valued grand-daughter for whom I have a special affection." Many years later, he would boast of her, "She merits anything I could have said of a good temper, a sound head and great range of information."[5]

One writer claims, "It may seem unfair to characterize Ellen as the most prized among Jefferson's granddaughters, but the historical record bears this out."[6] Yet, Ellen's sister Cornelia recalled that "Gran' papa" never showed signs of inconsistency in his treatment of the grandchildren. He was "always, in all things & at all times, with never a shade or shadow of change or variation, and without any one of us ever feeling that there was any difference in what he was for one from what he was for all & each of the rest."[7]

But one can see that Jefferson was lighthearted with Ellen, amusing in tone. In 1802, while Ellen was feeding her "bantams" (domestic fowls), a note arrived from the president of the United States. It read:

> Washington, Tuesday, July 20, 1802.
> My very dear Ellen
> I will catch you in bed on Sunday or Monday morning.
> Yours affectionately,
> TH. JEFFERSON.[8]

Surprising young Ellen in the early morning hours was customary for Jefferson; he teasingly alluded to it in other writings. Ellen rewarded Jefferson's devotion with, as she later put it, "all the affection of a child and something of the loyalty of a subject."[9]

Ellen's intelligence was evident at even the youngest age. By the time she had reached her fifth birthday, she had taught herself to read "by continually spelling out lines and putting them together and then reading them to who ever would listen to her."[10] Writing to five-year-old Ellen, Thomas Jefferson predicted, "You will become a learned lady and publish books yourself."[11] Ellen would fulfill her grandfather's promise of becoming a "learned lady." Her son would later note that Ellen had received "her education at the knees of the great philosopher. She had the education of a man, the morals and refinement of a woman."[12] But she would never publish her writings. Instead, she would preserve her letters and journals for her own reference and her family's legacy.

For a time, letters from Jefferson to Ellen far exceeded in number those from her to him. So, the president resorted to a bit of bribery to prompt her replies.

In a letter dated November 27, 1801, addressed to "Miss Eleanor Randolph," he wrote:

> My dear Ellen,
> I . . . am very happy to learn you have made such rapid progress in learning. When I left Monticello you could not read and now I find you can not only read but write also. I enclose you two little books as a mark of satisfaction. . . I hope you will . . . continue to be a very good girl, never getting angry with your playmates nor the servants, but always trying to be more good humored and more generous than they. If you find that one of them has been better tempered to you than you to them, you must blush, and be very much ashamed, and resolve not to let them excel you again. In this way you will make us all too fond of you, and I shall particularly think of nothing but what I can send you or carry you to show you how much I love you. . . I have given this letter 20 kisses which it will deliver to you: half to yourself, and the other half you must give to Anne.
> Adieu my dear Ellen. TH. JEFFERSON.[13]

It was no doubt from Jefferson and his letters that Ellen developed her own lyrical way with words. She learned quickly and was, in fact, an eager learner. For example, when she was just six, Jefferson sent her brother a French grammar book. Ellen then insisted that she too wanted to learn French.[14]

The earliest preserved letter from Ellen to her grandfather was written at age eight, on paper that her mother had ruled for her with lines. She wrote "in a large, round, regular hand, its occasional trembling betraying the great pains she took, as well as her lack of practice with a pen. In her eagerness . . . she forgot to dot her 'i's.'" The letter read:

> My dear GrandPapa:
> I recieved your letter and am very much obliged to you for it, as it is very seldom that I get one you cannot think how

glad I was at it. I am very much obliged to you for the bantams you promised me and will take great care of them. I go on very slowly with my French for I have got through but one book of Telemachus but I hope that I shall now go on better since Mamma's health is so much better that she is able to hear us our lessons regularly. Give my love to Papa and Mrs. H. Smith [whose acquaintance she had made in Washington during the winter of 1802]. Adieu my Dear GrandPapa believe me to be your affectionate GrandDaughter

ELLEN WAYLES RANDOLPH. Feb 22, 1805.[15]

By Ellen's ninth birthday, Jefferson was plying her with his love of fine arts, often sending her poetry to read.[16] And just as he had done for her brother, he instructed Ellen with his own life lessons, composing a persuasive letter on how to live a virtuous life. "Adore God," he advised her. "Reverence and cherish your parents. Love your neighbor as yourself, and your country more than yourself. Be just. Be true. Murmur not at the ways of Providence. So shall the life into which you have entered be the portal to one of eternal and ineffable bliss."[17] Jefferson went on to paraphrase Psalm 15:

THE PORTRAIT OF A GOOD MAN BY THE MOST SUBLIME OF POETS, FOR YOUR IMITATION. Lord, who's the happy man that may to thy blest courts repair; Not stranger-like to visit them, but to inhabit there? 'Tis he whose every thought and deed by rules of virtue moves; Whose generous tongue disdains to speak the thing his heart disproves. Who never did a slander forge, his neighbor's fame to wound; nor hearken to a false report, by malice whispered round.[18]

"The way to obtain love," Jefferson explained, was "never to quarrel or be angry with any body and to tell a story. Do all the kind things you can to your companions, give them every thing rather than to yourself. Pity and help anything you see in distress and learn your books and improve your minds."[19] According to one author, as his grandchildren "cultivated these character traits and their individual talents, Ellen seemed of all the grandchildren the most naturally inclined to improve her mind."[20] Indeed, when nine-year-old Ellen visited Washington in the winter of 1805–6, leading society figure Margaret Bayard Smith called her "without exception one of the finest and most intelligent children [she had] ever met with."[21]

At ten, Ellen studied Greek history, Latin, French, and mathematics and corresponded with her grandfather about topics as varied as the fine arts and natural history. Ellen clearly shared her grandfather's boundless intellectual curiosity. "I have often thought that the life of a student must be the most innocent and happy in the world," she said. To be highly educated, Ellen believed, was to be free and fulfilled: "The pursuit of knowledge unlike other pursuits is subject to no disappointments. It is a road where every step counts, where every advancement is secure, what you have acquired is beyond the risk of loss." She seemed to have learned this from her grandfather. "He was endlessly curious about subjects as wide-ranging as botany, architecture, [and] philosophy.[22]

It was also at age ten that Ellen entered into a "contest with her grandfather to see who could write the other the most letters." Jefferson confessed that he was woefully behind in this literary contest. "I believe it is true," he told her, "that you have written me 2. letters to my one to you. Whether this proceeds from your having more industry or less to do than myself, I will not say."[23]

When she was eleven, Jefferson sent her sheet music to play. ("It was much in vogue when I was your age," he said.) He also taught her useful Latin phrases and even conveyed his love of nature and gardening to her.[24] In fact, on Jefferson's return home to enjoy his long-sought retirement, his mind seems to have turned from politics to plants and flower beds. "For a man leaving the presidency $10,000 poorer than when he had taken office," writes one historian, "flowers had one great advantage over temples. They were cheaper. From the President's House he had sent his eldest granddaughter, Anne Cary Randolph, a plan of the beds that he intended to lay out on the west lawn."[25] Jefferson's plans showed a "winding walk surrounding the lawn before the house, with a narrow border of flowers on each side of the walk. The hollows of the walk would give room for oval beds of flowering shrubs."[26] Young gardeners Ellen and Anne took up Jefferson's new hobby with a zeal equal to their grandfather's. Ellen described the scene in a letter written to Jefferson's first biographer, Henry S. Randall:

> I remember the planting of the first hyacinths and tulips and their subsequent growth. The roots arrived, labelled each one with a fancy name. There was Marcus Aurelius and the King of the Gold Mine, the Roman Empress, and the Queen of the Amazons . . . Then, when spring returned, how eagerly we watched the first appearance of the shoots above ground . . . what joy it was for one of us to discover the tender green breaking through the mould, and to run to grandpapa to announce, that we really believed Marcus Aurelius was coming up, or the Queen of the Amazons was above ground![27]

Ellen, who proved to be Jefferson's most frequent pen pal, wrote him of many things at Monticello, including family news and gossip. The precocious Ellen even shared the rumor that her cousin Elizabeth Trist was going to marry the governor.[28] Ellen kept her grandfather informed about her new hobby—gardening—as well. She also wrote to him about the books she was reading, which included French texts and history.[29] "By 1809," comments one author, "Ellen was reading French fairly easily, and had been introduced to Homer."[30]

After his presidency, with Jefferson's formal retirement to Monticello in March 1809, Ellen's childhood letters ended. But when Patsy moved to Monticello to manage the household, Ellen's relationship with her grandfather grew much closer. In later letters, Ellen left an account of the contented years of Jefferson's retirement in her own words: "Repeat the same tale of love and kindness. From him seemed to flow all the pleasures of my life," she wrote.[31]

With Ellen's delightful help, Jefferson devoted himself to what he termed the seventh fine art: gardening, the skill of embellishing grounds by fancy. Ellen learned that the culture and placing of his flower garden gave Jefferson as much delight as his vast library. As one historian has concluded, "The one place where Jefferson was able to execute his landscaping ideas with complete freedom was within the confines of the first roundabout, the lawns and gardens immediately surrounding the house."[32] Jefferson told his oldest granddaughter, Anne, "I find that the limited number of our flower beds will too much restrain the variety of flowers in which we might wish to indulge, & therefore I have resumed an idea . . . of a winding walk surrounding the lawn before the house, with a narrow border of flowers on each side." Always the amateur architect, Jefferson sketched a drawing of the serpentine walk and flowerbeds on the perimeter of the lawn.[33] The gravel walk, flowerbeds, and a reflecting pool were laid out the following year. The oval flowerbeds proved to be a great source of joy for Jefferson and his grandchildren. Ellen wrote an account of how the grandchildren would help Jefferson plant hyacinth and tulip bulbs with such exotic names as "Roman Empress," "Queen of the Amazons," "Psyche," and "God of Love," and anxiously await "the surprisingly beautiful creations I should see arising from the ground when spring returned."[34]

By the time they reached their teens, Ellen and her sisters, Cornelia and Anne, were Jefferson's most frequent companions. The artistic Cornelia learned mechanical drawing from Jefferson. Ellen played chess with him. She also warmly recalled Jefferson humming to himself "between writing and reading chores, old Psalm tunes or Scotch melodies."[35]

Under her grandfather's tutelage, Ellen would develop from an adoring little girl picking flowers into an articulate and accomplished scholar, particularly in languages. "Later in life," wrote one author, "there was something special about Ellen's presence of mind that made her unusually adept in social settings, and an intelligent conversationalist."[36]

When Ellen turned nineteen, Abigail Adams took note of her, writing to Jefferson, "Your Grandaughter Miss Ellen Randolph['s] . . . praises are in the mouths, of all our northern Travellers, who have been so happy as to become acquainted with her."[37]

***

Jefferson's grandchildren carried fond memories of him. For instance, Jefferson often sent them books and bits of newspaper poetry for their scrapbooks whenever he wrote them through their maturing years. Ellen spoke of the many gifts that her grandfather had given to her: "My Bible came from him, my Shakespeare, my first writing table, my first Leghorn hat, my first silk dress."[38] On another occasion, as the story goes, another granddaughter tore a beloved muslin dress on the glass door connecting the hall to the portico. "Grand-papa was standing by and saw the disaster," the granddaughter recalled.[39] A few days later the former President glided into Patsy's sitting room, "a bundle in his hand" for his granddaughter. "I have been mending your dress for you," he announced.[40] Jefferson was equally generous with gifts to all his grandchildren.

When Ellen was fifteen, she asked for a small watch to know what time to accompany Jefferson to the garden. She describes what happened several weeks after her request:

> [I] knew the state of my father's finances promised no such indulgence. One afternoon the letter-bag was brought in. Among the letters was a small packet addressed to my grandfather. It had the Philadelphia mark upon it. I looked at it with indifference, incurious eye. Three hours after, an elegant lady's watch, with chain and seals, was in my hand, which trembled for very joy. What, in short, of all my small treasures did not come from him?[41]

In another of Ellen's many descriptive letters to biographer Henry Randall, she recounted:

> I was fond of riding, and was rising above that childish simplicity when, provided I was mounted on a horse, I cared nothing for my equipments . . . I was beginning to be fastidious, but I had never told my wishes. I was standing one bright day in the portico, when a man rode up with a beautiful lady's saddle and bridle before him. My heart bounded. These coveted articles

were deposited at my feet. My grandfather came out of his room to tell me they were mine.[42]

For all his emphasis on industry and good manners, Jefferson desired that his grandchildren enjoy themselves. He loved to give them presents at opportune times. His memorable gifts were numerous, and some had considerable value. He gave Virginia a guitar that cost $30, Ellen's elegant watch was valued at $135.[43]

Jefferson also enjoyed many games with the children.[44] It provided a mental break from the rigors of politics and his worry over his mounting debt. A visitor once saw the president sitting on the drawing room floor, surrounded by his captivated grandchildren, "so eagerly and noisily engaged in a game of romps" that they ignored the visitor for several minutes.[45] Virginia recalled that "cross questions" and "I love my love with an A" were two games she learned from Jefferson. After dinner, Jefferson would act as referee and gather everyone on the lawn, where he supervised their sprints. And the grandchildren would teach him some of their own games and foot races. As one writer described the scene:

> He arranged them by size, "gave the word for starting and away they flew," making a quarter-mile circle around the back lawn. The little girls "came panting and out of breath to throw themselves into their grandfather's arms, which were opened to receive them; he pressed them to his bosom and rewarded them with a kiss." Seated on the grass with the children, Jefferson happily consented to officiate at a second race, this one on the pavilion itself.[46]

Jeff and Ellen recalled the fun they had at "playtime" with Jefferson, when all the children gathered for games on Monticello's lawn in the warm summer months. Ellen remembered that she could hear frogs croaking in the afternoon rain leaking out of the oak trees when they played:

> About half-past three o'clock [h]e sat some time at table, and after dinner returned for a while to his room, from which he

emerged before sunset to walk on the terrace or the lawn, to see his grandchildren run races, or to converse with his family and friends. The evenings, after candle-light, he passed with us, till about ten o'clock. He had his own chair and his own candle a little apart from the rest, where he sat reading, if there were no guests to require his attention, but often laying his book on his little round table or his knee, while he talked with my mother, the elder members of the family, or any child old enough to make one of the family-party. I always did, for I was the most active and the most lively of the young folks, and most wont to thrust myself forward into notice.[47]

Jefferson preferred the heat of the Virginia summer over the frigid cold of winter throughout his life, claiming the sun was his "great physician." In the warmth, he could play for hours with the children, but not in the cold. "I have no doubt but that cold is the source of more sufferance to all animal nature than hunger, thirst, sickness, & all the other pains of life & of death itself put together . . . [W]hen I recollect on one hand all the sufferings I have had from cold, & on the other all my other pains, the former preponderate greatly."[48] Among many other references to cold weather, Jefferson wrote to John Adams, "During summer I enjoy it's [sic] temperature, but I shudder at the approach of winter, and wish I could sleep through it with the Dormouse, and only wake with him in spring, if ever."[49]

As if launched on a boyish lark from his own childhood, Jefferson would award fruit as prizes for the children, seeking "out the ripest figs, or bring down the cherries from on high above [their] heads with a long stick, at the end of which there was a hook and a little net bag."[50] Sometimes the grandchildren would gather with Jefferson in the south pavilion, a one-room structure built over a kitchen, the first brick building on the mountaintop. Here, the children would enjoy a "kick-up" with their grandfather—music and dancing until midnight. Jefferson would set up a chess table of his own design for a game with Ellen or Anne in the parlor on humid summer nights.[51]

Jefferson taught his grandchildren that chess was a game of skill "that appeals both to the intellect and to the architectonic imagination; it was one of his favorite amusements."[52] Chess had become popular among the intelligentsia in Europe during the time Jefferson was stationed there. One report noted that "Voltaire and Rousseau were passionate players. The coffee houses of London resounded with cries of 'Check!'"[53] According to one historian, Jefferson had been in France during the final years of the great French chess master François Philidor, "who astounded his countrymen by playing as many as three games simultaneously while blindfolded." In December 1801, Jefferson requested his son-in-law to send him "Philidor on chess, which you will find in the book room."[54] Jefferson had played chess in the salons of Paris while he was minister plenipotentiary, purchasing two chess sets in France. Often playing during his presidency, Jefferson once told a visitor to Monticello, "I played with Dr. Franklin at chess, and was equal to him at the game."[55]

When the days were cold and daylight was short in the winter months, Jefferson would gather the grandchildren around him before a roaring fire. This was the hour, a granddaughter wrote, "when it grew too dark to read," and so, "in the half hour before candles came in, as we all sat round the fire, he taught us several childish games, and would play them with us."[56]

The servants' lighting of glowing candles signaled an end to games and the beginning of quiet time for reflective reading and study. Everyone fell silent as Jefferson put on his spectacles and "took up his book to read."[57] "We would not speak out of a whisper lest we should disturb him," a grandchild recalled, "and generally we followed his example and took a book—and I have seen him raise his eyes from his own book and look round on the little circle of readers, and smile and make some remark to mamma about it."[58] As one author observed, Jefferson mainly read books on science, nature or philosophy, but "did not like the adventure-filled novels of Sir Walter Scott, though his granddaughters read and admired these as well."[59]

"His grandchildren loved him and revered him," wrote one observer. "They followed him on garden walks never, though, putting a foot on a garden bed, for that 'would violate one of his rules.'"[60] Jefferson never had to raise his voice with the children. "Their sense of his authority" made it unnecessary for him to "utter a harsh word to one of [them], or speak in a raised tone of voice, or use a threat . . . He simply said, 'do,' or 'do not.' And that was that."[61] These adored grandchildren repaid Jefferson in kind. "I can not describe the feelings of veneration, admiration, and love that existed in my heart towards him," insisted Virginia. Ellen was no less passionate: "I loved and honored him above all earthly beings."[62]

His grandchildren's adoration showed in their tender, expressive words about him:

> My grandfather's manners to us, his grandchildren, were *delightful*; I can characterize them by no other word. He talked with us freely, affectionately; never lost an opportunity of giving a pleasure or a good lesson. He reproved without wounding us, and commended without making us vain. He took pains to correct our errors and false ideas, checked the bold, encouraged the timid, and tried to teach us to reason soundly and feel rightly.[63]

Another grandchild remembered, "Our smaller follies he treated with good-humored raillery, our graver ones with kind and serious admonition. He was watchful over our manners, and called our attention to every violation of propriety. He did not interfere with our education . . . except by advising us what studies to pursue, what books to read."[64]

Perhaps, as most grandchildren do, Jefferson's grandchildren engaged in a bit of hero worship. One grandchild recalled a story about Jefferson's "medical" skills. While a "Mr. Fitzhugh" and a guest were strolling around the lawn at Ravensworth, "a servant ran up to tell them that a negro man had cut himself severely with an axe." Fitzhugh ordered the servant to quickly ride and bring back a physician. Jefferson suggested that the victim "might bleed to death before the doctor could arrive, and, saying that he himself had some little skill and experience in surgery, proposed that they should go and see what could be done for the poor fellow." Fitzhugh agreed. When they reached the man, they found he had a severe cut in the calf, bleeding profusely. Jefferson procured a needle and silk, stitched the wound with a surgeon's skill, and dressed and bandaged the man's leg. As they walked back from the slave's cabin, Jefferson remarked it had always "struck him as being strange that the thick, fleshy coverings and defenses of the bones in the limbs of the human frame were placed in their rear, when the danger of their fracture generally came from the front." The remark struck Fitzhugh "as being an original and philosophical one, and served to increase his favorable impressions of his friend's sagacity."[65] One historian commented that Jefferson could "calculate an eclipse, survey an estate, tie an artery, plan an edifice, try a cause, break a horse, dance a minuet, and play a violin."[66]

Granddaughter Virginia Randolph credited Jefferson with "all the small blessings and joyful surprises of my childish and girlish years."[67] According to one author, "Jefferson's nature 'was so eminently sympathetic,' that, with those he loved, he could 'enter into their feelings, anticipate their wishes, gratify their tastes, and surround them with an atmosphere of affection,' as [Virginia's] own father could never do."[68]

"Rather than regard . . . [his grandchildren] as a financial burden," one historian has explained, "Jefferson welcomed the opportunity to help raise the children, supervise their education, and surprise them with gifts."[69] The children adored this bonding time with Jefferson—Jeff and Ellen most of all. Jeff was literally at Jefferson's knee and "used to follow him about, and draw as near to him as [he] could."[70] Ellen paid homage to Jefferson, observing many years later in a letter to biographer Randall, "With regard to Mr. Jefferson's conduct and manners in his family, after I was old enough to form any judgment of it, I can only repeat what I have said before—I have never known anywhere, under any circumstances, so good a domestic character as my grandfather Jefferson's."[71] She described how she was "thrown most into companionship with him. I loved him very devotedly," she said, "and sought every opportunity of being with him."[72] Ellen fondly remembered that she used to "sit on his knee and play with his watch-chain. As a girl, I would join him in his walks on the terrace, sit with him over the fire during the winter twilight, or by the open windows in summer."[73]

Virginia was often distracted from her lessons by the arrival at Monticello of the latest novel of James Fenimore Cooper or Sir Walter Scott, and she found it difficult to study in a houseful of noisy guests.[74] Yet, amid this racket, Virginia found her quiet retreat: a "place over the parlour Portico into which the dome room opened." Having furnished it with a sofa, chairs, and tables, she boasted, "I have taken possession with the dirt daubers, wasps & bumble bees; and do not intend to give it up to anything but the formidable rats which have not yet found out this fairy palace."[75]

***

For many years, no one looked as intently, or as candidly, at the personal character of Thomas Jefferson than Ellen. This granddaughter enjoyed a special place in Jefferson's heart. Perhaps this was due to her own father's absence and erratic nature. Devoted to but coldly distant from her father, she described him with the greatest of tact: "With some noble qualities . . . and naturally warm affections, [he] was jealous, suspicious, irascible and violent."[76] Unlike her grandfather, it seems Thomas Mann Randolph had no time for or nurturing inclinations toward his own children, which stunted Ellen's emotional and intellectual growth. It was no wonder Ellen was closer to her grandfather, Thomas Jefferson, than she ever would be to her father.

Jeff's older sister, Anne, was also close to her grandfather. Their mutual interest in nature forged a strong bond. It was she who had tended the gardens at Monticello in Jefferson's absence, boasting to him of their growth. This would have delighted Jefferson, who wrote to a friend later in life, "Though an old man, I am but a young gardener."[77] Anne's "love of garden plants had been almost as ardent as his own."[78]

Another grandchild, Cornelia Randolph, also had fond recollections of Jefferson. "These remembrances are precious to me," she wrote, "because they are of him, and because they restore him to me as he then was, when his cheerfulness and affection were the warm sun in which his family all basked and were invigorated. Cheerfulness, love, benevolence, wisdom, seemed to animate his whole form. His face beamed with them. . . How active was his step, how lively, and even playful, were his manners."[79]

On one occasion, Ellen joined her grandfather when prominent artist Thomas Sully painted a magnificent, full-length portrait of Jefferson. Sully "succeeded admirably," Ellen told a cousin. "The upper part of the face is perfect, the eye is so full of life that you almost expect to see it roll. He is the first painter who has ever succeeded in catching the expression of Grandpapa's countenance, and rendering that mixture of dignity and benevolence which prevails in it."[80] Ellen thought there would be no more suitable rendering of Jefferson, "to whom future ages must look back with gratitude and admiration."[81]

Two years before Jefferson died, Ellen met the love of her life at Monticello. In fact, two of Patsy's daughters married men they had met at Monticello. Among the visitors in the spring of 1824 was a twenty-five-year-old Bostonian man who arrived in May with a letter of introduction to Jefferson from Harvard professor George Ticknor. Joseph Coolidge, who had recently completed a tour of Europe, attended the Boston Latin School and graduated from Harvard in 1817, after which he spent three years traveling through Italy, England, Ireland, and France. While on his travels, he suffered from "typhus fever," which almost killed him.[82] Washington Irving, his friend and occasional traveling companion, nursed Joseph back to health. While abroad, Joseph had learned of the death of Elizabeth Little, a young woman he had hoped to court and someday marry. Devastated, he lamented to his father that he had "given up all thought of ever being other than I now am, a single man," vowing to "turn his attention to business."[83]

Until he met Ellen Randolph.

Ellen and Joseph shared much in common, including a basic philosophy of life: a general sense that the conventional path would not be theirs. The year before they met, both had expressed the belief that they were destined to remain unmarried. Each had used the phrase *cui bono* in correspondence, which Ellen translated as "Of what use is all this?" to convey her sense of disquiet.[84] But by the end of Joseph's two-week stay at Monticello, it was clear that the two were smitten with each other.

After meeting Ellen, Joseph Coolidge immediately wrote to Jefferson asking permission to see her again.[85] The touching letter to Jefferson is still preserved, "the elegant blue paper and exquisitely written lines betraying the importance of his request":[86]

My dear Sir,

I have delayed to express the gratification which my visit to Monticello, during the last spring gave me, until called upon to ask you for further kindness. During the fortnight which I passed so agreeably in your family, the many valuable qualities of Miss Randolph made an impression upon me which, at parting, I did not attempt to conceal. I confessed to Mrs. Randolph the interest her daughter had inspired . . . and the correspondence which followed has perhaps assisted in showing us something of each other's character; it has certainly confirmed the high opinion I had formed of Miss Randolph's heart and understanding . . . and I now ask of you Sir, permission to return to Monticello, that my own character may become better known, by longer personal intercourse. The visit I am about to make does not involve Miss Randolph in any positive or implied engagement :—should she see fit to decline all connection but that of friendship, I should think less well of myself, but not of her: if she consent, after further acquaintance, to gratify my dearest wish, may I not hope, Sir, for the sanction of your approval? . . . Sir, as the cherished relation of one who, under every circumstance, will be dear to me, may I not be permitted to assure you of my individual, unfeigned regard?

J. COOLIDGE JR.

Boston:
October 13, 1824.
Thomas Jefferson, Esqre.[87]

"Jefferson's draught of his reply," comments one author, "with its many interlineations and scorings, mutely testifies to his affection for his granddaughter and his anxiety for her happiness":[88]

Dear Sir,

I should not have delayed a single day the answer to your interesting and acceptable letter of the 13th inst. but that it found me suffering severely from an imposthume under the jaw . . . I avail myself of the first moment of my ability to take up a pen to assure you that nothing could be more welcome to me than the visit proposed, or its object. During the stay you were so kind as to make with us, my opportunities were abundant of seeing and estimating the merit of your character insomuch as to need no further enquiry from others. Nor did the family leave me uninformed of the attachment which seemed to be forming towards my granddaughter Ellen. I learnt it with pleasure, because from what I believed of your, and knew of her, extraordinary moral qualifications, I was satisfied no two minds could be formed better compounded to make each other happy. I hold the same sentiment now that I receive the information from yourself, and assure you that no union could give me greater satisfaction, if your wishes prove mutual, and your friends consenting. . .

Your visit to Monticello and at the time of your own convenience will be truly welcome, and your stay whatever may suit yourself under any views of friendship or connection. My gratification will be measured by the time of its continuance.

TH. JEFFERSON.[89]

In effect, Jefferson gave Coolidge his full blessing.

Jefferson informed Joseph that the Marquis de Lafayette would be visiting Charlottesville in November and invited Joseph to be his special guest at the University of Virginia's dinner. On November 4, 1824, Joseph witnessed the historic reunion of the heroes of the Revolution on Monticello's lawn. The following evening he was among the four hundred dignitaries who dined in the university's rotunda. During Lafayette's historic visit, Joseph and Ellen became engaged. As one of Ellen's cousins recalled, the young couple's romance gained more attention than the two aging patriots:

> At the time of Genl. La Fayette's visit to Monticello (abt. the middle of November 1824) John Quincy Adams was President Elect. This festive occasion was graced by the presence of two lovers:—the lady, a member of Mr. Jefferson's family:—the gentleman, young, handsome, well educated, and recently returned from foreign travel —then a distinction —She was preeminently endowed—with talent of the highest order,—culture, such as few women have the opportunity to attain,—the beauty which belongs to statuesque features, and eyes which the soul speaks from. She possessed as a crowning attraction the most varied power as a converser,—an attraction which, I have before mentioned, was greatly prized in those good old times. To lookers-on the byplay of this love affair between two handsome young people, made an interesting episode amid all the novel and exciting material which each day brought.[90]

A year and a half later, Episcopal minister Frederick W. Hatch married Ellen and Joseph in the parlor at Monticello. Jefferson himself wrote the couple's marriage bond. They remained at Monticello for three weeks before departing northward to Boston, where Ellen would live with her new husband. But first, they undertook a six-week adventure through New England that covered over one thousand miles. Venturing farther from Virginia than she ever had before, Ellen was struck by the stark differences between the South and the North, not only in topography but in culture. She visited many of the same cities her grandfather had toured with James Madison, including Washington, DC, Philadelphia, and New York. She wrote to Jefferson:

> [Touring New England] has given me an idea of prosperity & improvement, such as I fear our Southern States cannot hope . . . whilst the canker of slavery eats into their hearts & diseases

the whole body by this ulcer at the core. . . I should judge from appearances that they are at least a century in advance of us in all the arts & embellishments of life; & they are pressing forward in their course with zeal and activity which I think must ensure success.[91]

Jefferson replied:

I have no doubt you will find also the state of society there more congenial with your mind, than the rustic scenes you have left: altho these do not want their points of endearment. Nay, one single circumstance changed, and their scale would hardly be the lightest. One fatal stain deforms what nature had bestowed on us of her fairest gifts.[92]

Although Jefferson was profoundly sad at Ellen's departure, he "demonstrably approved of Coolidge," according to one scholar, "and would not have thought of hindering their removal to New England." In a letter to Greek scholar and Massachusetts congressman Edward Everett, Jefferson affirmed his high opinion of Joseph Coolidge: "I have not been acquainted with a finer character than mr Coolidge, more amiable, more respectable or more worthy."[93] Yet, younger sister Virginia told Ellen of Jefferson's deep despair at Ellen's parting: "I fear he misses you sadly every evening when he takes his seat in one of the campeachy chairs, & he looks so solitary & the empty chair on the opposite side of the door is such a melancholy sight to us all, that one or the other of us is sure to go and occupy it, though we cannot possibly fill the vacancy you have left in his society."[94]

In the end, though, as one historian has written,

Ellen . . . never got to make the most of her abilities. In time, feminist-minded Americans would insist that the rhetoric of the Revolution be reconciled with the reality of women's abilities, but not soon enough for Ellen Randolph. In the early 1820s she both complained about her situation and resigned herself to it. "Was i a man," Ellen told her brother-in-law Nicholas Trist, and "could my studies have any object of sufficient importance to stimulate my exertions, i would now, even now [at age twenty-seven], commence my education... [But] [I] could promise myself no competent reward for so much trouble." [95]

Why? Because, unfortunately, in the eighteenth century, as the capable Ellen Randolph Coolidge expressed it, "I am nothing but a woman."[96]

5

LOVE

Harmony in the marriage state is the very first object to be aimed at.

—Thomas Jefferson (1798)

As touching as the preceding love story was, actually, Thomas Jefferson Randolph would find true love before his sister. The object of Jeff's affection was the beautiful and loyal Jane Hollins Nicholas, daughter of Thomas Jefferson's old and prominent friend Wilson Cary Nicholas, and Peggy Smith Nicholas of the influential mercantile Smith family of Baltimore.

Jane became Jeff's rock and vigilant supporter in the darkest days of his long life. Every day, Jane made him feel that somehow he was a gift in her life rather than the other way around. And if Jane ever had any fears, they were for Jeff's welfare, never for her own. Jane earned her way into Jeff's soul with unremitting kindness, loyalty, and a gentle love of the sort that Jeff's own mother had shown him.

To say Jane had come from good stock would be a vast understatement. Her father was a US congressman, senator, governor of Virginia, and political protégé of Thomas Jefferson. Born in Williamsburg, Wilson Cary Nicholas studied at the College of William and Mary until he joined the Continental army during the American Revolution. By 1784 he had been elected to the House of Delegates, serving until 1789. He befriended James Madison and consulted with Jefferson on many political issues. Nicholas was elected to the US Senate in 1799 and became a prominent "Jeffersonian." In 1814, he was a popularly elected governor of Virginia, serving through the end of the War of 1812. An ardent supporter of higher education, he later assisted Jefferson with his ambitious plans to construct a state university—-the University of Virginia.

Nicholas's ties to Jefferson continued throughout their lives. Jefferson often stayed at Nicholas's estate, Mount Warren, on his travels back from his Bedford County mansion, Poplar Forest. Much to Jefferson's dismay, however, Nicholas and his brother George became careless land speculators and found themselves deep in debt. As a consequence of the economic panic of 1819, Nicholas defaulted on a $20,000 note. The brothers turned to Jefferson for help, and he graciously agreed to co-sign another note with them—a fatal financial mistake for Jefferson. Years later, he alone would be saddled with repayment of the promissory note, deepening his own economic crisis.

To explain the cause of Jefferson's mounting debts is beyond the scope of this book. But allow me to stray from this chapter's topic momentarily for a brief explanation. Economic reality came at Jefferson in several overlapping waves, but the most important fact was that he was not an independent farmer but an indebted Virginia planter. "By the time of his retirement as secretary of state," notes one writer, "he owed about forty-five hundred pounds to English creditors in Bristol and another two thousand pounds to a Glasgow firm. The bulk of this debt had been incurred in the 1770s, when he inherited the burdened estate of his father-in-law, John Wayles."[1] But what Jefferson termed his "thralldom of debt" had been further complicated "by the wartime inflation that rendered his efforts at payment valueless, by the declining productivity of his lands during his long absences from Monticello from 1784 to 1794, as well as by his apparently constitutional inability to live within a budget."[2] Moreover, Monticello was under constant construction throughout the bulk of Jefferson's adult life. Bills came due for a congested construction site replete with broken bricks, roofless rooms, lumber piles and, at one time, more than a hundred workmen tearing and hammering away for years.[3] These circumstances, coupled with the fact that as patriarch Jefferson had generously agreed to provide guidance and financial support for an assortment of grandchildren, nieces and nephews rendered his financial picture bleak during his retirement years.

Five years had come and gone since Jeff Randolph had come home to work on his grandfather's farms. At twenty-two, Jeff yearned for a plantation and family of his own. Earlier in the year, Jefferson had told his granddaughter Elizabeth that Jeff had "found a lodestone at Warren," a plantation fifteen miles south of Monticello.[4] Jeff's "lodestone" was Nicholas's sixteen-year-old daughter, Jane. Jefferson believed "the attraction of the two bodies [to be] mutual." Their fledgling romance flourished over the next several months.[5] A year later, Jeff visited Jane's father to formally ask his consent and blessing for the marriage. Jeff understood the financial sacrifice Jane would be making because of his "pecuniary circumstances." She would be placed in a "a situation far below that which she had been accustomed to and had a right to expect". The value of his own property did not exceed $12,000.[6] Yet, truly in love with the grandson of a President, Jane eagerly accepted his marriage proposal.

On March 6, 1815, the couple married at Mount Warren. It was the happiest day of Jeff's life. Jane brought to the Jefferson family a "bright and radiant countenance and winning manner [from] her first moment."[7] The lavish wedding was performed by Martin Dawson. The Master of Monticello was more than pleased with Jeff's choice of a wife, gushing about Jane: "To our new friend whom you have brought into so close relation with this give assurances that we receive her as a member of our family with great pleasure and cordiality and shall endeavor and hope to make this an acceptable home to you both."[8] Artist and soldier Charles Wilson Peale congratulated Jeff on "fulfilling his duty to the community" and wished him a "great deal of happiness, numerous offspring, and a long life."[9]

At first, immediate family members had not shared Jefferson's favorable opinion of Jane. Petty family jealousies and malicious gossip had erupted between the two families. But the animus was directed more toward Jane's mother than toward Jane herself. According to author Joseph Carroll Vance, Jeff's sister Anne viewed Jane's somber mother, Peggy Smith, as "mercenary."[10] Further, she expressed "utter astonishment" over the fact that Jeff had visited the Nicholas estate. Allegedly, Jane's mother had made disparaging remarks about their own mother, Patsy. According to Anne's titillating gossip, Mrs. Nicholas had referred to their mother as a "very vulgar looking woman" and to Anne herself as "a poor stick." Hence, Anne had objected to the marriage between Jeff and Jane and urged her mother to call off the wedding over the slanderous remarks.[11]

Patsy Jefferson had initially shared her daughter's trepidation. But once the gossip had been cleared up, Jane won all hearts at Monticello with her gentle manner and compassionate nature. In time, she became "completely a child of" Patsy's and a "most affectionate sister to [Jeff's] brothers and sisters."[12] Patsy considered Jane "a blessing to the family" and ironically, Jane became "almost a mother to Anne's orphan children." Patsy was ashamed of her initial reservations about her.[13]

Jeff's sisters quickly warmed to Jane, embracing her fully as their own flesh and blood. In a letter to Jane two years after her marriage to their brother, Virginia would thrice refer to her as "Dear Sister."[14]

**

For the first two years of their marriage, the newlyweds lived in the third-floor Dome Room at Monticello, where eight circular windows looked out onto the majestic Blue Ridge mountains beyond. Monticello's octagonal dome room was Jane and Jeff's "temple of love." Life below the loving couple, however, was not harmonious. Jeff's sister Anne had married a violent alcoholic, Charles Bankhead. The Bankhead marriage, which had started so well, had by 1816 disintegrated into an abusive nightmare. Though a handsome man with a prominent family, Charles would prove to be, as Ellen bitterly described him, "a worthless . . . malignant drunkard."[15] This would set Jeff and Bankhead on a bloody collision course that would play out on the streets of Charlottesville later that year. But the Randolphs—Jeff and Jane—were happy. And it was a good thing.

"The women of [the eighteenth century] had high expectations from marriage," historian Thomas Fleming contends. "They wanted not only affection but respect as persons."[16] Things hadn't changed much in the nineteenth century. Jane's expectations were equally high, though in recent times, articles about unhappy marriages had been common in the newspapers, with one writer blaming these sour relationships on "women who spent too much of a man's money on luxury," and on "men who, for the sake of beauty or wealth, married [either] 'a fury' or an 'ideot [sic].'" Thomas Jefferson knew the importance of a happy marriage in a man's life, having spent five years in France, where he concluded that American marriage customs were far superior to French ones.[17] He did all he could to ensure Jeff and Jane's happiness under his roof.

Although comfortable and secure at the crowded mansion of Monticello, Jeff and Jane yearned for their own home and privacy. As Jeff grew in both age and experience, his share of family responsibilities increased, as did his family size. By the time Thomas Jefferson died, there would be seven daughters born to Jeff and Jane Randolph.

Eventually, the new family "colonized four miles off on the opposite side of the river." However, this arrangement did not sit well with Jefferson," who considered it too far away.[18] He became "restless and dreary" until Jeff "removed to a farmhouse of his one mile from Monticello on the same side of the river."[19] With their grandfather's consent, they soon moved to Jefferson's Tufton estate, one of Jefferson's quarter farms that bordered Monticello. The property at Tufton served as agricultural land, providing abundant crops and acting as an important food source for the Monticello plantation. The family remained there until after Jefferson's death.

When the Randolphs moved in, their Tufton home was an unfinished construction site, but Jefferson thought it would be "a very comfortable one when done in." Jane's sister did not seem impressed by Tufton and "would defy [anyone] to find a worse house . . . even the common comforts of plenty of meat and wood" were sometimes lacking.[20] At one point, this sister of Jane's "found it necessary to cook all the seed peas 'to keep the family from starving.' There was also a shortage of clothing."[21]

But Jane wanted her own household, preferring "such [a] house as Tufton to that of Monticello" and its attendant foot traffic.[22]

Beginning in 1817, Tufton came under Jeff's exclusive management. He built a sturdy log cabin there, then, later, a much bigger stone house for his growing family at Elk Hill.[23] Elk Hill had been inherited from Martha Jefferson's family. It turned out to be one of Jefferson's most profitable plantations, ideally located for both cultivation and transport.[24] As one writer described it:

Elk Hill plantation rolled gently toward the banks of the James River. The plantation house had none of Monticello's grandeur; it was a modest farmhouse with a pitched roof, set on a breezy eminence overlooking the plantation's 307 acres. In the little valley below, some of Jefferson's finest breeding horses were quartered in their stables. Barns were filled with corn and tobacco, slave cabins were scattered along the creeks, and cattle and sheep roamed through the grasses.[25]

Mistress of a fine estate and blessed with an accomplished husband—the grandson of a president—Jane found her family becoming prosperous. From Jeff's account books, his income seemed more than adequate for the day, accumulated from his father and grandfather's farms. This was later to be increased by the receipt of Jane's modest inheritance when her father died.[26] But Jane's priority was turning her house into a home. Jane had gained practical knowledge about working a plantation from her father, but she also depended on Patsy and Thomas Jefferson's gardening and farming expertise for growing food. In fact, the Jefferson family owned numerous books on gardening, farming, and planting, including *James on Gardening*, translated from Leblond's manual of the French formal style of gardening. Jane no doubt turned to these for advice.

Once fully settled at Tufton, Jeff began to manage more of his grandfather's financial and plantation matters. Jefferson proudly apprised his son-in-law, John Eppes, of Jeff's growing duties. "I am indeed an unschooled manager of my farms and sensible of this from its affects, I have now committed them to better hands, of whose care and skill I have satisfactory knowledge, and whom I have ceded the entire direction."[27] Indeed, Jeff was both capable and loyal to his grandfather. Once, he even sent a polite note to Jane's father, Wilson Cary Nicholas, gently asking him to remove a "certain stump of a limb that projected over the fairy sluice and obliged the old gentleman [Jefferson] to disembark from his carriage."[28]

Jane was equally loyal, and she cared deeply for the aging Thomas Jefferson. As one story goes, "it was a custom of the family . . . 'a sort of regulation imposed by his affection,' [historian] Henry Randall wrote—that whenever one of the young women of the family returned after a visit elsewhere, she would pay her respects to Jefferson at Monticello before going to her own home."[29] On one occasion, Jane had been away when Jefferson returned from Poplar Forest. By the time Jane made her way up the mountain, she had learned of her father's impending bankruptcy, which would directly affect Thomas Jefferson's finances. As noted earlier, Jefferson, as a favor to his close friend Wilson, Jane's father, had cosigned a note for $20,000 in 1819.[30] As one historian commented, "it was the act of a gentleman and a kinsman: a Nicholas daughter had married a Jefferson grandson." Sadly, "Nicholas was forced to default on the note, leaving the former president responsible for the debt."[31]

On Jane's first call at Monticello following news of the financial disaster, Jefferson took care to seek her out. When Jane arrived at Monticello around dinnertime, Jefferson emerged from his room and immediately called for her. "She heard his voice and flew to meet him," Henry Randall wrote. "Instead of the usual hearty hand-shake and kiss, he folded her in his arms. His smile was radiant." Jane was embarrassed over what her father's economic plight meant for Jefferson, but at dinner, Jefferson immediately put Jane at ease, conversing cheerfully with her. "Neither then nor on any subsequent occasion," wrote Randall, "did he ever by a word or look make her aware that he was even conscious of the misfortune her father had brought upon him."[32]

***

Despite the financial difficulties facing them, Jefferson's family remained eternally optimistic, like their patriarch. Patsy believed that "the country was beginning to recover" from the panic of 1819, pointing out that Jeff had "already arrested the progress of the debts, and the property was daily improving."[33] Jeff described his hectic life during these years as his grandfather's busy overseer and de facto agent as "the bad days with those which imperiously demanded my presence in each of these farms. I rarely failed," he wrote in his *Memoirs*. "Rain or snow was not recognized as an excuse. All our traveling was done on horseback, frequently on business to Richmond 80 miles and two in the state of my grandfather's in Bedford the same distance. I had a hearty temperament and could sleep anywhere, eating anything and never [tiring]."[34]

As Jeff worked more directly for his grandfather, Jane settled in at Tufton. Jeff relied on his wife to cheer his spirits amid his growing plantation and family duties. More and more, he sought solace in his loving wife's arms. "For godsake keep up your spirits," he begged her. "Without you, all events will be alike . . . a blank to me. With you only, I have known happiness. Your arms have been the haven of all my passions, hopes, & fears."[35]

Jane often visited Monticello to assist her mother-in law, directing both free and enslaved workers as they made thousands of bricks, cleared stumps, and dug out and graded the turnarounds for carriages. She also became a careful housekeeper herself, taking steps to ensure that Jeff's private world ran smoothly. She saw to fresh supplies of meat, eggs, butter,[36] and fruit, and supervised the making of soap, taught to her by Patsy, who had been taught by her own mother.[37] Jane also oversaw the slaughtering of ducks, geese, and hogs, and did some sewing each week. She took delight in personally directing the work of the kitchen with more sophisticated meals when Jefferson would visit. Jane also took a deep interest in the land at both Monticello and Tufton.

An Italian neighbor and good friend of Thomas Jefferson's, Phillip Mazzei, credited with naming Monticello (Italian for "little mountain),[38] had brought the Jefferson household several kinds of European seeds from his overseas trips. Mazzei recalled in his *Memoirs*, "In Virginia, and I think it is also true of other States, the wife is in full charge inside the house; the husband, outside; he does, however, see to the purchase of whatever provisions his wife tells him are needed."[39] Mazzei recounted that "hostesses just love to have their dinner guests find uncommon fare, especially early fruits or vegetables. Of their nine or ten varieties of Indian corn preferable to our own none mature as early as our fifty-day corn, and over there they make a very appetizing dish with corn that is not fully ripe. That is why the ladies were grateful to me for the fifty-day corn."[40]

While Jeff stayed chronically busy with management of his grandfather's estates, Jane would have overseen, at least in part, some of the stables and construction work at Tufton. As Jane herself was an accomplished rider, she would manage a stable of beautiful saddle mares and draft horses to make long trips in comfort. She likely would have also owned several mules, which were greatly valued for heavy field work. "In fact," said Mazzei, ". . . they were liked so much that their fame spread throughout the land."[41]

At Tufton, Jane had an abundance of land, encompassing a mountain, dense forest, and streams. While Jeff was away, she would supervise all varieties of animals that were sent to graze in the woods. Though she kept the breeding bulls and horses penned up for sale, the non-castrated ones were allowed to roam through the forest. One neighbor of the Jeffersons, "a certain Morris, a good but indolent man," had to be repeatedly warned "to pen up his mischievous young bull." Unfortunately, the warnings were to no avail.[42]

Life at Tufton took on a state of normalcy for Jane and her children. She and Jeff loved living near Monticello, which they could see on the distant mountain. Thomas Jefferson was often asked why he chose to live on an isolated mountaintop. His daughter recalled that she'd heard him say that he had "never wearied of gazing on the sublime and beautiful scenery . . . and that the indescribable delight he here enjoyed so attached him to this spot, that he determined when arrived at manhood he would here build his family mansion."[43] To Jefferson, and his inner family, including Jane, Monticello represented their cloistered oasis from harsh reality.

Jane Randolph soon became very much a product of her class. In fact, one historian commented that she seemed bred to be a plantation mistress, and during fifty years of married bliss with her husband, she worked hard at being a successful one.[44] The mistress of a Virginia plantation was expected to superintend her enslaved servants and their many household duties: preserving meat, dairy, and fresh foods; knitting or sewing bedding materials, linen, and their own clothing. Jane did all of this, and also taught the field hands how to make soap, candles, and dyes. She served as the plantation doctor too, along with her husband and his grandfather. As instructed by Jefferson, she tended to the illnesses of not only her own family, but the families of the house slaves too, inoculating them against smallpox as Jefferson had done with his own Monticello slaves.[45] As if that weren't enough, Jane also served as the ultimate mediator of the slaves' disputes.

The enslaved community also contributed to the family productivity and were very skilled gardeners. Focusing on one month of summer inventory, from August to September, records reveal an impressive sale of vegetables to Monticello, including watermelons, cabbages, potatoes, cucumbers, squashes, dozens of eggs, and chickens. "To ensure a steady supply," noted one historian, "the chicken-raisers among the slave community had to build and maintain nest boxes, food and water containers, brooding cages, and fenced chicken yards." And someone had to guard the chickens from snakes, wolves, raccoons, and stray dogs.[46]

Even though the cities on the Eastern Seaboard were growing, most women, like Jane, still lived on rural farms, producing everything they used and ate. "As towns sprouted up," observed one author, "women started specializing—one doing the soap making, another the cheese and butter churning, another the weaving. They bartered with each other for goods and services, creating an off-the-books economy entirely run by women."[47] Despite their lack of legal rights, most women carved out their niche in an elaborate view of male versus female "worlds."[48] The men were in the world sphere; a woman's place was the house, the "domestic sphere." The men handled politics and business, while the women managed pretty much everything else, suggests historian Cokie Roberts. "That's not to say that these women were unaware of the sphere outside of their homes, quite the contrary. Their letters and diaries are filled with political observations and, in the case of Abigail Adams, instructions. Newspapers and magazines of the day kept women as well as men up to date on the news, as well as the fashions, both at home and in England."[49]

Jane possessed distinct advantages over most post-colonial women. She had means, a prestigious family heritage, education, and the trust, confidence, and support of her loving father and devoted husband. Even so, life for women in her day was not easy.

In the harsh nineteenth century, childbearing was considered one of a wife's primary functions. As such, raising and educating her twelve children took up most, if not all, of Jane's time and energy. For a while, there was concern that there were no boys in the family, since Jane's first children were all girls. However, there would be "enough of both soon," said one relative.[50] Jane eventually would bear thirteen children—ten girls and three boys—over a twenty-three-year period. Her first son was born in 1829, and he was "called Tom to distinguish him from his father."[51]

By all accounts, Jane was a doting, devoted mother and wife. As one writer has commented, "Her children at home remained uppermost in her mind even on her infrequent trips outside the county, usually to visit her older children. At such times, she left positive instructions that should anyone become ill, she was to be notified immediately [and she] would depart for home on a moment's notice."[52] Still, Jane's letters to various relatives dramatically illustrate the drudgery that pervaded her severe plantation life. In one, she wrote that "the sameness and monotony of our lives necessarily leaves us but little to tell our absent friends, except that we are all very well, have good appetites and sleep sound of nights, rise at day light and go to work again without any prospect of any-thing of interest occurring."[53] Another told of being "up to the eyes in . . . hog killing."[54] And a third letter complained, "If you only knew the worry and toil of my life, you would not be surprised at my want of spirits to write anything."[55] In spite of this severe life, Jane's family noted Jane for her sunny personality, warmth, compassion, and work ethic.

During her childbearing years, Jane was pregnant almost every other year. But the size of Jane's family (thirteen children), and her mother-in-law's family (twelve children), was quite normal for the period. John Tyler, the tenth president of the United States, fathered fifteen children. He had eight with his first wife, Letitia, and seven more with his second wife, Julia Gardiner, who was thirty years younger than Tyler. In fact, nearly half of all plantation wives in the late eighteenth century had six or more children. Remarkably, one of every ten gave birth to twelve or more children. Due to the high infant death rate, however, mothers often lost as many children to disease and sickness as they bore.[56]

But no matter how many children Jane had, her clothing and style were expected to be dignified and tasteful, as part of a president's inner family, and Jane never disappointed. Although there were professional milliners and dressmakers in the larger towns—such as Williamsburg—clothing was typically purchased from England, and most plantation wives also knew how to sew. And whether or not Jane was in the habit of keeping accounts of her household expenses, she soon learned that Jeff expected that of her. In fact, she was already edified in the practice by her father, but she never came close to matching the monthly, detailed record keeping of her husband or Thomas Jefferson.

Jeff and Jane dined often with Jefferson, sometimes enjoying lavish French dinners. Patsy and her daughters kept handwritten recipe books they used to select specific menus and instruct the cooks. The younger Randolph women took their Monticello cookbooks with them when they married and established their own households. Nine recipes in Jefferson's own hand and manuscript cookbooks were compiled by his granddaughters Virginia and Septimia. Although Jefferson never ventured into the kitchen "except to wind up the clock," numerous recipes by his slave James Hemings, who was taught French culinary arts in Paris, have survived—including his recipe for "snow eggs," meringues in custard sauce. Several published cookbooks were used by Patsy and the cooks at Monticello, including the influential English work Hannah Glasse's *The Art of Cookery Made Plain and Easy* and a French work, *La cuisiniere bourgeoise*. Daniel Webster, a visitor to Monticello, recalled that "dinner [was] served in half Virginian and half French style in good taste and abundance."[57] With Jane's able assistance, Patsy Jefferson's table was set to accommodate both the diners and the fine meal. Jane and Patsy made sure their guests felt comfortable by avoiding politics as a topic. As usual, the dinner conversation was usually led by Jefferson, who employed wit, grace, and charming anecdotes. It was said that "in [dinner] conversation Mr. Jefferson [was] easy and natural."[58]

Monticello's kitchen and dining room matched each other in ingenuity. Jefferson had installed two unique devices both for convenience and to impress his dinner guests. The first, a dumbwaiter, modeled on those he had seen in France, carried bottles from the wine cellar up with a pulley and crank through shafts on either side of the dining room chimney. The bottles carried with them a scent of the cellar underworld. The second device was a door mounted on a central pivot that magically revealed shelves with fine china. Jefferson likely operated the dumbwaiter himself on occasion but most times had his personal butler, Burrell Colbert, perform this task, serving the wine "in the French manner."[59]

On formal dining occasions, with Jane's help, Patsy had the servants wheel in small carts beside each guest, so diners could serve themselves easily and without interrupting conversation. Aside from strangers who might stay overnight, or for a week, Monticello was generally full of relatives and friends, one of whom once observed that "with the family we seldom sit down to table fewer than twenty, beside those who eat at a side table."[60] Often, Patsy's daughter Virginia and her three sisters took over the housekeeping, each for a month, in rotation. Virginia complained of "the hardships of keeping house" at Monticello, and described herself to Nicholas as being "seated upon my throne in the kitchen, with a cookery book in my hand."[61]

On special occasions, Patsy wished these elegant dinners to be a supplement to polite social conversation. Of course, the food had already been prepared in a separate cookhouse a hundred feet or so down a covered pathway, then kept in a warming room downstairs. The dinner would be brought up in a dumbwaiter to a prep room next door. Then, depending on the occasion and the dinner, one of the house servants would carry the meal and set down each main course, from fish remoulade to wild duck to roast lamb to pudding. The elegant blue, shell-edged pearlware china was designed by the legendary Lowestoft, trimmed in blue and with the family crest and a small *J* in the middle. At special dinners, three different wines were served—each hoisted up from the cellar in the two dumbwaiters concealed at each end of the dining room mantelpiece.[62]

A less elegant, typical family meal could have consisted of fish, bread, fried apples, and bacon. A favorite dish was squab pie, always served when dignitaries were visiting Monticello. The Jefferson family also loved "spoon bread." Family lore says that on one very special occasion at Ashlawn-Highland, James Monroe's neighboring estate, in the cook's effort to make good mush, she heated it too long; thus "spoon bread" originated.

***

It appears that Jane ran her household at Tufton much as she had done at the Cary plantation, Warren. The size of the home and number of acres, farms, slaves, and visitors made her duties a considerable task, even with borrowed labor from Monticello, such as the trusted slaves Isaac Granger and his mother, Ursula, both trained as cooks. Tufton had gardens, orchards, and a smoke room, but not nearly as extensive as Monticello's. Still, Jane's life as a plantation wife was "not the romantic paradise of the traditional novel, nor was it usually even the pleasant existence remaining after the debunkers of that earlier tradition had had their say." In reality, as one historian has written,

> It was more often a drab and toilsome existence involving the care of the house, the family, the slave families, and, indeed, frequently the plantation itself, from which the average woman would have liked nothing better than escape. The lives of Jane, her relatives, and friends are certainly a case in point. With the shortage of money and sometimes even the lack of necessities attending the Tufton and Edgehill establishments, Jane's lot was an especially unenviable one.[63]

Jane was not a physically strong woman. She was small in stature and delicately featured. Twelve pregnancies and a war did not help her physical or emotional state. Even so, the phrase "unchequered happiness," as Thomas Jefferson described his own marriage, also aptly described Jeff and Jane's love story. Regardless of external troubles, and there would be many, no chasm separated them. One historian has argued that "many Virginia men found that their hopes and expectations of an affectionate, cheerful wife were realized, and that their mates created for them 'domestic happiness.'"[64] This was true for Jeff as well as for his father-in-law. Wilson Cary Nicholas could not have endured his impending financial collapse had it not been for his own wife. "With a good and affectionate wife, who chearfully bears her lot," he wrote, ". . . no reverse of fortune could happen to me, which I could not bear with fortitude."[65]

But in the nineteenth century—and today—a "good and affectionate" husband is needed too, and by all accounts, Jane was not disappointed in Jeff Randolph. He was a loving and kind husband, unlike his own abusive father. And so, at Tufton and Monticello, Jane's spirit soared in every direction. This was her home in every sense of the word, and it gave her a secure feeling to be in blooming nature and gardens that pleased both her mind and her eyes—with the man she loved.

In the winter months, Jeff and Jane enjoyed the crystal cool evenings, when the stars were clear and chimney smoke wafted in the white moonlight. On some of these nights, they would visit Jefferson, riding the short distance up the mountain to Monticello. Jefferson was comforted and attended in his old age by the couple. He saw himself as "living like an antediluvian patriarch among [his] children and grandchildren."[66]

Over their fifty-plus years together, Jeff and Jane raised and educated thirteen children, twelve of whom lived to adulthood. To ease the family's financial difficulties in their later years, the couple founded the Edgehill School. With the able help of Jane's mother-in-law, sisters-in-law, and later, three of own her daughters, the Edgehill School gained a reputation as one of the Southeast's most prestigious schools for young women.

In the serene setting of mountainous Virginia, Jeff and Jane's marriage lasted until Jane's death in 1871. Jeff would be disappointed in many people and circumstances throughout his long life, but not in love or marriage. It would be hard to imagine a more loyal couple than Jeff and Jane. One feels almost like an invader when reading a tender letter from Jeff to his wife. "Your affection and presence is all and everything to me," he once wrote her. "I would freely resign everything, never again to be separated from you. Every anxious thought and care is dissipated when I think of the moment that I am to clasp you to my heart."[67]

Indeed, so close had they become that a sister once accused Jane of "not being able to carry her hand to her head without consulting Jefferson."[68] But now she was gone. And so, as the rising patriarch of the Jefferson family that spanned all of Virginia, Jefferson Randolph must have taken solace in one comforting thought: someday his devoted sons and daughters would carry his remains up Monticello's mountain to the family graveyard, there to be buried by his cherished mother, his adored grandfather, and his devoted wife, Jane.

6

WAR AND DEATH

I think one war enough for the life of one man.

—Thomas Jefferson to John Langdon, 1808

In his *Memoirs,* Jeff Randolph offers rare and little-known details of the Revolutionary War that his mother, Patsy, and his grandfather shared with him. One of the most famous and harrowing episodes of the war involved Patsy as a little girl. Patsy related this story to Jeff as a remembrance of the war but also as a tribute to her father's courage and bravery. As a then nine-year-old during the war, Patsy Jefferson was eyewitness to the brutal British invasion of Monticello, and the near capture and hanging of her father, Thomas Jefferson.

Pasty also related another searing family memory to both Jeff and Ellen—the tragic and untimely death of Jefferson's wife and true love, Martha Jefferson, at age thirty-three. This loss was a deep emotional trauma from which, perhaps, neither Patsy nor Jefferson ever fully recovered.

***

During his first year and a half as a wartime governor, in 1777, Thomas Jefferson had managed a state that had not yet felt the lash of war. But the British were coming. Jefferson struggled to secure enough money, supplies, and soldiers to thwart the invaders, while receiving ominous reports from the northern front of the war. At the same time, he issued immediate requests for assistance from the Continental army.

For a short time, at least, his wife, Martha, age thirty-two, and his daughters Patsy and Polly, ages nine and three, respectively, were with him in Williamsburg. With Jefferson's consent, the legislature decided to transfer to Richmond, which they thought was deep enough within Virginia to be safe from British attack. Jefferson hurried Martha and the children to nearby Richmond and joined the lawmakers. Temporarily, he was encouraged by the good news that France had finally signed an alliance with the colonies, and the British army had been defeated in Philadelphia. With Washington's significant victory in the brutal battle at Monmouth, New Jersey, Jefferson hoped peace was at hand. He informed his friend Edmund Pendleton that he planned to retire from politics altogether after the war.

While retreating to Richmond, Jefferson knew that if he was captured by the British, he would be hanged as a traitor. Jefferson prepared Martha for the worst: the crime of "treason" against the British was punishable by not one formal execution, but three excruciating, torturous forms of capital punishment. After rebels were convicted of treason, they were marched to a public hanging. Hanging, however, was too easy a death for traitors to the Crown. After the condemned had suffered at the end of a rope, but before they were unconscious, they were cut down and then disemboweled, and their entrails were burned before their eyes. Then their savaged bodies were sliced into four large pieces and, finally, beheaded—hence the horrid term "drawn and quartered."[1]

During this time, one of the most horrific acts of British war atrocities took place. No doubt, Jefferson was aware of this, and perhaps Martha as well. Two soldiers in the Queen's Rangers had just robbed a home when they came upon a nine-year-old girl. According to journals and letters, the soldiers "ravished" the girl, diplomatic parlance for a brutal sexual assault. The commander of the Queen's Rangers investigated the incident and informed the British commander, Lord Cornwallis, "I have not the least doubt but that Jonathan Webster & Lewis Terrpan . . . of the Queen's Rangers, were guilty of a rape on Martha Dickinson yesterday."[2] After a brief trial, the two men were given an hour to prepare for their deaths. By order of Cornwallis, the men were then hanged "in the presence of the whole army." Rumors of the heinous offense spread through Virginia, terrifying women such as Martha Jefferson, who had young daughters of her own.[3]

Yet, the British were able to strike Richmond from their offshore fleet, with little resistance.[4] Governor Jefferson could do little to stop them. There, a British column appeared and cannonballs rained down, to the horror of fleeing Richmond citizens, who had time to escape. Isaac Granger, Martha's loyal and trusted slave, recalled that when the cannons boomed, "everybody knew it was the British" who were advancing. As cannonballs bashed the top off a butcher's house, "the butcher's wife screamed out and holler'd and her children too and all." According to one description of the scene, "the ensuing panic was instant and total. In ten minutes not a white man was to be seen in Richmond." Isaac remembered that his mother "was so skeered, she didn't know whether to stay indoors or out." The arrival of the invaders, with their beating drums, was terrifying: "It was an awful sight—seemed like the Day of Judgment was come," said Isaac. But his father, George, remained calm. He saved Jefferson's most valuable possessions, gathering all the silver, which he "hid . . . under a bed in the kitchen."

When the British finally came after, the Jeffersons had fled with the other servants to Monticello. Granger steeled himself. "Whar is the Governor?" demanded a soldier.

"He's gone to the mountains," Granger replied.

"Whar is the silver?"

"It was all sent up to the mountains," Granger bluffed.

The British then ransacked the house, smashed Martha's wine bottles, emptied the corncrib for horses, but did not find the precious, hidden silver. The next day, the British imprisoned little Isaac, and his mother too.

George Granger's bravery and loyalty may have led Jefferson to set him free years later. In his memoir, Granger's son, Isaac, said that his father "got his freedom" by his heroism. "But he continued to sarve [sic] Mr. Jefferson and had forty pounds from Old Master and his wife."[5]

In the fall of 1779, Martha and the children fled again from Richmond to their nearby plantation in Albemarle County, Elk Hill, while Jefferson tried to rally the state's militia. Barely two hundred men assembled, and "Jefferson had to sit helplessly on his horse on the south side of the James River and watch [Benedict] Arnold burn millions of dollars' worth of cotton, tobacco, and other property in Richmond."[6] In the midst of this tumult, Martha became pregnant again, adding another worry to her husband. In November of that year, in a small house Jefferson had rented from Martha's uncle, she gave birth to another daughter, whom they named Lucy Elizabeth.[7]

Sadly, on April 15, 1781, in the middle of the war, Martha and Thomas Jefferson were dealt another devastating emotional blow. "Our daughter Lucy Elizabeth died about 10 o'clock a.m. this day," Jefferson noted in his account of the five-month-old's death.[8] Martha seemed inconsolable. One cannot imagine her grief and depression at this tragedy, her third child to die within a few years, as a bloody war raged around her. Jefferson sent his political colleagues a letter explaining that Mrs. Jefferson's "situation" made it impossible for him to attend their legislative sessions—a letter that would haunt him later, when he was accused of cowardice as governor. In his refuge, Jefferson received a letter blaming him for everything that had occurred since the British invaded Virginia. The legislators informed him that an inquiry would be made into his wartime conduct, for he had failed to stop the British intruders. He had fled as Richmond was set aflame, they charged. Three days later, a distraught Jefferson bemoaned to a friend, "I mean shortly to retire."[9] He later told James Monroe, "I felt that these injuries . . . had inflicted a wound on my spirit which will only be cured by the all-healing grave."[10]

Even with more than fifty thousand militia on its official ledgers, Virginia was unable to stop the onslaught of only 180 British dragoons attacking in the heart of Virginia. No one had fired a single shot or offered even tepid resistance to these brutal raiders, in pursuit of Thomas Jefferson. "The British hunted Governor Jefferson fruitlessly," observed one scholar, raiding the plantation west of Richmond where he had hidden his family, only to find the quarry gone. After Jefferson placed Martha and the children at a farm deeper in the interior, the British withdrew to the east, carrying off many slaves, leaving Richmond a shambles, and permanently scarring Jefferson's reputation as a wartime leader.[11]

Martha's emotional distress deepened when a letter arrived, informing Jefferson that the Virginia legislature had launched a formal inquiry concerning his conduct as governor. The charge was dereliction of duty based upon Jefferson's perceived cowardly retreat from Williamsburg. Jefferson's former colleague and now heated political rival, Patrick Henry, had instigated this political vilification.

Henry, and others, may have been disappointed with Jefferson's performance, but it was also an opportunity to tarnish a future political opponent.[12] The assembly adjourned until the fall, leaving Jefferson's investigation dangling as they retreated to Monticello.

At this time, in May 1781, Monticello was a crowded eight-room house in the midst of yet another reconstruction project when Jefferson and several legislators arrived in flight from the British takeover of Richmond. Jefferson, Martha, "and their two daughters, along with servants and guests, crowded into rooms with exposed brick walls" during the next two weeks to discuss "the gloomy state" of the war.[13] Then, at dawn on June 4, 1781, Martha Jefferson's worst fears came true—her home and beloved family were in imminent danger. This was not some vague, distant assault that she feared, as in Richmond, months earlier. Now, a fierce strike force of British dragoons commanded by Lieutenant Colonel Banastre Tarleton, the most feared cavalry leader of the war, stormed toward Charlottesville to capture Jefferson and the legislature. Martha had good reason to fear Tarleton, the twenty-two-year-old officer "later known for bloodthirsty tactics in the South."[14] "Tarleton had a reputation for being charming with women and ruthless with enemies."[15]

Born in Liverpool, England, "the son of a wealthy merchant," Tarleton "was educated at Oxford. At nineteen he inherited a sizable fortune but lost most of it within a year due to gambling."[16] One scholar succinctly described Tarleton's bloody exploits:

> In May 1780, Cornwallis had been a leader of the British siege of Charleston. . . . He had ordered Tarleton to go after a nearby force of 350 Virginians led by Colonel Abraham Buford. Catching up to the Virginians at Waxhaws, near the border of North Carolina, Tarleton sent a message urging Buford to surrender or "the blood be upon your head." Buford responded that he would defend himself "to the last extremity." But after firing commenced, the Virginians hoisted the flag of truce.[17]

When Tarleton's horse was shot from under him, his troops believed he had been targeted in blatant violation of a cease-fire. In retaliation, they launched a savage attack against the Virginians. "'Slaughter was commenced before Tarleton could remount." Cornwallis later wrote that 172 Virginians were killed. As word of the grisly massacre spread, "Tarleton gained a reputation for being the most savage officer in the British army, earning the . . . nickname 'Bloody Ban' and prompting Americans to charge that he gave no quarter to pleas for mercy." Cornwallis cheaply boasted that the British victory had caused "inhabitants from every quarter" to "declare their allegiance to the King."[18]

In his pursuit of Jefferson, Tarleton had captured General Charles Lee, who had been hiding at a nearby Charlottesville tavern. When Lee spied Tarleton's horsemen outside his window, he gasped, "For God's sake, what shall I do?" The widow who owned the inn tried to conceal Lee above a fireplace as bullets ripped through the windows. After Tarleton threatened to burn down the inn, Lee surrendered in slippers and a filthy shirt." To make his degradation complete, the British didn't allow him to don a coat or a hat in the wintry weather. After all of his abrasive lectures to Washington, Charles Lee hadn't known how to protect himself, and his embarrassing capture proved the punch line of a grim joke. He would spend sixteen months in British captivity.[19]

Another legislator, Judge Lyons, was dragged from his room before he had finished dressing and shoved into the yard. When he appeared, the enormously rotund man "provoked gales of laughter from the assembled dragoons," according to one account. One of Tarleton's soldiers "found his cousin hiding at the Walker home. . . . [He] was unceremoniously taken away. . . According to family tradition, the Walker family did its part to save Jefferson. Dr. Walker had been the physician for Jefferson's father, Peter, and upon Peter's death had helped care for Thomas. A plot was hatched. Walker's chef, Dinah, cooked fried chicken for Tarleton, delaying his departure by crucial minutes."[20]

Now, riding fast, the British dragoons pursued Jefferson and his family, passing the Cuckoo Tavern in Louisa, Virginia. It was late—somewhere between nine and ten in the evening—when the British stormed by. A giant of a Virginia militiaman named Jack Jouett, six foot four and 220 pounds, was present at the same time. Jouett was described as "a flamboyant twenty-six-year-old who wore a feathered hat and fancied himself one of the best riders of the Blue Ridge." Jouett's father, a commissary to the Continental army, ran the Swan Tavern in Charlottesville, where the Virginia legislators had been lodging for days.[21]

The Jouett family knew Jefferson well, not just as the master of Monticello, but from having served him at the Swan Tavern. Jouett was aware that Jefferson had returned to Monticello after hours of meetings in Charlottesville.[22] It had been a dark, rainy day, but now the skies cleared to reveal a bright moon. Around 10:00 p.m., realizing that the enemy meant to capture Jefferson and his family, Jouett mounted his horse, "the best and fleetest of foot of any nag in seven counties," and crashed through the thick wilderness. Careering through the tangled woods, Jouett stayed clear of the main roads, which the British patrolled. According to one account, his face was "cruelly lashed by tree-branches as he rode forward, and scars which are said to have remained the rest of his life were the result of lacerations sustained from these low-hanging limbs."[23]

Finally, Jouett emerged from the woods in the early morning hours, riding with fury straight up the path to Jefferson's front porch. With calm and grace, Martha greeted Jouett with a glass of Madeira, trying to calm the man down. Having seen Jouett so agitated, it is not hard to imagine the stricken look on Martha's face. Not even at Monticello could she and her daughters be safe and secure. If they captured her husband, the British might hang him on the spot or take him to England for a political show trial. At the very least, the rampaging soldiers would loot and burn her beloved home, Monticello.[24] After speaking with Jouett, a calm Jefferson insisted that the mountains would delay the enemy and that there was time for breakfast. His plantation overseer, Edmund Bacon, explained later that he never saw Jefferson panic and he remained steadfastly calm. No matter what happened, Jefferson "always maintained the same expression . . . his countenance was perfectly unmoved."[25]

Such serenity in the face of chaos was a Jeffersonian trait, and Jefferson himself later recalled, "I ordered a carriage to be ready to carry off my family." Still in a weak state both physically and emotionally, Martha tried to remain as calm as Jefferson for the children's sake. She quickly prepared for the journey and her unknown future. She followed Jefferson's precise instructions, bundling up their two daughters, Patsy and Polly (or, Mary).[26] She packed for the long, rough carriage ride and said goodbye to Jouett. Jefferson shook Jouett's hand before he left and held it for a fraction longer than was necessary. He told Jouett to head back down to Charlottesville to warn the legislators. Once in Charlottesville, Jouett had barely sounded the alarm when another Virginian reported that Tarleton was minutes away from an attack. The lawmakers mounted horses and hurried in all directions, several barely clothed.[27]

At Monticello, Jefferson gave final instructions to the house servants; then a wild scramble ensued. Martha hurried their daughters into a carriage. Jefferson guided Martha, Patsy, and Polly with two slaves to an escape path, directing them to nearby Blenheim Plantation. Martha did not know if she would ever see Jefferson alive again.

Now Jefferson was alone except for two dutiful slaves who remained, so he tried to rescue his most important documents: "In preparing for flight, I shoved in papers where I could," he later recalled. The searing memory of his boyhood home, Shadwell, burning up with nearly all of his valuable books, may have played in the back of his mind.[28]

He had asked Martha to collect important personal papers and hide them in the woods. It was at this time that a twenty-three-year-old Virginia lieutenant, Christopher Hudson, happened to be traveling on the road about four miles east of Monticello. As Hudson rode, he encountered a man named Long, who told of British soldiers nearing Monticello. Long told him that Jack Jouett had gone to Charlottesville to warn the legislators. Hudson asked whether Jouett had also gone to Monticello to warn the Jeffersons. "Long replied that he did not know."[29]

Hudson hurried to Monticello and "found Mr. Jefferson, perfectly tranquil, and undisturbed." Hudson also noticed that Monticello seemed completely empty. "I was convinced his Situation was truly critical, since there was only one man (his gardener) upon the Spot." Hudson told Jefferson that Tarleton's men were riding up the hill. He begged Jefferson to quickly flee. Finally, "at my earnest request he left his house," Hudson recalled.[30]

As Martha and the children vanished down the road, Jefferson mounted his favorite horse, Caractacus, his six-year-old stallion and one of the fastest horses in Virginia. Jefferson kicked with his heels and whipped Caractacus through a dense thicket. He "knew that he would be pursued if he took the high road," so he "plunged into the woods of the adjoining mountain,"[31] cutting across his own property, to Carter's mountain. With his family now safely gone, Jefferson rode over to a nearby ridgeline and gazed down toward the valley below to try to locate the British dragoons.[32] As one historian described the scene:

> On Carter's Mountain, Jefferson resorted to his telescope again and saw no trace of Tarleton's green-coated horsemen. The telescope collapsed to 7 ¼ inches and extended in three draws to 20 ½ inches. At some point, the family had Jefferson's name etched into the silver plating that encircled the instrument. He peered through the spyglass but did not see a single English soldier. Perhaps it was all a false alarm. As he turned back, however, Jefferson's small sword cane fell from its sheath to the ground. As Jefferson went to retrieve the sword, he took one last look at Charlottesville. This time he noticed something glinting in the sun. Tarleton's dragoons were approaching the village.[33]

Jefferson was about to return to his estate when he saw that Charlottesville's streets swarmed with swordsmen chasing and capturing scurrying legislators. He rode fast down the other side of Carter's Mountain, escaping to join Martha and the girls at Blenheim Plantation. "Martha's anxiety remained acute," observed historian Thomas Fleming, "and so did Jefferson's mortification. Tarleton's incursion was a savage final commentary on his failed Governorship."[34] Jefferson would later make a cryptic notation about the day's extraordinary events for his memorandum book: "June 4, British horse came to Monticello."[35]

Mere minutes after Jefferson had fled, British Captain McLeod and his dragoons swamped Monticello. As slave George Granger had been the man to save the family silver in Richmond, that task now fell to twenty-six-year-old servant Martin Hemings. According to one of the most famous stories in Monticello lore, Tarleton's troops pounded up the mountain while Martin and another slave hid the silver beneath the planks of the steps of one of the front porticos. The British arrived just as they finished, and Martin slammed the planks down on the other man, who was trapped below. Bravely, Martin faced down armed soldiers.

They threatened to kill him if he did not tell them Jefferson's whereabouts. One of the dragoons jammed a pistol into Martin's chest. "Fire away, then," Martin replied, refusing to talk. As the story is told, he stood his ground, "fiercely answering glance for glance, and not receding a hair's breadth from the muzzle of the cocked pistol."[36] Unbeknownst to the British, the other servant, Caesar, lay in silence beneath their feet with the silver, for three nights without food.[37]

Martin escaped unharmed, and Tarleton's soldiers left Monticello largely undamaged, for reasons still unknown.[38] But one story, told by Jefferson's slaves, held that Tarleton's troops did loot Jefferson's beloved wine cellar. They destroyed his casks, smashed his expensive bottles with their swords, and flooded the dirt floor.[39] And British general Lord Cornwallis demolished Jefferson's Edge Hill plantation. Indeed, Cornwallis was in Jefferson's words, "the most active, enterprising and vindictive Officer who has ever appeared in Arms against us."[40] Cornwallis camped his army at Elk Hill for ten days. There he wrought his vengeance on Jefferson "in a spirit of total extermination." After first taking what he wanted, the British general destroyed all of Jefferson's corn and tobacco crops and burned all the barns. "He used, as was to be expected, all my stocks of cattle, sheep and hogs for the sustenance of his army," Jefferson lamented, "and carried off all the horses capable of service: of those too young for service he cut the throats, and he buried all the fences on the plantation, so as to leave it an absolute waste."[41]

There was also a human toll at Elk Hill. Some thirty slaves either were captured by Cornwallis, "joined [the] enemy," or simply ran away. Jefferson reviled Cornwallis for carrying off his slaves: "Had this been to give them freedom he would have done right, but it was to consign them to inevitable death from the small pox and putrid fever then raging in his camp."[42] Sadly, many of Jefferson's slaves died in British hands. Some returned or escaped to Elk Hill and Monticello, bringing with them smallpox, which they had contracted in British custody.[43] One historian tells of Cornwallis's later surrender at Yorktown. Slain black slaves captured by the British dotted the bloody battlefield:

> The next day soldiers waded across a hellish battlefield paved with cadavers, one recalling that "all over the place and wherever

you look [there were] corpses lying about that had not been buried." The majority of the bodies . . . were black, reflecting their importance on both sides of the conflict. Some of these black corpses likely belonged to runaway slaves who had sought asylum with Cornwallis, only to be stricken during the siege with smallpox or "camp fever"—likely typhus, a disease spread by lice and fleas in overcrowded camps.[44]

Historian Dumas Malone acknowledged the devastation at Elk Hill but argued that Jefferson's "supply of slaves was not seriously depleted, for he still had more than two hundred," including "his very special 'people,'" Jupiter and Suck, George and Ursula, "and the superior Heming [sic] of 'bright' mulattoes."[45]

***

Life at Monticello soon "resumed its normal character and tempo."[46] But the "normal character and tempo" of Martha Jefferson's life for the past two years had throbbed with death and loss. Yet, nothing had ever come close to this: her family physically threatened and a husband fleeing in disgrace.

It was a hard and frightening journey for Martha and her terrified young daughters over rough roads, guarded by the British. "Jefferson normally preferred to travel by longer routes if it meant he could avoid raking his carriage on bumpy mountain roads, especially when traveling with his wife and daughters, but there was no time for such a luxury," historian Michael Kranish observed. "The fastest route would take the Jeffersons along mountainous byways, over fast-moving streams, and through dense forests."[47]

Finally, Jefferson decided to move his family further into the dense Virginia countryside to the most isolated of his three plantations, Poplar Forest, in Bedford County, ninety miles away. Poplar Forest was a large estate of several thousand acres, which Martha had inherited from her father, John Wayles.[48] Poplar Forest (near present-day Lynchburg, Virginia) was an estate Jefferson and Martha had not visited in eight years, but the British would not find them there. Poplar Forest was bordered by the Bear and Tomahawk creeks and surrounded by enormous tulip poplar trees. Years later, Jefferson would build a magnificent house here, "an elegant octagonal structure with triple-sash windows and Palladian porticoes." At the time of their arrival, however, the property was sparse, having only barns, slave cabins, and a two-room cabin occupied by the overseer. A small, vacant cabin became the makeshift home for the Jefferson family over the next five weeks—far away from the comforts of Monticello, but safe and secluded from British dragoons.[49]

Arriving after the brutal journey, Jefferson rode out one morning on Caractacus. Unfortunately, the horse suddenly reared and threw Jefferson from the saddle, fracturing Jefferson's left wrist. Martha nursed Jefferson's hand back to health, but sensed that her husband was badly shaken up, not only by the fall but also by their harrowing escape from Monticello. It would take a full two months for Jefferson to regain the full use of his hand.

Rumors circulated as far as Europe that Jefferson was dead or had been captured by the British, greatly distressing John Adams.[50] But the family remained hidden at Poplar Forest for nearly two months. Diverting his mind from his escape and troubles as always, Jefferson began to write a formal response to the Virginia legislature on his actions as governor. In it, he declared that "he had been trying to defeat the British with a ragtag militia that was lucky to have a small number of men with real muskets, and a single armed boat."[51] According to one historian, Jefferson defended himself by asking if it was with this force that he, a man with no military training, was supposed to fight the greatest army and navy in the world? His defense shifted the blame away from him and put it squarely on the legislature's meager resources and the failure of militia to turn out.[52] In the end, the legislature offered to Jefferson what amounted to an "apology and offer of gratitude . . . It was the equivalent of a legislature on bent knee, asking forgiveness."[53] The resolution read:

> Resolved, That the sincere thanks of the General Assembly be given to our former Governor, Thomas Jefferson, Esq. For his impartial, upright, and attentive administration of the powers of the Executive, whilst in office; popular rumors gaining some degree of credence, by more pointed accusations, rendered it necessary to make an inquiry into his conduct, and delayed

that retribution of public gratitude, so eminently merited; but that conduct having become the object of open scrutiny, tenfold value is added to an approbation, founded on a cool and deliberate discussion. The Assembly wish therefore, in the strongest manner, to declare the high opinion which they entertain of Mr. Jefferson's ability, rectitude and integrity, as Chief Magistrate of this Commonwealth; and mean by thus publicly avowing their opinion to obviate all future, and to remove all former, censure.[54]

While in seclusion, Jefferson also started making partial notes in answer to a series of questions sent by a French aristocrat, the Barté-Martois, on the state of Virginia and the war. These now-famous notes, written under the most dreadful of circumstances, would later be published as the book *Notes on the State of Virginia*, written over a two-year period between 1780 and 1782.[55] One historian has aptly summed up the period: "Not only had Jefferson been driven from his home by British troops, he had been nearly censured by the Virginia legislature for failing, as the state's Governor, to prepare adequately for Cornwallis's invasion of 1781, two days after his thirty-eighth birthday. Then more tragic news struck the family—Jefferson's four-month-old daughter, Lucy Elizabeth, died, beginning a seventeen-month period of grief, complicated by Martha's seventh difficult pregnancy."[56]

The time of seclusion gave Jefferson his first real opportunity to inspect and survey his property at Poplar Forest. Accommodations were threadbare. Architectural historian Allen Chambers suggests that the family lodged with overseer Thomas Bennett, as Jefferson himself was later known to have done. In solitude, Jefferson had time to sketch a survey and plan a bigger house, even while working on *Notes*. He sketched out drawings on a large sheet, cobbled together from several pieces of paper made during the early 1780s, coinciding with his Poplar Forest seclusion.[57]

A month later, Cornwallis surrendered at Yorktown to the American and French coalition troops under Washington and Rochambeau. Months later, Jack Jouett, who had ridden through the night to warn Jefferson of the approaching army, was hailed a hero by the Virginia legislature for countering "the designs of the enemy." The assembly awarded Jouett a pair of pistols in 1783. But as one historian recounted, "it was a sign of Virginia's destitute finances that it took twenty years to fulfill a promise to present him with an 'elegant sword.' He moved west and became a leader in Kentucky's separation from Virginia."[58]

Toward the end of the war, Jefferson was asked to become one of the peacemakers in Europe. He declined, telling Edmund Randolph in a letter, "[I] have retired to my farm, my family and books from which I think nothing will ever more separate me."[59] Years later, Jefferson took a group of French officers and the Comte de Rochambeau, who had defeated Cornwallis at Yorktown, on a private tour of Monticello, pointing out the mountain trail where he had fled Tarleton's troops. "They discussed Jefferson's role in the revolution" and Tarleton's attack on Monticello, which had "much alarmed his family."[60] Jefferson never forgot this traumatic episode, and personal attack on his inner sanctum and those he loved.

Perhaps this explains a later event during his presidency.[61] It seems Jefferson took time to settle one score. At his first official meeting with British minister Anthony Merry, he was "not merely in undress, but actually standing in slippers down at the heels (as Merry described the scene to his King) and both pantaloons, coat, and underclothes indicative of utter slovenliness and indifference to appearances." Historian Fawn M. Brodie goes on to explain that "Jefferson compounded the insult later when Merry took his ostentatiously dressed wife to the President's House, only to see Jefferson ignore protocol and take into the dining room instead the woman he most enjoyed talking to—Dolley Madison." "This will be the cause of war!" whispered Spanish prime minister Carlos Martínez de Yrujo. This comment helped seal this as "one of the best remembered dinners in American diplomatic history," though Anthony Merry likely did not recognize that Jefferson was "paying off a personal as well as a national affront."

***

Martha Jefferson's death, four years later, was a heartbreaking tale. For Thomas Jefferson, perhaps, it was the worst day of his life.[62]

Inside the big mansion in 1782, Martha Jefferson's bedroom door was closed as she lay ill on her bed. She had grown so weak that summer that she spat up blood and could barely walk without assistance. By early August, she was confined to bed. Jefferson sensed she could not survive much longer.

The attending doctor opened the bedroom door and stepped into the hall to speak with Jefferson. He placed his hand on Jefferson's shoulder and gripped it firmly. The dreaded truth surged into the deepest recesses of Jefferson's soul. She would not last long.

Just a year earlier, and two days after Thomas Jefferson's thirty-eighth birthday, on April 15, 1781, his infant daughter, Lucy Elizabeth, had died. This had triggered a period of deep depression and grief for Martha, complicated by her seventh pregnancy. Martha's "desire to nurture a big family," six children in all, had ravaged her petite body. Her health had worsened with each difficult birth. The loss of so many children had shaken both her mental and her physical well-being. Already weak and emotionally drained, her final pregnancy was even riskier than the others. Martha had gained too much weight and was too sick to perform even the simplest of household tasks. She remained bedridden, relinquishing supervision of Monticello to her trusted house servants, the Hemings family.

When Martha's last baby was born, on May 8, 1782, Martha had named the child Lucy Elizabeth, in honor of her deceased daughter Lucy. And in spite of Martha's fragility, the baby was healthy, weighing an astonishing sixteen pounds at birth. But Martha's health had declined rapidly following the birth, prompting Jefferson to forward a somber letter to his friend James Monroe. "Mrs. Jefferson has added another daughter to our family. She has ever since and still continues very dangerously ill."

Around September 6, a few weeks short of her thirty-fourth birthday, Martha's health plummeted. She had never regained her vigor following the birth of Lucy Elizabeth, who, sadly, would die of whooping cough at age two. Of the six children born to Martha, only two daughters would survive to adulthood, Patsy and Polly. Tragically, Polly herself would die in childbirth in her twenties. Only Martha's oldest daughter, Patsy, would outlive her famous father. Death, it seems, followed the Jefferson family.

Day after day for three months, Jefferson had gazed into Martha's eyes, the color of blue glass. Her bright eyes were still unspoiled despite the stressful life that had been thrust upon her. Now, her light, loving eyes had sunk into drowsy sickness. In the middle of the night, Martha awoke with a burning sensation in her chest and a suffocating shortness of breath. It had been nearly four months since she had given birth to little Lucy, but Martha still had failed to gain any strength. Before retiring that night, Martha had refused the doctor's usual dose of laudanum. As she tried to sleep, she broke out in a sweat, nausea overwhelming her. Searing pain engulfed her. She gasped her husband's name in a strangled voice before she began to retch.

Hours later, her sister, Lisbet, tiptoed into the bedroom and took Martha's cold hand as the flaring light of the fire threw tall, dim shadows on the black walnut furniture. Martha managed to sit up. Two auburn braids fell on either side of her face. Her face was ashen.

Jefferson had stayed up all night with her now for several days. Once Martha was asleep, exhaustion overwhelmed him. He finally rested in the dressing room next to their bed. It had been Jefferson's habit in the afternoons to go riding, at Martha's insistence, then tend his cherished wife through the night, so as not to allow Martha's sisters to wear themselves out.

On the morning of September 6, 1782, it had started to rain, with the wind hastening decayed leaves from the magnolia trees. Martha did not have the strength to rise from her bed. She had spent her days drifting in and out, sleeping a good deal. The doctor had given her laudanum, which increased her fuzziness, but at least the pain in her chest had subsided. Betty Hemings, her faithful and loving servant since childhood, removed the warm cloth on her head, replacing it with a cool one. Betty, Nance, and Critta Hemings had taken loving care of Martha these last weeks. Betty spoke to Martha in a quiet voice, gentle and solicitous. She had nursed Martha Jefferson since she was two years old, becoming more of a surrogate mother to her than anyone else. Betty was a nurturer, not only to Martha, but to Martha's children as well.

Betty brought baby Lucy and held her close to her mother. Martha reached out and caressed Lucy's fine blonde fuzz. Dark hazel eyes gazed back at her. How sweet it was to Martha to breathe in Lucy's warm baby smell. Martha's four-year-old daughter, Polly, quietly entered the candlelit room. Martha took several breaths with great difficulty and grasped Polly's tiny hand. Little Polly was so gentle and kindhearted. She would be a lovely woman.

Martha drifted back to sleep and awakened to Patsy's small hand resting on her arm. "Miss Patt," her ten-year-old big girl, would one day capture this deathbed scene in correspondence and remembrances that would be read for many years to come.

Jefferson, now at her bedside, stroked Martha's soft hands as she drifted in and out of consciousness. His face paled at her sight. There was so much they had yet to do. They had talked of traveling to Paris and of building two new wings at Monticello. They'd talked of having another baby, a son. Of Martha playing her spinet, and of the digging in the garden together in the spring. Now, all Martha could do was stare into the depths of Thomas Jefferson's hazel blue eyes, where all boundaries between flesh and spirit were dissolved. Martha wept, but without tears; she had none left in her wasted body. She fell asleep in her husband's arms as she had done so often before, safe and warm.

Jefferson had spent the summer watching Martha slip away from him. He'd fed her food and medicine, and sat up with her during her final days, until finally he had to summon his sister, Martha Carr, and Martha's sister, Elizabeth Eppes, to assist him. Even then, he did most of the nursing himself, by now nearly as knowledgeable of medicine as the doctors. He sat beside Martha's bed for hours, reading to her from her favorite books when she was awake. While she slept, he retreated to a small room adjoining the bedroom, where he tried to work on the book he was finishing, *Notes on Virginia,* today considered by many "the most important American book written before 1800."[63]

Most of their conversations are lost to history, but throughout the summer Jefferson read to Martha from her favorite author, Laurence Sterne's, *Tristram Shandy*. Martha may have found in Sterne a confirmation of death's uncertainty, a theme that permeated her own life. Martha had survived the deaths of her father, her mother, and her precious babies. And Jefferson had endured the death of his father before he was twelve years old. It may have been with these deaths in mind that Martha scribbled some lines from Sterne's novel on a piece of paper that Jefferson saved for the rest of his life.

By Friday, September 6, 1782, the family and household servants sensed that Martha's death was imminent. The following account of the death scene is taken directly from Jefferson's daughter Patsy:

> As a nurse no female ever had more tenderness nor anxiety [than my father]... For four months that [my mother] lingered he was never out of calling; when not at her bedside, he was writing in a small room which opened immediately at the head of her bed. A moment before the closing scene, he was led from the room in a state of insensibility by his sister, Mrs. Carr, who, with great difficulty, got him into the library, where he fainted, and remained so long insensible that they feared he never would revive. The scene that followed I did not witness, but the violence of his emotion, when, almost by stealth, I entered his room by night, to this day I dare not describe to myself.[64]

Edmund Bacon, overseer at Monticello for many years, gave a slightly different account of Martha's death:

> The house servants were Betty Brown, Sally, Critta, and Betty Hemings, Nance, and Ursula . . . They were in the room when Mrs. Jefferson died . . . They have often told my wife that when Mrs. Jefferson died, they stood around the bed. Mr. Jefferson sat by her, and she gave him directions about a good many things that she wanted done. When she came to the children, she wept, and could not speak for some time. Finally she held up her hand, and spreading out her four fingers, she told him she could not die happy if she thought her four children were ever to have a stepmother brought in over them. [Bacon was wrong about the number of children—there were only three young daughters.] Holding her other hand in his, Mr. Jefferson promised her solemnly that he would never marry again. And he never did. He

was then quite a young man, and very handsome, and I suppose he could have married well; but he always kept that promise.[65]

Martha's "death bed" request—that Jefferson never marry again—is a psychological puzzle. Why would she ask such a thing of Jefferson? One historian suggested that Martha "may have been as possessive of him in death as she seems to have been possessive of him in life, as jealous of any future wife as she had been jealous of his 'passion' for politics."[66] But another explanation seems more likely. Martha herself had had to endure more than one stepmother. Perhaps this is why the thought of another woman replacing her as mother to her children was abhorrent. Most likely, the "promise" was not based on a selfish whim, but on her beloved children. She was worried that her girls would be raised by a controlling, harsh stepmother like Martha had experienced.[67]

At the end, Martha sank into a coma. Her breath became the shallow gasps of the dying. Jefferson literally blacked out as Martha took her last gasp. His sister called to the other women, still bending over Martha's lifeless body, "Leave the dead . . . come and take care of the living."[68] It took nearly an hour to revive Jefferson. His grieving was so out of character to the gathered women that their fear of his death was replaced by fear of his insanity. Patsy described her father's anguish:

> He kept his room three weeks, and I was never a moment from his side. He walked almost incessantly night and day, only lying down occasionally, when nature was completely exhausted, . . . on a pallet that had been brought in during his long fainting-fit. My aunts remained constantly with him for some weeks—I do not remember how many. When at last he left his room, he rode out, and from that time he was incessantly on horseback, rambling about the mountain, in the least frequented roads, and just as often through the woods. In those melancholy rambles I was his constant companion, a solitary witness to many a burst of grief, the remembrance of which has consecrated particular scenes of that lost home beyond the power of time to obliterate.[69]

This episode was the beginning of a deep and unshakable bond between father and daughter that became stronger and more meaningful to both of them with the passage of the years.

After Martha's funeral, on October 3, Jefferson wrote to his sister-in-law, Elizabeth, who had returned to her estate, Elk Hill. He told of Patsy riding with him and her determination to accompany him to Elk Hill when he was ready for a family visit. "When that may be . . . I cannot tell," Jefferson said. "Finding myself absolutely unable to attend to business." His grief poured out on the page as he added: "This miserable kind of existence is really too burdensome to be borne and were it not for the infidelity of deserting the sacred charge left to me, I could not wish its continuance for a moment. For what could it be wished?"[70]

He did not write another letter for eight weeks.

Martha Jefferson was buried beneath the great oak, near Jefferson's best friend, Dabney Carr, and her own lost children, in the eighty-square-foot graveyard Jefferson had set aside on his mountaintop in 1773, a year after his marriage. One historian is convinced that Jefferson's deep sense of privacy concerning Martha's life and death made him reluctant to "gratify the curiosity of posterity," but instead to veil his affection for his wife "from the vulgar gaze."[71] Hence, he destroyed all of their tender love letters, symbols of the soul's affections.[72] Jefferson even had the epitaph on Martha's gravestone inscribed in Greek:

> TO THE MEMORY OF MARTHA JEFFERSON, DAUGHTER OF JOHN WAYLES: BORN OCTOBER 19TH 1748 INTERMARRIED WITH THOMAS JEFFERSON JANUARY 1ST, 1772: TORN FROM HIM BY DEATH SEPTEMBER 6, 1782 THIS MONUMENT OF HIS LOVE IS INSCRIBED IF IN THE HOUSE OF HADES MEN FORGET THEIR DEAD YET WILL I EVEN THERE REMEMBER YOU, DEAR COMPANION.[73]

Those last words were a quotation from the *Iliad*.[74]

Martha's death was the proverbial straw that broke the camel's back for Jefferson. Perhaps he felt responsible for his wife's death. Had he sacrificed her to the Revolution he may have wondered. And what had he received in return? A blotted name, and accusations of cowardice from his foes, who claimed that he "preferred domestic pleasures" over serving his country.

At some point after the death of Martha Wayles Skelton Jefferson in September 1782, Jefferson destroyed all of their correspondence "in . . . fierce determination to gallop over his grief and obliterate its traces[;] he was a child of the eighteenth [century]. Those men and women believed that to discuss death was to invite stupor; to contemplate it, to succumb. As a result, they kept their descriptions of death and their letters of consolation brief."[75] Among the family relics discovered after Patsy's death in 1836 was a folded sheet of paper with a lock of her mother's hair and this notation in her handwriting: "A Lock of my Dear Mama's Hair inclosed [*sic*] in a verse which she wrote." The paper on which these lines were written was found after Jefferson's own death, forty-four years later, along with a lock of Martha's hair, in a secret drawer in Jefferson's private cabinet. "The condition of the note indicated that it had been folded, unfolded and read many times over the years."[76]

Later, Jefferson stoically recorded the sad occasion of Martha's death in his account book: "On September 6, 1782, My dear wife died this day at 11:45 a.m."[77] The most deeply felt dream of Thomas Jefferson's life was over. The figure who had stood "always in the forefront" of his happiness was now gone forever. The death of his young wife, Jefferson wrote, meant that "all [his] plans of comfort and happiness [were] reversed by a single event."[78] Perhaps, his destruction of their letters was a final communion that sealed against public intrusion or desecration. Martha Jefferson lived on in his mind, among the fleeting memories.

The rest is lost to history.

7

DOMESTIC VIOLENCE

With respect to [Charles] Bankhead, if ever he becomes a sober man, there will be no difficulty of reconciliation on Anne's account, but as long as he is subject to drink, his society is dangerous & we shall reject it.

—**Thomas Jefferson** to Craven Peyton (1821)

In the first months of Jefferson's return to Virginia after his presidency ended, he seemed in great cheer. The historical whirlwind that had carried him through scandal and his presidency now placed him in the *terra incognita* of retirement. He was finally home to his beloved oasis from politics, Monticello, and his beloved family. During his final packing at the White House, he wrote to Charles Wilson Peale of his joy in departing "to those scenes of rural retirement after which my soul is panting."[1] He declared to German naturalist Alexander von Humboldt, who had visited him in Washington, "Within a few days I shall bury myself in the groves of Monticello."[2] "Mr. Jefferson called last week, and dined here yesterday," Elizabeth Trist said to a friend in a letter in April 1809. "I never saw him look better nor appear so happy."[3] On her visit to Monticello, socialite Margaret Bayard Smith remarked that Jefferson seemed in a perfect state of mind. "The sun never sees him in bed, and his mind designs more than the day can fulfill, even his long day," she explained. "There is a tranquility about him, which an inward peace could alone bestow."[4]

Yet, Jefferson suffered briefly from retirement shock due to a lack of activity, argues one historian. He wrote to Dr. Benjamin Rush that "a retired politician is like a broken down courser, unfit 'for the turf, and good for little else."[5] A year after his retirement commenced, he told John Langdon, "Now, take any race of animals, confine them in idleness and inaction, whether in a stye, a stable or a state-room, pamper them with high diet, gratify all their sexual appetites, immerse them in sensualities, nourish their passions, let everything bend before them, and banish whatever might lead them to think, and in a few generations they become all body and no mind . . . Such is the regimen in raising Kings."[6]

Even so, Jefferson soon began to enjoy his leisure time. He told artist Charles Wilson Peale on May 5, 1809, "I am enjoying a species of happiness I never before knew, that of doing whatever hits the humour of the moment without responsibility or injury to any one."[7] To a neighbor, Jefferson observed that "the happiness of the domestic fireside is the first boon of heaven."[8] His slave Isaac later remembered that whenever Jefferson walked or rode about Monticello, he "was always singing . . . hardly see him anywhar out doors but what he was singin: had a fine clear voice, sung minnits [minuets] & sich: fiddled in the parlor."[9] Ellen, who now slept in the room right above her grandfather at Monticello, heard him humming old tunes, "generally Scotch songs but sometimes Italian airs or hymns."[10]

This tranquil domestic scene would soon change.

Every morning Thomas Jefferson walked across the sprawling West Lawn of Monticello, past willow trees and down the hill to the family graveyard. As were most things at Monticello, the cemetery was his own design. Here he had buried his mother, his wife, his babies, and his best friend. Here he would someday be buried. It seemed that death followed Jefferson throughout his long life, as in a Greek tragedy. In fact, sixty of Jefferson's *Commonplace Book* entries concerned death in one way or another.

A lifetime had taught Jefferson that the secret to happiness was the avoidance of despair by keeping busy, with your family drawn close. Home to stay after his years as president, Jefferson never again strayed far from his quiet mountaintop. His curious mind, however, was another matter. It never rested. Although he lamented the drained feeling of old age, Jefferson remained thoroughly engaged in his twilight years with gardening, farming, writing, reading, tinkering, mentoring, and visiting with family. Remaining cheerful, however, would soon become more difficult than the former president could have predicted. During the last seventeen years of his life, the Jefferson family had become emotionally fragile, vulnerable to death and the turmoil of the outside world, to failures of career and finances, to the convulsions that failed marriages created.[11] Thomas Jefferson's family had no greater special exemption from life's stress, grief, and misery than any other. In fact, Patsy's own sister-in-law became an impoverished and opium-addicted widow when she wrote her *Letters on Female Character*, a treatise that argued that women should be subordinate to generous men who could protect them.[12]

Yes, fate and family dealt Jefferson a series of savage blows that shattered his state of harmony. The Jefferson family hid their own dark secret—domestic violence and emotional turmoil. In the eighteenth century, Virginia was not a refined culture, nor a peaceable one. Violence was commonplace. In Jeff Randolph's prophetic words, it was not "the fashion of the day for men to restrain their tempers."[13] Jefferson had shuddered at the recent news that his beloved, erudite law professor and mentor, George Wythe, had been poisoned by a greedy nephew seeking an inheritance. The coming year, 1811, would prove to be another year of emotional turmoil for Jefferson, who had turned a fragile sixty-eight in the spring.

Patsy's abusive and volatile husband, Thomas Mann Randolph, was nearly penniless and estranged from his wife and children. Meanwhile, Jefferson's finances were distressed, despite Jeff's efforts to manage his extensive properties and pay off his loans. And Jefferson's oldest granddaughter, who suffered a failed pregnancy nearly every year, lived with an insolvent, violently drunk husband, while her younger sisters faced the bleak prospect of permanent spinsterhood.

Threaded through Thomas Jefferson's family woes was the tragic domestic violence involving Jeff's older sister, Anne Cary Randolph. She was Jefferson's eldest granddaughter and the first to marry. Jefferson fondly remembered morning walks with a ten-year-old Anne in the Monticello garden. He loved to reflect on that pleasures that nature offered. And the older he got, the more he delighted in sharing his enthusiasm for gardening. Many times, on these garden walks, he would be accompanied by his grandchildren—Meriwether Lewis Randolph, who had just turned nine, or the boy's sister, Septimia, who was five. In earlier years, however, Jefferson's companion on these outings had always been their much older sister, Anne, a delicate woman whose love of plants and flowers grew as passionate as Jefferson's.

On a beautiful September day in 1807, seventeen-year-old Anne, the gentle soul who delighted in tending flowers with her grandfather, had married the promising and handsome twenty-year-old Charles Lewis Bankhead at Monticello. In the eighteenth century, marriage was regarded more as a practical arrangement than as a vehicle for love, and the Bankhead marriage seemed to fit this pattern. No one at the time could have foreseen what an abusive and emotional disaster the marriage would become.

Anne was a slight, beautiful young woman. Her wavy light-brown hair was highlighted with long golden strands past her shoulders that might have given her an unkempt appearance if not for the meticulousness of her clothes and jewelry. In contrast, Charles was an enormous man, with a massive upper torso armored in muscle. A "fine looking man and a good father," he was unfortunately also "a terrible drunkard."[14] Charles would turn out to be "a man of violent temper even when sober," and "unquestionably abusive and dangerous when in a drunken state."[15]

Bankhead degenerated into a violent brute, beating Anne repeatedly, on one occasion right in front of her horrified mother. Anne, however, kept her dark secret well hidden from everyone but a select few family members. When finally revealed, the scalding reality of her violent marriage jarred the entire family—none more so than her protective brother, Jeff.[16]

At the time of Anne's marriage, Thomas Jefferson had had high hopes for the couple. Though he'd congratulated the beloved bride, he had asked her, "What is to become of our flowers? You must really make out a book of instructions for Ellen."[17] Anne's mother, Patsy, had been frazzled, having given birth only two months earlier to her ninth child. But Patsy had believed that Anne had found a good husband. Bankhead's father was a distinguished Virginia doctor, and Charles planned to study law under Jefferson. Before the marriage, the future brothers-in-law had been on fairly good terms. Bankhead had felt a "brotherly solicitude" for Jeff,[18] but this feeling would soon be dispelled. Although not privy to the brutal details, Jeff sensed his sister's anxiety, which turned out to be prescient.

Jefferson had anticipated that the couple would live with him for a time at Monticello, where Bankhead would avail himself of the former president's tutelage and law books. The first year of their marriage had shown promise, as both the Jefferson and Randolph families took the couple into their fold. In a letter to Anne, Jefferson expressed optimism for his granddaughter's future: "I trust it is Mr. Bankhead's intention to join us at Monticello in March and . . . take his station among my law books in the South pavilion . . . I hope therefore that he will consent to it, and that you will both ever consider yourselves as part of our family until you shall feel the desire of separate establishment insuperable. Salute him . . . in my name."[19]

However, not two months after the wedding, when the couple finally left the mountain to visit Charles's family, Patsy sensed trouble. She reported that Anne was "in a state of such extreme dejection at the separation from her family that it rendered the scene a very distressing one."[20]

For a few years, the young couple seemed happy enough. After losing her first baby, Anne gave birth to a son, John Warner Bankhead. "When Charles, who initially studied law with Jefferson, decided instead to become a [full-time farmer], he received 'a good many' slaves from his father and bought Carlton," an eight-hundred-acre farm on the west slope of Monticello's mountain.[21] Jefferson's patriarchal dream of keeping his family physically and emotionally close seemed to be coming to fruition.

It is not clear when Bankhead first began to abuse alcohol, but when he tried law, he tried farming, and nothing succeeded, the solution to his economic woes turned out to be a whiskey bottle. In the words of her sister, Anne's marriage was "the only thing . . . in our family history to which the word tragic might well be applied."[22] Patsy feared sharing her concerns with her husband, who himself was often morose and withdrawn from the family. She realized that a husband's treatment of his wife in colonial times was regarded as a private matter and "a manly right." As for the fiery and unstable Thomas Mann Randolph, the better course was to keep him oblivious to Anne's situation, for fear of an explosive confrontation. "These details," Jefferson confessed to Charles's father, Dr. Bankhead, "are very much unknown to Mr. Randolph."[23]

Family members, however, gossiped about Bankhead's alcoholism and volatile anger. "I heard too with great concern that Bankhead has turn'd out a great sot," complained Eliza Trist, a Jefferson cousin, "always frolicking and carousing at the taverns in the neighborhood. Poor Anne. I feel for her and Mr. R. [Thomas Mann Randolph] is so much involved that 'tis thought he can never be extricated from ruin, but this is between our selves."[24] The entire family considered the situation to be shameful, but a private matter between husband and wife.

In the beginning, Charles's repentance after his drunken tirades caused hope for his restoration, only to have those wishes crushed time and again. Despite the wealth of both families, the young couple's marital problems were magnified by financial struggles. Charles produced inferior tobacco crops that failed to sell every year. He began drinking heavily and selling his slaves to raise money. By 1815, he had become a hopeless alcoholic and a menace to his wife. Their respective fathers, Dr. Bankhead and Thomas Mann Randolph, were forced to assume the couple's morass of debt.[25] As a result, Charles and Anne signed over Carlton—along with its slaves, stock, and buildings—to their fathers as trustees. Jefferson, apparently concerned for Anne's financial as well as personal welfare, deeded to the trustees one hundred acres of land adjacent to Carlton. This property would be outside of Bankhead's financial control, Patsy explained to a family friend:

> Anne is living with Mrs. Bankhead where she will continue either one year or longer, should the payment of Mr. Bankhead's debts and other circumstances which perhaps you have heard, render it proper. Hers has been a hard fate, but thank God the property is secured to her self and children. Doctor Bankhead has behaved nobly and My Dear Father has added to her little property so as to make her independent; in case of the worst that could happen her children and her self can never want a home of their own.[26]

Anne's family grew more concerned as the months passed. Jefferson constantly corresponded with Charles's father, suggesting some sort of intervention between the two families. Dr. Bankhead could act in his capacity as a physician, Jefferson reasoned, with the goal of affecting a cure for Charles's alcoholism. Jefferson also reported that Charles' destructive behavior had detrimentally affected his estate and finances: [27]

> At his farm [Charles] destroyed all subordination of his negroes to their overseer . . . buying and bargaining again as if not sensible. When sober, he spoke of selling his farm here and moving elsewhere. Said he lost all consideration in this neighborhood and could never be happy here. But his habits would follow him wherever he went, except under your roof, and we have had too many proofs that his family would be safe nowhere else.[28]

Despite Bankhead's anemic attempts to sober up, Anne's marital misery continued. The family was appalled but seemed too perplexed to do anything but disapprove through letters. Jefferson sent Anne a copy of the novel *The Modern Griselda: A Tale*, by Maria Edgeworth, about a failing marriage.[29] "Mama and myself were so peculiarly unfortunate the other day . . . as to have an encounter with Mr. Bankhead in one of his drunkest moods," Mary told Ellen:

> Fortunately for us, there was no one present but the family, and we were spared the shame and mortification of such a meeting (which I know was premeditated on his part) in the presence of entire strangers. Aunt Cary and Wilson succeeded at last in carrying him home but not until he had offered to shake hands with us. I could not have given him mine and acted from impulse in withdrawing it, though I still think I was right in doing so, whatever impression his cry of unrelenting malice and persecution on the part of our family towards him.[30]

By now, Bankhead's local reputation had been ruined. He was considered a drunken rake who abused his wife, and he made a dangerous spectacle of himself both in Charlottesville and at Monticello. "I have seen his wife run from him when he was drunk and hide in a potato hole to get out of danger," recalled

Edmund Bacon, Monticello's overseer. He had also "seen him ride his horse into the barroom at Charlottesville and get a drink of liquor."[31]

Bankhead seemed to instigate fights, even when sober. One afternoon, Bankhead asked Bacon to accompany him home from Charlottesville, then abruptly stopped his horse on the road back to Carlton. There he lay in wait until William Fitzhugh Gordon, a Charlottesville lawyer, rode up with an acquaintance. Representing another party in a lawsuit that involved Bankhead, Gordon had allegedly made some offensive comments about Charles in court. Bankhead, seeking revenge, confronted the lawyer and ordered him to dismount. He threatened to shoot him if he refused. Gordon "had hardly touched the ground," Bacon recalled, "before at it they went and I never in all my life saw such a fight."[32] By the time Bacon separated the two combatants, they were "as bloody as butchers." Bankhead received the worst of it, Bacon recalled, with one eye badly swollen and bloody, "and I think never did get entirely over the hurt," Bacon added.[33]

After hearing this disturbing story from his overseer, Jefferson informed Dr. Bankhead that he was sending Charles back to him "as a medical subject . . . Nothing less than his good, and the hope of restoring happiness to his family and friends & to yourself particularly could have induced me to the pain of this communication," Jefferson lamented.[34] He listed a litany of Bankhead's transgressions, telling his father that Bankhead would return almost every night from Charlottesville in a drunken fury. Jefferson described "an assault on his wife of great violence" after which Bankhead "ordered her out of the room, forbidding her to enter it again and she was obliged to take refuge for the night in her mother's room. Nor was this a new thing."[35] Jefferson also retold the incident where Bankhead had stopped the man on the road from Charlottesville at gunpoint and forced him into a fight.

Chronically, Bankhead would repent the next day, but would repeat the same abuse. The family had talked of committing Bankhead to the hospital for the insane in Williamsburg, but felt that it was "but a temporary remedy." After a few weeks of rehabilitation at the "madhouse . . . he would be returned with renewed health to torment his family the longer,"[36] Patsy groused. Ever the mother, she felt that the solution might be to let Bankhead drink himself to death: "I really think the best way would be to hire a keeper for him . . . and let him finish himself at once."[37]

Bankhead's rage was not confined to his immediate family. It now infected Jefferson's serenity at Monticello. Another member of the household would soon be directly in the line of his wrath—Jefferson's personal butler, Burwell Colbert. As Jefferson's enslaved valet, Burwell was entrusted with the keys to Jefferson's coveted wine cellar. One night Bankhead became drunk and berated Colbert for refusing to hand over the keys to the liquor cabinet. Colbert "would not give him any more brandy," according to Edmund Bacon.[38] Patsy had tried to calm Bankhead but finally summoned Bacon for assistance, instead of her own husband, fearing Thomas's violent reaction. "She would never call on Mr. Randolph . . . at such a time, he was so excitable," Bacon confessed. Indeed, Jeff described his father as "more ferocious than the woulf and more fell than the hyena."[39]

Bacon described the ugly melee that ensued: "[Thomas Mann Randolph] entered the room just as I did, and Bankhead, thinking he was Burwell, began to curse him." Randolph seized a hot poker from the fireplace and struck Bankhead in the head, burning off a chunk of flesh. "[He] knocked [Bankhead] down as quick as I ever saw a bullock fall," Bacon continued. "The blow pealed [sic] the skin off one side of his forehead and face, and he bled terribly."[40]

Years later, Jeff Randolph, who was not at Monticello that night, acknowledged "that the incident had taken place, but diplomatically dismissed it as a mere 'row between two drunken men' who were 'immediately reconciled.'" [41] Even so, Jeff concluded from the encounter that Bankhead posed a direct threat to his sister's safety.

The final straw came when Bankhead, in a drunken rambling, wrote an abusive letter to Jeff's wife, which triggered a fateful encounter. The showdown must have long been brewing in Jeff's mind. The family attributed the violent confrontation to Bankhead, but on "Court Day," February 1, 1819, Jeff rode to Charlottesville armed with a horsewhip. Court Day was a time when men came together from their scattered plantations to settle their legal disputes, drink, socialize, politick—and fight.

On Court Day, the air had turned cold and smelled of burning wood as a winter dawn broke over the small town of Charlottesville. Public buildings and private homes glowed with candles and torches. Terrible winds and rain had swept through Charlottesville earlier that morning, dissolving the dirt streets into muddy pools. The small town smelled of tobacco, chimney smoke, and coffee mixed with crates of poultry. The tavern keepers and the livery stablemen had booked every available sleeping place weeks earlier. An enterprising wholesaler had stored quantities of flour in his cellar to await the bakers' inevitable shortage. Charlottesville bustled with drink and gossip, covering the town as thickly as the mud covered its sodden streets.

Witnesses later claimed they heard Bankhead threaten to kill Jeff on Court Day. What was about to happen would be impossible to conceal from Thomas Jefferson, or anybody else. As Jefferson caught up on his afternoon correspondence in his private study at Monticello, Bankhead rode into town and immediately purchased a large knife with a serrated blade. He had fought a searing hangover all morning with brandy and a chewable, wooden peppermint stick. Broad-shouldered with spearmint-green eyes, Bankhead had bought several knives in recent weeks, "ten or 12 of those Spanish knives in the course of a month," according to his cousin, Elizabeth Trist.[42] Each time he brought one of the weapons home, Anne managed to find and hide it. Yet, Bankhead was rarely unarmed. Sometimes he carried pistols, but he never left home without "a knife as long as a dirk."[43]

Bankhead searched for his prey—Jeff Randolph. When he noticed Jeff in the town square, his face darkened. Bankhead believed that the demon who had interfered in his marriage for the past few years would now be exorcised. He extended his hand, big and hard, the knuckles pronounced. He then made a gun figure with his two fingers, raised his hand, and pointed to Jefferson Randolph.

Jeff had ventured into Charlottesville that day to buy "snuffers" from Bell's store for his grandfather.[44] When he spotted Bankhead, his facial muscles hardened and he unleashed his leather horsewhip. Turning up his fur collar, he strode toward Bankhead, armed with his whip. But violence was not in his nature. Jeff had been raised as a gentle child at his grandfather's scholarly knee. A tall, skinny, and reserved boy, he had been intimidated by his father, who would bully and embarrass Jeff for his timid nature.

Bankhead had arrived armed, anticipating a public humiliation of a whipping, usually reserved for runaway slaves. Most accounts have Bankhead lying in wait, jumping on Jeff from behind a wagon, knife already drawn. According to one eyewitness, Jeff and Bankhead confronted each other in front of the courthouse. Bankhead brandished a large knife as he strode toward Jeff. Randolph drew his riding whip, demanding to know why Bankhead had written the insulting letter to his wife. Bankhead made no reply but continued to advance with his knife. Jeff gave ground, cracking the whip over Bankhead's head to keep him from drawing closer, then actually striking him with it. When Bankhead charged, Jeff fell backward. Before Bankhead could leap upon him, Jeff used the butt end of his whip and laid open Bankhead's head with "a pretty considerable gash in the side of his head."[45]

At close quarters, Jeff smelled alcohol and snuff reeking from his opponent. Bankhead's knife proved the more formidable weapon as the blade ripped down, making contact. Jeff felt the knife plunge into his left side, deeply cutting into his skin. Bankhead thrust the knife into Jeff's side again, slicing flesh and bone, stabbing Jeff twice above the hip and across his left arm. As Jeff fought not to pass out, he watched drops of his own blood run off his arm and break like small red stars in the dirt. Edmund Bacon rushed over and quickly separated the two men. "I think he [Bankhead] would have killed him," Bacon said, "if I had not interfered and separated them."[46]

Jeff's wounds appeared serious, but not mortal, though at first it appeared Jeff would not survive, as he was bleeding profusely. Bystanders rushed him into the counting room of Leitch's store. Four physicians dressed his wounds, surrounded by a cluster of people. Bankhead also sought medical attention and appealed to one of the doctors, but the crowd called out that he should not be attended until "Mr. Randolph was dress'd." [47]

Word quickly reached Monticello of the vicious clash. Jefferson had been in town earlier that day but had returned home before the violent brawl. A rider was dispatched up the mountain with the grim news. By the time Jefferson learned that Jeff had been severely wounded, the sun had set. The women at Monticello insisted that it was too dark for the seventy-six-year-old Jefferson to ride to Charlottesville. Ignoring their warnings, Jefferson ordered his horse be brought up. When the women objected, Jefferson repeated the order "in a tone which brooked no further opposition."[48] "He had Old Eagle brought up to the terrace so that he could be mounted from the height of the porch."[49] Jefferson eased himself into the saddle, assuming the straight posture of a natural-born rider, while the horse leaned patiently against the terrace wall. Jefferson prodded the horse, which bounded forward at a gallop. The women watched with anxiety as the horse approached "the notch," a gap in the dark woods with a steep descent. "With a clatter of hoofs," the horse and the frail former president of the United States disappeared down the mountain.[50]

Within the hour, Jefferson had ridden the four miles to Charlottesville, dismounted, and made his way to the back room of the store. He found Jeff inside "laid on a bale of blankets."[51] Nothing Jefferson had ever seen or done in life had prepared him for the sight of his dear grandson at the center of the most extreme of medical emergencies. The piercing smells of formaldehyde and laudanum filled Jefferson's nostrils. Blood was everywhere. An enormous purple bruise marked Jeff's forehead. Bandages covered his shoulder and stomach. Jefferson raised a fist to his trembling lips, then kneeled by his grandson's side. Tears bathed Jefferson's eyes. "I had borne myself with proper fortitude," Jeff later wrote, "but when [my grandfather] entered and knelt at my head and wept, I was unmanned."[52]

Jefferson's attention turned to Anne, fearing Bankhead might return to Carlton and wreak vengeance on his poor wife. Later that night, Jefferson returned to Monticello, sending several slaves with a letter to bring Jeff back to his mountain retreat. He would personally take charge of his medical care and recovery. However, "the doctors thought it would not be proper to move him for a day or two."[53] Jeff remained in the store the next day and then was moved to the home of Alexander Garrett, a lawyer and close friend of Jefferson's. Garrett had ridden up the mountain to reassure Jeff's wife, Jane, that the doctor believed her husband would survive, provided his infection subsided. Dr. Thomas Watkins remained at Jeff's side, dressing his wounds until nine the next morning. The infection did subside, but the injuries to Jeff's left arm were severe. There were fears that he might lose the use of the arm, "a deplorable loss to any man," Jane's sister-in-law reported, "but particularly so to a man of his industry and activity."[54] Garrett invited Jane to stay at his house in Charlottesville, where Dr. Watkins cleaned and dressed Jeff's wounds six times over the next nine days. There the wounds began to heal, but Jeff was unable to turn himself in bed, so "the young men in the town [sat] up with him every night."[55]

Concern for Jeff was not confined to his immediate family. Just as Thomas Jefferson had grown up alongside his slave Jupiter, Jeff Randolph had grown up alongside Jupiter's son, "little" Phil Evans, whom Jeff referred to as "my companion in childhood and friend throughout life."[56] When messengers were dispatched to inform the family that Jeff had been stabbed, one of these messengers was little Phil. Phil was intelligent, resourceful, and deeply devoted to Jeff. When he heard that Jeff was badly wounded, he rushed to the store. By the time he arrived, Jeff was feverish. Someone tried to help Jeff sit up, but he fainted. Moments later, when Jeff regained consciousness, Phil, with tears streaming down his face, cradled Jeff in his arms. He had even galloped to a distant town to summon Jefferson's personal physician, Thomas Watkins. Phil caught up with Watkins eighteen miles away in Fluvanna County, attending another patient. When he learned of Jeff's condition, he immediately set off with Phil. During Jeff's difficult recovery over the next few weeks, Phil Evans, his servant and boyhood friend, never left Jeff's side, nursing him back to health.[57]

The next day, Jane rushed to Charlottesville to comfort her husband. Over the next few weeks, the doctors became more optimistic about the crippling extent of Jeff's wounds. When his stab wounds were almost healed, he was able to ride to Monticello. But his grandfather feared that he would not recover the full use of his arm. Over time, however, Jeff healed enough to supervise light work on the plantations. Although his recovery had progressed enough that "he officiated as one of the managers" at a local ball in early March, Eliza Trist noted that Jeff's left arm was still crippled.[58]

As expected, the violent clash aroused much public gossip and interest. A sensational trial was anticipated. After the confrontation, Bankhead, whose injuries were not life-threatening, was detained and searched. The sheriff seized two more knives from him and brought Bankhead before two Albemarle justices of the peace. To the shock of many, the judges charged both Bankhead and Jeff with breach of the peace. A hearing was scheduled for a week later, when witnesses would testify, enabling the court to determine what charges were to be filed and against whom. Represented by attorney Alexander Garrett, Jeff was required to post a bond of $600. Bankhead was to secure a bond for $1,000. A hearing was set in February, but Jeff was not healthy enough to attend, so the court date was delayed until March.

With the exception of Anne, the family blamed Bankhead, insisting that he had been the aggressor. But in all of Anne Bankhead's documented letters and diaries over the years, there is but one minor comment on Bankhead's scurrilous behavior. Anne described Bankhead as having been "far from prudent" on Christmas Day, 1823—a reasonable interpretation being that Bankhead was either violent or intoxicated, or both.[59] After the brawl, Anne wrote to her parents several times, expressing her "great unhappiness at the event that took place" but insisted that Jeff had "brought it on himself by commencing hostilities."[60] Bankhead did not flee the county, she claimed. He had posted bond and gone to visit his father, as any reasonable person would have done. Even more surprising, a few days after the fight, a letter arrived at Monticello, personally addressed to Thomas Jefferson. "The course I now take in addressing you," Bankhead began, "is disapproved of by my wife, whose judgment but rarely errs; she thinks your time & feelings have already been too much encroached upon & excited." Bankhead went on to refute the charge that he had instigated the clash. Not "five minutes after the affray, when the minds of the people were warm and highly excited," Bankhead explained, every witness, "without the slightest variation in their testimony," had told authorities that Jeff "was the aggressor in the most unprovoked manner."[61] Before Bankhead could even draw his knife, he claimed, his head "was laid open to the skull in two places. . . It appears that [Randolph] rashly prefer[r]ed his horsewhip to any satisfaction that I could render," he said.[62] Bankhead concluded his letter to Jefferson, "I pray most sincerely and devoutly for his recovery."[63]

Needless to say, Jefferson did not reply. Two weeks later, in a letter advising James Madison of the next meeting of the University of Virginia's board of trustees, Jefferson explained that his grandson was "healing slowly" from wounds he had suffered in an "accident."[64]

Fearing prison, Bankhead retained four lawyers with the support of his father, who rode to Albemarle county. Apparently, Bankhead planned to bluff to a certain point and then escape if he faced serious punishment. In early March, Jefferson reported that Bankhead had forfeited his bail, and in his opinion, had fled the county for good. Jefferson wished for Bankhead to be sentenced to prison, but admitted, "The execution of the law is so lenient in our country . . . that altho' its provisions for personal safety are imperfect, enforcement of them is more so, and our citizens are, from this cause, left in the state of nature to save their own lives by taking that of another."[65] Not unexpectedly, the incident caused a major rift in the family. Jeff's mother-in-law did not want Bankhead sent to prison because he was so near a "family" connection. She reasoned that every member of the "family would feel that they partook in some measure of his disgrace."[66] It was her opinion that Bankhead would not return to Albemarle county, so the matter should be dropped.

By the end of February, officials had gathered enough evidence to charge Bankhead with "stabbing and attempted murder." Bankhead neglected to appear for his court hearing. Presumably, he had decided that "by staying out of Albemarle [county], he could escape prosecution, and so far, the sheriff had not tried to find him . . . That Bankhead would ever be tried, convicted, and imprisoned seemed doubtful," Jefferson told a friend.[67] The Jefferson family had hoped that such a violent public outburst would land Bankhead in jail.

Jefferson received a letter from Jeff's father-in-law, Wilson Cary Nicholas, who knew more about the violent skirmish than did most. "What, my Dear Sir, can be done to prevent the recurrence of a similar or more fatal misfortune than that which lately befell poor [Randolph]?" Nicholas asked. "I am in constant terror of that miserable man Bankhead perpetrating some dreadful deed or obliging some relation of his wife, her father or brother to kill him in their own defence." Bankhead's family "cannot be safe as long as they are in his power," Nicholas feared.[68]

In the end, neither man was prosecuted for the violent fight, and Bankhead never stood trial.

It seems incredible, but Anne and Charles continued to live together as husband and wife. When Bankhead fled the county, his family hoped Anne would remain with them at Monticello. But to their dismay, Anne accompanied her husband. One friend could not imagine how a "woman of delicacy" could "get into bed with a drunk." Another thought "there must be some thing wrong with a woman who could live with such a beast."[69] Anne's decision to remain with Charles Bankhead had made the friend "quite certain of it." Although no surviving letters document Patsy Jefferson's reaction to the altercation, years later she considered the episode her symbolic decline as mistress of Monticello. Beginning with Jeff's attack, Jefferson family problems had flourished. Patsy maintained a facade of good cheer as their personal woes increased, her own health and that of Jefferson declined, and economic troubles worsened. The violent affray was the first in a series of gripping episodes that would bring the Jefferson family pain and humiliation, resulting in the dissolution of the family and the ultimate loss of their beloved estate, Monticello.

Unfortunately, Charlottesville had not seen the last of Charles Bankhead. Within a few years he was back at Carlton, unrepentant and drunk. Five years after the encounter, Jeff was in Charlottesville, attending an exhibition by a ventriloquist who spoke in "11 tongues without moving his lips." Bankhead also attended. While there, he became drunk and behaved so atrociously that only the intervention of Anne and three other men prevented another fight.

Within two years, death had prematurely claimed Anne. Jeff's wife cared for Anne's children at their home, Tufton. Jeff magnanimously allowed Bankhead to visit them. Apparently, this new arrangement subdued the old hostilities, for there is no further evidence of strife between them. Patsy was even comforted that for several months Bankhead had "abstained from the vice which has caused so much unhappiness in the family," but still feared there might be "frequent relapses." Perhaps she could tolerate Bankhead only because his character had been "much softened from physical causes," and his "intemperance no longer produce[d] madness as it formerly did." In fact, she said, tht Bankhead's "feelings [were] entirely kind to every member of the family."[70]

"Perhaps it was fortunate," concluded one author, "that Jeff Randolph, still in Richmond on lottery business, was unable to return for his sister's burial. [Patsy] volunteered to raise the Bankhead children as her own, and Jeff Randolph expressed his eagerness to help care for his niece and nephew and their newborn brother."[71] "You will not be surprised to hear that Ellen Bankhead and the poor little infant will live with me," Patsy wrote. As for Jeff, he was "determined at once to make up their differences and [was] very anxious to have little Thomas Bankhead."[72]

But there was one person who could neither forgive nor forget what Bankhead had done to her dear brother: Ellen Coolidge. In a letter from Jeff's devoted sister to her mother in 1826, she mentioned Charles Bankhead by name, calling him "a drunken brute."[73]

The final chapter in the Charles Bankhead story was written in the summer of 1833, when Benjamin Franklin Randolph, Jeff's brother and a doctor, was summoned to Bankhead's bedside by an alarmed servant. Patsy described the events of that day:

> I got a letter from Ben informing me of the death of Charles Bankhead he went one night to Ben's room accompanied by his servant and told him he had been drunk for some days & was very ill. Ben immediately gave him what he thought the case required; & set up with him till two o clock when he said he was much better. Benjamin went to lie down in an adjoining room leaving him with his servant. at 6 o clock he had an apoplectick fit after which he lived about two hours in a state of absolute insensibility from which it was impossible to rouse him.[74]

Bankhead probably suffered a lethal stroke. With him died the family quarrel.

Jeff and Bankhead's children remained close, although Jeff carried the scars of his encounter to his grave.

***

Unfortunately for Thomas Jefferson, he had been too ill to visit his granddaughter Anne until the morning she died. By the time he arrived, Anne had lapsed into unconsciousness. Crushed by the burden of his debts and with his legendary health failing, Jefferson could hardly bear the death of his oldest granddaughter. Jefferson's doctor, Robley Dunglison, was present at Anne's passing and described Jefferson's reaction: "It is impossible to imagine more poignant distress than was exhibited by him. He shed tears, and abandoned himself to every evidence of intense grief."[75] Jefferson could hardly break the solemn news of Anne's death to Jeff, who had traveled to New York to raise funds for Jefferson's indebted home. "Bad news, my dear Jefferson, as to your sister Anne," he wrote. "She expired about half an hour ago. Heaven seems to be overwhelming us with every form of misfortune."[76]

Reading his grandfather's tragic letter, Jeff broke down. How tragic that the Jefferson family tree was watered, not with "the blood of patriots and tyrants,"[77] but with the blood of mothers.

8

MURDER: THE JEFFERSON NEPHEWS

He took up an axe and with a full two-handed swing sank it deep into George's neck. It was a mortal and nearly decapitating blow three inches deep and four inches wide.

—**Boynton Merrill Jr.,** *Jefferson's Nephews*,
on the murder of a slave named George

On a Sunday night, December 15, 1811, Thomas Jefferson's nephews, Lilburne and Isham Lewis, dragged a runaway slave named George into the kitchen cabin of their Kentucky plantation.[1] Lilburne, glowering and drunk, was sweating heavily, his clothing reeking of mildew. The intoxicated brothers stretched George out, binding him across a large wood cutting table situated in the middle of the dirt floor. Then they ordered the other slaves into the cabin. In the light of the searing yellow flames from the fireplace, Lilburne would teach his slaves a savage lesson about disobedience.

While guzzling from a whiskey bottle, two or three swallows at a time, Lilburne spotted a nearby meat ax. He set his bottle down, picked up the ax with both hands, and swung it with all his strength at the left side of George's neck, where it embedded, nearly decapitating the defenseless slave. The vicious blow severed his carotid artery. George wailed and writhed in pain, bleeding out on the dirt floor. Lilburne then forced one of the other slaves at gunpoint to dismember George's body and burn the pieces in the roaring fire.

This ghastly crime is a one of the most bizarre murder tales of the nineteenth century, involving two of Thomas Jefferson's nephews. The macabre murder story begins in Albemarle County, Virginia, where in the early 1740s, two families operated nearby plantations in what was then untamed wilderness. One family was that of Colonel Charles Lewis; the other was the family of Peter Jefferson, Thomas Jefferson's father. For three successive generations, there were numerous first-cousin marriages between the Lewis and Jefferson families. One of the first of these intermarriages was the union between Col. Charles L. Lewis and Lucy Jefferson, Thomas Jefferson's younger sister. Lucy was seventeen and Charles was twenty-two. If the ceremony was held at Shadwell, Jefferson's boyhood home, it was one of the last happy occasions there. Five months after the wedding, Shadwell burned to the ground, taking with it all of Thomas Jefferson's worldly possessions, including his important papers and cherished books.[2]

There is little reliable information about the personalities of Charles and Lucy Lewis, or the way they lived, but apparently, Colonel Lewis, like most gentry, took an interest in breeding horses. The records also indicate that the family was literate. Estate inventories demonstrate that they had some regard for books, but their collections were modest.[3] On several occasions they borrowed books from Jefferson's vast library at Monticello. Yet, there is no evidence that any of Lewis's sons attended college. When each boy reached the age of sixteen, Lewis made him a partner and assigned specific duties on his plantation, precluding a higher education for his sons. Lewis prospered for a while, but gradually fell into bad habits—gambling, drinking, and heavy borrowing, as well as a bitter depression at the turn of the century, took their toll.[4]

Thomas Jefferson was not close to his sister's family. In fact, it seems that Jefferson deliberately kept his distance from the entire Lewis brood, with the exception of occasional correspondence with his sister, Lucy. For example, when he went to France for five years, Jefferson did not leave his two young daughters in Charles and Lucy's care, but rather in his trusted sister-in-law, Elizabeth Wayles Eppes's. When it was necessary to delegate the management of his plantations, Jefferson did not choose any of the Lewises for these positions of power. Nor was Jefferson ever involved in any joint property or business dealings with them. Other than one dinner party, it seems doubtful that there was much socializing between Monticello and the extended Lewis family.[5] Apparently, Jefferson also had an aversion to Colonel Lewis's sister, Elizabeth Henderson, and her family. And writing of a brother-in-law of Colonel Lewis's, Jefferson complained, "I knew he was not to be depended on."[6] One of Charles Lewis's brothers-in-law became "overwhelmed with debt, stripped of his property, declared insane . . . and was placed in the asylum." For five years Jefferson had attempted to collect a debt from this man. Payment was never forthcoming.[7]

Yet, a more conventional Virginia gentry family than the Lewises could not be found. Like most Virginians, the Lewises seemed ordinary, not given to family drama. As the tumultuous eighteenth century ended, the Lewis family had acquired a modicum of wealth, most of it from land and slaves, but tough economic times were ahead. The Lewises suffered multiple crop failures. By 1807, Charles Lewis had been forced to sell his slaves and property, except for the portions he had previously given to his grown sons, Randolph and Lilburne. Both sons were now married and had growing families, leaving little inheritance left for the youngest son, Isham.

Randolph and Lilburne decided to seek their fortunes outside of Virginia. Packing up their families, they moved to Kentucky, not an uncommon venue during hard financial times. Their parents and three unmarried sisters decided to go along. The two sons had sold their property in Virginia and bought land on the Ohio River. For $9,100 Randolph bought nearly four thousand acres. Lilburne purchased nearly a thousand acres for $8,000, both tracts largely undeveloped. They sailed west in midwinter, down the Ohio River in flat boats. After a rough journey, marred with sickness, over rugged terrain, they arrived and established their homes. Lilburne built his house on a high bluff in the middle of his thousand-acre farm. He named it, appropriately, Rocky Hill.[8]

In spite of new opportunities on the frontier, the financial and personal difficulties the Lewises faced in the next years turned overwhelming. Chronic malaria was just one of many health problems the family suffered during these times. And money or revenue from any source was scant. Lilburne, being "land poor," accumulated multiple loans, deep debt, and lawsuits. It also appears that as self-styled aristocrats, the Lewises were resented by most of the other settlers. The family's financial misfortune was aggravated when, in 1809, Lilburne's beloved first wife, Elizabeth, died at age twenty-seven. A year later tragedy struck again when Lucy, Lilburne's mother, died as well, leaving three young daughters under her feckless husband's charge. Their oldest son, Randolph, and his wife and their eight children tried to raise Charles and Lucy's younger children.[9]

There was a promise to his fortunes when Lilburne married again, to Letitia Rutter, a member of a prospering family and lovely Southern belle. But tragedy returned when Randolph, the steady oldest son and head of the family, died from a snakebite. The Lewises' hopes for a Kentucky dynasty were quickly collapsing. As one historian has aptly concluded:

> One such aristocratic family, that of Charles Lewis of Albemarle County, brother-in-law to Thomas Jefferson, having lost most of his patrimony, emigrated to the western frontier of Kentucky in 1808, taking little with them except their pretensions. There on the frontier, where others thrived, the Lewis family experienced heartbreaking misfortunes, and at last met ruin in an incredible climax of horror, bloodshed, and natural upheaval.[10]

Despite the prestige of their presidential uncle, the Lewises' move to Kentucky did not elevate their reputation. Randolph fared best with appointments of local significance. When Randolph died, Lilburne became head of the family, his sickly father having abdicated in a downward spiral of drunkenness. The loss of his brother, mother Lucy, and his first wife—all within a stressful year—together with massive debt, added to his emotional anxiety. Marriage to Letitia did not improve his situation significantly. Lilburne fell in with a venal crowd and continued to consort with shiftless rakes like James McCawley and Richard Ferguson, who gouged out eyes in grudge fights, gambled, and cavorted with prostitutes. Isham often accompanied his older brother to McCawley's grog shop, which had the only pool table in town, where the brothers would end up roaring drunk, then bamboozled out of their money.[11]

A once-prominent citizen, Lilburne Lewis quickly acquired a depreciated reputation in his Smithland community. Although his mother, Lucy, was recognized and respected as Thomas Jefferson's younger sister, this connected family had severe financial problems, aggravated by unstable mental episodes and chronic drunkenness. Lilburne had reluctantly remarried Letitia. Although she was eight months pregnant, their marriage at "Rocky Hill" appears to be decidedly stressful and unhappy.

Beset with medical bills from a malaria outbreak, and obsessed with the memory of his first wife, Lilburne spent years trying to benefit from his relationship with his famous uncle, Thomas Jefferson—apparently to no avail.[12] Despite the family ties, Lilburne was unable to find steady work. And Isham, eager to learn a trade, even sent a letter to Jefferson on April 27, 1809, imploring his uncle to assist him in finding a career surveying the Louisiana Territory. It read, in part:

> Dear Sir,
> The great desire which I feel to be placed in some employ whereby, I may secure to myself the happiness derivable from the idea of enjoying the fruits of well spent industry and the difficulty I find in attaining this object unassisted by any influential friend has induced me to beg the favour of your endeavours in my behalf, I am in hopes you will be less disposed to think hard of this request when I assure you it is produced from necessity, brought on not from my own imprudences but those of an unfortunate father whose promises of wealth and neglect to bring me up in any useful pursuit has brought on me the want of the former and occasions me to deplore his inattention to the latter.[13]

On May 1, 1809 Jefferson coolly responded to his nephew:

> Dear Sir
> It is with real concern that I learn the disagreeable situation in which you are for want of employment, & the more so as I do not see any way in which I can propose to you any certain relief. As to offices under the government, they are few, are always full, & twenty applicants for one vacancy when it happens. They are miserable also, giving a bare subsistence without the least chance

of doing anything for the future. The army is full and, in consequence of the late pacification, will probably be reduced. [14]

If, however, Isham knew "common arithmetic, say multiplication and division," Jefferson could teach him the art of surveying if he moved back to Virginia.[15] According to one scholar's account, Isham did finally spend two weeks at Monticello:

> At the conclusion of this visit, Jefferson gave him two letters of introduction, the first of which described him as "a young man of excellent dispositions, correct conduct, & good understanding," though "little aided by education." The "shipwreck of the fortunes of his family" had thrown him back on his own resources and, having learned the rudiments of surveying, he wished "to try himself in that line." The second described Lewis as "possessing qualities which might render him useful and of value," including an eagerness to learn.[16]

Throughout the years, the Lewises had little shame about calling on their famous uncle for influence. As wartime governor of Virginia, Jefferson intervened to promote his brother-in-law Charles Lilburne Lewis, against the wishes of the troops. Then, years later, Charles, the colonel's firstborn, beseeched the president for a federal army commission, but he died in pestilence-ridden Louisiana in 1806.

Even though Jefferson seemed to take pity on Isham, his generosity was in vain. This "young man of excellent dispositions, correct conduct, & good understanding," as Jefferson had described him, escaped bad debts in Mississippi, caught malaria, and recuperated at Rocky Hill just in time to join Lilburne's corrupting downward descent.[17]

Jefferson's prescient dim view of his Kentucky relatives was based on good reasoning. In fact, the Lewises had tried to cheat one of Jefferson's friends, Craven Peyton, out of land rights in Albemarle County. Peyton had treated the Lewis family with generosity, and had come to their financial rescue several times.[18] Finally, Jefferson could no longer maintain his dignified silence. When Peyton asked his candid assessment, Jefferson was direct: "Not only the silence of C. L. Lewis on executing the deed to Peyton, but the import of the deed itself convicts him of gross fraud and disqualifies him from being a witness."[19]

By 1811 Lilburne's mounting debts, business failings, and angry mood swings had intensified with excessive drinking. He often turned moody and violent, taking out his problems on the family slaves, especially seventeen-year-old George,[20] the murder victim in this bizarre story. Little is known of George. One historian has noted, "Unfortunately, almost no traces remain of his life except a few sketchy comments written in the legend sources, and a comment or two about him handed down verbally as part of the Rutter family tradition."[21] George was described as an "ill-grown, ill-thrived" slave with a scar over one eye and "an independent nature."[22] He served Lilburne as a house servant, running general errands. It was reported that George disobeyed Lilburne on several occasions. But when Lilburne was drinking, George feared him and stayed away.[23]

On their final, fateful encounter, George had run away, returned, and while on an errand, broke a family heirloom, a treasured water pitcher of their mother's, infuriating Lilburne. According to historian Boynton Merrill's account, George was taken into a shed and bound for torture by Lilburne. The fire cast suffocating light and smoke in the small shed as Lilburne shouted at the slaves that he was going to teach them a lesson about defiance. He then raised a double-edged ax, and with both hands, slammed the blade down into George's neck. As one author described the ghastly murder:

> He took up an axe and with a full two-handed swing sank it deep into George's neck. It was a mortal and nearly decapitating blow three inches deep and four inches wide. If the spine was severed, and it probably was, then George's death was instantaneous. If it was not, and the carotid and jugular blood vessels were cut, then George would have remained conscious from ten to forty seconds, and it would have taken nearly a minute before George's heart pumped out most of the four or five quarts of his blood onto the cabin floor.[24]

As noted at the beginning of this chapter, Lilburne then ordered one of the other slaves to dismember George's body, starting with his feet, with each piece thrown into the fire to secrete the appalling crime.[25] Later that night, the severest earthquake in continental history destroyed the kitchen, collapsed the chimney, exposing the smoking remains of George's body. Lilburne ordered the slaves to quickly rebuild the chimney and seal up any unburned body parts in the masonry, "putting an end, it seemed, to the whole horrid ordeal."[26]

This account of George's murder may not be historically complete. The major sources of information about the murder seem to contradict each other. "This reconstruction of the crime," according to one author, "is a combination of what appears to be the most plausible . . . of the four written accounts."[27] There are other, more sensationalized accounts of this savagery, but most are considered less reliable. In 1824 the Lewis family pastor, Reverend William Dickey, described the crime in a letter as a premeditated homicide. According to Dickey, Lilburne chopped off the boy's feet, then his legs, thighs, and arms, in a much more deliberate and torturous manner than reported in most accounts. But many historians believe that as an abolitionist, Dickey purveyed the crime more graphically to garner abolitionist political support:[28]

> [Lilburne] called up George, who approached his master with the most unreserved submission. He bound him with cords, and by the assistance of his younger brother, laid him on the broad bench, or meat block. He now proceeded to WHANG off George by the ancles!! It was with the broad axe! — In vain did the unhappy victim SCREAM AND ROAR. He was completely in his master's power. Not a hand amongst so many durst interfere. Casting the feet into the fire, he lectured them at some length. He WHACKED HIM OFF below the knees! George roaring out, and praying his master to BEGIN AT THE OTHER END! He admonished them again, throwing the legs into the fire! Then above the knees, tossing the joints into the fire! He again lectured them at leisure. The next stroke severed the thighs from the body. These were also committed to the

flames. And so off the arms, head and trunk, until all was in the fire! Still protracting the intervals with lectures, and threatenings of like punishment, in case of disobedience, and running away, or disclosure of this tragedy. Nothing now remained but to consume the flesh and bones.[29]

Another author, William Courtney Watts, wrote a somewhat fictional account of the murder, *Chronicles of a Kentucky Settlement*. Dickey's version suggests that Lilburne chopped up George's body personally, but in Watts's version, the ax was wielded by a slave, on Lilburne's order. Here's his account:

That night, horrible to relate, Lilburne Lewis and his younger brother, Isham, caused most of the slaves on the farm to assemble in the cabin where George was bound, flat upon the floor, with each limb extended, and, with drawn pistols, forced one of the negro men to literally chop the bound boy to pieces, and, as joint by joint and limb by limb were severed from the body, they were cast into a roaring fire prepared for the purpose of consuming every trace of the body. When the hellish work was done, the assembled slaves were given to understand that such a fate as George's awaited any of them who should ever whisper a word about George's fate; and, if questioned regarding his disappearance, they were to answer that he had run away and had never been heard from. The cowed slaves were further told that should any of them ever run away they would, when captured, be treated as George had been. When the two drunken and fiendish brothers left the cabin and were returning to their house, a sudden and terrific rumbling noise was heard, and soon the surface of the earth seemed to rise and fall—rise and fall again like quick succeeding waves. To add to the horror of the phenomena, what appeared like a great blazing ball of fire darted hissing through the heavens, apparently close by.[30]

The last official account of the crime contains scant information—a one-paragraph newspaper article that appeared in the *Kentucky Gazette* in 1812: "Russellville, April 22. Murder! Horrid Murder!" Lilburne and Isham Lewis "had been taken to court 'for murdering a negro boy, (the property of the former) and burning him on a kitchen fire.'"[31]

To glean the most credible version of the murder, one must examine the exact language in the formal criminal indictment against the brothers:

> Lilbourn Lewis senior, farmer late of said County and (Isham Lewis yeoman late of said County not having the fear of God before their Eyes, But being moved & seduced by the Instigation of the Devil—with force and arms in & upon the body of a certain Negro Boy called George a slave the property of said Lilbourn Lewis senior . . . feloniously, wilfully, violently and of their malice aforethought an assault did make—and that he the said Lilbourn Lewis senior with a certain ax there & then had & held in both his hands of the Value of two dollars did strike cut and penetrate in & upon the neck of him the said Negro Boy George giving to the said Negro Boy, George then & there with the ax aforesaid in and upon the neck of him the said Negro Boy George one Mortal wound of the Breadth of four inches and of the Depth of three inches of which said mortal wound he the said Negro Boy George Instantly did die in the county of Livingston aforesaid and that the said Isham Lewis then & there feloniously wilfully Violently and of his malice aforethought was present aiding helping abetting comforting assisting and maintaining the said Lilbourn Lewis senior.[32]

Two hours after the murder and mutilation, the first massive earthquake, mentioned earlier, suddenly struck the region at an estimated magnitude of 8.1, literally jolting the family out of their beds. The next morning, there was an aftershock estimated at a magnitude of 7.4. Tremors every ten minutes violently shook the ground.[33]

After the murder, the town of Smithland, as well much of the central United States, still reeled from the latest of three massive earthquakes, with over two thousand lesser tremors centered around northern Arkansas and New Madrid, Missouri. The climax of the dire seismologic events, termed the New Madrid Earthquake, culminated in mid-December with jolting shocks, the most severe in recorded history on the North American continent. The epicenter of this catastrophic quake was a mere seventy-five miles southwest of Rocky Hill. The following summary was written by a scientist and is believed to be the most accurate description of the cataclysmic events:

> It is fairly well established that immediately before the earthquake unusual warmth and a thick oppressive atmosphere with occasional rain and unseasonable thunder showers prevailed over a wide area of country . . . A little after 2 o'clock on the morning of December 16, the inhabitants of the region were suddenly awakened by the groaning, creaking, and cracking of the timbers of the houses or cabins in which they were sleeping, by the rattle of furniture thrown down, and by the crash of falling chimneys. [34]

The third major quake, on the morning of February 7, 1812, was estimated to have been the ninth worst earthquake recorded in US history.[35] Even by today's standards, 1811 is considered an *annus mirabilis*, or "year of miracles." The reference to the *annus mirabilis* was drawn from the following 1835 account, documenting these unusual events:

> Many things conspired to make the year 1811 the annus mirabilis of the West. During the earlier months, the waters of many of the great rivers overflowed their banks to a vast extent, and the whole country was in many parts covered from bluff to bluff. Unprecedented sickness followed. A spirit of change and recklessness seemed to pervade the very inhabitants of the forest. A countless multitude of squirrels, obeying some great

and universal impulse, which none can know but the Spirit that gave them being, left their reckless and gambolling life and their ancient places of retreat in the North, and were seen pressing forward by tens of thousands in a deep and solid phalanx to the South. No obstacles seemed to check their extraordinary and concerted movement. The word had been given them to go forth, and they obeyed it, though multitudes perished in the broad Ohio, which lay in their path. The splendid comet of that year long continued to shed its twilight over the forests, and as autumn drew to a close, the whole valley of the Mississippi, from the Missouri to the Gulf, was shaken to its centre by continued earthquakes.[36]

To add to this misery, the entire state of Kentucky, including the Lewis plantation, suffered from severe drought. During the strange summer and fall of that year, in addition to the great squirrel migration mentioned in the preceding quotation, the passenger pigeon population exploded. People reported that the woods were darkened by thousands of the birds as they stripped bare oak, chestnut, and hickory trees.[37] The comet of that year, a dazzling twin-tailed comet named Tecumseh's Comet, dotted the sky for almost two years. It was "reckoned" by native Americans that the Tecumseh comet had collided into the Ohio River, causing the devastating earthquakes. According to lore, the comet foretold a coming war with the Indians at Tippecanoe.[38]

The intensity of these brutal earthquakes cannot be understated. The massive waves of the Mississippi River were beyond belief. Above New Madrid, the river bottom rose and formed a six-foot waterfall that cut savagely across the river. Boats were swept away by crashing rapids. Other boats were tossed about by thirty-foot walls of water.[39] Some accounts have the Mississippi River actually flowing backward, forming two new, giant waterfalls. Deafening thunderclaps and thick black smog intensified the cataclysmic weather phenomenon.[40] Of the earthquakes between January 23 and February 4, an Eliza Bryan wrote:

> The earth was in continual agitation, visibly waving as a gentle sea. On that day there was another shock, nearly as hard as the preceding ones. Next day four such, and on the 7th at about four o'clock, A. M., a concussion took place so much more violent than those which had preceded it, that it is denominated the hard shock. The awful darkness of the atmosphere, which as formerly was saturated with sulphurous [sic] vapor, and the violence of the tempestuous thundering noise that accompanied it, together with all the other phenomenon mentioned as attending the former ones, formed a scene, the description of which would require the most sublimely fanciful imagination.[41]

In his mental delusions, Lilburne interpreted the massive earthquake as a sign from the heavens of the wrath of God. As the lightning flashed, Lilburne muttered, "It's only the devil in [hell] rejoicing over having got hold of George!" His neighbors seemed to agree with this biblical interpretation. One account explained that "many thought that the devil incarnate had actually arrived, and was shaking the earth with his great wheel. Some took to the woods, while others stood in motionless stupor, victims of absolute fright."[42] Others thought the quakes were a warning of God's rage, believing he would return to punish the wicked.[43] In New Madrid, a gaggle of unkempt religious fanatics marched around town, shrieking, "Praise God and repent!" Some of the residents were not impressed by these street preachers, one noting that "more repulsive, ill-timed visitors a hospitable community never had."[44]

Shortly after the murder, another tremor crumbled Lilburne's chimney again. Sometime before dawn, a dog, perhaps Lilburne's own hound, Nero, came by and carried off part of George's remains from the debris. Two months later, as a farmer named Hurley rode his horse through the earthquake-damaged settlement of Smithland, he noticed a stray dog carrying something in its mouth. Hurley thought the dog may be rabid. The dog dropped the object and started gnawing on it. Curious, Hurley approached. To his horror, he saw that the dog was chewing on the charred human head of a black man.[45]

Wondering if the charred skull was the result of the earthquakes, Hurley tried to locate the local sheriff, Robert Kirk. Finding him alive and uninjured, Hurley returned, bringing Kirk with him, and examined the head. Recognizing what seemed to be a large scar over one eye, Sheriff Kirk recalled that a teenage house slave named George belonging to Lilburne Lewis had disappeared the previous December. Kirk remembered that George had had a similar scar.[46]

The identity of the man who found George's head is not known for certain, for the discovery is attributed to two different men. One of these men was Jonah Hibbs, whose farm adjoined the Rocky Hill plantation. "One day as Mr. Jonah Hibbs was enroute to Smithland," the story goes, ". . . he noticed a dog gnawing a peculiar looking bone and on examination it proved to be a human skull. He reported it to the authorities."[47] The other man was the aforementioned Dickson Hurley. Mr. Grady Rutter, the great-grandson of Letitia's brother, James, gave the following account of the grisly discovery:

> Dick Hurley was a neighbor of the Lewis family. He lived between Birdsville and Salem. It was Dick Hurley who found George's head. My grandfather told me that Hurley was riding his horse on the road to Salem and saw a dog gnawing on the head which was lying near a cattle trough in the field by the road. He recognized the head because George had a large scar over one of his eyes. Hurley was the one who reported it to the law. Several years ago one of my relatives was traveling in Memphis, Tennessee, and saw a restaurant sign that said Dick Hurley was the owner. This member of my family went in and asked the proprietor for whether he knew anything about Livingston County, Kentucky. Mr. Hurley smiled and said: "Yes, I do. It was my grandfather who found the head and he told me about it."[48]

With the discovery of the charred human head, Sheriff Kirk had enough evidence to arrest Lilburne and Isham. He charged them both with murder. In western Kentucky at that time, murdering a slave was illegal. The discovery of the head proved that the crime was never reported. George had been decapitated and his body burned in an attempt to cover up the heinous crime, evidence of premeditated murder, Kirk reasoned.[49]

It was a Monday morning when the circuit court opened in between earthquake tremors, with the required sixteen "housekeepers" needed to compose a grand jury. Judges Ford and Givens set bail at $1,000 for Lilburne and $500 for his brother Isham. While the prosecutor petitioned the trial to proceed immediately, the judges continued the hearing until the next session, three months later. After finding five men to sign their bail securities, Lilburne and Isham were released and returned home to Rocky Hill.[50]

Letitia, Lilburne's second wife, could not be forced to testify against her husband, Lilburne, but could testify against Isham. Knowing this, or perhaps for other reasons, she fled from Rocky Hill with her infant son, born a week after the murder. Literally crazed from fear and humiliation, Lilburne, free on bond, plotted his own death. Writing his "cruel but beloved" Letitia, he pledged "forgiveness to your connections" and claimed to "die on account of your absence & my dear little son James."[51] At no time did Lilburne ever acknowledge his guilt or remorse for the crime. Nor did he feel that Letitia had good reason to leave him. She had been considered the sole witness to the events because the slaves, although they, too, had witnessed the crime, could not testify against their owner. Letitia, spoiled and shrewish as she was, had dreaded the return of her erratic husband. Fearing for both her and their two-month-old baby's safety, she may also have worried that Lilburne would falsely implicate her as an accomplice to George's murder. So she fled, traveling sixteen miles to her father's estate in Salem. Lilburn was enraged by his wife's abandonment of him.[52]

Lilburne had now become a pariah in his own community. "He had lost all of the things that make up a sense of identity and worth in a man," commented one historian:

> His prestige was gone. The nature of Lilburne's crime was so heinous that he could expect sympathy from no one except the lowest class of social scum. He was the defendant in two unsettled court cases, one for a substantial debt, and another for

murder. His own nephew was to testify against him, and his wife might implicate his brother. He had lost his political influence and could not even obtain the position of justice of the peace. His wife, whom he loved, had deserted him out of fear and taken their infant son away with her.[53]

The last blow to Lilburne's fragile psyche was that the men who had originally signed his initial bail money refused to secure a second bond for his release. William Dickey described Lilburne's feelings: "Now he saw that his character was gone, his respectable friends believed that he had massacred George; but, worst of all, he saw that they considered the life of the harmless Letitia was in danger from his perfidious hands. It was too much for his chivalry to sustain. The proud Virginian sunk under the accumulated load of public odium."[54]

Letitia's desertion was the excuse Lilburne gave for the final insane decision of his life. In despair and facing hanging on the murder charge, he persuaded Isham to enter into a suicide pact. As the trial date drew near in April 1812, the doomed brothers went to the graveyard on the crest of Rocky Hill, where Lilburne's first wife was buried in a thirty-foot-square plot of ground. As one writer described the scene, "Clouds covered the sky, and a few miles downriver, the Ohio overflowed its banks. Just before noon, the ground shook again, and for some ten minutes, witnesses swore, compass needles did not point north. The brothers met in the Rocky Hill graveyard."[55] Each brother stood with his back to the inside of the cedar fence that kept the cows from flattening Elizabeth's gravesite. Lilburn brought a copy of his will, a suicide note on the back addressed to his lawyer:

> Rocky Hill Apl. 9 1812. Mr. James MCawley I have fallen a victim to my beloved but cruel Letitia. I die in the hope of being united to my other wife in Heaven. Take care of this Will & come here that we may be decently buried. Adieu. L. Lewis.[56]

Lilburne even included a clause in the will for his serendipitous dog: "My dog Nero I do hereby bequeath to my beloved father. L. L."[57] As Boyd Merrill commented, "His handwriting, which once was fluid and graceful, had become as chaotic and disorderly as his mind."[58]

The brothers were now determined to "present a gun at each [other's] breast" and, at a word, fire.[59] But the plan went amiss. Isham asked Lilburne what to do if his weapon failed to fire. Lilburne showed Isham how to reprime the rifle, rest the butt on the ground with the muzzle pointed at his chest, and push the trigger with a stick. "Lilburne told Isham to get a small branch and cut it off about two feet long, which he did, and handed it to Lilburne. Lilburne then leaned forward slightly, holding the stick in his other hand."[60] But in demonstrating to his brother, Lilburne accidentally touched the trigger, firing the gun into his own chest and blowing his torso open. He was killed instantly.

Horrified by the bizarre accident and the ensuing blood that splattered Elizabeth's grave, Isham panicked and sprinted from the cemetery.[61]

The next day, news of the shooting reached the town coroner, John Dorroh. After certifying Lilburne's death, Dorroh appeared before a local justice of the peace, William "Baptist Billy" Woods in Salem. Woods was an old friend of the Lewis and Jefferson families. Lilburne had even named him as one of his executors of his estate. He was called "Baptist" Billy because he had been a minister in the Baptist Church in Virginia. Woods was regarded, as one historian recorded, as "a man of real ability and genuine magnetism. It is said that in his younger days he was tall and handsome and that he long retained his manly beauty. He was considered wealthy, and always rode a splendid horse accompanied by his faithful body servant, Ben."[62]

Be that as it may, whether out of friendship or lack of evidence, Woods immediately acquitted Isham as an accessory in the death of his brother, Lilburne. However, Woods was overruled by a local judge, and Isham was rearrested. He was held in jail as an accomplice in both George's murder and Lilburne's suicide.[63]

On May 5, Isham somehow escaped from the rickety Salem jail and fled the county forever. For many years Isham's fate was unknown, but in 1986, records were found that documented his final years. According to one author, six weeks after escaping the Salem jail, and the day before the United States declared war against England in the War of 1812, Isham enlisted for five years in a US infantry company. On July 8, 1813, he transferred to the Ninth Company of the Seventh

Regiment, where he rose to the rank of sergeant. During the half-hour battle of New Orleans on December 31, 1814, according to one account, "only eight Americans were killed. One of the eight to fall at New Orleans was Isham Lewis, Jefferson's disgraced nephew. After escaping from jail in Kentucky in 1812, Lewis had taken a new name and, under this alias, enlisted in [Andrew] Jackson's army. Jefferson may never have learned of his death."[64] Isham was buried in a military grave on the battlefield, while his widow was granted $6.50 per month by his military pension for the next five years.[65]

Although there is no evidence that Thomas Jefferson ever commented on the bizarre murder involving his nephews, he was well aware of the "melancholia" and mental instability that ran in the Lewis family. Privately, he may have believed that this hereditary, erratic mental condition had contributed to Lilburne's state of mind, prompting his insane, murderous act. In 1812, three years after Meriwether Lewis's (of Lewis and Clark fame) mysterious death along Tennessee's Natchez Trace at the age of thirty-five, and a year after Lilburne's horrific crime, Jefferson wrote in a telling letter, "Governor Lewis had from early life been subject to hypochondriac affections. It was a constitutional disposition in all the nearer branches of the family of his name, and were more immediately inherited by him from his father."[66]

One historian argues, however, that consanguinity may have led to genetic and mental aberrations in the Lewis family, due to the intermarriages among the family. Lilburne and Isham were offspring of a first-cousin marriage, and Mary (Randolph), their grandmother, had sprung from the tangle of Randolph crossbreeding.[67] Yet, the historical record demonstrates that Lilburne's premeditated murder of a defenseless slave owed less to genetic malignancy than to his own savage and malicious nature. Lilburne Lewis, from all accounts, was a venal pettifogger with an inability to cope with family troubles, anxiety, and stress. "The confusion of identity," wrote one historian, "and a separation of self from true contact with innermost feeling probably had much to do with southern violence and Lilburne's crime, factors born within the family structure."[68]

"Thomas Jefferson surely knew of these macabre events," wrote author and journalist Allen Pell Crawford. "He remained in contact with the sisters of Isham and Lilburne for several years afterward. As their poverty deepened, these nieces of Jefferson's tried to borrow money from him, without success."[69] Yet, there is no evidence that Jefferson ever acknowledged or discussed his nephews' depraved actions.[70] Per his custom and nature, regret and remorse were noticeably absent from his private letters, and he maintained a stoic silence concerning family scandals, leading one author to conclude, "The enigmatic masks he . . . learned to wear were essential additions to his public persona."[71]

9

THE "FAMILY DENIAL"[1]

A refutation can never be made.

—J. T. Callender, 1802

During Thomas Jefferson's presidency, his daughters and other family came to Washington for Christmas visits. In 1802, Patsy and Polly traveled together by carriage to visit their father at the White House. One of Washington's premier socialites, Margaret Bayard Smith, was the wife of Samuel Harrison Smith, a Republican newspaperman and founder of the *National Intelligencer*.[2] Mrs. Smith spent time with both daughters during their visit and wrote of the eldest, "[Patsy] gave me an account of all her children, of the character of her husband and many family anecdotes. She has that rare but charming egotism which can interest the listener in all one's concerns."[3]

These pleasant family visits were about to be rudely interrupted by a major political scandal. In the midst of Jefferson's launch of his reelection bid for the presidency in 1802, a muckraking journalist rocked the entire Jefferson family, alleging that Jefferson had had a sexual affair with one of his slaves, Sally Hemings.[4] From that point on and for the rest of his life, his grandchildren, most notably Jeff and Ellen, would play central roles in the Sally Hemings scandal, becoming Jefferson's fiercest defenders against what they considered a vile political smear that, for him, was morally impossible.[5]

Thomas Jefferson's mental impressions, especially when they came to his slave Sally Hemings, are almost totally hidden from historians. As was his way, he made no public comment on the allegations. One historian has written that "as in the temple a veil covered the sanctuary, so the doors of [Jefferson's] private apartments were locked, and shuttered porches were set up at the windows, that no profane eye might search his secret study."[6] But it was not so with his family. Jeff and Ellen mounted a vigorous defense of their grandfather's reputation, with Jeff often quoting Jefferson's own words regarding the sexual allegation: "All should be laid open to you without reserve, for there is not a truth existing which I fear, or would wish unknown to the whole world."[7] Thomas Jefferson went even further, writing a private, tacit denial of the allegation to James Madison, declaring there is "nothing that Callender knows about me, that I would not broadcast to the world."[8]

Thus, to understand Jeff and Ellen's defense of their grandfather's legacy, the sexual allegation against Jefferson and its origin needs to be placed in historical context. The scurrilous allegation began with James Callender, the eighteenth-century version of a Hollywood tabloid reporter, who printed the allegation in a Richmond newspaper. Months earlier, in a heated dispute, Callender's own attorney, a "Mr. Hay," had beaten Callender repeatedly on the forehead with a walking stick. For a year, the flammable personality of Callender had staggered in and out of Richmond's finest taverns, slurring words of rage against President Thomas Jefferson. Finally, on a Sunday in June 1803, a coroner heaved Callender's alcohol-infused body onto an autopsy table. The cause of death was registered: drowning. Amid rumors of foul play, the formal inquest noted that Callender had been drunk, his waterlogged body recorded as drowned in three feet of water. The coroner then scrawled a name on the death certificate: *James Thomson Callender*. Ten days later, the *Examiner* reported Callender's death as a drunken suicide. "This unfortunate man had descended to the lowest depths of misery after having been fleeced by his partner."[9] His onetime collaborator recalled years later that Callender had resorted to "unwarrantable indiscretions" begun amid "paroxysms of inebriety."[10] And so the foul life of the most ignoble James Callender came to an end.

But this is where the embryo of the "Sally Hemings" accusation against Jefferson begins—as well as Jeff and Ellen's defense of their grandfather. Jefferson's grandchildren were direct: they argued to friends and biographers alike that the alleged relationship between Jefferson and Hemings was invented by the fractured psyche of an alcoholic hack journalist. Jeff and Ellen, as well as their mother, Patsy, knew that Jefferson's fierce political enemies lacked a substantial issue to use against the president as he sought reelection. The country was prosperous and peaceful, and the historic Louisiana Purchase had just been concluded. So Jefferson's political opponents turned personal and venal. The previous election, between incumbent John Adams and Jefferson, had descended into a vicious affair in which Federalists attacked Jefferson's character in a fevered pitch. Jefferson had cheated British creditors, they charged, obtained property by fraud, and robbed a widow of 10,000 pounds. The Federalist *Connecticut Courant* even alleged that if Jefferson were reelected, "murder, robbery, rape, adultery, and incest will openly be taught and practiced."[11]

James Callender surged onto the scene and represented, as one historian aptly commented, a "darker and more personal kind of trouble for the President."[12] He distinguished himself by the scurrility of his attacks on Jefferson, as well as John Adams and Alexander Hamilton. In 1802, the sexual accusation against Jefferson first appeared in a slashing article, a full-blown campaign of political vilification written by Callender. Published in the *Richmond Recorder* on September 1, 1802, Callender alleged:

> It is, well known that the man, whom it delighteth the people to honor, keeps and for many years past has kept, as his concubine, one of his own slaves. Her name is Sally. The name of her eldest son is Tom. His features are said to bear a striking although sable resemblance to those of the president himself. The boy is ten or twelve years of age. His mother went to France in the same vessel with Mr. Jefferson and his two daughters . . . By this wench Sally, our president has had several children.[13]

"With the aid of a lying renegade from Republicanism, the Federalists have opened all their sluices of calumny," Jefferson complained.[14] Among other things, Callender's racist diatribe referred to Sally as an "African Venus," a "black Venus," "dusky Sally," a "wooly-headed concubine," and a member of Jefferson's "Congo harem" who had a "complection between mahogany and dirty greasy yellow."[15] The tawdry accusation was released into a receptive political world of Jefferson foes. The president's involvement with "Black Sal," they argued, made him morally unfit for high office. Ultimately, to his critics' chagrin, Jefferson won the 1804 election in a landslide, capturing all but two states and 92 percent of the electoral vote.

As for Callender's background, he was a political refugee from Scotland who began his career as a blistering writer in the 1780s. He was one of those men "who never in his life beheld with equanimity a greater than himself."[16] Full of pride and jealousy, Callender embarked on writing political pamphlets, leading to *The Political Progress of Britain*, which criticized powerful British politicians. He libeled Lord Gardenstone, his mentor, as well as noted English writer Dr. Samuel Johnson, and the Crown itself. Callender, hearing rumors of his imminent arrest for his traitorous writings, fled Britain in 1793. He escaped to the New World, leaving behind his wife and child to fend for themselves.

On May 27, 1800, Callender's muckraking brand of writing resulted in his arrest under the Sedition Act for attacking President John Adams as a "hoary headed incendiary and a man who had deserted and reversed all principles."[17] Callender was put on trial in Richmond. Having learned of the indictment and coaxed by his vehement opposition to the sedition laws, Jefferson told James Monroe, "I think it essentially just and necessary that Callendar [sic] should be substantially defended."[18] Jefferson associated with Callender against his own better judgment, not because he approved of Callender, but because he needed Callender to rebut newspaper attacks on his political policies. In June 1800, Judge Samuel Chase fined Callender $200.00 and sentenced him to nine months in jail under the Sedition laws.

When Jefferson became president, he pardoned Callender, due to Jefferson's vehement contempt for all sedition laws that sanctioned censorship. Jefferson also allowed Callendar to claim compensation for his fine and incarceration. The muckraker then began to solicit Jefferson for money and a presidential appointment to postmaster of Richmond. He complained to James Madison that "Jefferson has not returned one shilling of my fine. I now begin to know what Ingratitude is."[19] Jefferson denied Callender his appointment to postmaster, concluding that he was "unworthy."[20] Callender turned to Monroe, who tried to "tranquilize his mind" but Monroe began to suspect that Callender would attack the "Executive." Monroe had a sharper eye to Callender's potential threats than did Jefferson. He advised Jefferson to "get all the letters however unimportant from him . . . Your resolution to terminate all communication with him is wise, yet it will be well to prevent even a serpent doing one an injury."[21] Madison also became suspicious of Callender's motives, observing, "It had been my lot to bear the burden of receiving and repelling [Callender's] claims . . . [I]t is impossible to reason concerning a man, whose imagination and passions have been so fermented."[22] Jefferson refused to become any closer to Callender, whom most readers recognized as a "bitter, ranting mercenary."[23] He sent Callender fifty dollars, a sum that incensed Callender as paltry "hush money." Jefferson, in turn, severed his relationship. "I am really mortified at the base ingratitude of Callender," he wrote. "It presents human nature in a hideous form. It gives me concern because I perceive that relief which was afforded him on mere motives of charity, may be viewed under the aspect of employing him as a writer.[24]

Callendar's political idol, Jefferson, had spurned his efforts to cultivate their friendship or procure a job for him. The perceived slight stirred his desire for political revenge.

In August 1802, one of Jefferson's political allies accused Callender of causing his wife's death from a venereal disease. Callender counterattacked with a defamation of character charge and accused Jefferson of keeping a slave as his "concubine." He denigrated Sally as a "[s]lut common as the pavement," who was "romping with half a dozen black fellows," and having "fifteen, or thirty gallants of all colours."[25] Callendar referred to Jefferson as a man who would lecherously summon Sally from "the kitchen or perhaps the pigsty," comparing Jefferson's mixing of the races with bestiality.[26] Callender excoriated Jefferson in the *Richmond Recorder*. The sensational accusations spread rapidly, appearing in the cheering Federalist press—the *New York Evening Post*, the *Washington Federalist*, and the *Gazette of the United States*. Although sexual abuses by masters inflicted on female slaves were common in the Old South, the widower Jefferson had never before been suspected or accused of such amoral behavior. Callender's scandalous revelation dramatically changed Jefferson's political perception.

Callender himself was not only a "drunken ruffian," but a racist,[27] referring to Sally as, among other things, "Black Sal" and a "mahogany colored charmer." "If eight thousand white men in Virginia followed Jefferson's example," he wrote, "you would have FOUR HUNDRED THOUSAND MULATTOES in addition to the present swarm. The country would no longer be habitable."[28] Callender believed that accusing Jefferson of miscegenation (race mixing) would fatally ruin his political career. As one author commented, "Jefferson's offense was held to be mixture of the races, and Callender and his fellow scandalmongers strummed the theme until it was dead tired."[29] At one point, Callender boasted that he had done more harm to Jefferson's reputation in five months than all of Jefferson's critics in ten years—a prophetic statement. John Quincy Adams wrote of Callender, "He writes under the influence of personal resentment and revenge, but the effect of his publications upon the reputation of the President has been considerable."[30]

Callender's libel was not limited to Jefferson. He called John Adams a "repulsive pedant," a "gross hypocrite," and in his "private life, one of the most egregious fools upon the continents." He further said that Adams was a "hideous hermaphroditical character who has neither the force and firmness of a man, nor the gentleness and sensibility of a woman."[31] The blunt and irascible Adams had no use for Callender, either. "I believe nothing that Callender said any more than if it had been said by an infernal spirit. I would not convict a dog of killing sheep upon the testimony of two such witnesses," Adams blustered, concluding that Callender's charges against Jefferson were "mere clouds of unsubstantiated vapour."[32] Jefferson's allies also hurried to his defense. "I would at this time only remark that as to the case of the lady there is not a gentleman in the U. States of either party who does not hold in detestation the pitiful propagations of so pitiful a tale," Robert Smith, his secretary of the Navy, wrote Jefferson. "Your country by their approving voice at the last election have passed sentence on all the allegations that malice has exhibited against you."[33] Edward Coles, a friend and neighbor of Jefferson's, referred to the allegations as "vacuous."[34] And Socialite Margaret Smith defended Jefferson's reputation, declaring emphatically, "I have seen, I have listened to, one of the greatest and best of men . . . truly a philosopher, and a truly good man, and eminently a great one."[35]

In additional to Callender himself, two potential sources for Callender's charges also had a clear motive against Jefferson: Callender's informants, David Meade Randolph and his wife, Mary (Molly), who were disaffected, distant cousins of Jefferson's. Before the appearance of Callender's articles, Jefferson had fired David from his position as federal marshal in Richmond, allegedly for rigging the Callender jury. Randolph's dismissal outraged him, and the couple's grandiose lifestyle disintegrated. They became outspoken enemies of Jefferson and fed hearsay and scalding gossip to Callender and others. Yet, Elijah Fletcher, a visitor from Vermont, believed Callendar's sexual allegation and left a harsh description of Jefferson and his slave mistress:

> Mr. Jefferson is tall, spare, straight in body. His face not handsome but savage—I learnt he was but little esteemed by his neighbors. . . . The story of Black Sal is no farce—That he cohabits with her and has a number of children by her is a sacred truth—and the worst of it is, he keeps the same children slaves—an unnatural crime which is very common in these parts—This conduct may receive a little palliation when we consider that such proceedings are so common that they cease here to be disgraceful.[36]

How, and what, did Callender know of Sally Hemings? In fact, who was Sally Hemings, and what is known about her life? Almost nothing. There is so little information about Sally Hemings from which to work. "One could probably write everything that we really know about her on an index card," notes prominent Jefferson historian Robert Turner.[37] Excluding Jefferson's various listings of slaves he owned, and distribution lists for blankets and other supplies (in which Sally was treated like all of her relatives at Monticello), there are but a few brief descriptions of Sally: for instance, of her being "mighty near white" and "very handsome" or "decidedly good looking."[38] Noting money for clothes and a smallpox vaccination while Sally was in Paris, Jefferson appears to have made reference to Sally in only four of the twenty-five thousand letters he penned. There is no evidence that Jefferson ever wrote to her directly or received mail from her (or that she could have read them had he written). The references that do exist consist of a note that "Maria's maid" (which may not have been Sally Hemings) had a baby, as well as two letters suggesting that "if Bet or Sally's children" came down with the measles, they should be sent off the mountain. Finally, there is a note concerning a "d.o. Sally" notation in the margin of a letter stating that Jefferson was sending the bedding of Sally's older brother, James Hemings, back to America.[39]

The only credible surviving descriptions of Sally Hemings's abilities are found in two 1787 letters from Abigail Adams, wife of US minister to Great Britain John Adams. The Adamses kept the fourteen-year-old Sally—and Jefferson's eight-year-old daughter, Polly—for two weeks when they arrived from Virginia on their ocean voyage to join Jefferson in Paris. Abigail described Sally as being "quite a child" and said that she "wants more care than the child [Polly], and is wholly incapable of looking properly after her, without some superiour [sic] to direct her."[40] Indeed, Sally is a historical enigma. As biographer John C. Miller commented, "We know virtually nothing of Sally Hemings, or her motives [and] she is hardly more than a name."[41] One account says that Sally was born in 1773 at a Charles City plantation and was the alleged illegitimate daughter of John Wayles, Jefferson's father-in-law, who was a well-known businessman, lawyer, and occasional slave trader for a British supplier. Her mother was Betty Hemings, a "chattel" of Wayles. It was rumored that Wayles took his slave Betty as his "concubine," thus making Jefferson's wife, Martha, Sally's half sister.[42] Betty also served as surrogate mother to Martha when Martha's own mother tragically died in childbirth.

When Wayles died, Thomas Jefferson inherited, on his wife's behalf, all of Betty Hemings's family, (including the infant Sally) as well as several large parcels of land and 135 slaves from Wayles. At Martha's direction, most of the Hemingses, including Betty, became trusted house servants at Monticello, which seemed to confirm their special status to Martha. It seems clear that the Hemingses were valued and loyal servants to the entire Jefferson family as nannies, cooks, carpenters, dressmakers, and seamstresses who supported Monticello.[43] Historian Donald Jackson explains this special relationship:

That the Hemings matriarchy was well thought of by the Jefferson family made the children and grandchildren more conspicuous than the other slaves in the Monticello neighborhood. Add the facts that miscegenation [race mixing] did exist in the South; that men of such probity as George Washington were falsely but commonly believed to engage in it; and that Sally and her children were all but white in appearance, and it is little wonder that Jefferson's opponent would eventually produce a story conferring on him the paternity for those children.[44]

It appears that Sally was illiterate, and one can only speculate as to the relationship she had with the Jefferson family. A reasonable inference would be that Sally must have left Monticello after it was sold in 1828. By 1830, she was living with her sons, Madison and Eston, in or around Charlottesville. Interestingly, in one census, Sally was listed as free and in another she was designated "white."[45] Some historians have speculated that Sally lived inside the house at Monticello or had a secret room at the main house. This is neither accurate nor supported by any historical documentation. After her return from Paris as maid to Jefferson's daughter, Sally lived with her older sister, Critta, on Mulberry Row, the slave quarters closest to the big house. Four years later, they moved, in all probability, into one of the three new log cabins built in 1793. The three log dwellings, more comfortably furnished than typical slave dwellings, replaced the slave quarters in the 1790s and likely housed several Hemings family members, including parlor maid Critta and her son, James, and house joiner John and his wife, Priscilla, a valued nurse to Jefferson's children.[46] Finally, between 1803 and 1807, Sally moved into a masonry room near the "south dependency," then the kitchens and stables. There is not a shred of historical evidence that Sally lived inside Monticello or occupied some secret rendezvous room there.[47]

Sally died in 1835 or 1836, at age sixty-two, ten years after Thomas Jefferson's death. She had no burial marker or obituary in the newspaper. There is no recorded evidence or letters suggesting that she ever addressed her relationship, if any, with Thomas Jefferson. Nor is there any evidence about her activities in the post-Monticello period. If Sally was Jefferson's sexual partner, there is no indication that she was approached by anyone on this subject.[48] Based on historical evidence, Sally Hemings appears to have been a very minor figure in Thomas Jefferson's life.

And this is where Jeff and Ellen came to Jefferson's defense. Both grandchildren knew Sally, and played a central role in what has been labeled derisively by some historians as "the family denial." Jefferson's friends vehemently denied the sexual accusation in print, but the president himself bore this vilification without public comment or letters. Privately, he informed Jeff, Ellen, and others that a formal refutation was beneath his dignity. "I have determined to contradict none," he emphatically informed Monroe.[49] A statement made to George Logan indicates Jefferson's mature judgment with regard to the slurs against him: "As to federal slanders, I never wished them to be answered, but by the tenor of my life . . . The man who fears no truths has nothing to fear from lies."[50] Jefferson further explained his avowed silence to William A. Burwell:[51] "Many of the [Federalist] lies would have required only a simple denial, but I saw that even that would have led to the infallible inference, that whatever I had not denied was to be presumed true. I have, therefore, never done even this, but to such of my friends as happen to converse on these subjects, and I have never believed that my character could hang upon every two-penny lie of our common enemies."[52]

Jeff Randolph knew that his grandfather's muteness on the subject was in accord with his resolve not to respond to newspaper attacks, as Jefferson had reiterated: "Their approbation has taught a lesson, useful to the world . . . I should have fancied myself guilty had I condescended to put pen to paper in refutation of their falsehoods, or drawn to them respect by a notice from myself."[53] In a letter to Samuel Smith of Maryland, Jefferson said, "At a very early period of my life, I determined never to put a single sentence into any newspaper. I have religiously adhered to the resolution through my life . . . were I to undertake to answer the calumnies of the newspapers, it would be more than all my own time and that of twenty aids could affect. For while I should be answering one, twenty new ones would be invented."[54] In 1806 Irish poet Thomas Moore published verses hinting at the rumors about Jefferson and Sally Hemings: "The weary statesman for repose hath fled / From halls of council to his negro's shed, / Where blest he woos some black Aspasia's grace, / And dreams of freedom in his slave's embrace!"

Shown the "obnoxious passages," Jefferson simply gave a dismissive laugh, ending any discussion with his code of silence.[55]

Privately, Jeff urged his grandfather to vigorously deny the charges in a public forum, and, apparently, Jefferson considered his grandson's advice. "I know," Jefferson explained to a friend in Connecticut, "that I might have filled the courts of the United States with actions for these slanders, and have ruined, perhaps, many persons who are not innocent. But this would be no equivalent for the loss of character. I leave them, therefore, to the reproof of their own consciences. If these do not condemn them, there will come a day when the false witness will meet a judge who has not slept over his slanders."[56] After all, Jefferson had once reasoned, if a historian "speaking of a character well known and established on satisfactory testimony imputes to it things incompatible with that character, we reject them without hesitation, and assent to that only of which we have better evidence."[57]

Two years before his own death in 1826, Jefferson reflected on Callender's allegations and seemed to pity him: "He was a poor creature, sensible [oversensitive], hypochondriac, drunken, penniless & unprincipled."[58] But Dumas Malone, the most respected Jeffersonian scholar, accepted no such excuses, concerned only that "the evil that [Callender] did was not buried with him: some of it has lasted through the generations."[59]

Even so, Jefferson left the zealous defense of his reputation to his family, especially Jeff Randolph, and his political allies. Historian Henry Randall, who had interviewed Jeff, later recorded, "Col. Randolph said that he 'slept within sound of [Jefferson's] breathing at night.' Jeff said that 'he had never seen a motion, or a look, or a circumstance which led him to suspect for an instant that there was a particle of familiarity between Mr. Jefferson and Sally Hemings—and that no person ever at Monticello dreamed of such a thing.'"[60] In his 1874 biography of Jefferson, James Parton quoted Jeff Randolph as telling Randall that "there was not the shadow of suspicion that Mr. Jefferson in this or any other instance had commerce with female slaves."[61]

Jeff also related further details to Randall, implicating Jefferson's nephews as the true culprits in the sexual episode:

> Mr. Jefferson had two nephews, Peter Carr and Samuel Carr whom he brought up in his own house. They were the sons of Jefferson's sister and her husband Dabney Carr . . . who died in 1773 . . . Sally Hemings was the mistress of Peter and her sister Betsey (she was actually the daughter of Sally's half sister) the mistress of Samuel—and from these the progeny which resembled Mr. Jefferson. . . . Their connection with the Carrs was perfectly notorious at Monticello, and scarcely disguised by the latter—never disavowed by them. Samuel's proceedings were particularly open.[62]

Jeff's sister Ellen went even further. She admitted that there were mixed-race children at Monticello, but insisted that Sally was "pretty notoriously the mistress of a married man, a near relation of Mr. Jefferson's." Ellen identified Jefferson's nephew Samuel as that near relation. "There is a general impression that the four children of Sally Hemmings were all the children of Col. Carr, the most notorious good-natured Turk that ever was master of a black seraglio kept at other men's expence. His deeds are as well known as his name."[63] She further insisted that the "tender, considerate, refined" grandfather she knew so well was the least likely person to "carry on his low amours," with a slave while so closely watched by an adoring family.[64]

Dabney Carr, the Carr brothers' father, had been Jefferson's best boyhood friend, but had died tragically when he was only thirty years old. Thereafter, Jefferson had acted as protective guardian and helped raise his sons, Samuel and Peter Carr. They often visited Monticello and are now scientifically confirmed suspects for fathering Sally's and, most likely, her sister, Mary's, children (see epilogue). In fact, the Carr brothers stood directly accused by Jeff, and according to Randall's account, they admitted their sexual complicity with Sally. Jeff said, "To my knowledge and the statements of other gentleman made to me 60 years ago the paternity of these parties was admitted by two other persons."[65] In fact, the recorded evidence shows that the Carrs were present at Monticello during Sally's daughter Harriet's conception in 1795, when the second Harriet was conceived in 1800, and when Eston (the 1998 DNA match) was conceived in 1807.

Contradicting historian Fawn Brodie's claim that the Carr brothers had left the Monticello area when Sally became pregnant is Jefferson's own account book, made early in the year 1795, when Harriet was conceived:

> Feb. 11 Gave S. Carr to Pay Clarkson&c.
> Knitting 2 pr stockgs., 2 Dollars.
> Mar 2. Gave P. Carr to send by S. Carr to
> Dabney Carr 8 Dollars.[66]

Commenting on his interview with Jeff, historian Henry Randall remarked that he could give much more evidence," fifty more facts were there time and were there any need of it, to show Mr. Jefferson's innocence of this and all similar offenses against propriety."[67] And the only reason he did not include the allegation against the Carr brothers in his biography, *Life of Jefferson,* was because Jeff had prohibited him from naming the Carr nephews, warning, "You are not bound to prove a negative. If I should allow you to take Peter Carr's corpse into Court and plead guilty over it to shelter Mr. Jefferson, I should not dare again to walk by his grave: he would rise and spurn me."[68] Jefferson was "deeply attached to the Carrs," Randall wrote, "especially to Peter. He was extremely indulgent to them and the idea of watching them for faults or vices probably never occurred to [Jefferson]."[69] Indeed, Jefferson had loved Peter as a son and had held great hopes for him. A man of character and honor, he would never attempt to absolve himself by implicating his sister's son though that son had greatly disappointed him.

There appears to be some confusion over which Carr brother was supposedly the lover of Sally Hemings. According to one historian, Randall said that Jeff Randolph had identified Peter as Hemings's lover, but in Ellen Coolidge's 1858 letter to her husband, she identified Samuel. It is likely that they both had Samuel in mind. Ellen wrote her letter immediately after her conversation with Jeff, when her memory of the details would have been fresh. Randall wrote his letter twelve years after his conversation with Jeff Randolph; he probably got the brothers mixed up. "But to further complicate the issue, in an 1873 letter Jeff wrote, 'The paternity of these persons was admitted by two others,' meaning both of the Carr brothers."[70]

Historian Frank Berkley, curator of historical manuscripts for twenty-nine years at the University of Virginia and former Monticello board member, agrees with Jeff's indictment of both Carr brothers, but specifies Peter as Sally's true lover:

> [The nephews] were very much involved in this . . . I don't think Samuel had too much to do with Sally, but Peter did . . . Everybody knew she [Sally] was living with Peter . . . and Samuel had a mistress at Monticello too . . . the reason I am so persuaded of that relationship . . . that Peter being seen daily at [Sally's cabin] . . . what was he doing there? I think he had a long time love affair with her . . . I think it was a genuine love affair.[71]

Israel Jefferson, another Monticello slave, echoed Callendar's story of a sexual liaison between Sally and Thomas Jefferson. Shortly after Israel's story was published in the *Pike County Republican* newspaper, Jeff Randolph penned a scathing six-page rebuttal letter to the editor, pointing out many factual errors in Israel's account (and, of course, denying the allegation). For example, Israel did not even live at Monticello until he was eight years old, long after Sally Hemings's last child was born.[72] Israel also claimed that he was the only slave that had kindled Thomas Jefferson's fire, yet, fifteen years earlier, historian Henry Randall had included as an appendix to volume 3 of his *Life of Thomas Jefferson* a letter from Jeff that directly contradicts Israel's claim: "[Jefferson] always made his own fire." Four years later, another book published this statement by former Monticello overseer Edmund Bacon: "He never had a servant make a fire in his room in the morning, or at any other time, when he was at home. He always had a box filled with nice dry wood in his room, and when he wanted fire he would open it and put on the wood."[73]

Israel's interview also included bitter remarks about Jeff, whom he claimed to have encountered after the Civil War. He'd found the "proud and haughty Randolph in poverty, at Edge Hill" in 1868, he had said.[74] This is the same Jeff Randolph who, according to Madison, presided over the Republican political convention of 1872. In Jeff's stinging rebuttal to the newspaper, he wrote, "Israel is made to revive and confirm of his own knowledge a calumny generated in the hot bed of party malice." Jeff also declared that the other slaves had been bitterly jealous of the Hemingses because, he presumed, of their "very superior intelligence capacity and fidelity to trusts." Finally, he stated that those who were slandering his family were simply "pondering [sic] to a ferocious hate of the southern white man."[75]

Perhaps most important, one other direct observer of happenings at Monticello corroborated Jeff and Ellen's version of "the family denial." In a reminiscence first recorded in 1862, perhaps the most convincing historical evidence that exists that Jefferson was innocent of the sexual allegation, Edmund Bacon denied that Sally Hemings's daughter (presumably Harriet) was Jefferson's daughter, stating bluntly, "She was not his daughter, she was _____'s daughter. I know that."[76] Exactly how he knew that will be discussed momentarily in the next chapter.

Notwithstanding the denial of the Hemingses' paternity allegation by Jeff and Ellen, and eyewitnesses to life at Monticello, the accusation has survived in the oral traditions of several American families who claimed descent from Jefferson and Sally Hemings. These included the descendants of Madison Hemings, Sally's child, and the descendants of Thomas Woodson, who claimed to be the "love child" Jefferson had fathered in Paris with Sally. It was Callender who first alleged that there was a "love child," identifying him as "Tom" in his original article. But the sexual allegation was given new life when Madison Hemings's "memoir" was resurrected.[77]

Madison Hemings was Sally's second son, born in 1805 at Monticello.[78] He lived there until Jefferson's death in 1826. Both Madison and his younger brother, Eston, were freed by Jefferson's will. According to the terms of the will, both were apprenticed to their uncle, John Hemings, as cabinetmakers until they reached the age of twenty-one. The freeing of the Hemingses was nothing out of the ordinary, as some historians have claimed. Rather, Jefferson provided for their release because he believed they could sustain themselves as freed men by their carpentry skills. He also emancipated James Hemings because he was confident he could take care of himself with an occupation. And there were other male slaves whom Jefferson had freed or let "run away."[79]

Madison's accusations derived from his "interview" in the *Pike County (Ohio) Republican* on March 13, 1873, under the title "Life Among the Lowly, No. 1.," (Harriet Beecher Stowe's subtitle to her book, *Uncle Tom's Cabin*), in which Madison declared that he was Thomas Jefferson's son.[80] Madison was sixty-eight when he was interviewed, so his recollection of events may have dimmed over time. Betty Hemings, his mother, died when Madison was quite young. Moreover, Madison said that during Sally's stay in Paris, she became Jefferson's "concubine"—the exact word used by Callender seventy years earlier. Madison declared that when Jefferson returned to Virginia from Paris, Sally was *enceinte* (French for "pregnant"). "Soon after their arrival, she gave birth to a child, of whom Thomas Jefferson was the father. It lived but a short time. She gave birth to four others, and Jefferson was the father of all of them."[81]

Madison's testimony strains common sense, as well as the historical facts. For example, there is no evidence in the interview that Sally herself claimed Jefferson as the father of any of her children. In fact, Madison Hemings's statements so closely resemble the original Callender allegations from 1802, almost verbatim. For example, they both identically misspelled John Wayles's name. It seems obvious that he (or the editor, Wetmore) based his story solely on Callender's newspaper story. Madison's interview was heavily edited, if not written altogether, by the editor, S. F. Wetmore, a fervent abolitionist from New England who had a bias against Jeffersonian Democrats. For example, notice the extraordinary vocabulary used by a former slave who "induc[ed]" the white children to teach him his "letters." The interview included specific words, such as "demurred," "compunctions of conscience," "aristocratic," "interment," and "viz."[82]

Wetmore's suggestive editing is exemplified by sophisticated, specific phraseology, not likely to be used by the semi-literate Madison. For instance, Madison's sister married a white man, but she was never suspected of being "tainted with African blood." Beverly's daughter was never suspected of having any "colored blood coursing in her veins." Madison's interview is laced with racial commentary. He asserted that white slave masters had no "compunctions of conscience [against] parting mother and child" and that "many [false] promises of white folks [were made] to the slaves."[83] Finally, his use of the French phrase *"enceinte,"* or pregnant, raises suspicions: is this the editor's sophisticated word or that of a poorly educated ex-slave like Madison?[84]

Preeminent Jefferson historian Julian Boyd notes that Madison's testimony "was obviously prompted by someone . . . shaped and perhaps even written and embellished by the prompter." Dumas Malone assigns it a place in "the tradition of political enmity and abolitionist propaganda."[85] Biographer Willard S. Randall agrees: "I wish I knew what Madison Hemings said. The piece was written, and rewritten and rewritten by an abolitionist journalist after the civil war when Jefferson and the South were in disrepute . . . We don't have Madison Hemings's words. We have a doctored version by a disreputable journalist. The problem is that this is oral tradition; it is not written history."[86]

Madison's account also revealed a new tangent—Sally refused to return with Jefferson from Paris without some quid pro quo. When Jefferson returned to the United States and brought Sally (and her brother, James) back to Monticello, she "demurred," according to Madison. He recalled that Sally began to learn French, and in Paris she was free (slavery was outlawed in France, and a slave could sue for freedom), while in Virginia she would be "re-enslaved." According to Madison, to "induce" Sally to return, Jefferson promised her "extraordinary privileges" and made a "solemn pledge" that her children would be freed at the age of twenty-one. "In consequence of his promises, on which she implicitly relied, she returned with Jefferson to Virginia."[87] As one Jefferson scholar, Virginius Dabney, has concluded, "the notion that a sixteen-year-old slave would defy her master and seek to drive a hard bargain with him is incredible on its face."[88]

Madison was very young at the time he described. He likely heard this second-hand version from his older siblings, Beverly and Harriet. Madison was only seventeen when Harriet and Beverly "ran away," implying they were freed with Jefferson's acquiescence. More telling is that Madison is the *only one* of Sally's children to commit his accusations to record. None of Madison's brothers or sisters ever made any claim against Jefferson. Indeed, none spoke or wrote for the record. In fact, Eston's family claimed descent from a "Jefferson Uncle" (Randolph Jefferson, Jefferson's younger brother, was known as "Uncle Randolph"). Eston himself was asked about his possible lineage to Jefferson while he lived in Ohio. Apparently, the interviewer thought Eston resembled a statue of Jefferson that he had seen in Washington. Strangely, Eston replied, "My mother was never married." He could have easily replied yes if he had believed he was Jefferson's son, but he did not.[89]

In his interview, Madison alleged that "[u]nlike Washington [Jefferson] had but little taste or care for agricultural pursuits."[90] This is monumentally wrong, as Jefferson's voluminous *Garden Book* would attest. Jefferson delighted in that "the greatest service which can be rendered any country" is to "add an useful plant to its culture."[91] Farmers, Jefferson believed, were the "chosen people of God."[92] The Virginian was a skilled botanist, farmer, gardener and inventor. He mastered many elements of horticulture and applied the best techniques to the raising of crops. His "plants gracefully curved away, in keeping with the undulating horizons beyond" Monticello.[93]

In essence, then, the historical record is mixed, but Jeff and Ellen made a strong, perhaps irrefutable case for Jefferson's innocence of the sexual allegation. Three eyewitnesses intimately knew both Sally and Jefferson. Patsy, Ellen Coolidge, and Jeff Randolph all found the accusations inconceivable and never witnessed any hint of a sexual liaison. In fact, there is not a scintilla of proof of "cohabitation" or any physical intimacy between Jefferson and Sally during the thirty-seven years she lived, on and off, at Monticello. Most important, at least four witnesses assert that Jefferson was not in physical proximity of Sally for fifteen months before the birth of her son who most resembled Jefferson: Patsy Jefferson, Thomas Jefferson Randolph, George Wythe Randolph, and biographer Henry Randall.

As Jeff explained in the "family denial," the sexual allegation was preposterously out of character for Jefferson. The grandchildren also knew firsthand that Jefferson's health, especially in the last decade of his life, would have physically prevented him from engaging in a vibrant sexual relationship with Sally Hemings, a fourteen-year-old servant. His severe migraines, diarrhea, rheumatoid arthritis, and emotional distress over his finances and the death of his wife and daughter had contributed to deteriorating physical and mental health for a man who was sixty-four at the time of Eston's conception. According to Jeff and Ellen, it is simply beyond common sense to believe their grandfather was having an ongoing sexual affair at his age and in his condition.

When it came to women, Thomas Jefferson's nature was sheepish, some would say awkward and "geekish," but certainly not lustful. Noted historian Dumas Malone opines that Jefferson "was not bold toward women and . . . was much more in character as a devoted husband and kind father than as an aggressive lover, and it is hard to believe that he would have persisted in the face of rebuffs at any age."[94] Scholar E. M. Halliday echoed Malone's viewpoint by alluding to "the certainty, from all that is known about him, that aggressive sexual advances upon a woman who had given no signal of invitation were contrary to his nature and his code of conduct."[95] Jefferson's marriage proposal to his first love, Rebecca Burwell, in 1763 illustrates this point. The future president and author of the Declaration of Independence became so nervous and awkward that he could barely utter his words. He later reflected on his disastrous experience in the famous Apollo room at the Raleigh tavern: Jefferson had been overwhelmed with "strange confusion" that deteriorated into "a few broken sentences."[96] Later in life, he was cloistered in his tranquil home life with his wife, Patty, and then deeply conflicted over his deep romantic feelings for the married Maria Cosway.[97] The Hemings allegation of sexual misconduct is contrary to Jefferson's refined and reticent nature toward women.

Thus, some prominent historians are quick to dismiss the "family denial" and instead believe that Jefferson engaged in rape and was a brutal slave "master," thus making the sexual allegations true. Yet, when Thomas Jefferson arrived at Monticello from Paris after a five-year absence, his slaves were so ecstatic to see him that they unhitched his horses and pulled his carriage up the last ridge of the mountain, then carried him in their arms into his house, laughing and crying with joy. "It seemed impossible to satisfy their anxiety to touch and kiss the very earth which bore him," Patsy Jefferson said.[98]

WILLIAM G. HYLAND JR.

JEFFERSON'S GRANDCHILDREN PLAYING ON MONTICELLO'S LAWN—PAINTING BY JANE BRADDICK PETICOLAS (1825)

THOMAS JEFFERSON

MONTICELLO

WILLIAM G. HYLAND JR.

UNIVERSITY OF VIRGINIA

THOMAS JEFFERSON

PATSY JEFFERSON RANDOLPH

THOMAS JEFFERSON RANDOLPH

THOMAS JEFFERSON

ELLEN RANDOLPH COOLIDGE

THOMAS MANN RANDOLPH

JEFFERSON'S LIBRARY

WILLIAM G. HYLAND JR.

JEFFERSON'S BEDCHAMBER

ANNE CARY RANDOLPH BANKHEAD

POPLAR FOREST

THOMAS JEFFERSON

MARIA COSWAY

10
"UNCLE RANDOLPH": THE UNKNOWN BROTHER

As to Randolph, I think it would not be improbable . . . He was clearly an earthbound farmer of no intellectual interest whatsoever. He liked hunting and fishing and that was about the size of it . . . I could imagine such a man doing this, but [Thomas] Jefferson was exactly the contrary.

—**Historian Frank Berkley**[1]

A minor figure of little historic interest, Thomas Jefferson's intellectually challenged younger brother, Randolph Jefferson,[2] has been ignored by most historians. Most scholars know little of Randolph, and major biographers mention him only in passing, if at all. Few people even know that Jefferson had a younger brother.

So, who was Randolph Jefferson, and what was his relationship to his older and more famous brother? Through the fifty or more letters that passed between the brothers, as well as Jeff's and Ellen's letters, observations, and descriptions of "Uncle Randolph," we can cobble together a profile of Randolph Jefferson.[3] Even with less than half of their correspondence available to historians, there is little difficulty drawing a clear picture of Randolph and his relationship with Jefferson, Ellen, and Jeff Randolph. Randolph emerges, at best, an unenlightened and simple dirt farmer, albeit one with an appreciable slave force and valuable lands. For example, one is moved by Randolph's somewhat illiterate pleas and requests to his brother for a watch (which both brothers refer to as a "she"), or a loan (Jefferson loaned his brother $6.50) or simply a letter.

Unfortunately, according to Jefferson's Summary Journal of Letters, there are approximately twenty letters missing between the two brothers for the period 1793–1806.[4] But throughout the paltry correspondence available, Jefferson remains the superior but sympathetic and generous brother, who was adept at supplying Randolph with dogs for his farm, seed, and medical advice—an admonition to use a "bougie" (a catheter for the prostate) even though it might be extremely painful.[5] Yet, the correspondence between the brothers illustrates that great contrasts exist between members of the same family and illuminates Jefferson as a caring and tender older brother.[6]

Unfortunately, neither a portrait nor a physical description of Randolph exists. But Jefferson described his younger brother after his death in an 1815 deposition, involving a dispute over Randolph's estate, saying "that he considered his said brother as not possessing skill for the judicious management of his affairs, and that in all occasions of life a diffidence in his own opinions . . . and an easy pliancy to the wishes and urgency of others made him very susceptible of influence from those who had any views upon him."[7]

Randolph was twelve years younger than Jefferson, an age gap that may have accounted for their lack of intimacy. Growing up, Jefferson's closest relationship among his siblings was his older sister, Jane, his "constant companion when at home, and the confidant of all his youthful feelings." They shared common passions for nature, the wilderness, and playing music. Jane sang hymns for Jefferson. Together, they would sing psalms "many a winter evening, round the family fireside . . . accompanied by the notes of his violin, thus ascending together."[8]

Perhaps Jefferson's best friend in his young life was not Randolph or his sister, but his friend and fellow student at Reverend James Maury's elementary school, Dabney Carr. Carr became the central figure of Jefferson's youth—almost a surrogate brother. The two young men shared a love of literature, learning, and the rolling landscape of the Blue Ridge mountains. When at Shadwell, Jefferson's boyhood home, the two took their books and climbed through the woods of the mountain Jefferson later named Monticello. The two would play together, coming to rest at the base of an oak tree near the top of the mountain. They promised each other they would be buried on this spot, and years later this is where Jefferson designed the family cemetery. Carr was the first to be buried there. To Jefferson, Dabney was the best of friends. No man, Jefferson said later, had "more of the milk of human kindness, of indulgence, of softness, of pleasantry of conversation and conduct."[9] Unfortunately, Dabney died when he was only twenty-nine, leaving a wife and two small children to raise. Later in life, Jefferson became a mentor and guardian to his two young sons, Peter and Samuel Carr.

Although Jefferson and his younger brother were not close, they both grew up as the sons of a prosperous, cultured, and sophisticated family. The Jeffersons dined with silver, danced with grace, and entertained guests.[10] Their father, Peter Jefferson, an accomplished surveyor by trade, worked in his study on the first floor of their house.[11] Jefferson greatly admired, almost worshipped, his father and enjoyed their precious time together. Peter Jefferson was six foot four and strapping—the kind of man people noticed. He was an imposing, wealthy, well-liked man known for his feats of strength and his hunting adventures. One of Thomas Jefferson's favorite stories about his father, according to one writer, was that he was "a man of prodigious strength . . . [who] once directed three husky slaves to pull down an old outbuilding with a rope. After they had repeatedly tried and failed, Jefferson's father 'bade them stand aside, seized the rope and dragged down the structure in an instant.'"[12]

Peter had amassed large tracts of land and hundreds of slaves in and around what became Albemarle County, Virginia. There, along the Rivanna River, he built his family home, Shadwell, named after the London parish where his wife, Jane, had been baptized.[13] As a surveyor and a planter, Peter thrived. Jefferson sensed that his father was a man whom other men admired. Biographer Henry Randall described Peter's life and influence on young Jefferson: "After the wearisome and often stirring events of a day of border life were passed, he spent the evening in reading historians, essayists, and even poets. Addison, Swift and Pope were prime favorites with him—but Shakespeare was his great favorite!"[14] Together with his wife, Jane, they raised a family of seven children, owned slaves, managed a plantation, and became rising Virginia gentry.[15] Although Peter often traveled on surveying trips, he handsomely provided everything his family needed. Jane, in turn, made the Jefferson home a welcoming place, where children knew their place and minded their manners.[16]

It is unfortunate that Peter died at the young age of forty-nine of some unknown illness. Jefferson was only fourteen, and his brother, Randolph, was barely two. Randolph would never enjoy a father figure in his life and would struggle to come to terms with Peter's death for the rest of his own life. Thomas Jefferson was devastated at the loss of his beloved father, his mentor and leader in life, who had imparted to his oldest son a regard for learning and devotion to family. Peter's influence on young Jefferson cannot be understated. Jefferson would always speak of and describe his father in a positive, loving light. As we have seen, his father's untimely death was but one of many tragic deaths that Jefferson mourned throughout his long life.

After his father died, the teenage Jefferson propelled through his grief into the role of man of the house. He recalled the transition with great anxiety. "At 14 years of age the whole care and direction of myself was thrown on my self entirely, without a relative or friend qualified to advise or guide me." There would be no more intimate evenings spent in the first-floor study with his father, studying maps, listening to stories of brave expeditions, tinkering with Peter's surveying tools. That time with his father was now a loving memory. And Randolph, a toddler when Peter died, would not know his father at all.[17]

Jefferson's younger brother, Randolph, was born on October 1, 1755, at Shadwell in Albemarle County. With his twin sister, Anna Scott—or Nancy, as she was known in the family—he was the last of ten children born to Peter and Jane Jefferson. When Randolph was born, Jefferson was on the verge of attending college. He was nearly seventeen when he arrived at Chatsworth, his cousin Peter Randolph's house on the James River. During the visit, Peter advised young Jefferson to enroll at the College of William and Mary in Williamsburg, by far one of the wisest decisions Jefferson would eventually make. "By going to the College," he later said, "I shall get a more universal acquaintance which may hereafter be serviceable to me. . . . [and] I can pursue my studies in the Greek and Latin as well there as here, and likewise learn something of the mathematics."[18] Jefferson took Peter's advice and left Albemarle County, bound for Williamsburg, the capital of Virginia, and home to the House of Burgesses, to theaters, to taverns—to a transformed life.

Randolph, one of two twins, was four years old at the time of Jefferson's departure. Randolph was raised, for the most part, by his mother, Jane, and his three older sisters. Randolph's young life, as well as Jefferson's, was to be dominated by their mother, who exerted as great an influence on her children as the legend of their father. In many social and economic ways, Jane was fortunate. Peter had left her a viable legacy: an elegant and thriving plantation free from debt, and children old enough to support their mother. But losing her husband left Jane brokenhearted. Literate, social, and fond of the finer things, at thirty-seven Jane became head of a household to eight surviving children. From various descriptions, one of her children, Elizabeth, appears to have been mentally challenged.[19] Jane's fortitude, however, was remarkable, as one author argues: this was a woman "who had crossed an ocean and lived in half a dozen houses, borne ten children, buried two of her babies, cared for a mentally disabled daughter, and managed two households and dozens of people, and had remarkable power to endure."[20]

The sudden death of a strong father can shatter a family. Fortunately, Peter had left his financial affairs in good order. At the time of his death, he was one of the wealthiest men in Albemarle County, and the second-largest slaveholder in the county. Unlike many Virginia planters, he left behind little accumulated debt. According to one scholar, "Jane was spared the fate of so many widows who were ruined by their husbands' massive debt." There was enough money to pay for her sons' educations and board them at private school, for well-designed furniture, for jewelry and silk corsets for the girls, and dancing lessons for all the children. Jane continued life as a widow, visiting family and friends, and raising her children amid her heartache.[21] A vigilant mother, she personally taught her daughters to read and write and had them take singing and music lessons. Thomas Jefferson and his sister Jane were particularly fond of music, as noted earlier. They played together, Jefferson on the violin, Jane on a spinet. After the family's move back to Shadwell, Jane hired a tutor to instruct her daughters as well as her youngest son, Randolph. Both Thomas and Randolph received more formal education than their sisters, but the young Jefferson women were unusually well versed for their time, due solely to their mother's appreciation of a good education. Jane's great-granddaughter described her as "a woman of a clear and strong understanding."[22] She was "an agreeable, intelligent woman, as well educated as the other Virginia ladies of the day."[23]

While Jefferson was being boarded and taught by the Reverend James Maury, Randolph was being tutored by Benjamin Snead. Snead's school was located a few miles southeast of Shadwell. During these years, the accounts of John Harvie, Peter Jefferson's executor, show payments for Randolph's board and tuition to Snead. Meanwhile, Jefferson moved on to the College of William and Mary, then studied and began the practice of law. In that year, Harvie died and Jefferson, with a brotherly affection, started to look after Randolph's interests, which would continue the rest of their lives. Jefferson's memoranda and fee books provide excellent financial records of the relationship of the two brothers. Their entries concern Randolph's education, sale of his tobacco crops, and various other business transactions. They also reflect the personal interest Jefferson took in his younger brother's affairs both before and after he came of majority age.[24] At sixteen, Randolph was also dispatched to Williamsburg for his further education. It is not clear from the records (which include the bursar's books at the College of William and Mary) whether he attended the grammar school, the college, or both.[25] According to Jefferson's records, Randolph left Shadwell for Williamsburg on October 1, 1771, arriving in time to begin his instruction with Reverend Thomas Gwatkin, professor of natural philosophy and mathematics. After ten months with Gwatkin, Randolph entered the grammar school, then headed by Josiah Johnson, with its less rigorous curriculum. College records only reveal that Randolph was in school in 1771 and 1772. Unfortunately, they fail to say in which schools. Of Randolph's scholastic record nothing is known, but his later letters to Jefferson, with many misspellings and flaws in grammar, evinces that he was not learned, like his brother.

Through their adult years, Jefferson and Randolph remained friendly, but not emotionally close. Jefferson was refined, erudite, and a thirsty intellectual. Randolph seemed content to be an earthbound farmer. One scholar described him as being "less than mediocre in talent and native intelligence," and another as being "mentally ill."[26] Historian Dumas Malone described Randolph as a "very amiable man" who "never amounted to anything much" even though the brothers were similarly educated and reared. Author James Bear, one of the foremost Jeffersonian experts, comments, "Randolph emerges, at best, as an unenlightened and simple dirt farmer."[27] Author Nathan Schachner concludes that Randolph's "mind was limited and his world circumscribed to the narrow confines his daily routine."[28] Historian Forrest McDonald described Randolph more bluntly: a "half wit."[29] Some historians have speculated that both Randolph and his twin sister, Anna, suffered mild brain damage during birth, forever affecting their mental faculties.[30]

Yet, Jefferson always treated his brother with tenderness and respect. The two always wrote affectionately, addressing one another as "Dear Brother." Jefferson helped Randolph patiently in all the minutiae that troubled the younger man. When Randolph would scrawl semi-literate notes to Jefferson, Jefferson would reply, writing of family events within Randolph's limited world.[31] Take for example, Jefferson's letter to Randolph on the eve of the French Revolution, which began, "The occurrences of this part of the globe are of a nature to interest you so little that I have never made them the subject of a letter to you."[32]

Although it appears Randolph briefly attended college and managed his own plantation with Jefferson's sage advice, no doubt he suffered in comparison to his brilliant older brother. Although the two were not close companions, Jefferson was always ready to assist Randolph through financial and personal difficulties. Consider the sworn affidavit that Jefferson provided in connection with a dispute over Randolph's estate involving his sons. "That the testator [Randolph] was always in the habit of consulting this deponent [Thomas Jefferson] in all cases of importance respecting his interests, and he knows of no such case in which he did not consult him, except that of his last marriage."[33]

When Randolph turned eighteen, he inherited 2,200 acres of prime farmland and enough slaves to make a nice living. Randolph seemed to be a substantial farmer. His taxes for 1782 reveal an assessment based on thirty slaves, six horses, forty-two head of cattle, and 2,000 acres of land. Letters between the brothers indicate that he was moderately healthy for the time, but that he experienced a few serious illnesses, one of which was the "gravil," a reference to kidney stones.

Although Thomas Jefferson did not fight in the Revolutionary War, Randolph served and was commissioned a captain in the Buckingham militia. He was routinely referred to as "Captain Randolph" in the community. During the revolution, he fought as a soldier in General Thomas Nelson's corps of Virginia Light Dragoons.[34] In 1778, Randolph also saw active duty as a member of a troop of Albemarle County light horse in the northwest. It was in this militia that Randolph served with a number of white men who were involved in interracial relationships with slaves—two of whom, William Fosset and Joseph Nielson, were hired workers at Monticello. Fosset and Nielson cohabitated with members of the infamous Hemings family. Mary Hemings (Sally's sister) was Fosset's mistress, and Nielson fathered a child with Betty Hemings, Sally's mother.[35]

Apparently, Randolph "had a drinking problem."[36] Randolph's letters to his brother even admit he had an alcohol problem.[37] At one point, Jefferson advised his younger brother to address the issue, and in a letter written on Jefferson's sixty-ninth birthday in 1812, Randolph wrote, "I have not put a drop of any kind of spirits in My Mouth since I saw you."

In 1780, Randolph married Anna Jefferson Lewis, his first cousin, and they produced five sons and one daughter. By his second wife, Randolph had only one son, John. The cause of Randolph's death at age sixty remains yet another of his secrets. But perhaps, the stress of his dismal financial state was partly to blame for a premature death. Randolph was a poor businessman and frequently asked Jefferson for loans. From young adulthood, Randolph was often in debt (as was his brother), and his second wife was an extravagant and difficult woman who ran up excessive bills. His last years were distressed by the severe estrangement between his second wife and his sons. The latter were angered when their stepmother forced Randolph to write a new will, to their financial detriment. Before Randolph's death, his sons urged Jefferson to visit Snowden to persuade their father to change his will, but to no avail. In the legal dispute that continued long after Randolph's death, his sons obtained a deposition from Jefferson. The sons argued that their father had not consulted Jefferson when changing his will, as he had "in all cases of importance respecting his interests. The one exception being his second marriage to Mitchie B. Pryor."[38]

The Monticello slaves were so familiar with the younger brother that they referred to him as "Uncle Randolph." This seems to confirm that Randolph was a frequent visitor. In a letter to her father, Patsy remarked on "Uncle Randolph" being "in the house" and giving a "dram" to a sick slave, which made him feel better.[39]

Unlike his accomplished brother, Randolph had little interest in science or world affairs, and thus he probably would not have found great pleasure in sitting around Jefferson's mansion after dinner, listening to his brilliant brother entertain visitors with accounts of travels and government affairs.[40] As one historian has opined, "Perhaps Randolph would take his leave after dinner and seek pleasure elsewhere on the mountain. Fortunately, we need not speculate on this point, as we have reliable eyewitness accounts that confirm this fact."[41] In 1847, Charles W. Campbell recorded a lengthy narrative from former Monticello blacksmith Isaac Jefferson. Later published in 1951 under the title *Memoirs of a Monticello Slave*, this document provides the following explanation of Randolph's behavior while visiting Monticello: "Old Master's brother, Mass Randall [*sic*], was a mighty simple man: used to come out among black people, play the fiddle and dance half the night; hadn't much more sense than Isaac."[42] Isaac confirms that Randolph was a man of limited capacity and saw him playing his fiddle with and for the slaves on several occasions. Interestingly, Randolph took classical violin lessons from Francis Alberti, who had also instructed Thomas Jefferson. But unlike Jefferson's passion for the classical violin, Randolph's preference was the "folk" fiddle music that was popular among the Monticello enslaved community.[43]

According to professor of law Robert Turner, a retired Jefferson scholar at the University of Virginia, Randolph probably fathered children by his own slaves and spent social time with the slaves at Monticello.[44] Randolph, according to Turner, is far more likely than Thomas Jefferson to have engaged in a sexual relationship with any slave. As noted above, Randolph visited Monticello often, and his years as a widower corresponded with the years during which Sally Hemings had children. "We know that Randolph had a habit of socializing at night with the slaves," Turner added, and he "would fiddle and dance in slave quarters."[45] Although we do not know of Randolph's temperament or how he treated his own slaves, there is one disturbing report that an enslaved woman, Hannah, was sent to Randolph's Snowdon plantation and was beaten to death by the overseer there,

Isaac Bates. Thomas Jefferson, on the other hand, seemed amiable and pleasant, but was nonetheless "a man of almost impenetrable emotional reserve."[46] Jefferson separated himself physically and emotionally from his slaves, and by some historical accounts early in his career, considered them intellectually inferior due to their degraded conditions. Jefferson suffered from a conceptual blind spot about slavery, tending to regard it as a fair economic exchange: hard work for food, shelter, clothing, and safety. As author Andrew Burstein comments, "He was a fair master, but not uncomfortable in the role of master."[47]

Did Randolph Jefferson know Sally Hemings? A review of Thomas Jefferson's voluminous papers, Randolph's correspondence, and Jefferson family genealogies have helped determine the identities and whereabouts of other male members of Jefferson's family during Sally Hemings's pregnancies, and this huge cache of historical writings provides a myriad of compelling reasons why Randolph was most likely one of Sally's sexual partners and the father of some of her children:[48]

- Randolph was expected to visit Monticello during Eston Hemings's precise conception period. A specific letter from Jefferson to his brother confirms Randolph's visit.

- Randolph had the same Jefferson Y chromosome as his older brother, Thomas Jefferson, and other Jefferson males. Randolph had the same parents as Thomas and carried the same genes that determine one's appearance.

- Randolph had a reputation for socializing with Jefferson's slaves and was counseled about his abuse of alcohol, a habit that can lower one's inhibitions and affect one's choices.

- Randolph lived fewer than twenty miles from Monticello and had a pattern of visiting his brother in the spring and late summer, coinciding with all of Sally's pregnancies. Randolph and his sons owned more than enough horses for them to visit Monticello.

- In 1807, Randolph was a widower and only fifty-one years old, in contrast to the frail sixty-four-year-old Thomas Jefferson, who was in declining health. All of Sally's children were born between 1795 and 1808, when Randolph was single. Shortly after Eston's birth, Randolph married again and Sally had no more children. Randolph's new wife was considered "a controlling woman," more than capable of ending Randolph's inclinations for Sally or any other woman.[49]

- Randolph made his will at Monticello six days after the birth of Eston, leaving his estate to his five legitimate sons, apparently severing any future paternity claims.

- Randolph produced all male children—six sons. Jefferson, on the other hand, produced all girls with his beloved wife, Martha ("Patty"). The 1998 DNA was to a male descendant.

- The heirs of Eston Hemings had been told by their parents and grandparents that they were descendants of an "uncle" of Thomas Jefferson. Though Randolph was not Jefferson's uncle, but his brother, oral history confirms that his father was some Jefferson "uncle."

Clearly, Eston could not have been fathered by either of Thomas Jefferson's paternal uncles, as both had been dead for several decades when Eston was conceived. So, as the "uncle" story was passed down through generations, Eston might have eventually been told that, in fact, "Uncle Randolph" was his father. Randolph was certainly known by Jefferson's grandchildren as "Uncle Randolph."[50] In a letter to her father, dated January 30, 1800, Patsy referred to Randolph as "Uncle Randolph," and four months before Eston was conceived, Jefferson received a letter from his granddaughter Ellen that noted, "Uncle Randolph Jefferson is with us."[51] It is easy to reason how such an oral history as Eston's Jeffersonian paternity began: Randolph was the paternal uncle of daughters Patsy and Polly and was referred to as "Uncle Randolph" when he visited Monticello. If the grandchildren called him "Uncle Randolph," it would seem reasonable that Sally Hemings would also have referred to him by this moniker.

One of the most interesting assessments of Randolph's possible paternity is found in a 1958 letter from historian Pearl Graham to the editor of *The Papers of Thomas Jefferson*, published at Princeton University Press.[52] Long before any DNA test, Ms. Graham was convinced that Thomas Jefferson was the father of Sally Hemings's children. She had conducted extensive research on the paternity issue—including interviewing two granddaughters of Harriet Hemings, Sally's daughter.[53] Noting the reported physical resemblance of Hemings's children to Thomas Jefferson, Graham also explored alternative theories: "Among his paternal relatives, the possibilities could be narrowed down to three—his brother, Randolph, and two nephews, Samuel and Dabney Carr. A study of the known facts about these three convinced me that, while some one of them might have fathered one of Sally's children, a liaison advering [sic] well over ten years was not in the realm of possibility."[54]

According to Graham, a further item would seem to implicate Randolph Jefferson: one of Harriet's granddaughters had told Graham that Jefferson's younger brother "also" had "colored children." At a minimum, this letter shows that Randolph was discussed as a serious alternative to Thomas Jefferson for the paternity of Sally Hemings's children. This appeared four decades before the 1998 DNA tests were made public, from by a source who was persuaded that Jefferson was the father of Sally's children.[55] There is also an important documented letter from Thomas Jefferson, dated August 12, 1807, inviting Randolph to visit Monticello. The historical correspondence makes it clear that, again, Randolph was present at Monticello at the time of Eston's conception, almost nine months before his birth (the 1998 DNA match):

> Dear brother
> I did not receive your letter of July 9 till the 8th. inst. and now, by the first post inclose you 20.D. to pay for the clover and greenswerd seed; which goes by post to Warren. The greenswerd seed I wish to have here; but the white clover seed is to go to Bedford. I must thereefore get you to make interest with Mr. Crouch to have it conveyed to the care of Mr. Brown mercht. of

Lynchhburg for Burgess Griffin at Poplar Forest. This he can do I expect by his batteaux which go to Lynchburg.

Our sister Marks arrived here last night and we shall be happy to see you also. I salute you affectionately.

Th:Jefferson [56]

According to one scholar, "This letter places Randolph, with his sons most probably, at Monticello within Sally's conception time frame. Since the trip to Monticello was less than a day's ride from Randolph's estate (twenty miles away), this was an easy journey in good weather."[57] In fact, there was no need for them to hurry to Monticello. They had seventeen days to travel the one-day ride to Monticello, most likely arriving on or about August 29, 1807—the most probable conception date of Sally Hemings's son Eston. Jefferson had, in fact, sent Randolph money to buy the grass seed, with the expectation that Randolph would deliver it.[58] As one historian has explained: "There were instances where Randolph sent regrets due to bad roads or health issues, so it is reasonable to assume the widower Randolph came to visit . . . his brother this particular August."[59]

Jefferson's letter also refers to the arrival of Randolph's twin sister, Anna Scott Marks, at Monticello. Randolph seemed particularly close to his twin sister and probably wanted to visit with her anytime he could. August was also a good time for Randolph to visit because the fields would have been plowed and the crops planted, but it was not yet harvesttime. Randolph had also promised to deliver the grass seed to Monticello. According to Jefferson scholar Eyler Coates, a former assistant librarian of Congress,[60] "An invitation should be enough evidence, because there just weren't those kinds of records kept on family visits. Only when something special happened, like when Thomas Jefferson made out Randolph's last will and testament, do we have actual documented evidence that Randolph was present. Ordinary visits would be noted only incidentally."[61]

Other documented correspondence suggests that Randolph was also present at Monticello when Sally's first daughter, Harriet, was conceived in January 1795. While it is generally presumed that Randolph was a regular visitor to Monticello, as noted in the preceding letter, such routine visits by close relatives were apparently not thought remarkable enough by Jefferson to make note of them in his various record books. One historian concludes, "Indeed, throughout his life, although Randolph may well have made the twenty-mile trip to see his brother and other family members at Monticello several times each year, there are only four visits actually documented in Jefferson's surviving records—each of these because of some business that was transacted in connection with the visit. This indicates that Randolph's visits were considered so routine as to not be noteworthy.[62]

Perhaps, more important in the paternity debate was Randolph's marital status at the time of all of Sally's Hemings pregnancies. When Randolph's youngest son was born in 1789, it seems he had produced children about every two years. As noted above, Randolph was between wives when Sally became pregnant with her first child. Randolph remarried, without consulting Jefferson's sage advice, in 1808 to an abusive "shrew"—the kind of woman who would not tolerate her husband wandering down to the slave quarters for a night of socializing.[63] Randolph's new wife proved extravagant and emotionally distressing to his sons. "Poor Randolph," one author noted, "fell under her domination, had to sell lands to pay her debts and finally, on his brother's advice, informed the local merchants that she was to receive merchandise only on his written order. Thereupon she forged the orders. Thus harassed, Randolph quietly died in 1815."[64]

The year 1809 is of major importance in the sexual scandal controversy: Jefferson had retired from the presidency and returned to Monticello, where he could have had access to Sally Hemings every night if he had so desired. Meanwhile, Randolph had recently remarried, and Randolph's twenty-seven-year-old son, Thomas Jefferson Jr., had also married, in 1808. After these marriages, Sally Hemings had no more known children. Is all of this a coincidence? Perhaps, but that the dates of Randolph's widower status coincide exactly with Sally's childbearing years cannot be ignored.[65] And it had been more than five years since Sally had arrived at Monticello from Paris with Jefferson.[66] But no pregnancies resulted in those years. Randolph married his second wife the very next year and had a child, John, proving beyond all doubt that he was sexually active and potent. Most interesting, perhaps, is that three of Sally's children, "Harriet, Beverly, and Eston the latter two not common names, were given names of the family of Randolph Jefferson's mother, the Randolphs, after whom he was named."[67]

Other historical evidence also seems to implicate Randolph as one of Sally's sexual partners. Author and historian Rebecca L. McMurray, whose family resided in Charlottesville during Jefferson's time, affirmed her family's oral history that Randolph was the father of Sally's "yellow" children:

> Her grandmother lived for the first several years of her married life about 15 miles north of Monticello. Though these events had taken place decades earlier, her "in-laws" had purchased items at the great sales at Monticello and Montpelier . . . My mother continued, saying the rumors concerning the father of Sally Heming's children had placed the blame on Jefferson's "half-wit brother," though commenting that the "Carr boys" were "too familiar" with her as well.[68]

Some scholars have concluded that Sally's children had more than one father, and this is now scientifically confirmed by the new 2021 DNA results (see epilogue). The stark physical differences between Sally's children also strongly suggests this: the short, tan-skinned Madison Hemings (Sally's third child) looks markedly different from his tall younger brother, Eston (Sally's last child and the 1998 DNA match), who had reddish hair and bore a striking resemblance to the Jeffersons. This fact casts further doubt on the assertion by some prominent scholars, such as Annette Gordon Reed, that Sally Hemings never had sexual relations with anyone except Thomas Jefferson. Further fueling this doubt are the recollections of a French visitor, Comte de Volney, who spent three weeks at Monticello in 1796 and noted the sexual atmosphere: "Women and girls . . . do not have any censure of manners," he commented in his journal, "living freely with the white workmen of the country or hired Europeans, Germans, Irishmen and others."[69] Another French visitor made similar remarks regarding Monticello's enslaved community.

Notably, Sally's Hemings's mother, Elizabeth (Betty) Hemings, also had multiple fathers for her children, both white and black. Betty had six children, it was alleged, by Jefferson's father-in law, John Wayles, and eight more by other fathers, some white, some black, after she came to live at Monticello.[70] In fact, Sally's mother had at least two or possibly three lovers, at least one of whom was white: Englishmen Joseph Nelson (or Neilson, a white carpenter at Monticello), who fathered most of her twelve children. Betty produced two more children (John or "Johnny" and Lucy) after her arrival at Monticello by Nelson. As one scholar has detailed, "During his stay at Monticello, Neilson's joinery was not limited to woodwork; he also fathered, with Betty Hemings, Jefferson's talented slave carpenter, John Hemings. Indeed, there are probably still sections of woodwork at Monticello shaped by two sets of hands, father and son, white and black, free and slave, Neilson and Hemings—a continuity of craft, of generation and race, of old house and remodeled house."[71]

This is not a moral judgment, but as Sally's mother was the most important person in her life, and her role model, it seems highly probable that she, too, had several lovers and more than one father for her children.[72] Perhaps it is not hard to envision Randolph—and Sally—participating in the late-night revels Comte de Volney described.[73]

Finally, there is the crucial eyewitness account by Jefferson's overseer, Edmund Bacon—briefly mentioned in the last chapter—that must be considered.[74] Bacon was Jefferson's overseer for fifteen years during Sally's pregnancies. He had also worked for Jefferson before becoming overseer. Jefferson admired and trusted this hardworking individual: "He is an honest, correct man in his conduct, and worthy of confidence in his engagements."[75] This testimony on Bacon's behalf indicates that intimacy and trust existed. Bacon was elderly, about seventy-six, when he gave an interview to the president of Cumberland College, Reverend Hamilton Pierson, published in 1862. This interview is monumental because Bacon personally identified Sally's true lover—and it was not Thomas Jefferson:

> Mr. Jefferson freed a number of his servants in his will. I think he would have freed all of them if his affairs had not been so much involved that he could not do it. He freed one girl some years before he died, and there was a great deal of talk about it.

She was nearly as white as anybody and very beautiful. People said he freed her because she was his own daughter. She was not his daughter; she was _____'s daughter. I know that. I have seen him come out of her mother's [Sally's] room many a morning when I went up to Monticello very early.[76]

The identification of the man Bacon witnessed leaving Sally's room "many a morning" was deleted by Reverend Pierson before publication, and his original manuscript has not been located. It is reasonable to venture that the name was omitted out of respect for Jefferson's family and because Bacon resided in Trigg County, Kentucky—adjacent to Todd County, where Isham's (Randolph Jefferson's son) family lived. This historical correspondence is significant because Bacon was there to witness a man leaving Sally's room during the period when Eston Hemings was conceived. Bacon was in a unique position to witnesses these comings and goings—Sally lived near the blacksmith shop and nailery, so it would be reasonable for Bacon to have witnessed someone leaving Sally's room. Was it Randolph or the nephews Peter and Samuel Carr? Or someone else altogether? Whoever that person was that Bacon witnessed, we know now it was not Thomas Jefferson.

Although Randolph Jefferson is little noted in history books, he now plays a major role in the Jefferson–Hemings sexual controversy. The most likely and undeniable historical evidence, direct and circumstantial, identifies him as the father of Sally's son, Eston Hemings. Eston was the 1998 DNA match that most historians interpreted as implicating Thomas Jefferson as Sally's sexual partner. While historians have learned not to repudiate such sexual allegations against Thomas Jefferson with knee-jerk rigidity, his paternity seems highly doubtful based on the historical record, which points to "Uncle Randolph," not Thomas Jefferson, as the most probable paternity candidate.

11

THE "ACADEMICAL" VILLAGE

His greatest artwork was the cluster of buildings in Charlottesville that he called his "academical village." There he launched and completed what was the largest construction project since the development of the federal city itself.

—**Garry Wills**, *Mr. Jefferson's University*

When Jefferson retired from public life after his presidency, "he became more . . . localist than he had ever been before. He had always prided himself on his cosmopolitanism," notes historian Gordon Wood, "yet upon his retirement from the presidency he returned to Virginia and never left it. In fact, he almost never again lost sight of his beloved Blue Ridge. He cut himself off from many of the current sources of knowledge of the outside world and became, as one of his visitors, George Ticknor, recounted, 'singularly ignorant & insensible on the subjects of passing politics.'"[1] Jefferson took only one newspaper, the *Richmond Enquirer*, and he seemed to have little interest in receiving mail. He differed from his political protégé and friend James Madison, who was said to have received "multitudes of newspapers" and kept "a servant always in waiting for the arrival of the Post," intently noting "all passing events."[2]

Thomas Jefferson's retirement from the presidency led to stunning new construction work at Monticello and his retreat home at Poplar Forest. With age, noted one author, "his grasp grew firmer, his vision clearer. Working at a strenuous pace from 1817 to 1826, he passed from his seventy-fourth to his eighty-third year in this final creative act. As his own body's fabric was disintegrating, he poured his spirit into a physical expression of intellectual activity."[3] In fact, his Bedford County retreat, Poplar Forest, was to become one of the architectural triumphs of his old age. Poplar Forest was begun when Jefferson was sixty-three, the University of Virginia when he was seventy-four,[4] while the rotunda at the university was actually built when Jefferson turned eighty.[5]

During his stay in Paris as minister plenipotentiary to France, Jefferson studied continental architecture every chance he could. "Although he admired much of what he saw in France," commented one historian, "he was particularly taken by a new style of architecture that abandoned multistoried houses in favor of single-story, horizontal dwellings... One reason Jefferson functioned so comfortably in this cultural environment was that the intellectual garments of the age fit so perfectly his personal identity—he was most satisfied and secure when he was saving, measuring, counting, or timing."[6] For measuring, he utilized his surveying equipment, a pocket sextant, a thermometer, a barometer, a pedometer, and a wind vane for recording wind directions at Monticello.[7]

With the able assistance and support of grandson Jeff Randolph, Jefferson focused his entire efforts on the final project of his life—one that he was, perhaps, most proud of: building the University of Virginia. It became a university so much his own design that it simply become known as "Mr. Jefferson's" university.[8] Jefferson's love of books, education, and architecture spurred this crowning achievement: one of his three major accomplishments that he wished engraved on his tombstone. "I look to the diffusion of light and education," he confirmed, "as the resource most to be relied on for ameliorating the condition, promoting the virtue and advancing the happiness of man."[9] In a letter Jefferson transmitted to Thomas Cooper, he admitted, "I have long had under contemplation and been collecting materials for the plan of a university in Virginia which should comprehend all the sciences useful to us, and none others."[10] Jefferson further explained the importance of a state university that he would now champion: "Were it necessary to give up either the Primaries or the University, I would rather abandon the last. Because it is safer to have a whole people respectably enlightened, than a few in a high state of science and the many in ignorance. This last is the most dangerous state in which a nation can be. The nations and governments of Europe are so many proofs of it."[11]

And Jefferson wanted the university situated in Charlottesville, when other cities were being considered for its location: "The situation of Charlottesville is in a mountainous, healthy, fertile country, delicious climate, good water, cheap subsistence, an independent yeomanry, many wealthy persons, good society, and free as air in religion and politics."[12] These remarks echoed Jefferson's earlier praise of his home, central Virginia: "A genial climate, a grateful soil, gardens planted by nature, liberty, safety, tranquility and a very secure and profitable revenue from whatever property we possess."[13]

Once Jefferson had trained his considerable focus upon constructing a university in the shadow of Monticello, the idea of a state university consumed him.[14] But Jefferson could not complete this project without the aid and assistance of his stalwart grandson. Jeff served as both his eyes and his ears, chief negotiator with the legislature and dynamic courier, overseeing the plans and the implementation of Jefferson's university. In fact, Jeff later became one of the first rectors and trustees of the University of Virginia.

The retired Jefferson succeeded in giving life to the "child of his old age." "The one bright spot," explains one scholar, "amid the deepening sense of gloom about public affairs was provided by the project taking shape a few miles away in Charlottesville, barely visible on a clear day from his mountaintop, which Jefferson called his 'academic village.'"[15] Now known, of course, as the University of Virginia and recognized by the American Institute of Architects as "the proudest achievement of American architecture in the past 200 years," it became Jefferson's major retirement project in 1817.[16] As one historian has eloquently written, "Jefferson is the only president of the United States who was also a great artist. Other presidents have noodled at the keyboard or daubed at easels. But Jefferson was a building architect of large ambition and achievement, as well as a landscape architect and an interior designer. There are no exact parallels, at least in Western culture, for this combination of political and aesthetic prominence."[17]

Jefferson's fascination with design and architecture was a lifelong pursuit. Knowing his acumen in the field, in 1785 the commission appointed to supervise the construction of the capitol in Richmond appealed to Jefferson for advice. Jefferson describes, in his autobiography, his response:

> Thinking it a favorable opportunity of introducing into the State an example of architecture in the classic style of antiquity, and the Maison Quarree of Nismes, an ancient Roman temple, being considered as the most perfect model existing of what may be called Cubic architecture, I applied to M. Clerisseau, who had published drawings of the Antiquities of Nismes, to have me a model of the building made in stucco, only changing the order from Corinthian to Ionic, on account of the difficulty of the Corinthian capitals. . . To adapt the exterior to our use, I drew a plan for the interior, with the apartments necessary for legislative, executive, and judiciary purposes; and accommodated in their size and distribution to the form and dimensions of the building. These were forwarded to the directors in 1786, and were carried into execution.[18]

It was not until March 1787 that Jefferson saw the actual building at Nimes. While in Paris as *ministre plénipotentiare des États Unis d' Amérique,* Thomas Jefferson studied European architecture with a keen eye. He would often perch on a wall of the Tuileries Garden overlooking the Seine river, gazing across the river at a building under construction—the Hotel de Salm, an elegant new residence in Paris. Later, he wrote that he had been so "violently smitten" with the house that he visited the Tuileries Garden daily, straining his neck "to view the object of [his] admiration."[19] As he gazed across the river, "he could see the construction site teeming with workmen-masons in their leather aprons cutting and dressing the great blocks of white stone that faced the building, carpenters constructing scaffolding."[20] While in Paris, Jefferson also visited the ruins of a third-century Roman arena and, as one author commented, "given as he was to making constant comparisons, measured the height, width, and thickness of the bricks."[21] In a letter to the Comtesse de Tesse, a cousin of Lafayette, Jefferson wryly commented on his architectural passion:

> Here I am, Madam, gazing whole hours at the Maison Quarree, like a lover at his mistress. The stocking weavers and silk

> spinners around it consider me a hypochondriac Englishman about to write with a pistol the last chapter of his history. This is the second time I have been in love since I left Paris. The first was with a Diana at the Chateau de Laye-Epinaye in Beaujolais, a delicious morsel of sculpture by M. A. Slodtz. This, you will say, was in rule, to fall in love with a female beauty; but with a house! it is out of all precedent.[22]

Jefferson hoped the university would be the beginning of a broader system of public education throughout Virginia and ultimately the nation. Sixty years removed from his college days, Jefferson proposed a dynamically new and innovative educational model, incorporating a new seat of higher learning and a novel teaching method. He set his sights on small regional college as his cornerstone for his vision of the university. Central College, as it was called then, was soon to become the University of Virginia, Jefferson's "academical village."[23] In 1788 James Monroe had purchased an eight-hundred-acre farm in Charlottesville to be close to his friend and colleague Thomas Jefferson, as well as to establish his law office. In 1799 the Monroes moved to their new Highland plantation adjacent to Monticello and sold the first farm. In 1817, the board of visitors of Central College purchased 43.75 acres of Monroe's old farm, for the lawn and the ranges of the "academical village" that Jefferson was planning to build with private contributions.

Jefferson's prototype for his new method of teaching had percolated in the back of his mind for fifteen years. An earlier letter, written to the trustees of East Tennessee College in 1810, reveals Jefferson's innovative plans:

> I consider the common plan followed in this country, but not in others, of making one large and expensive building, as unfortunately erroneous. It is infinitely better to erect a small and separate lodge for each separate professorship, with only a hall below for his class, and two chambers above for himself; joining these lodges by barracks for a certain portion of the students, opening into a covered way to give a dry communication between all the

schools. The whole of these arranged around an open square of grass and trees, would make it, what it should be in fact, an academical village, instead of a large and common den of noise, of filth and of fetid air.[24]

During Jefferson's long life he had much to say about education because he was erudite and highly educated himself. It was said that as a student Jefferson studied fifteen hours a day in Williamsburg. Throughout his life he never tired of yearning for knowledge—from science to farming, arts, literature, and music. From the Renaissance philosophers, Jefferson had learned the need for education in order to fully embrace man's rationale mind. In his native state of Virginia, land and aristocracy had been the only criteria used to select political leaders. Jefferson wanted to change these artificial criteria to include one's own natural talents fostered through a liberal arts education. If every man was able to promote himself through education, then he could become a leader regardless of wealth or family status. Education, Jefferson believed, could edify any man on the valuable lessons of history, its triumphs and its failures. More importantly, higher education and study taught an informed citizenry to oppose all forms of autocracy over mankind's natural rights and freedoms. With Jeff's assistance, he crafted detailed plans to implement his ambitious educational design in a time when most people were barely literate.

***

The university project was conjured up in typical Jefferson fashion: a grandiose notion, but, in practicality, difficult to consummate. In an 1814 meeting of the board members of Albemarle Academy, a Charlottesville preparatory school chartered in 1803, the elder statesman proposed his idea of his expansive state university. In time Jefferson gained the institution's promotion to Central College, thus placing the school under the province of the Virginia legislature. After much financial wrangling by Jeff, together with John Hartwell Cocke and Joseph Cabell in Richmond, the Virginia legislature appointed a commission to study the plan with a meeting date in 1818 at Rockfish Gap, Virginia. Jefferson committed to attend the meeting.[25]

He left his mountain for a twenty-five-mile journey to the Mountain Top Tavern in Rockfish Gap between Nelson and Augusta counties in the Blue Ridge. There Jefferson and others approved a plan for a university to be built in Charlottesville. The formidable gathering included, Jefferson, Madison, Marshall and other notable Virginia politicians. Jefferson was clearly in charge and relished the role.[26]

Jefferson had himself and Madison appointed to the commission. He dominated the recommendations and personally wrote the Rockfish Gap Report that recommended the creation of a state university. Jefferson then instructed Jeff to assist him in a vigorous fundraising campaign to start the university, including the construction of buildings, the hiring of faculty, and the designing of an academic curriculum. Dispatched back and forth to Richmond, Jeff had several difficult negotiating rounds with the legislators. It is ironic that in spite of Jeff's own lack of higher education, he, more than anyone else except Jefferson himself, worked tirelessly to advance the realization of the university. As noted in previous chapters, for years Jeff resented his sullen father for not sending him to a university to complete a higher education. Psychologically, this was deep motivation for his involvement in a university now. Slowly but surely, the legislature approved sufficient seed money. Central College in Charlottesville would finally evolve into a reality: the University of Virginia.[27]

Jefferson's academic philosophy dated back to his college years. First as governor of Virginia and then in his *Notes on Virginia,* Jefferson had proposed a state educational system that would rival those of the New England states:

> As president he had taken on George Washington's favorite scheme for a national university, presumably located in the nation's capital. Soon after his retirement from the presidency his broodings assumed the more tangible form of a master plan for Virginia. Each county would be divided into a series of local "hundreds" or "wards" modeled on the New England townships. Then each county would contain an academy or secondary school where the best graduates of the ward schools could learn their Latin and Greek and the rudiments of science, the

poorer students at public expense. The capstone of the plan was a state university where the best graduates of the county academies would receive the best education available in America.[28]

As a student, Jefferson had been profoundly disappointed by his academic experience at William and Mary, preferring his informal dinners with such Renaissance mentors as George Wythe, William Small, and the cultured royal governor Francis Fauquier—who introduced Jefferson to fine French wine. These men had taught him natural philosophy and the classics through informal events. In his five years in France, Jefferson had studied the European educational models, with their emphasis on tutoring students through "reading." Jefferson found this method superior to the traditional American method of teaching. "Paris is the only place where a man . . . not obliged to do anything will always find something amusing to do," Jefferson told William Short.[29] Now, Jefferson had "a determination to place his idealized university at a healthier, more central location where he could give its creation and development his personal attention."[30] The details of these plans led to Jefferson's goal to institute higher education in Virginia, and his clarion call for a "national university."[31]

His architectural plan for his university did not resemble William and Mary's structured brick buildings, like the Wren building. Instead, Jefferson envisioned a more compact university situated around a broad lawn, a university with a strict "honor code," where "every professor would be the Police officer of the students adjacent to his own lodge, and might be at the head of their table, if, as I suppose, it can be reconciled with the necessary economy to dine them in smaller and separate parties, rather than in a large and common mess."[32] Jefferson's plan for a university was now his highest importance: "I know of no safe depository of the ultimate powers of the society, but the people themselves: and if we think them not enlightened enough to exercise their control with a wholesome discretion, the remedy is, not to take it from them, but to inform their discretion by education. This is the true corrective of abuses of constitutional power."[33]

By 1817, the former president, through Jeff's numerous rides to Richmond, had managed to convince the state to initially fund his educational dream. The execution of the University of Virginia called on Jefferson's greatest political, intellectual, and architectural talents and powers of persuasion. He wrote numerous letters to friends and acquaintances for financial support. He urged Joseph Cabell not to "desert" the effort to create the university. "Continue with us in these holy labors until, having seen their accomplishment, we say with old Simeon, *Nunc dimittis, Domine*."[34] As one historian concluded, "The Declaration of Independence's words lived on past him. The Louisiana purchase lived on past him. And the university would as well." With the dutiful help of his grandson, having the university financed, built, and into practical operation lasted the rest of Jefferson's days.

"I think by far the most important bill in our whole code is that for the diffusion of knowledge among the people," Jefferson had written his old mentor George Wythe. "No other sure foundation can be devised for the preservation of freedom and happiness."[35] "This institution will be based on the illimitable freedom of the human mind," he wrote elsewhere.[36] Echoing sentiments in his first inaugural address, Jefferson stated, "For here we are not afraid to follow truth wherever it may lead, nor to tolerate any error so long as reason is left free to combat it."[37] He was determined that Virginia would have a prestigious university. "If our legislature does not heartily push our University we must send our children for education to Kentucky or Cambridge," Jefferson warned in 1820, alluding to Transylvania College in Kentucky and to Harvard. "The latter will return them to us fanatics and tories, the former will keep them to add to their population."[38]

Jefferson envisioned a superlative state university that would eventually earn a national reputation. No one could dissuade him from his tenacious goal. Jeff had even installed a telescope for his grandfather on the terrace at Monticello so Jefferson could watch the daily construction and progress of his university.[39] Eliza House Trist noted that Jefferson was so determined to build the university that he rode one day through "a perfect hurricane . . . to visit the college."[40]

On October 6, 1817, the Virginia political dynasty consisting of Thomas Jefferson, grandson Jeff Randolph, accompanied by President James Monroe and former president James Madison, ceremoniously laid the cornerstone for the university's first building, Pavilion VII. As one writer described the historic scene:

About a mile from the tiny village of Charlottesville, Virginia, there was an odd thronging of people through an open field. It would not take an acute observer long to see what the occasion was. Freemasons were there, in full regalia, in a procession of the sort reserved for laying important cornerstones. On they came, in graded ranks—tile-layers with swords drawn, apprentices, fellows, masters, past masters, stewards, deacons, secretaries, treasurers, wardens, visiting masters, substitutes, and the grand master and chaplain. Following them were bearers of the corn and oil and wine used in the Masonic ceremonies, and a designated orator (Valentine Southall), and a marching band. This might seem a disproportionately grand way to begin constructing one building for a regional academy (Central College), one no different from other local schools in Virginia, Hampden-Sidney say, or Washington College (it would later be Washington and Lee). The humpbacked site was cut and scarred with ongoing efforts to grade it, placing the new building asymmetrically on the western edge of a ridge of land more carefully leveled. Piles of freshly kilned bricks stood ready for use.[41]

Workers and slaves milled around the large crowd, waiting for it to disperse so they could go to work. The Masonic grand master handed "the implements used by our ancient fraternity"—the square, the plumb, and the level—to the man who would formally lay the cornerstone—President James Monroe.[42] Monroe was a member of the six-man board of Central College, as were two former presidents who also attended the ceremony. William Thornton, the architect of the United States Capitol, commented after the ceremony, "I was also pleased to see an account of the meeting of such distinguished characters as the three presidents of the United States on so praiseworthy an occasion. How different to the meeting of the three emperors on the continent of Europe, after a bloody battle!"[43]

As buildings went up rapidly, Jefferson dispatched a curt note to James Madison, one of the original members of the board of visitors for the university. Madison was still trying to disengage himself from the end of his presidency, but had missed the first meeting of the planning committee to the university: "A detention at Washington I presume prevented your attendance... Circumstances which will be explained to you make us believe that a full meeting of all visitors, on the first occasion at least, will decide a great object in the State system of general education; and I have accordingly so pressed the subject on Colo. Monroe [the incumbent president replacing Madison] as I think will ensure his attendance, and I hope we shall not fail in yours."[44]

Jefferson seemed irritated at his protégé's absence. He wrote that he expected Madison to attend the next conference as "a full meeting of all."[45] Once Madison began to attend the meetings of the board of visitors on a regular basis, he recognized that the university was an embodiment of Jefferson's political personality. With Madison's direction, all members of the board followed Jefferson's lead, displaying "unaffected deference . . . for his judgment and experience."[46] One historian noted Jefferson's zealous commitment to the university project: "Jefferson's total immersion in his new educational and architectural venture; it never occurred to him that the outgoing and incoming presidents of the United States might have more important things to do."[47]

With Jeff's untiring assistance, Jefferson immersed himself in the planning and building of the university with the same passion and energy he had infused into the construction of his beloved mansion, Monticello. "It was the perfect building project to keep him busy," declares one historian. "But it was also much more, since it involved cajoling the Virginia legislature for money, selecting a faculty, building a library, shaping a curriculum, in effect creating a model American university in his own image and likeness."[48] For this task, he greatly depended on his *Godsend*, Jeff Randolph.

Jeff also saw to the execution of the details of Jefferson's plan with a meticulous mastery of financial detail to prevent cost overruns. Together, they rode to town and surveyed the site for the Charlottesville campus themselves. Jeff personally laid out the stakes. For the rotunda, which was to be the architectural centerpiece, Jeff suggested something similar to Monticello. Jefferson selected the Pantheon of Rome as his model and designed it to serve as both the library and a planetarium, with movable planets and stars on the interior. Architecturally, both grandfather and grandson decided that the university would mirror Monticello's classical designs—Tuscan, Doric, Ionic, Corinthian, Composite.[49]

With Jeff's assistance and voracious letter writing campaign to the state legislature on his grandfather's behalf, Jefferson worked four hours each day to assemble the catalog for the library of 6,860 volumes. Jeff estimated the cost of acquisition of the books at $24,076.[50] After Jeff's visits with the Virginia legislature, they authorized the board of visitors to borrow $60,000 for the university project. But the main rotunda construction proved more expensive than Jefferson had anticipated. He instructed Jeff to revise the estimate to a significantly higher amount of $162,364. The following year, facing stinging criticism from the legislature for the inflated costs, Jefferson revised the estimate to $195,000, which would cover the cost of the rotunda's final completion.[51]

The hiring of the specific faculty presented a quandary for Jefferson. He seemed equivocal as to what final model of instruction would be used at the university—a European model or a more traditional American model. "As both a den of political iniquity and the cradle of all learning," wrote one author, "he insisted that only European scholars could provide the high level of intellectual distinction necessary for a truly first-rate university, so he persuaded a reluctant Board of Visitors to dispatch Francis Gilmer, a bright young Virginia lawyer, to recruit prospective faculty in England, France and Germany."[52]

Jefferson insisted on the significance of a classical, liberal education for informed minds: "The learning of Greek and Latin, I am told, is going into disuse in Europe. I know not what their manners and occupations may call for: but it would be very ill-judged in us to follow their example in this instance."[53] In 1821, when the construction of the campus rapidly proceeded, Jefferson made one of his goals clear: to give the students a classical liberal arts education. He prepared a list of standard texts to be required in the classes: law and government; the Declaration of Independence, the *Federalist Papers*, the Virginia Resolutions of 1799, and George Washington's inaugural and farewell addresses. Madison had his own, supplemental suggestions. Political and religious creeds needed to be considered, he argued. Jefferson, after all, would not want to be viewed as dictating his own political "values in the manner of a priest or pope."[54] Jefferson agreed, editing his list of required documents on Madison's recommendation. He led his list with the following academic specialties: botany, chemistry, zoology, anatomy, surgery, medicine, and natural philosophy.[55]

As buildings ascended, Jefferson's grand vision of a national university was supplanted by a southern college as an alternative to Harvard and Yale. Jefferson viewed those institutions dimly. "Here was yet another manifestation of his 'Virginia-writ-large' version of patriotism toward the end," writes one historian: "Two truly distinctive features of the university were very much a projection of Jefferson's personality. First, most of the traditional rules and curricular requirements that governed the operation of all other American colleges were completely abandoned. There were no distinctions among freshmen, sophomores or upperclassmen. Jefferson also wanted 'to leave everyone free to attend whatever branches of instruction he wants, and to decline what he does not want.'"[56]

Indeed, no specific courses would be mandated. It was a wholly elective system. Nor was there any separate executive administration, such as a formal president of the university. The school was to be controlled exclusively by the faculty but overseen by the board of visitors. Jefferson insisted that the university be devoted to the principle of "self-government"—an "honor code." This mindset lay behind the student culture that Jefferson imagined for the entire university. "We studiously avoid too much government," Jefferson explained to Ellen. "We treat them as men and gentlemen, under the guidance mainly of their own discretion."[57] Knowing the stakes of youth and the weight of their duty to the future of the Republic, Jefferson expected the students, one scholar contended, to set themselves as honorable gentlemen.[58]

Jefferson had hoped to live long enough to see his grandson, Jeff, attend the university. But in 1825, when the first students began to attend classes, Jeff had already finished his education and busied himself managing his grandfather's farm while supporting his own burgeoning family. But Jeff's younger sons, James and Ben, would soon join the student body. Although none of Jefferson's grandsons became as serious a scholar as Jefferson, the young men were fortunate enough to enroll in the university, though they were more noted for their family heritage than their academic excellence. Ironically, one of Jefferson's distant cousins was expelled after a drunken student "riot."[59]

Consulting with his grandson, Jefferson proposed that students could dine in separate dining halls or "hotels," instead of the traditional assembling for meals. When Jefferson had attended William & Mary, food was provided by private vendors but paid for directly by the students. Breaking the university into a collection of small "villages," Jefferson eliminated the formal establishment he had known as a student at William and Mary.[60] Jefferson also planned to have the professors and students cluster in close quarters, with each professorial house bordered by student dorm rooms along the now famous "colonnade." His goal was to create a "family" environment, with the professors serving as sage mentors to the students. Jefferson reasoned that his academical "village" embodied the essence of an ordered society. With family as the center component of his village, mutual affection could congeal with education. Jefferson's three-sided designed colonnade captured his vision of the teacher as mentor and parental figure to the student, bridging the emotional distance between the two.[61]

Jefferson had always relied on books in forming his previous architectural designs, such as Monticello and Poplar Forest, his octagonal Bedford retreat. He understood that "the major advantage of the octagon over the square in an age before electricity was that it eliminated dark corners. The corner of a square room in an eighteenth-century house was lost space for anything requiring decent light."[62] However, Jefferson realized his University of Virginia project was much too big and intricate for simple books on design. Jefferson turned to professional architects and experts for assistance in designing the seventeen buildings he had in mind. He discussed his architectural plans with two men, William Thornton and Benjamin Latrobe, soliciting their written suggestions. Jefferson relied more on the accomplished Latrobe, who was occupied as the supervising architect of the Capitol in Washington. Latrobe responded to Jefferson with a letter dated June 28, 1817, containing his proposed sketches of the university grounds. Latrobe penned an elevation of the north end of the campus, molding Jefferson's suggestion of a centrally located domed building that resembled Palladio's Villa Rotunda, flanked by pavilions with massive columns. Jefferson immediately accepted this idea: "Latrobe followed up his first response with a letter written four days later: 'I have found so much pleasure in studying the plan of your college that the drawings have grown into a larger bulk than can conveniently be sent by the mail. I have put the whole upon one very large sheet, which I am very unwilling to double."[63]

With Latrobe's extensive design help, Jefferson's final architectural plans incorporated four rows of buildings for his academical village, with Tuscan columns. The columns' original color was different from what it is today, as was the dome.[64] Marble was quarried locally for some of the structures, "but Jefferson reported that it was of poor color and not able to 'bear the chisel for delicate work.'"[65] The inner two rows consisted of ten "Pavilions (professors' homes and classrooms), five on either side of a central Lawn, leading up to the high Rotunda that would hold the library . . . The two outer rows (Ranges) had "six 'hotels' (service buildings), three on each side. The buildings on all four rows were connected by a small row of student rooms," Jefferson's "dormitories," with an elongated colonnade on the Lawn. One scholar described "the rows of dormitories/ colonnades/ arcades [as] the ligaments that tie the whole together organically."[66] As one author has aptly described: "The design of the place—an imposing Pantheon, contrasting with an open lawn and a set of buildings where students and instructors could be close together—was a balance between dignity and intimacy. As far as possible, it was not to be a Virginian university, but the Virginia branch of the universal enlightenment."[67]

According to one author, at Jeff's recommendation, Jefferson decided that the professors were to live in the individual pavilions separated from one another by student dormitories. He specifically designed the pavilions and student dorms into an open campus so that additional buildings "might be erected successively and occasionally, as the number of professors and students should be increased, as the funds become competent." This allowed for academic growth of the university. Jefferson viewed the pavilions as distinctive to his college campus, "exemplars of correct taste for a new generation of architectural patrons and practitioners." Believing the university would draw a student body from different states, "Jefferson attempted to make it the incubator of high aspirations of his new republic. Thus, each of the buildings rendered an order from some renowned example of architecture. The result," one historian added, "was an open-air catalog of architectural forms with a variety of appearances, no two alike, so as to serve as specimens of orders for the architectural lecturer. From the abstract domain of the printed page, Jefferson projected classical knowledge into the concrete realm of experience—empirical learning of the sort that became a touchstone of enlightenment thought."[68]

Charlottesville was lively that spring of 1824, Jefferson's granddaughter, Virginia, reported to her fiancée, Nicholas Trist. Some of the newly hired professors had begun to arrive at the university, scheduled to open the next February, 1825. "We shall have as much gaiety in our neighbourhood as we have hitherto had moping. I dare say the young ladies begin already to prepare for execution, and aspire to the bellehood which want of beaux has deprived them of heretofore." Virginia went on to share the progress of the university buildings, describing in eloquent detail the beautiful figures and vases in alabaster imported from Italy. "There are among these things two elegant vases of marble intended for a portico . . . I thought how much they would embellish our portico's which Grand-Papa is just completing."[69]

The University project seemed to infuse eighty-two-year-old Jefferson with a new energy, and he became as active as he could physically manage. Yet, notes one author, his grandchildren were ever on his mind. "His cheerful and affectionate interest in all that concerned his grandchildren was unchanged."[70] Jefferson planned to give Nicholas Trist, his son-in-law, one of the pavilions for a study, to help him with reading of law. Virginia and Nicolas had planned to live at Monticello until Nicholas was ready to practice in Charlottesville. "You could attend the courts laced in a Cossack jacket or ranibelt, and be as much of a dandy as my heart can wish," Virginia teased.[71]

According to Jefferson's educational philosophy, the professor held a leading position, but not one of absolute power. Jefferson advocated that each student would attend classes or lectures under his specific instructor, which would, as noted earlier, cultivate a mentor-student bond. He eliminated the raised desks of the professors, which he had witnessed at William & Mary, projecting an elevated position over the students. This Jeffersonian model gave his university a new character, molded on mutual respect between professor and student, while invoking the aforementioned "honor" system. Students were "a compleat [sic] police of their own, tempered by the parental attentions of their tutors."[72] Except in the case of major violations, sanctions were to be handed down by a board of six student "censors." Jefferson said this system was needed "from times of old, from the regular annual riots & battles between the students of William & Mary with the town boys, before the revolution, *quorum pars fui*."[73] Jefferson's university, as one historian has commented, "embodied the ideal of an extended, patriarchal family, . . . organized and governed from a single locus of authority. Jefferson's father-son model evoked a different sort of family . . . the "sentimental" family."[74]

When the university construction was nearly completed, Jefferson turned to the task of hand-picking the first faculty members. He was meticulous and considered twelve candidates to teach law at the university before hiring John Tayloe Lomax. Why was it so difficult to find the right person for the job? "Most law professors at that time were also sitting judges, so there was not necessarily a great deal of prestige to holding the professor of law position," explained Professor Gordon Hylton. "Law teaching as a career did not really exist in 1824, when Jefferson began his search for the first law professor at UVA."[75] Jefferson may have had difficulty hiring a law professor, but recruiting other university professors "actually went pretty smoothly. The first faculty members as a whole proved to be quite distinguished," Hylton noted.[76]

One of those first faculty members was Dr. Robley Dunglison. As the story goes, Dunglison was a young doctor whose prospects were favored by the medical establishment of London, but who needed money to marry the woman he loved. Travel cash was promised by Jefferson's negotiator, Francis Gilmer, as an advance on Dunglison's proposed salary.[77] This, along with the pledge of free lodging in one of the new Pavilions on campus, tempted Dunglison. When Gilmer made his formal offer of employment to Dunglison,

> the Scot said that his response would depend on his fiancée's agreeing to cross the ocean with him. He rushed to her house, but could not immediately ask her since she was entertaining some prominent friends of her father. But as soon as he could get her aside and assure himself of her agreement, he returned to a relieved Gilmer and accepted the professorship. The marriage had to be rapidly concluded for him to reach Virginia for the opening session—but then he and his bride spent the first three

and a half months of their marriage on a ship immobilized or making slow progress toward their future.[78]

Remembering his days as a young man in Williamsburg, Jefferson usually invited several students for dinner on Saturday or Sunday at Monticello, surrounding a little table in the tearoom. He treated them as fledgling peers.[79] "We receive and treat our students as gentlemen and friends," Jefferson declared. "Every weekend," explained one observer, "five or six boys from the Classic School with their knapsacks trudged up the mountain to Monticello; every Saturday night, with Mr. Jefferson's warm approval, they danced with the girls in the south pavilion to the music of a [slave] fiddler."[80] Night after night, Patsy recounted that she accommodated men and women who came to admire her father. The opening of the university sped the flow of unannounced visitors. "Our lives," Patsy said, "are literally spent in the drawing room." Good naturedly, she delighted the guests and supervised the lodging of as many as fifty people a night:[81]

> Toward the end of the summer of 1819, some students performed a feat at their boarding house in Charlottesville "which displeased the old patriarch [Jefferson] very much." Their landlord, "a thin mean looking frenchman" named LaPorte, was unfortunately a protege of Mr. Jefferson, "who had eaten some soup at his house and immediately concluded that he would be the very man to introduce the French way of living." The boys did not share the old patriarch's opinion of LaPorte's cooking. To show their disapproval, seven of them, "after getting pretty tovy" on wine spiked with whiskey, stoned the Frenchman's house. LaPorte "went prancing up to Monticello in his wrath" and Mr. Jefferson wrote notes to the students desiring not to be honored with their company. We were all in the fidgets for two or three days, between the fear of being prosecuted and, what was a thousand times worse, Mr. J's anger." Mrs. Randolph, however, intervened on behalf of the boys and Mr. Jefferson relented.[82]

Jefferson was aware of the pranks of some raucous students at other colleges, including South Carolina College, where rocks were thrown through the president's office window. This is why Jefferson created strict "honor" rules for the students, which required them to be courteous and act like "gentlemen" toward their professors and one another.

The long-awaited opening of the university on Monday, March 7, 1825, "appears to have been entirely unceremonious," Dumas Malone has written, "and could not have been impressive." This might have been intentional, considering Jefferson's distaste for pageantry, but there is no record to that effect. About thirty students began their studies—the number would triple by the fall—under five instructors, three recruited from the British Isles. A sixth, George Tucker, a William and Mary product, would teach moral philosophy.[83]

Several weeks earlier, however, there had been an unruly party in one of the dormitories. Bringing liquor into a dormitory was an honor violation. Though the professors had been somewhat lenient up to this time, they now suspended two students. When petitioned by the students after an apology, the students returned to good standing. The incident, however, had left a "growing concern over the problem of student misconduct." Dr. Dunglison, a professor and later Jefferson's personal physician, called this event to the attention of the visitors.[84] The subsequent incidents of the nights of Friday, September 30, and Saturday, October 1, were much more serious. On the first night, a student, whom Jefferson's daughter described as "a rich fool,'" threw a bottle and a pack of cards through a window occupied by a Professor Long. According to Jeff Randolph, the student cursed the foreign professors and threatened to take them "to the pump."[85] Since the student's identity was unknown, this episode did not receive the attention of the visitors at their meeting. Their attention was focused on the events of Saturday night, when fourteen masked students created a "riot" on the lawn.[86]

At their meeting, the visitors of the university agreed that the professors should enforce the rules and regulations. In the minutes of this meeting it is recorded, presumably in Jefferson's words, that "this loose principle in the ethics of schoolboy combinations, is unworthy of mature and regulated minds." But the minds of the students were not as mature as Jefferson had expected. They were obviously not ready to police themselves.[87] Jefferson, accompanied by Jeff, rode down to Charlottesville to attend the final meeting. When he arrived, the octogenarian Jefferson took his place in the rotunda, flanked by Madison and Monroe—the Virginia dynasty and all former presidents.[88] One of the students, Henry Tutwiler, described what happened. Jefferson rose to admonish the students. He began emotionally by stating that this was one of the most painful days of his life.[89] One writer described the setting:

> The students filed in, and among those suspected of having assaulted their professors sat the nephew of one of Jefferson's own grandchildren. Jefferson rose to address the students but, by one version of events, he recognized this young face in the crowd and was too overcome to go on. In George Tucker's somewhat different account, an uncharacteristically passionate Jefferson seethed with anger. "The shock which Mr. Jefferson felt when he, for the first time, discovered that the efforts of the last years of his life had been fouled and put in jeopardy by one of his family was more than his own patience could endure," Tucker recalled, "and he could not forbear from using, for the first time, the language of indignation and reproach."[90]

According to one account, Jefferson became so overcome with emotion that he soon gave up the attempt to speak. Chapman Johnson, a leader of the bar, then rose to speak. In response to his indictments of the student, the fourteen masqueraders arose and admitted their part in the disorderly events.[91] Afterward, they appeared before the faculty for their academic punishments. Three students were expelled, and academic sanctions were imposed on eleven others.[92] Writing Ellen's husband, Joseph Coolidge Jr., in Boston about a week after the meeting, Jefferson characterized the recent "riot" as serious. But the university student body had been strengthened by the show of authority, convinced that the rules would now be enforced. Jefferson believed that "the vigilance of the faculty and energy of the civil power" would prevent another violent event.[93] Jefferson proclaimed that they had a fine body of youths, but that they were "much obstructed by about a dozen of vicious and worthless scape-graces whom we shall endeavor to ferret out and get rid of as soon as we can."[94]

In the end, when Jefferson corresponded with his granddaughter Ellen, he insisted that the university had made the best of a bad situation. "Everyone is sensible," Jefferson believed, "of the strength which the institution has derived from what appeared at first to threaten its foundation."[95] In August, Jefferson wrote to Ellen that the university "has been a model of good order and behavior."[96] The students were treated as adults, "under the guidance mainly of their own discretion."[97]

This blissful portrait was not quite accurate. In fact, a few weeks earlier, granddaughter Cornelia Randolph had given her sister a different portrayal of life at the university. "There is a really shocking scandal afloat," Cornelia wrote. One young lady, "whom you may remember as a very bold impudent girl was missing one night & found at twelve o'clock in one of the dormitories of the students & it is said that it is not one but many that she visits, but really this is scandal of too black a dye to write."[98]

Three years after Thomas Jefferson's death, Jeff was appointed to the empty seat on the university's board of visitors. J. A. G. Davis, who would later become a professor and then be scandalously murdered by a student, was pleased with the choice of Jeff Randolph. For the next twenty years, Jeff's major assignments on the board were to the committees of inspection and finance. In addition, Jeff served on the executive committee, which could take action during the absence of the whole body. At such times, he worked with James Madison, John Hartwell Cocke, and Joseph C. Cabell, all major supporters of the University project.[99] Throughout his later years, Jeff remained one of the most active members of the board. In 1857, he was elected to succeed the late Andrew Stevenson as rector, a position he held until 1864. His retirement brought to an end his thirty-five years of dedicated service on the board of visitors—and to the university his grandfather had lovingly founded.[100]

Nine years earlier, John Adams had written that Jefferson's southern university would not survive. He now humbly apologized to Jefferson, recognizing Jefferson was on the verge of a monumental accomplishment: "I congratulate you and Madison and Monroe on your noble employment in founding a university. From such a noble triumvirate, the world will expect something very great and very new. But if it contains anything quite original, and very excellent, I fear the prejudices are too deeply rooted to suffer it to last long, though it may be accepted at first. It will not always have three such colossal reputations to support it."[101]

Not only did Jefferson's university survive—the "colossal reputations" survived as well. James Madison succeeded Jefferson as rector upon his death, and Jefferson's son-in-law Nicholas Trist served as Madison's enthusiastic secretary. Former president James Monroe served on the board of visitors of the college until his own death in 1831.[102] And the local newspaper actively supported the new institution. "Let us no longer pause," said the editor, "but carry the University into effect—educate our sons for public life, and save the sinking character of 'the old Dominion.'"[103]

To say that Thomas Jefferson was emotionally tied to creating this university would be a vast understatement. He wrote, "This institution will be based on the illimitable freedom of the human mind. For here we are not afraid to follow truth where it may lead, nor to tolerate any error so long as reason is left free to combat it."[104] Jefferson was so proud of this achievement that he chose to list the university as one of his accomplishments on his tombstone. He left explicit instructions for Jeff that only three achievements be placed on his grave "and not a word more. . . . He did not put there that he was a member of the Continental Congress, governor of Virginia, minister to France, the nation's first secretary of state, its second vice president, its third president. For his tombstone he restricted himself to a more personal list, to the things that mattered most to him, to his identity, to his comfort as he thought of the gains among all his life's losses."[105]

Jeff Randolph followed his grandfather's explicit instructions. The marble obelisk over Jefferson's grave is inscribed with the following words:

> Here was buried
> Thomas Jefferson,
> Author of the Declaration of American Independence,
> of the Statute of Virginia for religious freedom
> & Father of the University of Virginia.[106]

12
JEFFERSON'S HEALTH

There is a ripeness of time for death.

—**Thomas Jefferson to John Adams**, 1816

Thomas Jefferson's world seemed to darken around him in the final years of his life.[1] His daughter, Patsy, who tenderly cared for him and for Monticello's household, was now in her fifties, overworked, with twelve children to raise, and often fell ill. Her absentee husband, Thomas Mann Randolph, bordered on the brink of insanity, convinced that his own son had cheated him out of his estates. Jeff had confided to Jefferson's doctor, Robley Dunglison, that his father had even threatened to kill him in an insane rant.[2] Tom Randolph's paranoia had even led him to believe that Jefferson had infected the minds of his wife and children against him.[3]

And now Jefferson was dying from a wasting internal infection. For the last decade of his life, his health had declined at an accelerated pace, affecting two of his physical passions: hunting and horseback riding.[4] As the story goes, one of his true delights almost cost him his life. "We all had a dreadful shock," wrote his granddaughter Virginia, "at an accident which was near proving fatal to my dear Grand-Father the other day in the river; and are more miserable than ever at his persisting in the practice of riding without a servant to attend him, while his arm is still in a sling and quite helpless. His horse mired in the river and fell, confining

Grand-Papa's legs under him, and although not hurt by that, he would inevitably have been drowned had not the rapidity of the current carried him down to a much shallower place, where by reaching the bottom of the river with his hand he was enabled to rise on his feet & get out."[5]

As one author further explained, "It was an accident that might well have been fatal to a man of eighty; yet the old statesman's only remorse for his imprudence arose from his 'decent respect to the opinions of mankind.' According to Virginia, he said that 'it would have been thought by every one that visited the spot, if he had been drowned, that he had committed suicide.'"[6]

By May 1808, Jefferson had lived to an age that was double the life expectancy for men born in 1743. But as chronicled by both Jeff and Ellen, Jefferson's age, illnesses, prescribed treatments, stress level, habits, and lifestyle had an adverse impact on his physical and emotional well-being through his remaining years.[7] And though Jefferson did not endure any life-threatening illnesses, he was plagued with chronic diarrhea and intestinal disorders, prostrate trouble, and rheumatism most of the last decade of his life. He also continued to suffer from chronic migraine headaches, which he had already suffered for years and which confined him to darkened rooms for weeks at a time.[8] Let us examine those headaches more closely, along with his other afflictions, before moving on to Jefferson's final years.

One historian dates Jefferson's migraines to his awkward, stuttering marriage proposal to his first love, Rebecca Burwell, when he was only twenty. Her rejection seemed to have triggered the onset of Jefferson's first headaches. Jefferson recorded a "violent headache" in March 1764.[9] In their article "*Thomas Jefferson's Headaches: Were They Migraines?*," Drs. Gary L. Cohen and Loren A. Rolak corroborate this historian's conclusion, citing another scholar: "At eleven o'clock at night on March 20, 1764, racked by 'a violent head ache' with which he had been afflicted for two days, Jefferson wrote of the finality of his loss."[10] In time, Jefferson's headaches would become so severe that they would incapacitate him for days and even weeks at critical times in American history.

Dr. Cohen writes that a second headache occurred when Jefferson's mother died, in the spring of 1776, when he was in his early thirties. Historian Dumas Malone describes Jefferson's emotional distress: "This was just about the time that he had expected to return to Congress, but in the meantime he himself fell ill and was incapacitated for some five weeks longer. The report got around that he was suffering from an inveterate headache which had a hard name; probably it was what we now call migraine."[11] Jefferson himself described his mother's death in one brief sentence: "My mother died at 8 o'clock this morning in the 57th year of her age." Her death, coupled with angst over his wife's complications from a previous pregnancy, spun him into a health collapse. In fact, he was so sick, both physically and mentally, that he did not return to Congress for a full six weeks.[12] Jefferson himself described another headache at Natural Bridge, the famous rock formation in southwest Virginia, that was likely around this same period: "Looking down from this height about a minute," he said, "gave me a violent head ach."[13]

Dr. Cohen documented a third headache at the end of Jefferson's Paris years. In Paris, Jefferson became infatuated with the beautiful artist Maria Cosway. Maria was described as "a wisp of a woman, soft and delicate with deep blue eyes set in an oval face, with a head of frothy golden curls."[14] It is widely thought that Maria fell in love with Jefferson. One author wrote that Maria "loved Paris, and, in the handsome, intelligent, and charming American diplomat, she found the perfect man to paint her into her exquisite new world. For six weeks she was happy."[15] In the month that followed, Jefferson saw or heard something beautiful with Maria Cosway nearly every day.[16] And he was smitten with the cultured Maria, even though she was married at the time to a degenerate artist, Richard Cosway. As one observer described the foppish Cosway:

> His relentless ambition, his physical appearance and extravagant attire, and his sexual tastes were lightning rods for satire and ridicule. "Although a well-made little man," a friend recalled, Cosway was "certainly very like a monkey in the face. Writing to a friend who was touring Europe, Cosway expressed his lust for Italian women with the vulgar bravado of a man seeking to proclaim his masculinity. Among the more exotic of Richard's close friends was the transvestite Charles Beaumont, chevaliere

d'éon, a former French diplomat notorious for demonstrating his fencing skills in exhibitions dressed as a woman.[17]

Knowing her marriage was an arranged farce, Jefferson attempted to woo Maria away. But as one author has argued, "That does not mean he fell into Maria Cosway's arms in the promiscuous atmosphere of Paris. Intellectual passion and the power of his imagination seem to have brought him to the verge of satisfying his physical needs, but the power of his conscience likely constrained him from realizing his private fantasy."[18] If, as some historians contend, Jefferson did succumb to moments of passion, "the consciousness of these acts must have riddled him with guilt, as he returned to a friendship marked by controlled passion."[19]

As one story is recounted, trying to impress Maria, Jefferson performed a dangerous stunt while strolling with her along the Seine River. Unfortunately, he broke his right wrist, which caused a lifetime of suffering in his writing hand. One author described it this way: "The day before yesterday Mr. Jefferson dislocated his right wrist when attempting to jump over a fence in the Petit Cours. The wrist is in place all right but he has suffered a great deal and I do not see how he can write for another month."[20] French doctors set the fracture carelessly. Jefferson's hand developed atrophic changes and was a source of intermittent "rheumatism" for the rest of his life, prompting him to write with his left hand.

When Maria chose to return to her strange husband in England, Jefferson suffered another prolonged, excruciating headache. One historian defined the onset of this headache: "On September 2 [Jefferson] said goodbye to John Trumbull, whom he had asked to become his secretary.... One hour after Trumbull left for London Jefferson was in bed seriously ill. The old migraine was back for the first time since he had set foot on French soil. It lasted six days."[21]

In time, Jefferson's migraine headaches were accompanied by painful arthritis. Both Jefferson and George Washington suffered from debilitating rheumatoid arthritis. Washington's was so severe in his later years that he could not roll over in bed without pain and resorted to sleeping with one arm in a sling.[22] According to Jefferson historian Cynthia Burton, at fifty-one, Jefferson had severe soreness in his joints, which progressed to a debilitating case of chronic rheumatism and kept him bedridden for weeks. Jefferson complained of such rheumatism as early as 1785 (age forty-two), and expressed his dislike for cold, damp weather because of the suffering it inflicted upon his joints. While at Monticello, Jefferson would frequently travel to a friend's home to dine in the afternoon, then spend the evening at their home to avoid the night air on his arthritis.[23] From Paris he informed James Monroe, "I have had a very bad winter, having been confined the greatest part of it . . . The air is extremely damp and the waters very unwholesome. We had for three weeks past a warm visit by the sun (my almighty physician) and I find myself almost reestablished."[24]

Jefferson's fourth known episode of prolonged headaches occurred in the spring of 1790, when he returned to America to become secretary of state. The fifth recorded time of severe headache, according to Drs. Cohen and Rolak, occurred during the winter of 1790–91, as Jefferson continued to have personal and political differences with Alexander Hamilton. His headache seemed to blind him during the day, forcing him to read and write at night by soft candlelight. One physician aptly noted that "in the clinical literature of our own time one reads that migraine sufferers . . . are generally 'anxious, striving, perfectionist, order-loving, rigid persons, who, during periods of threat or conflict, become progressively more tense, resentful, and fatigued.'"[25] This is a perfect description of Jefferson, especially during this season.

After leaving Washington's cabinet in 1793, declaring permanent retirement from politics, he had no more headaches for a decade, until after his election as president. Even so, he remained unhealthy. Historian and Jefferson researcher Cynthia Burton notes that "Jefferson's health has been completely overlooked."[26] She is correct, and this is hard to even explain, because Jefferson's health was so poor in 1794, not much more than fifty years old, that he told Abigail Adams that he expected "not to live a Dozen [more] years."[27] In 1795, Jefferson wrote to James Madison, "My health is entirely broken down . . . my age requires that I should place my affairs in a clear state."[28] The next year, he complained to another friend, "I begin to feel the effects of age. My health has suddenly broken down, with symptoms which give me to believe I shall not have much to encounter of the *tedium vitae*."[29] Although he lived three more decades after this letter, at the time he felt he had but a few years remaining.

In addition to the aforementioned conditions, Jefferson also experienced urinary tract issues. A February 1799 entry in *Jefferson's Memorandum Book* records a payment to a Dr. Physick in Philadelphia. Jefferson's family had begged the former president to consult Dr. Physick during his last illness when he suffered from urological and prostate problems. Jefferson probably saw Dr. Physick for urological complaints in 1799 while in Philadelphia; there are no published letters from Jefferson to his daughters from February 7 to March 8, 1799, when he returned home to Monticello.[30] He would also endure chronic urological problems during his last decade of life.[31]

Once Jefferson was elected president, in 1801, his jarring headaches made a reappearance and continue throughout his presidency, through 1809. His arthritis also worsened during this period. In a letter in 1801, he complained that "cold is the source of more sufferance to all animal nature than hunger, thirst, sickness, & all the other pains of life & of death itself put together . . . When I recollect on one hand all the sufferings I have had from cold, & on the other all my other pains, the former preponderate greatly."[32] While in Washington, he even declined a dinner invitation from Dr. William Thornton in 1801, declaring it had been his practice for the past ten years to avoid evening engagements due to health considerations,[33] which would surely have included arthritis. Yet there was still another health problem he would face.

In December 1801, Jefferson confided in Dr. Benjamin Rush about his nagging physical complaints. "My health has always been so uniformly firm, that I have for some years dreaded nothing so much as . . . living too long," he wrote. "I think however that a flaw has appeared which ensures me against that."[34] Jefferson revealed that his complaint was diarrhea, a serious illness in the eighteenth century, which so weakened him that he found it necessary to seek Dr. Rush for relief.[35] On one occasion, it was so severe that Jefferson crumpled over in excruciating pain.

In his *Medical Lexicon: A Dictionary of Medical Science*, Dr. Robley Dunglison, who years later would attend Jefferson at the time of his death, described diarrhea as a "disease characterized by frequent liquid . . . evacuations and generally owing to inflammation or irritation of the mucous membrane of the intestines."[36] It could be "acute or chronic," and in some cases fatal "because like hectic fever it seems to obtain habitual possession of the constitution to operate upon it with scarcely any perceptible intermission, and, in general, to defy the most powerful remedies."[37] "The affliction," wrote one author, "would trouble Jefferson for the rest of his life." [38]

An expert anesthesiologist, in reviewing Jefferson's medical history, concluded that Jefferson "might have had an autoimmune disease, possibly Crohn's disease, as this involves colitis and arthritis, possibly reflex sympathetic dystrophy from the fracture of his wrist and certainly prostatitis."[39] According to medical experts, Crohn's disease fits some of Jefferson's symptoms. For example, the disease is a chronic inflammatory disease of the intestines. It primarily causes ulcerations (breaks in the lining) of the small and large intestines but can affect the digestive system. Crohn's disease is related closely to another chronic inflammatory condition that involves only the colon, called ulcerative colitis. Together, Crohn's disease and ulcerative colitis are frequently referred to as inflammatory bowel disease. Ulcerative colitis and Crohn's disease have no medical cure. Once the diseases begin, they tend to fluctuate between periods of inactivity (remission) and activity (relapse).[40]

Some doctors speculate that Jefferson also suffered from chronic prostatitis that led to benign prostatic hypertrophy (BPH). Chronic prostatitis is "an inflammation of the prostate gland that develops gradually" with subtle symptoms, such as low back pain, painful urination, and painful ejaculation. Some degree of BPH is thought to occur in 80 percent of all men over forty years old.[41]

Jefferson's health was so bad at times that it stirred rumors of his impending death. Once, when he arrived at Monticello in late summer 1802, it was reported that Jefferson was so sick that he required the constant attention of half a dozen doctors.[42] In 1804, Jefferson wrote to James Madison, "The motion of my blood no longer keeps time with the tumult of the world. It leads me to seek for happiness in the lap and love of my family."[43] But his agony lingered on.

A few years later, Jefferson made a payment to a Dr. Patterson that evidences that Jefferson likely battled rheumatism or sciatica during the summer of 1807. Patterson prescribed a remedy for the joint pain in his legs involving wrapping them with flannel. Jefferson told his granddaughter Ellen that he could not attend the races by "an attack of rheumatism. It is precisely the same as that which I had at Monticello . . . I keep up but can scarcely walk, and that with pain. I suppose it will take the same course as it did at Monticello, and that I shall be well at the meeting of Congress."[44] Hearing of his complaints of pain, Patsy wrote to Jefferson two days later. "I am truly concerned to hear that your rheumatism has fixed in so dreadful a part of the back. You will be obliged to try flannel next to the skin in which I have a very great confidence, particularly as you never abused the use of it."[45]

Evidently, Jefferson's arthritis was also aggravated by a drop in barometric pressure and rising humidity preceding stormy weather at Monticello.[46] Humid August evenings exacerbated Jefferson's pain, what modern medicine would categorize as "atmospheric pressure changes that alter the pressure within a person's joints."[47] In fact, there was significant rainfall in that region in the summer of 1807. Even George Washington commented on the storms and rain during the August summers: "The Rains have been . . . more abundant since the first of August than ever happened in a summer within the memory of man."[48] One author notes that there was extensive flooding damage to Jefferson's mills shortly after Jefferson's arrival at Monticello that year.[49] According to one historian, Jefferson "experienced his debilitating rheumatism, especially during the warm months at Monticello. Other significant bouts of rheumatism mentioned in Jefferson's correspondence were in spring 1797, summers of 1802 and 1806, August 1811, August 1813, August 1818, and August 1819. He wrote that these attacks affected his back, hips, and thighs, and kept him from walking."[50]

In 1808 Jefferson was struck with another debilitating headache. For nearly three weeks, he wrote, he was "obliged to be shut up in a dark room from early in the forenoon till night, with a periodical head ach."[51] The headache coincided with a stressful time in Jefferson's life: the collapse of the treaty negotiations with Great Britain, his son-in-law's life-threatening illness, and the impending treason trial of Aaron Burr.[52]

Preeminent history professor and Jefferson scholar Forrest McDonald notes that in his midsixties, Jefferson suffered severe migraine headaches while undergoing a foreign policy crisis in the midst of his second, less-successful presidential term. "You can cut the mustard when you're 65, but you can't do it when you're 65 and have migraines," McDonald added. "It just doesn't happen."[53]

Some have suggested that Jefferson's headaches were not migraines, but rather "tension" headaches (TTH's) triggered by stress.[54] However, Drs. Cohen and Rolak note that Jefferson's headaches meet most of the formal requirements of the International Headache Society's criteria for "migraine without aura" (also known as a common migraine with no warning signs).[55] Jefferson's own description of his headaches as "violent" and "blinding" is also more suggestive of migraines than of the less severe TTHs that most patients describe. His eldest daughter, Patsy, also had migraine headaches, suggesting a hereditary component found in the majority of migraine patients. On balance, the doctors conclude, the diagnosis of migraines fits Jefferson best.[56]

And there was more. In addition to his neurological, skeletal, urological, and digestive issues, by the time Jefferson returned to Monticello at the end of his stressful presidency, he was also likely impotent. Certain drugs, such as laudanum-related medications, reduced libido and decreased potency. So did prolonged horse riding. Jefferson was an avid horseman. He made many long trips on horseback (e.g., from Philadelphia to Georgetown before Beverly Heming's conception), and he generally rode his horse a minimum of three to four hours a day, as he felt it was therapeutic. He continued riding until the age of eighty-three, when he "was so weak that he could only get into the saddle by stepping down from the terrace."[57] One historian remarked, "Medical studies of the last thirty years link impotency, infertility, and erectile dysfunction to . . . horseback riding caused by saddle compression to arteries and nerves. Jefferson's medical history and lifestyle would indicate he probably had significant sexual loss as early as the 1790s, when he began complaining regularly about his symptoms associated with aging."[58]

Further, according to a professor and male reproduction expert in the Department of Urology at the University of Virginia Medical Center, "a 50–60 year old male in the late 1700's and early 1800's was likely a much 'older' male than is presently the case, much more worn down by the salts of disease, the stresses of lifestyle, and the inadequacy of medical care."[59] In short, male fertility starts to decline after age thirty-five, so Jefferson's fertility had likely been waning for thirty years by 1808.[60]

After his presidency, Jefferson discovered that private life could be more distressing than public life. His daughter Patsy, as discussed in earlier chapters, had married an abusive, erratic man. Her eldest daughter, Anne, had married a violent alcoholic, Charles Bankhead, who, you will recall, nearly killed Jeff. These things weighed heavy on Jefferson's mind. And all the while, the "periodical head ach," as he called it, continued to plague him too.[61]

By 1812, Jefferson had even more physical problems. In January, Jefferson revealed in a letter to his brother that on the advice of a doctor, he had brought home from Philadelphia some "lunar caustic" (bougies/catheter) that were commonly used for urinary strictures. Jefferson clearly knew firsthand of the severe pain these instruments caused when he warned Randolph, "The pain will be great." Dr. Robley Dunglison had to use bougies to dilate Jefferson's urethra during his last illness, which may have caused a fatal infection.[62]

As one historian argues, when Jefferson described his health as good, he judged it according to his age. With undue optimism, he wrote to Abigail Adams in 1813 that he was suffering from "rheumatism" but added that "excepting for this I have enjoyed general good health; for I do not consider as a want of health the gradual decline and increasing debility which is a natural diatheses of age."[63]

Jefferson suffered more than physical ailments. His emotional state had been declining ever since his days as secretary of state, as he constantly worried about his family's well-being and finances. He also fretted about his mental deterioration, reporting to Dr. Rush that he had "forgotten much" of his mathematical knowledge. He found that he could remember what he had forgotten but with difficulty. Jefferson feared that his mental acuity would force him to retire from public life—an unfounded fear, as it turns out. "The fear of becoming a dotard, and of being insensible of it, would of itself have resisted all solicitations to remain."[64] Author Gore Vidal notes that "in old age [Jefferson] said he read only one newspaper and promptly forgot what he had just read."[65]

Mentally, Jefferson also suffered from profound grief and depression over his daughter Polly's untimely death in March 1804 from complications of childbirth. His emotional state exacerbated his rheumatism pain. Jefferson continued to suffer from periodic bouts of dejection and despair, during which he was full of "gloomy forebodings" about his future. On one occasion, Jefferson had lain for six weeks in ill health at Monticello, paralyzed by a mysterious "malady." Similar emotional and physical symptoms occurred during stressful periods in his life, often accompanied by violent headaches, the worst of these presenting after his wife, Martha, died in 1782.

By 1815, when his brother Randolph died, Jefferson had suffered the emotional loss of his wife, five of their children, two grandchildren, and the deaths of five siblings and numerous friends.[66] This emotional distress certainly played an adverse role in his health. Jefferson also experienced a constant state of emotional distress over all the money he owed. Deep in debt when he left the presidency, he teetered on the edge of bankruptcy. He worried about leaving his family debt-ridden and also distrusted the banks. One historian contends that "Jefferson did not believe that any one personal failing had brought on his financial crisis, but a far-reaching defect preexisting in the realm of economy."[67] But his "financial crisis" only aggravated his physical ailments.

Returning for a moment to the Hemings sexual allegations, all of the above—Jefferson's age, his stress level, his painful arthritis, his urological issues and likely impotence, and his emotional state of mind—make the notion that Jefferson had carried on a vibrant sexual affair with Sally Hemings all the more dubious. Medical science would deem it improbable if not impossible.[68] Ellen and Jeff made use of all of these factors in their denial of the allegations.

***

Jefferson managed to live to the ripe old age of eighty-three—a remarkably old age for the early nineteenth century. And for most of his life, he had been keenly interested in his own health. His exercise regimen, begun as a student at William and Mary, had included running at twilight a mile out of Williamsburg and back again.[69] He was also adamant about a proper diet, writing in 1819 that he preferred to eat "little animal food, and that not as an aliment so much as a condiment for the vegetables, which constitute my principal diet." He also enjoyed a moderate, daily amount of "weak wine" and drank little water.[70] Jefferson also liked to conduct his own experiments with regard to his health and diet.

Jefferson was equally interested in holistic cures. The gardens at Monticello had allowed him to combine his interests in botany and self-care. In 1794, for instance, he listed sixteen medicinal herbs in his gardening journal, including peppermint, lavender, chamomile, thyme, and rue.

Yet, in spite of his good habits, in Jefferson's final decade his health declined rapidly. His disabilities made walking through his garden or even rising from a chair more difficult.[71] The arthritis in his wrists and fingers had worsened with age, too, and Jefferson grumbled, "The unceasing drudgery of writing keeps me in unceasing pain and peevishness."[72]

As recorded by Jeff and Ellen, their grandfather's final years were a series of maladies. On August 7–21, 1818, Jefferson visited Warm Springs for his arthritis and left seriously ill. Jefferson's self-treatment for the body abscesses he had developed from the Springs—an oral mercury compound— almost killed him.[73]

In 1822, at the age of seventy-eight, Jefferson fell from a crumbled step leading down from a terrace at Monticello, badly breaking his left wrist and arm. As the bones healed slowly, his wrist swelled and stiffened in pain, just as his right wrist had thirty years before in Paris. "Crippled wrists and fingers make writing slow and laborious," he informed John Adams. "But, while writing to you, I lose the sense of these things, in the recollection of antient times, when youth and health made happiness out of every thing. I forget for a while the hoary winter of age, when we can think of nothing but how to keep ourselves warm, and how to get rid of our heavy hours until the friendly hand of death shall rid us of all at once."[74]

By this time, an enlarged prostate gland and swelling in his legs made walking ever more difficult, but Jefferson still continued to ride, one of his few remaining pleasures. In fact, his rides may have eased his pain. "I am too weak to walk further than my garden without suffering," he complained to Charles Wilson Peale that same year, "altho' I ride without fatigue 6 or 8 miles every day."[75] It was his reliable horse Eagle, his steadfast companion with a white spot on its nose, that he so greatly enjoyed riding. As one historian related, once his horse stumbled in a torrent and Jefferson fell. His crippled wrists caught in the reins and he barely escaped drowning in the deep creek. But he passed off the incident to his family as of little consequence. When George Ticknor visited him in December 1824, he found the former president still riding ten to fifteen miles a day. "Mr. Jefferson seems to enjoy life highly, and very rationally," Ticknor reported, "but . . . said 'When I can neither read nor ride, I shall desire very much to make my bow.'"[76]

Jefferson's health had suffered during his years of work on the University of Virginia, and by 1825, he was eighty-two years old and feeling his age. That year, Dr. Dunglison, his English physician, made his first professional visit to Monticello.[77] As Jefferson's health grew worse, his thoughts turned to death, and he described how he wished to be buried. He wanted a simple grave on the mountainside below his house. He even sketched an obelisk headstone that he wanted at his gravesite.[78]

On May 11, Jefferson received a memorandum from his physician advising him that he was suffering from dysuria, a stricture and inflammation of the urinary canal apparently brought on by the enlargement of his prostate. Dr. Dunglison rode scores of times from the University of Virginia to Monticello that summer. Jefferson commented to Dunglison with grim humor that he had one foot in the grave and the other uplifted to follow.[79]

Jefferson was deathly afraid of senility. It was never so evident as when he reported to John Adams that Charles Thomson, one of the signers of the Declaration of Independence, at ninety-three, was "so much without memory that he scarcely recognises the members of his household."[80] Yet Jefferson found that his own memory failed on several occasions, and he had lost many a friend to the grave. "Is this life?" Jefferson asked. "It is at most but the life of a cabbage; surely not worth a wish."[81] He told a friend, "When I look back over the ranks of those with whom I have lived and loved, it is like looking over a field of battle. All fallen."[82] A few months before his death he lamented that "those who have no claims upon me, will at length advert to the circumstances of my age and ill health."[83] He had also complained that his hearing had become so impaired that he could barely make out the conversation at his dinner table.[84]

Jefferson's advanced age and physical frailty had made it impossible for him to keep his cherished Monticello in proper repair. The mansion had shown signs of decay long before his death. In 1826 he proposed a lottery to benefit his survivors. Under the plan, citizens across the country could buy chances to win a prize consisting, originally, of acreage Jefferson owned in Bedford County. He hoped to raise $60,000 this way. Unfortunately, before the Virginia legislature approved the plan, Jefferson would have to offer Monticello itself as collateral. When he heard this news, Jefferson "turned quite white," a relative recalled, but he agreed nonetheless.[85] That same year, the bursar of the University of Virginia observed, "Mr. J's health is rather better than it has been for some weeks past. Yet his spirits are much worse than I have ever known them. Indeed, it is wonderful that he retains any under the many distressing circumstances under which he now labors."[86]

The date that marked the beginning of Jefferson's final illness was June 24, 1826, when he summoned Dr. Dunglison, who had visited him a month earlier for troubled diarrhea. Jefferson's small reserve of strength seemed depleted, and his doctor saw little chance of recovery. In fact, Dr. Dunglison remained at Monticello during the last week of Jefferson's life.[87] Dunglison saw the end coming soon, as constant diarrhea tortured Jefferson. The doctor warned James Madison that there was little time left for a visit with Jefferson: "I much fear that, without some speedy amelioration, my worst apprehension must soon be realized."[88] Jefferson lapsed into unconsciousness the night of July 2 and he awakened only a few times thereafter: "On one or more of those occasions," wrote Malone, "he inquired if it was the fourth of July. Dr. Dunglison's response was that it soon would be . . . When the hands reached twelve they knew that the old patriot's wish to live until the day he had done so much to make glorious had been granted. The end came at fifty minutes past noon. It was remarked afterwards that the Declaration of Independence was presented to the Continental Congress at approximately that time."[89]

Sadly, six months after his death, Jefferson's family was forced to sell much of their furniture and almost all of the slaves at public auction to pay his enormous debts. They huddled in a drafty, deteriorating shell of a house that leaked when it rained until the family sold Monticello in 1831.[90]

13

"IS IT THE FOURTH?"

The loss of Mr. Jefferson is one over which the whole world will mourn. He was one of those ornaments and benefactors of the human race, whose death forms an epoch, and creates a sensation throughout the whole circle of civilized man.

—**Dabney Carr Jr., Thomas Jefferson's nephew**

One advantage both Jeff Randolph and his sister Ellen had as favored grandchildren was their ability to meet and converse with some of the most famous people of the times: John Adams, James Madison, James Monroe, and Abraham Lincoln. In fact, one of Jefferson's last letters to John Adams was the one in which he introduced him to his grandson Jeff. In the letter, he wrote that if his grandson did not meet Adams on his New England trip, he would "think he had seen nothing."[1] Ellen's husband, Joseph Coolidge Jr., accompanied Jeff to Quincy, and their pleasant visit was reported by Adams. "The old patriot was pleased with the manners of the young Virginian and much impressed with his stature," said one historian.[2] As for the letter Jeff brought with him from Jefferson, Adams described it as one of the most delightful he had ever received. "This was not the first time he complimented one of his letters from Monticello, but it was the last time, for he never wrote his comrade of 1776 again."[3]

As one story goes, Ellen met Dolley Madison when the University of Virginia visitors convened. Dolley would always accompany the former president to Monticello. She did not sleep well in Jefferson's built-in beds and admitted that she preferred the four-poster bed at James Monroe's Ashlawn plantation to "lodging in the recesses at Monticello."[4] Ellen seemed impressed with the vivacious Dolley and remarked on "the constant sunshine of mind which she seems to enjoy."[5] Less of a joy was Dolley's temperamental son, Payne Todd. Explained Virginia, "The visitors of the University met three days ago, and . . . Mr. Todd . . . has been detained here ever since by bad weather. I really expect," she added, "that poor Mr. Todd will hang himself if it rains again tomorrow . . . We have not time to employ in vain endeavours to amuse this unhappy victim of ennui, and consequently he is left to his fate which appears to hang upon the weather-cock."[6]

Perhaps most poignantly for his grandfather, Jeff was able to meet the famous French patriot and hero of the Revolution, the Marquis de Lafayette, when he visited Monticello two years before Jefferson's death.[7] On the morning of November 4, 1824, a coach drawn by four gray horses and accompanied by two carriages, a wagon, and a small military escort traveled along the Three Notched Road, heading west toward Charlottesville. Before his journey to Monticello, Jeff had ushered Lafayette into a tavern, "where refreshments were served at noon. Lafayette was helped into an elegant landau dispatched by Jefferson, who waited at Monticello." Then, as "members of the welcoming committee," Jeff and Rives climbed in, and the landau took off.[8]

With revolutionary banners waving, the procession made its way up the mountain road. When the coach, "fleet as the wind," crossed into Albemarle County just after 11 a.m., the Marquis de Lafayette arrived at Monticello for the first time in nearly thirty years:[9]

> After he climbed down from the coach and received an official greeting from U.S. congressman William Cabell Rives, . . . a gouty Lafayette was helped down from the landau. Jefferson, who found it impossible to walk farther than his garden, emerged from the house and gingerly descended the steps. The old friends, forgetting their aches and pains, caught each other's eye and advanced. [Jeff] Randolph watched as his grandfather, "feeble with age," broke "into a shuffling quickened gait." "Ah,

Jefferson!" Lafayette called out. "Ah, Lafayette!" his host replied, and "they threw themselves with tears into each other[']s arms."[10]

Jeff, who had helped organize the patriotic reunion, wrote that "of the 3 or 400 persons present not a sound escaped except an occasional suppressed sob, there was not a dry eye in the crowd—altho' invited into the house none would enter."[11] Fifty-two-year-old Patsy Jefferson stood beside her father and son, welcoming the Marquis de Lafayette. The French diplomat was accompanied by one of his sons, whom he had named George Washington. "The General was led up the steps by Mr. Jefferson, & introduced to Mrs. Randolph, whom he remembered as a school girl . . . and then as the mistress of her father's house in Paris." One observer saw Lafayette kiss Patsy's hand and speak "many kind words" to her.[12] "The aging French hero," writes one scholar, "who was touring the United States to commemorate the fiftieth anniversary of American independence, kissed her hands and offered kind words, while his hostess, according to one report, "received him with a grace peculiarly her own.""[13]

The meeting of the old patriots was primarily arranged and directed by Patsy. One historian concluded of Patsy during this grand reunion, "[She] presided over a celebration that showcased the Virginia gentry's gracious style of living and traditional rites of southern hospitality. After receiving Lafayette on Monticello's columned portico, twenty 'ladies & gentlemen,' including several of her own 'white robed' daughters and nieces, enjoyed a pleasant dinner indoors. By all accounts, the food was good and the company was congenial."[14]

After receiving Lafayette on Monticello's columned portico, Patsy arranged a sumptuous French dinner for the dignitaries:

> Jefferson sat next to Lafayette at one end of the table in Monticello's spacious dining room; George Washington Lafayette, son of the marquis, sat at the other end, between Martha and her daughter Ellen. Three other Randolph daughters and several of their "young lady relatives," along with Nicholas Trist, Joseph Coolidge, and two members of the governor's council who had accompanied Lafayette from Richmond

to Albemarle, constituted the remainder of the company. James Madison arrived to join the group as dessert was being served.[15]

As the aging revolutionaries renewed their acquaintance, nostalgia filled the air and the "glory of the setting sun shone from behind the many tinted mountains behind which it was sinking."[16] After dinner, the two old patriots retired to the comforts of Monticello "in profound silence."[17] As the sun set behind the distant Blue Ridge Mountains, Jeff and Patsy "basked in the nostalgic glow of the reunion of the old revolutionaries."[18]

The next night, a formal dinner was held in the partially finished rotunda at the University of Virginia. Jefferson had arranged the menu himself with *champignons farcis and tournedos*, coupled with the best French wine from Monticello's cellar.[19] Patsy's husband, Thomas, was notably missing from the festivities. As one historian explained, "[Randolph's] status in Albemarle remained sufficiently high to warrant his being chosen to chair the committee that orchestrated the local reception of the Marquis de Lafayette. By early November, however, when the old revolutionary hero arrived in Albemarle, Tom had left Monticello, and he participated in neither the formal activities the welcoming committee had planned nor the more intimate gatherings at Jefferson's house."[20]

No women were present among the four hundred guests at the dinner in Lafayette's honor. As per custom, the ladies were entertained outside, in the galleries and arcades of the pavilions. "It was an occasion of almost religious awe," wrote one author.

After the cloth had been removed and the wine served, the younger guests, Joseph Coolidge and Ellen among them, gathered round, listening to the conversation of the two old men. Four hundred guests were fed at tables placed in three concentric circles under the dome of this recently completed building at Jefferson's University. The most important toast of that day was "To Thomas Jefferson and the Declaration of Independence—alike identified with the cause of liberty."[21]

Valentine Southall, as presiding officer at the dinner, read Jefferson's speech, for Jefferson contended that his voice was too weak. "Born and bred among your fathers," Southall began,

> led by their partiality into the line of public life, I labored in fellowship with them through that arduous struggle which, freeing us from foreign bondage, established us in the rights of self-government . . . inspired by the visit of this our ancient distinguished leader and benefactor . . . To these effusions for the cradle and land of my birth, I add, for our nation at large, the aspirations of a heart warm with love of country, whose invocations to heaven for its indissoluble union, will be fervent and unremitting while the pulse of life continues to beat, and, when that ceases, it will expire in prayers for the eternal duration of its freedom and prosperity.[22]

Jefferson then offered a heartfelt appreciation for Lafayette's services to the feeble American Republic. Jefferson modestly declared that he had only "held the nail while Lafayette drove it. Among the many who proposed 'volunteer' toasts" to the aging patriots were Jeff Randolph, Francis W. Eppes, Nicholas Trist, and Charles Bankhead, who had been banished from Monticello five years earlier. James Dinsmore, a skilled carpenter, also proposed a toast solely to "Thomas Jefferson, founder of the University of Virginia."[23]

In the following days, Jeff, Patsy, and the two old comrades took carriage rides, driven by the slave Israel Gillette, down to see Jefferson's fledgling university.[24] Accompanied in the landau by Jeff Randolph and Valentine Southall, and escorted by the Albemarle Lafayette Guards, the general set out for Orange County to visit James Madison. Lafayette's party had enjoyed Jefferson's hospitality for ten days. It was said that Jefferson had to replenish his stock of red wine after their departure.[25]

Three decades had passed since Lafayette had seen Jefferson. In 1789, when Lafayette had first visited Jefferson, the Master of Monticello was a vigorous forty-seven years old. Now, Jefferson would soon turn eighty-two, although he exhibited "an extraordinary degree of health" for a man his age. But Jefferson's hearing had begun to fail, and "a number of voices in animated conversation confuses it." Successive rides over rough roads, however, had taken its toll on his bones and health. Because of the pain he suffered, Jeff increased his grandfather's daily dose of laudanum from eighty-five to one hundred drops. Jefferson told his longtime secretary, William Short, that due to his age, infirmity, and increasing deafness, he was no longer able to perform many everyday tasks.[26]

Jefferson's health had not recovered by early October, when he had an alarming experience at the hands of a sculptor. "John H. I. Browere was supposed to be adept at making life masks but was described by Jefferson's granddaughter Virginia as a 'vile plasterer.'"[27] After covering Jefferson's face and neck with plaster in the process of making a life mask for Jefferson, Browere left it on for an hour, instead of the usual twenty minutes, nearly smothering Jefferson. Jefferson had to bang on a table near his sofa, where his servant, Burwell Colbert, rushed to his aid, probably saving his life. The plaster became so hardened that a chisel and hammer had to be used to remove it.[28] Though Jefferson later made light of the nearly fatal episode, he emitted anguished moans during the extraction of the suffocating plaster. His daughters excoriated the sculptor and spread the story of Browere's negligence to others. To ease the wound to the sculptor's reputation, Jefferson later gave him a modest testimonial.[29] In fact, James Madison described the finished bust as a most faithful likeness.[30] The traumatic episode of the life mask seemed to have no ill effect on Jefferson's overall health. One observer, Daniel Webster, said in 1824 that Jefferson's "general appearance indicates an extraordinary degree of health, vivacity, and spirit"—and this was two years before Jefferson's death.[31]

In May 1824, a traveling book peddler named Samuel Whitcomb paid a visit to Monticello. Jefferson answered the door himself. According to the peddler, Jefferson was,

> tall and very straight excepting his neck which appears limber and inclined to crook. His hair is long and thin. His eyes light and weak, but somewhat severe. . . He is more positive, decided and passionate than I had expected. I should think him less of a philosopher than a partizan. His manners are much the most agreeable part of him. They are artifical [*sic*], he shrugs his shoulders when talking, has much of the Frenchman, is rapid,

varying, volatile, eloquent, amusing. I should not think him (did I not know his age) much over 60 or 65 years.[32]

But Jefferson realized that his time on earth was coming to an end and did not seem troubled about it. He informed Benjamin Waterhouse, "Should a stumble, a fall, cut short life and relieve me from the evils of dotage, death would not be a tragedy."[33] And realizing that his mental faculties were also in rapid decline, he declined to comment on a code of laws, not out of laziness but from "an approvable caution for the age of fourscore and two. . . . The misfortune of a weakened mind," he said, "is an insensibility of its weakness."[34]

Jefferson continued to experience painful rheumatoid arthritis, but now these episodes became somewhat longer. He left the mansion only for an occasional ride, and still depended on laudanum. Jefferson realized that at his age, some chronic pain was inevitable. As his doctor treated him on a regular basis, Jefferson thought this might be a good time to pay Dr. Dunglison's full bill for his faithful services. Dunglison graciously refused Jefferson's offer of payment, explaining to the former president that he had not kept a bill for his medical services. Though his health was stable at the moment, Jefferson recognized that the "fragment of life" remaining could be in severe illness. Unwilling to trust any other doctor's advice, he explained that he could not accept Dunglison's services without making at least some nominal payment to him. He enclosed fifty dollars, hoping to satisfy his bill. Dr. Robley Dunglison, friend, doctor, and one of the first professors at Jefferson's university, tended the old sage to the very end.[35]

In vintage fashion, Jefferson was ever the optimist, whether it came to his declining health or his mounting debt. "My temperament," Jefferson once said, "is sanguine. I steer my bark with Hope in the head, leaving Fear astern. My hopes indeed sometimes fail; but not oftener than the forebodings of the gloomy. I have often wondered for what good . . . the sensations of Grief could be intended."[36] But he was also realistic and fully understood the gravity of his impending financial troubles. Taxes were coming in as "an approaching wave in a storm; still," he said, "I think we shall live as long, eat as much, and drink as much, as if the wave had already glided under the ship. Somehow or other these things find their way out as they come in, and so I suppose they will now.[37]

The future, Jefferson believed, was on his side, as was the democratic society he had helped invent.[38] In Jefferson's last letter to Adams, written in 1826, just before he descended into his final illness, Jefferson asked if his grandson and namesake, Thomas Jefferson Randolph, might pay a visit to the Sage of Quincy during Jeff's visit to Boston. "Like other young people," Jefferson explained, "he wishes to be able, in the winter nights of old age, to recount to those around him what he has heard and learnt of the Heroic age . . . and which of the Argonauts particularly he was in time to have seen."[39] Like mythical gods, as one historian aptly expressed, Jefferson and Adams had become living statues to the next generation. Their correspondence, over three hundred letters, preserved for posterity the spirit of 1776.[40]

In his last months, Jefferson attempted to write his autobiography, but only half completed it, complaining, "I am already tired of talking about myself."[41] He disdained those in history who had published their memoirs with a haste he found self-aggrandizing, thus abandoning the project. His final death sentence came in the summer of 1826. But shadows loomed over his final surrender. The first came from those fields and farms he inspected every day. For visitors, Monticello was a mansion, a national shrine with a majestic view from the top of his mountain. Yet, two distressing issues preoccupied Jefferson on his daily rides in his final months: what could be done with his land to transform it into a cash profit, and what should be done with those who "labored for his happiness": his slaves.[42] Looming bankruptcy, family distress, and his enslaved community occupied his final thoughts in that summer of his death.

As life wound down for Jefferson at Monticello, Jeff brought him a variety of visitors for the last time. One was the Washington socialite, Mrs. Margaret Bayard Smith. The conversation was at first limited to the "commonplace topics of the day." But "before I was conscious of it," Mrs. Smith reported, Jefferson had drawn her "into observation of a more personal and interesting nature." She was entranced by the flow of Jefferson's wit, beautiful manners, and penetrating insights. "I know not how it was," she said, "but there was something in his manner, his countenance and voice that at once unlocked my heart."[43] Mrs. Smith wondered whether the possessor of this "benignant and intelligent" face and "almost femininely soft and gentle" voice could really be the "vulgar demagogue," the "bold atheist," the "profligate man" she had read about in the political newspapers.[44] On another occasion when she met Jefferson, at the inauguration ball of James Madison, and Madison had shaken Margaret's hand, Smith was nonplussed at the diminutive and bookish Madison. "It was when I saw our dear and venerable Mr. Jefferson that my heart beat," she said.[45] When Jefferson noticed her, "he advanced from the crowd, took [her] hand affectionately and held it five or six minutes."[46] While Jefferson paid some attention to Dolley Madison's "plain cambrick dress with a very long train," and "bonnet of purple velvet and white satin with plumes," Smith intently gazed at the departing president. Madison was "extremely pale and trembled excessively when he first began to speak, but soon gained confidence and spoke audibly."[47] Then Smith watched Jefferson, graceful and relaxed, obviously happy in his successor. "I do believe father never loved son more than he loves Mr. Madison," she wrote. After the ceremony, when Smith insisted on following the crowd of friends to the president's house, her husband teased her openly: "Saying to Jefferson that 'the ladies would follow him,' Jefferson replied with a wistful reminiscence: 'That is right, since I am too old to follow them. I remember in France when his friends were taking leave of Dr. Franklin, the ladies smothered him with embraces and on his introducing me to them as his successor, I told him I wished he would transfer these privileges to me, but he answered, "You are too young a man.""[48]

Even facing his own mortality, Jefferson grew more whimsical as he aged. As mentioned in the prologue, he had a favorite mockingbird, which sang to him when Jefferson took his nap and which he believed possessed an "affectionate disposition."[49]

In his final months, Jefferson resumed his correspondence with his brief romantic companion in Paris, Maria Cosway. Her history, since her dalliance with Jefferson, had also been full of distress. Maria's daughter had died at the age of six. Her eccentric and bisexual husband, Richard, never recovered from the emotional loss. Cosway had a nervous breakdown, preserving his daughter's embalmed body in the house, where it lay in a sarcophagus. Maria returned to England to nurse her husband in his last mental illness, but by this time he bordered on insanity. He babbled to Maria that he had found a fragment of Noah's ark and a feather from the phoenix, and had persuaded the Blessed Virgin to model for him in his studio.[50]

Jefferson described to Maria his plans for the university. "I am laying the foundation of a University in my native state . . . I have preferred the plan of an academical village rather than that of a single massive structure. It's within view, too, of Monticello, so it's a most splendid object, and a constant gratification to my sight."[51] Maria replied, "I have had my saloon painted with the representation of the 4 parts of the World, & the most distinguished objects in them." But she was "at a loss for America." She hoped Jefferson would favor her "with some description" of the new nation's capital. "Washington town," she said, "is mark'd in the Seminary."[52]

***

Soon after this correspondence, Jefferson became constricted to his bed. He continued to read, however: the Bible, Sophocles, and Euripides, reflecting on the great tragedy of life as illness enveloped him.[53] The date which marked the beginning of Jefferson's last illness was June 24, 1826, when Jeff Randolph urgently summoned Dr. Dunglison, who had visited Jefferson a month earlier for troubled diarrhea. Jefferson's small reserve of strength waned. Dunglison saw little hope of recovery. In fact, at Jeff's request, Dr. Dunglison remained on call at Monticello during the last week of Jefferson's life.[54] Dunglison consulted another doctor, Dr. Watkins, who prescribed "castor oil, warm water, rest, and a mild diet. For the pain, he advised a half grain of opium with one grain of calomel at night."[55]

Jefferson's granddaughter Virginia urged her family members to hasten their journey to Monticello. She wrote to Cornelia, "Oh! How I wish you were all here."[56] Henry Lee, son of Light-Horse Harry Lee, also called on Jefferson during his last days. Learning Lee was on hand, Jefferson, lying in his bed, sent for his visitor. "My emotions at approaching Jefferson's dying bed I cannot describe," Lee poignantly remembered. "You remember the alcove in which he slept. There he was extended, feeble, prostrate; but the fine and clear expression of his countenance not all obscured."[57] The Sage recognized Lee and warmly offered his hand. "The energy of his grasp, and the spirit of his conversation, were such as to make me hope that he would yet rally—and that the superiority of mind over matter in his composition, would preserve him yet longer."[58] Jefferson spoke philosophically on his impending doom. "He alluded to the probability of his death," what Jefferson termed as "that eternal sleep which, whether with or without dreams, awaits us hereafter."[59] Jefferson had even composed a posthumous poem for Patsy, alluding to his heavenly reunion with his departed wife and daughter, Patty and Polly. Jefferson enclosed the lines in a small locket Patsy discovered the day after his death:

> Life's visions are vanished, its dreams are no more;
> Dear friends of my bosom, why bathed in tears?
> I go to my fathers, I welcome the shore
> Which crowns all my hopes or which buries my cares.
> Then farewell, my dear, my lov'd daughter, adieu!
> The last pang of life is in parting from you!
> Two seraphs await me long shrouded in death;
> I will bear them your love on my last parting breath.[60]

While Jefferson slipped closer to death, Jeff pondered a way out of Jefferson's deep monetary problems to save Monticello from foreclosure. When he returned from a trip from Richmond, he found Jefferson deeply worried about the future of his daughter Patsy. "It is an agony," he told Jeff, "to leave her in the situation she is now in. She is sinking every day under the suffering she now endures; she is literally dying before my eyes."[61] He made Jeff promise never to leave his mother, that he would always be on hand to give her any comfort and assistance that he could. Jeff promised he would.

Jefferson's personal doctor, Robley Dunglison, watched over Jefferson in his final days. Dunglison's detailed memoirs provide intimate details of Jefferson's final illness and excruciating pain. Dunglison was a distinguished American medical educator, brought to this country from England in 1825 to serve as the professor of medicine at the newly founded University of Virginia. "Not long after my arrival at the University," Dunglison wrote,

> Mr. Jefferson found it necessary to consult me in regard to a condition of great irritability of the bladder under which he had suffered for some time, and which inconvenienced him greatly by the frequent calls to discharge his urine. Few, perhaps, attain that advanced age without suffering more or less from disease of the urinary organs. This condition interfered, however, materially with his horseback exercise to which he had been accustomed on his excellent and gentle horse Eagle—long a favourite with his illustrious master.[62]

Dunglison went on to note that "Mr. Jefferson was considered to have little faith in physic," and "has often told me he would rather trust to the unaided, or rather uninterfered with, efforts of nature than to physicians in general."[63] But whatever may have been Jefferson's notions of physicians, Dunglison wrote, "He was one of the most attentive and respectful of patients. He bore suffering inflicted upon him for remedial purposes with fortitude; and in my visits shewed me by memoranda the regularity with which he had taken the prescribed remedies at the appointed times. From the very first, indeed, he kindly gave me his entire confidence and at no time wished to have anyone associated with me. It was about this time that Mr. Short wrote to him urging that he should consult Dr. Physick in Philadelphia."[64]

Dunglison described in graphic detail his last days with Jefferson at Monticello: "I generally visited him at Monticello two or three times a week and always had my seat at table on his left hand. His daughter Mrs. Randolph or one of the granddaughters took the head of the table; he himself sat near the other end, and almost always some visitor was present. The pilgrimage to Monticello was a favourite one with him who aspired to the rank of the patriot and philanthropist; but it was too often undertaken for idle curiosity."[65]

In February 1826, Dunglison had noted that more ominous symptoms had surfaced in the former president. His bowels had begun to constantly bother him, a fatal medical sign that the end was near. "An habitual diarrhea in a very old man was at that time death[']s herald," Dunglison noted. "The griping pains undermined all the patient's vital strength, and he began to rot inwardly."[66]

In March, Jefferson made his last will and testament. Toward the end of June, he composed his last letter in anticipation of the fiftieth anniversary of the Declaration of Independence. "The golden day was to be celebrated in less than a fortnight," reported Dunglison. "He dearly wished to see it." The letter Jefferson composed was a valediction, Dunglison declared, the last statement of Jefferson's belief that "the mass of mankind has not been born with saddles on their backs, nor a favored few booted and spurred, ready to ride them legitimately, by the grace of God." It is said that, during the last days, he "spent much time reading the Greek dramatists and the Bible." But he looked, too, to another source for inspiration. During his long life Jefferson had often dipped into the records of the Roundheads, the annals of seventeenth-century English Protestantism, for a model and a muse. In his last letter he turned again to the language of the Puritan saints. The boots and spurs were borrowed from an old soldier of Cromwell's army, Richard Rumbold.[67]

By July, Jefferson was on the threshold of death. Intervals of lucidity were followed by long periods of sleep. The near approach of death was now evident to Jeff and Patsy. Monticello teemed with extended family awaiting the sad end. On the morning of July 3, Jefferson sipped a cup of hot tea. Jeff noticed that Jefferson's hand quivered. Reading and studying to the end, volumes of Aristotle and Seneca lay on Jefferson's reading table, as well as two French pamphlets. He dozed drowsily for the rest of that day. When he woke in the evening, he thought that he had slept through the night. "This is the fourth of July," he asked, though it was still the third. Later, when he was again awake, he was pressed to take his laudanum. "No, nothing more," he told Dr. Dunglison with finality. After taking his opium, Jefferson's sleep became "disturbed and dreamy."[68] Jeff stayed constantly at his grandfather's deathbed during his final hours. Until the very end, Jefferson spoke freely of his death and "made all his arrangements with his grandson in regard to his private affairs."[69] Jeff wrote later that "his mind was always clear—it never wandered. He conversed freely, and gave directions as to his private affairs."[70] Jefferson informed his grandson about the exact details for his coffin and funeral service. "There was to be nothing showy or grand," observed one writer. "He would take his leave of the world with a simple Episcopal service and be laid to rest in the cemetery on the western slope of Monticello, where he had interred Dabney Carr so many decades before—and then his mother, and then his wife."[71]

As a house servant waved a wooden paddle to stir the soggy air, every breath Jefferson took seemed labored, pain etched on his face. After realizing Jefferson's grave condition, Dr. Dunglison stepped into the hallway. The young doctor hung his head and stood for a moment. Then he raised his eyes and stared at the frozen figure of Jefferson Randolph, six feet four, with massive shoulders and eyes like charcoal-colored smoke. As he turned and walked toward Jeff, grief flooded Dr. Dunglison's eyes. The doctor placed his hand on Jeff's granite shoulder in a hard grip. Dunglison's voice tried for professional calm. Death was near, he told Jeff. Over the next few hours, Jeff tried to rally his grandfather's sprits. He told Jefferson that he was looking better. Jefferson waved a hand in dismissal. "Do not imagine for a moment that I feel the smallest solicitude about the result," he said in a weak voice. "I am like an old watch with a pinion worn out . . . until it can go no longer." Jefferson knew he was dying. A hint of a resolved smile grooved his cheeks. "A few hours more, Doctor, and it will be all over," he murmured.[72] To a great-granddaughter, Jefferson quoted a line from the Gospel of Luke: "Lord, now lettest thou thy servant depart in peace."[73]

Jefferson steeled himself to stay alive until the fourth, but he was in so much pain. He took some laudanum in grog, then was given tea three hours later and brandy four hours after that.[74] Throughout the night, Jeff sat on a sofa near the bed, peering at the hands of the clock, "which, it seemed to me, would never reach the point at which I wished to see them." At 4:00 a.m., Jefferson awoke, summoning his house slaves "with a strong and clear voice," though what he said to them went unrecorded. At 10:00 a.m., conscious again, Jefferson "fixed his eye intently upon [Jeff] indicating some want, which most painfully," Jeff lamented, "I could not understand."[75] More sensitive to Jefferson's wishes, Burwell Colbert noticed that Jefferson's head was not as raised as he preferred it, shifting his pillow for him. Jefferson nodded, and seemed to relax.

At eleven, Jefferson again looked to Jeff, moving his lips to indicate that his mouth was dry. Jeff applied a wet sponge to his mouth, "which he sucked and appeared to relish."[76]

Jeff caressed Jefferson's warm cheek, which had not felt a razor in days. From this point forward, Jeff watched "from hour to hour to a close of the scene."[77] "With intervals of wakefulness and consciousness," Jefferson found the strength to speak. He told Patsy of his gift for her in a pocketbook that could be found in a specific drawer after his death. Jefferson also spoke with each member of the family, urging them "to pursue virtue, be true and truthful." As eight-year-old great-grandson George Wythe Randolph took in the mournful gathering, Jefferson managed a weak smile. "George does not understand what all this means."[78]

Jeff later wrote sadly to his dear wife, Jane, at Tufton, informing her the end was coming soon: "After passing a very good night my grandfather sank rapidly. My mother perfectly conscious of his situation. I hope will bear it. I will hang out a white towel or sheet upon the thorn bush upon the brow above Priscilla's house to let you know when it is over."[79] At the end, Jefferson rallied and composed himself: "I commit my soul to my God," he told Jeff, "and my child to my country."[80] Patsy stayed at his side during the day, but Jeff would not permit her to sit up at night, traditionally the task of the men of the family—specifically, Jeff, Nicholas Trist, and of his servant Burwell.

At 11:45 a.m., the grim doctor told Randolph that Jefferson had only minutes left to live, and to gather the family quickly. Summoning his last reserves of strength through a stupendous act of willpower, Jeff roused his grandfather to take his laudanum, but Jefferson protested in a final, raspy voice. For the last three days, he had exhibited the prodigious stamina and granite resolve of his Revolutionary War days. At 12:50 p.m. on the Fourth of July, fifty years to the day that the Declaration of Independence was signed, Jeff Randolph felt a soft squeeze of his grandfather's hand and stared into Jefferson's hazel blue eyes. He touched Jefferson's cooling forehead. It was over. Thomas Jefferson never uttered another word.[81] He simply "ceased to breathe" and died with his eyes open peacefully in his bed, three miles from Shadwell, his boyhood home.[82]

Dr. Dunglison detailed the death scene with firsthand observations:

> Until the 2nd and 3rd of July he spoke freely of his approaching death; made all his arrangements with his grandson, Mr. Randolph, in regard to his private affairs, and expressed his

anxiety for the prosperity of the University; and his confidence in the exertions in its behalf of Mr. Madison and the other visitors. He repeatedly, too, mentioned his obligations to me for my attention to him. During the last week of his existence, I remained at Monticello; and one of the last remarks he made was to me. In the course of the day and night of the 2nd of July, he was affected with stupor; with intervals of wakefulness and consciousness; but on the 3rd, the stupor became almost permanent. About seven o'clock in the evening of that day, he awoke, and seeing me standing at his bedside, exclaimed "Ah! Doctor are you still there?" in a voice, however, that was husky and indistinct. He then asked "Is it the 4th?" to which I replied "It soon will be." These were the last words I heard him utter. In Mr. Wirt's eulogy of him, it is said that he clasped his hands and said *"Nunc dimittis."* No such expression was heard by me; and if any other person had heard it, it would certainly have been communicated to me. Until toward the middle of the day—the 4th—he remained in the same state, or nearly so; wholly unconscious to everything that was passing around him. His circulation was gradually, however, becoming more languid; and for some hours prior to dissolution, the pulse at the wrist was imperceptible. About one o'clock, he ceased to exist.[83]

Nephew Nicholas Trist quietly clipped a few small locks of Jefferson's sandy gray hair, relics for the family. The wooden coffin, built by slave John Hemings, was already made. The body of the third president was transferred to it, and the coffin taken to the parlor to rest in state.[84] Then, using his signal, Jeff draped a white sheet over a thornbush on Mulberry Row, near the Monticello slave quarters. The sheet, visible at Tufton, told his wife, Jane, that death had come. Alexander Garrett, a lawyer and family friend present at Jefferson's death, described this final scene to his wife:

> Mr Jefferson is no more, he breathed his last 10 minutes before 1 Oclock today allmost without a struggle. no one here but Col. Carr & myself, both of us ignorant of [. . .] shrouding, neither never having done it, ourselves or seen it done, we have done the best we could, and I hope all is right. his remains will be buried the day after tomorrow at 2 5 oclock, PM no invitations will be given, all comeing will be welcome at the grave. I understand Mrs R. [Patsy] bears the loss as well as could be expected, perhaps better, she has not as yet shed a tear, could she do so it would go better with her, the rest of the family are much distressed I learn, all however is silence about the house.[85]

As the Charlottesville church bells tolled, Jeff tried to compose himself, but utterly broke down in stricken grief. His grandfather, surrogate father, the man he loved with every fiber of his bones, was now gone forever. As he wept, Jeff's volatile and moody father, Thomas, rode up the mountain. Tom Randolph had not been to Monticello in weeks, either to comfort his wife, Patsy, or pay his last respects to his father-in-law. Now, noticing that Patsy was not crying, Randolph berated her, accusing her of being too cold to shed a tear. Telling Dr. Dunglison that Patsy's failure to grieve must be the result of a "morbid condition," Randolph ordered the doctor to prescribe medicine to induce tears. "Nothing as a matter of course could be done," Dunglison replied testily, "but to enjoin quiet which she was not likely to obtain." "That excellent lady," Dunglison reported later, referring to Patsy, "and her equally excellent daughters were in the deepest distress, whilst Governor Randolph was taunting her for not shedding a tear."[86]

This was too much for the exhausted and grief-stricken grandson. Jeff lost his granite self-control, on the verge of a physical fight with his own father at Jefferson's deathbed. Dr. Dunglison reported the ugly details: "A singular scene presented itself," he said. Jeff accused his father of "hating [Jefferson] in life [and] neglecting him in death." He defended his mother's honor against an abusive father, a father who had literally abandoned his own wife and family. As father and son yelled at each other, a "dreadfully distressed" Patsy looked on, then fled the appalling scene, her nerves and emotions shattered beyond the pale. Jeff quickly followed her, embracing and comforting his beloved mother.[87]

Jeff saw his beloved grandfather die in a manner that befit his life: with grace, dignity, and a deep regard for his remaining family. Per Jefferson's wishes, Jeff instructed Wormley Hughes, the gardener, to dig Jefferson's grave on the western side of the mountain.[88] Through blades of rain clouds, Jefferson would have appreciated the view to the Blue Ridge Mountains. It was glorious. University students trekked up the mountain with their teachers, under a threat of rain, to watch as their rector was buried.

The only known eyewitness account of Jefferson's funeral was provided by Andrew K. Smith years later. Smith, having seen a death notice for Jeff Randolph, wrote to the *Washington Republican*, recounting his memories of the Jefferson funeral. As Smith recalled, a contingent from Charlottesville was supposed to proceed up to the mountain from the courthouse, but there was a dispute about the funeral procession. Smith and others grew impatient, so they headed for Monticello:

> The time of the funeral was fixed for 5 o'clck, P. M., July 6, and it was arranged that the procession should form on the courthouse square at 4 o'clock, but a difference of opinion arose as to whether the citizens or students were entitled to the right in the procession, and much time was lost, and several of us, becoming tired of the discussion, turned our horses' heads to the mountain. On arriving at the cemetery, we found that the coffin had been removed from the house and was resting on narrow planks placed across the grave, (with a view of enabling the great number expected to have a better opportunity of seeing it.) Ex-Governor Thomas Mann Randolph (who was not on good terms with Mr. Jefferson,) thought it the duty of his son to inform the clergyman that they were awaiting the arrival of the citizens, professors and students, and his son, deeming it the duty of his father to do so kept silent [and] the services went on to the close of the same. The grave was filled up, and the

thirty or forty persons who witnessed the interment started for home, and met the procession, numbering about one thousand five hundred persons, coming up the mountain.[89]

Smith's *Account of Thomas Jefferson's Funeral* for the *Charlottesville Weekly Chronicle* noted one famous attendant at the funeral, then a student at the university: "Among the students present at the funeral, I recollect seeing Edgar A. Poe, a high-minded and honorable young man, though easily persuaded to his wrong."[90]

"The loss of Mr. Jefferson," mourned his nephew Dabney Carr, "is one over which the whole world will mourn."[91] After Jefferson's death, Carr noted:

> There were found in a drawer in his room . . . some little packages containing locks of the hair of his deceased wife, daughter, and even the infant children that he had lost. . . . They are labelled in his own handwriting. One, marked *"A lock of our first Lucy's hair, with some of my dear, dear wife's writing,"* contains a few strands of soft, silk-like hair evidently taken from the head of a very young infant. Another, marked simply *"Lucy,"* contains a beautiful golden curl.[92]

When Jefferson's will was read, it was found that he had bequeathed to his political protégé James Madison a very special gift: "I give to my friend James Madison of Montpellier my gold mounted walking staff of animal horn, as a token of the cordial and affectionate friendship which for now near half a century has united us in the same principles and pursuits of what we have deemed for the greatest good of our country."[93] After Jefferson's funeral, Jeff wrote Madison to inform him of the gift: "Dr Dunglison is the bearer of a cane a legacy left you by my dear grandfather, as a token of that intimate friendship which had so long existed between you . . . May I ask in the name of my mother and her family that in your visits to the University that you will continue to make Monticello your head quarters. Accept the assurance of my highest admiration and my most devoted attachment."[94]

Madison immediately replied to the distraught grandson upon receipt of the gift:

> The Article bequeathed to me by your Grandfather, had been delivered by Dr Dunglison, and received with all the feelings due to such a token of the place I held in the friendship of one, whom I so much revered & loved, when living, and whose memory can never cease to be dear to me. I must beg you, my dear Sir, to assure your excellent and dear mother that I shall be happy in every opportunity of proving the value I put on the kind invitation you have communicated, and to be assured yourself of my great & affectionate esteem.[95]

After twenty-five years of faithful service to his grandfather, Jefferson Randolph now became the head of the entire Jefferson family. Their welfare and financial security were held in his capable hands.

14

A TROUBLED TWILIGHT

His house is rather old and going to decay; appearances about his yard and hill are rather slovenly.

—**A visitor's description of Monticello, May 31, 1824**

The death of Thomas Jefferson was cataclysmic for all at Monticello: Jeff; his mother Patsy; and the extended Jefferson family, as well as the house servants and slaves. At the time of Jefferson's death, at least fourteen people, spanning four generations, ages two months to eighty-three years, lived under one roof at Monticello. Grief quickly turned to apprehension about the future of the family's welfare and finances. The slaves, whose entire lives had centered around Jefferson and his world at Monticello, were anxious about their fates, having lost their benevolent leader of thirty years.

After Jefferson's death, it fell to Jeff Randolph to manage and solve the financial crisis his family had inherited. Jefferson had known he was leaving a financial disaster to his family, but was at a distinct loss on how to solve his debt problems, lamenting, "It is part of my mortification to perceive that I had so far over-valued myself . . . I see in the failure of this hope, a deadly blast of all my peace of mind, during my remaining days . . . I am overwhelmed at the prospect of the situation in which I may leave my family."[1] He went on to describe his shame: "My dear and beloved daughter, the cherished companion of my early life and nurse of my age, and her children, rendered as dear to me as if my own had lived with me from their cradle, left in a comfortless situation, hold up to me nothing but future gloom, and I should not care if life were to end with the line I am writing; were it not that in the unhappy state of mind which your father's misfortunes have brought upon him, I might yet be of some avail to the family."[2]

When Jeff showed his grandfather's letter to his cousin, Randolph Harrison, Harrison threw it down, half-read, and burst into tears.[3] One scholar has posed "a nagging question about Jefferson's finances: How could a man who recorded every penny he earned or spent, who kept accounts as rigorously as a banker, allow himself to slip so deeply into debt? The explanation by the editors of Jefferson's *Memorandum Books* is as surprising as it is insightful: he rarely ever knew how badly in debt he actually was. Through much of his life in public service, they write, 'Jefferson was profoundly ignorant of his own financial condition.'"[4]

Jeff labored heroically to save Monticello from debt and foreclosure, all to no avail. "I served my grandfather, mother and her children," he later said, "with as much fidelity as I could have served my God."[5] But Thomas Jefferson was $100,000 in debt, which in modern currency equates to over $2,000,000. The last few months of Jefferson's life had been grim, with Jeff embarking on one final effort to rescue his grandfather's burdened Monticello for his heirs. Yet, the mountain of debt was simply too much to resolve. Jefferson would be dead and gone on that cold January day two years later when Jeff oversaw Monticello's sale and dismemberment.

Jefferson's financial troubles had begun a decade earlier, with ill health and grinding anxieties. Historian Edmund Morgan has said that "Jefferson's concern with the perniciousness of debt was almost obsessive."[6] Perhaps, as one scholar has speculated, Jefferson did not want to be seen by his family as a miserly parent or grandparent, either in emotion or in money. This may have been a reflection on his mother, Jane, who had held a tight rein on Jefferson's life and money after the death of his own father. So, Jefferson conferred money constantly and without concern, which included to his wasteful brother, the three sons of his sister, and even the rake Charles Bankhead.[7] But in 1819 a series of crop failures destroyed Jefferson's hopes that he could climb out of the morass of debt. His chronic optimism failed to save him from increasing insolvency, slipping toward bankruptcy. He had been forced to borrow $8,000 just to liquidate his debts when he left the presidency. In April 1815, after the British burned the entire Library of Congress in the War of 1812, Jefferson offered to sell his library of 6,400 volumes for $23,990, a fraction of its real value, to constitute the new Library of Congress.[8] But Jefferson found his empty bookshelves depressing. "I cannot live without books," he once declared to Jeff, who immediately started a campaign to replenish Jefferson's library on meager funds. One diplomat, Augustus John Foster, was shocked that Congress did not vote Jefferson the money for his new library, calling it "another great slur upon the character of Congress."[9] Jefferson's account book showed that he spent $480.80 to reconstitute his library over several months, a significant sum for books in that day.[10]

When Jefferson was still alive, visitors and relatives had continued to visit and stay at Monticello. Feeding and housing them also became a burden on Jefferson's finances. His fame, one historian noted, "brought hundreds of uninvited visitors to Monticello during his presidency, even these measures proved insufficient in establishing his privacy. On too many occasions, Thomas Jefferson Randolph recalled, his grandfather was plagued by 'parties of men and women [who] would sometimes approach within a dozen yards, and gaze at him point-blank until they had looked their fill, as they would have gazed at a lion in a menagerie.'"[11]

Jeff Randolph could see the future bankruptcy of both his father and his grandfather. He desperately tried to persuade Jefferson to turn the Edgehill plantation over to raising tobacco for quick money. Jefferson was cool to the idea, knowing how tobacco eventually ruined the Virginia soil. He had written to Thomas Mann Randolph in 1809, "I consider it much better to sell this property than my slaves. I have raised many of them myself and know them all well."[12] In the end, both the Edgehill and Varina plantations belonging to Tom Randolph had to be sold to pay creditors. Jefferson became distressed that the slaves he had given to Patsy as her dowry could be sold at auction.[13] But the Monticello slaves were not sold during Jefferson's lifetime—he absolutely forbade this action, somehow managing to pay off the amount owed for the slaves. He planned to leave them as "capital" for Patsy and her children, knowing that Tom Randolph would probably leave a paltry sum to his family.[14]

As for Jefferson's dwindling finances, during his two terms as president, the office had provided a reasonable salary for the time: $25,000. From this, however, he had to pay the White House staff, his own secretary, and all his travel and entertainment expenses. The fine French food and wine served at Jefferson's lavish dinner parties became renowned, but was expensive. As he prepared to leave the presidency, Jefferson was shaken to learn, by calculating "rough estimates in [his] head," that he had exceeded his salary, which meant he had a debt of $10,000.[15] A discreet loan was arranged. Although he had informed Patsy of the "gloomy prospect of retiring from office loaded with serious debts," he maintained his eternal optimism: "I nourish the hope of getting along."[16] No doubt, Jefferson despised his bleak economic circumstances, but he lived with crushing debt almost all of his adult life. As president, he was proud of reducing the national debt. But his personal finances were an abysmal failure.

Before Jefferson died, as Jefferson lay awake in pain one night, he and Jeff brainstormed over how to save Monticello. Finally, they conceived of the idea of a "lottery" to sell some of Jefferson's property to pay off the debt. Under the plan, Jefferson would offer up specific land tracts, with winning lottery holders having their choice of offerings. Jeff firmly believed that if the Virginia legislature approved such a lottery, he might not only pay his grandfather's debts, but provide a permanent home for his mother and the family. Jefferson agreed, reasoning that if allowed to conduct a lottery rather than an outright sale, his mills on the Rivanna River would cover his debts and leave Monticello as an inheritance for his family.[17] Jeff hurriedly took the lottery suggestion to the legislature. Patsy hoped that Jeff's success would prolong the life of her "dearest father who . . . would have had his heart broken by his difficulties and ourselves reduced to abject want."[18]

Jefferson, like all Virginia farmers at the time, had experience with these types of lotteries when he helped coordinate one for his cousin, George Jefferson, in 1768.[19] Jefferson set to work immediately on a lottery petition for Jeff to carry to Richmond. In January 1826, "Thomas J. Randolph attend[ed] the legislature on a subject of ultimate importance to [Jefferson's] future happiness."[20] Jeff's objective in Richmond was the passage of the lottery bill. Jefferson himself reasoned , "My application to the legislature is for permission to dispose of property . . . in a way which, bringing a fair price for it, may pay my debts, and leave a living for myself in my old age, and leave something for my family. Their [the legislators'] consent is necessary. It will injure no man, and few sessions pass without similar exercise of the same power in their discretion . . . I think it just myself . . . To me it is almost a question of life and death."[21]

However, there were significant political hurdles in the Virginia legislature to the lottery proposal, where lotteries could only be commenced with formal state sanction. Political animus still simmered against Jefferson and his anti-federalist views. Staunch allies like Joseph C. Cabell knew that Jefferson was spending his last ounce of energy establishing the state's university. Jeff and Cabell fought on behalf of Jefferson's lottery, but met stiff political opposition. To Jefferson, already suffering with his final illness, this was an emotional blow. To Cabell, Jefferson expressed his fears about the crushing debt: "If refused [permission for the lottery] I must sell everything here, perhaps considerably in Bedford, move thither with my family where I have not even a log hut to put my head."[22]

Jefferson's financial situation became public when Jeff presented his lottery petition to the Virginia legislature on February 8, 1826. Expressions of disbelief greeted the petition: How could a former president be in such a poor financial position? *The Baltimore Patriot* said it was shocking that the famous author of the Declaration of Independence should be on the verge of bankruptcy. Similar sentiments were published in the *Richmond Enquirer*. Some legislators objected due to old political arguments, while some argued that the lottery would stain Jefferson's reputation.[23]

After much cajoling and persuading by Jeff and Cabell, the lottery passed but was tethered with two significant conditions: an inspection and appraisal of Jefferson's properties would be required, and Monticello itself would be included as collateral in the lottery plan.[24] Unfortunately, Jefferson's initial optimistic calculation that his mills and their surrounding tracts would raise enough money to pay his debts was vastly underestimated.

Once the lottery bill passed and the property was appraised, Jeff engaged lottery brokers Yates and Mcintyre of New York. There were to be 11,477 tickets offered at $10 each—the prizes to be the Monticello estate, the Shadwell mills, and one-third of Jefferson's Albemarle County lands. When word of Jefferson's desperate financial situation spread, concerned citizens of New York City persuaded Jeff that the money could be raised other than with a humiliating lottery.

Financial committees were formed in New York, Philadelphia, and Baltimore. Approximately $16,500 was raised, a paltry sum compared with Jefferson's total debt of more than $100,000. Yet, it gratified Jefferson immensely that the citizens had not forgotten the old patriot. With the prospect of public donations, the lottery scheme was abandoned. More money might have been raised, but with Jefferson's death, the contributions faded.[25]

According to one account, Jefferson was said to have been conscious before he died when $7,500 arrived from admirers in New York. Later, Jeff reported his grandfather's death in a gracious letter in which he acknowledged this generous gift. A newspaper printed Jeff's letter, saying that the gift "had smoothed the patriot's way to the grave."[26]

After Jefferson's death, and with little revenue from any other source, Jeff Randolph had solely to deal with his grandfather's indebted estate, as well as his dysfunctional family. With extraordinary fortitude, it was Jeff who managed the emotionally wrenching sale of Monticello and its slaves. His mother, Patsy, was basically left homeless, with Jefferson's heirs heavily indebted. Patsy, her estranged husband, Thomas, and their children are the main characters in these final depressing years with Jeff. Fortunately, Ellen had married the successful Joseph Coolidge and escaped to a comfortable lifestyle in Boston. Ellen would live a full and active life of travel with her family, but helped Jeff and her mother as much she could from a distance.

Thomas Jefferson lived out the final months of his life in a house full of unpaid bills, overburdened women, and small, demanding children. That he remained at Monticello at all, given the rising call of his creditors, was a matter of immense relief to the family, due in large part to the Herculean efforts of one man: Thomas Jefferson Randolph. His efforts were not lost on his mother. Patsy poured her heart out to Ellen in an emotional letter, detailing the uselessness and ruin of her husband, and the approaching financial disaster at Monticello.[27]

Jefferson's generosity with money cannot be overstated. In 1824, after Lafayette's visit to Monticello, Jefferson had become aware that the "hero of two continents" was now himself in perilous financial straits. Jefferson discreetly urged that Congress make a financial bequest to Lafayette. Lafayette was generously awarded "$200,000 and a township of land" for his heroics in the

American revolution. Remarkably, no similar financial gesture was ever made by Congress to Thomas Jefferson or his strapped family. Creditors hounded the former president even more in his final years. It seemed as if he would be forced into bankruptcy—Monticello would be lost.[28]

In the end, Jeff desperately tried to salvage any financial shred of his grandfather's legacy, but understood that time had run out. They would have to sell Monticello "and as many negroes as would pay the debts," then relocate to Poplar Forest. He could barely bring himself to propose the idea to his mother, but if they delayed any longer, they would lose everything. Patsy had never seen Jeff "so much agitated as he was."[29]

Thomas Jefferson's will held no surprises for the family. On March 16, 1826, he had drafted and signed his will, but added a codicil the next day, four weeks before his eighty-third birthday. Both documents, observed one historian, are in his strong, clear handwriting. After describing in precise detail the land he was giving Francis Eppes at Poplar Forest, he bequeathed his residual estate in trust to his daughter Patsy. He was careful and precise to leave his affairs in the care and control of three valued trustees: his grandson Jeff, his grandson-in-law Nicholas Trist, and Alexander Garrett, bursar of the university. The purpose of this arrangement, as he wisely planned, was to avoid the property falling into the hands of the creditors of his insolvent son-in-law, Thomas Mann Randolph.[30]

Jefferson bequeathed Monticello, its furnishings, and surrounding land to his daughter Patsy.[31] Two years after his death, Monticello's exterior, like Jefferson's fortune, had greatly deteriorated.[32] Jefferson's once fine landau was now referred to as "that dreadful carriage." When Nicholas Trist was soon to return to Monticello for a final time, his wife, Virginia, could only promise him a riding horse, "old Blucher, that time has deprived of his sight almost entirely, without improving his gait."[33] By this time, Jefferson had already given his Poplar Forest estate to grandson Francis Eppes, the only surviving child of Jefferson's deceased daughter, Polly. Jefferson may have had second thoughts on Poplar Forest had he fully understood the dire circumstances that would soon plague Patsy. The rest of his property was left in trust for Patsy, under the trusteeship of Jeff, Nicholas Trist, and Alexander Garrett, to prevent the claims of Tom Randolph's creditors. Jefferson understood that creditors would have a potential lien against any property in Patsy's name. Jeff, who eventually took over these debts, soon was appointed the sole executor of his grandfather's estate, making all the final, difficult financial decisions.[34]

Thomas Mann Randolph, livid that he had not been named executor of Jefferson's estate, swore he would never visit Monticello again. He refused to acknowledge the "executor," as he now referred to his own son. Nicholas, who had married Jefferson's granddaughter, Virginia, in the autumn of 1824, was tasked with the mundane daily upkeep of Monticello. With Patsy's reluctant agreement, Jeff finally decided that the furniture and slaves must be sold for financial survival—the Jefferson family had simply run out of time and money.[35]

Fortunately, Jeff spared his mother the sight of Jefferson's loyal house servants on the auction block.[36] At the time of the slave sale, Patsy was far away from Monticello, visiting Ellen in Boston.[37] But she was all too familiar with the sight of humans being sold. "'The discomfort of slavery I have borne all my life,' she had written Ellen at the moment when Thomas Mann Randolph's slaves were sold, 'but it's [sic] sorrows in all their bitterness I had never before conceived. . . . The country is over run with those traffickers [sic] in human blood the negro . . . buyers . . . [H]ow much trouble and distress y[ou] have been spared My beloved Ellen by your removal, for nothing can prosper under such a system of injustice.'"[38] Patsy further lamented to her family about her financial worries: "My life of late years has been such a tissue of privations and disappointments that it is impossible for me to believe that any of my wishes will be gratified, or if they are, not to fear some hidden mischief flowing even from their success."[39]

Patsy would never recover emotionally from Jefferson's death. Heartbroken and nearly penniless, she shuttled between her children's homes in Boston, Philadelphia, and Virginia. As one author has described her plight, "Her poverty was scandalous"—so scandalous, in fact, that "in 1827, the state legislature of South Carolina voted to give her a ten-thousand-dollar pension, much to the relief of her indigent children. The state of Louisiana would shortly follow suit."[40]

On November 3, 1826, four months after Jefferson's death, Jeff announced in the *Richmond Enquirer* an auction of "the whole of the residue of the personal estate of Thomas Jefferson":

> On the fifteenth of January, at Monticello, in the county of Albemarle; the whole of the residue of the personal property of Thomas Jefferson, dec., consisting of 130 valuable negroes, stock, crop, &c. household and kitchen furniture. The attention of the public is earnestly invited to this property . . . The household furniture, many valuable historical and portrait paintings, busts of marble and plaister of distinguished individuals; one of marble of Thomas Jefferson, by Caracci, with the pedestal and truncated column on which it stands; a polygraph or copying instrument used by Thomas Jefferson, for the last twenty-five years; with various other articles curious and useful to men of business and private families . . . Thomas J. Randolph Executor of Th. Jefferson, dec.[41]

The formal sale of Monticello's furnishings was held on January 15, 1827. By this time, Patsy had departed for Boston while Cornelia and Mary stayed on at the Tufton farm. For five anguishing days they heard every raw detail of the sale, happy that their mother did not witness the sad and depressing scene.[42] On a bitter-cold day in January, the dismantling of Monticello began. The house was now unoccupied. The women of the family stayed home while crowds of buyers and onlookers made their way up Jefferson's sacred mountaintop.[43]

Before the sale, Jeff turned down many offers to purchase the servants, especially the Hemings, one from a plantation owner who wanted to buy fifty slaves to work a harsh cotton plantation in Georgia. Jeff knew this would be hard labor and would break up many of the slave families. He flatly turned the man down.[44] Just before the Monticello sale, the wife of medical professor Robley Dunglison, Jefferson's doctor, had written to Jeff about purchasing some of the house servants: "I have felt so much interested for Fanny as she has once lived with me, for fear she may be sent to a distance, that the Doctor has permitted me to try to obtain her at the sale as well as her youngest child, should they go at a reasonable price." The Dunglisons did purchase Fanny Hern and her youngest child, Bonnycastle, who was named after another professor, Charles Bonnycastle. Thirteen years later, Jefferson's granddaughter Virginia, writing from France, asked her sister-in-law to remember her "most kindly" to all their old servants. David and Fanny Hern were two of the eight men and women she named.[45]

The five-day sale began on January 15, when, despite frigid temperatures, a large crowd turned out. Jeff's deeply lined face showed complete exhaustion. Forlorn, he looked on at the sale of his boyhood home that held many fond memories. Almost everything went under up for sale: elegant pieces of furniture that Jefferson had purchased in Paris; prints and maps, wine glasses, candlesticks, grandfather clocks, and saddles. Jeff held on to the most valuable family heirlooms, paintings, and busts, including the magnificent Jefferson portrait by artist Gilbert Stuart. Some of Jefferson's clothes were saved and later stored at Edgehill. Jefferson's "polygraph" machine, a complex machine of two pens that produced a duplicate copy of writing, was also saved until 1875, when it was presented as a gift to the University of Virginia. Nicholas Trist wrote to James Madison afterwards that "the furniture sold very well . . . The whole was disposed of with the exception of that of [Jefferson's] apartment and a couple of chairs. Everything was sold at 12 months credit without interest." Even some of Jefferson's prized portraits had to be sold when Jeff became "wrung to the quick for every dollar" that he could raise.[46]

When the slaves were led away by their new owners, Jeff became emotionally undone, eager to be finished with "this dreadful business." The "sale and dispersion of [the] slaves was a sad scene," Jeff observed years later. "I had known all of them from childhood and had strong attachments to many. I was powerless to relieve them."[47] Jeff compared the scene to "a captured village in ancient times when all were sold as slaves."[48] By this time, commented one historian:

> Sally Hemings had been freed and was living with her sons Madison and Eston in a small rented house near Monticello.[49] When the terrible, tearing asunder—the sale and slave auction of 1829—came to the great house in which she had spent almost the whole of her life, she was fifty-six. In 1830, the US Census of Albemarle County, Virginia, listed Eston Hemings as head of a family and as a white man. The other members of this family were listed under his name by age and sex only,

as was traditional at the time. There is a listing of a woman—fifty to sixty years of age—described as white. This was Sally Hemings.[50]

Despite the severe weather, bidding at the auction of Monticello continued to be brisk over five days—even worn chairs brought top dollar, because they had been owned by the famous author of the Declaration of Independence. The slaves were sold for amounts averaging 70 percent more than their appraised value.[51] Jeff's sister Mary, who stayed two miles away at Tufton during the sale, wrote to Ellen the following week: "Thank heaven the whole of this dreadful business is over, and has been attended with as few distressing occurrences as the case would admit. . . You may imagine what must have been the state of our feelings, such a scene passing actually within sight and every hour bringing us fresh details of everything that was going on."[52]

During the next few months, Jeff's mother gathered the remaining family at Monticello. Together they huddled in parts of the sprawling house they could manage without servants. Jeff knew the state of decay at Monticello, advising his mother to move in with his family at Tufton. During Patsy's absence, serious structural damage had already been inflicted on Monticello "by the numerous parties who [went] to the place." Patsy's "choicest flower roots" as well as "everything and anything that they fancied" had been carted away.[53] Visitors to Monticello were appalled. "The first thing that strikes you," one antebellum tourist observed, "is the utter ruin and desolation of everything."[54]

Patsy accepted Jeff's advice and moved in with his family. One sister believed that knowing Patsy was safe and secure with Jeff would "be a relief to brother Jeff's difficulty," and a comfort to the entire family.[55] With Monticello's final sale, Patsy Jefferson turned somewhat bitter, castigating an ungrateful citizenry for not financially assisting Jefferson's family. "Supporting a large family in genteel society, upon very limited means" was a challenge, she complained, even in her rented town house in Washington. Supporting her single daughters was also a source of financial drain for Patsy. She earned some money by making dresses, "at which," she said, "I am quite a proficient."[56] Some winter days found the whole family packed around the same warm fire, "without the possibility of enjoying elbow room or quiet or privacy even for an hour in the day," Patsy wrote.[57]

Knowing his mother's plight, Jeff regretted Jefferson's decision to pursue the lottery, which he felt left his family exposed to public embarrassment: "How often have I bitterly regretted that my dear grandfather had not taken my advice and asked nothing of the legislature but have given up his property to his creditors and looked to his children for support and not leave his family the mortification of neglect from an ungrateful country."[58]

According to one account, a "vulgar herd" would flock to Monticello on Sundays. They behaved so raucously that Jeff placed a notice in the *Charlottesville Gazette* asking visitors not to steal plants. Burwell Colbert, who looked after the mansion, said the vandalism became even worse after Jeff's notice. As one scholar has written, "The house and outbuildings fast became eyesores. Slave cabins were in 'little heaps of ruin everywhere,' Cornelia said, and Henry Gilpin, a Philadelphia lawyer who visited Monticello that year, described the mansion as 'dark & much dilapidated with age & neglect.' No monument had yet been placed over Jefferson's grave and, with 'one or two exceptions,' the graves were marked 'by a board stuck in at the head with initials painted or cut in it.'"[59]

Margaret Bayard Smith, who had last seen Monticello just after Jefferson retired from the presidency, paid a second visit two years after his death. "How different did it seem from what it did eighteen years ago!" she observed. "No kind friend with his gracious countenance stood in the Portico to welcome us, no train of domestics hastened with smiling alacrity to show us forward. All was silent. Ruin has already commenced its ravages—the incisures, the terraces, the outer houses."[60]

"Met at the door by 'a little negro girl poorly dressed,' Mrs. Smith and her party found the entrance hall 'once filled with busts and statues and natural curiosities to crowding, now empty! Bare walls and defaced floor, from then into the drawing room, once so gay and splendid, where walls were literally covered with pictures . . . bare and comfortless."[61] Then Patsy appeared, "with open arms and affectionate countenance." It was as if "the spirit of the place, that had survived its body." Patsy summoned the family, and Mrs. Smith counted fifteen members of the household: Patsy, four daughters, four sons, four grandchildren, son-in-law

Nicholas, and Nicholas's mother. Always the host, Patsy apologized that there were not enough chairs for her visitors. "You will excuse all that is wanting," she said. "You know all that has passed."[62]

One account described a snowy February day in 1830, four years after Jefferson's death. Anne Newport Royall, a novelist and travel writer, visited Monticello. When no one answered their knock, Royall and her party let themselves in. Seated by a dimly lit fire in the house, they discovered "a great coarse Irish woman" who offered to show them around for fifty cents. "A bust of Jefferson still stood in the otherwise deserted entrance hall," said one observer. "The parlor was empty except for massive mirrors on either side of the door. Although Jefferson's bedroom was sealed off, the visitors glimpsed his bed through a window. On the third floor, Mrs. Royall's friends found a broken spinet among heaps of "coffee-urns, chinaware, glasses, globes, chairs and bedsteads." As the carriage began its descent, Mrs. Royall noticed a bare patch of grass south of the house. The plot "appeared to have been a garden," Royall sadly observed, "but hardly a vestige of it remained."[63]

Jeff's sisters yearned for their days back at Monticello, with its lush lawn, flowers, and gardens. For Jeff and his siblings, the mountain had been a comfortable, almost mythical world apart from reality. Patsy herself had experienced the rolling Virginia hills surrounding Monticello as her tender succor to an otherwise harsh life. She had been her father's sole companion on long rides with him after her mother's tragic death. When she gazed out from the terraces of Monticello, she felt that "all the Kingdoms of the world, and the glory there of" lay spread before me." She wrote to her daughter that "every feature of that landscape has its own spell upon my heart, can bring back the living breathing presence, of those long mingled wither moved from these bittersweet scenes."[64] Ellen said that when she dreamed of Monticello, "I never find myself within the house; I am always wandering through the grounds or walking on the terrace."[65] There, in her dreams said Ellen, "glorious prospect lays open before me. I seem to have 'leaped a gulf' of fifteen years, to have retraced my steps, and losing sight of all present ties, forgetting even my children, to be what I was at sixteen."[66]

While the Randolph women could be sentimental about Monticello, they also felt deep bitterness about their poor circumstances. "In July 1832," wrote one observer, "Meriwether Lewis Randolph, Cornelia's twenty-two-year-old brother, visited the property—now occupied by Dr. Barclay—and regretted having done so."[67] "The prospect sickened me to the heart," Randolph wrote. "Every thing so changed. Corn growing to the verge of the Lawn." Except for "a few miserable looking, ghostlike trees, where the beautiful Scotch broom delighted the eye," all the other trees were dead. "The savage burnt them," Randolph said. "At each turn you are insulted by a monument of the destroying hand of the Gothic barbarism."[68] Had the Randolphs not retained ownership of the family cemetery, Barclay's plow would "have visited its walls & violated the sanctity of that soil which alone on this earth calls forth my admiration."[69] Meriwether did not venture into the mansion itself, he explained, for that would have shown respect to its owner. He closed his account, declaring "I most sincerely pray that before I leave the neighbourhood my eyes may be gladdened with the sight of the House wrapped in flames, and that every vestige of building be swept from the top of the Mountain."[70]

One writer commented:

> The family was making do as best it could, crowded together in makeshift households, scrimping on coffee and sugar and firewood, depending mostly on Cornelia's harried brother, [Jeff] Randolph, to house them and feed them and fend off the creditors and the scavengers . . . Cornelia confided that she hated "dependance[,] particularly dependance on brother Jeff.[71]

The complete sale of Monticello with an adjoining 552 acres was finally completed in November 1831. Its enslaved community had already been sold, as well as parcels of land, household furniture, and livestock. Jefferson's art collection was sent to the Boston Athenaeum for sale there, but it garnered little interest. The precise amount of the debt paid by these sales is not known, but it was much less than Jefferson's total debt. The decrease in Monticello's advertised price can be attributed to its severe decay and disrepair. In spite of desperate efforts to sell Monticello, there were initially no takers. Patsy expressed her racked emotions at the loss of her beloved Monticello: "There is some prospect of selling Monticello but I do not wish the thing spoken of yet. I thought I had made my mind up upon that subject and I find when it comes to the point, that all my [sorrows] are renewed and that it will be a bitter, bitter heartache to me its going out of the family."[72]

In 1826, Monticello was offered for sale at $26,000. Five years later the price dropped drastically to $11,000. Monticello sat empty and the victim of souvenir hunters and vandals for three years before it was finally sold in 1831 for a mere $7,500, to a wealthy druggist, James Barclay. Barclay's enthusiasm for the historic property waned when his "dubious scheme of raising silkworms on the estate for the manufacture of silk" failed miserably.[73] He did little to maintain either the mansion or its grounds, and Monticello was once again offered for sale.

In 1834, the mansion was sold again to Uriah Phillips Levy, a native Philadelphian and an admirer of Jefferson. Levy purchased the decaying mansion for $2,500. A lieutenant in the navy, Levy wanted to own a southern estate. But more important, his goal was to preserve Jefferson's legacy when he moved into and restored Monticello in 1836. Although his naval career kept him away from the mansion for months, a small staff maintained the grounds. Levy added his own furniture to Monticello, keeping much of Jefferson's memorabilia. He also entertained his friends and important visitors, showing off the patriotic estate.[74]

Monticello remained in the Levy family for an incredible ninety years, longer than Jefferson had originally owned it. In 1858, Levy moved back to New York, leaving Monticello to be tended to by an overseer. He died in 1862, the same year that the Confederacy seized Monticello. In 1863, Levy's heirs successfully contested his will, which had left Monticello to the federal government on condition that the mansion be preserved as a school for orphans of navy veterans.[75] After years of litigation, Levy's nephew, Jefferson Monroe Levy, bought out the other heirs, repairing some of the damage done by years of inattention. But even the Levy family had its critics. Jefferson Levy was condemned before Congress as "a rank outsider" subjecting what should be a national memorial to "the desecration of being lived in."[76] Among the criticism, "the Levy family had the audacity to hang their own portraits on the walls of Monticello."[77] When a congressman visited Monticello in 1878, he recounted, "There is scarcely a whole shingle upon it, except what have been placed there within the last few years. The windows are broken, everything is left to the mercy of the pitiless storm."[78] David Culbreath, visiting in 1872, left Monticello depressed: "Everything observed," he mourned, "belonged to a passed generation, had apparently seen its day of usefulness, and was on the rapid road to extinction. No one, seemingly, was left with sufficient means, interest or patriotism to stay the inroad of decay."[79] In 1882, Congress provided some financial assistance by appropriating $10,000 for a monument to be erected over Jefferson's grave and for maintenance of the family cemetery and grounds. Finally, in 1923, private groups, which advocated public ownership of Monticello, merged to establish the Thomas Jefferson Memorial Foundation. After a hurried fundraising drive, the foundation bought Monticello within the year by paying $100,000 of the $500,000 purchase price.[80]

If Jefferson's crushing economic distress was not enough for Jeff, he also had to deal with the final years of his father's bizarre behavior and his hounding creditors. After Jefferson's death, Jeff and his father battled over ownership of the Edgehill plantation. Years earlier, Jeff had hired William B. Phillips and Malcolm F. Crawford, a local mason and skilled carpenter, to rebuild Edgehill in the style of Monticello, which could be viewed in the distance. Jeff intended to grow tobacco on the property to pay down Jefferson's debts. He could also raise some money by selling his own property at Pantops. "How can I wish him success in that scheme?" his father asked. Father and son were not "within a thousand years of agreement," and the more they discussed these matters, the worse things grew. Patsy made her choice between the two. In her letter to Nicholas Trist, she agreed with the decision to leave Jefferson's property in the care of Jeff and the trustees, to avoid Randolph's creditors.[81]

Bitter and depressed, Randolph isolated himself from Monticello during the day, only to return at night to harangue Patsy and verbally abuse his son. Relatives and neighbors described him as "more cruel, barbarous and fiend-like than ever."[82] Francis Gilmer found him "broke to atoms, in mind, body and estate."[83] The only legal authority he had left was over the minor children. He forbade Patsy and the children to visit Jeff's family at Tufton. Although Randolph succeeded in obtaining a temporary injunction against Jeff's sale of the Edgehill mansion, the property was finally sold on January 2, 1826. The buyer, as he had suspected, was his son, Thomas Jefferson Randolph.

In fairness to Randolph, he had suffered deep depression after two emotional deaths in the family, one on February 11, 1826, his firstborn child, daughter Anne Cary Bankhead, who was married to an abusive husband who would beat her. Two weeks later, Francis Walker Gilmer, a friend of the family and Randolph's protégé, died of tuberculosis.[84] Randolph spent his last solitary days in North Milton. He saw nothing of Thomas Jefferson during the last dying weeks of the old man's life. From all accounts, he made no effort toward reconciliation with his father-in law. Although friends and family members constantly attended to Jefferson as he died, Randolph was nowhere to be found. Patsy kept a vigil at her father's bedside, and Jeff stood within call, "but Thomas Mann Randolph did not come forward to have a last word with a man who had been his patron, philosopher and party chief."[85]

Tom Randolph returned briefly to live in seclusion at the small room in Monticello's North Pavilion. He required "undisturbed solitude" and was "completely separate" from the family, he complained to son-in-law Nicholas.[86] A dejected Randolph recalled his life as forty years of misery. The isolation was required by a "state of Mind so influenced by no very pleasing associations with Monticello during the last short interval of [his] residence there, almost constant from Dec. 1789."[87] He had written Trist saying, "I do not consider myself a member of the family at all, and cannot reside at Monticello again."[88] But it was Patsy's determination, moral obligation as she saw it, that brought Randolph back to Monticello—as far as the North Pavilion, where he remained in seclusion.

On Sunday, June 19, John Hemings came over from Edgehill to see the sick man. On Monday morning, Randolph pleaded with Patsy to summon Jeff. He wished to have his final say with all the men of the family—his last effort at atonement. Patsy described the emotional scene in a letter to Ellen: "He offered and begged of him [Jeff] mutual forgiveness. He said it was folly for a dying man to talk of forgetting, but that *he* [Jeff] would live for many years, and begged that everything might be forgotten. He said in presence of us all 'an honester man exists not.'"[89] Randolph pleaded for pardon for the errors and blunders, as he called them, of his wasted life. Patsy told Ellen weeks later, "After the first burst of grief was over tranquility was soon restored . . . I think with you that returning health would have brought with it the same passions and jealousies, and that confidence, so completely destroyed, could never have revived."[90]

Randolph's stay in the North Pavilion was brief—in three months, death finally relieved him of misery. Although Patsy had nursed him devotedly during his final days, from five in the morning till nine at night, it had been out of marital duty, not love. Patsy reflected on her tumultuous marriage in a July 1828 letter:

> Every unkind feeling has been buried in the grave of the sufferer; no longer an object of terror or apprehension, he became one of deep sympathy, or rather commiseration and kind feeling; and affection itself could not have watched with more attentive and patient kindness over every motion forward; but the habits of intercourse with his family were so completely broken, the bonds of affection so much weakened by the events of the last years of his life, that after the first burst of grief was over, tranquility was soon restored.[91]

In mid-October 1829, Patsy lived in Washington. DC: "[A]gain I shall be a mistress of a home, though a rented one," Patsy informed Nancy Morris, her cousin and Gouvernor Morris's wife, "and where I have to learn the art of supporting a large family in genteel society, upon very limited means. . . . Nicholas & Virginia, Browse, & Burwell, will all live with me, each furnishing their portion to the general expenses." [92]

Initially Patsy had contemplated opening a women's finishing school in Charlottesville to earn some money. She knew that possibility might "mortify" her friends and family. She was in such a desperate financial state, however, that she admitted, "Our circumstances are so well-known that I feel no shame but for anything that might appear like mismanagement or want of attention."[93] After Monticello was finally gone, Patsy suffered "a complete prostration of health, strength, and spirits" during the 1826–27 Boston winter while living with Ellen. The "doubt and uncertainty" about the future had "preyed" upon her health, but the family's prospects looked "much brighter" in the spring. It seemed that a generous donation might pay Patsy's old debts. She declared, "[That money,] well managed . . . might save me from the horrors of keeping a boarding school . . . which in the country where I should have had the trouble of boarding with all it's [*sic*] teasing consequences, in addition to tuition, would have been a very severe trial in my feeble state. I can conceive of none more so."[94]

Patsy was saved from the humiliation of running a school by a charitable gift of $10,000 from the state of South Carolina. This money allowed to her to settle in Washington, DC, "where," she said, "living is cheap, and we are known, and of course where wealth will not enter on a scale of our importance."[95] Patsy could also take care of her small staff of house servants for far less money. Meat for the servants would only cost them twenty-five cents a day: "I do not speak of the choice pieces but such as we would think very tolerable in the country."

Patsy's daughter Cornelia expressed the family's distress on leaving Monticello when it was finally sold. Everyone, except for Patsy, she wrote, wanted to leave Virginia: "[W]hether to Louisiana or Vermont, to the west or the east, when people's inclinations are so different & yet all wish to hang together, is hard to say . . . I hope what Virginia & the poet say is true."[96] Cornelia also cherished her time at Monticello, fondly reliving past memories. A springtime walk on the mountaintop was one of her "greatest pleasures," because "the place is so lovely & in this beautiful season too, that if it was not for our affection to it would be a pleasure to come." The house was refreshingly cool, compared to Tufton; "old remaining chairs, & marble tables . . . set in order" welcomed them; and the "robin sung his sweetest song" just as on the day Ellen was wed. Memories of those times were bittersweet—stirring a "mixture of pleasure & pain."[97]

As in most families, minor squabbles over money occurred among the siblings. Several of his sisters questioned Jeff's financial decisions as executor of their grandfather's estate. Ellen considered it "unaccountable that having been compelled by his necessities to sell books," Jeff had sent them to what Ellen "considered the wrong place [Washington] without a catalog at a time when Congress was out of town!"[98] Boston, with its wealth, cultural centers, and prestigious colleges, would be a better home for Jefferson's books, she contended to Jeff.[99] Ellen's impatience boiled over: "Send all the books—and take the responsibility upon yourself[;] do not wait to consult," she instructed brother-in-law Nicholas Trist.

Noble as intentions were for his family's economic welfare, Jeff was vexing to his sisters Cornelia, Mary, and Virginia, with his hyper-frugality and constant hounding. He would inspect their housekeeping expenses doggedly. This made Cornelia all the more intent upon becoming independent of big brother. Inspired by her grandfather's example, she wrote, "We are his children, and the energy he has shewn in public affairs, is in our blood & we will shew it in our private affairs. [W]e will never despair, we will never be cast down by difficulties, we will bear ourselves bravely & be cheerful in the midst of misfortunes, & if we are thrown upon our own resources we will find them in ourselves."[100]

After Ellen arrived in Washington, she recalled, "Mama pointedly told Jeff he was under a strange misapprehension when [he said] 'the girls took every thing worthy of retention.'" Patsy meticulously inventoried each family heirloom. Included was a "large trunk" she could not part with containing "old gloves, old shoes, leather straps broken . . . old rusty tin boxes & & &." Seeing them gave her "pain," yet she could not "destroy" them." [101]

In April 1834, Patsy, then living in Washington, where the Trists made their home, became ill one night. In sudden alarm and perhaps delirious, Patsy thought of her house servants Sally, Wormley and Betsey, slaves who had never been formally freed. In the middle of the night, Patsy dictated a will to her daughter Virginia:

> APRIL 18TH 2 O'CLOCK IN THE MORNING FRIDAY
> To my five daughters I wish to bequeath my property in funds. To Benjamin and Lewis the two negroes now in Benjamin's possession. Emily I wish liberated as soon as you break up housekeeping here; Patsy Ann at the death of her old grandmother, in the meantime to live with her and take care of her. To Betsy Hemings, Sally and Wormly I wish my children to give their time. If liberated they would be obliged to leave the state of Virginia. To my dear George I have nothing but my love to leave, and in any division made of my books that he should have a share. In dividing the plate among you, I wish Jefferson to have the casseroles, and Mr. Coolidge the

duck. To Nicholas I leave my father's clock. written by Mama's request.[102]

This is virtually the same will as her more detailed, formal will, created in January 1836.

Patsy was fortunate to have raised children who loved her deeply, who could provide shelter, comfort and emotional support in her last stressful years. As she drifted from place to place, Patsy left behind the vestiges of her father's legacy: the few people she still nominally owned. Among those individuals was Sally Hemings. Sally was also fortunate enough that she could depend on her children for support. After Jefferson's death, she moved to Charlottesville, into a house owned by her sons, Madison and Eston Hemings. The three were listed in the 1833 parish censuses as "free people of color," though Sally had never formally been freed.[103]

Sally died in Charlottesville in 1835, believing that she had been free, informally, since 1826. She was buried in an unknown grave.[104]

Indeed, the Hemings family, as well as the entire enslaved community, was drastically affected by the sale of Monticello. According to one scholar, "the feelings of these slaves that were most impacted by 'this dreadful business' must have been preceded by years of anxious speculation."[105] The fate of the vast majority of those enslaved at Monticello is unknown. We know that Jeff Randolph had refused an offer from a plantation owner in Georgia to buy a large number of the Monticello slaves. Jeff rightly feared that the slave families he had come to know for two decades would be separated. As one historian has commented, "sale to the Deep South was a nightmare scenario for most enslaved people, and there was great relief that this did not happen." The price of some of the slaves may have been reduced purposely by Jeff so that other Jefferson family members could buy and keep them together.[106]

Ironically, Burwell Colbert, Jefferson's faithful servant who was given his freedom by Jefferson, was the only one to attend the sale at Monticello in 1827. Burwell spent over fifty dollars at the sale of his old home, purchasing a carving knife, tea china, and portrait engravings of Thomas Jefferson and the Marquis de Lafayette.[107] His most expensive purchase was a mule, for thirty-one dollars. The fate of Burwell's children, the property not of Jefferson but of Patsy Randolph, were not at risk. Unfortunately, every other slave feared the possibility of being sold and separated from their families.[108]

In the end, the Jefferson family, as did several of Virginia's dynasties, "had to witness the ignominious decline of their beloved Old dominion in the early nineteenth century: in agriculture, manufacturing, national political influence, and reputation." Visitors were mortified at the neglected roads, decrepit houses and ramshackle farms. Many families moved west of the Blue Ridge Mountains or out of state to Kentucky.[109] In 1833, Patsy lamented, "Virginia is no longer a home for the family of Thomas Jefferson."[110] She was right, one author has aptly written: "Many of the families occupying Virginia's great houses watched their fortunes decline alongside the prospects of their state. Thomas Jefferson and Dolley Madison were financially ruined at the end of their lives, but they were hardly alone. James Monroe kept Oak Hill afloat by selling land and slaves and borrowing money. He went badly into debt to the Bank of the United States, but, lucky for him, the bank was loath to bring suit."[111]

In 1809, Henry "Light Horse Harry" Lee, the brilliant cavalry leader, remained in a jail cell for failing to pay some debts.[112] The history the Jefferson family shaped to explain their family's financial decline emphasized Jefferson's severe sacrifices for the nation. As one historian has succinctly argued, they could not hide their economic ruin, but explained it in patriotic terms: "Just a few months after Jefferson's death, Ellen and Joseph Coolidge found themselves quizzed by a potential biographer who 'wished to know exactly the causes of the embarrassment of his pecuniary affairs.' In response, Ellen and [Patsy] laid out a story of personal sacrifice for political service. Jefferson had neglected his plantation because he was busy building a nation. To secure the Republic he lost Monticello."[113]

In the end, Thomas Jefferson had lived in a world of comfort, nurturing women and loyal slaves. Yet, it was one man who persevered in his sphere until the bitter end. No doubt, more than anyone else, Jeff Randolph knew his grandfather had lived in relative luxury and left his family in penury. It would take Jeff and his stalwart wife, Jane, another twenty years of painful sacrifices, but Thomas Jefferson's debts would ultimately be paid to the last penny. The effort required years of backbreaking toil and the sacrifice of all luxuries. Jeff would be short of money for many years, burdened paying Jefferson's relentless creditors: "His rapidly increasing family, the new home at Edgehill, the education of his brothers, his involvement in Virginia politics (to the neglect of his own affairs, his family insisted), and of course the depressed agricultural situation in Virginia, added to his financial woes." In addition, his door was "always open to [his] relations on both sides of the house."[114]

To his credit, Jeff always placed his family and his grandfather's legacy first, in spite of his lack of money and time. And, most importantly, he managed to erect, at his own expense, a magnificent stone monument at the Monticello graveyard, in strict conformity with Thomas Jefferson's wishes.

15
A FIRE BELL IN THE NIGHT[1]

Slavery . . . gave me a disgust of the whole system and made me an abolitionist.

—**Jeff Randolph**, *Memoirs* (1874)

In 1825, some neighbors of Jeff Randolph's urged him to become a candidate for a seat in the Virginia state legislature. This venture into politics "so distressed" Thomas Jefferson that Jeff had to promise his grandfather that he would not think of public life as long "as Jefferson lived."[2] But there was one gnawing issue that would eventually pull Jeff into the political arena after Jefferson's death: slavery.[3]

For most of their lives, slavery dominated both Jeff Randolph and Thomas Jefferson's everyday existence. In fact, the two men's evolving views on slavery played a vital role in their political arc regarding racial relations in general. Thomas Jefferson owned slaves—he inherited 175 upon the deaths of his father and father-in-law. One scholar opined, "How Jefferson's noble, altruistic words, his liberal sentiments, his immense plans for doing good coexisted with this institution [slavery] is a mystery we shall never wholly understand."[4] The answer is, perhaps, unknowable. However, one philosopher's words may be helpful in our interpretation of Jefferson and the issue of slavery. French critic and historian H. A. Taine said, "When you consider with your eyes the visible man, what do you look for? The man invisible. . . You consider his writings, his artistic productions, his business transactions or political ventures . . . All these externals are but avenues converging to a center; you enter them simply in order to reach that center; and that center is the genuine man . . . the inner man."[5]

When it came to the institution of slavery, Jefferson understood two contradictory truths: (1) slaveholding violated his republican principles, and (2) his family's financial well-being depended on it.[6] In fairness, however, one must judge Jefferson's entire record on the issue of slavery, not fragments or piecemeal correspondence. "It was Jefferson," observes one scholar, "who in 1769 drafted the law that, when enacted three years later, permitted the freeing of Virginia slaves."[7] In his 1776 draft of the Declaration of Independence, Jefferson denounced King George III for transporting "a distant people who never offended him" into slavery in America. Henry Wiencek, writing for *Smithsonian* magazine, noted, "In his original draft of the Declaration, in soaring, damning, fiery prose, Jefferson denounced the slave trade as an 'execrable commerce . . . this assemblage of horrors,' a 'cruel war against human nature itself, violating its most sacred rights of life & liberties.'" As historian John Chester Miller put it, "the inclusion of Jefferson's strictures on slavery and the slave trade would have committed the United States to the abolition of slavery."[8] The language, however, was deleted to keep South Carolina and Georgia from scuttling the Philadelphia convention.

It was Jefferson who authored a bill that outlawed the importation of new slaves into Virginia. Enacted in 1778, it was ignored by the majority of slave traders. According to historian Robert Turner, "Five years after writing the Declaration of Independence, Jefferson authored his only book, *Notes on the State of Virginia*. He denounced the evils of human bondage, asserting: 'I tremble for my country when I reflect that God is just and that his justice cannot sleep forever . . . The Almighty has no attribute which can take side with us in such a contest.'" Jefferson referred to slavery as a "moral depravity" and an "abominable crime."[9] "Never," he wrote in 1811, "have I ever been able to conceive how any rational being could propose happiness to himself from the exercise of power over others."[10]

At the beginning of Jefferson's political career, he fully understood the hypocrisy of slavery. More important, perhaps a strong case could be made that Jefferson's wife, Martha, profoundly influenced Jefferson's views on slavery. When we analyze Martha's background, the closest person to a loving mother that she knew was a slave, Betty Hemings, who cared for and nurtured Martha most of her life. The nature of this relationship was not lost on Jefferson, whose own life at a young age was also associated with a slave—his body servant, Jupiter.[11] In 1743, both men were born at Shadwell, a newly opened plantation of Virginia's western frontier. "As boys," notes historian Lucia Stanton, "they may have fished in the Rivanna River, set trap lines along its banks, and shared hunting escapades in the surrounding woods. As young men they traveled the length and breadth of Virginia together and found wives on the same planation near Williamsburg."[12] Jupiter frequently "accompanied Jefferson on his travels and acted as his personal attendant while he studied law in Williamsburg." Later, Jefferson described Jupiter's duties: "Shave, dress, and follow me on horseback."[13] In the colonial capital, Jupiter wandered down the Duke of Gloucester Street, purchasing Jefferson's books and wig powder for him. When Jefferson was short of money, Jupiter lent him a small amount for tips to the other slaves, domestic servants of his Williamsburg colleagues.[14]

Thus, it is not mere coincidence that both Martha and Thomas Jefferson had a close personal attachment with two trusted slaves, Betty Hemings and Jupiter. This semi-filial connection undoubtedly influenced their views on slavery. As one historian argues, "Jefferson . . . saw the behavior of Jupiter . . . in terms of their 'fidelity.'"[15] In fact, Jefferson freed several of his most trusted slaves in his will:

> Give also to my good servants John Hemings and Joe Fosset, their freedom at the end of one year after my death; and to each of these respectively, all the tools of their respective shops or callings; and it is my will that a comfortable log house be built for each of the three servants so emancipated on some part of my lands convenient to them with respect to the residence of their wives, and to Charlottesville and the University where they will be mostly employed . . . of which houses I give the use of one, with a curtilage of an acre to each, during his life or personal occupation thereof.[16]

Jefferson's early distaste for slavery was accompanied by his sympathy for mulattoes, whom he considered especially victimized by the colonial system.[17] Early in his career, in the 1780s, Jefferson worked hard to have slavery abolished in the new western territories. As historian Thomas Fleming has commented:

> In his early days as a lawyer, Thomas Jefferson revealed an almost instinctive dislike of slavery. At the age of twenty-one, he had inherited 5,000 fertile acres and 52 slaves, making him a member of Virginia's ruling class. But slavery offended his sense of justice in a deep and intensely personal way. In one of his first law cases, Jefferson had maintained that a mulatto grandson of a white woman and a black slave should be considered a free man. His argument, which the astonished judge dismissed out of hand, declared slavery a violation of every person's natural right to freedom.[18]

Before 1776 and the war, the Virginia Assembly passed two laws regarding slaves, which the king did not approve. The first prohibited their importation; the second authorized owners to set them free. "The veto of the first was probably due to the great profit accruing to the London Africa Company from that inhuman and infamous traffic," said Philip Mazzei, a Jefferson friend and neighbor near Monticello. "As for the second, I would not know what to attribute its veto to."[19] Mazzei recounted in his *Memoirs* that

> Jefferson declared that he did not go in for palliative remedies but for what was essential; that he would move for abolishing slavery entirely since both humanity and justice demanded it; that to keep in bondage beings born with rights equal to our own and who differed from us only in color was an injustice not only barbarous and cruel but shameful as well while we were risking everything for our own freedom [during the Revolutionary War]. He concluded by saying that it would be preferable to run the risk of having to till the land with our own hands.[20]

Mazzei was quick to point out Jefferson's adamant views against the institution of slavery:

> Beginning with Jefferson, they all were convinced by the reasons advanced by Mr. Mason and myself. Hence it was agreed to propose the two laws vetoed by the present King of England and to begin spreading the word that another would be enacted compelling slave owners to send black children to public schools in every county in order to learn reading, writing, and arithmetic and how to make good use of the freedom that their owners were determined to give all those who would so behave as to deserve it. The two laws were passed as soon as they were proposed.[21]

To understand Jeff Randolph's view of slavery, we must look at Jefferson's complicated views of the institution, even though a thorough discussion of the topic is beyond the scope of this book. In fairness, recent biographies have not fully and accurately reflected Jefferson's real angst regarding the issue. In his last years with Jeff as his trusted confidant, Jefferson's views on slavery radically changed for a number of reasons. Perhaps this is a testament to Jeff and his most important historical legacy—to fully voice Thomas Jefferson's lifelong dilemma regarding the abolishment of slavery.[22]

Rightly or wrongly, Jefferson could not fully express his real opinions and anxieties over slavery in the political arena. But his daughter and grandson could. Patsy Randolph would eventually influence Jeff's strong abolitionist views. Thankfully, when Monticello and its slaves were eventually sold, she "had been spared the sight" of her servants "on the auctioneer's block."[23]

Essentially, Thomas Jefferson knew slavery was diametrically opposed to the very document he had penned, the Declaration of independence. But he was in a conundrum for years on how to abolish slavery without destroying the entire southern economy. So, he basically washed his hands of the issue in his lifetime, leaving it to Jeff's generation to solve. In a letter to his colleague Edward Coles,

Jefferson tried to clarify his thoughts: "Mine on the subject of the slavery of negroes have long since been in possession of the public, and time has only served to give them stronger root. the love of justice & the love of country plead equally the cause of these people, and it is a mortal reproach to us that they should have pleaded it so long in vain, and should have produced not a single effort, nay I fear not much serious willingness to relieve them & ourselves from our present condition of moral and political reprobation."[24]

Jefferson declared to Coles that an abolitionist movement would "do honor to both the head and heart of the writer [Jefferson himself]."[25] Yet, he lamented that he could not do more to abolish slavery in his lifetime, explaining:

> I had always hoped that the younger generation receiving their early impressions after the flame of liberty had been kindled in every breast, & had become as it were the vital spirit of every American, that the generous temperament of youth, analogous to the motion of their blood, and above the suggestions of avarice, would have sympathized with oppression wherever found, and proved their love of liberty beyond their own share of it. But my intercourse with them, since my return has not been sufficient to ascertain that they had made towards this point the progress I had hoped.[26]

As early as 1776, Jefferson had agreed with his colleague Charles Thomson, who wrote from Philadelphia, "This is a cancer that we must get rid of. It is a blot on our character . . . that must be wiped out. If it cannot be done by religion, reason and philosophy, confident I am that it will one day be by blood."[27] As author Jon Meacham observed:

> The man who believed in the acquisition and wielding of power—political power, intellectual power, domestic power, and mastering life from the fundamental definition of human liberty in the modern world down to the smallest details of the wine he served and the flowers he planted—chose to consider himself

powerless over the central economic and social fact of his life . . . Slavery was the rare subject where Jefferson's sense of realism kept him from marshaling his sense of hope in the service of the cause of reform.[28]

Writing to a correspondent who had asked Jefferson if he had a formal plan to emancipate the slaves of Virginia, the sage responded, "This, my dear sir is like bidding old Priam to buckle the armor of Hector . . . This enterprise is for the young . . . It shall have all my prayers, and these are the only weapons of an old man."[29] During General Lafayette's visit with Jefferson at Monticello in 1824, one visitor overheard the conversation between the two statesmen on slavery. Lafayette declared that the slaves should be freed—that no man could rightfully own another human being. In direct terms, he told Jefferson that he fought on behalf of the American cause for a great principle—the freedom of mankind.[30] Jefferson replied that he thought slaves would gain complete emancipation, but could not predict when or how. Allegedly, he also told Lafayette he favored teaching slaves how to read, for newspapers and to gain information. But he drew the line at teaching them to write, for this might lead to the forging of papers.[31] Jefferson explained further to one of Lafayette's colleagues his position on the abolition of slavery:

> At the age of eighty-two, with one foot in the grave, and the other uplifted to follow it, I do not permit myself to take part in any new enterprises, even for bettering the condition of man, not even in the great one which is the subject of your letter, and which has been through life that of my greatest anxieties. The march of events has not been such as to render its completion practicable within the limits of time allotted to me; and I leave its accomplishment as the work of another generation . . . The abolition of the evil is not impossible; it ought never therefore to be despaired of. Every plan should be adopted, every experiment tried, which may do something towards its ultimate object.[32]

Fairly or unfairly, it is Jefferson's views on black Americans and slavery that has made him most vulnerable to moral censure in the twenty-first century. The contrast between Jefferson's declarations of equality and his lifelong ownership of slaves is at monumental odds with each other. As one historian explained the conundrum:

> No historical figure can bear this kind of symbolic burden and still remain a real person. Beneath all the images, beneath all the allegorical Jeffersons, there once was a human being with every human frailty and foible. Certainly Jefferson's words and ideas transcended his time, but he himself did not.

Jefferson believed that his "self-evident" truths would eventually implode the institution of slavery—but when was the question. Jefferson did not know. "Where the disease is most deeply seated, there it will be slowest in eradication," he said in 1815.[33] But a year before his death, he wrote more optimistically, "I am cheered when I see that . . . the abolition of the evil is not impossible: it ought never therefore to be despaired of. Every plan should be adopted, every experiment tried, which may do something towards the ultimate object."[34]

In reality, a multiracial society was beyond Jefferson's political imagination, but this viewpoint slowly changed over his last years. "Nothing is more certainly written in the book of fate than that these [black] people are to be free. Nor is it less certain that the two races, equally free, cannot live in the same government."[35]

The issue of slavery was dividing the country in half. Jefferson's dire predictions now seem prescient. "I fear," said he, "that much mischief had been done already [Missouri Compromise of 1820], but if they carry matters to extremities again at the approaching session of Congress, nothing short of Almighty power can save us."[36] Jefferson even predicted a civil war over the issue of slavery, lamenting that "as it is, we have the wolf by the ears, and we can neither hold him, nor safely let him go. Justice is in one scale, and self-preservation in the other."[37] Elsewhere, he predicted:

The Union will be broken. All the horrors of civil war embittered by local jealousies and mutual recriminations will ensue. Bloodshed, rapine and cruelty will roam at large, will desolate our once happy land and turn the fruitful field into a howling wilderness. Out of such a state of things will naturally grow war of extermination toward the African in our land. Instead of improving the condition of this poor, afflicted, degraded race, terminating, in the ordering of wisdom, in equal liberty and enjoyment of equal rights (in which direction public opinion is advancing in rapid strides) the course pursued, by those who make high professions of humanity and of friendship for them, would involve them as well as us in certain destruction.[38]

From all accounts, Jefferson was extremely benevolent to his enslaved community: "I have my house to build, my fields to form, and to watch for the happiness of those who labor for mine."[39] Jefferson even allowed some slaves to escape and not return to Monticello, as noted in an earlier chapter. As Ellen Coolidge recalled, at least four "runaway" slaves were not pursued: "Their whereabouts was perfectly known but they were left to themselves—for they were white enough to pass for white."[40]

Jefferson also had his enslaved community inoculated against smallpox.[41] He and Patsy also did their best to keep Monticello's slave families together and to provide good food, clothing, and medical treatment for them.[42] Jefferson also provided liquor to his slave laborers. "Field workers were given whiskey in cold weather, or for sickness, and also during harvests," one writer explained. "Each worker received about four ounces of whiskey a day at harvest during the workday. A cart followed the harvesters from field to field periodically doling out liquor."[43] Jefferson even paid some of his enslaved workers, a practice unheard of on other plantations. His personal servant, Burwell Colbert, was paid an annual "gratuity" of ten dollars, later increased to twenty dollars until Jefferson's death. Jefferson also paid his head carpenter, John Hemings, fifteen dollars annually, "to wit the wages of one month in the year, which I allow him as an encouragement." This was increased the next year to twenty dollars and continued until the end of Jefferson's life.[44] Despite few references to Robert Hemings, "over the years, Jefferson thought highly of Hemings, proclaimed him extremely intelligent, and extolled his capabilities to others."[45] One historian notes that even though Jefferson did not name him personally, the "servant of great intelligence and diligence" was Peter Hemings, "who had been taught brewing by a London brewer who had relocated to Virginia."[46]

Patsy declared that she felt an "awful responsibility" for her slaves, confessing that she had "no right to sacrifice the happiness of a fellow creature black or white."[47] She took particular care in dressing her maids in fine clothing, personally selecting dresses and outfits for the house servants. Jefferson wrote Patsy from Philadelphia in 1791 that he had "just put on board Capt. Stratton a box with the following articles for your three house-maids: 36 yds callimanco [calamanco: 'a woolen stuff of Flanders, glossy on the surface, and woven with a satin twill and chequered in the warp, so that the checks are seen on one side only' (Oxford English Dictionary)] 13½ yds calico of different patterns 25. yds linen 9. yds muslin 9. pr cotton stockings thread."[48] Jefferson's grandchildren were so close and familiar with the house servants that they sometimes referred to them as their own "aunts" or "uncles." In a letter from Ellen to her mother, she first speaks of Burwell Colbert's (Jefferson's personal valet) child who had been ill. "Critty's child is pretty much as it was, if there is any change it is for the worse, but Aunt Bet [Betty Brown] who keep it at her house and nurses it, desired me to ask you to tell Burwell, that it is just as . . . he left it."[49] Another granddaughter of Jefferson's, Cornelia Randolph, was more direct: she considered slavery "unjust & tyrannical," and had come to loathe this "dreadful state of things where self defense makes men feel toward their fellow creatures as if they were bears & wolves & treat them accordingly."[50]

One story has Jefferson's son-in-law, Thomas Mann Randolph, performing emergency surgery on one of the slaves, who had been attacked by another. As the account goes, "the boy Cary, irritated at some little trick from Brown, who hid part of his nailrod to teaze him . . . took a most barbarous revenge." He raised his nail hammer and struck Brown "with his whole strength upon the skull." Brown went into convulsions, then a coma, and a doctor operated on him to relieve the pressure from a piece of skull that had embedded in his brain. "Warlaw and myself arriving nearly at the same time," Randolph wrote, "I acted as his assistant in the operation which he performed by means of the trephine (the saw which works both ways or with the motion of the wrist only) with the greatest boldness, steadiness and skill." He sent Cary to jail, and Jefferson told him to leave the slave there "under orders not to permit him to see or speak to any person whatsoever" until a buyer could be found so far away that "it would be to the others as if he were put out of the way by death. Brown fully recovered and learned the brickmason's trade. Three years later, Jefferson sold him to the brickmason John Jordan, so Brown could live with his wife, whom Jordan already owned."[51]

More important, there is no historical or documentary evidence Jefferson ever personally whipped or tortured his slaves.[52] He firmly believed that whipping slaves was cruel, counterproductive and restrained such brutality.[53] Jefferson agreed with Washington on this position. "General Washington has forbidden the use of the whip on his blacks," a French visitor to Mount Vernon later averred, "but unfortunately his example has been little emulated."[54] In fact, writing in 1814, Jefferson said, "My opinion has ever been that until more can be done for them [slaves] we should endeavor with those whom fortune has thrown on our hands to feed & clothe them well, protect them from ill usage, require such reasonable labor only as is performed voluntarily by freeman, and be led by no repugnancies to abdicate them, and our duties to them."[55]

However, there is one letter where it appears Jefferson sanctioned the punishment of a slave. In his letter to Reuben Perry on April 16, 1812, Jefferson wrote that he had hired Isham Chisolm to find a runaway slave named James Hubbard, who was accused of theft. Chisolm found the slave, "got upon his tract, & pursued him into Pendeleton county, where he took him and brought him here in irons. I had him severely flogged in the presence of his old companions, and committed to jail where he now awaits your arrival," Jefferson told Perry.[56] In fairness, this is the only letter among Jefferson's nearly fifty thousand that he penned or received that a slave's whipping is even mentioned, and runs counter to his consistently humane and compassionate treatment of his slaves. Most historians examining the complete historical record have agreed that "nevertheless, the allegation is at odds with the many known examples of Jefferson's benevolent treatment of his slaves."[57] As one noted scholar aptly concludes, "There is abundant information that Jefferson's slaves loved him, worshiped him even, would have given their lives for him. Yet we know that extremes of degradation and veneration sometimes meet. The darkness of a slave plantation is never wholly penetrable."[58]

Despite the fact that Jefferson was unable to free his slaves under Virginia law, he remained a national symbol advocating eventual emancipation. He helped turn the nation's culture into a direction that would allow equal civil rights, regardless of race. For this reason, some blacks viewed Jefferson in a much more favorable light. One of the earliest and most important black Americans to acknowledge Jefferson's evolving views on slavery was the brilliant Benjamin Banneker. Banneker was a self-taught mathematician and astronomer known for his popular almanac predicting the weather and locust swarms. Jefferson had secured employment for him, a job assisting the army engineer in surveying Washington, DC.[59] Banneker and Jefferson began a series of little-known, but revealing correspondence in 1791 on the issue of slavery. Banneker wrote, "[I] hope I may safely admit in consequence of the report which hath reached me that you are a man far less inflexible in sentiments of this nature than many others—that you are measurably friendly and well-disposed towards us and that you are willing to lend your aid and assistance for our relief from those many distresses and numerous calamities to which we are reduced."[60]

Banneker appealed to Jefferson to actively involve himself for the political cause of complete emancipation:

> Now, sir, if this is founded in truth, I apprehend you will readily embrace every opportunity to eradicate that train of absurd and false ideas and opinions which so generally prevails with respect to us; and that your sentiments are concurrent with mine, which are that one universal Father hath given being to us all, and that He hath . . . made us all of one flesh [Acts 17: 26] . . . Sir, if these are sentiments of which you are fully persuaded, I hope you cannot but acknowledge that it is the indispensable duty of those who maintain for themselves the rights of human nature and who possess the obligations of Christianity to extend their power and influence to the relief of every part of the human race

from whatever burden or oppression they may unjustly labor under.[61]

Having explained to Jefferson the degraded condition of blacks nationwide, Banneker sent Jefferson "a copy of an almanac which I have calculated for the succeeding year . . . in my own handwriting."[62] Jefferson was extremely impressed with Banneker's eloquence and thought-provoking letters. He quickly responded to Banneker's kind gift:

> Thank you sincerely for your letter of the 19th instant and for the almanac it contained. Nobody wishes more than I do to see such proofs as you exhibit—that nature has given to our black brethren talents equal to those of the other colors of men, and that the appearance of a want [lack] of them is owing merely to the degraded condition of their existence both in Africa and America. I have taken the liberty of sending your almanac to Monsieur de Condorcet, Secretary of the Academy of Sciences at Paris and member of the Philanthropic Society, because I considered it as a document to which your whole color had a right for their justification against the doubts which have been entertained of them. I am with great esteem, sir, your most obedient humble servant.[63]

When Jefferson forwarded Banneker's almanac to the Marquis de Condorcet, a leading antislavery advocate in France, he extolled him to the Marquis: "I am happy to be able to inform you that we have now in the United States a Negro . . . who is a very respectable mathematician. Add to this that he is a very worthy and respectable member of society. He is a free man. I shall be delighted to see these instances of moral eminence so multiplied as to prove that the want [lack] of talents observed in them [blacks] is merely the effect of their degraded condition."[64]

Jefferson admitted to Banneker that his own parochial experience with blacks had been confined to his slaves at Monticello. Jefferson acknowledged that most slaves had been denied one of the things he cherished most in life:

education: "To our reproach, it must be said that though for a century and a half we have had under our eyes the races of black and of red men, they have never yet been viewed by us as subjects of natural history. I advance it, therefore, as a suspicion only that the blacks . . . are inferior to the whites in the endowments both of body and mind." Jefferson also explained that "[i]t will be right to make great allowances for the difference of condition, of education, of conversation, of the sphere in which they move."[65]

Remarkably, Jefferson admitted to Banneker that slavery had inflicted an unfair measure of the black man's intellect. This was a monumental change in Jefferson's thinking. He invited Banneker to provide him with evidence to disprove his "suspicion only." "Nobody wishes more than I do to see such proofs . . . that nature has given to our black brethren talents equal to those of the other colors of men, and that the appearance of a want [lack] of them is owing [due] merely to the degraded condition of their existence both in Africa and America."[66]

Jefferson made his same views on slavery known to Henri Gregoire, a Catholic priest and fervent abolitionist in the French Revolution. Gregoire had sent Jefferson a book with the literary compositions of blacks to demonstrate their equal intellect. Jefferson's reply to him is telling:

> Be assured that no person living wishes more sincerely than I do to see a complete refutation of the doubts I have myself entertained and expressed on the grade of understanding allotted to them by nature, and to find that in this respect they are on a par with ourselves. My doubts were the result of personal observation on the limited sphere of my own state, where the opportunities for the development of their genius were not favorable, and those of exercising it still less so. I expressed them therefore with great hesitation; but whatever be their degree of talent, it is no measure of their rights. Because Sir Isaac Newton was superior to others in understanding, he was not therefore lord of the person or property of others.[67]

There is no historical question that Jefferson, as well as Washington, Madison, and other Virginia planters, acknowledged the immorality of slavery while admitting perplexity as to how to abolish the institution without causing financial ruin to Virginia's economy. "When denouncing British behavior on the eve of the American Revolution," wrote historian Ron Chernow, "Washington made clear the degrading nature of the system when he said that, if the colonists tolerated abuses, the British 'will make us as tame and abject slaves as the blacks we rule over with such arbitrary sway.'"[68] "To get some historical balance," argues historian Gordon Wood, "it is important to remember that by the time of the American Revolution slavery had existed in Virginia and in America for more than a century without substantial criticism or moral censure. Therefore by condemning slavery and putting the institution morally on the defensive, Jefferson and many of his fellow revolutionaries did confront the slaveholding society in which they had been born and raised. It was an accomplishment of the Revolution that should never be minimized."[69]

Some scholars have argued that Jefferson's role as an owner of men was thrust upon him. Born into a slave system, some contend, he made the best of a bad situation by behaving as a benevolent master. Indeed, the most competent and scholarly biographer of Jefferson contends that "if the master himself erred [in handling his slaves] he did so on the side of leniency."[70] There was, however, one highly significant area in which Jefferson held that blacks were every bit the equal of whites: they possessed a "moral sense."[71] As historian Winthrop Jordan points out, "for Jefferson to deny this would have been tantamount to excluding blacks from membership in the human species. He defended blacks against the charge that they were thievish, attributing this to their degraded station in life rather than to "any depravity of the moral sense."[72]

Jefferson repeatedly expressed his dislike for the commerce of slavery. He tried to avoid selling his slaves, except for gross misbehavior. In 1787, in debt due to assuming his inheritance from his father-in-law, Jefferson told his plantation manager:

> I have sold too much of them already, and they are the only sure provision for my children, nor would I willingly sell the slaves

> as long as there remains any prospect of paying my debts with their labor. In this I am governed solely by views to their happiness which will render it worth their while to use extraordinary exertions for some time to enable me to put them ultimately on an easier footing, which I will do the moment they have paid the debts due from the estate, two thirds of which have been contracted by purchasing them.[73]

Only two and a half years before his death, Jefferson reiterated his long-held belief that emancipation of the slaves was imperative for the sake of the nation. In historian Alexander O. Boulton's analysis of Jefferson's slavery record, he insists that Jefferson, "throughout the entire course of his life, maintained an abiding faith in an antislavery philosophy in his words and actions. It is difficult to understand Jefferson's ardent critique of all forms of authority and oppression without including his fervent antislavery beliefs."[74]

It is also interesting to note how the slaves themselves viewed both Thomas Jefferson and Jeff Randolph. One slave wrote:

> Mr Jefferson used to hunt squirrels & partridges; kept five or six guns; oftentimes carred Isaac wid him. My old master was as neat a hand as ever you see to make keys & locks & small chains, iron & brass;" he kept all kind of blacksmith and carpenter tools in a great case with shelves to it in his library—an upstairs room. Mr Jefferson was a tall strait-bodied man as ever you see, right square-shouldered: nary man in this town walked so straight as my old master: neat a built man as ever was seen in Vaginny, I reckon or any place—a straight-up man: long face, high nose. Jefferson Randolph (Mr Jefferson's grandson) nothing like him, except in height—tall, like him: not built like him: old master was a Straight-up man. Jefferson Randolph pretty much like his mother. Old master wore Vaginny cloth & a red waistcoat, (all the gentlemen wore red waistcoats in dem days) & small clothes: arter dat he used to wear red breeches too.[75]

As one historian has succinctly concluded: "Thomas Jefferson was imperfect . . . But one of the things that set him apart from most of his southern contemporaries was his politically courageous public opposition to slavery. Jefferson's articulate condemnation of slavery ultimately contributed to the end of slavery throughout America. For that he deserves our respect and our gratitude."[76]

Like his grandfather and perhaps his father, Jeff Randolph came to believe there was no compromise with his contemporaries' "new morality which tolerates perpetuity of slavery."[77] To Jeff's father, Thomas Randolph, slavery was "ungrateful to all human and liberal feelings . . . All men," Randolph contended, "have a right to liberty, and if forced to yield it in exchange for life . . . may legitimately resume it whenever an opportunity offers, without commission of crime." He argued that "the failure to apply this basic American concept to the Negro would lead inevitably to the dissolution of the Union and civil war."[78]

Jeff Randolph's opinions on slavery were strongly influenced by his boyhood friendship with some of the slaves. "Having no companion of my own age, I associated entirely with the slaves and formed early and strong attachments,"[79] he wrote. He reflected in his 1874 memoirs that during his youth, his slaves would "take [him] on their backs by turns. We were taught to treat them with this much courtesy and kindness as if they were our equals," he wrote.[80] Jeff remembered one particular event while riding in the country with this grandfather. "On riding with Mr. Jefferson when Pres. we met a Negro [who] bowed to us. Mr. Jefferson returned the salute. I did not. He turned to me after we had passed and asked if I permitted a Negro to be more of a gentleman than myself."[81]

Jeff also fondly remembered the slaves who had cared for him, especially after he was attacked by his alcoholic brother-in-law: "When I was injured in Charlottesville by a brutal attack made by Charles Bankhead, Phil [a slave] came to me of his own accord as soon as he heard of it that night . . . on being raised up I fainted. When revived Phil was holding me in his arms with his eyes streaming with tears."[82]

Jeff made a dramatic and courageous admission for the time: "Slavery gave me a disgust to the whole system and made me an abolitionist. I had slave companions of my age. . . . Little Phil (John Jupiter), Amon, Philip Evans, a year or two older than myself, small, active, intelligent, much of a humor, were my companions in childhood and friends through life."[83]

***

After Jefferson died, and Jeff's duties as editor and executor of his estate were nearly completed, his major preoccupation became Virginia politics. His wife, Jane, echoed Thomas Jefferson's distaste for politics and was thrown "into a great wrath."[84] Jane's mother feared that a political race would "occupy more of [Jeff's] time than his circumstances and private business [would] admit of with safety."[85] Anne Maury, who visited Edgehill around this time, considered it a pity that "he should desire to be a politician," when his talents lay elsewhere. According to her, he was an "excellent farmer," a very "affectionate parent," and a "lively, good hearted man" generally.[86] As one historian explains, "Like his father and his grandfather before him, Thomas Jefferson Randolph aspired to a career in public service, but the women in his family greeted the prospect with dread."[87] "I [am] in despair," Patsy lamented. "It's a paltry business."[88]

To a large extent, the circumstances of the Randolph family made a political career impossible. The deaths of his father and grandfather, the burden of their debts, and the pressing family responsibilities of providing for his own children made politics a luxury. Yet, civic duty and politics ran in his blood, coupled with a gnawing political issue in the back of his mind: slavery. In 1831, Jeff allayed his wife's qualms, winning a seat in the House of Delegates. In Jeff's *Memoirs* he wrote, "I became a member of the legislature for my County in 1832. I was too poor to think of a career public life, for Virginians after a life of public service had always left office with clean and empty hands. It was not then considered meritorious to amass vast fortunes from public service. It was not deemed a merit, but common honesty for men to be as honest in public his private life. My previous habits of life have prepared me for it."

Soon, he became involved in two monumental political issues—emancipation and nullification. "His stand on these issues," wrote one historian, "as well as his alignment with the democratic elements of western Virginia, would alienate most of his fellow planters in Albemarle. His stand on the burning issues of the time was clearly motivated by his determination to champion the ideas of his grandfather, as he understood them. The espousal of these principles of an earlier day would cause him to stand forth as a political heretic in the society in which he had been born. Certainly Randolph was sincere in his convictions. He must have been, for the course he chose was the least expedient he might have pursued to achieve his ambition of becoming a power in Virginia politics.[89]

That same year, Jeff proposed a gradual emancipation of Virginia's slaves. He tried to realize a viable solution to the problem that had tormented his grandfather most of his life.

Jeff's first term in the House was historically important because he proposed a national plan of emancipation of slaves. Six feet four, with massive shoulders, the thirty-nine-year-old Jeff was still deeply devoted to his grandfather's political legacy. Jeff suggested that a law be passed that the children of all female slaves who were born in Virginia on or after the Fourth of July, 1840 would become the property of the commonwealth, but would eventually be freed to leave the state.[90] Jeff explained: "I felt no hesitation in bringing forward a proposition for the gradual abolition of slavery upon the first rate principal. It ostracized me for life beyond the limits of my native County. That in my democratic principles, that is attachment to popular liberty, these majorities were restricted to minorities and individuals protected by constitutional law."[91]

From the moment of his election, Jeff's desire for the abolition of slaves grew. In 1834 he visited Kentucky and Missouri, encountering a fervent anti-slavery climate. "All looked," he said, "to the first rate plan is given the least shock to society in the gradual and imperceptible introduction of the slave to his freedom and the gradual establishment of the race to themselves and some congenial climb."[92] Jeff's abolitionist views were met with a smattering of sympathetic support, but significant visceral opposition in Virginia. Jeff recalled, "My relationship to Mr. Jefferson gave me many empty civilities, but many bitter enemies and detractors."[93]

For advice in developing an emancipation plan, Jeff conferred with Edward Coles, a native of Albemarle County.[94] As a young man, Coles had urged Thomas Jefferson to lead an emancipation movement in Virginia. Jefferson deferred, urging the younger generation to take that mantle. Coles saw little hope of success of emancipation in Virginia. Instead, he took his slaves to Illinois and freed them. A few years later, he was elected governor of Illinois and opposed all who wanted to make Illinois a slave state. Coles ultimately supported Jeff's slavery plan.[95]

As a formal emancipation proposal, Jeff's plan appeared fairly anemic. He suggested no measures to prohibit the sale of slaves in the South, but the plan had its fervent supporters at the beginning. Antislavery supporters joined Jeff with their denunciations of slavery. George I. Williams of Harrison County warned his listeners that "the poorest tattered Negro, who tills the planter's field . . . feels within him that spark which emanates from the deity—the innate longing for liberty." Samuel McDowell Moore of Rockbridge declared that liberty was one of those inalienable rights belonging "to the whole human race."[96] Charles Faulkner of Berkeley County feared that western Virginia would become an outlet of the Tidewater's increasing slave population driving out "our native, substantial, independent yeomanry . . . distinguished for an elevated love of freedom—for morality, virtue, frugality and independence." Eloquently, he cried out, "Sir, tax our lands—vilify our country . . . but spare us, I implore you, spare us the curse of slavery!"[97]

Trying to compromise, Jeff recognized the legal property rights of slaveholders, but argued that the state had the right to remove any property deemed injurious to society. As one writer has concluded, "But economic considerations cannot be overlooked in Jeff's vote. His planting operations were not at the time very profitable and thus did not threaten his antislavery inclinations. His chief political support came from the farmers, who would have profited by the deportation of slaves."[98]

Optimistic at the end of the slavery debate that "a revolution has commenced which cannot go backward," Jeff seemed to prove his prediction was right when he won reelection by a wide margin. Joining Jeff's emancipation petition, William Henry Roane, a grandson of Patrick Henry, submitted a petition calling for emancipation as a topic the legislature should discuss. A violent debate erupted. Those opposed to emancipation suggested that the mere idea of freedom for the slaves would foment an uprising more violent than Nat Turner's bloody rampage.[99]

Clearly, Turner's bloody slave revolt was still fresh on their minds. Alan Pell Crawford tells the story: "On the night of August 21, 1831, near the town of Jerusalem in Southampton County, Virginia, 140 miles southeast of Charlottesville, a slave named Nat Turner and several cohorts broke into the home of Joseph Travis, Turner's owner, murdering Travis and his family in their sleep." Over the next thirty-six hours, Turner and some sixty to eighty followers—"a parcel of blood-thirsty wolves," according to the *Richmond Enquirer*—"stabbed, shot, and beat to death nearly sixty whites, including twenty-four children." Over the next six weeks, as Turner eluded capture, terror gripped the Virginia countryside. "In a wave of retribution, some two hundred blacks were murdered by white militia and mobs. Some of the slaughtered blacks' severed heads were displayed on poles as a warning to would-be insurrectionists."[100]

Indeed, Nat Turner's bloody slavery revolt had stirred fear, including in Jeff Randolph's wife, Jane. As for many Virginia women, fear of slave riots had all but vanished from her mind when Turner's eruption occurred. The violent uprising now injected Jane, and others, with great anxiety "to the most agonizing degree."[101] It even led Jane and Jefferson's granddaughters to talk of leaving Virginia, throwing off the problem of slavery completely. But in the end, they could not bear to leave their beloved state.[102]

Jeff presented his own plan of emancipation to the legislature: he recommended that beginning on July 4, 1840, all the slaves born in Virginia would become the property of the state government when they reached maturity. The slaves would be hired out to earn the cost of transporting them "beyond the limits of the United States." It was far from a complete solution to slavery—but it was a start. Jeff's speech explaining his plan was not well received. Later, he would confess that when he rose to speak, his words had vanished "as mist before the sun." Unfortunately, he had inherited Thomas Jefferson's shortcomings as a dynamic orator. He meekly read Thomas Jefferson's letter to Edward Coles—proof of his wish for abolition of the institute of slavery.[103]

The race war that had resulted in the murders of every white person in the French half of Santo Domingo during Jefferson's presidency was, perhaps, a gruesome reminder for the Virginia legislators. The eastern delegates ridiculed Jeff's plan, calling it "monstrous and unconstitutional." They claimed Virginia's slaves were "as happy a laboring class as exists upon the habitable globe." Finally, committee chairman William Broadnax intervened, concluding there was little chance the committee would approve Jeff's bold emancipation plan. But Broadnax disagreed with those delegates who blocked slavery as a topic of discussion. He argued that a political solution to slavery was already being debated in all parts of the civilized world.[104] Great Britain deliberated the problem of slavery in her West Indies colonies—a discussion that ended in the slaves' peaceful liberation.[105] Senator Broadnax was one of Jeff's most ardent supporters, firmly believing that slavery was immoral and a "transcendent evil." If anything was to be done about it, he argued, it had to meet three conditions: freed slaves had to be removed from Virginia; private property rights had to be upheld; and, no slave could be freed without "ample compensation" to the owner. Unfortunately, in Broadnax's view, Jeff's plan did not meet his criteria, so he dismissed it as "nauseous to the palate."[106]

With little debate, the committee's report declared it was "inexpedient" at this time to enact legislation for abolition. The report was sustained by a vote of 67–60, with Jeff voting against it, amazed by the close vote. A shift of opinion by four delegates would have defeated the measure.[107] Watching this reversal of his hopes, Jeff became more discouraged. Uncharacteristically, he exploded in a speech that was printed in the *Richmond Enquirer*. Without any hope of freedom, he argued, Virginia's slaves may revolt on a scale far larger than Nat Turner's:

> There is one circumstance to which we are to look as inevitable in the fullness of time; a dissolution of this union. God grant that it may not happen in our time, or that of our children; but sir, it must come, sooner or later; and when it does come, border war follows it . . . this [slave) population, tampering with it in your bosom, when your citizens shall march to repel the invader, their families butchered and their homes destroyed in their rear .

. . Suppose an invasion by your enemy, in part with black troops . . . burning with enthusiasm for the liberation of their race . . . Is it not wise policy, while the evil is still within our grasp, when we can gradually obliterate it . . . to prepare way for better prospects to our children.[108]

For his abolitionist views, Jeff went down to electoral defeat in April 1833. His opponents sought revenge for his unpopular views, defeating him by sixty votes. He was "vilely traduced on the court-green as being guilty of every base act that man could be accused of," his wife, Jane, said.[109]

Disappointed by his political career, worried about the lack of money from his crops, Jeff considered moving his family out of Virginia. Jane, still fearful of a slave rebellion, was eager to move to a state without slavery. But in the end, they could not bring themselves to leave their beloved Virginia. Perhaps the eventual revival of the economy, as well as his political reelection, contributed to his decision. By 1850, in Jeff's successful campaign for election to the state constitutional convention, he declared his continuing angst regarding the issue of slavery: "The conflict in all civilized society is between capital and labor, [which] are probably more blended under our peculiar institutions than in any States without slave labor."[110]

Jeff continued his political career and his clarion call fight for emancipation. He returned to Albemarle County, determined to continue his fight for gradual abolition. He stood for the legislature again, and slavery became the paramount issue in the spring election. Again, Jane was "thrown into despair" upon learning that her husband had announced his intention of standing for reelection. What a "Mad Man," wrote Peggy Nicholas, but she advised Jane to acquiesce with "a good grace," as anything which she could say would "have no other effect than to worry him."[111] Jeff defeated a former US congressman who ran against him on a proslavery platform, but Jeff soon grew discouraged with his legislative defeats and abandoned his emancipation campaign.[112] Between 1831 and 1843, he was successfully elected six times to the General Assembly. Yet, a year later, Jeff was at an end with politics, writing to Jane, "I wish to God I was quietly by my own fireside with you. I am worried out with this business."[113]

Soon, enraged Virginians would not tolerate a discussion of how to eliminate slavery. Jeff knew that "the hope for a rational debate about how to solve Virginia's—and the nation's—most grievous problem had vanished forever.[114]

And now, as Thomas Jefferson had predicted forty years before, a devastating civil war over slavery would follow.

16

BOSTON TO LONDON[1]

[Joseph] Coolidge was the man who at last succeeded where so many others had failed. It was as Mrs. Joseph Coolidge that Ellen Randolph was finally persuaded to leave Olympus for that other intellectual mecca, Boston, Massachusetts.

—**Elizabeth Langhorne,** *Monticello* **(1987)**

Whatever her private trials, successes, or failures, when Ellen Randolph was young and lived with her grandfather at Monticello, she continued to charm visitors, "particularly those enlightened ones from the cooler northern climes."[2] Ellen's glowing reputation had, in fact, spread to Boston: "A young visitor, Elliot Cresson, shown around Monticello by Ellen, was absolutely overcome by her charm but felt it would be "insane to venture" a proposal. A sort of quiet self-possession had been the fruit, after all, of that rigorous struggle with her own restlessness. It was not to be long before another visitor, Joseph Coolidge, was to find himself considerably bolder."[3]

When Ellen married Bostonian Joseph Coolidge in 1825, she left behind her secluded life on a Virginia plantation for a bustling city. Now a part of a prominent and prosperous mercantile family, Ellen assumed the role of wife to a successful businessman with trade interests around the globe. When she moved to Boston, the city had tripled in size since the Revolution, with an active cultural life and thriving economy. The 1830 federal census found more than sixty thousand people living in Boston, making it the fourth largest city in the United

States (after New York, Baltimore, and Philadelphia), emerging as a modern urban center.[4] Although Ellen's early impressions of Boston were not favorable, she embraced Joseph's urbane social circle, living in a three-story Federal-style house among their elite neighbors. Ellen made a warm home for her husband and growing family, choosing "unostentatious elegance" and domestic comfort. Indeed, Boston's affluence impressed her brother, Jeff, when he visited Ellen for the first time. Jeff reported to his wife that he had washed his feet "in a plain basin that cost $30 [and] had the water deep enough I might have taken a swim."[5] Although Ellen missed her home and family, she sometimes wished that Bostonians "were a little more sentimental & roma[ntic]," like Virginians. Her letters depicted Bostonians as hardworking, well educated and devoid of one thing: slave labor. In contrast to Virginia, the Massachusetts Supreme Court had abolished slavery decades earlier.[6]

Before Ellen's departure to Boston, the slave John ("Johnny") Hemings, made her an elegant wooden writing desk as a wedding present from her grandfather. Hemings was a cabinetmaker of remarkable skill. Tragically, the writing desk, along with most of Ellen's personal belongings, was lost at sea when the boat carrying them caught fire, burned, and sank into the Atlantic. Ellen lost everything she had packed to bring from Monticello to Boston, including the handcrafted writing desk. Jefferson shared Ellen's anguish at the distressing news: "The documents of your childhood, your letters, correspondencies, notes, books, &c. &c., all gone! And your life cut in two, as it were, and a new one to begin, without any records of the former."[7] Jefferson told Ellen that Johnny had also taken the news badly: "John Hemmings was the first who brought me the news... He was au desespoir! That beautiful writing desk he had taken so much pains to make for you! Everything else seemed as nothing in his eye, and that loss was everything. Virgil could not have been more afflicted had his Aeneid fallen a prey to the flames. I asked him if he could not replace it by making another? No. His eyesight had failed him too much, and his recollection of it was too imperfect."[8]

Patsy added, "The writing desk Johnny insists upon it that he has no longer eye sight to execute. He actually wept when he heard of the loss."[9] Johnny's eyesight was indeed failing—three years earlier Jefferson had given him a pair of spectacles he had made himself.[10] Besides Ellen's desk, Johnny had once built an elegant carriage to Thomas Jefferson's precise specifications. He also repaired and handcrafted Polly's harpsichord after her death. When plagued by agonizing arthritis in his lower back while at Poplar Forest, Jefferson sent for his "siesta chair" from Monticello, handcrafted by Johnny Hemings.

Ellen once wrote that Johnny was a favorite of hers. The loving sentiment seemed to be reciprocated.[11] As one historian has concluded, "The lost wedding gift symbolizes the personal connection Hemmings felt for the Jeffersons."[12] As a valuable replacement, Jefferson sent Joseph Coolidge the writing desk on which he had composed the Declaration of Independence. According to the story, the desk, or "writing box" as Jefferson called it, was crafted from Jefferson's own design by one of Philadelphia's most respected cabinetmakers, Benjamin Randolph. "Mr. Coolidge must do me the favor of accepting this," Jefferson wrote.[13] For Coolidge, it was far superior to any dowry that Jefferson could afford. Jefferson believed that one day, the desk may be "carried in the procession of our nation's birthday, as the relics of the saints are in those of the church."[14] That, wrote one historian, "was the comment of a man who was well aware of his own place in history."[15]

With Ellen in Boston, her sisters back at Monticello started to ignore "the cost-conscious Jeff Randolph's protests" against what he considered extravagant spending. For example, they ordered a new pianoforte, selected by the Coolidges in Boston, which Jeff insisted the family could not afford. When it arrived, Jefferson was so impressed with "the cleanness and sweetness of the tone," Patsy told Joseph Coolidge, that as soon as the "lottery" money came in, he planned to buy one of his own.[16] "How his crippled fingers would ever play the pianoforte, Jefferson failed to say," one author wrote. "That he seems to have thought he could accomplish such a feat is further evidence of the man's remarkable sense of possibility, which, while it might from time to time have wavered, would persist to the end."[17]

Yet, Ellen constantly worried about her family's continued economic plight back home. At the bottom of one of her letters, she added, "My sisters are losing heart . . . poverty was approaching with withering strides. The first great evil is sin, the second disease, the third pecuniary difficulty. My sisters wish to work for their own support, but [they are] the granddaughters of Thomas Jefferson."[18]

When her family left Monticello for the final time, Ellen advised her sister to be stalwart and to reject martyrdom:

> The most disinterested and self-sacrificing people are sometimes the least able to deny themselves the dangerous gratification of musing & melancholy recollection. they have relinquished so much, they think, done so much, and suffered so much, that it is hard they should be refused the luxury of regret. but the cup which they cannot dash from their lips is drugged; although the best feelings of our nature, our best affections are mingled in the draught, it is only the more alluring, for being so compounded. drink deeply and often if you would become useless, enervated, repining, unfit for the situation in which you are placed & incapable of its duties.[19]

One historian notes that hard economic times "had doomed most Virginians, men and women alike, to that which they dreaded: a life of dull work and limited pleasure. A life of independence, comfort, and ease presupposed leisure, yet the kind of independent life nineteenth-century Virginians desired precluded the hard work . . . necessary to procure that rest." Even Ellen sometimes "felt like a weary thing to live on with so many cares and so few enjoyments, but," she added, "I presume this is the history of more lives than mine . . . It is a poor consolation to be compelled to acknowledge that we are ourselves far more to blame than our destinies."[20] One scholar concludes, "There is more than a little irony in the fact that the first generation of Americans to commit themselves to the pursuit of happiness would find so much sadness instead."[21]

Ellen's marriage and her arrival in Boston did not deprive Jefferson of her attention during the last year of his life. Frequent gifts and constant letters passed between them. Their strong shared emotional bond was palpable in Ellen's first letter from Boston. She wrote to Jefferson, "One of my first cares, is . . . to thank you for all the kindness I have received from you, & for all the affection you have shewn me, from my infancy & childhood, throughout the course of my maturer years: the only return I can make is by gratitude the deepest and most enduring and love the most devoted; and although removed by fortune to a distance from you, yet my heart is always with you."[22]

With her mother's encouragement, Ellen had chosen the traditional marriage path, reluctantly relocating to her husband's home state of Massachusetts. Patsy admired her son-in-law's intelligence and impeccable manners, rejoicing that Ellen, at age twenty-nine, had finally found such a loving and promising husband. Although Ellen and Joseph moved permanently to Boston, they maintained close ties with their Monticello family, but did not return for a visit until after Jefferson's death. One of the reasons was Coolidge's dislike of Ellen's father, Thomas Mann Randolph. Joseph had met Randolph briefly during two short visits to Monticello, finding him erratic, moody, and unstable. He thought that Randolph possessed none of the good qualities that he attributed to his brother-in-law, Jeff—stability, forbearance, frugality, and undying loyalty to his family.

Knowing her Virginia family missed Ellen dearly, Joseph wrote often to Patsy and Thomas Jefferson. In one letter, he said that the journey to Boston had given Ellen "an idea of prosperity and improvement, such as I fear our Southern States cannot hope for, whilst the canker of slavery eats into their hearts and diseases the whole body by this ulcer at the core."[23] Still, Jefferson missed his granddaughter dearly and longed for Ellen's company: "We did not know, until you left us," he wrote to her, "what a void it would make in our family . . . I have no doubt that you will find . . . the state of society there more congenial with your mind, than the rustic scenes you have left: although these do not want their points of endearment."[24]

After Ellen's marriage at Monticello, the newlyweds traveled through upstate New York, Vermont, Connecticut, and Massachusetts.[25] Eventually, they arrived at Joseph's parents' home on affluent Bowdoin Square. In her first months settling into Boston, Ellen had trouble adjusting to her cold and wet new city, a far cry from her quiet and bucolic Monticello mountaintop. "I do not think that she is so much pleased with Boston or its inhabitants, as I thought she would have been," Joseph admitted to Jefferson. Indeed, Ellen seemed extremely homesick for Monticello, her sisters, and her mother. "Like every Virginian who has left home," one author commented, "she was always to feel herself an exile, a happy and fortunate one, perhaps, but an exile nonetheless."[26]

Ellen told her mother of Boston's "nabobs, one of whose incomes, taken separately, would restore tranquility to my dearest friends, & brighten the hopes of so many loved ones."[27] She lamented Boston's seeming inequality of wealth, class, and station but noted "that these very persons have made themselves what they are & risen superior to all the obstacles which poverty & obscurity & original insignificance would accumulate in their paths."[28] Ellen held out hope "that the younger branches of my family may one day achieve the fortunes to which they were born."[29]

Although Ellen had been raised, for the most part, as a Deist, she now turned toward a deep sense of faith to protect her mother, sisters, and ailing grandfather back home:[30] "For those who from sex or age are condemned to a passive endurance of whatever may happen, I cannot help hoping that brighter days are in store . . . for I feel a stronger confidence in the doctrine of an immediate providence, & greater trust in its interference with the affairs of men than I think I used to."[31]

When her mother finally visited Ellen, Joseph made Patsy feel loved and welcomed. He knew how important this woman was to his wife. However, he was glad that Tom Randolph had not traveled with her. The sullen Randolph had been more than Coolidge could take. Coolidge was a businessman with a reputation in Beacon Hill for respectability, coupled with a worthy family lineage.[32] The idea of the volatile Randolph's arrival, he told Nicholas Trist, made him "shudder. The object should be to keep Him from Monticello . . . and Her here with her children," he said.[33] Coolidge's enmity toward Randolph was evident again when he wrote to Ellen's brother, Jeff: "[Patsy] submits implicitly to what is proposed [to her], excepting that she wishes to pledge herself that, at a future day, [Randolph] shall again be received at Monticello, and that she shall, even now, contribute to his support: against such a pledge I have earnestly protested!"[34]

Coolidge's resentment was not unfounded. Thomas Mann Randolph continued to irrationally rail against even his own son, forbidding his children from ever visiting Jeff and their cousins at Tufton. The "very moment they cross the threshold" of his son's house, Randolph threatened, he would hold Patsy responsible and take the children from her.[35]

But Randolph only knew of Patsy's and the children's plans to travel to Washington, and then return soon. She had not told him of her plans for Boston.

After a few weeks in Washington, however, Patsy failed to return to Monticello, and traveled by train to Boston, where she lived for the next two years. Ultimately, Patsy was unhappy in Boston, the result not only of her financial worries but her deep grief and depression over her father's death. "I have lost all sensibility to pleasure or pain," she told Jeff, adding that she could no longer "comprehend the possibility of better days."[36]

Had Patsy remained in Virginia, she would have been even more disheartened. Four months after Thomas Jefferson's death, Jeff announced in the *Charlottesville Central Gazette* an auction at Monticello of "the whole of the residue of the personal estate of Thomas Jefferson, dec, consisting of 130 VALUABLE NEGROES, Stock, Crop, &c. Household and Kitchen Furniture." He went on to claim that the slaves were the most valuable ever offered at one time in the state.[37] Patsy could not have endured this anguishing scene.

At the time of her grandfather's grave illness, Ellen was on her way from Boston to Charlottesville when the devastating news of Jefferson's death reached her in New York.[38] Unfortunately, she arrived at Monticello long after Jefferson's funeral was over. To Ellen, Monticello without Jefferson seemed like a lonely, foreign land. "He was gone," she wrote biographer Henry Randall many years later, recalling the painful memory of her return visit. "His place was empty. I visited his grave, but the whole house at Monticello, with its large apartments and lofty ceilings, appeared to me one vast monument."[39] Ellen half-expected her loving grandfather to appear one last time for a final game of chess, one last walk through his pruned garden. "I wandered about the vacant rooms as if I were looking for him," she wrote. "Had I not seen him there all the best years of my life? . . . I passed hours in his chamber. It was just as he had left it. There was the bed on which he had slept for so many years—the chair in which, when I entered the room, I always found him sitting—articles of dress still in their places."[40] She longed for days gone by with her grandfather:

> For days I started at what seemed the sound of his step or his voice, and caught myself listening for both. In the dining room where, in winter, we passed a good deal of time, there was the low arm chair which he always occupied by the fireside, with

his little round table still standing as when it held his book or his candle. . . . In the tea-room was the sofa where, in summer, I had so often sat by his side—In the large parlor, with its parquet floor, stood the Campeachy chair . . . where, in the shady twilight, I was used to see him resting. In the great Hall, with its large glass doors, where, in bad weather, he liked to walk, how much I liked to walk with him!—Everything told of him. An invisible presence seemed everywhere to preside![41]

"Finally she left the house," one writer commented, "and the estate, never to return. Her grandfather lived, for her, in her heart and mind."[42]

When she returned to Massachusetts, Ellen bemoaned how foreign her lifestyle and culture in Boston seemed from what she had known in Virginia. She wrote her mother that she lived in "perpetual fear of violating some established rule, of sinning against the laws of propriety as they are understood here. . . . I am sure I often do or say things which I ought not, & it grieves me the more that Joseph . . . should now be evidently uneasy as to the impression I make upon his family & friends, & think it often necessary to check or advise me. . . . I weigh every word before I utter it, curb every sally of imagination, regulate my very countenance, & try to look, speak, walk, & sit just as I ought to do."[43] Perhaps she felt herself unprepared for her many duties as a wife and mother in harsh Boston. Her southern upbringing and genteel manners stood in marked contrast to the direct and brusque nature of Bostonians.[44] "I never knew how deficient I was in useful qualities until called on for the exercise of them," she wrote. "I am constantly trying by the sacrifice of my brilliant qualities to acquire those of ordinary usefulness."[45] She attributed her "present uneasiness" to her "unfortunate education . . . I was brought up far too tenderly, rendered unfit for an ordinary destiny . . . Nature gave me a timid and affectionate temper, great flexibility and docility, quick feelings, & a lively imagination."[46] Though as a child, Ellen was "a darling with all," as an adult, she castigated herself as "a sluggard, fond of ease, averse to any employment which does not happen to fall in with the humor of the moment."[47]

How at odds this tendency in contrast with her grandfather's constant energy and motion. Jefferson had always advised Ellen and Jeff that indolence was to be avoided. When the mind was idle—"snaggle-toothed laziness"—one's "being becomes a burthen, and every object about us loathsome." Furthermore, idleness, Jefferson had warned, "begets ennui," and "ennui the hypochondria."[48] Showing inexhaustible energy even in his old age, Jefferson's vigor was what one writer would refer to as "the power of doing whatever we do at all, with the same spirit and promptness which we exercise in doing what is agreeable to us."[49] It was Jefferson's dynamism, one historian argues, "that [Ellen had] lacked as a child, but she could make up for her deficiency by giving it to her children."[50] Ellen resolved, "I will try to give my children the habit of energy, for it should be a habit, not an occasional impulse, so should be all our virtues. So is all Virtue, for nothing deserves the name which is not steady in its course."[51]

Ellen would later attribute her "fond of ease" to Virginia's peculiar institution: slavery. Northern girls, she declared, picked up after themselves, whereas southern girls knew that their servants would put away their belongings for them.[52] She admonished her son, "Your success in life will depend as much upon the habits formed in youth as in your natural talents and disposition. How many men of fine and excellent dispositions are lost for want of the early habits of self command and industry."[53] Such good habits, Patsy told Ellen, "are more rarely to be met with to the south than they ought to be. the number of slaves make people indolent and idle, and consequently encourage a habit of self indulgence as ruinous to the moral character as to one's fortune."[54]

Ellen eventually acclimated to her new environs. She impressed her Boston neighbors as well as dignitaries, conversing with "fluency, cheerfulness and a visible interest upon almost any topic."[55] John Adams, a shrewd judge of character, assured Thomas Jefferson that "Mrs. C [Coolidge] deserves all the high praises I have constantly heard concerning her. She entertained me with accounts of your sentiments of human life, which accorded so perfectly with mine that it gave me great delight."[56] Ellen "commanded in conversation," one historian noted, "with delicacy and good deportment in equal portions. [Ellen was] armed with all the qualities of female competence that her exacting grandfather wished for . . . in the young woman he . . . regarded as the principal heir to his tastes and affections."[57]

Joseph was equally adroit in social conversation, especially when it came to the lucrative, foreign trade business.[58]

As Ellen grew accustomed to living in Boston, there were some things she missed terribly, namely, southern "comfort" food. The New England diet of fish, pudding, and potatoes paled in comparison to the sumptuous French dinners at Monticello.[59] Furthermore, books were rarely discussed in her new social environment, the weather was frigid and harsh, and her toilette proved difficult to manage without the luxury of a personal servant. Perhaps most frustrating to Ellen was the fact that her grandfather's politics (anti-Federalism) were completely and "utterly misunderstood" in her new setting.[60] Yet, Joseph held out hope for "making [Ellen] something of a Yankee."[61] He promised Patsy that Ellen's view of the North would improve once she toured the city's magnificent buildings and museums and used Harvard's impressive library. Patsy tried to assuage her daughter from afar, persuading Ellen to acclimate to her new city. She sent Ellen a cookbook, *Le Cuisinier Royal*, with five pages of handwritten notes and favorite recipes. Patsy also enclosed two thick, fur capes that the explorer Meriwether Lewis had given Patsy after his expedition, to warm Ellen in the "tremendous winters of [her] new country."[62]

By November 1825, the couple had established themselves in a fine house on Sumner Street, on the wealthy side of Beacon Hill. Joseph entered into a mercantile partnership with his cousin Thomas Bulfinch, and the following spring Ellen gave birth to their first child, a daughter they named Ellen. Four months later, the senior Ellen's sister Cornelia came to visit and help with Ellen's newborn.[63]

For seven years after Jefferson's death, Ellen and Joseph were closely involved in the settlement of his estate. In particular, the Coolidges managed the sale of Monticello's magnificent art collection. Joseph believed that the art market in Boston offered the top prices, and arranged for Jefferson's art to be viewed at the prestigious Boston Athenzum. The near insolvency of Jefferson's estate also meant that Patsy and her children—seven in all, ranging from ages eight to twenty-seven—were without a primary home. They shuffled between the Coolidges in Boston and Jeff in Virginia.

Meanwhile, while Ellen mourned the loss of her grandfather, her own family was growing. Over the next six years, she gave birth to six children, including a set of twins, finding herself confined to the nursery. She yearned for the assistance of one of her faithful servants from Monticello—Sally Cottrell—rather than the brassy Boston maids Joseph had hired. Visits from her family buoyed Ellen, particularly those from Patsy and her sisters. The two single sisters who were closest to her, Mary and Cornelia, became valued confidants and nurses to her children. The two sisters also became involved in Boston society, perhaps looking for suitable husbands. They spent months living either with the Coolidges or in a rented house in the countryside of Cambridge.[64]

Ellen's growing family presented another challenge for Joseph: money. When he found himself still relying on his wealthy parents for financial support, he chose a remedy that would turn out to be one of the wisest choices of his life. He joined a lucrative business and overseas trading firm. In 1832, against his mother's wishes, Joseph went to work for Russell & Company, one of three Boston firms that maintained a branch office in China. His success over the years there led to his travel to Bombay in 1833, where he took part in "the great trade in Opium & Cotton grown in that country and sent to China for sale on consignment." "My object," he told his parents, "is to become acquainted with the Native Merchants, and to take advantage of peculiarly favorable circumstances in securing a portion of this valuable trade to the House of Russell & Co." Joseph carried with him "large funds & unqualified letters from Houqua, and the House."[65]

Hardworking and diligent, a year later Joseph became a full partner at Russell & Company, along with John Forbes and John Green, at the invitation of Augustine Heard, a retired shipmaster who was a senior partner with the firm. Heard left China after securing the partnership and returned to Boston with a promise to Joseph to carefully tend to Ellen and their family while Joseph remained overseas. Heard became a favorite with Ellen, who hoped that he might be a suitable husband for one of her sisters. Heard helped manage and direct the Coolidges' move into a sprawling new house on Bowdoin Square that Joseph's grandfather had owned. Ellen sent a description of her spacious new house to her sister Virginia:

> It is rather a gloomy situation on the north side of the hill and at a distance from the cheerful & more fashionable part of the

town, but I prefer it greatly, notwithstanding these disadvantages, to any other house I could have commanded. All my early associations are in favor of space and I so much dislike the cramped and confined houses, with their narrow, dark entries and steep interminable stairs, which it is now the fashion to build in Boston that I rejoice in the prospect of elbow room for myself and play room for my children.[66]

The year after her relocation to Boston, Ellen sat for her first portrait by the Boston artist Francis Alexander. In a letter to Heard, she expressed worry about her portrait: "I wish the hundred dollars you will have to pay on Joseph's account for this ugly daub were appropriated to some better purpose. . . . [As] far as I can see my presentiment on the subject is as gloomy as the ill-favored countenance which, I am told, is to be worked up into a resemblance of my own. I hope it will take a great deal of work to bring the likeness about, for a more faded, haggard and care-worn face I have seldom seen."[67]

Ellen's elegant portrait shows a striking resemblance to her grandfather, and as one historian has commented, "While Ellen was often self-deprecating, especially in correspondence with her family and Heard, her description of Alexander's portrait hints at the growing feelings of despair and exhaustion that arose during Joseph's 'dreaded absences.'"[68]

Ellen was waiting for Patsy's return in 1836 after a summer spent at Edgehill, when she received devastating news: Patsy had died suddenly. It was a crushing, emotional loss for Ellen, compounded by the fact that Joseph was out of the country at the time. Ellen had been particularly close with her mother and was probably Patsy's favored child. As her sister Virginia had described their mother, "She is *our sun* and when she thinks how many live in her *light & warmth* she must guard [her health] carefully."[69] Patsy had been Ellen's last thread to her grandfather's memory.

Months earlier, Jeff had written a sobering letter to Ellen, detailing Patsy's fragile health. Not long after her children had gathered at her bedside during some illness, Patsy's health improved dramatically. Jeff had informed his wife that his mother's voice was stronger and her pulse better, though she still had a fever, lacked an appetite, and was "excessively weak" overall. Her forehead appeared wrinkled in a way that reminded him of his grandfather's "last moments." Days later, Jeff reported that Patsy's fever had diminished, but he believed that her "age and debility" would prevent a full recovery.[70] He was right—six months later Patsy would be dead.

Patsy's death struck the family as hard as Jefferson's had ten years before. A stricken daughter, Virginia, described the "bitter . . . pangs of parting" to her husband Nicholas.[71] Patsy's youngest daughter collapsed when she heard of her mother's death. She and Nicholas cried for half an hour, holding each other. Her youngest son, eighteen-year-old George, was jolted when Jeff told him the grim news. "Even now, I can hardly realize that I am without a mother," he wrote, two days after receiving Jeff's letter. "So accustomed am I to think of her that there is a blank in my very existence which I can't fill up."[72] Ellen never suspected that her mother's "sweet parting smile" at the Boston train station the previous spring would be her last of the one she said had "loved me better than any other being on earth. No other love is like that of a mother."[73]

Surprisingly, in a decade when newspaper obituaries touted the legacies and family heritage of famous women, Patsy's death notice bordered on the perfunctory: "Died, suddenly, at the residence of Thomas Jefferson Randolph . . . Mrs. Martha Randolph, the widow of the late Thomas Mann Randolph, and the daughter of Thomas Jefferson," began the curt, two-sentence obituary of the Richmond newspaper. "The character of this distinguished lady must be drawn by an abler hand than ours."[74] There was nothing more.

Sadly, Joseph was still absent when his own mother died the following February, but he returned to Boston in October 1837. He had planned to move himself and Ellen, if not the entire family, to London. But the economic depression in Europe and America, which caught him "wholly ignorant," delayed their travel plans.[75] Joseph's plan now was for Ellen to accompany him to China, after a brief stay in London. The Coolidges' youngest son, Thomas, recorded in his *Autobiography*, "In 1839 my parents went to China, my father to take charge of the house of Augustine Heard & Co., and my mother to keep him company, as far as that was possible. No ladies being admitted to Canton, she remained two years at Macao."[76]

Ellen's joy at her husband's return was tempered by the untimely death of her younger brother, Meriwether Lewis Randolph. By this time Ellen was, in her sister Cornelia's words, "broken down" by Boston's climate and by "anxiety & fatigue." Joseph wrote to Jeff that Ellen's "health of body and mind requires, absolutely, rest and change: she is feeble, thin, nervous and worn—the sea, and a new world, will do more for her than medicine." On March 24, 1838 Joseph left for London ahead of Ellen, carrying the letter of authorization from Augustine Heard to start a new business firm in the case of an emergency.[77]

Two months later, Ellen met Joseph in London for an extended visit, arriving in England at the start of Queen Victoria's new monarchy. During her nine-month stay, Ellen fastidiously kept a detailed diary of her travels abroad as well as her loving memories of when she lived with her grandfather at Monticello. Ellen wrote extensively in her diary of London's docks, theaters, parks, public buildings, and museums as she and Joseph toured and discovered their new city. Because of her famous grandfather, Ellen was admitted into some of London's most privileged social circles, viewing more than four hundred works of art of the Dutch masters. Ellen was permitted exceptional social access, especially for a woman at this time period. "The result," concludes one scholar, "is a rare diary—equal parts travelogue and introspection. Ellen's diary conveys London's atmosphere in the summer of 1838, when a new queen inspired the people."[78]

In her diary, Ellen's tells of her literary discussions with writers such as Samuel Rogers, Thomas Carlyle, and Anna Jameson.[79] She also details the opening of Parliament by the new queen. Ellen recorded in her diary, as well, the songs her grandfather had sung while working in his study. And like her grandfather, Ellen preserved her private letters and journals as gifts to her family—and to us all. One prominent scholar commented on Ellen's illuminating diaries, "In an era when many educated women living in elite households kept diaries, Ellen's still stands apart, distinguished by her remarkable education and perspective. Corresponding regularly with her famous grandfather—even during his presidency—Ellen [had] developed an exceptional aptitude for writing and observation."[80] This same historian writes that Ellen had "also participated in what she called the "feast of reason" at Jefferson's Monticello, where she lived from the age of thirteen until her marriage at twenty-eight. Her diary makes clear that Jefferson was not the sole beneficiary of the intellectual and social riches he gathered around his mountaintop home."[81]

When Ellen arrived in England, sixty-two years had come and gone since Thomas Jefferson had authored the Declaration of Independence. In her diary, Ellen defended Jefferson's view of freedom and independence, and justified the colonies' break from England, even while admitting her love of London. This was Ellen's first trip outside the United States, while Joseph waited for her at Fenton's Hotel on St. James's Street. With their five children safely in the care of trusted family and superior boarding schools, the couple planned to explore London for two months before sailing to China, where Joseph had pressing, lucrative business interests. But their temporary visit to London lasted nearly a year. Ellen kept her fastidious diary from the beginning of her London adventure, filling four full notebooks. Writing on various topics that ranged from London's politics to its thick fog, impressive museums, and theaters, Ellen captured the city that had entered into a brand-new political era. Her diary is "the voice of an exceptional student of the world, a woman whose life and education began in Virginia under the care of her maternal grandfather, Thomas Jefferson."[82]

When Ellen initially left Boston for London, she thought her stay would be so brief that she did not carry any diplomatic letters of introduction or recommendation with her. Thus, her initial activities changed significantly during the course of the year in London. Ellen began by visiting the popular "tourist" sites, such as the Tower of London, the river Thames, the British Museum, and St. Paul's Cathedral, "often with a guidebook in hand." However, the American ambassador in London, Andrew Stevenson, was an old family friend from Virginia. His wife, Sally Coles Stevenson, was also Ellen's distant cousin. Through the Stevensons' social connections they introduced the Coolidges to the exquisite salons of English artists and politicians. Mrs. Stevenson said she was pleased to have "the advantage of introducing [Ellen] to these fastidious people as the grand daughter of our immortal Jefferson. Ellen has rather taken here," she added. "The desire to see Mr Jefferson's Granddaughter extends to all classes— torys & radicals & I whisper around, very like him—educated by him, &c, Sec.[83]

By the spring of 1839, Ellen had transformed from tourist to vising dignitary: "I am beginning to make acquaintance with persons, to see something of society, and as I am a stranger and belong to no particular set or circle, I have gained admittance to several, and can compare the different styles."[84] The Coolidges met with several famous authors and collectors, and even attended the wedding of the Belgian ambassador to the daughter of an American financier.[85] Ellen also witnessed "Queen Victoria's opening of Parliament in February 1839." It was an event for which coveted cards of admittance were rarely obtained by Americans. Ellen became reacquainted with Harriet Martineau, whom she had met in Washington, D.C., and just as she finished reading Anna Jameson's newly published *Winter Studies and Summer Rambles* in Canada, Ellen met the author and went with her to call on the writer Joanna Baillie. Thomas Carlyle welcomed the Coolidges into his home on several occasions; after one such visit, they carried away manuscript pages of his French Revolution as a souvenir.[86]

Mrs. Stevenson introduced Ellen to art collector James Morrison, who accompanied Ellen to exclusive auction rooms and private estates. Joseph and Ellen even dined with the president of the Royal Academy of Art. Ellen paid two visits to the home of another collector, retired coachmaker Benjamin Godfrey Windus, who owned more than two hundred dazzling watercolors and sketches. Admiring great art, as Jefferson had done, became one of Ellen's happiest pastimes while in London. Her diary mentions over four hundred works of art that she and Joseph viewed in more than forty public and private collections. Ellen was fortunate enough, she wrote, that when visiting the studio of the sculptor Sir Francis Chantrey, "the clay model of his bust of Queen Victoria was delivered—still wet—from the queen's sitting for the artist at Buckingham Palace."[87]

Some of the British political debate at the time was familiar to Ellen. Unlike many of her English acquaintances, Ellen had an experience with slavery that was far from abstract. Ellen commented that "though born . . . [and] brought up in a Slave State I was early taught to abhor an odious system."[88] When politics was raised, of course, her grandfather's name was always mentioned. Ellen met both British and American men and women who fondly recalled Jefferson. As one author has noted:

> Lady Charlotte Lindsay, the daughter of Frederick North, Britain's prime minister during the American Revolution,

became an unexpected friend and model. During Ellen's time in London Lady Charlotte was celebrated in the press and society for a letter she sent to her father's biographer in which she recounted her "impressions of my father's private life," including her family's rejoicing when North resigned as prime minister. Ellen invoked Lady Charlotte's example twenty years later when she, too, sought ways to work with a biographer and the press to illuminate Jefferson's character and repair his image by sharing her own anecdotes and observations.[89]

While she was abroad, Ellen still longed for her days in Virginia. British landscapes outside of London reminded her of the Monticello mountaintop. The aroma of the tobacco warehouses brought back memories of her grandfather's tobacco crops in Virginia. Her trip to Scotland, she recorded in her diary, evoked precious memories of the Scotch tunes Thomas Jefferson had sung while working in his private study just below Ellen's room. Certain social connections also prompted Ellen's reminiscences of Patsy's schoolgirl friends from Paris, "women who had become intellectual icons in Patsy's rearing of her own children."[90] But these memories were bittersweet, one author commented: "Ellen transcribes them in her diary, sharpening as they do the keenness with which she still feels Patsy's, as well her grandfather's, absence. When Ellen was nineteen her mother had written, 'Ellen fulfills the promises of her childhood she is a nurse to me in sickness a friend and companion in health and to her grand Father "the immediate jewel of his soul."[91]

As another author has explained: "It was only after she had arrived in England and had the luxury to reflect on her life that Ellen found herself assuming her mother's role as matriarch while fully mourning her death . . . In spite of tiring of the task of keeping a diary, Ellen continued the habits of her youth by putting pen to paper to record news large and small for those she held dear and from whom she was absent."[92]

Ellen's journey to London marked the beginning of nearly ten years of constant travel for her and the family. Ellen, Joseph, and their son Thomas Jefferson Coolidge arrived back in Boston in 1839. Weeks later, Ellen and Joseph departed again, sailing directly for Canton. As noted previously, however, Chinese regulations mandated that Ellen live in the Portuguese settlement at Macao. She only saw Joseph a few times during her entire eighteen-month-stay.[93]

With Augustine Heard as their chaperone, Thomas Coolidge and his three brothers also set sail in 1839 to Geneva, where Ellen had enrolled them in Alphonse Briquet's prestigious boarding school. Ellen and her daughter later joined the four boys in Europe. When Joseph retired from the China trade in 1844, the entire family remained in Europe for another three years. Upon their return to Boston, their sons Joseph and Thomas enrolled at Harvard, following their father's legacy. Another son, Algernon, graduated from Harvard Medical School. And Sidney Coolidge received an honorary master's from Harvard in 1857 for his work and study in astronomy.[94]

By 1850, Ellen and Joseph had moved once again, this time to 12 Pemberton Square on Beacon Hill. In the 1870s they settled into what would be their final home, at 184 Beacon Street in Boston's Back Bay. Tragically, they lost their son Sidney in the bloody Civil War but had gained fifteen grandchildren over thirty years.[95]

During the 1876 celebration of the centennial of the Declaration of Independence, Ellen presented her grandson Thomas Jefferson Coolidge Jr. with one of the few copies of the original Declaration, accompanied by an engraving of Thomas Jefferson's inaugural address.[96] She had found both valuable documents among Jefferson's papers at Monticello. Years later, Ellen's grandson wrote a letter of gratitude to her, providing a vivid portrait of Ellen:

> I remember my Grandmother . . . who was especially kind and fond of me, perhaps on account of my holding the name of her greatly loved and respected grandfather, Mr. Jefferson. Her knowledge was so great and her memory so perfect that when any question arose, whether in history or in literature or about any other subject, if it could not be solved by reference to the encyclopedia, we would be sent to Grandmother Coolidge to get the information required, and it was seldom that she was not able at once to give it. Such another mind I have never known.

In addition to showing this wonderful knowledge, which she had undoubtedly acquired by having lived for many years at Monticello and having often enjoyed the privilege of presiding at Mr. Jefferson's table surrounded by the many distinguished visitors constantly paying their respects to him, she had the charming faculty of endearing to herself her grandchildren and all others who surrounded her.[97]

Ellen's husband, Joseph, passed away in 1879. "My father died after a week of unconsciousness," his son Thomas wrote in his diary, adding a curious comment on his father's faith at the end of his life. Perhaps, it represented Thomas's own secular upbringing: "He was a little over eighty-one years of age. I never heard him express an opinion about his religious feelings and do not know what they were; but I have known several men of distinction who lived to past eighty . . . and I have found them all agnostics as if their faith had become weakened by years, or because they considered it no longer necessary to pretend to a belief they had never held."[98]

Ellen had died peacefully three years earlier. Thomas related the details of his mother's death in his diary: "I met . . . with the greatest misfortune of my life in the death of my mother, who expired April 21, 1876, after a painless struggle with pneumonia." He recalled that "on the twenty-fifth we all attended the funeral at Mount Auburn. She was about eighty years old and had kept her faculties perfectly until the last, taking an interest in her grandchildren and in all that went on in literature and science. I wish I had profited more by her example."[99] Thomas touchingly described his mother's enduring family legacy: "Through a long life, in which she met many tribulations, she showed such gentleness with so much courage, such intelligence, united with such devotion for her husband and children, as to excite in their minds the most unbounded love and admiration. During my whole life I have never met her equal in a woman, whether in cultivations of the mind or in the performance of her duties."[100]

One of Ellen's grandchildren wrote of her death, "Her loss was felt by all, young and old, and she continues to be referred to in the family as a splendid example of her generation."[101]

Ellen Randolph Coolidge, granddaughter of the author of the Declaration of Independence, led a full and complete life that Thomas Jefferson would have been most proud of.

17
A CARRIAGE ACCIDENT

[Thomas Jefferson Randolph] was educated under the eye and care of his illustrious grandfather, and was one of his constant associates when the latter reached the presidency.

—**Eulogy for Jeff Randolph**

Like those of his grandfather, Thomas Jefferson Randolph's final years were marred with tragedy and heartache, beginning with the death of his parents and ending with the devastating aftermath of reconstruction following the Civil War. In between these two sad events, Jeff managed to become the first editor of Jefferson's private papers and opened a school for young women, managed by his wife, Jane, and their three daughters. But with "the failure of the subscription and lottery schemes," one historian has written, "Randolph, as Jefferson's sole executor,' was left with the unenviable task of salvaging something for his family from the wreck of his grandfather's estate."[1] As Jeff wrote to one colleague, Jefferson's "debts were of such magnitude that, considering the depressed price of land in Virginia, the income from an immediate sale of the estate, the bulk of which was in land, would leave his mother 'turned out and pennyless upon the world.'"[2] Even Jeff's wardrobe suggested desolation: "a coat, thin black waistcoat, a pair of thin and another of thick pantaloons, all black."[3]

With Thomas Jefferson's death, the family also became fragmented, with several moving out of state. George Wythe Randolph, Jeff's younger brother, left the Navy to study law at the University of Virginia. Eventually he moved to

Richmond, where he developed a successful law practice. He later served briefly as the Confederacy's secretary of war. Both Jeff and his brother Ben stayed in Albemarle County, where Ben became a doctor. Ben bought 642 acres and inherited eighteen slaves by his marriage to Sally Carter, of the famed King "Carter" family of Virginia. Jeff himself thought briefly about moving out of Virginia, perhaps out West. "Ever since the decline of Virginia agriculture in the 1820's," one writer commented, "Jeff had been entertaining serious ideas of migrating. Probably he was in agreement with another grandson of Jefferson, Francis Eppes, who could not make a success of farming in Virginia. Eppes declared, 'let me squeeze through this scrape and damn me if you will ever find me in another.'" Eppes eventually moved to Florida, departing "right old Virginia." He had never been able to make money in his home state, he complained, nor could anyone "for quite a while to come."[4]

Jeff took complete possession of Edgehill, an estate of 1,500 acres that was home to his own large family of unmarried daughters, the students at the Edgehill Academy, and an enslaved workforce.[5] He continued to live a gentleman farmer's life in Albemarle County, while editing Jefferson's official papers. He wrote of his life in and around Charlottesville around this time, "The country is what we call well inhabited . . . The society is much better than is common in country situations, perhaps there is not a better country society in the U. S. But do not imagine this a Parisian or academical society. It consists of plain, honest and rational neighbors, some of them well informed, and men of reading, all superintending their farms, hospitable and friendly, and speaking nothing but English."[6]

Since Jefferson's death in 1826, many different compilations of his letters and writings have been published. But the first formal editing of his papers was completed by Jeff three years after Jefferson's death, in 1829. When his grandfather died, Jeff was in his early thirties and presented "a striking appearance. He resembled his great grand-father, Peter Jefferson, in the size and frame, and his grandfather, Thomas Jefferson, in the imposing dignity of his bearing."[7] According to one account, Jeff "boasted of 'a decision of character and confidence' in himself, which he certainly would need as he assumed his new duties as Jefferson's first official editor."[8]

Jeff compiled Jefferson's daunting correspondence with his mother's and sisters' able assistance. He had reason to feel optimistic about the proposed edition and publication of Jefferson's papers. An Albany publishing house suggested that forty thousand subscriptions could be obtained and offered its literary agents to Jeff. Jeff was elated at this prospect "and enjoyed visions of the estate settled, his mother provided for, and himself with a comfortable income."[9] His wife Jane was jubilant too, "not having felt so easy about [their] affairs since Jefferson's purchase of Edgehill. Under this stimulus Randolph soon was 'working right hard' at the task of selecting manuscripts for the forthcoming volumes and hoped to 'have the "prospectus" out by Xmas.' The bright prospects with the Albany group did not materialize. April, 1828 found him in Philadelphia, dejected, where he was again unable to 'effect anything' with the publishers."[10]

Finally, Jeff decided to publish the papers himself. He applied himself to editing Jefferson's papers with steady dedication, his memory consistently retentive. In Charlottesville, Jeff arranged with F. Carr and Company to print the work. Events moved rapidly with the publication of the first volume. Numerous people, including James Madison, assisted Jeff in the final editing project. An eloquent preface written by Madison was sent to Jeff with a request that he revise it for the selected correspondence Madison had read. At major stages during publication, Jeff sought Madison's editorial advice and skills before the papers went to final print.[11]

Jeff's most valuable aid came from the women in his family, primarily his sisters, who did a majority of the laborious transcription for the manuscripts. "One of these young scribes wrote [Nicholas] Trist that they each devoted 'about as much time every day' to the task as Trist spent at his desk in the Department of State, and in addition they had 'a good deal of necessary needlework to do.' [Patsy] joined them daily for a 'sitting of 5 hours' and found it trying, especially with the 'press copies,' which were considerably faded. She was soon 'convinced that none less interested than the family would have undertaken them at any price.'" The work was so tedious that the women had trouble keeping ahead of the printer.[12]

According to one account:

Not all the manuscripts were transcribed at Edgehill. Some at least in the early stages of the project, were prepared in Charlottesville under the supervision of J. A. G. Davis, later Professor of Law at the University of Virginia, where he was fatally shot by a student. Davis bitterly complained about the assistance he was getting and wished that Trist could have been there to help him. One copyist, according to Davis, was especially incompetent, making "as many mistakes as [Davis] should in copying a Hebrew book." This resulted in costs of several dollars a week for corrections in the print. However, "the ladies at Edgehill" planned to proof-read the work in the future, and Davis anticipated an improvement.[13]

Jeff published Jefferson's private papers in four volumes, titled *Memoir, Correspondence, and Miscellanies: 4 volumes, The Memoir, Correspondence, and Miscellanies: From the Papers of Thomas (1829)*. It was the first publication of Thomas Jefferson's papers after his death, and the only one available until Henry A. Washington's edition was published in 1853 and 1854.[14] Jeff's compilation of his grandfather's papers was initially published by F. Carr in Charlottesville in 1829, with subsequent editions printed in London, Boston, and Paris. The documents included were selected, transcribed, and meticulously edited by Jeff himself in an effort to shape his grandfather's legacy. The money he received would also relieve some of Jefferson's debt. Ever vigilant regarding his grandfather's reputation, Jeff carefully edited the papers to avoid any controversial subjects.

Jeff made some surprising discoveries about his family's lineage when he read his grandfather's papers. Historian Henry Randall recounts Jeff opening a trunk of documents at Edgehill and discovering that Peter Jefferson, Thomas Jefferson's father, had been a colonel and a member of the Virginia House of Burgess. That fact had not been part of the oral family tradition. In fact, Jeff wondered if Jefferson had known these facts about his own father, but then, according to Jeff, his grandfather had always preferred not to take credit for accomplishments or elected offices, and left them out of family tradition.[15] He would be just as likely not to boast about his father.

After Jeff's publication, George Tucker's *Life of Thomas Jefferson* was published in 1837, followed in 1858 by the major work of historian Henry S. Randall. Randall also used Jeff's book for his own seminal biography, *The Life of Thomas Jefferson*, published in three volumes in 1858. Randall was the only biographer permitted to interview Jefferson's immediate family, detailing "the family denial" involving Sally Hemings. Finally, Sarah Randolph, Jeff's daughter, added her own personal life stories to the image of Jefferson with her poignant and personal book, *The Domestic Life of Thomas Jefferson*, published in 1871.

In the midst of this editorial project, Jeff's father, Thomas Mann Randolph, died on June 20, 1828, at age sixty. Now thirty-five, with a strong, pragmatic character, Jeff exercised total control over the Jefferson family finances. Patsy relied heavily on her stalwart son for almost everything, as well as her deep religious faith during these lean times. She spent a severe winter with Jeff's family at Edgehill, where deep snow buried their house for weeks. Together, mother and son worried about the family's finances, causing Patsy to take out a bank loan to pay her bills. In fact, her situation was so dire that her daughter Virginia offered to hire out Ellen, the family house servant, for extra money. Virginia suggested that Patsy delay her return trip back to Washington until the fall "on account of the great embarrassments she is under for money."[16] More emotional pain was inflicted from the sudden death of Patsy's second oldest son, twenty-eight-year-old James Madison Randolph. James had recently lost his farm due to financial difficulties and was living at Edgehill with Jeff and Jane. A reticent man, James was described as "patient, disinterested & affectionate . . . innocent and helpless like a lamb."[17] James's death, as one author has explained, "profoundly affected [Patsy], who blamed herself at least in part for her son's demise. 'He was too good for this world,' she confided to Nancy Morris, 'and I too poor to have shielded him from the blight of poverty which had nipped him in his early youth' and would have 'crushed his gentle spirit' had he survived the loss of his 'little farm.'"[18]

Virginia believed that Patsy's depression and her chronic financial troubles had aged her tremendously. She described Patsy's health as "far from good" and "so delicate [that] the least trifle . . . gives her a fever."[19] Patsy, at sixty-two, was "broken down" and showing "the infirmities of age," gazing out her window most days where she could see Monticello in the distance.[20] On her final day of life, Patsy gazed at the back lawn of Monticello, already fallen into deep shade. The soft wind flattened the azalea petals on the bushes. From her bedroom window on the southwest corner of Edgehill, Patsy wrote her final farewell to her beloved father, who had been gone for nearly ten years: "I will still think of thee, as in times gone by when I looked from the terrace of Monticello and thought 'all the kingdoms of the world and the glory thereof' lay spread before me. Every feature of that landscape has its own spell upon my heart, can bring back the living, breathing presence of those long mingled with the clods of the valley, can renew (for a moment) youth itself. Youth with its exquisite enjoyments, its ardent friendships, and Oh! dearer than all, its first, purest, truest love!"[21]

In the final years, Patsy depended on her deep religious beliefs to comfort her in her misfortune. Deeply devout, she still prayed on her knees every night. Then, on the night of October 9, 1836, Patsy suddenly fell sick with a severe headache accompanied by nausea, and became bedridden. For much of her adult life, she had suffered from headaches similar to those that afflicted Thomas Jefferson. Since the illness "appeared to us to be one of her accustomed sick headaches," Ellen later wrote, the family did nothing more "than apply the usual palliatives."[22] Patsy's daughters attributed her illness to exhaustion as she prepared to move again to Boston, to visit Ellen. Cornelia, Mary, and Virginia tended their mother, whose pain seemed to increase over the day. When night came, Patsy fell asleep. The sisters retired to bed believing their mother's illness was not grave. Mary remembered that her mother "passed a bad night but this was so usual a thing in these indispositions."[23] Her daughters, however, believed there was no cause to send for a doctor. The next morning, however, Patsy's pain grew intense, so excruciating that Cornelia sent for her brother Jeff to summon a doctor. Moments after Jeff entered the room, Patsy stared intently at her son for the last time. She had waited for him, then experienced a "spasm," her face having turned "a blue shade."[24] Surrounded by her daughters, her daughter-in-law Jane, and some grandchildren, Patsy managed to speak to Jeff but "immediately after became sick," Ellen said, "heaved convulsively, fell forward into his arms and drew her last breath."[25] Jeff would later write that his mother had "died of apoplexy caused by the rush of blood to the head"—in modern medical terms, a probable stroke.[26]

Jeff penned a formal eulogy for Patsy, who was buried in the family graveyard at Monticello two days after she died. "She met death as a relief from the infirmities and melancholy of old age," Jeff wrote.[27] In a brief summation of his mother's life, Jeff praised Patsy's superior intellect, along with her maternal and nurturing nature. "She possessed a mind strong and cultivated; mild and gentle temper; warm affection," he observed, noting that she was "disinterested and self-sacrificing in the discharge of her duties."[28] Ellen also paid tribute to her mother for her "deep affection, her high principles, her generous & magnanimous temper, her widely diffused benevolence, her sound judgment and glowing imagination, her highly cultivated understanding and fascinating manners."[29] She spoke of Patsy's years in Paris with Jefferson—the "gay circles of Paris," remarking that "the young Martha could not have imagined 'a greater contrast between her single & her married life!'" Ellen noted that her mother "bore the change with true female heroism, which is made up of resistance to small evils and cheerful courage and patient endurance under domestic grievances. In bearing these burdens and other 'calamities,' she was 'equal to all.'"[30]

Ellen ended her loving tribute, writing an eloquent, touching epitaph: "It may be told for a while in the neighborhood of her and her father's home, that a daughter of Thomas Jefferson sleeps by his side in that neglected burying ground at Monticello, but of who or what she was, otherwise than the daughter of Thomas Jefferson, a well-known statesman & great political leader, no tradition will after one generation remain."[31]

***

Over the next ten years, Jeff was determined to pay Jefferson's creditors "to the last copper," as he would write in his memoirs, whether legally obligated to do so or not. He chose this course, he said, to guarantee "that a character like [Jefferson's] should not be tainted with having failed to comply with his obligations."[32] And because he knew that is what would have made his mother happy. While Jeff and Jane struggled to pay off the family debt, their children blossomed into mature adults. Jeff was nearly fifty when Sarah Nicholas Randolph, their youngest child, was born at Edge Hill in 1839. Sarah would eventually write a family biography, a loving tribute to her great-grandfather. *The Domestic Life of Thomas Jefferson* was compiled from private family letters and reminiscences, published in the summer of 1871 by Harper & Brothers. In 1872, a second edition of Sarah's work appeared, and in 1939, a third edition was published. In the foreword to this 1939 edition (Cambridge, MA: University Press) appears a touching note of dedication that, perhaps, Sarah would have treasured: "This Edition is a Memorial to the Thomas Jefferson Randolph family of Edge Hill, Albemarle County, Virginia. Colonel Thomas Jefferson Randolph, His Wife Jane Hollins Nicholas and their children."

In her book, Sarah painted a vibrant portrait of life at Monticello with her parents and siblings, especially her sisters. She notes that all of her sisters were remarkable women of talent. Several became teachers at the girls' school her father had chartered. Her sisters possessed the attributes that made them successful mentors to the young students: "breeding, culture, charm, high mindedness. They were greatly beloved by the girls under their care, and were honored by all who knew them."[33]

During his long life, Jeff Randolph was engaged in a variety of undertakings, but he considered himself primarily a farmer. Jeff had taken his grandfather's comment, "Those who labour in the earth are the chosen people of God," to heart.[34] But both men, as one writer has commented, "had an equal respect for laborers whose lives were spent mastering and practicing a useful trade. Late in life, passing the house of a neighbor, Jesse Lewis, an old blacksmith who had still worked at his forge even though he had become a man of means, Jefferson had noted, "It is such men as that who constitute the wealth of a nation, not millionaires."[35] But Jeff found farming particularly agreeable to his temperament and talked about it at length with Jefferson and others. Like George Washington, Jeff was a yeoman farmer, toiling by the backbreaking sweat of his labor. Jeff certainly would have agreed with Washington, who had written that "the life of a husbandman, of all others, is the most delectable . . . To see plants rise from the earth and flourish by the superior skill and bounty of the laborer fills a contemplative mind with ideas which are more easy to be conceived than expressed."[36] Farming, instead of politics, was a safe topic of conversation for both Washington and Jeff Randolph, because it was their true passion.[37]

As a farmer, Jeff came to be highly regarded in his county. He had started his agricultural career, however, in a depressed economic period in Virginia. He wrote many times that his land had been ruined by Virginia's tobacco culture, commenting also on the harsh Albemarle soil:

> Farming on high lands at that time in Virginia was not profitable . . . Every thunder shower carried off the soil loosened . . . Tobacco was made exclusively on virgin soils the first and second years after clearing; leaving the land in the best condition to raise corn for the support of the plantation . . . Then corn was planted every year on these virgin soils, turned fresh from tobacco, until the washing of rains had impoverished it. It was then abandoned to gullies, broom straw, and briers. In 1804 nine tenths of the cleared land in my neighborhood was in this condition.[38]

The affluent tobacco market was a now in the distant past. Decades of planting the Virginia mainstay had depleted Virginia's rich soil. "As a result," explained one author, "the advantage with tobacco was on more fertile lands to the west. Consequently, well before the Revolution, many planters, small and large both, shifted to grain production, where an expanding market promised a good return. Yet growing cereals was not the stuff of grand fortunes."[39]

For these reasons and others, some of Jeff's neighbors fled Virginia to pursue the virgin earth in the West Indies: "After every dry year the roads would be thronged with emigrants" heading to some other venue. For those who stayed behind it was a struggle, exacerbated by the troubles plaguing the farmers. Jeff began to practice a new method of revitalizing the soil to end the crop erosion. Soon his farms became productive and turned a profit. He noted that the Piedmont area of Virginia "was advancing rapidly in wealth and prosperity."[40] Then, the destructive Civil War followed, ruining his chance for even a modicum of wealth. With a war looming, Jeff accurately predicted that Virginia's agricultural economy would not recover for decades, if ever.

While Jeff was absorbed in settling Jefferson's estate, to the neglect of his own farms, he produced two thousand bushels of wheat in a year, but within a few years he had more than doubled production. By 1860 Jeff had harvested eight thousand bushels from the same land. Other factors contributed to this degree of success. In 1830 he had owned seventy-six slaves, but only thirty-one of those were over twelve years old. By the end of the decade, Jeff's enslaved force had increased to forty-six and his horses from twenty to thirty-two. During this period he owned approximately twenty-five hundred acres, only a part of which was being tilled.[41]

While Jeff was away in Richmond and Williamsburg on business or politics, the management of the plantation frequently fell to Jane, who had her own overwhelming domestic tasks. Jane wrote that it was even difficult to hire a competent overseer to assist her and Jeff.[42] The economic depression of 1837 forced the couple to struggle with money, as the residue of Jefferson's loans plagued the couple for years. Yet, Jeff's economic prospects slowly brightened. Like his grandfather, he believed the answer to most problems in life was hard work, confiding in one letter to his mother, "If a man is . . . slothful he had better go and hang [himself], as the only evidence which he can give of being useful to his fellow man is by getting out of the way."[43] The 1840s saw dramatic improvement in Jeff's farms, finances, and prospects for the future. His thousand acres increased in value, resulting in the highest taxes in the county. As a result, he sold some land to his new son-in-law, Frank Ruffin, who had married Cary Anne. Jeff even helped build the couple's new house. Ruffin's payments enabled Jeff to pay off many of Jefferson's lingering debts.[44]

In the 1830s affordable transportation was essential to a crop farmer like Jeff Randolph. Shrewdly, this is why he sought to improve the method of transportation in his own county. To understand Jeff's life of near isolation before the railroad, it is necessary to study the outdated methods of passage of the day.[45] "The latter is illustrated," suggests one historian, "by George W. Randolph, who, in trying to allay the fears of a niece in connection with a duel which he might have to fight, pointed out that he would be in no more danger than that attending a trip by stagecoach. A strained comparison, of course, but with at least a grain of truth."[46] In fact, roads were rocky, little more than unpaved dirt craters—the main streets of Charlottesville were little better. As one story goes, Thomas Jefferson had planned a quick trip to visit a local man at the courthouse in Charlottesville, then decided that "it would be easier to write a letter than ride half a dozen miles and wade in the mud of the court yard."[47]

It was the advent of the railroad that made the Jefferson "family fortunes appear to be taking a turn" for the better.[48] Jeff's financial situation was brightened when he bid and won the contract to build a rail section through Edgehill and Shadwell for the new train station. This golden opportunity employed and paid fifty-one of Jeff's laborers. The train station would be important to the Randolph family in another way. In 1848, Jeff wrote that soon "you can step off the [railroad] cars within a pleasant walk of Monticello."[49] In the next decade the economic value of Jeff's Edgehill property continued to increase: it was valued at $74,437 in 1852, and then $89,475 in 1861. At this time, Jeff still owned 68 slaves of working age, 26 horses, 330 cattle, three "pleasure carriages," $400 worth of gold and silver plate, and the household furniture, valued at $4,600.[50] Interestingly, even in the troubled economic times, Jeff's one-half acre ownership of the Monticello family graveyard was worth an estimated $425. From 1838 until Virginia joined the Confederacy, this graveyard was taxed at three cents. At that time, it rose to ten cents. In 1862, the tax increased to fifteen cents, then as high as twenty-five cents in 1863, and settled at thirteen cents by 1870, resulting in a net worth of the cemetery of nearly $6,000.[51]

To supplement his income, Jeff had another ingenious idea that would sustain the family for years. As he had assisted his grandfather with the founding of the University of Virginia, Jeff had the notion of opening a young women's school at Edgehill. In fact, an elite school for girls, staffed and taught by the Randolph women, had been brewing in his mind since his grandfather's death. Jeff's daughter later wrote that it was natural that we "should make education their life work—they were all at home in such matters and wonderfully gifted; the talk at table was [of] a liberal education, had we younger ones listened and heeded."[52] Jeff's school at "Edgehill" began before the Civil War, established primarily for the neighbors' daughters. After the Civil War, the school was greatly expanded. According to Sarah, it would eventually become "the best school in the South, much sought after and patronized by all sections of the country as well as by well-known Southern families. The standard of the school was high, as to character and scholastic attainment. The text books used were for the most part those used by the University of Virginia—six miles away. Miss Mary B. Randolph, the oldest sister, was the Principal of the school. Colonel Randolph had no part in the school, but was much beloved by the girls, all of whom called him 'Grandpa.'"[53]

Sarah taught and took part in all matters concerning the schoolwork. After her mother's death, Carolina Randolph had charge of the housekeeping and was assisted by a niece, Eliza Ruffin, an adopted daughter of the house.[54]

In 1827, Jeff's design and plans for the school had been completed, with the idea that Jane was to be its headmistress. By the spring of 1829, Jeff's "sixth scholar," a student, had arrived, bringing with her the much-needed tuition. Jane assisted in teaching, entering into the music department with "great spirit."[55] She was also able to hire another teacher, a Miss Hannah Starnes. "Miss Starnes proved an able teacher and was quite attracted to the neighborhood. She especially enjoyed her walks, which brought her, 'through the vista of poplars and locusts . . . a view of 'sweet Monticello.'"[56] The school continued to grow, and its curriculum became more formal. In the early 1840s, a student described her regular school day: "I go to school at eight, read one chapter in the Testement [sic], then I write, then I say my dictionary, then my geography, then I get my lessons that I say to sister Cary Anne, which are my verb translations [and] arithmetic. When I know them I come out and say them. Then I cipher till twelve. After twelve I read, then draw the rest of my time till half past two."[57]

Before 1850, Jane's daughters had taken over most of the teaching duties, much to Jane's relief. Jane suggested to Jeff that they reduce the number of students, but he was "so much shocked at the idea" that she did not bring the subject up again.[58] The tuition money was greatly needed by the family, he explained to Jane. A married daughter, who lived away from Albemarle, remembered that Jane was "shackled with the vile school."[59] To help relieve his wife, Jeff took a more active part, acting as an informal admissions director, acquainting the parents of potential students with the rules and regulations. He praised the virtues of the small student body, declaring that only twenty students would be allowed at the school for a valuable education. By 1850 the school's academic reputation had grown, and they had admitted thirty girls. But Jane complained that she was "sick & tired of the whole concern," though she knew the income was "indispensable" to the family.[60] The school flourished until the devastating Civil War destroyed most of Virginia. The academy opened again in 1867, tended exclusively by Jeff's daughters. It remained open during most of the nineteenth century, earning an excellent reputation in Virginia, and the region, as a fine school for young ladies.[61]

With increasing age and the approach of the Civil War, Jeff Randolph grew closer to his own neighbors and townspeople in Charlottesville. Like so many Southerners, he rallied to support and defend his native state, Virginia, from the verbal attacks and denigration of the South by Northerners. Famed author Harriet Beecher Stowe irritated Jeff by what he considered her unfair and defamatory portrayal of the South. "In his devotion to the Union he was unswerving," wrote one author, "until John Brown's murderous raid, strengthened by the antagonism of the North against the South. Jeff announced his decision to support his state should she secede from the union."[62]

Abraham Lincoln's election powered the belief by Jeff, and most Southerners, that Lincoln would subjugate entire state power to the massive federal government. Virginia would be dictated to by Washington politicians. Early in 1861, Jeff served on a statewide committee to advise Virginia on seceding from the Union. He was convinced that the only alternative to secession was a violent, slave riot caused by Northern propaganda. For his own part, Jeff prepared to defend his family at Edgehill with his very blood. On the day Lincoln took office, Jeff ordered "six shooters of the Navy size," which he expected to be delivered to his plantation.[63] Although a colonel in the militia, Jeff was too elderly to take the battlefield. When the brutal fighting started, he was nearly seventy and too feeble for combat. The fighting was left to Jeff's son, Meriwether Lewis, who reported from his company in May 1861 that he was "in good health and spirits and regularly embarked in a soldier's life."[64] Fortunately, Meriwether escaped serious injury during the bloody war. Jeff later wrote that Meriwether served as a confidential scout for Generals Lee and Jackson, and "escaped unscathed from twenty general actions" and a hundred skirmishes.[65]

Jeff raised as much money as he could for the Confederacy and supplied food, shelter, and provisions for the Virginia Army. A soldier stopping by Edgehill in early 1865 recalled Jeff as "the giant form of Col. Randolph" and "in the tales he spun of the olden days of Virginia, of his illustrious grandfather and of the legislature of Virginia in 1832."[66] A few months later, another soldier saw the family when Union general Sheridan savaged the Virginia countryside. He found that Jeff and his family had fled to the mountains for safety, where a slave boy supplied them with food and water.[67]

During the Civil War, the Confederate government confiscated Monticello, utilizing it as a wartime hospital. However, the greatest damage to the house did not occur during the war. But it was afterward when the Levy family, who had purchased the mansion, was embroiled in a twenty-year lawsuit over ownership. The house had been left in the care of a negligent overseer, Joseph Wheeler, who rented it out for money and parties. Wheeler had even allowed his cattle to roam in Monticello's basement during winter. As one visitor reported, "in the beautiful drawing salon with its handsome parquet floors, Wheeler had a granary where he set up a hand fanning mill and winnowed his grain."[68] Under Wheeler's reckless care, Monticello and its grounds badly decayed. Everything but the finished porticoes became deteriorated, tattered, and peeled. Monticello's furniture and lush curtains faded; its orchards and gardens became overgrown with weeds. As one historian eloquently concluded, "Jefferson's Monticello is irretrievably lost, for the soul of the house perished with its owner-builder. Just as the evolution of Monticello paralleled the patterns of Jefferson's intellectual and emotional life, its disintegration was appropriately parallel to his own. At his death, with the dispersal of his family and the sale of his possessions, Jefferson's Monticello ceased to exist."[69]

Jeff's sister Cornelia felt the loss of Monticello as deeply as Jeff did. She had her own private, special memories of what she considered her lifetime home. Cornelia warmly reminisced sitting on the stones at the end of the barn, gazing at "the pillars of the house gleaming from the deep shade of the trees." Monticello spoke to her in eternal memories: "Whether in the morning when the landscape is covered by a soft mist and you look to the east and see the blue horizon disappear behind those beautiful Edgehill and Shadwell mountains, or in the evening when the deep indigo and bold outline of the Blue Ridge shows against the bright gold colored or orange western sky."[70]

The Civil War lasted four grisly years and resulted in more than six hundred thousand deaths, half of them lost to disease. Confederate general Robert E. Lee finally surrendered the Army of Northern Virginia to Union general Ulysses S. Grant at the Court House in Appomattox, Virginia, effectively ending the war. But other rebel armies, according to one historian, continued the cause: "Some Confederate sympathizers mourned the outcome of the war—the 'lost cause'—would forever change the Southern way of life, including slavery. Many Southerners were unwilling to give up the lost cause, believing they could continue to fight and eventually win, or die trying. It was a dangerous place and time. With Lee's surrender, soldiers shed their uniforms, turned in their weapons, and rode or walked home to resume their lives."[71]

The end of the fierce war came and Albemarle County, like most of Virginia, took stock of its ravaged land and economy, beginning the arduous task of "reconstruction." As familiar forms of government were reinstituted, Jeff traveled to Washington as a "dignitary" of Virginia. There he told President Andrew Johnson that the submission of Virginia to the Union was absolute. He requested Johnson to safeguard his beloved state, and "protect them against the Radicals." Johnson urged Jeff to "send representatives to help sustain him against the Radicals."[72]

Jeff's plight during Reconstruction in Virginia was little different from that of most of Virginia's families left shattered by the war. Needless to say, emancipation of the slave workforce wreaked havoc on Virginia's economy and its entrenched social order. Jeff, with his deeply held abolitionist views, made the adjustment better than most of his fellow Virginians. After the war, he returned to what he knew best—farming, producing a large amount of wheat instead of tobacco. Remarkably, within several years, he had his farm running smoothly and turned a profit.[73] Fortunately, as head of an extended family of unmarried sisters, he had ample food for his family, even though other luxuries were sorely lacking. When his mother lived with Jeff and Jane, Patsy was impressed with the bountiful table that was set at Edgehill. She reported to Ellen in 1834 that "Jefferson is an excellent manager and provider. Meats, vegetables, milk, butter and everything that a rich and well managed farm can supply we have in good abundance."[74] Patsy enthused about the warmth she had received on her stays with Jeff and Jane. "Jefferson and Jane are two of the very best tempered and most kindhearted people I ever saw in my life. They will be kind to you, kind to your children, kind to your nurse, and every child in the house will wait on you and yours with the utmost good humor and affection."[75]

In 1871, after fifty-six years, the marriage of Jeff and his beloved wife Jane ended with Jane's death at age seventy-three. Jane, who was still grieving for a son who lay dying in Georgia, collapsed, rallied a short while to speak to her family, and then peacefully died from a stroke. "The death of one lady had been marked by more feeling in the community," Jeff wrote. A large group attended the funeral services for Jane at the church, then followed the body to the graveyard at Monticello.[76] "There 'her former slaves asked to be allowed to sing a hymn,' and, with 'tears trickling down their cheeks' broke into a 'spiritual' which 'deeply touched the "hearts of all present.""[77] Similar to Thomas Jefferson's grief at his own wife's death, Jeff's profound sorrow seemed overwhelming. For over half a century he and Jane had been a devoted and loving couple, raising twelve children, enduring family drama and financial distress. Jane had been his rock and his tender succor in life.

But the aging widower did not have long to bear his sorrow. Jeff himself rapidly declined in the last few years of a "'vigorous and beautiful old age,' only occasionally marred by an 'alarming attack of palpitations of the heart.'"[78] For most of his life, Jeff had sustained good health, like his grandfather. In fact, his health suffered less in his later years than did Jefferson's. He avoided colds, which usually afflicted him when he visited Richmond, with a regular morning cold foot-bath, a habit Jefferson had taught him. Jeff controlled overeating by chewing on "rheubarb" before he slept. Jane had recorded that he drank very little, but he himself gave a detailed report on the contents of "the case" that always accompanied him to Richmond, mostly for his fellow legislators: "4 qauart [sic] bottles of whiskey, 3 full, one not half used. 2nd, 4 ditto champagne brandy, 2 full, one empty, 1 half full—say 1 1/2 used. 4 ditto maderia [sic] wine, emptied once, 1 1/2 of the second [filling] used."[79] And at eighty, Jeff could still ride "15 miles on horseback with little fatigue."[80]

Even in Jeff's old age, a visitor to Edgehill had described him as "6 feet 4 1/2 inches, treads as lightly as a young man, has no ailments, and is as active a planter as a man of five and 20."[81] His last public appearance happened when he was chosen interim chairman of the Democratic National convention in 1872. This convention nominated Horace Greeley, one of "the shortest and dullest in the parties history,"[82] as its presidential candidate. When the "Honorable Jefferson Randolph" came onstage, Jeff was still "a towering figure, venerable appearance, and white locks made him an object of immediate interest and he was soon surrounded."[83] August Belmont, chairman of the national executive committee, made a long speech, then nominated Jeff: "'I have the honor to propose to you as your temporary chairman a distinguished and venerable citizen of Virginia, grandson of the patriot and statesman, Thomas Jefferson. It is an auspicious omen that a scion of the author of the Declaration of Independence is to inaugurate the struggle of the democracy for freedom and equality for every American citizen and against oppression and tyranny in our fair land.' . . . The *Richmond Dispatch* assured its readers that 'the fine gentleman made a brief, sensible address in response.'"[84]

In 1875, the last year of his life, Jeff traveled to Hot Springs, Virginia, seeking relief from his weary bones and nagging arthritis. He was accompanied by his son Wilson, a physician. On the road back to Edgehill, their carriage suddenly broke down, slamming the old man violently against the side of the coach. According to the *Charlottesville Chronicle,* for the rest of the way, "[Jeff] lay in his son's arms, suffering great pain and in a fainting condition."[85] Once home, Jeff asked to sit near a window that would allow him to look, for the last time in his life, at Monticello. His sons moved him to the small etched window. Jeff nodded toward Monticello with the sunshine streaming into his window. He realized that the end was near and accepted it with the "utmost composure."[86] Neither morbid nor mournful, Jeff faced his mortality. His sensible nature never deserted him. Perhaps, boyhood memories of Monticello and Grandfather Jefferson flooded his thoughts. His youth was now a decayed memory. Attended by eight sons and grandsons, Thomas Jefferson Randolph took his final breath and died peacefully on October 7, 1875, at the age of eighty-three—the same age of his beloved grandfather.[87]

A small company of men rode out from Charlottesville to accompany Jeff's body to the church. All the shops and business in the town closed. The funeral procession was joined by a crowd of townspeople, professors, and students from the University of Virginia, where Jeff had served as rector. After church services, a large group accompanied him on his last trip up Monticello mountain, where he joined his earthly trinity—his wife, his mother, and his beloved grandfather, Thomas Jefferson. The fitting obituary for Jeff declared that "Col. Randolph was a man of commanding presence, genial and courteous in his manners, boundless in his hospitality and a fine type of the old Virginia gentleman":

> Thomas Jefferson Randolph died at his home near Charlottesville Virginia on the seventh. . . age 83 years. The deceased was the eldest son of Gov. Thomas Mann Randolph and Martha Jefferson, the daughter of Thomas Jefferson and was born in 1792. He was educated under the eye and care of his illustrious grandfather, and was one of his constant associates when the latter reached the presidency. Col. Randolph made his debut in political life in 1832 as a delegate from Albemarle County Virginia and the general assembly of that state. He was a man of strong natural powers and fine educational training in early obtained a leading position in the councils of his native state. The resolutions for the abolition of slavery were introduced they met with the full and earnest support of Col. Randolph and notwithstanding this fact he was reelected to the next session, although Albemarle was one of the largest slaveholding counties in the state. Upon the organization of the Whig party in Virginia Col. Randolph was beaten in 1833- 1835 for the legislature. But in 1836 he and Judge Rives were elected over Gov. Gilmer and South Hall and reach shows in the following year. After this. Col. Randolph remained upon his farm until he was elected delegate to the convention which amended the Constitution of Virginia previous to the war of 1861. After the end of the war, Randolph again came upon the surface of public life was a delegate to

the Baltimore Democratic convention which nominated Mr. Greeley and temporary president of that body. This ended Col. Randolph's public life. Thomas Jefferson made Col. Randolph his executor and in him was confided the public and private papers of his grandfather. Four volumes of Mr. Jefferson's works were afterwards published by him.[88]

In the end, Jeff was laid beside the man he had been in the unique filial position to observe the "real" Thomas Jefferson.

With Jefferson, in his writings and in his life, there remained a veil of mystery to the public. Jeff saw firsthand Jefferson the father, grandfather, architect, gardener, host, letter writer, and educational statesman. His admiration of Jefferson was unmatched. He knew that men like Jefferson and Washington "built their homes upon the mountain tops" and thus "had a breadth of vision, a singleness of purpose, a loftiness of ideals, a love of humanity, a moral fibre, a grace of life, [and] a chivalry of deeds."[89] But, Jeff also recognized the Oracle of Monticello as a brilliant but flawed man. Writing in his memoirs, Jeff kept his grandfather in his own time and place.[90] For better or worse, Thomas Jefferson and Thomas Jefferson Randolph were worshipped by the people who knew them best—their family.

And in the end, that was all that mattered to them.

EPILOGUE:
DNA REDUX: SALLY HEMINGS

This whole affair's been conducted by amateurs. I include myself.
—**Dr. Eugene Foster, who performed the DNA test in 1998**[1]

Most historians believe that Thomas Jefferson is the most prolific, hypocritical liar in American history. Some, however, contend that he is the victim of the most profane 250-year-old defamation of character allegation in legal annals. Apparently, there is no gauzy middle ground in this historical tableau.

Many recent historians—some very prominent—have utterly dismissed Jeff and Ellen Randolph's "family denial" of the alleged affair between Thomas Jefferson and Sally Hemings. They have rejected notable historians such as Dumas Malone and Winthrop Jordan who argued that "despite the utter disreputability of the source, the charge has been dragged after Jefferson like a dead cat through the pages of formal and informal history."[2] Some historians now declare that the 1998 DNA conclusively proved that Sally Hemings and Thomas Jefferson had a sexual liaison.

The 1998 DNA finding that a male in the Jefferson line fathered one of Sally Hemings's children led to a scholarly reevaluation of the entire question of the Jefferson-Hemings relationship. The then-president of Monticello and the Thomas Jefferson Foundation, Daniel P. Jordan, tasked a committee with examining the issue. "Although paternity cannot be established with absolute certainty, our evaluation of the best evidence available suggests the strong likelihood that Thomas Jefferson and Sally Hemings had a relationship over time that led to the birth of one, and perhaps all, of the known children of Sally Hemings," Jordan opined when the committee's report was published in 2000. He went on to conclude that, "We recognize that honorable people can disagree on this subject, as indeed they have for over two hundred years. Further, we know that the historical record has gaps that perhaps can never be filled and mysteries that can never be fully resolved."[3]

In fact, the release of DNA evidence tying one of Sally Hemings's children to a Jefferson father, and the subsequent report has led to widespread misperception. This misperception permeates both the academic community and the public, holding that science has conclusively proven that Thomas Jefferson had a sexual relationship with one of his slaves. Even though the sexual rumors were promoted by Jefferson's Federalist enemies, they have now been accepted by most historians through gossip, distorted scientific results, and offered to the public as "fact." But what is presented as historical fact is based on a singular misleading headline in the 1998 science journal *Nature*: "Jefferson Fathered Slave's Last Child."[4] There is now convincing biographical evidence, as well as new DNA evidence, that Jefferson was not a man of such appetites. It is extremely unlikely he carried on any type of sexual liaison with a fourteen-year-old slave girl.

Two hundred and fifty years after the political smear was started, the Sally Hemings story intersected with a Charlottesville woman by the name of Winifred Joyce Bennett. Bennett's name should be registered in every history book. Who was she and what did she have to do with Thomas Jefferson and Sally Hemings? While studying philosophy and art history at New York University, Bennett, with her honey blonde hair and stunning good looks, modeled for the Ford agency. In 1993 the refined socialite divorced her husband of thirty years and moved to Charlottesville, where, as an amateur historian, she put her inquisitive mind to work. One evening in 1996, over a casual dinner at the home of Dr. Eugene Foster, a retired pathologist, the conversation turned to DNA. For years, a Charlottesville woman had claimed to be Anastasia, the long-lost daughter of Russian Czar Nicholas II. Years later, DNA testing debunked her claim. Mrs. Bennett wondered whether DNA might resolve the Thomas Jefferson-Sally Hemings controversy.[5]

Thus, the tumultuous DNA Project was launched by Dr. Eugene A. Foster, a pathologist working at the University of Virginia Hospital. Foster was urged to undertake the 1998 DNA investigation by a "friend," later revealed to be Winifred, who was planning a book about the controversy. After some study, Foster embarked on a search for male candidates for testing.[6]

One of the biggest misconceptions of the controversy is that the DNA sample (blood) was drawn from Thomas Jefferson himself. This is absolutely false. Jefferson had no male surviving children, so Foster turned to five male-line descendants of Jefferson's uncle, Field Jefferson. With the assistance of a Jefferson family historian and genealogist Herbert Barger, a wizened former Air Force and Pentagon official, they located the individuals to be tested and included the descendants of the Carr family (Jefferson's nephews, both of whom were alleged to be Sally's lovers by Jeff and Ellen Randolph) and the Woodson family (the baby "Tom," supposedly fathered by Jefferson in Paris).[7]

At the University of Virginia, DNA was extracted from the blood samples. After Foster tried to negotiate a publication deal with *Science* magazine (which refused to publish his article), the extracts were then flown to England by Dr. Foster in December 1997. Foster said that he rode a bus from Heathrow airport to Oxford and handed over his samples to a researcher, who stored them in a refrigerator, after which the two "toddled" off to a pub.[8] Three laboratories at Oxford performed the analysis, and some tests were performed as far away as the Netherlands (Leiden University). The results were completed in June 1998 and published in *Nature* magazine on November 5, 1998.

Not one historian reviewed the findings, or the article, on behalf of *Nature* before it was published. According to Dr. Foster, the results were threefold: (1) the analysis found *no match* between the DNA of Jefferson and Woodson descendants—thus, Woodson was not fathered by *any* Jefferson, debunking any notion that Jefferson and Sally had a sexual relationship in Paris; (2) no match was found between the DNA of the Carrs (Jefferson's nephews) and the Hemings descendant—thus exonerating the Carr brothers, Peter and Samuel, as the father of Eston Hemings *only*; and (3) most controversial, the Y-chromosome "haplotypes" of the descendants of Field Jefferson (Jefferson's uncle) and Eston Hemings did match, implicating *a male* Jefferson (though not Thomas Jefferson, as the public was led to believe) as the father of Eston.[9]

Most leading historians then concluded that since there was no DNA match to the Carr brothers, the historical case was proven beyond a reasonable doubt that Jefferson alone had a sexual relationship with Sally Hemings. Yet, the misleading and sensationalized headline in *Nature* pronounced Jefferson guilty: "Jefferson fathered slave's last child." The *Nature* article was signed by Dr. Foster and six other European biologists, none of whom were United States board-certified doctors, molecular scientists, or historians. Foster later wrote that he was embarrassed by the blatant spin of the *Nature* article, but had to admit that he had negotiated the text with the magazine, including the lead—"Jefferson fathered slave's last child." Had the headline stated, "A male Jefferson fathered slave's last child" it would have been accurate, but as Foster himself was quick to point out, the published version was misleading. Nevertheless, the damage had been done. Although in some early reports the press conveyed the speculative and limited nature of the DNA study, the subtleties were gradually lost. Matters were complicated by revisionist historians spreading the word that Jefferson's paternity was now scientific fact.[10]

After the study was completed, Mrs. Bennett, Dr. Foster's friend who had prompted him to undertake the DNA tests, read in the newspaper that Foster had published the results in *Nature*. Much to her surprise, Foster did not give her any credit for her contribution, which she had planned to take to the official Jefferson Memorial Foundation (legal owners of Monticello) for financial support, research and a possible book. In a later conversation with Foster, Mrs. Bennett questioned why Foster would do such a thing. *"Gene, what is it that you want? Do you want money?"* Foster replied, *"No, I want fame."* Mrs. Bennett related these statements to Jefferson family historian Herbert Barger, adding: "Well, he was just willing to sacrifice me for his fame."[11] Barger also related an interesting side note to the controversy:

> After several months of research I was able to locate and identify a second Hemings DNA source, William Hemings, a son of Madison Hemings [Sally's eldest son], in a Veteran's Cemetery in Leavenworth, Kansas. I notified the Hemings family, gave them forms and urged them to permit a gathering of that valuable DNA. At the same time I advised Monticello President

Dan Jordan, and suggested he urge the Hemings to permit the gathering of a second Hemings DNA. He [Jordan] refused to contact them, suggested that I contact them, but cautioned me against undue pressure. All eight Hemings family members refused to permit the test and their spokesperson, Shay Banks-Young, informed me that they are happy with their oral family history and will never give permission.[12]

"My family doesn't need to prove themselves," said Shay Banks-Young, fifty-five, a great-great-great-granddaughter of Madison Hemings, who lives in Columbus, Ohio. "If they dig up Thomas Jefferson at the same time, maybe I'll reconsider."[13] The Woodson family was particularly critical of Dr. Foster. They allege that he rejected their requests for certain assurances. They wanted the blood samples to be independently tested for accuracy. Apparently, Dr. Foster circumvented their requests and found people who claimed they were male-line descendants of Thomas Jefferson through Thomas Woodson.

The Woodson DNA result is of extreme historical significance, and often overlooked or marginalized by most historians: if Tom Woodson was Sally's Paris-conceived son, and shown to have the Jefferson Y chromosome, it would be a *certainty* that Jefferson was his father, since he was the only Jefferson in Paris. But there was no match. In fact, the one thing the DNA proves beyond all doubt is that whoever was Woodson's father, his Y chromosome was one common among white Europeans, not sub-Saharan blacks. Thus, Tom's father was surely someone Sally had met in France—but not Thomas Jefferson.[14]

Foster was obviously conflicted by his role in the subsequent rush to judgment maelstrom, as indicated in the following correspondence to Barger in 1998:

> Dear Mr. Barger:
> I continue to understand your distress at what has happened with the media, but I would like you to understand my role more fully. First of all, you must understand that I had no control over the headline in Nature and had no knowledge whatever of the content of Ellis and Lander's companion piece. The title of our piece submitted to NATURE was "Genetic Evidence That

Thomas Jefferson Fathered a Slave Child . . . When NATURE accepted the article they told me that the format of the Scientific Correspondence articles required a very short title. The galley proof they sent me was titled, "Jefferson fathered his slave's child" . . . I regret that they chose the title they did, but I did my best to have a title that more accurately reflected the content of the article. Furthermore, we stated that we understood that there were other possible explanations. The discussion of the other possible explanations has to be left to historians . . . As you know, I have said publicly, both before and after publication of our article, that our results could not be conclusive. I have already sent you a copy of my letter to the New York Times in which I repeat that message . . . My experience with this matter so far tells me that no matter how strongly I say that the study is not conclusive and no matter how often I repeat it, it will not stop the media from saying what they want to in order to try to increase their circulation. And I truly regret that. In fact, I am angered by it . . . Your evidence on Randolph Jefferson and his sons, now that it has been made public, will be evaluated by other historians and will eventually be accepted if it is found to be valid. Eventually, and I don't think it will be soon, there will be enough solid scientific and historical evidence for people to be able to make an informed judgment . . . It has been painful to me to see my work over interpreted and sensationalized by the media. *But I know that this will all die down [emphasis added], that sober reconsideration of the issues will take place over the years, and that new scientific and historical knowledge will be accepted...*
Sincerely,
Gene Foster[15]

More importantly, a blue-ribbon panel of Jefferson scholars reexamined the sexual allegation issues carefully and authored a public report in 2001, and later a book in 2011. The "Scholars Commission" included some of the nation's leading historians on Thomas Jefferson. Several members had written one or more biographies on Jefferson. Most of the members had either chaired their departments, and several served or had served as "eminent" or "distinguished" professors. The thirteen scholars came from prominent universities spread from southern California to Maine and then as far south as Alabama. They were trained in such diverse disciplines as history, political science, law, economics, and biochemistry. Most of the historians had studied Thomas Jefferson and his era for at least two decades and held teaching or research appointments at Harvard, Yale, Stanford, Brown, Virginia, North Carolina, Kentucky, Indiana, Bowdoin, and many other institutions of higher learning.[16]

The group of historians began their inquiry with diverse opinions on the sexual liaison issue. Some members of the commission were admirers of Thomas Jefferson, others were not. At least one of the historians, Professor Forrest McDonald, (whom I interviewed before his death) had assumed the allegations of a Jefferson-Hemings relationship were true. Though it received little coverage in the mainstream press, the detailed and lengthy report (later published as a book) concluded:[17]

> In the end, after roughly one year of examining the issues, we find the question of whether Thomas Jefferson fathered one or more children by his slave Sally Hemings to be one about which honorable people can and do disagree. However, it is our unanimous view that the allegation is by no means proven; and we find it regrettable that public confusion about the 1998 DNA testing and other evidence has misled many people into believing that the issue is closed. *With the exception of one member . . . our individual conclusions range from serious skepticism about the charge to a conviction that it is almost certainly untrue. (emphasis added)*[18]

Until the 1998 DNA test, most historians dismissed the allegations, as noted by prominent historian Joseph Ellis: "Within the scholarly world, especially within the community of Jefferson specialists, there seems to be a clear consensus that the [SALLY] story is almost certainly not true."[19] Ellis went on to explain that (pre-DNA):

> Within the much murkier world of popular opinion, especially within the black community, the story appears to have achieved the status of a self-evident truth. If either side of this debate were to file for damages in a civil suit requiring a preponderance of evidence as the standard, it is difficult to imagine an impartial jury finding for either plaintiff. Jefferson's most ardent defenders still live under the influence of what might be called the Virginia gentleman ethos (i.e., this is not something that a Virginia gentleman would do), which increasingly has the quaint and charmingly naive sound of an honorable anachronism.[20]

Thus, contrary to popular misconception, the DNA testing did not prove Thomas Jefferson fathered Eston Hemings, or any other child of Sally Hemings. The Scholars Report noted in detail that although Jefferson did not directly deny the sexual charges, he penned many letters impliedly denying the charge that was beneath his dignity to even respond. In fact, Jefferson delegated his Presidential Secretary, William Burwell, to answer various repetitive attacks on his character. Burwell, writing under a pseudonym, said of the slave-paramour charge that it was "below the dignity of a man of understanding." The newspaper, *The Republican Watch Tower*, denounced it as a "damnable lie." And Jefferson's allies in Richmond "set out with a sturdy denial of Sally's existence. They had been in this country their whole lives. They had never heard a word of her. How then could Callender get hold of the story? Depend upon it, sir, the whole thing must be a lie. It cannot possibly be true."[21]

The Scholars report also noted that there was evidence that other slaves were jealous of the Hemings special treatment, and this may have been the catalyst for the sexual allegation rumor. Jeff Randolph said the Hemings family was "a source of bitter jealousy to the other slaves who liked to account for it with other reasons than the true one viz. superior intelligence, capacity and fidelity to trusts."[22]

Their special treatment caused rivalry with the other servants, and probably was a source for the "Sally" rumor.

Author Allan Pell Crawford suggests in his book *Twilight at Monticello*, that Jefferson had some sort of secret room or a staircase installed so "Sally . . . could easily have entered Jefferson's private chambers at any time of day or night, without being seen or heard."[23] Crawford probably based this assumption on an article written by Helen Leary in the *National Genealogical Society* quarterly that speculated: "These porticles may not have been built specifically to facilitate Sally's nocturnal visits, but they certainly would have concealed them."[24] This is not accurate. There are only two ways to gain access to Jefferson's bedroom. Through the side door, off the main entrance, which would be clearly visible to everyone in the house. Or two, a circuitous route up from the slave quarters, over the south pavilion, through the green house window, through another window to Jefferson's summer study (southwest porticle), through the French doors and into his bedroom. All of which could have been heard throughout the house. Moreover, Crawford describes that the "porticles" (blinds) and staircase were added at the same time. This, again, is not accurate. They were built at two different times—porticles in 1805 and the staircase in 1796. The staircase he refers to leads into a hallway, not directly into Jefferson's library.[25] Another ladder leads to a narrow storage closet over Jefferson's bed, used for out of season clothes and legal papers. There was no other entrance to this closet.[26]

A small universe of historians contends that whether the consanguinity allegations are true is a peripheral issue, since the renown of Jefferson as a votary of liberty is so monumental that nothing can affect it. Perhaps. Yet the "Sally" charges have permeated the national consciousness and remain a demonizing blot on Jefferson's character. The 1998 DNA findings darkened the portrait of "Jefferson, the man" that has been incubating ever since. Conservative writer Dinesh D'Souza describes a conversation he had with several college students: "On Jefferson, the three were agreed: he was, in various descriptions, a 'hypocrite,' a 'rapist'..., and a 'total racist.' Jeffersonian principles of individualism, reason, science, and private property, all become tainted."[27]

I have attempted to research and evaluate every scholarly book, article, committee report, eighteenth century letters, and ancillary material relevant to the singular, inflammatory subject of whether Thomas Jefferson had an exotic, sexual liaison with his "servant" Sally Hemings.[28] I conducted personal interviews and corresponded with two Jeffersonian experts intimately involved in the initial 1998 DNA test: Dr. White McKenzie (Ken) Wallenborn, a former professor at the University of Virginia medical school and tour guide at Monticello,[29] and genealogist Herbert Barger.[30] Both gentlemen are Jefferson "insiders" intimately involved in the distorted DNA study and the subsequent misleading report. They reveal how evidence was manipulated into a censored, predetermined "official" conclusion, giving a false stigma of Jefferson's guilt to the American public.[31]

Moreover, Jeff and Ellen Randolph offered Jefferson's first biographer, Henry Randall, a whirlpool of salient facts, making a strong historical case that bolsters the so-called "Family Denial" linking the Carr nephews to Sally Hemmings:

- the one credible eyewitness to this sexual allegation was Edmund Bacon, Jefferson's overseer at Monticello, who saw another man (not Jefferson) leaving Sally's room "many a morning." Bacon wrote: ". . . I have seen him come out of her mother's room many a morning when I went up to Monticello very early."[32]

- Jefferson's deteriorating health would have prevented any such sexual relationship. He was sixty-four at the time of the alleged affair and suffered debilitating migraine headaches which incapacitated him for weeks, as well as severe intestinal infections and rheumatoid arthritis. He complained to John Adams: "My health is entirely broken down within the last eight months."[33]

- Jefferson owned three different slaves named Sally, adding to the historical confusion.

- He never freed his supposed lover and companion of thirty-seven years, "Sally Hemings," from her enslavement nor mentioned her in his will.

- Randolph Jefferson, his younger brother, would have had the identical Jefferson Y chromosome as his older brother, Thomas, that matched the DNA. Randolph had a reputation for socializing with Jefferson's slaves and was expected at Monticello *approximately nine months* before the birth of Eston Hemings, Sally's son who was the DNA match for a "male Jefferson."

- Until 1976, the oral history of Eston's family held that they descended from a Jefferson "uncle." Randolph was known at Monticello as "Uncle Randolph."

- Unlike his brother, by taste and training Thomas Jefferson was raised as the perfect Virginia gentleman, a man of refinement and intellect. The personality of the man who figures in the Hemings soap opera cannot be attributed to the known nature of Jefferson. Having an affair with a house servant would be preposterously out of character for him.

Unfortunately, the Sally "allegation" is one fraying legend that truth may never catch up to. Even when facts contradict a salacious story, it is the story that usually survives. Betsy Ross may have her American flag, so we can let Sally have Thomas Jefferson's love child. Joseph Ellis, an award-winning historian, proclaimed in 1996 (pre-DNA) that: ". . . the likelihood of a liaison with Sally Hemings is remote . . . ," and the story is "a tin can tied to Jefferson's reputation . . . that has rattled through the ages and pages of history books ever since."[34] After the DNA study, however, Ellis veered and enthused to *Newsweek*: "For all intents and purposes, this ends the debate." Ellis also referred to Jefferson as a "white supremacist" in the *New Republic* and *William & Mary Quarterly*.[35]

During his grandfather's volatile re-election campaign for the presidency in 1804, Jeff Randolph knew better than most that history, now as then, has become politicized in America, as illustrated by the widespread acceptance of the Jefferson-Hemings legend as historical "fact." It seems that a period of self-analysis for the history profession is in order—at least under the portico that shelters Jeffersonian scholars. As much as this controversy has been about DNA's attempt to solve a time-shrouded mystery, it should be an occasion for reflection on the all-too-human failings of a few historians.[36]

For many scholars of race relations that promote "critical race theory" in America, the Jefferson-Hemings story provides further evidence of the "systemic racism" they say permeates American society. Indeed, for many, acceptance of Jefferson's guilt has become a kind of litmus test for "social justice": those scholars who continue to question the paucity of facts supporting the Hemings allegation have been stigmatized as racially insensitive or white supremacists.[37] This is intellectually stultifying, dishonest, and misdirects the focus of the controversy from the evidence.[38] The Jefferson controversy is no longer a scholarly investigation about a sexual affair, but a muscular, social analysis on slavery. That is fundamentally unfair to Jefferson's legacy, and to the specific historical record challenging the allegation. Social justice and cultural agendas are, and should be, entirely irrelevant to the historical facts.

"Critical race theory" is the latest battleground in the culture war. Since the murder of George Floyd last year, critical race theory's key concepts, including "systemic racism," "white privilege," and "white fragility," have become ubiquitous in America's elite institutions, according to author Christopher F. Rufo.[39] And Thomas Jefferson has been caught in the middle of this debate about the history of slavery and racism. Recently, The National Archives' task force on racism claimed in a little-noticed report to the top librarian that the Archives' own Rotunda—which houses Jefferson's Declaration of Independence, the US Constitution and the Bill of Rights—is an example of "structural racism" and that the Founding Fathers and "other white, historically impactful Americans are portrayed too positively." The National Archives' task force suggested a website on American "milestone documents" be less celebratory of historically impactful Americans like Thomas Jefferson. "For example, a search of Thomas Jefferson in OurDocuments.gov brings up 24 results. He is described in this sample lesson plan as a 'visionary' who took 'vigorous action' to strengthen the 'will of the nation to expand westward,'" the report continues. 'The plan does not mention that his policy of westward expansion forced Native Americans off their ancestral land, encouraged ongoing colonial violence, and laid the groundwork for further atrocities like the Trail of Tears,' it added."[40]

In 2018, President of the University of Virginia Teresa Sullivan, a university Thomas Jefferson founded, commissioned a ninety-six-page report regarding

Jefferson and the issue of slavery. The introduction of the report included this statement: "The President's Commission on Slavery and the University is not a South African truth and reconciliation commission, but we have been deeply informed by a similar restorative justice model." The commission was convened in 2013 by the then president to examine the university's "racist past."[41] The report details the university's history with slavery and acknowledges Jefferson's participation in slavery.[42] According to accounts, Sullivan received criticism from students and faculty members for invoking Jefferson without acknowledging his racism.[43] In November 2016, she sent two emails calling for respect and civility during the volatile 2016 election. In the correspondence, she suggested that students and staff look to Jefferson's actions after the election of 1800 to inspire unity and respect. Noelle Hurd, a psychology professor at UVA, wrote to Sullivan expressing her disappointment at the "use of Thomas Jefferson as a moral compass." Hundreds more students and employees signed the letter.[44] "Tensions have risen even higher since the 2016 election, especially after the Unite the Right rally that descended on UVA's campus and the surrounding city of Charlottesville last August," one newspaper reported.[45] "A month afterward, students gathered to protest the university's ineffectual response to the white nationalists and shrouded the Jefferson statue on campus in black. On the university's founders' day last April, the words "racist + rapist" were spray painted at the base of the [Jefferson] statue."[46]

At the University of Virginia, it is no longer a debated issue for the students whether Jefferson fathered children with Sally. It is accepted fact in the history department. *The Cavalier Daily*, the student newspaper, quoted the former chair of the History Department, Professor Peter Onuf: "The argument is so overwhelming that we need to move on to other more fruitful sites of inquiry."[47]

This social justice, cultural climate of critical race theory is not confined to the University of Virginia. Agenda driven courses taught at Wesleyan University and Bridgewater College require students to accept as historical fact that Jefferson fathered children by Sally. Canisius College had a senior seminar which was described as a wide range of infamous scandals in American history, including sexual hijinks, shady financial practices, political corruption, and sports fixing. "Among other episodes, we will read about Thomas Jefferson's relationship with his slave,

Sally Hemings; . . . the alleged adultery of the Rev. Henry Ward Beecher; . . . the Clinton-Lewinsky affair. By examining such episodes, the course will reveal the seamy underside of American cultural, financial, and political values." That Jefferson had a "relationship" with Hemings is a prerequisite that the student must accept. The only issue is where that "relationship" ranks with the other examples of sexual misconduct and financial fraud.[48]

The Jefferson-Hemings debate has been turned into cultural symbolism for people of various political persuasions. As Timothy Sandefur notes in his essay *Anti-Jefferson, Left and Right,* "What damns Thomas Jefferson in conservative and multiculturalists eyes alike is his appeal 'to all men and at all times,' and not to the considerations of race, class, and sex, of which the left approves, or to the 'whispers of dead men' that the conservative hears."[49] The Hemings story permits some to see Jefferson's whole political life as "bound up in the sexual exploitation of a slave," Sandefur adds. "Jefferson's position as the Enlightenment figure in America can thus be seen as inseparable from his ownership and exploitation of slaves."[50]

Take, for example, this pugilistic exchange between a prominent author and genealogist Herbert Barger, which exemplifies this cultural battle ground:

> Mr. Barger . . . I must tell you that I find it difficult to understand your utter and complete contempt for the history of the slaves at Monticello . . . I am fully aware that the Monticello Association, along with historians friendly to their point of view, has spent the last 100 years or so putting the blame for the fatherhood of Sally Hemings' children on one or the other of the Carr brothers. Now that the DNA results have effectively ruled out the Carr brothers as possible fathers of Sally's children, you are going about the despicable business of trying to place the blame elsewhere . . . In addition, I found your entire efforts to exonerate Mr. Jefferson from any potential fatherhood of Sally's children, while at the same time seeking to place the blame elsewhere—indeed, anywhere but upon Jefferson himself—to be absurd and racist and beneath contempt. Do not look to me for

support for your pathetic efforts in this regard . . . My advice to you, Mr. Barger, is to get a grip . . . [51]

History Professor David Mayer gives a tangible name to this heated Jefferson-Hemings debate: "Presentism." The term presumes that the historical past can be judged by the contemporary standards of the present.[52] Presentism, Mayer argues, plagues historical discussions of the past by its inability to make allowances for prevailing historical conditions.[53] "The rise of three related phenomena in higher education, the 'political correctness' movement, multiculturalism, and post-modernism explain why the Jefferson-Hemings myth has become so readily accepted today, not only by the American general public but also by scholars who should know better."[54] What began on behalf of diversity, Mayer argues, has devolved into a social movement merged with disturbing distortions in scholarship and public discourse.[55]

According to Mayer, the historical profession today has lost much of the standards by which evidence can be objectively weighed and evaluated in the search for historical facts. Taken together, political, social and cultural agendas have created an environment in the academic arena in which scholars feel pressured to accept the Jefferson-Hemings myth. "White scholars in particular" Mayer argues, "fear that by challenging the dubious Hemings narrative, they will be called racists. Questioning the Hemings allegation has been equated with the denigration of African Americans and their place in American history."[56] This argument is intellectually dishonest, unfair, and morally bankrupt, Mayer reasons:

> Some historians in the debate have ceased to function as an historian and instead have manipulated history, carefully marshaling every piece of evidence in favor of the desired interpretation. As to the evidence against the allegation, some scholars have carefully doctored all the evidence to the contrary, either by suppressing it when that seemed plausible, or by distorting it when suppression was not possible. It is far more likely that some historians involved in this debate are engaged in revisionism at its best—that is to say, the prostitution of scholarship for political

ends. Some historians have turned this entire issue from one of scholarly evidence and interpretation, to a discussion on slavery and Jefferson's racial views.[57]

Julian Boyd, renowned editor of the *Jefferson Papers*, seems to agree and summed up the revisionist movement: "[The] despairing, ambivalent, indecisive and guilt-ridden Jefferson may be soothing to those who eagerly embrace the concept of collective guilt, who project our views of the rights of women and blacks into the past . . . but it is assuredly not scholarship, and the resultant Jefferson—unless I have wasted thirty of the best years of my life in studying all his recorded actions—is only an imaginative creature and, in my view, a rather repulsive one."[58]

As columnist Edwin Yoder has noted, "Since the hack journalist and thwarted office-seeker James Callender first published his scurrilities, the Jefferson/Hemings controversy has had a run of nearly two centuries. And the longer it continues, the more it carries the marks of a *kulturkampf:* a culture war."[59] As Yoder concludes, "That there is slight evidence of this alleged liaison, and much negative evidence, seems to make little or no difference. The pseudo-historical drama is now deeply inscribed in public consciousness by movies, televised 'docudrama,' sloppy journalism, and historical polemics. It conforms to a mythic pattern, and such patterns are in their nature resistant to prosaic facts, especially when tinged by romance."[60]

Yoder echoes Professor Mayer's views on historical revisionism, holding that "the tissue of hearsay and distortion that characterizes popular versions of the 'affair' is to be expected now that historical analysis is a fading art."[61]

I have found logical, plausible, sensible explanations for the paternity of Sally's children that do not inculpate Thomas Jefferson.[62] In my view, belief in the paternity allegation is literally a concocted myth, a symptom of a disconcerting trend injected not only into the Jefferson-Hemings controversy, but academia as well. I was particularly troubled in my research by the fact that some biographers have mangled professional standards in seizing upon the emotionally charged DNA results. Any knowledgeable Jefferson historian knows full well that he was accused of the "crime against nature" that he most abhorred—miscegenation (race mixing).[63] In fact, only six months before he died in 1826, Jefferson explained his "aversion" to "the mixture of colour."[64]

Some partisan historians have abjured the potent testimony of Jefferson's grandchildren, his own private denials of the charge, the fact that this behavior would be in fundamental contradiction to his towering character, and his massive powers of self-control. In the process, a few prominent scholars negligently presumed, ignored, omitted, or misrepresented the findings that exonerate Jefferson, to mine their own simmering dyspepsia about slavery. As one historian of slavery has unfairly declared: "White historians were determined not to listen to Madison Hemings, a historical figure who said things they did not want to hear."[65] This is monumentally wrong as the most prominent Jeffersonian historian, Dumas Malone, explained: "To me the story would be no more credible (and no more creditable) if the supposed object of Mr. Jefferson's amours had been white. So far as I am concerned, the question of race is entirely irrelevant."[66] Malone added, perhaps, the most important point in the entire controversy: "From my understanding of [Jefferson's] character, temperament, and judgment I do not believe that he would have done that with a woman of any sort. If I find the story unbelievable it is not because of Sally's color."[67] Historian Virginius Dabney agreed with Malone, declaring: "To charge him with that degree of imprudence and insensitivity requires extraordinary credulity . . . Quite obviously the truth must be sought in the life he actually lived, not in what political enemies or social reformers have said about that life for their own purposes, good or bad."[68]

One of the foremost Jefferson scholars, Professor Merrill Peterson, grasped the nettle: "American history has sometimes seemed a protracted litigation—hearings, negotiations, trials, and appeal in endless number—on Thomas Jefferson."[69] Unfortunately, most have presumed "Mr. Jefferson" guilty of the paternity charge. Yet, what troubles me most about the remnants of this "revisionist Sally" mood, is that some of Jefferson's most interesting accomplishments have been obscured:[70]

—Jefferson was the president who abolished the slave trade with Africa.

—the indefatigable Virginian taught himself to read and write Spanish, while on his nineteen-day voyage across the ocean to France.

—Jefferson was the first president to celebrate the Fourth of July at the White House, when he held a festival complete with horse races, food, and music from the United States Marine Band.

—Though born a wealthy man, he died a debtor, having spent the majority of his time on launching our nation, a stark contrast to today's politicians.

—In 1814, after British warships burned the White House and the Library of Congress, Jefferson sold the majority of his personal books to the library to jumpstart its recovery.

Commenting on the Kennedy assassination in 1967, famed CBS anchorman and journalist Walter Cronkite observed: "Only in fiction do we find all the loose ends neatly tied. Real life is not all that tidy."[71] And neither is the Jefferson-Hemings case. Obviously, a large number of people, for various cultural or political reasons, passionately want to believe they have a place in American history: that Thomas Jefferson fathered Sally Hemings's children. But it is not the role of historians to make people feel good about their widespread family stories. The role of historians is simply to explain the past by following objective methodology and the historical evidence, however upsetting this conclusion may be.[72]

Coming to terms with Jefferson in the twenty-first century is not easy for some. Jefferson was no saint, but none of his biographers claimed he was. His changing opinions about race and slavery cannot be glossed over. No one will deny that the facts about the paternity of Sally's children are repulsive evidence of one of the worst aspects of the slave system—the manner by which some enslaved women were sexually abused by their masters or others. Nevertheless, whether Jefferson or others at Monticello were "racists" as defined by twenty-first-century standards is an entirely different scholarly issue than whether he had sexual relations with a fourteen-year-old slave girl.[73]

The Hemings myth has now come full circle. In 1840, Citizens of Albemarle County passed a resolution "vindicating the memory of Mr. Jefferson from posthumous slanders" with regard to his private character. These individuals were his neighbors, who "had an opportunity of personally knowing the true state of facts."[74] The Marquis de Lafayette said that Jefferson was "everything that is good, up right, enlightened and clever, and is respected and beloved by everyone that knows him."[75]

On his deathbed, Jefferson spoke of the slanders and libel against him, uttering: "[T]hey had never known him. They had created an imaginary being clothed with odious attributes, to whom they had given his name."[76] Finally, only two people know the absolute truth: one was Sally Hemings, who wrapped herself in the mantle of silence her entire life on the accusation. Perhaps she believed that it deserved nothing more. The other was Thomas Jefferson, who privately denied the charge to friends and colleagues, declaring that "truth is . . . great and will prevail if left to herself . . . she is the proper and sufficient antagonist to error."[77]

Quite obviously, the debate over Jefferson-Hemings will continue. As the prominent historian C. Vann Woodward commented: "The sad probability is that as long as the majestic bronze figure stands in its marble temple near the Potomac, some version of the old Sally story will be periodically hung round its neck."[78] Yet the truth about Thomas Jefferson must be gleaned in the life he led, not what his political enemies poured into his life as a tonic for their own purposes. Let a sensible, fair-minded, informed public decide where the truth lies, mindful of Jefferson's own words:

When tempted to do anything in secret, ask yourself if you would do it in public; if you would not, be sure it is wrong.[79]

APPENDIXES
"THE FAMILY DENIAL"[1]

Ellen (Eleanora) Wayles Randolph Coolidge to her husband, Joseph Coolidge, Jr.

Edgehill 24 October 1858

I am just from church, a church originally planned by Grandpapa, where I hear a good sermon from an Episcopalian Clergyman, a young man, the Revd. M Butler.

I have been talking freely with my brother Jefferson on the subject of the "yellow children" and will give you the substance of our conversation, with my subsequent reflections.

It is difficult to prove a negative. It is impossible to prove that Mr. Jefferson never had a coloured mistress or coloured children and that these children were never sold as slaves. The latter part of the charge however is disproved by it atrocity, and its utter disagreement with the general character and conduct of Mr. Jefferson, acknowledged to be a humane man and eminently a kind master Would he who was always most considerate of the feelings and the well-being of his slaves, treat them barbarously only when they happened to be his own children, and leave them to be sold in a distant market when he might have left them free--as you know he did several of his slaves, directing his executor to petition the Legislature of Virginia for leave for them to remain in the State after they were free. Some of them are here to this day.

It was his principle (I know that of my own knowledge) to allow such of his slaves as were sufficiently white to pass for white men, to withdraw quietly from the plantation; it was called running away, but they were never reclaimed, I remember four instances of this, three young men and one girl, who walked away and staid away. Their whereabouts was perfectly known but they were left to themselves--for they were white enough to pass for white. Some of the children currently reported to be Mr. Jefferson's were about the age of his own grandchildren. Of course he must have been carrying on his intrigues in the midst of his daughters family and insulting the sanctity of the home by his profligacy. But he had a large family of grandchildren of all ages, older & younger. Young men and young girls. He lived, whenever he was at Monticello, and entirely for the last seventeen years of his life, in the midst of these young people, surrounded by them, his intercourse with them of the freest and most affectionate kind. How comes it that his immoralities were never suspected by his own family--that his daughter and her children rejected with horror and contempt the charges brought against him. That my brother, then a young man certain to know all that was going on behind the scenes, positively declares his indignant belief in the imputations and solemnly affirms that he never saw or heard the smallest thing which could lead him to suspect that his grandfather's life was other than perfectly pure. His apartments had no private entrance not perfectly accessible and visible to all the household. No female domestic ever entered his chambers except at hours when he was known not to be in the public gaze. But again I put it to any fair mind to decide if a man so admirable to his domestic character as Mr. Jefferson, so devoted to his daughters and their children, so fond of their society, so tender, considerate, refined in his intercourse with them, so watchful over them in all respects, would be likely to rear a race of half-breeds under their eyes and carry on his low amours in the circle of his family.

Now many causes existed which might have given rise to suspicions, setting aside the inveterate rage and malice of Mr. Jefferson's traducers.

The house at Monticello was a long time in building and was principally built by Irish workmen. These men where known to have had children of whom the mothers were black women. But these women were much better pleased to have it supposed that such children were their master's. "Le Czar m'a fait l'honneur de me faire cet enfant." There were dissipated young men in the neighborhood who sought the society of the mulatresses and they in like manner were not anxious to establish any claim of paternity in the results of such associations.

One woman known to Mr. J. Q. Adams and others as "dusky Sally" was pretty notoriously the mistress of a married man, a near relation of Mr. Jefferson's, and there can be small question that her children were his. They were all fair and all set free at my grandfather's death, or had been suffered to absent themselves permanently before he died. The mother, Sally Hemmings, had accompanied Mr. Jefferson's younger daughter to Paris and was lady's maid to both sisters.

Again I ask is it likely that so fond, so anxious a father, whose letters to his daughters are replete with tenderness and with good counsels for their conduct, should (when there were so many ocher objects upon whom to fix his illicit attentions) have selected the female attendant of his own pure children to become his paramour? The dining will not bear telling. There are such things, after, as moral impossibilities.

The habit that the Southern slaves have of adopting their master's names is another cause of misrepresentation and misapprehension. There is no doubt that such of Mr. Jefferson's slaves as were sold after his death would call themselves by his name. One very notorious villain who never had been the property of Mr. Jefferson, took his name and proclaimed himself his son. He was as black as a crow, and born either during Mr. Jefferson's absence abroad, or under some other circumstances which rendered the truth of his assertion simply impossible.

I have written thus far thinking you might chuse to communicate my letter to Mr. Bulfinch. Now I will tell you in confidence what Jefferson told me under the like condition. Mr. Southall and himself young men together, heard Mr. Peter Carr say with a laugh, that "the old gentleman had to bear the blame of his and Sam's (Col. Carr) misdeeds."

There is a general impression that the four children of Sally Hemmings were all the children of Col. Carr, the most notorious good-natured Turk that ever was master of a black seraglio kept at other men's expense. His deeds are as well known as his name.--I have written in great haste for I have very little time to write. We sat down sixteen at my brother's table today, and are never less than twelve--children, grandchildren, visitors, friends--I am in a perfect whirl. Yet this is the way in which I lived during all my girlish days, and then it seemed the easiest and most natural thing imaginable. Now I wonder how any head can bee it long. But Jefferson and Jane are the most affectionate parents and the kindest neighbors that I know.

****

The second part of the "Family Denial" is a letter from Henry S. Randall, reporting a conversation between himself and Thomas Jefferson Randolph in which Randolph stated that Peter Carr had fathered Sally Hemings's children. This letter was published in full in MILTON E. FLOWER, JAMES PARTON–THE FATHER OF MODERN BIOGRAPHY 236-39 (1951), and printed in Fawn Brodie's biography of Jefferson:

> *Dear Sir [to James Parton],*
> *Courtland Village, N.Y. June 1, 1868*
>
> The "Dusky Sally Story"– the story that Mr. Jefferson kept one of his slaves, (Sally Hemings) as his mistress and had children by her, was once extensively believed by respectable men, and I believe both John Quincy Adams and our own Bryant sounded their poetical lyres on this very poetical subject!
>
> Walking about mouldering Monticello one day with Col. T. J. Randolph (Mr. Jefferson's oldest grandson) he showed me a smoke blackened and sooty room in one of the colonnades and informed me it was Sally Hemings' room. He asked me if I knew how the story of Mr. Jefferson's connection with her originated. 1 told him I did not. "There was a better excuse for it, said he, thanyou might think: she had children which resembled Mr. Jefferson so closely that it was plain that they had his blood in their veins." He said in one case the resemblance was so close,

that at some distance or in the dusk the slave, dressed in the same way, might have been mistaken for Mr. Jefferson. He said in one instance, a gentleman dining with Mr. Jefferson looked so startled as he raised his eyes from the latter to the servant behind him, that his discovery of the resemblance was so perfectly obvious to all. Sally Hemings was a house servant and her children were brought up house servants that the likeness between master and slave was blazoned to all the multitudes who visited this political mecca.

Mr. Jefferson had two nephews, Peter Carr and Samuel Carr whom he brought up in his house. They were the sons of Jefferson's sister and her husband Dabney Carr, that young and brilliant orator described by Wirt, who shone so conspicuously in the dawn of the Revolution, but who died in 17--. Peter was peculiarly gifted and amiable. Of Samuel I know less. But he became a man of repute and sat in the State Senate of Virginia. Col. Randolph informed me that Sally Hemings was the mistress of Peter, and her sister Betsey the mistress of Samuel and from these connections sprang the progeny which resembled Mr. Jefferson. Both the Heming girls were light colored and decidedly good looking. The Colonel said their connection with the Carrs was perfectly notorious at Monticello, and scarcely disguised by the latter never disavowed by them. Samuel's proceedings were particularly open. Col. Randolph informed me that there was not the shadow of suspicion that Mr. Jefferson in this or any other instance had commerce with female slaves. At the periods when these Car, children were boon, he, Col. Randolph, had charge of Monticello! He gave all the general directions, gave out their clothes to the slaves, etc., etc. He said Sally Henings was treated, dressed, etc., exactly like the rest. He said Mr. Jefferson never locked the door of his room by day:

and that he (Col. Randolph) slept within sound of his breathing at night. He said he had never seen a motion, or a look, or a circumstance which led him to suspect for an instant that there was a particle more of familiarity between Mr. Jefferson and Sally Hemings than between him and the most repulsive servant in the establishment and that no person ever living at Monticello dreamed of such a thing. With Betsy Hemings, whose children also resembled him, his habitual meeting, was less frequent and the chance of suspicion still less, and his connection with her was never indeed alleged by any of our northern politicians, or poets.

Col. Randolph said that he had spent a good share of his life closely about Me Jefferson at home and on journeys in all sorts of circumstances and be fully believed him chaste and pure as "immaculate a man as God ever created." Mr. Jefferson's oldest daughter Mrs. Gov. Randolph, took the Dusky Sally stories much to heart. But she never spoke to her sons but once on the subject. Not long before her death she called two of them the Colonel and George Wythe Randolph to her. She asked the Colonel if he remembered "– Henings (the slave who most resembled Mr. Jefferson) was born." He said he could answer by referring to the book containing the list of slaves. He turned to the book and found that the slave was born at the time supposed by Mrs. Randolph. She then directed her son's attention to the fact that Mr. Jefferson and Sally Hemings could not have met -were far distant from each other for fifteen months prior to such birth. She bade her sons remember this fact, and always to defend the character of their grandfather. It so happened when I was afterwards examining an old account book of Jefferson's I came pop on the original entry of this slaves birth: and I was then able from well known circumstances to prove the fifteen months separation–but those circumstances have faded from me memory. I have no doubt I could recover them however did Mr. Jefferson's vindication in the least depend upon them.

Colonel Randolph said that a visitor at Monticello dropped a newspaper from his pocket or accidentally left it After he was gone, he (Colonel Randolph) noticed the paper and found some very insulting remarks about Mr. Jefferson's mulatto children. The Colonel said he felt provoked. Peter and Sam Carr were lying not far off under a shade tree. He took the paper and put it in Peters hands, pointing out the article. Peter mad it, tears coursing down his checks, and then handed it to Samuel. Samuel also shed tears. Peter exclaimed "Ar'nt you and I a couple of____ pretty fellows to bring this disgrace on poor old uncle who has always fed us! We ought to be_____ by _____.

I could give fifty more facts were there time and were there any need of it, to show Mr. Jefferson's innocence of this and all similar offenses against propriety.

I asked Col. Randolph why on earth Me. Jefferson did put these slaves who looked like him out of the public sight by sending them to his Befond [Bedford] estate or elsewhere. He said Mr. Jefferson never betrayed the least consciousness of the resemblance and although be (Col. Randolph) and he had no doubt his mother, would have been very glad to have them removed, that both and all venerated Mr. Jefferson too deeply to broach such a topic to him. What suited him, satisfied them. Mr. Jefferson was deeply attached to the Carrs especially to Peter. He was extremely indulgent to them and the idea of watching then for faults or vices probably never occurred to him.

Do you ask why I did not state, or at least hint the above facts in my Life of Jefferson? I wanted to do so, but Colonel Randolph, in this solitary case alone, prohibited me from using at my discretion the information he furnished me with. When I rather pressed him, on the point, he said, pointing to the family graveyard, "You are not bound to prove a negation. If I should allow you to take Peter Carr's corpse into Court and plead guilty over it to shelter Mr. Jefferson, I should not dare again to walk by his grave: he would rise and spurn me." I am exceedingly glad Col. Randolph did overrule me in this particular. I should have made a shameful mistake. If I had unnecessarily defended him (and it was purely unnecessary to offer any defense) at the expense of a dear nephew and a noble man hating a single folly.___

I write this currente calamo, and you will not understand that in telling what Col. Randolph and others said, I claim to give their precise language. I give it as I now recall it. I believe I hit at least the essential purport and spirit of it in every case.

Do you wonder that the above explanations were not made by Mr. Jefferson's friends when the old Federal Party were hurling their villanes at him for keeping a Congo Harem. Nobody could have furnished a hint of explanation outside the family. The secrets of an old Virginia Manor house were like the secrets of an Old Norman Castle. Dr. Dungleson, and Professor Tucker had lived years near Mr. Jefferson in the University and were often at Monticello. They saw what others saw. But Dr. D. told me that neither he nor Prof. T. ever heard the subject named in Virginia. An awe and veneration was felt for Mr. Jefferson among his neighbors which in their view, rendered it shameful to even talk about his name in such a connexion. Dr. D. told me that he never heard of Col. Randolph talking with anyone on the subject bot [sic] me. But he said in his own secret mind he had always believed the matter stood just as Col. Randolph explained it to me.

You ask if I will not write a cheap Life of Jefferson of 600 pages, to go into families who will not purchase a larger work. I some years ago commenced such a condensed biography. I suspended the work when the storm of Civil War burst over the land. I have not again resumed it. I may yet do so hereafter–I have been strongly urged to the work by a prominent publishing house, and if I find time I may again mount my old hobby.

I must again express my regret that I cannot send you a fine autograph letter of Mr. Jefferson on some interesting topic but I am stripped down to those his family expected me to keep. But I send you some characteristic leaves—one from his draft of his Parliamentary Law.

Very truly yours,
Henry S. Randall

James Parton, Esq.

APPENDIX B [2]
MINORITY REPORT BY DR. WALLENBORN

DATE: March 23, 2000
TO: Readers of the Attached Reports
FROM: Daniel P. Jordan, President, TJF
SUBJECT: Dr. Wallenborn's Minority Report

White McKenzie (Ken) Wallenborn, M.D., was a conscientious member of the *ad hoc* staff committee that I appointed in late 1998 to review, comprehensively and critically, all the evidence, scientific and otherwise, relating to the relationship of Thomas Jefferson and Sally Hemings and to report its findings and recommendations to me in a timely manner. Twice in the spring of 1999, during and after the conclusion of the work of the committee, Ken expressed some reservations to me, and I encouraged him to write up his concerns. It was my understanding at the time that he wanted his report to be for my review and consideration, not general circulation, but Ken now feels that it should be distributed more broadly -- and I agree. I subsequently learned that Ken gave a copy to the committee chairman.

For the record, Ken's concerns were reviewed and considered systematically and seriously. I believe the issues he raised are addressed in the research report of the committee, and I concur with the findings of the committee. **I would** encourage anyone interested in the general subject to read both reports and draw their own conclusions.

I recognize that honorable people can disagree on this subject, as indeed they have for over two hundred years. Further, we know that the historical record has gaps that perhaps can never be filled, and mysteries that may never be fully resolved. The Foundation stands ready to review any fresh evidence at any time and to reassess our understanding of the matter in light of more complete information. In the meantime, while respecting fully Ken's opinions, I stand by the research report as circulated.

Thomas Jefferson Foundation
DNA Study Committee
Minority Report
April 12, 1999

Preface:

When Daniel P. Jordan, President of the Thomas Jefferson Foundation, convened the DNA Study Committee on 12/21/98, he asked the committee to evaluate the DNA study (Eugene Foster et al) in context of all evidence, to assess the impact on historical interpretation at Monticello, and to formulate a course of action for the Thomas Jefferson Foundation. As a result, numerous meetings of the committee were held. Voluminous material was presented and studied, outside opinions were obtained, a discussion meeting was held with the African American Advisory Committee, and discussion and debate freely occurred between members of the committee. As the DNA Study Committee began to formulate its report to Mr. Jordan, certain areas of disagreement became apparent and this has prompted the preparation of a minority report. Because there were many areas of agreement among all of the committee members, these will not be included in the minority report.

Areas of Disagreement:

Historical Evidence

The DNA Study Committee majority appears to agree that the DNA study showed that Eston Hemings direct male line descendants had an identical DNA haplotype to that of Field Jefferson's direct male line descendants and that assuming that Thomas Jefferson's DNA haplotype was identical to his uncle's descendants DNA haplotype, this would prove that Thomas Jefferson was related to Eston Hemings (Sally Hemings youngest son). The DNA Study Committee agrees that this finding alone does not prove that Thomas Jefferson was the father of Eston Hemings. However the majority of the committee feels that in view of multiple strands of documentary and statistical evidence combined with the DNA findings substantiates the paternity of all the children listed under Sally Hemings name in Jefferson's Farm Book. The minority report agrees that there is significant historical evidence that would show that Thomas Jefferson could be the father of Eston Hemings but also strongly feels that there is significant historical evidence of equal statue that indicates that Thomas Jefferson was not the father of Eston Hemings (or any of Sally Hemings' children).

These events happened more or less two hundred years ago and only four or possibly five people (Thomas Jefferson, Sally Hemings, Randolph Jefferson, Peter Carr, and Samuel Carr) would have known the truth about the paternity question. Only one of them has left us direct evidence in their own words and handwriting. On July 1, 1805, Thomas Jefferson wrote a letter to Robert Smith, Secretary of the Navy, in which he said: "The inclosed copy of a letter to Mr. Levi Lincoln will so fully explain it's own object, that I need say nothing in that way. I communicate it to particular friends because I wish to stand with them on the ground of truth; neither better nor worse than that makes me. You will perceive that I plead guilty to one of their charges, that when young and single, I offered love to a handsome lady. I acknowledge its incorrectness. It is the only one founded on truth among all their allegations against me ... "This has to be a very straight forward denial of all the Federalist charges which included the report of a sexual liaison with Sally Hemings (that he had fathered Sally Hemings' children). Some feel that this statement is ambiguous but how can it be? Mr. Jefferson and his cabinet members Robert Smith and Levi Lincoln certainly knew all of the Federalist charges against the president. Thomas Jefferson was not known to issue falsehoods to his intimate associates. The minority report maintains that this statement by Thomas Jefferson is a significantly powerful denial.

In a letter to Dr. George Logan (Penn.) in 1816, Thomas Jefferson said "As to Federal slanders, I never wished them to be answered, but by the tenor of my life, half a century of which has been on a theater at which the public have been spectators and competent judges of its merit. Their approbation has taught a lesson, useful to the world, that the man who fears no truths has nothing to fear from lies. I should have fancied myself half guilty had I condescended to put pen to paper in refutation of their falsehoods, or drawn to them respect by any notice of myself."

In the courtroom-like atmosphere of this committee study, the defendant has made two rather significant denials in his own words and handwriting of the Federalist charges against him. None of the others who would have had first hand knowledge of the facts have put down statements in their own handwriting and their own words.

Edmund Bacon (born March 28, 1785 near Monticello) had the title of overseer at Monticello from September 29, 1806 until about October 15, 1822 (sixteen years). Edmund Bacon was interviewed at length (several weeks) by the Rev. Hamilton Wilcox Pierson, president of Cumberland College, Princeton, WVA around 1861 or 1862 at Mr. Bacon's home. Mr. Bacon recalled that he went to live with Mr. Jefferson on Dec. 27, 1800 and was with him precisely twenty years but Mr. Jefferson recorded his employment as overseer for sixteen years. Possibly Mr. Bacon had started working as early as age sixteen but was not hired as overseer until age twenty and if so would have been working at Monticello when Harriet Hemings was conceived and born. Mr. Bacon's recollections and letters from Thomas Jefferson provided a remarkable record of the years that he was at Monticello. At times his memory was not absolutely accurate on minor matters. Mr. Bacon had many observations about Mr. Jefferson including: "his skin was very clear and pure-just like he was in principle." He also commented on William C. Rives, a youngster, who would stay and play at Monticello with the other boys (most likely the Randolphs, Carrs, and Maria's son, Francis)...Willie would stay with Mr. Bacon rather than at the house (Monticello) because the other boys were too intimate with the negro women to suit him. Bacon also said "he (TJ) could not bear to have a servant whipped, no odds how much he deserved it."

Edmund Bacon also shed some light on the Sally Hemings controversy. "He freed one girl some years before he died, and there was a great deal of talk about it. She was nearly as white as anybody and very beautiful. People said he freed her because she was his own daughter. She was not his daughter, she was ___'s daughter (Rev. Pierson apparently left the name blank to protect that individual.). I know that. I have seen him come out of her mother's room many a morning when I was up to Monticello very early." Bacon had to be referring to Harriet Hemings. If Bacon had actually come to live at Monticello at age sixteen, on December 27, 1800 (before Th. Jefferson was inaugurated for his first term as president), he would have been working at Monticello during the time of conception and birth of Sally Hemings last three children -- Harriet, Madison, and Eston. Bacon's observations are certainly valid information and do strongly suggest that another male was having a sexual liaison with Sally Hemings.

Thomas Jefferson Randolph (1792-1875) was the oldest grandson of Thomas Jefferson and was Mr. Jefferson's farm manager and later executor of his estate. T.J. Randolph is a primary witness who was involved directly and who saw a past situation with his own eyes according to Douglas Adair.

Thomas Jefferson Randolph emphatically denied that Mr. Jefferson had commerce with Sally or any other of his female slaves. Since he "had spent a good share of his life closely about Mr. Jefferson at home and on journeys-in all sorts of circumstances," he could testify that his grandfather was in sexual matters "chaste and pure" -- indeed as "immaculate a man as God ever created." Randall as quoted in Adair's treatise said that Col. Randolph said that he "Slept within sound of his (TJ's) breathing at night." He said that "he had never seen a motion, or a look, or a circumstance which led him to suspect for an instant that there was a particle of familiarity between Mr. Jefferson and Sally Hemings than between him and the most repulsive servant in the establishment --and that no person ever at Monticello dreamed of such a thing."

Thomas Jefferson Randolph also told Randall "Mr. Jefferson had two nephews, Peter Carr and Samuel Carr whom he brought up in his own house. They were the sons of Jefferson's sister and her husband Dabney Carr...who died in 1773...Sally Hemings was the mistress of Peter and her sister Betsey (she was actually the daughter of Sally's half sister) the mistress of Samuel -and from these the progeny which resembled Mr. Jefferson. Both Hemings girls were light colored and decidedly good looking...Their connection with the Carrs was perfectly notorious at Monticello, and scarcely disguised by the latter-never disavowed by them. Samuel's proceedings were particularly open." Col. Randolph told Randall that his mother, Mrs. Gov. Randolph took the Dusky Sally stories much to heart, not long before her death she called two of them-the Colonel and George Wythe Randolph-to her. She asked the Colonel if he remembered when _____ Hemings (the slave who most resembled Mr. Jefferson) was born. The Col. turned to the book containing the list of slaves and found his birthdate. Martha Jefferson Randolph directed her sons attention to the fact that Mr. Jefferson and Sally Hemings could not have met and were far distant from each other-for fifteen months prior to such a birth. Col. Randolph later while examining an old account book of Jefferson's came on the birthdate again and was able from well known circumstances to prove the fifteen months separation. T.J. Randolph never recorded those circumstances.

Now if those circumstances confirming the fifteen months separation between Mr. Jefferson and Sally Hemings before the birth of _____ Hemings who most resembled Mr. Jefferson--and this by most accounts would be Eston Hemings--this would dramatically change the thinking in regards to the DNA studies...Thomas Jefferson would not be the father of Eston. Another Jefferson DNA Haplotype carrier would be the father of Eston and the stories about Peter Carr and Sally Hemings would probably indicate Peter as the father of Sally's other four children. Intensive research by outstanding historical investigators may be able to uncover this answer.

The Monte Carlo Simulation:

This is an interesting simulation to determine the probability that the timing of Th. Jefferson's known visits to Monticello were related to the conception dates of Sally Hemings five children (the study used six children but the significant evidence indicates only five children) as opposed to the null hypothesis that they were unrelated. According to the results obtained, there is only a 1% chance that Sally Hemings's conceptions are coincidental to TJ's presence at Monticello. Based on the Monte Carlo Evaluation, the fact that all 6 conceptions occur during TJ's visits is 100 times more likely if TJ or someone with the same pattern of presence and absence at Monticello is the father.

Comments from the minority:

Statistics can be misleading. The basis for the numbers used in calculating statistical results has to be proven as true representations. In this simulation, two of the three proofs necessary are probably reliable...conception dates and timing of Mr. Jefferson's visits to Monticello. The third proof cannot be proven...Sally Hemings presence at Monticello is not accurately recorded and her presence or absence cannot be proven as also coinciding with Mr. Jefferson's presence.

A good example would be that if Martha Jefferson's message to her sons that Mr. Jefferson was not in the presence of Sally Hemings for fifteen months prior to the birth of Eston (assuming that she was referring to Eston), the odds that were one hundred to one that TJ was the father would be meaningless.

Also because it is impossible to determine the timing of the presence or absence of other males with the Jefferson DNA haplotype at Monticello, you have no way to compare the probability of their being the father of Sally Hemings children with the probability that Mr. Thomas Jefferson was the father. This evidence just is not there for vital comparison studies.

Wetmore's "Memoirs of Madison Hemings":

The minority feels that Madison was telling the truth as he remembered it in his interview by Mr. Wetmore. However it appears that Mr. Wetmore might have harmed his case because of the use of journalistic license. Mr. Madison Hemings admittedly had no formal education but in the memoirs, Mr. Wetmore has Madison using an amazing vocabulary and grammar, and having a remarkable knowledge of history. All of this was remembered some thirty five or forty years after he was at Monticello. Wetmore's use of direct quotes instead of paraphrasing would have helped make the memoirs more believable. As far as the minority can tell, Wetmore's handwritten notes covering his interview have not been found and as a result it is hard to tell when the words were Madison's or Wetmore's.

Summary:

The results of the DNA studies enhance the possibility that Thomas Jefferson was the father of one of Sally Hemings children, Eston Hemings, but the findings do not prove that Thomas Jefferson was the father of Eston. This is a very important difference.

There is historical evidence of more or less equal statue on both sides of this issue that prevent a definitive answer as to Thomas Jefferson's paternity of Sally Hemings' son Eston Hemings or for that matter the other four of her children. In fairness to the descendants of Sally Hemings and the descendants of Thomas Jefferson and Martha Wayles Jefferson, the Thomas Jefferson Foundation should continue to encourage in depth historical research in hopes that accurate answers to very sensitive questions may be found.

In regards to the historical interpretation of Thomas Jefferson and his family, Monticello, and slavery at Monticello, The Thomas Jefferson Foundation should continue to present a properly weighted historical interpretation to visitors. As new historical evidence is found, it should continue to be incorporated into interpretive presentations. However, historical accuracy should never be overwhelmed by political correctness, for if it is, history becomes meaningless. Construction of historically inaccurate buildings on the mountaintop at Monticello would detract from the historically accurate picture that the Thomas Jefferson Foundation is trying to portray.

In summary, the Thomas Jefferson Foundation should continue to seek the truth. If the truth is not known, it should be so stated. The minority feels that it would be improper to accept that portion of the DNA Study Committee's report that says "the DNA study when combined with the multiple strands of documentary and statistical evidence, substantiates Thomas Jefferson's paternity of all the children listed under Sally Hemings name in Jefferson's Farm Book."

The historical evidence is not substantial enough to confirm nor for that matter to refute his paternity of any of the children of Sally Hemings. The DNA studies certainly enhance the possibility but to repeat, do not prove Thomas Jefferson's paternity. These events happened almost two hundred year ago and there were four (five) people who might have known the truth about this issue. Only one of them has answered in his own handwriting and words. Thomas Jefferson denied all the allegations except for the "Walker" affair which he admitted.

Respectfully Submitted,
White McKenzie Wallenborn, M.D.
Author of the Minority Report

APPENDIX C [3]

Reply to Thomas Jefferson Foundation Response to the Minority Report to the DNA Study Committee.

Reply by White McKenzie Wallenborn, M.D.
Author of the Minority Report
Former Clinical Professor, University of Virginia School of Medicine
Former Historical Interpreter, Monticello
June 2000

This is the reply to the response to the Minority Report of the DNA Study Committee by the Thomas Jefferson Foundation through Lucia C. Stanton. With respect to the introductory comments by Mr. Daniel P. Jordan, President of the Thomas Jefferson Foundation, on March 23, 2000 presenting the "Minority Report": Mr. Jordan's invitation to the public to read both reports (DNA Study Committee and Minority Report) and draw their own conclusions has produced an immense positive response to the "Minority Report" from Jefferson scholars, historians, physicians, scientists, statisticians, active and retired college professors, attorneys, genealogists, and the general public. Many of those who have taken the time to read the TJMF report have been shocked to see the evidence that the committee used to reach their conclusions.

Several opening comments should be recorded before beginning the point by point discussion. The Foundation response by Ms. Stanton said that the committee as a whole did not feel the Minority Report was of sufficient weight to warrant a different conclusion. *This statement is anything but the truth because the committee as a whole did not see the Minority Report until well after the release of the final committee report on January 27, 2000. In other words, the chair of the committee did not share the dissenting report (which was submitted on April 12, 1999) with the complete committee.* As a matter of fact, the committee as a whole did not even see the final DNA Study Committee report until 72 hours prior to the release of this report to the public and there was no time to discuss the contents at that time (the committee had finished its deliberations in April 1999 - nine months earlier). There will be more comment about the elastic conception of the truth in section 1.

1. Jefferson denied the relationship (and Ms. Stanton says: "and by implication, Jefferson would not lie.").

In the fall of 1802, James Thomson Callender in a series of scandalous articles in a pro-Federalist weekly newspaper, the "Richmond Recorder" charged Thomas Jefferson with three basic misdeeds. These were as follows: 1) he had a son called Tom by his slave Sally; 2) that he had an affair with a married woman; and 3) that he had paid off a loan with devaluated currency. Although the Federalists continued to attack Mr. Jefferson most of his public life and throughout his retirement, primarily their charges echoed Callender's charges of 1802. The Federalists used them repeatedly against Jefferson.

Callender's allegations concerning the Walker affair with a reference to the "sable damsel", to whom Mr. Jefferson supposedly turned to after he was rejected by Mrs. Walker, were revived and printed again in 1805 in northern papers. This brought about a national political debate about Th. Jefferson's morality in the cases of Mrs. Walker and the concubinage of Sally Hemings.

Usually the Walker story and the Sally affair were lumped together in the same articles which confirm his distinct denial in the following letter. On July 1, 1805, Thomas Jefferson wrote a cover letter to Robert Smith, Secretary of the Navy, and enclosed a copy of a letter to Mr. Levi Lincoln, the Attorney General. In this letter Mr. Jefferson pled guilty to one of the Federalists' charges, that when young and single, he offered love to a handsome lady. He acknowledged the incorrectness of the act but said that it is the only one founded on truth among all their allegations against me. There is no element of ambiguity in Jefferson's denial. The other allegations were well known to all.

In his letter to Dr. George Logan in 1816 he uses the exact phrase and capitalization as James T. Callender used, e.g. "As to Federal slanders, I never wished them to be answered, . . .Their approbation has taught a lesson, useful to the world that the man who fears no truths, has nothing to fear from lies. I should have fancied myself half guilty had I condescended to put pen to paper in refutation of their falsehoods, or drawn to them respect by any notice of myself." So it would appear that in this denial he was again specifically referring to Callender's slanders as picked up by the Federalists.

Ms. Stanton quotes Joanne Freeman as saying Mr. Jefferson had an *elastic conception* of the truth, when he believed the stakes of the nation were high. We are not talking about the stakes of the nation here but the private communication between Th. Jefferson and two of his close personal and political friends. There is no proof, that I am aware of, that would show that Mr. Jefferson told anything but the truth to any of his adult family, friends, or close political associates.

Ms. Stanton also states: "We know Jefferson's rationalizing talents and can imagine ways he could find a fairly comfortable place for this relationship in his view of himself." This statement belies all of Mr. Jefferson's professions of morality, his assertions that a slave master must not abuse those under his control, and especially his strong and well known feelings about miscegenation. An even less scholarly comment was referenced by Ms. Stanton that Jefferson might have considered a sexual liaison with a slave necessary for his health as he had books on the subject of health and sexual activity. This is preposterous . . .in my library are books by Fawn Brodie and Annette Gordon-Reed but by no means do I agree with them nor should anyone make a supposition that I do just because they are in my collection. Th. Jefferson himself never wrote about or was quoted as saying anything that would give credence to these statements.

Robert McDonald writing in "Southern Cultures" said that Callender's allegations had *"scant credibility"* to readers, and even *"Jefferson's reticence which regularly characterized his responses to attacks"* did nothing to enhance their believability.

In summary, the 1805 letter to Robert Smith is both an incisive and direct denial by a primary subject and is certainly not fraught with ambiguity or falsehood. Daniel P. Jordan, President of the Thomas Jefferson Foundation, said in reference to Ms. Stanton's responses *"Her views reflect my own"* but in commenting on the possibility of Mr. Jefferson having a sexual relationship with a slave said in an interview for the Ken Burns documentary on PBS-TV: *"My own belief is that, as one of the contemporaries of Jefferson said, it would be morally impossible for that to have occurred."*

2. Edmund Bacon denied the relationship (and Ms. Stanton says: "and by implication, Bacon too would not lie").

Edmund Bacon said in his interview with Rev. H. Pierson that he began working for Mr. Jefferson on Dec. 27, 1800 and had the title of overseer from Sept. 29, 1806 until Oct. 15, 1822. In Thomas Jefferson's *Farm Book* and *Garden Book* there are at least two references to Bacon having several jobs at Monticello before he became overseer in 1806. His father had apparently done some contract jobs for Mr. Jefferson and so Edmund Bacon was known to Mr. Jefferson well before 1806. In his interview with Rev. Pierson, Mr. Bacon produced letters of Mr. Jefferson's to him, bills from Monticello, etc. to back up some of his remarks. Thomas Jefferson provided a letter of recommendation for Mr. Bacon when he went West looking for land and employment. Whether or not he was at Monticello at Harriet's or Madison's conception is not nearly as important as his observation that Sally's male companion was not Thomas Jefferson. Remember that he was there by all accounts when Eston was conceived (if Eston was conceived at Monticello). There are no secrets on a farm and Monticello was no different, so Edmund Bacon would have been aware of who was having an affair with Sally Hemings even if the affair had been going on before Bacon's arrival. Edmund Bacon, being a primary witness, gives a significant observation that Mr. Thomas Jefferson was not involved with Sally Hemings at least for one of her conceptions.

Now again we see undocumented assumptions on the part of the TJMF responder with an attempt to read the mind of Edmund Bacon. Ms. Stanton says: "First we have to consider reasons Bacon might have had for absolving Jefferson of the Hemings connection (he was talking to a clergyman in 1860, when mores were decidedly different from those of 1800; he was deeply loyal to Jefferson and proud of his association with a great man, and so forth)". Of course the main reason Bacon had for absolving Mr. Jefferson was that he was telling the truth about the situation. As to the mores being different in 1860 from those of 1800, it is doubtful that telling a truism (or a falsehood) to a clergyman in 1860 would be different from telling one in 1800. And what would be wrong with being proud of your association with a great man as long as you are willing to tell the truth about him? There just is no good reason for Mr. Bacon to tell lies during his interview. Being forgetful on minor points is understandable after not being around Mr. Jefferson for thirty eight years. *As a primary witness, Edmund Bacon's revelations are of significant value in discrediting the purported Jefferson-Hemings affair.*

3. Thomas Jefferson Randolph denied the relationship (and Ms. Stanton says: "and by implication, Thomas Jefferson Randolph would not lie").

Actually the DNA evidence may have strengthened Thomas Jefferson Randolph's version of the events. The DNA applies only to Eston Hemings and not to Sally Hemings other four children and in no way eliminates Peter or Samuel Carr from being the father of those four children. The DNA evidence indicates that Eston's father was someone carrying the Jefferson Y-Chromosome. Thomas Jefferson Randolph (and Henry S. Randall) reported that Thomas Jefferson and Sally Hemings could not have met-were far distant from each other-for fifteen months prior to the birth of the Hemings who looked most like Thomas Jefferson and this most likely would have been Eston . . .and here Ms. Stanton erroneously gives these dates as July 1806 to September 1807 when these dates of 15 months separation should be February 1807 to May 1808 (see section 4 of the response). Thus if Eston's father was a Jefferson and Mr. Jefferson was not around Sally for fifteen months prior to Eston's birth, then the most likely father would be Randolph Jefferson or one of his sons. Eston is said to be the son of Sally that most resembled Thomas Jefferson. He was six feet one inch tall and decidedly very light skinned. Madison Hemings was five feet seven inches and a darker mulatto. Beverly's appearance is only vaguely described. Eston was noted by one person in Cincinnati to look just like a Jefferson bust in Washington, thus it would appear that Eston was most likely the one referred to in TJR's comments to Henry S. Randall.

In response to Ms. Stanton's statement that "we know, however, from the Memorandum Books and other sources that Jefferson was at Monticello at the right time to father all of Sally Hemings children". A study of the Memorandum Books, the Farm Book, the Garden Book, and the Monticello Research Staff's Chronology Record of time and location of Mr. Jefferson do not support Ms. Stanton's statement. We do know the dates of Mr. Jefferson's departures from Philadelphia and Washington and the dates of his departures from Monticello to return to those cities. However it is difficult to pinpoint his presence at Monticello on or near the estimated dates of conception. Mr. Jefferson was a man on the move when he returned to Monticello and would make visits overnight or for longer periods to places such as Poplar Forest, Enniscorthy, Warren, Scottsville, Montpelier, Natural Bridge, etc. We do know that he was at Monticello on April 17, 1804 which is ten days before the estimated date of Madison Hemings's conception. He was there at the time of the death of his younger daughter, Maria Jefferson Eppes. She was the daughter that looked most like Th. Jefferson's wife and died from the same cause, late complications of childbirth. It is extremely unlikely that he would show his grief at that time with all of the family around by having a sexual liaison with Sally Hemings ten days after Maria's death. As to Sally's presence or absence from Monticello, there is only sketchy evidence of her whereabouts prior to 1801. From 1801 until 1810, there is almost no evidence bearing on this matter. While Mr. Jefferson was serving as President (1801-1809) and away from Monticello, the house was kept locked. During this time he leased some of his slaves out and it would not be unreasonable to think that Sally and some of the other house staff might have been loaned out to neighbors or nearby relatives at Edgehill, Snowden, Varina, Farmington, etc.

In summary, Thomas Jefferson Randolph's comments to Henry S. Randall were quite candid and were most likely closer to the truth on these matters. *And because he was a primary witness, they are very meaningful.*

4. There is insufficient information about Sally Hemings and other Jeffersons to make a valid statistical estimate of probability.

This was discussed in point three but to be more specific let me give here the estimated dates of conception (EDC), F. Neiman's dates that Th. Jefferson was supposed to be at Monticello (FND), and the dates that the Farm Book, Garden Book, Memorandum Books, and Monticello Research Department's Chronological Record can give Mr. Jefferson's exact location on specific date. *He was known to be at Monticello on April 17, 1804 because this is the date that his daughter Maria died at Monticello.

There are some striking coincidences which also add to the perplexity. For example, when Jefferson finally came home after his second term as President, for some reason Sally quit having children. Randolph Jefferson (TJ's brother and a possible father of Eston) was widowed probably as early as 1796 but as soon as he remarried in late 1808 or early 1809, Sally had no more children. Thomas Jefferson, Jr. (Randolph's son and a possible father of Eston) married on Oct. 3, 1808 and after this date, Sally had no more children. Obstetrical calculations are notoriously fallible and coupled with early or late deliveries being entirely possible, throw more doubt on the Monte Carlo Simulation studies based on these factors. At any rate, Neiman's statistics cry out for valid comparative studies of the other Jefferson males who might have fathered Eston and in the absence of these comparisons, the results are inconclusive. Because no accurate records were kept of these other Jefferson male visits to Monticello, no comparisons can be performed. And given the fact that there is no proof of Sally Hemings's presence at Monticello when Eston was conceived, the picture really becomes muddled.

(A chronology of Jefferson's whereabouts throughout his life compiled by former Monticello Curator, James A. Bear, Jr., lists Jefferson at Monticello on many more dates than Dr. Wallenborn notes. The chronology is available at Monticello's Jefferson Library in Charlottesville, VA.)

5. Madison Hemings recollection lacks credibility because of language used (Ms. Stanton says: "amazing grammar and vocabulary") and his age 68.

Wetmore's article about Madison Hemings can not be called an "accurate reflection of Hemings's statements" as there are not direct quotations of Madison Hemings before and/or subsequent to the publication that reaffirm Wetmore's opinions. To make such a statement without access to Wetmore's interview notes just is not acceptable. Madison Hemings did not sign the original document or at least there is no record of a signature to affirm concurrence with Wetmore's statements. There can be no doubt that the language is Wetmore's and whether or not he changed the content to fit his (Wetmore's) strong political agenda is unknown but becomes suspect. *In other words, this document is very problematic and should not be considered as a primary source of evidence.*

In response to Ms. Stanton's statement that "Hemings would not have forgotten who his father was, no matter his age", it is almost impossible for anyone to say with absolute certainty who his father was. DNA can rule out paternity but does not prove it as we have seen in the case of Eston Hemings. Your parent(s) can tell you who your father is but even this is sometimes wrong, as is seen in the case of Thomas Woodson, who certainly did not know who his father was. If you read Wetmore's article carefully, at no time does Madison Hemings say that his mother told him that Thomas Jefferson was his father.

In final response to Ms. Stanton's comment that "the details of language and historical facts are irrelevant to the main issue: paternity", the entire questionable composition of Wetmore's publication, coupled with the fact that Madison never acknowledged the source of his information as to whom his father was, are very relevant to the main issue of paternity.

The author of the Minority Report of the DNA Study Committee would like to conclude with a statement: If the Thomas Jefferson Foundation and the DNA Study Committee majority had been seeking the truth and had used accurate legal and historical information rather than politically correct motivation, their statement should have been something like this: *"After almost two hundred years of study including recent DNA information, it is still impossible to prove with absolute certainty whether Thomas Jefferson did or did not father any of Sally Hemings five children."* This statement is accurate and honest and it would have helped discourage the campaign by leading universities (including Thomas Jefferson's own University of Virginia), magazines, university publications, national commercial and public TV networks, and newspapers to denigrate and destroy the legacy of one of the greatest of our founding fathers and one of the greatest of all of our citizens.

White McKenzie Wallenborn, M.D., Second Revision: June 29, 2000

SELECTED BIBLIOGRAPHY

The following abbreviations are used in the notes:

AGR, *Hemingses*	Annette Gordon-Reed, *The Hemingses of Monticello* W.W.Norton, 2008
AGR, *Sally*	*Thomas Jefferson and Sally Hemings: An American Controversy*, Charlottesville: University Press of Virginia, 1997.
Anas	The Complete Anas of Thomas Jefferson, ed. Frank B. Sawvel
Betts GB	Thomas Jefferson's Garden Book: 1766–1824, With Relevant Extracts from His Other Writings, ed. Edwin Morris Betts
Bear, *Monticello*	James A. Bear, Jr. Jefferson at Monticello. Charlottesville, 1967
Burstein, *Inner*	Andrew Burstein, *The Inner Jefferson: Portrait of a Grieving Optimist*. Charlottesville: University Press of Virginia, 1995.
Burstein, *Secrets*	Andrew Burstein, *Jefferson's Secrets: Death and Desire at Monticello* (2005).
Brodie, *Intimate*	Brodie, Fawn M. *Thomas Jefferson: An Intimate History*. New York: W. W. Norton, 1998.

Burton, *JV*	Cynthia Burton, *Jefferson vindicated: Fallacies, Omissions and Contradictions in the Hemings genealogical search* (2005)
Cappon, *Letters*	Lester J. Cappon, ed. *The Adams-Jefferson Letters.* Chapel Hill, 1959.
Domestic Life	*Sarah N. Randolph. The Domestic Life of Thomas Jefferson, Compiled from Family Letters and Reminiscences by His Great-Granddaughter.* 1871. Reprint, Charlottesville, 1985.
FL	Edwin M. Betts and James A. Bear, Jr., eds. Family Letters of Thomas Jefferson. Charlottesville, 1986.
FB	Thomas Jefferson's Farm Book: With Commentary and Relevant Extracts from Other Writings, ed. Edwin Morris Betts
Ford, Writings	Paul Leicester Ford, ed. The Writings of Thomas Jefferson. New York 1904-05.
Garden Book	Edwin M. Betts, ed. Thomas Jefferson's Garden Book, 1766-1824. Philadelphia, 1944.
History	Henry Adams, History of the United States of America During the Administrations of Thomas Jefferson
JHT, I-VI	Dumas Malone, Jefferson and His Time LOC Library of Congress
Jefferson *Papers*	Julian P. Boyd et al., eds. Papers of Thomas Jefferson. Princeton, 1950-.34 vols. to date.

MB, I-II	Jefferson's Memorandum Books: Accounts, with Legal Records and Miscellany, 1767–1826, ed. James A. Bear, Jr., and Lucia C. Stanton Parton, Life
Myth,	Coates, Eyler Robert, Sr., ed., *The Jefferson-Hemings Myth: An American Travesty*, Charlottesville, 2001. (Essays by John H. Works, Jr.; Rebecca L. McMurry and James F. McMurry, Jr., M.D.; Herbert Barger; David Murray, PH.D.; White McKenzie Wallenborn, M.D.; C. Michael Moffitt, PH.D.; Eyler Robert Coates, Sr.; Richard E. Dixon; and Bahman Batmanghelidj.)
Parton,	*Life of Thomas Jefferson*
PTJ, I-XXXIX	*The Papers of Thomas Jefferson*
PTJRS, I-VIII	The Papers of Thomas Jefferson. Retirement Series
Randall, *Life* I-III	Henry S. Randall. *The Life of Thomas Jefferson*. 3 New York, 1858.
TDLTJ	Sarah N. Randolph, The Domestic Life of Thomas Jefferson
TJ	Thomas Jefferson TJF The Thomas Jefferson Foundation
VTM	Merrill D. Peterson, Visitors to Monticello
Writings	Thomas Jefferson, Writings, ed. Merrill D. Peterson (Library of America)

SHORT TITLES

CSmH	The Huntington Library, San Marino, California
DLC	Library of Congress
FLP	Family Letters Project, Thomas Jefferson Foundation
JMB	*Jefferson's Memorandum Books*, 2 vols. eds. James A. Bear, Jr. and Lucia C. Stanton (Princeton, NJ: Princeton University Press, 1997)
JFL	*The Family Letters of Thomas Jefferson*, eds. Edwin Morris Betts and James A. Bear, Jr. (Charlottesville, VA: University Press of Virginia, 1986 paperback edition)
MHi	Massachusetts Historical Society
MoSHi	Missouri Historical Society, St. Louis
NHi	New York Historical Society, New York City
PPAmP	American Philosophical Society, Philadelphia
PTL	*Papers* The Papers of Thomas Jefferson, 34 vols. through 2007, eds. Julian Boyd, et al. (Princeton, NJ: Princeton University Press, 1950)
	Papers, RS The Papers of Thomas Jefferson: Retirement Series, 4 vols. through 2007, eds. J. Jefferson Looney, et al. (Princeton, NJ and Oxford, UK: Princeton University Press, 2004 -)

TJF	Thomas Jefferson Foundation, Charlottesville, Virginia
ViHi	Virginia Historical Society, Richmond
ViU	University of Virginia, Charlottesville
WMQ,	William and Mary Quarterly.
Works	*The Works of Thomas Jefferson* (Federal Edition), ed. Paul Leicester Ford (New York: G. P. Putnam's Sons, 1904-05), available at http://oll.libertyfund.org/title/1734.
Writings	*The Writings of Thomas Jefferson* (Library Edition), 20 vols., eds. Andrew A. Lipscomb and Albert E. Bergh (Washington, D. C.: The Thomas Jefferson Memorial Foundation, 1903

ELECTRONIC SOURCES/DIGITAL ARCHIVES

FOUNDERS ONLINE: https://founders.archives.gov/--CORRESPONDENCE AND OTHER WRITINGS OF SEVEN MAJOR SHAPERS OF THE UNITED STATES: George Washington, Benjamin Franklin, John Adams (and family), Thomas Jefferson, Alexander Hamilton, John Jay, and James Madison. Over 184,000 searchable documents, fully annotated, from the authoritative Founding Fathers Papers projects.

At the **Library of Congress**, there are of course the Thomas Jefferson Papers, all of which are accessible online here: https://www.loc.gov/collections/thomas-jefferson-papers/about-this-collection/. There is also a large collection of Nicholas Philip Trist papers, MSS 43232. Letters are arranged by correspondent, so there are separate files for Ellen W. Randolph Coolidge and her husband Joseph, as well as files for letters between Trist and Thomas Jefferson Randolph. You can access information about this collection here: https://

findingaids.loc.gov/db/search/xq/searchMfer02.xq?_id=loc.mss.eadmss.ms006012&_faSection=overview&_faSubsection=did&_dmdid=

The **University of North Carolina at Chapel Hill** has digitized their extensive collection of Nicholas Philip Trist papers, MSS 02104, where you'll find letters between Trist, the Coolidges, and TJR. The finding aid and all of the digitized materials are accessible here: https://finding-aids.lib.unc.edu/02104/

The Charles Bulfinch Papers of the **Boston Athenaeum**, also note this item: "The collection also includes: a manuscript by Ellen Wayles Randolph Coolidge (1796-1876), Thomas Jefferson's granddaughter, reminiscing about Monticello, Jefferson's personal traits, his ability to entertain and his death." I have not yet seen this manuscript but it sounds fascinating. The catalog entry for the collection is here: https://catalog.bostonathenaeum.org/vwebv/holdingsInfo?bibId=375315

Letters from both Coolidge's can be found in the extensive collection of Joseph Coolidge's business partner and long-time friend Augustine Heard and his family in the **Baker Library at Harvard University**. Information for that collection can be found here: https://hollisarchives.lib.harvard.edu/repositories/11/resources/575/collection_organization

Finally, with regard to the Coolidges, the **Massachusetts Historical Society** has a small collection of letters from Joseph Coolidge to his parents, MSS N-92, catalog entry here: http://balthazaar.masshist.org/cgi-bin/Pwebrecon.cgi?v1=18&ti=11,18&Search%5FArg=Joseph%20coolidge&Search%5FCode=FT%2A&CNT=10&PID=JsqfcB3UTwj6haXHQlCWTbMe4RREA&SEQ=20210427135208&SID=1 and Ellen Coolidge's London diaries, MSS N-1027, catalog entry here: http://balthazaar.masshist.org/cgi-bin/Pwebrecon.cgi?v1=4&ti=1,4&SC=Author&SA=Coolidge%2C%20Ellen%20Wayles%20Randolph%2C&PID=olyMzNw8tmz6lnrSibw2ZHay8vTT2&SEQ=20210427135327&SID=2 and "her book of reminiscences containing 'Virginia Legends' and 'Negro Stories' includes fables, folklore, and favorite stories that Ellen recalled from her youth at Monticello," is part of the Coolidge-Lowell family papers, MSS N-2404, entry and finding aid here: http://balthazaar.masshist.org/cgi-bin/Pwebrecon.cgi?v1=1&ti=1,1&SC=Author&SA=Coolidge%2C%20Ellen%20Wayles%20Randolph%2C&PID=o1yMzNw8tmz6lnrSibw2ZHay8vTT2&SEQ=20210427135327&SID=2

PRIMARY BOOKS CONSULTED

Barton, David, *The Jefferson Lies: Exposing the Myths You've Always Believed About Thomas Jefferson* (Nashville, Tenn., 2012).

Bear, James A., Jr. *Jefferson's Cannons of Conduct.* 73 vols. Vol. 8, *Monticello Keepsake Collection.* Charlottesville, VA: Thomas Jefferson Foundation, Inc., 1964.

--------*Jefferson's Advice to His Children and Grandchildren on Their Reading.* Charlottesville, VA: The University of Virginia, 1967, ed. *Jefferson at Monticello.* Charlottesville, VA: The University Press of Virginia, 1967.

Bear, James A., Jr., and Lucia C. Stanton, eds. *Jefferson's Memorandum Books.* 2 vols, The Papers of Thomas Jefferson, Second Series. Princeton, NJ: Princeton University Press, 1997.

Bear, James A., Jr., ed. *Jefferson at Monticello.* Charlottesville: University of Virginia Press, 1967.

Bedini, Silvio. *The Life of Benjamin Banneker.* New York: Scribner, 1972.

Beran, Michael Knox. *Jefferson's Demons: Portrait of a Restless Mind.* New York: Free Press, 2003.

Betts, Edwin Morris, and James A. Bear, Jr., eds. *The Family Letters of Thomas Jefferson.* Paperback edition. Charlottesville, VA: University Press of Virginia,

1986.; *The Family Letters of Thomas Jefferson*. Ed. by Edwin Morris Betts and James Adams Bear, Jr. Columbia: University of Missouri Press, 1966, (457-458).

Birle, Ann Lucas, and Lisa A. Francavilla, eds. *Thomas Jefferson's Granddaughter in Queen Victoria's England: The Travel Diary of Ellen Wayles Coolidge*, 1838–1839. Boston, 2011

Boyd, Julian P., Lyman H. Butterfield, Mina R. Bryan, and et. al., eds. *The Papers of Thomas Jefferson*. 34 vols. thru 2007. Princeton: Princeton University Press, 1950-

Brodie, Fawn M. *Thomas Jefferson: An Intimate History*. New York: W. W. Norton, 1998.

Bullock, Helen Duprey. *My Head and My Heart: A Little History of Thomas Jefferson and Maria Cosway*. New York: G. P. Putnam's Sons, 1945.

Burstein, Andrew. *Sentimental Democracy*. New York: Hill and Wang, 1999.

--"Jefferson in Retirement," in Cogliano, ed., A Companion to Thomas Jefferson

Jefferson's Secrets: Death and Desire at Monticello. New York: Basic Books, 2005.

Burstein, Andrew, and Nancy Isenberg. Madison and Jefferson. New York: Random House, 2010.

"Jefferson's Rationalizations." The William and Mary Quarterly, 3rd Series 57, no. 1 (2000): 183-197; available from http://www.jstor.org/ (February 1, 2006).

Burton, Cynthia *Jefferson Vindicated: Fallacies, Omissions and Contradictions in the Hemings genealogical search* (2005)

Cappon, Lester J., ed. *The Adams-Jefferson Letters*. 2 vols. Chapel Hill: The University of North Carolina Press, 1959.

Coolidge, Ellen Wayles Randolph. Correspondence of Ellen Wayles Randolph Coolidge, 1810-1861 Special Collections, University of Virginia, Charlottesville, VA. Accessions 38-584, 9090, 9090-cL.

-------Ellen Wayles Coolidge (Author), Ann Lucas Birle (Editor), Lisa A. Francavilla (Editor),*Thomas Jefferson's Granddaughter in Queen Victoria's England: The Travel Diary of Ellen Wayles Coolidge, 1838–1839* (Massachusetts Historical Society, 2013).

Coolidge, Ellen Wayles. (Ann Lucas Birle and Lisa A. Francavilla, eds.) *Thomas Jefferson's Granddaughter in Queen Victoria's England: The Travel Diary of Ellen Wayles Coolidge, 1838-1839*. Boston: Massachusetts Historical Society and the Thomas Jefferson Foundation, Inc., 201

Correspondence of Ellen Wayles Randolph Coolidge, 1810-1861, Accession #38-584, 9090, 9090-c Special Collections, University of Virginia Library, Charlottesville, VA. [http://ead.lib.virginia.edu/vivaxtf/view?docId=uva-sc/viu00095.xml]; "Extracts from Ellen W. Randolph (Coolidge) to Martha Jefferson Randolph, 24 August 1819," *Founders Online,* National Archives, https://founders.archives.gov/documents/Jefferson/03-14-02-0592. [Original source: *The Papers of Thomas Jefferson*, Retirement Series, vol. 14, *1 February to 31 August 1819*, ed. J. Jefferson Looney. Princeton: Princeton University Press, 2017, pp. 631–634.]

Crawford, Alan Pell. *Unwise Passions: A True Story of a Remarkable Woman and the First Great Scandal of Eighteenth-Century America*. New York: Simon & Schuster, 2000.

--Twilight at Monticello

Dabney, Virginius *The Jefferson Scandals: A Rebuttal* (New York: Dodd, Mead, 1981

Dunglison, Robley. *Medical Lexicon: A Dictionary of Medical Science*. 5th ed. Philadelphia: Lea and Blanchard, 1845.

Durey, Michael. *With the Hammer of Truth: James Thomson Callender and America's Early National Heroes*. Charlottesville: University Press of Virginia, 1990.

Ellis, Joseph J. *American Sphinx: The Character of Thomas Jefferson*. New York: Vintage Books, 1996.

Fleming, Thomas, *A Disease in the Public Mind,* New York: Da Capo Press, 2013.

---*The Intimate Lives of the Founding Fathers* New York: Harper Collins, 2009.

Ford, Paul Leicester. *The Works of Thomas Jefferson* (Federal Edition) G. P. Putnam's Sons, 1904-05 [cited Various. Available from http://oll.libertyfund.org/title/1734.

Francavilla, Lisa A. "Ellen Randolph Coolidge's "Virginia Legends" and "Negro Stories": Antebellum Tales from Monticello." *Massachusetts Historical Review.* Volume 17, 2015, 99-151.

Gaines, William H., Jr. *Thomas Mann Randolph: Jefferson's Son-in-Law*. Baton Rouge: Louisiana State University Press, 1966.

Glover, Lori, *Founders as Fathers*, New Haven: Yale University Press, 2014.

Gordon-Reed, Annette. *The Hemingses of Monticello: An American Family.* New York: W. W. Norton, 2008.

———. *Thomas Jefferson and Sally Hemings: An American Controversy.* Charlottesville: University Press of Virginia, 1997.

Halliday, E. M. *Understanding Thomas Jefferson.* New York: HarperCollins, 2001.

Hitchens, Christopher. *Thomas Paine's Rights of Man.* Books That Changed the World. New York: Atlantic Monthly Press, 2006.

Hyland, William G., *In Defense of Thomas Jefferson* (St. Martins 2009).

Martha Jefferson: An Intimate Life with Thomas Jefferson (Rowman and Littlefield 2014).

Long Journey with Mr. Jefferson (Potomac 2013).

Jefferson, Thomas. *Notes on the State of Virginia.* Edited by Frank Shuffleton. New York: Penguin Books, 1999.

Jefferson, Thomas. *The Complete Anas of Thomas Jefferson.* Edited by Franklin B. Sawvel. New York: Round Table Press, 1903. Reprint, LaVergne, Tenn.: BiblioLife, 2009. Page numbers are to the 2009 edition.

——— *Jefferson Abroad.* Edited by Douglas L. Wilson and Lucia Stanton. New York: Modern Library, 1999.

——— *The Jefferson Bible: The Life and Morals of Jesus of Nazareth,* Extracted Textually from the Gospels in Greek, Latin, French and English. With essays by Harry R. Rubenstein, Barbara Clark Smith, and Janice Stagnitto Ellis. Washington, D.C.: Smithsonian Books, 2011.

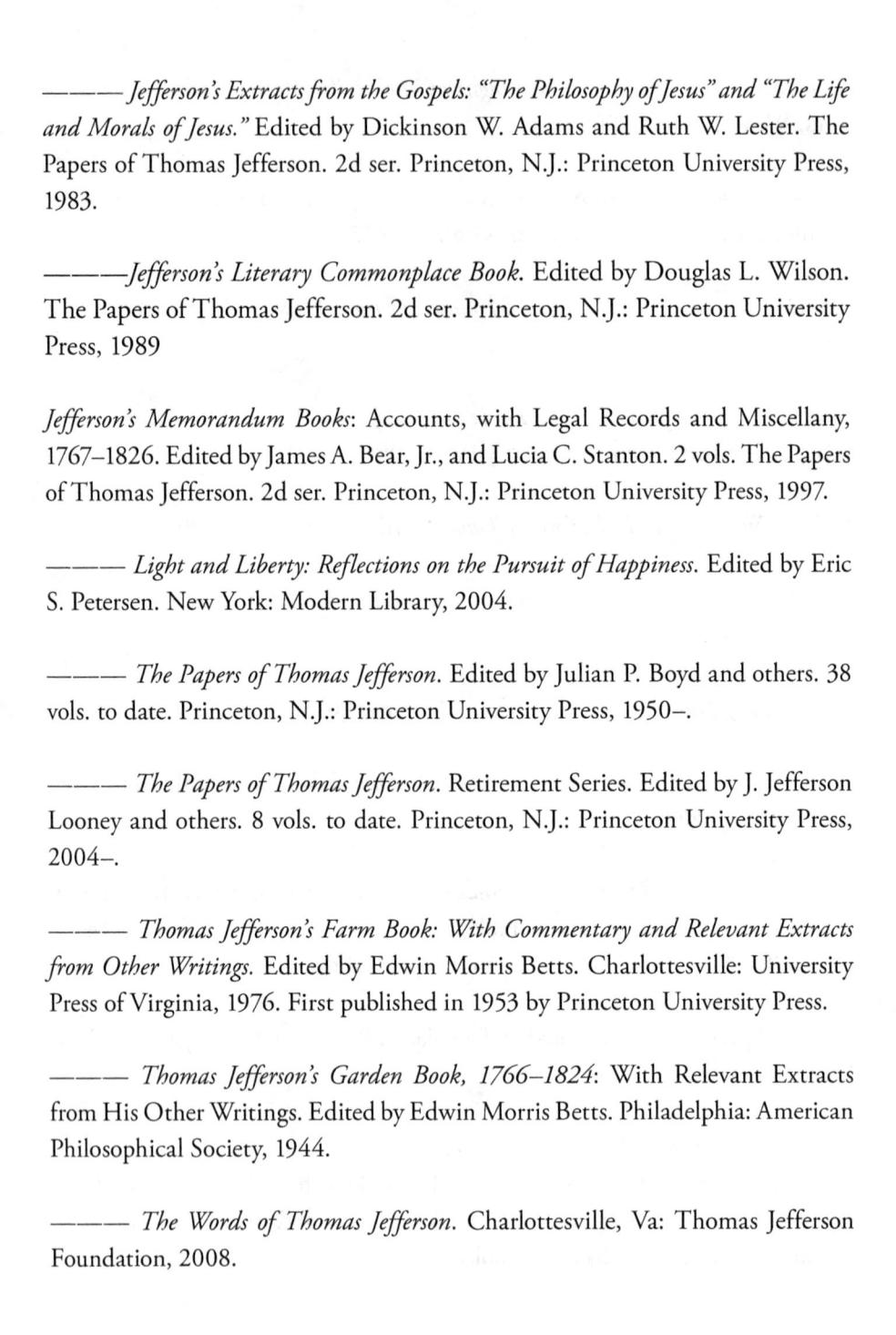

———— *Jefferson's Extracts from the Gospels: "The Philosophy of Jesus" and "The Life and Morals of Jesus."* Edited by Dickinson W. Adams and Ruth W. Lester. The Papers of Thomas Jefferson. 2d ser. Princeton, N.J.: Princeton University Press, 1983.

————*Jefferson's Literary Commonplace Book.* Edited by Douglas L. Wilson. The Papers of Thomas Jefferson. 2d ser. Princeton, N.J.: Princeton University Press, 1989

Jefferson's Memorandum Books: Accounts, with Legal Records and Miscellany, 1767–1826. Edited by James A. Bear, Jr., and Lucia C. Stanton. 2 vols. The Papers of Thomas Jefferson. 2d ser. Princeton, N.J.: Princeton University Press, 1997.

———— *Light and Liberty: Reflections on the Pursuit of Happiness.* Edited by Eric S. Petersen. New York: Modern Library, 2004.

———— *The Papers of Thomas Jefferson.* Edited by Julian P. Boyd and others. 38 vols. to date. Princeton, N.J.: Princeton University Press, 1950–.

———— *The Papers of Thomas Jefferson.* Retirement Series. Edited by J. Jefferson Looney and others. 8 vols. to date. Princeton, N.J.: Princeton University Press, 2004–.

———— *Thomas Jefferson's Farm Book: With Commentary and Relevant Extracts from Other Writings.* Edited by Edwin Morris Betts. Charlottesville: University Press of Virginia, 1976. First published in 1953 by Princeton University Press.

———— *Thomas Jefferson's Garden Book, 1766–1824*: With Relevant Extracts from His Other Writings. Edited by Edwin Morris Betts. Philadelphia: American Philosophical Society, 1944.

———— *The Words of Thomas Jefferson.* Charlottesville, Va: Thomas Jefferson Foundation, 2008.

―――― *Writings.* Edited by Merrill D. Peterson. The Library of America, no. 17. New York: Literary Classics of the United States, 1984.

―――― *The Writings of Thomas Jefferson.* Edited by Paul Leicester Ford. 10 vols.

Justus, Judith. *Down from the Mountain: The Oral History of the Hemings Family. Are They the Black Descendants of Thomas Jefferson?* Fremont, Ohio: Lesher Printers, Inc., 1990.

Kern, Susan. "The Material World of the Jeffersons at Shadwell." William and Mary Quarterly 62 (April 2005): 213–42.

―――― *The Jeffersons at Shadwell.* New Haven: Yale University Press, 2010

Kierner, Cynthia. *Beyond the Household: Women's Place in the Early South, 1700-1835.* Ithaca, NY: Cornell University Press, 1998.

"Hospitality, Sociability, and Gender in the Southern Colonies." *The Journal of Southern History* 62, no. 3 (1996): 449-480; available from http://www.jstor.org/ (March 31, 2005).

Kierner, Cynthia, *Martha Jefferson Randolph, Daughter of Monticello: Her Life and Times.* Chapel Hill. University of North Carolina Press, 2012.

Kimball, Marie. *Jefferson: The Road to Glory, 1743–1776.* New York: Coward-McCann, 1943.

――――. *Jefferson: The Scene of Europe, 1784–1789.* New York: Coward-McCann, 1950.

――――. *Jefferson: War and Peace, 1776–1784.* New York: Coward-McCann, 1947.

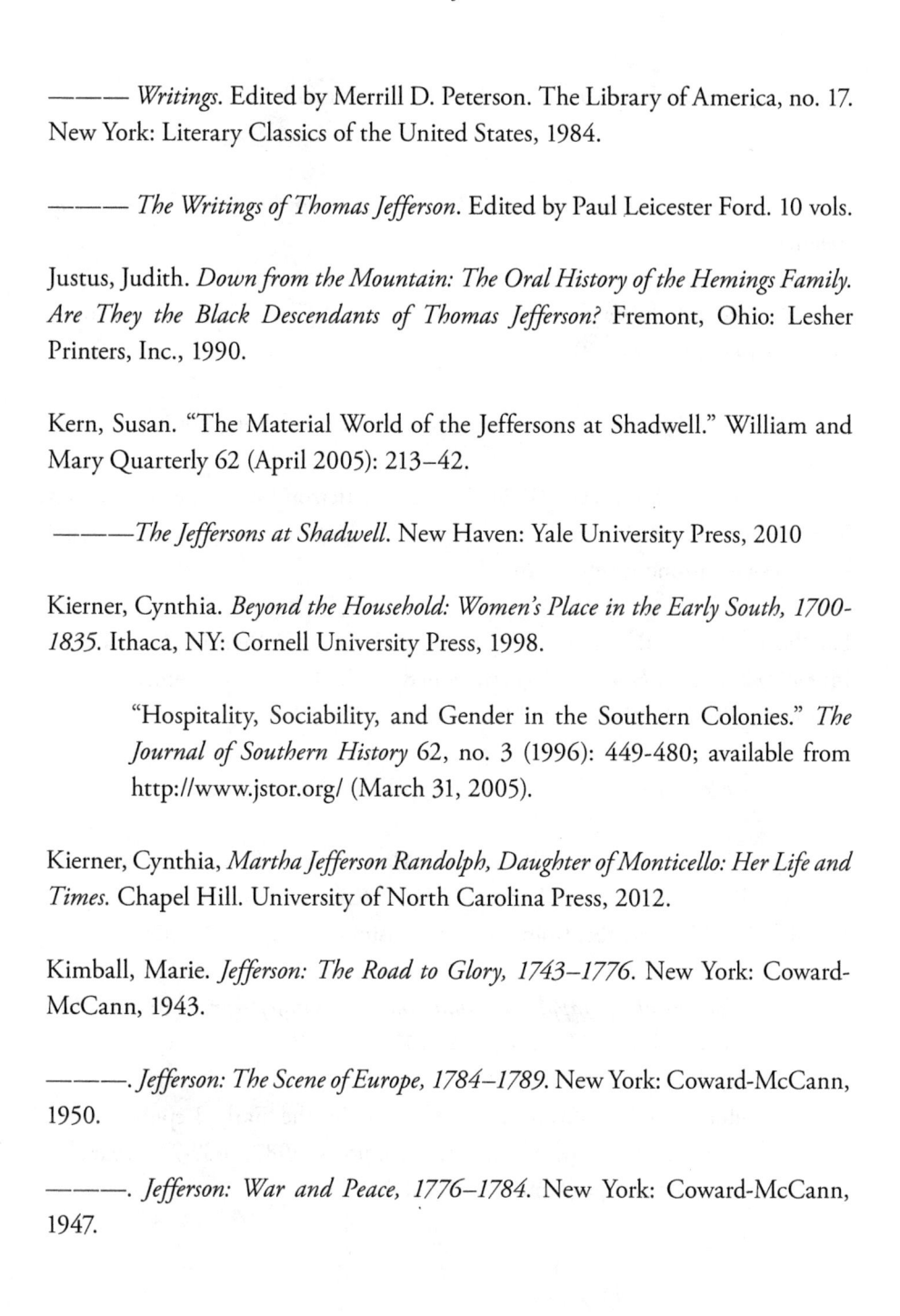

———. *Thomas Jefferson's Cook Book.* Charlottesville: University Press of Virginia, 1976.

———. *A Wilderness So Immense: The Louisiana Purchase and the Destiny of America.* New

Kranish, Michael. *Flight from Monticello: Thomas Jefferson at War.* New York: Oxford University Press, 2010

Kukla, Jon. *Mr. Jefferson's Women.* New York: Alfred A. Knopf, 2007.

Lafayette's Visit to Monticello (1824)." Thomas Jefferson Encyclopedia, Thomas Jefferson Foundation. http://www.monticello.org/site/research-and-collections/lafayettes-visit-to-monticello-1824.

Langhorne, Elizabeth. "Black Magic and Tales from Jefferson's Monticello." In *Folklore and Folklife in Virginia,* edited by Jr. Charles L. Perdue, 60-67. Charlottesville, VA: Virginia Folklore Society, 1979.

----*Monticello: A Family Story.* Chapel Hill, NC, 1989.

Lewis, Jan. "Domestic Tranquility and the Management of Emotion among the Gentry of Pre-Revolutionary Virginia." *The William and Mary Quarterly* 39, no. 1 (1982): 135-149; available from http://www.jstor.org/ (April 22, 2005).

---*The Pursuit of Happiness: Family and Values in Jefferson's Virginia.* New York: Cambridge University Press, 1983.

"The Republican Wife: Virtue and Seduction in the Early Republic." *The William and Mary Quarterly,* Third Series 44, no. 4 (1987): 689-721; available from http://www.jstor.org/ (January 23, 2004).

"The Blessings of Domestic Society: Thomas Jefferson's Family and the Transformation of American Politics." In *Jeffersonian Legacies,* edited by Peter Onuf, 109-146, 1993.

"Jefferson, the Family, and Civic Education." In *Thomas Jefferson and the Education of a Citizen,* edited by James Gilreath, 63-75. Washington, D. C.: Library of Congress, 1999.

Lipscomb, Andrew A., and Albert E. Bergh, eds. *The Writings of Thomas Jefferson.* Library Edition. 20 volumes Washington, D. C.: The Thomas Jefferson Memorial Association, 1903.

McCullough, David. *The Greater Journey: Americans in Paris.* New York: Simon and Schuster, 2011.

———. *John Adams.* New York: Simon and Schuster, 2001.

———. *1776.* New York: Simon and Schuster, 2005.

McLaughlin, Jack. *Jefferson and Monticello: The Biography of a Builder.* New York: Henry Holt, 1988.

Malone, Dumas. *Jefferson and His Time.* 6 vols. Boston: Little, Brown and Company, 1948-1981.

Malone, Dumas, ed. *Correspondence between Thomas Jefferson and Pierre Samuel Du Pont De Nemours.* Boston: Houghton Mifflin Company, 1930.

"Polly Jefferson and Her Father." Virginia Quarterly Review 7, no. January (1931): 81-95; available from http://pao.chadwyck.co.uk (December 9, 2007).

Meacham, Jon. *Thomas Jefferson: The Art of Power*. New York: Random House, 2012.

Merrill, Boynton, Jr. *Jefferson's Nephews: A Frontier Tragedy*. Lincoln: University of Nebraska Press, 2004. First published in 1976 by Princeton University Press.

Miller, John Chester, *The Wolf By The Ears: Thomas Jefferson and Slavery*. Charlottesville: The University Press of Virginia, 1991.

Mockingbirds." Thomas Jefferson Encyclopedia, Thomas Jefferson Foundation. http://www.monticello.org/site/research-and-collections/mockingbirds.

"Monticello Dining Room." Thomas Jefferson Encyclopedia, Thomas Jefferson Foundation. http://www.monticello.org/site/house-and-gardens/monticello-dining-room.

"Monticello (House) FAQ." Thomas Jefferson Encyclopedia, Thomas Jefferson Foundation. http://www.monticello.org/site/house-and-gardens/monticello-house-faq#rooms.

Morgan, Edmund S. *American Slavery, American Freedom: The Ordeal of Colonial Virginia*. New York: W. W. Norton, 1975.

Onuf, Peter S., ed. *Jeffersonian Legacies*. Charlottesville, VA: University Press of Virginia, 1993.

Parton, James. *Life of Thomas Jefferson*. The American Scene, Comments and Commentators. New York: Da Capo Press, 1971. First published in 1874 as *Life of Thomas Jefferson, Third President of the United States* by J. R. Osgood.

Peterson, Merrill D., ed. *The Portable Thomas Jefferson*. Paperback ed. New York: Penguin Books, 1975. ed.

---*Visitors to Monticello* (Charlottesville: University of Virginia Press, 1989)

---*Jefferson in the American Mind*

"Physical Descriptions of Jefferson." Thomas Jefferson Encyclopedia, Thomas Jefferson Foundation. http://www.monticello.org/site/research-and-collections/physical-descriptions-jefferson/

Pierson, Hamilton W., ed. *Jefferson at Monticello: The Private Life of Thomas Jefferson from Entirely New Materials.* 1862. Reprint, Stratford, N.H.: Ayer Company, 1971.

Randall, Henry S. *The Life of Thomas Jefferson.* 3 vols. The American Scene. New York: Da Capo Press, 1972. First published in 1858 by Derby and Jackson.

Randolph Family Papers, 1829-1978. Tallahassee, FL: State Library and Archives of Florida, [cited November 8 2007]. Available from http://www.floridamemory.com/.

Randolph, Sara N. "Mrs. Martha Jefferson Randolph." In *Worthy Women of Our First Century,* edited by Mrs. **0.** J. Wister and Miss Agnes Irwin, 9-70. Philadelphia: J. **B.** Lippincott & Co., 1877.

Randolph, Sarah N. *The Domestic Life of Thomas Jefferson.* Reprint of 1871 edition published by Harper, New York. Charlottesville, VA: The University Press of Virginia, 1978.

Roberts, Cokie. *Founding* Mothers, New York, Harper Perennial; Reprint edition 2005.

Scharff, Virginia. *The Women Jefferson Loved.* New York: Harper Collins, 2010.

Shuffelton, Frank. "Binding Ties: The Public and Domestic Spheres of Jefferson's Letters to His Family." In *Thomas Jefferson and the Education of a Citizen,* edited by James Gilreath, 28-47. Washington, D. C.: Library of Congress, 1999.

Smith, Margaret Bayard. *The First Forty Years of Washington Society in the Family Letters* of Margaret Bayard Smith. Edited by Gaillard Hunt. American Classics. New York: Frederick Ungar, 1965. First published in 1906 by Charles Scribner's Sons

Stanton, Lucia. *Free Some Day: The African-American Families of Monticello.* Monticello Monograph Series. Charlottesville, Va.: Thomas Jefferson Foundation, 2000.

———*Slavery at Monticello.* Monticello Monograph Series. Charlottesville, Va.: Thomas Jefferson Memorial Foundation, 1996.

Stanton, Lucia. *"Those Who Labor For My Happiness": Slavery at Thomas Jefferson's Monticello.* Charlottesville and London: University of Virginia Press, 2012.

Stein, Susan R. *The Worlds of Thomas Jefferson at Monticello.* New York: H. N. Abrams, in association with the Thomas Jefferson Memorial Foundation, 1993.

The Thomas Jefferson Heritage Society, *The Jefferson-Hemings Myth: An American Travesty* (2001)

Turner, Robert ed. *The Scholars Commission Report,* Carolina Academic Press, 2011.

Wallace, Benjamin. *The Billionaire's Vinegar.* Broadway Books, 2008.

Wiencek, Henry. *Master of the Mountain: Thomas Jefferson and His Slaves.* New York: Farrar, Straus, and Giroux, 2012.

--Wiencek, Henry. *An Imperfect God: George Washington, His Slaves, and the Creation of America*. New York: Farrar, Straus and Giroux, 2003

Wills, Garry. *Inventing America: Jefferson's Declaration of Independence*. America's Political Enlightenment. Garden City, N.Y.: Doubleday, 1978.

------------ Garry Wills, *Mr. Jefferson's University* (Washington, DC: National Geographic Society, 2002).

Wilson, Douglas L. *Jefferson's Literary Commonplace Book*. Princeton: Princeton University Press, 1989.

Wood, Gordon S. *The Radicalism of the American Revolution*. New York: Alfred A. Knopf, 1992.

—————. *The Birth of the Republic, 1763–89*. Rev. ed. Chicago History of American Civilization, no. 14. Chicago: University of Chicago Press, 1977.

—————. *The Gentle Puritan: A Life of Ezra Stiles, 1727–1795*. New Haven, Conn.: Published for the Institute of Early American History and Culture, Williamsburg, Va., by Yale University Press, 1962.

—————. *Inventing the People: The Rise of Popular Sovereignty in England and America*. New York: W. W. Norton, 1988.

—————. *Virginians at Home: Family Life in the Eighteenth Century*. Williamsburg in America Series, no. 2. Charlottesville, VA: Dominion Books, 1963. First published in 1952 by Colonial Williamsburg, Williamsburg, Va.

—————. *Revolutionary Characters: What Made the Founders Different*. New York: Penguin Press, 2006.

ARTICLES, ESSAYS, REVIEWS AND WEB SOURCES

A Memorial of Col. Thomas J. Randolph," *Charlottesville Chronicle*, October 22, 1875 Alderman Library, University of Virginia.

"America During the Age of Revolution, 1764–1775." Documents from the Continental Congress and the Constitutional Convention, 1774–89. Library of Congress, American Memory. http://memory.loc.gov/ammem/collections/continental/timeline1e.html (accessed March 25, 2012).

"Appendix H: Sally Hemings and Her Children." Thomas Jefferson Foundation. http://www.monticello.org/site/plantation-and-slavery/appendix-h-sally-hemings-and-her-children (accessed May 18, 2012).

Ayres, S. Edward. "Albemarle County, Virginia, 1744–1770: An Economic, Political, and Social Analysis." *Magazine of Albemarle County History* 25 (1966–67): 37–72.

Ayers, Edward L. Scot A. French and, "The Strange Career of Thomas Jefferson: Race and Slavery in American Memory, 1943–1993," in Jeffersonian Legacies, ed. Peter S. Onuf (Charlottesville: University Press of Virginia, 1993), 418–456.

Bear, James A., Jr. "The Last Few Days in the Life of Thomas Jefferson." *Magazine of Albemarle County History* 32 (1974): 63–79.

———. "Wine." Thomas Jefferson Encyclopedia, Thomas Jefferson Foundation. http://www.monticello.org/site/research-and-collections/wine (accessed March 24, 2012).

Bear, James A., Jr. "Thomas Jefferson and the Ladies." *Augusta Historical Bulletin* 6, no. 2 Fall (1970).

Bear, James A., Jr. "The Last Few Days in the Life of Thomas Jefferson." *Magazine of Albemarle County History* 32 (1974): 63–79.

Boyd, Julian P. "Two Diplomats Between Revolutions: John Jay and Thomas Jefferson." *Virginia Magazine of History and Biography* 66 (April 1958): 131–46.

Bullock, Helen D., ed. "A Dissertation on Education in the Form of a Letter from James Maury to Robert Jackson, July 17, 1762." *Papers of the Albemarle County Historical Society* 2 (1941–42): 36–60.

Cockerham, Anne Z., Arlene W. Keeling, and Barbara Parker. "Seeking Refuge at Monticello: Domestic Violence in Thomas Jefferson's Family." *Magazine of Albemarle County History* 64 (2006): 29–52.

Cohen, Morris L. "Thomas Jefferson Recommends a Course of Law Study." *University of Pennsylvania Law Review* 119 (April 1971): 823–44.

Cohen, William. "Thomas Jefferson and the Problem of Slavery." *The Journal of American History* 56 (December 1969): 503–26.

"Crops at Monticello." Thomas Jefferson Encyclopedia, Thomas Jefferson's Monticello. http://www.monticello.org/site/plantation-and-slavery/crops-monticello (accessed April 8, 2012).

Dabney, Virginius. "Jouett Outrides Tarleton, and Saves Jefferson from Capture." *Scribner's Magazine,* June 1928, 690–98.

Dabney , Virginius, "Jack Jouett's Ride," American Heritage, XIII (Dec. 1961), 56–59;

"Dabney Carr (1743–1773)." Thomas Jefferson Encyclopedia, Thomas Jefferson Foundation. http://www.monticello.org/site/research-and-collections/dabney-carr-1743–1773 (accessed March 23, 2012).

"Debt." Thomas Jefferson Encyclopedia, Thomas Jefferson Foundation. http://www.monticello.org/site/research-and-collections/debt (accessed April 8, 2012).

"Dinner Etiquette." Thomas Jefferson Encyclopedia, Thomas Jefferson Foundation. http://www.monticello.org/site/research-and-collections/dinner-etiquette (accessed April 7, 2012).

"Dome Room." Thomas Jefferson Encyclopedia, Thomas Jefferson Foundation. http://www.monticello.org/site/house-and-gardens/dome-room (accessed April 7, 2012).

Dumbauld, Edward. "Thomas Jefferson and the City of Washington." *Records of the Columbia Historical Society* 50 (1980): 67–80.

"Entrance Hall." Thomas Jefferson Encyclopedia, Thomas Jefferson Foundation. http://www.monticello.org/site/house-and-gardens/entrance-hall (accessed April 7, 2012).

"Expedition Timeline." Thomas Jefferson Foundation. http://www.monticello.org/site/jefferson/expedition-timeline (accessed April 4, 2012).

"Firearms." Thomas Jefferson Encyclopedia, Thomas Jefferson Foundation. http://www.monticello.org/site/research-and-collections/firearms (accessed April 2, 2012).

"Fishing." Thomas Jefferson Encyclopedia, Thomas Jefferson Foundation. http://www.monticello.org/site/research-and-collections/fishing (accessed April 2, 2012).

"Francis Fauquier (bap. 1703–1768)." *The Dictionary of Virginia Biography.* http://www.encyclopediavirginia.org/fauquier_francis_bap_1703–1768 (accessed March 24, 2012).

Founders Online, https://founders.archives.gov/volumes/Jefferson/03-12

"Gallatin, Albert, (1761–1849)." Biographical Directory of the United States Congress, 1774–Present. http://bioguide.congress.gov/scripts/biodisplay.pl?index=g000020 (accessed March 24, 2012).

"George Wythe House." Colonial Williamsburg, Colonial Williamsburg Foundation. http://www.history.org/almanack/places/hb/hbwythe.cfm (accessed March 25, 2012).

"House and Gardens." Thomas Jefferson Foundation. http://www.monticello.org/site/house-and-gardens (accessed April 7, 2012).

Howard, Seymour. "Thomas Jefferson's Art Gallery for Monticello." *Art Bulletin* 59 (December 1977): 583–600.

"Hunting." Thomas Jefferson Encyclopedia, Thomas Jefferson Foundation. http://www.monticello.org/site/research-and-collections/hunting (accessed April 2, 2012).

Jefferson, Thomas. "Jefferson's Confidential Letter to Congress." Thomas Jefferson Foundation. http://www.monticello.org/site/jefferson/jeffersons-confidential-letter-to-congress (accessed April 4, 2012).

"Jefferson: The Scientist and Gardener." Thomas Jefferson Foundation. http://www.monticello.org/site/house-and-gardens/jefferson-scientist-and-gardener (accessed May 18, 2012).

Johnson, Ludwell H., III. "Sharper Than a Serpent's Tooth: Thomas Jefferson and His Alma Mater." *Virginia Magazine of History and Biography* 99 (April 1991): 145–62.

Jones, Gordon W., and James A. Bear. "Thomas Jefferson's Medical History." Unpublished manuscript. Thomas Jefferson Foundation, Charlottesville, Va.

Kern, Susan. "The Material World of the Jeffersons at Shadwell." *William and Mary Quarterly*, 3rd ser., 62 (2005): 213–42.

Ketchum, Richard M. "Men of the Revolution: 11. George Rogers Clark." *American Heritage* 25, no. 1 (December 1973): 32–33, 78.

Kimball, Fiske. "The Life Portraits of Jefferson and Their Replicas." *Proceedings of the American Philosophical Society* 88 (December 28, 1944): 497–534.

Kimball, Marie. "A Playmate of Thomas Jefferson." *North American Review* 213 (February 1921): 145–56.

"Lafayette's Visit to Monticello (1824)." Thomas Jefferson Encyclopedia, Thomas Jefferson Foundation. http://www.monticello.org/site/research-and-collections/lafayettes-visit-to-monticello-1824 (accessed April 8, 2012).

Looney, J. Jefferson. "Thomas Jefferson's Last Letter." *Virginia Magazine of History and Biography* 112, no. 2 (2004): 178–84.

"Martha Wayles Skelton Jefferson." Thomas Jefferson Encyclopedia, Thomas Jefferson Foundation. http://www.monticello.org/site/jefferson/martha-wayles-skelton-jefferson

Mayer, David "The Thomas Jefferson - Sally Hemings Myth and the Politicization of American History, Individual Views of David N. Mayer, Concurring with the Majority Report of the Scholars Commission on the Jefferson-Hemings Matter," April 9, 2001 at http://www.ashbrook.org/articles/mayer-hemings.html

"Meriwether Lewis." Thomas Jefferson Encyclopedia, Thomas Jefferson Foundation. http://www.monticello.org/site/research-and-collections/meriwether-lewis (accessed April 4, 2012).

"Mockingbirds." Thomas Jefferson Encyclopedia, Thomas Jefferson Foundation. http://www.monticello.org/site/research-and-collections/mockingbirds (accessed April 2, 2012).

"Monticello Dining Room." Thomas Jefferson Encyclopedia, Thomas Jefferson Foundation. http://www.monticello.org/site/house-and-gardens/monticello-dining-room (accessed April 7, 2012).

"Monticello (House) FAQ." Thomas Jefferson Encyclopedia, Thomas Jefferson Foundation. http://www.monticello.org/site/house-and-gardens/monticello-house-faq#rooms (accessed April 7, 2012).

"Monticello South Square Room." Thomas Jefferson Encyclopedia, Thomas Jefferson Foundation. http://www.monticello.org/site/house-and-gardens/south-square-room (accessed April 7, 2012).

Neiman, Fraser D. "Coincidence or Causal Connection? The Relationship between Thomas Jefferson's Visits to Monticello and Sally Hemings's

"North Octagonal Room." Thomas Jefferson Encyclopedia, Thomas Jefferson Foundation. http://www.monticello.org/site/house-and-gardens/north-octagonal-room (accessed April 7, 2012).

Oberg, Barbara. Review of *Thomas Jefferson,* by Joyce Appleby. *The Pennsylvania Magazine of History and Biography* 128 (October 2004): 406–8.

Parkinson, Robert G. "First from the Right: Massive Resistance and the Image of Thomas Jefferson in the 1950s." *Virginia Magazine of History and Biography* 112, no. 1 (2004): 2–35.

"Parlor." Thomas Jefferson Encyclopedia, Thomas Jefferson Foundation. http://www.monticello.org/site/house-and-gardens/parlor (accessed April 7, 2012).

Peterson, Merrill D. "Thomas Jefferson and Commercial Policy, 1783–1793." *The William and Mary Quarterly*, 3d ser., 22 (October 1965): 584–610.

"Physical Descriptions of Jefferson." Thomas Jefferson Encyclopedia, Thomas Jefferson Foundation. http://www.monticello.org/site/research-and-collections/physical-descriptions-jefferson (accessed March 31, 2012).

"Plantation and Slavery." Thomas Jefferson Foundation. http://www.monticello.org/site/plantation-and-slavery (accessed April 2, 2012).

"Printer and Binder." Colonial Williamsburg, Colonial Williamsburg Foundation. http://www.history.org/almanack/life/trades/tradepri.cfm (accessed March 24, 2012).

Rahe, Paul A. "Thomas Jefferson's Machiavellian Political Science." *The Review of Politics* 57 (Summer 1995): 449–81.

Rakove, Jack N. "Presidential Selection: Electoral Fallacies." *Political Science Quarterly* 119 (Spring 2004): 21–37.

Randolph, John. "Letters of John Randolph, of Roanoke, to General Thomas Marsh Forman." *Virginia Magazine of History and Biography* 49 (July 1941): 201–16.

Reagan, Ronald. "Remarks and a Question-and-Answer Session at the University of Virginia in Charlottesville," December 16, 1988. The American Presidency Project. http://www.presidency.ucsb.edu/ws/?pid=35272 (accessed April 8, 2012).

"Report of the Research Committee on Thomas Jefferson and Sally Hemings." Thomas Jefferson Foundation. http://www.monticello.org/site/

plantation-and-slavery/report-research-committee-thomas-jefferson-and-sally-hemings (accessed March 23, 2012).

Roosevelt, Franklin D. "Address at Jefferson Day Dinner in St. Paul Minnesota," April 18, 1932. The American Presidency Project. http://www.presidency.ucsb.edu/ws/?pid=88409 (accessed April 8, 2012).

Rosano, Michael J. "Liberty, Nobility, Philanthropy, and Power in Alexander Hamilton's Conception of Human Nature." *The American Journal of Political Science* 47 (January 2003): 61–74.

Self, Robert L., and Susan R. Stein. "The Collaboration of Thomas Jefferson and John Hemings: Furniture Attributed to the Monticello Joinery." *Winterthur Portfolio* 33 (Winter 1998): 231–48.

Stanton, Lucia. "Looking for Liberty: Thomas Jefferson and the British Lions." *Eighteenth-Century Studies* 26 (Summer 1993): 649–68.

"Tea Room." Thomas Jefferson Encyclopedia, Thomas Jefferson Foundation. http://www.monticello.org/site/house-and-gardens/tea-room.

"Thomas Mann Randolph." Thomas Jefferson Encyclopedia, Thomas Jefferson Foundation. http://www.monticello.org/site/jefferson/thomas-mann-randolph.

Vance, Joseph Carroll. "Thomas Jefferson Randolph." Ph.D. diss., University of Virginia, 1957.

Wenger, Mark R. *Thomas Jefferson, the College of William and Mary, and the University of Virginia Source:* The Virginia Magazine of History and Biography, Vol. 103, No. 3 (Jul., 1995), pp 339-374 Published by: Virginia Historical Society Stable URL: http://www.jstor.org/stable/4249522 , Accessed: 12-05-2018 15:46 UTC

"William Small." Thomas Jefferson Encyclopedia, Thomas Jefferson Foundation. http://www.monticello.org/site/jefferson/william-small (accessed March 24, 2012).

"Wine." Thomas Jefferson Encyclopedia, Thomas Jefferson Foundation. http://www.monticello.org/site/research-and-collections/wine

Wilson, Douglas L. "The Evolution of Jefferson's 'Notes on the State of Virginia.'" *Virginia Magazine of History and Biography* 112, no. 2 (2004): 98–133.

Wylie, John Cook, "Writings About Jack Jouett and Tarleton's Raid on Charlottesville, in 1781," The Magazine of Albemarle County History, vol. 17 (1958–1959), 49–56.

Wilson, Gaye. "Horses." Thomas Jefferson Encyclopedia, Thomas Jefferson Foundation. http://www.monticello.org/site/research-and-collections/horses (accessed April 2, 2012).

"Wren Building." Colonial Williamsburg, Colonial Williamsburg Foundation. http://www.history.org/almanack/places/hb/hbwren.cfm (accessed March 24, 2012).

Young, Alfred F. "English Plebeian Culture and Eighteenth-Century American Radicalism." In *The Origins of Anglo-American Radicalism,* edited by Margaret Jacob and James Jacob, 185–212. London: Allen and UnWIN, 1984.

DISSERTATIONS

Gaines, William, *Thomas Mann Randolph of Edgehill*, University of Virginia, (1950).

Kern, Susan, *The Jeffersons at Shadwell*, The Social and Material World of a Virginia Family A Dissertation Presented to The Faculty of the Department of History The College of William and Mary in Virginia (2005).

Vance, Joseph Carrol, *Thomas Jefferson Randolph,*, University of Virginia, (1957).

Wayson, Billy Lee, *Martha Jefferson Randolph: The Education of a Republican Daughter & Plantation Mistress,* 1782-1809 A Dissertation Presented to The Faculty of the Curry School of Education University of Virginia In Partial Fulfillment of the Requirements for the Degree Doctor of Philosophy, May, 2008.

ILLUSTRATION CREDITS

1. Jefferson's grandchildren playing on Monticello's lawn—painting by Jane Braddick Peticolas (1825), courtesy of Author's Private Collection and Courtesy of Wikimedia Commons.

2. Monticello, Courtesy of Author's Private Collection.

3. University of Virginia, Courtesy of Author's Private Collection.

4. Patsy Jefferson Randolph, Courtesy of Thomas Jefferson Foundation at Monticello.

5. Thomas Jefferson Randolph, Courtesy of Thomas Jefferson Foundation at Monticello.

6. Ellen Randolph Coolidge, Courtesy of Thomas Jefferson Foundation at Monticello.

7. Thomas Mann Randolph, Courtesy of the Encyclopedia Virginia and the Library of Virginia.

8. Jefferson's Library, Courtesy of Wikimedia Commons.

9. Jefferson's Bedchamber, Courtesy of Wikimedia Commons.

10. Anne Cary Randolph Bankhead, Courtesy of Wikimedia Commons.

11. Poplar Forest, Courtesy of Authors Private Collection.

12. Maria Cosway, Courtesy of Wikimedia Commons.

ABOUT THE AUTHOR

WILLIAM G. HYLAND JR., a native of Virginia, is the author of four widely praised historical biographies, including ***IN DEFENSE OF THOMAS JEFFERSON*** (St. Martin's/Thomas Dunne Books), which was nominated for the Virginia Literary Award.

Mr. Hyland is a seasoned litigation attorney with a national law firm, with nearly 30 years of high profile trial experience. A former prosecutor, he is licensed to practice law in the District of Columbia, Florida, Alabama, Colorado and before the United States Supreme Court. Mr. Hyland is also a former Adjunct Professor of Law at Stetson University College of Law. His professional lectures include televised speeches at the National Archives, the Colonial Williamsburg Foundation, the University of Virginia, CSPAN, BOOK TV (https://www.c-span.org/video/?463476-1/george-mason) and The Federalist Society. He is a member of the Virginia, Massachusetts and New York Historical Societies and serves on the Board of Directors of the Thomas Jefferson Heritage Society. He holds a B.A. from the University of Alabama and a J.D. from Samford University's Cumberland School of Law. Before law school, Mr. Hyland held a TOP SECRET security clearance and worked for the Arms Control and Disarmament Agency.

ENDNOTES

List of Important Names

1   Julian P. Boyd, ed., *Papers,* 10:453n. "The Head-Heart letter has been justly described as one of the notable love letters in the English language. Its distinction, however, derives not only from what it reveals about Thomas Jefferson, but from what it discloses about those who read it. Like most works of art, it is richly ambiguous, arguing with equal persuasiveness for the ascendancy of intellect and of feeling. The conflict between head and heart is like modern warfare, where victory by either side is destruction for both." Jack McLaughlin, *Jefferson and Monticello: The Biography of a Builder* (New York: Henry Holt, 1988), 215.

2   "The substantial recollections of four men were recorded: Isaac (Granger) Jefferson (1775–ca. 1850), reprinted as 'Memoirs of a Monticello Slave,' in Bear, 3–24; Madison Hemings (1805–1877), in Pike County [Ohio] *Republican,* 3 Mar. 1873, reprinted as 'The Memoirs of Madison Hemings,' in Annette Gordon-Reed, *Thomas Jefferson and Sally Hemings: An American Controversy* (Charlottesville, 1997), 245–248; Israel Gillette Jefferson (1800–1873+), in Pike County [Ohio] *Republican,* 25 Dec. 1873, reprinted as 'The Memoirs of Israel Jefferson,' in Gordon-Reed, *Thomas Jefferson and Sally Hemings,* 249–253; and Peter Fossett (1815–1901), in *New York World,* 30 Jan. 1898, and in an unidentified Cincinnati newspaper." Stanton, *"Those Who Labor for My Happiness,"* 885.

3   "Patty Jefferson was previously married to Bathurst Skelton, whom Jefferson had known in college; the couple had one child, a boy who died shortly before Jefferson married the widow Skelton in 1772." Burstein, *Secrets,* 298n29.

4   "Jane Jefferson has long been depicted as a riddle, a mystery at the heart of the story of Thomas Jefferson. There are several reasons for this. For one, Jefferson appears to have spoken more often and more fully about his father than about his mother, leaving more family stories that, combined with the extant public records available for leading colonial men (who held office and left more traces than women of the day), have given us a more detailed sense of Peter Jefferson than we have had for Jane Jefferson. Another reason is the Shadwell fire in 1770 destroyed family papers that may have shed light on the relationship between mother and son. And another reason lies in Jefferson's larger reticence about the women in his life. Evidence of Jefferson's musing about either his mother or his wife is sparse. The relatively thin traditions about Jane Jefferson have led some writers to speculate that mother and son were estranged. . . . [Jane was a] very great influence which he deeply resented, and from which he struggled to escape." Brodie, *Intimate,* 43. Reflecting on Merrill Peterson's observation that "by his own reckoning she was a zero quantity in his life." More recent scholarship has attempted to revise the estrangement interpretation, most notably Susan Kern, *The Jeffersons at Shadwell* (New Haven, CT: Yale University Press, 2010); Virginia Scharff, *The Women Jefferson Loved* (New York: Harper-Collins, 2010), 3–57; Merrill D. Peterson, *Thomas Jefferson and the New Nation: A Biography* (London: Oxford University Press, 1970); and Jon Meacham, *Thomas Jefferson: The Art of Power* (New York: Random House, 2012).

5   Bertram Wyatt-Brown, *Southern Honor: Ethics and Behavior in the Old South* (Oxford University Press, 1982), 310. To add to the confusion of names, Thomas Jefferson's brother and favorite grandson were named, respectively, Randolph Jefferson and Jefferson Randolph. While the grandson went by the name Jeff, his full name was Thomas Jefferson Randolph, which causes still more confusion because his father was Thomas Mann Randolph, who had a half brother also named Thomas Mann Randolph. Both Thomas Mann Randolph and Thomas Jefferson Randolph were occasionally referred to as "Col. Randolph."

Introduction

1   Thomas Jefferson, *Letters and Addresses of Thomas Jefferson*, ed. William B. Parker (Buffalo: National Jefferson Society, 1903), 43.

2   *The Papers of Thomas Jefferson*, Retirement Series, vol. 6, *11 March to 27 November 1813*, ed. J. Jefferson Looney (Princeton, NJ: Princeton University Press, 2009), 193–95.

3   Ellen W. Randolph Coolidge to Henry S. Randall, 1856.

4   Michael Knox Beran, *Jefferson's Demons* (New York: Free Press, 2003), Apple Books ed., 702, quoting Victor Hugo's, *Les Misérables*. All Beran citations are from the Apple Books edition.

5   Randall, *Life*, 3:349; see Jon Meacham, *Thomas Jefferson: The Art of Power* (New York: Random House, 2012), Apple Books ed., 872; *TDLTJ*, 381–83, for the Old Eagle story and the various injuries suffered in falls. Malone, *JHT*, volume 6 is the final volume in the authoritative biography covering these final years.

6   Jefferson to George Washington, May 14, 1794, Lipscomb and Bergh, *Writings*, 9:288.

7   Jefferson, "his face like a lion, told the ferrymen 'in tones of thunder' to row for their lives or he would pitch them into the stream." Brodie, *Intimate*, 21.

8   Ellen W. Coolidge to Joseph Coolidge, October 24, 1858, Ellen W. Coolidge Journal, Ellen W. Coolidge Papers, ViU.

9   Brodie, *Intimate*, 21.

10 Burstein, *Inner*, 1.

11 Burstein, 1.

12 "Margaret Bayard Smith was born in 1778; her father was Colonel John Bayard, a Pennsylvania statesman and member of the Continental Congress. Her family included James A. Bayard, a Federalist lawmaker and diplomat from Delaware, who was to play a noted role in Jefferson's election to the presidency in February 1801." Meacham, *Jefferson*, 34.

13 Brodie, *Intimate*, 27.

14 Burstein, *Inner*, 291.

15 Malone, *Sage*, 498.

Prologue

1. My effort at a realistic rendering of this scene draws upon multiple accounts; see also Boynton Merrill, *The Jefferson Nephews: A Frontier Tragedy* (Lincoln: University of Nebraska Press, 2004).

2. "Shadwell and Monticello are adjacent and were part of the same tract of land that Jefferson inherited from his father. The Thomas Jefferson Foundation (formerly The Thomas Jefferson Memorial Foundation), which operates Monticello, owns both properties today." Susan Kern, *The Jeffersons at Shadwell*, introduction, Kindle edition, n. 2, 5469, n. 2; "Monticello" encompassed Jefferson's entire five-thousand-acre operation in Albemarle County. It included the farms of Monticello and Tufton south of the Rivanna River and Shadwell and Lego on the north side. "The name Monticello can be applied to a house, a farm, and a plantation. When used here without qualifiers, it applies to Jefferson's five-thousand-acre Albemarle County plantation, which consisted of several discrete farms (Monticello, Tufton, Shadwell, and Lego), as well as other contiguous properties that were not farmed." Stanton, *"Those Who Labor for My Happiness": Slavery at Thomas Jefferson's Monticello* (Charlottesville: University of Virginia Press, 2012), 891n3.

3. Malcolm Kellsall, *Jefferson and the Iconography of Romanticism: Folk, Land, Culture and the Romantic Nation* (London, 1999), 115.

4. Bear, *Monticello*, 70; see also Jefferson to Frances Wright, August 7, 1825, Jefferson to William Gordon, January 1, 1826, Jefferson to Thomas Jefferson Randolph, February 8, 1826, Ford, *Writings* X, 344, 358, 374–75; and Joseph J. Ellis, *American Sphinx* (Vintage Books, 1998), Apple Books ed., 60. Painter-playwright William Dunlap recorded in his diary in 1806, "Thomas Jefferson, is a tall man, say 6 feet & thin. His hair which has been red is now grey & is worn in negligent disorder, tho not ungracefully. His complexion is ruddy & his eye (a hazle) very animated. He converses with ease & vivacity, possessing true politeness, which places his guests perfectly at their ease." See *Diary of William Dunlap (1766–1839)* (New York, 1930), 2:388; Burstein, *Secrets*, 818n23.

5. Bear, *Monticello*, 71.

6. Jefferson suffered from debilitating migraine headaches through his adult life; see Edmund Pendleton to Jefferson, Williamsburg, VA, May 24, 1776; Jefferson to Thomas Nelson, Philadelphia, May 16, 1776.

7. "Although the tragedy in Kentucky was published in the press at the time, several eminent students of [Jefferson's] life and work assured me, when I was working on the first version, that they could find no reference by him to the Kentucky story, and one scholar even went so far as to state in a letter 'his feeling that Jefferson could not bring himself to discuss—or perhaps even to face—the appalling episode.'" Robert Penn Warren (1953), foreword to his *Brother to Dragons*, robertpennwarren.com, accessed August 30, 2021, http://www.robertpennwarren.com/Bro%20to%20Dragons-Foreward.htm. Other Jefferson scholars disagree, inferring that through Woods, or others, Jefferson was surely made aware of the murders by his own nephews.

8. Alan Pell Crawford, *Twilight at Monticello: The Final Years of Thomas Jefferson* (New York: Random House, 2008), 64; hereinafter *Twilight*.

9   Crawford, 81. "After the murder, much of the central United States still reeled from the latest of three massive earthquakes, with over 2,000 lesser tremors centered around Northern Arkansas and New Madrid, Missouri. The climax of the dire seismologic events came in mid-December with the first terrible shocks of the New Madrid earthquake, the most severe in the recorded history on the North American continent."

10 Crawford, 144.

11 McLaughlin, *Jefferson and Monticello*, 20.

12 McLaughlin, 20.

13 "It was not until 1804, during his first term as President, that [Jefferson] replaced the cumbersome copying press and its often illegible facsimiles with a polygraph manufactured by the artist Charles Wilson Peale. The polygraph was based on the mechanical principle of a seventeenth century invention, the pantograph, a series of rigid rods in the form of a parallelogram with two pens attached. When one pen was used to draw or write, the other pen produced an exact duplicate. The refinement of this device into the polygraph by Peale and John Isaac Hawkins, a Philadelphia inventor, made it possible for Jefferson to produce nearly perfect copies of his vast correspondence. He was infatuated with this machine, owned several versions of it during his lifetime, and collaborated with Peale over a number of years to eliminate the failings of a delicate and fussy instrument with tolerances too fine for the hard labor that Jefferson's writing schedule imposed on it. He kept a polygraph in his private suite at Monticello, and another at Poplar Forest, and it is to these instruments that we owe the historical treasure." McLaughlin, 370.

14 Benjamin Wallace, *The Billionaire's Vinegar* (New York: Three Rivers, 2008, 2009), 12.

15 McLaughlin, *Jefferson and Monticello*, 375.

16 James A Bear Jr., "The Last Few Days in the Life of Thomas Jefferson," *Magazine of Albemarle County History* 32 (1974): 63–79; Meacham, *Thomas Jefferson*, Apple Books ed., 861.

17 "There were a number of clocks at Monticello; each of the public rooms had a decorative clock on the mantelpiece, and Jefferson kept a clock on a bracket in his bedroom sleeping alcove. . . . A conversation piece, in Jefferson's day and still so, was the Great Clock' over the entrance hall doorway, with a face on the outside portico and another in the hall." McLaughlin, *Jefferson and Monticello*, 813; *MB*, April 27, 1793.

18 McLaughlin, *Jefferson and Monticello*, 371.

19 "But whether I retire to bed early or late, I rise with the sun," he wrote Utley. Meacham, *Thomas Jefferson*, 1121. "He said in his last illness that the sun had not caught him in bed for fifty years," grandson Thomas Jefferson Randolph recalled to biographer Henry S. Randall. Randall, *Jefferson*, 3:675. Visiting Monticello in December 1824, when Jefferson was eighty-one, Daniel Webster wrote, "Mr. Jefferson rises in the morning as soon as he can see the hands of his clock, which is directly opposite his bed, and examines his thermometer immediately, as he keeps a regular meteorological diary." *VTM*, 98; Bear, "Last Few Days in the Life of Thomas Jefferson," 68, 7; "Notes on Jefferson's Bed Chamber," Memorandum of Susan R. Stein to author Jon Meacham; Meacham, *Thomas Jefferson*.

20 McLaughlin, *Jefferson and Monticello*, 372.

21 "It undoubtedly was designed for mockingbirds, Jefferson's favorite bird. He had always admired the song of this bird, and at various times purchased mockingbirds. It was not until he went to France, however, that he was able to compare it to the legendary song of the nightingale. He advised his daughter Martha to become acquainted with the nightingale's song 'that you might be able to estimate its merit in comparison with that of the mockingbird.' The latter has the advantage of singing thro' a great part of the year, whereas the nightingale sings but 5. or 6. weeks in the spring, and a still shorter term and with a more feeble voice in the fall." During his presidency he kept mockingbirds at the President's House. Margaret Bayard Smith described his affection for one of them: "He cherished [it] with peculiar fondness, not only for its melodious powers." Bear, "Last Few Days in the Life of Thomas Jefferson," 68; "A Long Forgotten Arabian Prince"; Jefferson's Ubiquitous Mockingbirds "Notes on Jefferson's Bed Chamber," Memorandum of Susan R. Stein to author Jon Meacham.

22 Brodie, *Intimate*, 425–26. "On his return to Monticello, he wrote to his steward at the President's House, Etienne Lemaire, 'My birds arrived here in safety & are the delight of every hour.'" McLaughlin, *Jefferson and Monticello*, Apple Books ed., 713.

23 *TDLTJ*, 338; Meacham, *Thomas Jefferson*, Apple Books.

24 *PTJRS*, 8:544. Bear attributed Jefferson's habit to a reading of Sir John Floyer's and Edward Baynard's popular two-part book, *Psychrolousia: Or, the History of Cold Bathing*. "In a volume that Jefferson owned and read, the English physician Edward Baynard recommended cold-water baths as both a preventive measure for head colds and a cure for headaches." See Baynard, *[Psychrolousia]; or, The History of Cold Bathing . . .* , 3rd ed. (London, 1709), 138, 365–66. Jefferson owned Baynard's 2nd ed. (London, 1706); E. Millicent Sowerby, comp., *Catalogue of the Library of Thomas Jefferson*, 5 vols. (Washington, DC, 1952–59), 1:417.

25 Meacham, *Thomas Jefferson*, Apple Books ed., 1121.

26 *MB*, 1:771.

27 Marie Kimball, *Thomas Jefferson's Cook Book* (Hartsville, OH: James Direct, 2007), 103.

28 McLaughlin, *Jefferson and Monticello*, 9.

29 McLaughlin, 9–10. Lemaire's pancakes were made with egg yolks, cream, and flour, and with whipped egg whites in place of baking soda." See "Kimball, *Thomas Jefferson's Cook Book*, 103.

30 Randall, *Jefferson*, 3:450. Isaac Jefferson "never heard of his being disguised in drink." Bear, *Monticello*, 13.

31 Boynton Merrill Jr., Kentucky Newspaper, *A Chapter of Horrors*; Summer 1998, "Constructing *Jefferson's Nephews*: A Speech to the Kentucky Library Association, Lexington, Kentucky, November, 1979," *Kentucky Review* 14, no. 1, art. 3 (Summer 1998).

32 "Jefferson's grandson, Thomas Jefferson Randolph remembered that Colbert was the only person, besides the maid who cleaned the room and made the bed, who ever entered

Jefferson's bedroom, to which he brought wood and water during the family breakfast. He accompanied Jefferson on his overnight visits to friends or on journeys to Richmond and to Poplar Forest. It was at the latter place, in 1819, that a series of calamities caused Jefferson's granddaughters to provide the fullest surviving accounts of Colbert." Stanton, *"Those Who Labor for My Happiness,"* 519–20.

33 TJR, *Memoirs*, 6.

34 "Burwell Colbert was a skilled painter and glazier and Monticello's butler for many years. Colbert, freed in Jefferson's will, also attended the 1827 Monticello sale, purchasing a mule and portrait prints of his former master and of Lafayette." Stanton, *"Those Who Labor for My Happiness,"* 565n34.

35 "His eyes, which were of hazel-gray, were beaming and expressive; and his demeanor gave assurance of a gentle heart, and a sympathetic, inquisitive mind." Meacham, *Thomas Jefferson*, Apple Books ed., 19; "Later, Jefferson's eyes are described as blue or light gray. They perhaps 'changed color in the light.'" Beran. *Jefferson's Demons*, 403.

Chapter 1

1 "Lines Copied from Tristram Shandy by Martha and Thomas Jefferson, [before 6 September 1782]," *Founders Online*, National Archives, https://founders.archives.gov/documents/Jefferson/01-06-02-0185.

2 The story of the deathbed promise first appeared in print in George Tucker, *The Life of Thomas Jefferson*, 2 vols. (Philadelphia, 1837), 1:158; Joseph J. Ellis, *American Sphinx: The Character of Thomas Jefferson* (New York: Vintage Books, 1996), Apple Books ed., 583.

3 On the much-neglected subject of Patsy Randolph, I found myself gratefully dependent upon Cynthia Kierner, *Martha Jefferson, Daughter of Monticello: Her Life and Times* (Chapel Hill: University of North Carolina Press, 2012; hereinafter *MJR*); and Virginia Scharf, *The Women Jefferson Loved* (New York: Harper-Collins, 2010); see also Brodie, *Intimate*, 287–300.

"Martha still awaits a biographer who can see her as the most important woman in Jefferson's life and not just as a footnote to Sally Hemings." Ellis, *American Sphinx*, Apple Books ed., 787n31.

4 Israel Jefferson recollections, AGR, *Sally*, 252. No reference to this deathbed promise has yet been found in the papers of Jefferson or his Randolph and Eppes descendants. William G. Hyland, Jr., *Martha Jefferson: An Intimate Life with Thomas Jefferson* (Lanham, MD: Rowman & Littlefield, 2015), 1.

5 Burstein, *Secrets*, Apple Books ed., 12; William G. Hyland Jr., *In Defense of Thomas Jefferson: The Sally Hemings Sex Scandal* (New York: St. Martin's, 2009), 75; Burton, *JV*, 12.

6 Hyland, *In Defense of Thomas Jefferson*, 75; Burstein, *Secrets*, 12; see also Burstein, *Inner*; Walter Kirn, "Life, Liberty and the Pursuit of Thomas Jefferson," *Time*, July 5, 2004; taped interview with Frank Berkley and Herb Barger, March 29, 2000.

7   *Autobiography, Writings*, 1:80; Thomas Jefferson, "Autobiography," July 27,1821, Thomas Jefferson Papers 1606 to 1827, LOC Manuscript Division, loc.gov/collections/thomas-jefferson-papers; Merrill D. Peterson, ed., *Writings*, 17:46.

8   E. M. Halliday, *Understanding Thomas Jefferson* (New York: Harper Perennial, 2001), 29.

9   Planning to return to Virginia quickly, Jefferson left his two small children with his sister-in-law.

10 *MJR*, 8.

11 *MJR*, 276.

12 Barbara Mayo, "Twilight at Monticello," *Virginia Quarterly Review* 17, no. 4 (Autumn 1941): 505, https://www.vqronline.org/essay/twilight-monticello.

13 Marie Kimball, *Jefferson: The Scene of Europe, 1784–1789* (New York: Coward-McCann, 1950), 5–9, offers one of the best descriptions of Jefferson's arrival in France and, more generally, the fullest coverage of the Paris years. See also Malone, *JHT* 2:3–6.

14 See Kierner, *MJR*, chap. 8.

15 *MJR*, 274.

16 *TDLTJ*, viii.

17 *MJR*, 8.

18 *TDLTJ*, quoted in *MJR*, 275.

19 *TDLTJ*, quoted in *MJR*, 275.

20 TJR, *Memoirs*, 19.

21 Jan Lewis, *The Pursuit of Happiness: Family and Values in Jefferson's Virginia* (New York: Cambridge University Press, 1983).

22 See Billy Lee Wayson, "Martha Jefferson Randolph: The Education of a Republican Daughter & Plantation Mistress, 1782–1809," (PhD diss., ViU, 2008); hereinafter "Education."

23 *MJR*, 43.

24 *MJR*, 41.

25 Wayson, "Education," 91.

26 Wayson, 91.

27 *TDLTJ*, 69.

28 Jon Meacham, *Thomas Jefferson: The Art of Power* (New York: Random House, 2012), 349.

29 Meacham, 348–49.

30 Lorri Glover, *Founders as Fathers: The Private Lives and Politics of the American Revolutionaries* (New Haven, CT: Yale University, 2014), 136.

31 Glover, 136.

32 Thomas Jefferson to Martha Jefferson Randolph, March 28, 1787, in Julian Boyd, ed., *The Papers of Thomas Jefferson*, vol. 11, *1 January 1787 to 6 August 1787* (Princeton, NJ: Princeton University Press, 1955), 251.

33 Thomas Jefferson to Martha Jefferson Randolph, April 4, 1790, Randall, *Life*, 622.

34 McLaughlin, *Jefferson and Monticello*, 367.

35 Elizabeth Langhorne, "Black Magic and Tales from Jefferson's Monticello," in *Folklore and Folklife in Virginia*, ed. Charles L. Perdue Jr. (Charlottesville: Virginia Folklore Society, 1979), 74.

36 Benjamin Wallace, *The Billionaire's Vinegar* (New York: Three Rivers, 2008, 2009), 8.

37 Wallace, 21.

38 *TMR*, 28–32.

39 McLaughlin, *Jefferson and Monticello*, 192.

40 McLaughlin, 192.

41 PTL, 8:436.

42 Catherine Kerrison, *Jefferson's Daughters* (New York: Ballantine Books, 2018), Apple Books ed., 112

43 Wallace, *The Billionaire's Vinegar*, 10.

44 Wallace, 9.

45 Wallace, 16.

46 *MJR*, 8.

47 *MJR*, 13.

48 Bear, *Monticello*, 83.

49 Wallace, 18.

50 Wallace, *The Billionaire's Vinegar*, 19.

51 "For a complete list of items brought back from France see *Papers*, 18:34–39." McLaughlin, *Jefferson and Monticello*, 454n364.

52 Wallace, *The Billionaire's Vinegar*, 19.

53 "Memoirs of a Monticello Slave as Dictated to Charles Campbell," in Bear, *Monticello*, 5.

54 Jefferson to Count de Volney, Washington, DC, February 8, 1805; Beran, *Jefferson's Demons*, 412n29.

55 *MJR*, 77.

56 *MJR*, 77.

57 *TMR*, 13–24.

58 *TMR*, 28–31.

59 *MJR*, 79.

60 *MJR*, 79.
61 *MJR*, 45.
62 *TMR*, 25–34.
63 *MJR*, 226.
64 Kierner, 145.
65 Henry Wiencek, *Master of the Mountain: Thomas Jefferson and His Slaves* (New York: Farrar, Straus, and Giroux, 2012), 88.
66 Henry S. Randall, *The Life of Thomas Jefferson*, 3 vols., rev. ed. (New York: Da Capo Press, 1972).
67 *Papers*, vol. 16, *November 1789 to July 1790* (1961), 191.
68 *MJR*, 81.
69 McLaughlin, *Jefferson and Monticello*, 264; emphasis in the original.
70 *TDLTJ*, 343–44.
71 *FL*, 51.
72 TJ to Martha Jefferson Randolph, February 9, 1791, in Henry S. Randall, *The Life of Thomas Jefferson*, vol. 2 (Philadelphia: J. B. Lippincott· 1871), 15
73 Glover, *Founders as Fathers*, 162.
74 Glover, 374 (Apple Books).
75 Martha Jefferson Randolph to Thomas Jefferson, January 16, 1793, in Crawford, *Twilight*, 28.
76 Crawford, 29.
77 *MJR*, 100.
78 Lucia Stanton, *Free Some Day: The African American Families of Monticello* (n.p.: Thomas Jefferson Foundation, 2000), 28.
79 Noble E. Cunningham Jr., *In Pursuit of Reason: The Life of Thomas Jefferson* (New York: Ballantine, 1987), 136.
80 Langhorne, *Monticello*, 206; *FL*, 51.
81 *MJR*, 90, iBooks ed.
82 TJ to Thomas Mann Randolph, January 18, 1796, in Langhorne, *Monticello*, 63.
83 Wayson, "Education."
84 Wayson, 280.
85 Edge Hill, also known as Edgehill and Edgehill Farm, is a historic house located near Shadwell in Albemarle County, Virginia. "William Randolph of Tuckahoe acquired 2,400 acres as a land grant from King George II in 1735, and it was inherited by his son Thomas Mann Randolph Sr. of Tuckahoe. In 1790, he gave it and his Varina

plantation near Richmond to his son Thomas Mann Randolph, Jr. as a wedding gift when the younger Randolph" married Patsy. Preferring the cooler mountain air of Albemarle County, the younger Randolphs "built a one-story, wood-frame structure on the property about 1799," but they actually lived mostly at Monticello (a far more sophisticated and cozier building). Randolph Jr. ran this new plantation and acted as an overseer at Jefferson's plantation, but he also ran up great debts. "The property passed out of the Randolph family in 1902, following the death of Carolina Ramsay Randolph. It was added to the National Register of Historic Places in 1982." Wikiwand, s.v. "Edge Hill (Shadwell, Virginia)," accessed August 31, 2021, https://www.wikiwand.com/en/Edge_Hill_(Shadwell,_Virginia).

86   Wayson, *Education*, 280.
87   PTL, 37, *4 March to 30 June 1802* (1950), 247.
88   PTL, 37:247.
89   Margaret Bayard Smith, *The First Forty Years of Washington Society in the Family: Letters of Margaret Bayard Smith*, ed. Gaillard Hunt (New York: Charles Scribner's Sons, 1906), 34.
90   *MJR*, 252.
91   Mayo, "Twilight at Monticello," 505.
92   *MJR*, 100.
93   Martha Jefferson Randolph to TJ, March 31, 1797; *MJR*, 100–101.
94   *MJR*, 101.
95   *MJR*, 103.
96   *MJR*, 103.
97   *MJR*, 103.
98   *MJR*, 104.
99   *MJR*, 104.
100 *MJR*, 105.
101 *MJR*, 115.
102 *MJR*, 115.
103 *MJR*, 123.
104 Mrs. Smith, quoted in Katharine Susan Anthony, *Dolley Madison: Her Life and Times* (Garden City, NY: Doubleday, 1949).
105 *MJR*, 189. On caning, see Greenberg, *Honor and Slavery*, 123. Although some historians cite this statement about Tom's violent temper as evidence of his abusiveness toward his son (and possibly toward Jane), Jeff was actually describing his father's supposed hostility toward Jefferson during the last year of the latter's life.

106 "Extract from Ellen W. Randolph Coolidge to Henry S. Randall," 1856, https://tjrs.monticello.org/letter/1964.

107 Scharff, *The Women Jefferson Loved*, 382.

108 Glover, *Founders as Fathers*, 154.

109 Glover, 154.

110 TJR, *Memoirs*, 4.

Chapter 2

1 Thomas Mann Randolph served as governor of Virginia from 1819 to 1822 and was also a colonel. The latter fact has caused some historians to confuse him with his eldest son, Colonel Thomas Jefferson Randolph; I am grateful for the sterling research done and the excellent biography of Thomas Mann Randolph by William Gaines, "Thomas Mann Randolph" (PhD diss., ViU, 1950), as well as Gaines's book based on his dissertation, *Thomas Mann Randolph: Jefferson's Son-in-Law* (Baton Rouge: Louisiana State University Press, 1966); hereinafter *TMR*.

2 Jon Meacham, *Thomas Jefferson: The Art of Power* (New York: Random House, 2012), Apple Books ed., 901.

3 For a sketch of Jeff Randolph's ancestry and an excellent biography of Thomas Mann Randolph, see Gaines, "Thomas Mann Randolph," as well as Gaines's book based on this dissertation (see note 1).

4 *TMR*, 26.

5 Jack McLaughlin, *Jefferson and Monticello: The Biography of a Builder* (New York: Henry Holt, 1988), 242.

6 McLaughlin, 242.

7 *TMR*, v–vii.

8 Brodie, *Intimate*, 458.

9 See *TMR*, chap. 11.

10 Gaines, "Thomas Mann Randolph," 274; See also *TMR*, 181–83.

11 TJR, *Memoirs*, 3–4.

12 *TMR*, 3

13 *TMR*, 7.

14 *TMR*, 12.

15 *TMR*, 12

16 *TMR*, 12.

17 "From Thomas Jefferson to Thomas Mann Randolph, Jr., 27 August 1786," Founders Online, National Archives, https://founders.archives.gov/documents/Jefferson/01-10-02-0226.
18 *TMR*, 18–21.
19 *Papers*, 11:293.
20 *Papers*, 11:557.
21 *TMR*, 22–25.
22 *TMR*, 21–22.
23 *Papers*, 15:156.
24 *TMR*, 23–25.
25 Noble E. Cunningham, *The Life of Thomas Jefferson* (New York: Ballantine, 1987), 136.
26 *TMR*, 25–35.
27 *TMR*, 25–35; "Thomas Jefferson to Marbois, 5 December 1783," Founders Online, National Archives, https://founders.archives.gov/documents/Jefferson/01-06-02-0297; see also "Letters of Thomas Jefferson to Marbois," *American Historical Review* 12, no. 1 (October 1906): 76.
28 Thomas Mann Randolph Sr. of Tuckahoe (1741–93) was the father of fifteen children and gave his name to a son by each of his two wives: Thomas Mann Randolph of Edgehill (1768–1828), Patsy's husband; and Thomas Mann Randolph of Tuckahoe (1791–1851).
29 *TMR*, 32.
30 *TMR*, 32.
31 *TMR*, 32.
32 *TMR*, 32.
33 *TMR*, chaps. 3–4.
34 *TMR*, 61–63.
35 *TMR*, 61.
36 TMR, 61.
37 *TMR*, 62.
38 TJR, *Memoirs*, 20; Beran, *Jefferson's Demons*, 350.
39 Catherine Kerrison, *Jefferson's Daughters* (New York: Ballantine Books, 2018), 165.
40 Lorri Glover, *Founders as Fathers: The Private Lives and Politics of the American Revolutionaries* (New Haven, CT: Yale University Press, 2014), 164.
41 TJ to Maria Jefferson, June 14, 1797, in *FL*, 148; TJ to Martha Jefferson Randolph, June 8,1797, in *FL*, 146

42 TJ to Martha Jefferson Randolph, June 8, 1797, *FL*, 148, 146; Glover, *Founders as Fathers: The Private Lives and Politics of the American Revolutionaries* (New Haven, CT: Yale University, 2014), 148.

43 McLaughlin, *Jefferson and Monticello*, 264.

44 McLaughlin, 264.

45 Beran, *Jefferson's Demons*, 314.

46 Beran, 350.

47 Beran, 350–51.

48 *TMR*, 57.

49 *TMR*, 57.

50 *TMR*, 61–63; chaps. 3–4.

51 Beran, *Jefferson's Demons*, chap. 5.

52 Beran, 340.

53 *TMR*, 97, 99; TJR, *Memoirs*, 304; *MJR*, 904.

54 *TMR*, 793

55 Crawford, *Twilight*, 228; See also https://www.monticello.org/.

56 Jefferson to Catherine Church, 1799, in *TDLTJ*, 264.

57 *TMR*, 45.

58 *TMR*, 45.

59 See Brodie, *Intimate*, chap. 32; 430.

60 Brodie, 430

61 Martha Jefferson Randolph to TJ, November 18, 1801, in Boyd, *Papers* 35:690; *MJR*, 598.

62 *TMR*, chap. 9.

63 *TMR*, 134

64 *TMR*, 137.

65 *TMR*, 138–39.

66 *TMR*, 155–60.

67 Brodie, *Intimate*, 394.

68 Brodie, 458.

69 Gaines, "Thomas Mann Randolph," 119; *TMR*, 155–60.

70 *TMR*, 155–60.

71 *TMR*, 155–60.

72 *TMR*, 155–60.

73	*TMR*,
74	Scharff, *Women Jefferson Loved*, 323
75	*TMR*, 28; chaps. 9–10; 155–60.
76	*TMR*, 57.
77	*TMR*, 57.
78	*TMR*, 57–60.
79	*TMR*, 65–66.
80	*TMR*, 66.
81	*TMR*, 66–67.
82	*TMR*, 48, 66–67.
83	*TMR*, 48.
84	*TMR*, 48.
85	*TMR*, 48.
86	Jan Lewis, "Domestic Tranquility and the Management of Emotion among the Gentry of Pre-Revolutionary Virginia." *WMQ* 39, no. 1 (1982): 135–49, 3.
87	*TMR*, 155–60.
88	John Randolph to Francis Walker Gilmer, 21 June 1825, John Randolph of Roanoke Papers, LOC; Gaines, "Thomas Mann Randolph," 251; *MJR*, 921. Thomas Jefferson Randolph to Jane Randolph, 14 February 1825, Edgehill-Randolph Papers, Special Collections, ViU.
89	*TMR*, 44.
90	Crawford, *Twilight*, 209.
91	*TMR*; John Randolph to Francis Walker Gilmer, 2 July 1825, John Randolph of Roanoke Papers, LOC; Gaines, "Thomas Mann Randolph," 251.
92	*TMR*; Randolph to Gilmer, 2 July 1825; Gaines, "Thomas Mann Randolph," 251.
93	Jefferson to Randolph, 9 July 1825, Edgehill-Randolph Papers, Special Collections, ViU
94	See Virginia Scharff's excellent book, *The Women Jefferson Loved* (New York: Harper Collins, 2010), 268; Scharff devotes detailed chapters to Jefferson's mother, wife, daughters, and granddaughters, focusing on their relationships with him and how their connection to Jefferson came with costs and benefits; see also *MJR*.
95	Virginia Randolph Trist to Ellen Randolph Coolidge, 19 March 1828, Jefferson Papers, ViU; Randolph to William Cabell Rives, 3 May 1828, William C. Rives Papers, LOC.
96	Berna, *Demons*, 319-320.
97	Brodie, *Intimate*, 395.
98	Brodie, 395.

99   "Ellen W. Randolph Coolidge to Henry S. Randall," March 13, 1856, https://tjrs.monticello.org/letter/1984.

100 Glover, *Founders as Fathers*, 154.

101 Glover, 154.

102 Brodie, *Intimate*, 430.

103 Ellen W. Randolph Coolidge to Henry S. Randall, Boston, March 13, 1856.

104 *TMR*, chaps. 9–10.

105 Ellen Coolidge to Henry Randall, March 27, 1856, Ellen Wayles Coolidge Randolph Papers, Accession #9090, ViU.

106 Coolidge to Randall, March 27, 1856.

107 Langhorne, *Monticello*, 428.

108 *MJR*, 455-456.

109 Kierner, *MJR*, 455; Martha Jefferson Randolph to Ellen, June 30, 1828.

110 *TMR*, chap. 11.

111 Edgehill-Randolph Papers, Special Collections, ViU

112 Ellen Nicholas to Jane Randolph, 12 January 1827, Edgehill-Randolph Papers, Special Collections, ViU; TJR, *Memoirs*.

113 Crawford, *Twilight*, 192.

114 *TMR*, 186–88.

Chapter 3

1   Merrill Peterson, quoted in Brodie, *Intimate*, 470.

2   Garry Wills, *Mr. Jefferson's University* (Washington, DC: National Geographic Society, 2002), Apple Books ed., 103

3   Brodie, *Intimate*, 470.

4   Mayo, "Twilight at Monticello," 502.

5   Mayo, 502.

6   Jon Meacham, *Thomas Jefferson: The Art of Power* (New York: Random House, 2012), Apple Books ed., 1134.

7   Meacham, 1134.

8   TJR, *Memoirs*, 2–5.

9   Thomas Jefferson Randolph recollections, ViU, 1837; Lucia C. Stanton, *"Those Who Labor for My Happiness": Slavery at Thomas Jefferson's Monticello* (Charlottesville: University of Virginia Press, 2012), Apple Books, n. 6, 891.

10 TJ to Wistar, June 21, 1807, in Ford, *Writings*, 10:423.

11 Lorri Glover, *Founders as Fathers: The Private Lives and Politics of the American Revolutionaries* (New Haven, CT: Yale University Press, 2014), 120.
12 Glover, 120.
13 Glover, 120.
14 TJR, *Memoirs*, 18.
15 Monticello website and plaque at Monticello.
16 McLaughlin, *Jefferson and Monticello*, 366.
17 McLaughlin, 366.
18 Stein, *Worlds of Thomas Jefferson at Monticello*, 50; Meacham, *Thomas Jefferson*, Apple Books ed., 868.
19 Randall, *Life*, 3:349. 62.
20 See TJR, *Memoirs*.
21 See TJR, *Memoirs*.
22 Crawford, *Twilight*, 69.
23 Martha Jefferson Randolph, [Monticello], to Thomas Jefferson, 18 November 1792, Edgehill-Randolph Papers, Special Collections, ViU; Joseph Carroll Vance, "Thomas Jefferson Randolph," PhD diss., University of Virginia, 1957, republished as Monticello West, *Favorite Grandson: Thomas Jefferson Randolph* (Lulu.com, 2017), https://www.google.com/books/edition/Favorite_Grandson_Thomas_Jefferson_Rando/VHMnDwAAQBAJ?hl, 4.
24 Vance, "Thomas Jefferson Randolph," 3–5.
25 Thomas Jefferson, Monticello, to Martha Jefferson Randolph, 22 January 1795, Edgehill-Randolph Papers, Special Collections, ViU; Vance, "Thomas Jefferson Randolph," 5.
26 Thomas Jefferson, Monticello, to Martha Jefferson Randolph, 22 January 1795, Edgehill-Randolph Papers, Special Collections, ViU.
27 TJ to Martha Jefferson Randolph, January 25, 1796, in *The Papers of Thomas Jefferson*, vol. 28 ed. John Catanzarini (Princeton, NJ: Princeton University Press, 2000): 599.
28 Vance, "Thomas Jefferson Randolph," 5–6.
29 Vance, 5–6.
30 Vance, 6; TJR, *Memoirs*, 26.
31 Vance, "Thomas Jefferson Randolph," 11.
32 McLaughlin, *Jefferson and Monticello*, 228.
33 McLaughlin, 228.
34 McLaughlin, 228.

35 McLaughlin, 228. "This history of Jefferson's dining habits includes a collection of modernized recipes taken from the Monticello cookbook copied by generations of Jefferson grandchildren and great-grandchildren." (p. 421).
36 McLaughlin, 238.
37 McLaughlin, 232
38 Langhorne, *Monticello*, 186.
39 Burstein, *Secrets*, Apple Books ed., 498, n. 23.
40 Anna Eliot Ticknor and George Stillman Hillard, eds., *Life, Letters and Journals of George Ticknor* (Boston: Houghton Mifflin, 1909), 1:34 seq., 806.
41 Langhorne, *Monticello*, 186.
42 Langhorne, *Monticello*; Ticknor and Hillard, *Life, Letters and Journals*, 1:34 seq., 806.
43 Thornton Diary, September 19, 1802, *DLC*.

Jefferson was not the only Founding Father who was fond of wine. Franklin, for one, kept a substantial cellar in Paris and called wine "proof that God loves us and that he likes to see us happy." But Jefferson, who had been ordering wine for many years, had recently acquired an unmatched breadth and depth of knowledge about the subject.

Not only had he learned which were the best wines, but he had also become savvy about the mischief to which an unwary consumer might fall prey. In his 1788 letter to the owner of Lafite, Jefferson spelled out his concern directly: "If it would be possible to have them bottled and packed at your estate, it would doubtless be a guarantee that the wine was genuine, and the drawing-off and so forth well done." Wallace, *The Billionaire's Vinegar*, 8.

44 McLaughlin, *Jefferson and Monticello*, 235.
45 McLaughlin, 235.
46 McLaughlin, 235–36.
47 Langhorne, *Monticello*, 299; Ticknor and Hillard, *Life, Letters and Journals*, 1:34 seq., 806.
48 TJR, *Memoirs*, 26–28
49 Vance, "Thomas Jefferson Randolph," 7.
50 TJR, *Memoirs*, 30–31 ; Vance, "Thomas Jefferson Randolph," 12–13.
51 TJR, *Memoirs*, 30–33.
52 Langhorne, *Monticello*, 567.
53 Vance, "Thomas Jefferson Randolph," 12; TMR, *Memoirs*, 32.
54 Vance, "Thomas Jefferson Randolph," 7; TJR, *Memoirs*, 7–8.
55 TJR, *Memoirs*, 8.
56 TJR, *Memoirs*, 8.

57   TJR to Martha Jefferson Randolph, ca. 30 November 1809, ViU, http://tjrs.monticello.org/letter/584ViU.

58   *MJR*, 501; TJR, *Memoirs*, 4, 6–7.

59   TJR, *Memoirs*, 3-4.

60   Martha Jefferson Randolph to Thomas Jefferson, 31 January 1801, in Boyd, *Papers*, 32:527; *MJR*, 503.

61   *Papers*, 32:52..

62   Thomas Jefferson to Martha Jefferson Randolph, 5 February 1801, *FL*, 195; Scharff, *Women*, 1191.

63   Scharff, *Women*, 324–25.

64   Thomas Jefferson to Martha Jefferson Randolph, February 5, 1801, in *The Papers of Thomas Jefferson*, ed. Barbara B. Oberg, vol. 32, *June 1800 to February 1801* (Princeton, NJ: Princeton, University Press, 2005), 556.

65   Scharff, *Women*, 325.

66   "From Thomas Jefferson to Thomas Jefferson Randolph, 24 November 1808," *Founders Online*, National Archives, https://founders.archives.gov/documents/Jefferson/99-01-02-9151 (this is an Early Access document from The Papers of Thomas Jefferson. It is not an authoritative final version); Glover, *Founders as Fathers*, 136. For additional examples, see " From Thomas Jefferson to Ellen Wayles Randolph, 27 November 1801," Founders Online, https://founders.archives.gov/documents/Jefferson/01–35-02-0561; Patrick Henry to Betsy Aylett, 20 August 1796, PHC, 2:571; and George Mason to Thomas Jefferson, 26 May 1788, *PGM*, 3:1044.

67   Thomas Jefferson to Anne Cary Randolph, Thomas Jefferson Randolph, and Ellen Wayles Randolph, March 2, 1802, in Glover, *Founders as Fathers*, 133.

68   Thomas Jefferson to Martha Jefferson Randolph, January 5, 1808, in *FL*, 320.

69   Jefferson to Cornelia Jefferson Randolph, undated, The Thomas Jefferson Papers, Special Collections, ViU Library, in "Canons of Conduct," https://www.monticello.org/site/research-and-collections/canons-conduct. Transcription of extract available online at Jefferson Quotes and Family Letters, https://tjrs.monticello.org/?_ga=2.241767366.559297922.1634932835-1355971884.1634932834.

70   Thomas Jefferson to Anne Cary Randolph, Thomas Jefferson Randolph, and Jefferson to Cornelia Jefferson Randolph, undated, The Thomas Jefferson Papers, Special Collections, ViU Library. Transcription of extract available online at Jefferson Quotes and Family Letters. Ellen Wayles Randolph, 7 March 1802, *Founders Online, National Archives*, https://founders.archives.gov/documents/Jefferson/01–37-02-0017.

71   Thomas Jefferson to Thomas Jefferson Randolph, 24 November 1808, Founders Online, National Archives, https://founders.archives.gov/documents/Jefferson/99-01-02-9151.

72   Thomas Jefferson, Washington, to Dr. [Caspar] Wistar, 12 October 1808, Founders Online, National Archives; Gaines, *TMR*, 79, chap. 3–4.

73 Thomas Jefferson to Thomas Jefferson Randolph, 13 October 1808, Founders Online, National Archives, https://founders.archives.gov/documents/Jefferson/99-01-02-8852.

74 Burstein, *Jefferson's Secrets* (New York: Basic Books, 2011), Apple Books ed., 529n48.

75 Thomas Jefferson to Randolph Washington, 21 February 1803, Thomas Jefferson Papers, 1606 to 1827, Manuscript Division, LOC.

76 Thomas Jefferson to Thomas Jefferson Randolph, 24 October 1808, Founders Online, National Archives, https://founders.archives.gov/documents/Jefferson/99-01-02-8933.

77 Thomas Jefferson to Randolph Washington, 24 November 1808, Founders Online, National Archives, https://founders.archives.gov/documents/Jefferson/99-01-02-9151.

78 Peterson, *Writings*.

79 Vance, "Thomas Jefferson Randolph," 45.

80 TJR, *Memoirs*, 48.

81 Thomas Jefferson, Monticello, to Thomas Z. Randolph, 14 November 1813, Thomas Jefferson Papers, LOC; Vance, "Thomas Jefferson Randolph," 45

82 Sarah E. Nicholas to Jane Randolph, 12 February 1841, Edgehill-Randolph Papers, Special Collections, ViU.

83 Vance, "Thomas Jefferson Randolph," 13.

84 TJR, *Memoirs*, 10.

85 McLaughlin, *Jefferson and Monticello*, 43

86 TJR, *Memoirs*, 22–23.

87 Beran, *Demons*, 29–31.

88 Beran, 31; letter to George Ticknor, 16 July 1823, in Andrew A. Lipscomb and Albert E. Bergh, eds., *The Writings of Thomas Jefferson* (Library Edition), 20 vols. (Washington, DC: The Thomas Jefferson Memorial Foundation, 1903), 15: 455.

89 Vance, "Thomas Jefferson Randolph," 6

90 TJR, *Memoirs*, 20.

91 TJR, *Memoirs*, 3–4, 6–7.

92 Martha Jefferson Randolph to Thomas Jefferson, 31 January 1801, Massachusetts Historical Society; Martha Jefferson Randolph to Thomas Jefferson, 16 April 1802, Jefferson Papers, Coolidge Collection, Massachusetts Historical Society; Vance, "Thomas Jefferson Randolph," 9.

93 Martha Jefferson Randolph to Thomas Jefferson, 31 January 1801, Massachusetts Historical Society; Martha Jefferson Randolph to Thomas Jefferson, 16 April 1802, Jefferson Papers, Coolidge Collection, Massachusetts Historical Society; Vance, "Thomas Jefferson Randolph," 9

94 Vance, "Thomas Jefferson Randolph," 13; TJR, *Memoirs*, 10.
95 John W. Eppes to Francis Eppes, 20 June 1816, John W. Eppes Papers; Vance, *Thomas Jefferson Randolph*.
96 Vance, "Thomas Jefferson Randolph," 22–23.
97 Vance, "Thomas Jefferson Randolph," 23.
98 TJR, *Memoirs*, 38-39.
99 Vance, "Thomas Jefferson Randolph," 20.
100 Vance, 24.
101 Vance, 29–30.
102 Vance, 30.
103 Thomas Jefferson in Washington, D.C., to Benjamin Rush, 3 January 1808, Jefferson Papers, Alderman Library, Reprinted in Mayo, *Jefferson Himself: The Personal Narrative of a Many-Sided American* (Boston: Houghton Mifflin and Bernard Mayo, 1942), 272; Vance, "Thomas Jefferson Randolph," 26–27.
104 Vance, "Thomas Jefferson Randolph," 30.
105 TJR, *Memoirs*, 40–41.
106 Vance, "Thomas Jefferson Randolph," 27–28.
107 Crawford, *Twilight*, 53.
108 Crawford, 55.
109 Crawford, 56.
110 Vance, "Thomas Jefferson Randolph," 33. "Actually Randolph was deputy collector and his father the collector. Apparently the work was done by the deputy." Tax receipt to Thomas Jefferson, 23 January 1814, Jefferson Papers, Coolidge Collection, Massachusetts Historical Society, in Vance, 33.
111 Langhorne, *Monticello*, Apple Books ed., 300.
112 Vance, "Thomas Jefferson Randolph," 33.
113 Elizabeth Trist to Nicholas Trist, 9 February 1821. Trist Papers; Cornelia Randolph to Coolidge, 18 March 1826.
114 Mayo, "Twilight at Monticello," 507.
115 Ellen Wayles Randolph Coolidge's memories of trips to the Poplar Forest, written in 1856 and printed in Randall, *Life*, 3:343–44; *Twilight at Monticello*; Mayo, "Twilight at Monticello," 502, 507.
116 Cornelia Randolph to Virginia Randolph Tristan, 17–19 August 1817, Trist Papers; Coolidge to Jane Jefferson Randolph, 13 September 1820, Correspondence of Ellen Wayles Randolph Coolidge, Special Collections, ViU.
117 Virginia Randolph to Nicholas P. Trist, 17 September 1823, Trist Papers, LOC, in Vance, "Thomas Jefferson Randolph," 166.

118 Vance, 168.
119 Meacham, *Thomas Jefferson,* Apple Books ed., 871.
120 Jefferson to Thomas Mann Randolph, Jr., 18 October 1820.
121 Virginia Randolph, Monticello, to Trist, 6 December 1823, Nicholas Philip Trist Papers, Manuscript Division, LOC; in Vance, "Thomas Jefferson Randolph," 53.
122 Gaines, *TMR,* 158.
123 Gaines, 131.
124 *TDLTJ,* 346.
125 Glover, *Founders as Fathers,* 162.
126 TJR, *Memoirs,* 52.
127 Thomas Jefferson, Monticello, to Elizabeth Trist, 1 February 1814, Jefferson Papers, Coolidge Collection, Massachusetts Historical Society.

Chapter 4

1 Burstein, *Jefferson's Secrets* (2011), Apple Books ed., 133
2 Burstein, *Jefferson's Secrets,* Apple Books ed., 133.
3 Burstein, 130.
4 Marie Kimball, "A Playmate of Thomas Jefferson," *North American Review* 213, no. 783 (February 1921): 145.
5 Burstein, *Secrets,* 134; Kimball, "A Playmate of Thomas Jefferson," *145–46.*
6 Burstein, *Jefferson's Secrets* (2011), Apple Books ed., 133–34.
7 Burstein, 133; Cornelia Randolph to Lizzie Rivinus, June 7 1864.
8 Kimball, "A Playmate of Thomas Jefferson," 145.
9 Kimball, 146.
10 Oberg, *Papers,* 37:247.
11 Kimball, "A Playmate of Thomas Jefferson," 146.
12 Coolidge, *Autobiography,* 17.
13 Kimball, "A Playmate of Thomas Jefferson," 146.
14 Scharff, *Women Jefferson Loved,* 327.
15 Kimball, "A Playmate of Thomas Jefferson," 147.
16 Burstein, *Jefferson's Secrets* (2011), Apple Books ed., 135.
17 Meacham, *Thomas Jefferson,* Apple Books ed., 942; Randall, *Jefferson* 3:524–25.
18 Meacham, 943.
19 Glover, *Founders as Fathers,* 133.

20. Glover, 133.
21. Glover, 133.
22. Glover, 133–34.
23. Beran, *Jefferson's Demons*, n.p.
24. Burstein, *Jefferson's Secrets* (2011), Apple Books ed., 135.
25. Langhorne, *Monticello*, 248.
26. Langhorne, 248.
27. Extract from Ellen W. Randolph Coolidge to Henry S. Randall; Tr in Letterbook (ViU: Ellen W. Randolph Coolidge Correspondence), in Henry S. Randall, *Life of Thomas Jefferson* (New York, 1858), 3:346–49, https://tjrs.monticello.org/letter/1434.
28. *MJR*, 596.
29. Kierner, 596.
30. Burstein, *Jefferson's Secrets*, 76
31. Kimball, *A Playmate of Thomas Jefferson*, 154.
32. McLaughlin, *Jefferson and Monticello*, 355.
33. McLaughlin, 355.
34. McLaughlin, 355–56.
35. McLaughlin, Apple Books ed., 778.
36. Burstein, 133–34
37. Burstein, 134; Abigail Adams to TJ, December. 15, 1816.
38. *TDLTJ*, 345
39. Meacham, *Thomas Jefferson*, Apple Books ed., 871–72; Randal, *Jefferson* III, 350.
40. Meacham, *Thomas Jefferson*. Apple Books ed., 871–72.
41. *TDLTJ*, 345.
42. Langhorne, *Monticello*, Apple Books ed., 265.
43. Malone, *Sage*, 298.
44. *TDLTJ*, 350; see *VTM*, 53–54, for Margaret Bayard Smith's reminiscence of his grandfatherly games.
45. Meacham, *Thomas Jefferson* Apple Books ed., 742; Smith, Forty Years, 396.
46. Crawford, *Twilight*, 69.
47. *TDLTJ*, 343.
48. Jefferson to Dunbar, 12 January 1801, in Paul Leicester Ford, ed., *The Works of Thomas Jefferson*, Federal Edition (New York, 1905).
49. Jefferson to Adams, 1 June 1823, reprinted in Cappon, *Letters*, 578.

50 Randall, *Jefferson, III*, 349, 65, 69; Langhorne, *Monticello*, 714; Randall, *Life of Jefferson*, 3:350.
51 Meacham, *Thomas Jefferson*, Apple Books ed., 870; Ellen Coolidge to Henry Randall, February 22, 1856.
52 McLaughlin, *Jefferson and Monticello*, 26.
53 McLaughlin, 26.
54 McLaughlin, 26.
55 McLaughlin, 26.
56 Randall, *Life*, 3:350.
57 Randall, 3:350.
58 Randall, 3:350.
59 See Randall, 3:448; Burstein, *Jefferson's Secrets*, Apple Books ed., 518n33. MJR to TJ, Nov. 24, 1808.
60 Meacham, *Thomas* Jefferson, 449.
61 Meacham, 449.
62 Glover, *Founders as Fathers*, 162.
63 Ellen Coolidge to Henry Randall, in *TDLTJ*, 344, emphasis in original.
64 Coolidge to Randall, in *TDLTJ*, 344.
65 Randolph, 282.
66 Parton, *Life*, iii, 165.
67 Cornelia Randolph to Henry S. Randall, quoted in Crawford, *Twilight*, 135.
68 Crawford, 135.
69 Crawford, *Twilight*, 135.
70 Randall, *Life*, 348.
71 Randall, 347.
72 *TDLTJ*, 344.
73 *TDLTJ*, 344.
74 Kimball, "A Playmate of Thomas Jefferson," 510.
75 Kimball, "A Playmate of Thomas Jefferson," 510.
76 Langhorne, *Monticello,* Apple Books ed., 348.
77 Merrill D. Peterson, *Visitors to Monticello* (Charlottesville, University of Virginia Press, 1989), 203.
78 Crawford, *Twilight*, xviii.
79 *TDLTJ*, 295.

80 Ellen to Francis Eppes, April 5, 1821, in Burstein, *Jefferson's Secrets* (2011), Apple Books ed., 138.
81 Burstein, 138.
82 Birles and Francavilla, *Thomas Jefferson's Granddaughter*, xx–xxii.
83 Birles and Francavilla, xx–xxii.
84 Birles and Francavilla, xx–xxii.
85 Birles and Francavilla, xx–xxii.
86 Kimball, "A Playmate of Thomas Jefferson," 155.
87 Kimball, 155.
88 Kimball, Marie, *A Playmate of Thomas Jefferson*, The North American Review, Feb., 1921, Vol. 213, No. 783 (Feb., 1921), pp. 145--156, University of Northern Iowa; Stable URL: https://www.jstor.org/stable/25120674, p.
89 Kimball, Marie, *A Playmate of Thomas Jefferson*, The North American Review, Feb., 1921, Vol. 213, No. 783 (Feb., 1921), pp. 145--156, University of Northern Iowa; Stable URL: https://www.jstor.org/stable/25120674,
90 "Lafayette's Visit to Monticello (1824): An Article Courtesy Of The Thomas Jefferson Encyclopedia," The Jefferson Monticello, accessed October 29, 2021, https://www.monticello.org/site/research-and-collections/lafayettes-visit-monticello-1824.
91 To Thomas Jefferson from Ellen Wayles Randolph Coolidge, 1 August 1825, *Founders Online*, National Archives, https://founders.archives.gov/documents/Jefferson/98-01-02-5424.
92 From Thomas Jefferson to Ellen Wayles Randolph Coolidge, 27 August 1825, https://founders.archives.gov/documents/Jefferson/98-01-02-5493.
93 Burstein, *Jefferson's Secrets* (2011), Apple Books ed., 131.
94 Virginia Randolph Trist to Ellen, June 27, 1825, in Burstein, 131.
95 Glover, *Founders as Fathers*, 163; Ellen Wayles Randolph to Nicholas Trist, 30 March 1824, FLDA
96 Ellen W. Randolph (Coolidge) to Nicholas P Trist, March 30, 1824, "Jefferson Quotes," The Jefferson Monticello, https://tjrs.monticello.org/letter/970.

Chapter 5

1 Ellis, *American Sphinx*, Apple Books, 390.
2 Ellis, 390–91.
3 Ellis, 408–9.
4 Thomas Jefferson, Monticello, to Elizabeth Trist, 1 February 1814, Jefferson Papers, Coolidge Collection, Massachusetts Historical Society.

5   Thomas Jefferson, Monticello, to Elizabeth Trist, 1 February 1814, Jefferson Papers, Coolidge Collection, Massachusetts Historical Society; 3.

6   Crawford, *Twilight*, 115.

7   Martha Jefferson Randolph, Edgehill, to Ellen W. Randolph Coolidge, 10 June 1833, Additional Papers of the Randolph Family of Edgehill, Albert and Shirley Small Special Collections Library, ViU; Vance, "Thomas Jefferson Randolph."

8   Vance, "Thomas Jefferson Randolph," 39–40

9   Charles Willson Peale to Thomas Jefferson, 2 May 1815, in Vance, 40.

10 Vance, "Thomas Jefferson Randolph," 39.

11 Vance, 39–40.

12 Vance, 39.

13 Vance, 39–40.

14 See Virginia J. Randolph (Trist) to Jane H. Nicholas Randolph, September 16, 1817, Jefferson Quotes and Letters, https://tjrs.monticello.org/letter/738.

15 Brodie, *Intimate*, 458.

16 Thomas Fleming, *The Intimate Lives of the Founding Fathers* (New York: Harper Collins, 2009), 16–18.

17 William G. Hyland Jr., *Martha Jefferson: An Intimate Life with Thomas Jefferson* (Lanham, MD: Rowman & Littlefield, 2015), 85; Fleming, *Intimate Lives*, 16–18.

18 Vance, "Thomas Jefferson Randolph," 46.

19 Vance, 46.

20 Vance, 46–47.

21 Vance, 47; Sarah E. Nicholas to Jane Randolph, 12 February 1841, Edgehill-Randolph Papers, Special Collections, ViU.

22 Vance, 46.

23 See "Tufton: An Article Courtesty of the Thomas Jefferson Encyclopedia," The Jefferson Monticello, https://www.monticello.org/site/research-and-collections/tufton.

24 Michael Kranish, *Flight from Monticello: Thomas Jefferson at War* (New York: Oxford University Press, 2010), 287; see also Ellie Weeks, "'Elk Hill': Thomas Jefferson's Plantation on the James," *Goochland County Historical Society Magazine* 3, no. 1 (1971): 6–11

25 Kranish, *Flight from Monticello*, 287.

26 James Parton, *Life of Thomas Jefferson*: *The American Scene, Comments and Commentators* (New York: Da Capo Press, 1971), 103. First published 1874 by J. R. Osgood as *Life of Thomas Jefferson, Third President of the United States*. All subsequent citations refer to 1971 edition.

27 *TDLTJ*, 364.

28 Vance, "Thomas Jefferson Randolph," 55.

29 Crawford, *Twilight at Monticello*, 179.

30 Randall, *Life*, 3:533–35.

31 Meacham, *Thomas Jefferson*, Apple Books ed., 940

32 Meacham, 940.

33 Vance, "Thomas Jefferson Randolph," 55, 56.

34 Vance, 49.

35 Lewis, *Pursuit of Happiness*, xiii.

36 Because dairy products were scarce during the first two years of Jane's residence at Monticello, she probably made regular purchases of butter from the slaves or the Monticello overseer. Yost, review of *Thomas Jefferson's Cook Book*. In fact, by the fall of 1816, large quantities of butter were being brought to Monticello from Jefferson's Bedford plantation, Poplar Forest.

37 Jane, assisted by her servants, became adept at the messy and unpleasant task of making soap for the family. Soap was produced by adding assorted fats to lye that had been made by leaching water through ashes gathered from the plantation fireplaces. The lye was strong enough and determined ready for use if an egg floated in it. The lye and fat were boiled, usually in a large kettle over an open fire outdoors. Making soap was normally a cold weather task, when fire ashes were ample. Hard soap, made by adding salt to the lye, was used for general cleaning of your person as it is today. Jane's soft soap, with a consistency much like butterscotch pudding, was utilized used for the plantation laundry. McLaughlin, Jefferson and Monticello, 181–82.

38 Philip Mazzei, *My Life and Wanderings*, ed. Margherita Marchione, trans. Eugene Scalia (Morristown, NJ: American Institute of Italian Studies, 1980), 14.

39 Mazzei, *My Life and Wanderings*, 209.

40 Mazzei, 209.

41 Mazzei, 213–14.

42 Mazzei, 61n406.

43 Giacomo [James] Leoni, trans. *Architecture of A. Palladio*, 4 vols. 3rd ed. (London, 1742), 56; 1 Quattro Libri dell'Architettura, Venetia, 1570, book 2, 46). Earlier, Leon Battista Alberti had recommended an elevated site as ideal for health. Giacomo [James] Leoni, *Architecture of Leon Batistta Alberti* (London, 1726), 2:79; see Fiske Kimball, *Thomas Jefferson Architect* (New York: Da Capo Press, 1968), 5n20; David Irwin, *Winkelmann: Writings on Art* (London: Phaidon, 1972), 42–43, 61, 107–8, 113–14; Gene Waddell, "The First Monticello," *Journal of the Society of Architectural Historians* 46, no. 1 (March 1987): 5, 29, http://www.jstor.org/stable/990142.

44 Genevieve Yost, review of *Thomas Jefferson's Cook Book*, by Marie Kimball, *WMQ*, second series, 19, no. 2 (April 1939): 238–39, http://www.jstor.org/stable/1922859.

45 "The chief danger" for people in that region "was malaria, known as intermittent fever, marsh fever, or autumnal fever. It was not yet known that it was transmitted by mosquitoes. Washington, which became the nation's capital in June 1800, was considered particularly unhealthy because it was situated on a swamp." McLaughlin, *Jefferson and Monticello*, 272; Hyland, *Martha Jefferson*, 170.

46 Wiencek, *Master of the Mountain*, 156.

47 Roberts, *Founding Mothers*, 91.

48 Roberts, 91.

49 Roberts, 48–49.

50 Vance, "Thomas Jefferson Randolph," 154.

51 Vance, 154.

52 Vance, 155.

53 Jane Randolph to Virginia R. Trist, ca. 1835, quoted in Vance, 156–57.

54 Jane Randolph to Peggy Nicholas, 1836, in Vance, 157.

55 Jane Randolph to Virginia R. Trist, 12 January 1841, in Vance, 157.

56 *Tampa Bay Times*, Ask the *Times*, March 30, 2014, 5.

57 Hyland, *Martha Jefferson*, 173.

58 Yost, review of *Thomas Jefferson's Cook Book*; Hyland, *Martha Jefferson*, 173.

59 Hyland, *Martha Jefferson*, 174; Burwell Colbert attended the auction at Monticello after Jefferson's death. "In addition to spending thirty-one dollars for a mule, he bought "a carving knife, tea china, and portrait engravings of Jefferson and the Marquis de Lafayette." Colbert had numerous children, but because his deceased wife, Critta, had belonged to Martha Randolph, they were not part of Jefferson's estate. We do not know whether he had yet received his three-hundred-dollar legacy. Given the appraised value of the younger, more productive members of the Hemings family, his bequest would not have been much help. In addition, he did have children of his own to think of. His mother, Betty Brown, was listed as having no value and was in no immediate danger of being moved from her cabin on Monticello. He had no reason to fear for his aunts Critta and Sally, who were not part of the auction either. He may have already known that Francis Wayles Eppes intended to purchase the freedom of Critta Hemings, his nurse for a brief period and the half sister to his mother, so that she could live with her husband, Zachariah Bowles." AGR, *Hemingses*, 1053.

60 Kimball, "A Playmate of Thomas Jefferson," 509.

61 Kimball, 509.

62 Burns, *Enslaved*, 2.

63 Vance, "Thomas Jefferson Randolph," 152–54.

64 Lewis, *The Pursuit of Happiness*, 193.

65 Lewis, 193.

66 Beran, *Demons*, 619.
67 Vance, "Thomas Jefferson Randolph," 40.
68 Vance, "Thomas Jefferson Randolph," 40.

Chapter 6

1   *My Thomas*, 8.
2   Hyland, *Martha Jefferson*, 154.
3   Kranish, *Flight from Monticello* 274.
4   The following account is taken from Wiencek, *Master of the Mountain*, 39–40 (see chap. 1, n. 74).
5   Wiencek, 42.
6   Fleming, *Intimate Lives*, 968.
7   Mary Beacock Fryer and Christopher Dracott, *John Graves Simcoes, 1752–1806: A Biography* (Toronto: Dundurn, 1998), 75.
8   Kranish, *Flight from Monticello*, 238.
9   Thomas Jefferson to Timothy Matlack, 18 April 1781, in Boyd, *Papers*, 1:589; Fleming, *Intimate Lives*, 969.
10 TJ to James Monroe, May 20, 1782, *Papers of Thomas Jefferson*, 6: 184-187.
11 Wiencek, *Master of the Mountain*, 40.
12 Yet, to be historically fair, no person has ever accused Samuel Adams or John Hancock of similar cowardliness in fleeing from Lexington when warned by Paul Revere that the British were coming. Some historians have overlooked the fact that Jefferson was a county lieutenant before he was governor and head of the local militia. He was entitled to be addressed as "colonel," as his father had been, and occasionally he was, but the title did not hold. Jefferson did not take up arms in the struggle for American independence, but he went to war as truly as any civilian could.
13 Kranish, *Flight from Monticello*, 269.
14 Ron Chernow, *Washington: A Life* (New York: Penguin, 2010), 267.
15 Kranish, 257.
16 Kranish, 257.
17 Kranish, 258.
18 Kranish, 258.
19 Chernow, *Washington*, 167.
20 Kranish, *Flight from Monticello*, 277.

21. Kranish, 275. See also Virginius Dabney, "Jack Jouett's Ride," *American Heritage* 13, no. 1 (December 1961), https://www.americanheritage.com/jack-jouetts-ride; John Cook Wylie, "Writings about Jack Jouett and Tarleton's Raid on Charlottesville, in 1781," *Magazine of Albemarle County History* 17 (1958–1959): 49–56
22. Kranish, *Flight from Monticello*, 274.
23. Meacham, *Art of Power*, 297.
24. Kranish, *Flight from Monticello*, 269.
25. Kranish, 269.
26. Kranish, 279.
27. Kranish, 279.
28. Meacham, *Art of Power*, 298; PTJ 6:84
29. Kranish, *Flight from Monticello*, 283.
30. Kranish, 283.
31. Kranish, 283.
32. Kranish, 279.
33. Kranish, 279.
34. Fleming, *Intimate Lives*, 975.
35. Kranish, *Flight from Monticello*, 284.
36. "McLaughlin, *Jefferson and Monticello*, Apple Books ed., 375.
37. TJR, *Memoirs*, 18. "Caesar was a farm laborer whom Jefferson was later to characterize as 'being notorious for his rogueries.'" McLaughlin, *Jefferson and Monticello*, 413.
38. Scharff, *The Women Jefferson Loved*, 141.
39. Wallace, *The Billionaire's Vinegar*, 9.
40. Boyd, *Papers*, 6:24.
41. Scharff, *Women*, 141–42.
42. Scharff, 142.
43. Kranish, *Flight from Monticello*, 283–87.
44. Chernow, *Washington*, 704.
45. Dumas Malone, *Jefferson the Virginian*, vol. 1 (Boston: Little, Brown, 1948), 391.
46. Malone, *Jefferson the Virginian*, 391
47. Kranish, *Flight from Monticello*, 285.
48. Thomas Jefferson and Norma B. Cuthbert, "Poplar Forest: Jefferson's Legacy to His Grandson," *Huntington Library Quarterly* 6, no. 3 (May 1943): 333–56, http://www.jstor.org/stable/3815767.

49 Kranish, *Flight from Monticello*, 295–96.

50 David McCullough, *John Adams* (New York: Simon and Schuster, 2001), 316.

51 Kranish, *Flight from Monticello*, 299.

52 Kranish, 299; TJ, *Jefferson's Notes on the State of Virginia*, ed. William Harwood Peden (Chapel Hill: University of North Carolina, 1954), 91.

53 Kranish, *Flight from Monticello*, 314.

54 Kranish, 314.

55 Kranish, 283–87.

56 Douglas Anderson, "Subterraneous Virginia: The Ethical Poetics of Thomas Jefferson," *Eighteenth-Century Studies* 33, no. 2 (Winter 2000): 241, http://www.jstor.org/stable/30053684. Recent biographical accounts by Andrew Burstein and Conor Cruise O'Brien appear to confuse the first Lucy Elizabeth Jefferson with her necronymically christened sister, whose birth in May 1782 marked the beginning of Martha Jefferson's fatal illness. Fawn Brodie's controversial biography provides a more complete and sensitive rendering of Jefferson's personal predicament in this period. See Brodie, *Intimate*, 135–71.

57 Kranish, *Flight from Monticello*, 318.

58 Kranish, 329.

59 "From Thomas Jefferson to Edmund Randolph, 16 September 1781," *Founders Online*, National Archives, https://founders.archives.gov/documents/Jefferson/01-06-02-0112..

60 Kranish, *Flight from Monticello*, 316; Evelyn M. Acomb, ed., The *Revolutionary Journal of Baron Ludwig von Closen, 1780–1783* (Chapel Hill: University of North Carolina Press, 1958), 186–87.

61 The following story and quotations are taken from Brodie, *Intimate*, 412–13.

62 The following narrative is adapted from Hyland, *Martha Jefferson*, chapter 15. Quotations in the remainder of this chapter, unless otherwise noted, are from this source.

63 Robert Forbes, "*Notes on the State of Virginia* (1785)," In *Encyclopedia Virginia*, January 12, 2021, https://encyclopediavirginia.org/entries/notes-on-the-state-of-virginia-1785. "The Founding Father wrote only one full-length book, *Notes on the State of Virginia*, a book he neither originally intended to write, nor when completed, to publish widely or even under his own name. It was, in a manner of speaking, a 'cultural accident.' Still, this accidental creation has been called the 'best single statement of Jefferson's principles, the best reflection of his wide-ranging tastes and talents.'" "Notes on the State of Virginia," *Thomas Jefferson Encyclopedia*. Accessed November 2, 2021, https://www.monticello.org/site/research-and-collections/notes-state-virginia.

64 *TDLTJ*, 63.

65 Bear, *Monticello*, 99–100. "Another of Monticello's former slaves, Israel Jefferson, affirmed 'that it was a general statement among the other servants at Monticello, that Mr.

Jefferson promised his wife, on her death bed, that he would not again marry.'" See 'Life Among the Lowly, No. 3,' *Pike County* (Ohio) *Republican*, 25 Dec. 1873, reprinted in Annette Gordon Reed, *Thomas Jefferson and Sally Hemings: An American Controversy* (Charlottesville, 1997), 252; Jon Kukla, *"Mr. Jefferson's Women* (New York: Alfred A. Knopf, 2007), Apple Books ed., 489n57.

66 Brodie, *Intimate*, 168.
67 AGR, *Hemingses*, 266–67.
68 *TDLTJ*, 63.
69 *TDLTJ*, 63.
70 Jefferson to Elizabeth Wayles Eppes, October 3, 1782, in *Papers*, 6:198.
71 Brodie, *Intimate*, 26.
72 Bursten, *Optimist*, 3; "Language—symbol of the soul's affections, as Aristotle put it."
73 Brodie, *Intimate*, 26.
74 Homer, *The Iliad*, trans. A. T. Murray (Cambridge, MA: Harvard University Press, 1925), bk. 22, 1.389–90, p. 483.
75 Lewis, *the Pursuit of Happiness*, 70.
76 Brodie, *Intimate*, 165-168
77 MB, 6 September 1782; see also Malone, 1, 396–97.
78 Kranish, *Flight*, 318.

Chapter 7

1 Brodie, *Intimate*, 424.
2 Brodie, 424–25.
3 Trist to Elizabeth Kortwright Monore, April 3, 1809, in Meacham, *Thomas Jefferson*, Apple Books, 873.
4 Meacham, 873.
5 Brodie, *Intimate*, 428.
6 Brodie, 428.
7 Brodie, 429.
8 Brodie, 429.
9 Brodie, 429
10 Brodie, 429.
11 *MJR*, 20

12 *MJR*, 20; Cynthia A. Kierner, "Virginia Randolph Cary (1786–1852)," in *Dictionary of Virginia Biography* (Library of Virginia, 1998; 2006), http://www.lva.virginia.gov/public/dvb/bio.asp?b=Cary_Virginia_Randolph.

13 Crawford, *Twilight*, 7.

14 Bear, *Monticello*, 94. PTJRS, 3:633–34. See also Anne Z. Cockerham, Arlene W. Keeling, and Barbara Parker, "Seeking Refuge at Monticello: Domestic Violence in Thomas Jefferson's Family," *Magazine of Albemarle County History* 64 (2006): 27.

15 Malone, *Sage*, 299.

16 "Of 47 cases of marital conflict in the records of three Virginia counties between 1675 and 1750, '3 focused on the husband's physical cruelty.'" Kukla, *Mr. Jefferson's Women*, Apple Books ed., 485n25, quoting Kathleen M. Brown, *Good Wives, Nasty Wenches, and Anxious Patriarchs: Gender, Race, and Power in Colonial Virginia* (Chapel Hill, NC: 1996), 464–65, nn. 39, 44. "Forty-two percent of women who petitioned for divorce in antebellum Virginia were battered wives. Although "women from across Virginia and from every class and rank in society sought divorces on the grounds of battery.... Battering husbands tended to come from lower socioeconomic levels than their wives." Kukla, 485n25, quoting Thomas E. Buckley, *The Great Catastrophe of My Life: Divorce in the Old Dominion* (University of North Carolina Press, 2003), 168. "Carol Shammas's observation about New England—where 'doubts have been raised as to how frequently town officers actually prosecuted wife beating, because recorded cases are so rare"—is surely applicable to Virginia as well; "Anglo-American Household Government in Comparative Perspective, *WMQ*, 3d ser.,52 (1995): 117.

17 Letter from Thomas Jefferson to Anne Randolph Bankhead, 1808; Thomas Jefferson to Anne Randolph Bankhead, 29 December 1809; *FL*, 394; Langhorne, *Monticello*, 176.

18 Vance, "Thomas Jefferson Randolph," 62.

19 Anne Z. Cockerham, Arlene W. Keeling, and Barbara Parker, "Seeking Refuge at Monticello: Domestic Violence in Thomas Jefferson's Family," *Magazine of Albemarle County History* 64 (2006): 29–52.

20 Cockerham, Keeling, and Parker, 29–52.

21 *MJR*, 159.

22 Ellen Wayles Coolidge Memoir, Correspondence of Ellen Wayles Randolph Coolidge, 1810–1861, Special Collections, ViU; Langhorne, *Monticello*, 329.

23 Thomas Jefferson to Dr. John Bankhead, 28 October 1815, Edgehill-Randolph Papers, Special Collections, ViU; Langhorne, *Monticello*, 821; See also TJR, *Memoirs*.

24 Langhorne, *Monticello*, 831; See also *Magazine of Albemarle County History*.

25 *MJR*, 604; Langhorne, *Monticello*, 610–11; See also Olivia Taylor, "Charles Lewis and Anne Cary Randolph Bankhead," in *The Collected Papers of the Monticello Association*, ed. George Green Shackelford (Princeton: Princeton University Press, 1965), 71–73; Pierson, *Private Life*, 94–96; Anne Cary Randolph Bankhead to Martha Jefferson Randolph, 2 February 1810, Nicholas P. Trist Papers, Southern Historical Collection,

University of North Carolina Library; Archibald Robertson to Thomas Jefferson, 16 May 1812, Papers of Thomas Jefferson: Retirement Series, Thomas Jefferson Foundation, 5:51; Elizabeth Trist to Catharine Wistar Bache, 28 December 1810, 7 May 1811, 22 August 1814, FLDA; Household accounts maintained by Anne Cary Randolph, 1805–1808, http://memory.loc.gov/ammem/collections/jefferson_papers/ser7v011.html.

26 Cockerham, Keeling, and Parker, "Seeking Refuge at Monticello," 36.

27 Cockerham, Keeling, and Parker, 36–37.

28 Cockerham, Keeling, and Parker, 37.

29 Meacham, *Thomas Jefferson: The Art of Power*, Apple Books ed., 901.

30 Martha Jefferson Randolph to Ellen Coolidge, 11 September 1825, Ellen W. Coolidge Papers, ViU.

31 Crawford, *Twilight*, 75.

32 Crawford, 162.

33 Crawford, 162; Bear, *Monticello*, 95.

34 Crawford, *Twilight*, 127.

35 Crawford, 127.

36 Crawford, 134.

37 Martha Jefferson Randolph to Thomas Jefferson, 11 November 1816, in *FL*, 417; Crawford, *Twilight*, 502.

38 Meacham, *Thomas Jefferson*, 466.

39 Thomas Jefferson Randolph to Dabney S. Carr, 11 July 1826, Carr-Cary Family Papers, Accession 1231, Special Collections Department, ViU Library; Meacham, *Art of Power*, 901; Gordon-Reed, *The Hemingses of Monticello*, 417.

40 Bear, *Monticello*, 94.

41 Crawford, *Twilight*, 162.

42 Crawford, 162.

43 Hetty Carr to Dabney S. Carr, 15 February 1819, Nicholas Philip Trist Papers, Manuscript Division, LOC.

44 Thomas Bell to Thomas Jefferson, 12 June 1797, in Boyd, *Papers*, 29:427; Stanton, *Monticello to Main Street*, 123. Although Bell's grandson's recollections refer to visits that would have taken place after Bell's death, it is apparent from the tenor of the two men's letters, and the fact that Bell's store was attached to his home, that TJ visited Bell's home in the 1790s as well. Thomas Jefferson to Thomas Bell, 16 March 1792, in Boyd, *Papers*, 20:758–59; Thomas Jefferson to Archibald Stuart, 2 December 1794, in Boyd, *Papers*, 28:214; Thomas Jefferson to Thomas Mann Randolph, 20 August 1795, in Boyd, *Papers*, 28:214, 439; James Madison to Thomas Jefferson, 25 December 1797, in Boyd, *Papers*, 29:591.

45 Crawford, *Twilight*, 165.

46 Brodie, *Intimate*, 459.
47   Vance, "Thomas Jefferson Randolph," 67.
48 Crawford, 1.
49 Joseph J. Ellis, *American Sphinx: The Character of Thomas Jefferson* (New York: Knopf, 1997; New York: Vintage, 1998), 274. Citation is from the Vintage edition. Edmund Bacon had bought Eagle on Jefferson's behalf in November 1820, when the horse was six years old. See Bear, *Monticello*, 62; Memorandum Books, 2:1371.
50 Crawford, *Twilight*, 1.
51 Burstein, *Secrets*, 71.
52 Langhorne, *Monticello*, 191
53   Vance, "Thomas Jefferson Randolph," 68.
54 Crawford, *Twilight*, 167.
55 Vance, "Thomas Jefferson Randolph," 68.
56 TJR, *Memoirs*, 4
57 Crawford, *Twilight*, 166.
58 Vance, "Thomas Jefferson Randolph," 69.
59 Ann Cary Randolph Bankhead diary, 26 November 1820–27 Nove,ber 1825, *FLDA*, cited in Kierner. *MJR*, 539n58.
60 Crawford, *Twilight*, 168.
61 Crawford, 168.
62 Crawford, 168–69.
63 Crawford, 169.
64 Crawford, 169.
65 Crawford, 171.
66 Peggy Nicholas, quoted in Vance, "Thomas Jefferson Randolph," 71.
67 Crawford, *Twilight*, 171.
68 Wilson Cary Nicholas to Thomas Jefferson, in Crawford, 170.
69 Crawford, *Twilight*, 168.
70 Crawford, 231.
71 Crawford, 231.
72   Crawford, 231.
73 Ellen Wayles Randolph Coolidge to Martha Jefferson Randolph), January 23, 1826, quoted in "Charles Lewis Bankhead,")," an article courtesy of the *Thomas Jefferson Encyclopedia*, The Jefferson Monticello, accessed November 3, 2021, https://www.monticello.org/site/research-and-collections/charles-lewis-bankhead.

74 Martha Jefferson Randolph to Ellen Wayles Randolph Coolidge, June 14, 1833, quoted in "Charles Lewis Bankhead," *Thomas Jefferson Encyclopedia*.

75 Randall, *Life*, 549.

76 Burstein, *Secrets*, 14.

77 See "The Tree of Liberty . . . (Quotation)," an article courtesy of the *Thomas Jefferson Encyclopedia*, The Jefferson Monticello, accessed November 3, 2021.

Chapter 8

1 This chapter is largely based on Boynton Merrill Jr.'s conscientious and scholarly account in his book *Jefferson's Nephews: A Frontier Tragedy* (Princeton, NJ: Princeton University Press, 1976). Merrill is now the owner of much of the Lewis estate. I owe a tremendous debt to his painstaking research. In addition, this chapter also leans heavily on the epic poem about the tragic events, titled *Brother to Dragons* by Robert Penn Warren (New York: Random House, 1953).

2 Jefferson wrote to John Page following the fire, lamenting the loss "of every pa[per I] had in the world, and almost every book." He estimated the value of the books at £200 sterling, and wished he had only lost that sum in money, rather than in books. *Papers*, 1:34–35; Merrill, *Jefferson's Nephews*, 12.

3 Merrill, *Jefferson's Nephews*, 12.

4 Merrill, 38–48.

5 Merrill, 79-81.

6 Merrill, 79.

7 Merrill, 79.

8 Boynton Merrill Jr., "Constructing *Jefferson's Nephews*: A Speech to the Kentucky Library Association, Lexington, Kentucky, November, 1979," *Kentucky Review* 14, no. 1, art. 3 (1998), https://uknowledge.uky.edu/cgi/viewcontent.cgi?article=1018&context=kentucky-review.

9 Dale M. Brumfield, "Murder among the Earthquakes: The True Story of Lilburn and Isham Lewis, Thomas Jefferson's Murdering Nephews," October 22, 2018, Medium, https://dalebrumfield.medium.com/murder-among-the-earthquakes-c786a38a9a44.

10 Merrill, Speech, "Constructing *Jefferson's Nephews*."

11 Bertram Wyatt-Brown, "*Jefferson's Nephews* and Other Murderers: Thoughts on Southern Violence," *Reviews in American History* 5, no. 2 (June 1977): 203–10, https://www.jstor.org/stable/2701631.

12 Brumfield, "Murder among the Earthquakes."

13 Brumfield.

14 Brumfield.

15 Crawford, *Twilight*, 65.

16 Crawford, 65.
17 Crawford, 65; Bertram Wyatt-Brown "Jefferson's Nephews and Other Murderers," 203–10
18 Merrill, *Jefferson's Nephews*, 315.
19 Merrill, 316.
20 Merrill, 315–16.
21 Merrill, 256.
22 Brumfield, "Murder among the Earthquakes."
23 Merrill, *Jefferson's Nephews*, 256
24 Merrill, 257.
25 Brumfield, "Murder among the Earthquakes."
26 Crawford, *Twilight at Monticello*, 82.
27 Merrill, *Jefferson's Nephews*, 249.
28 Brumfield, "Murder among the Earthquakes."
29 Merrill, *Jefferson's Nephews*, 260.
30 Merrill, 261.
31 Merrill, 263.
32 Merrill, 249.
33 Brumfield, "Murder among the Earthquakes."
34 Merrill, *Jefferson's Nephews*, 249.
35 Brumfield, "Murder among the Earthquakes."
36 Charles Joseph Latrobe, *The Rambler in North America*, vol. 1 (New York, 1835).
37 Brumfield.
38 Brumfeld. Tecumseh's Comet is not scheduled to return until the year 3775
39 Merrill, *Jefferson's Nephews*, 251.
40 Brumfield, "Murder among the Earthquakes."
41 Lorenzo Dow, *The Dealings of God, Man, and the Devil, as Exemplified in the Life, Experience, and Travels of Lorenzo Dow, in a Period of More Than a Half Century* (Norwich, Wm. Faulkner, 1833), 292.
42 Merrill, *Jefferson's Nephews*, 253.
43 Merrill, 253.
44 Merrill, 254.
45 Brumfield, "Murder among the Earthquakes."
46 Merrill, *Jefferson's Nephews*, 267–68.

47 Merrill, 267.
48 Merrill, 267–68
49 Merrill, 267–68.
50 Brumfield, "Murder among the Earthquakes."
51 Wyatt-Brown, "*Jefferson's Nephews* and Other Murderers."
52 Wyatt-Brown.
53 Merrill, *Jefferson's Nephews*, 292.
54 Merrill, 285.
55 Crawford, *Twilight*, 82.
56 Richard Taylor, *Three Kentucky Tragedies* (Lexington: University Press of Kentucky, 1991), n.p.
57 *Filson Club History Quarterly* 9–10 (1935): 244.
58 Merrill, *Jefferson's Nephews*, 295.
59 Merrill, 297.
60 Merrill, 296.
61 Brumfield, "Murder among the Earthquakes."
62 Merrill, *Jefferson's Nephews*, 298.
63 Brumfield, "Murder among the Earthquakes."
64 Crawford, *Twilight*, 120.
65 Brumfield, "Murder among the Earthquakes."
66 Meriwether Lewis, a relative of Jefferson's, was rumored to have suffered from depression and may have committed suicide. Jefferson admired Lewis and wrote of his death, "His courage was undaunted; his firmness and perseverance yielded to nothing but impossibilities; A rigid disciplinarian, yet tender as a father of those committed to his charge; honest, disinterested, liberal, with a sound understanding and a scrupulous fidelity to truth." "There is some evidence, which does not strike me as necessarily convincing, that Meriwether was murdered. But certainly there was in the Lewis blood a strain of what Jefferson referred to as "hypo-V chondriacal affection," as is well evidenced by Lilburne. In any case, Jefferson believed that the death was by suicide committed in despair at the injustice of the charges brought against him as Governor of the Louisiana Territory." Robert Penn Warren, *Brothers to Dragons* (New York: Random House, 1953).
67 Wyatt-Brown, "*Jefferson's Nephews* and Other Murderers,". 203–10.
68 Wyatt-Brown, 203–210.
69 Crawford, *Twilight*, 82.
70 Brumfield, "Murder among the Earthquakes."
71 Ellis, *Sphinx,* 126.

Chapter 9

1. The 1998 alleged DNA match to a Jefferson is thoroughly discussed in this book's epilogue.

2. "Mrs. Smith's recollections of Washington society life in the early nineteenth century constitute one of the major sources of information on Jefferson's social life as President. After Jefferson's retirement from political life, Smith visited him at Monticello. Her account of this visit is another fruitful source of information on Jefferson's daily life and family." "Margaret Bayard Smith: An Article Courtesy of the Thomas Jefferson Encyclopedia," The Jefferson Monticello, https://www.monticello.org/site/research-and-collections/margaret-bayard-smith.

3. Meacham, *Thomas Jefferson*, Apple Books ed., 741.

4. For Callender's career, see Michael Durey, *With the Hammer of Truth: James Thomson Callender and America's Early National Heroes* (Charlottesville: University of Virginia Press, 1990); Jefferson to James Monroe, May 26, 1801, and July 15, 1802, Ford, *Writings*, 8:57–58.

   The story that Jefferson was the father of slaves by Sally Hemings was first published by James Thomson Callender in the *Richmond Recorder* in the fall of 1802. It was carried through the nineteenth century in Federalist attacks, British critiques of American democracy, and abolitionist efforts to end slavery. Fawn Brodie's biography of 1974 revived the claim and suggested a romantic dimension—that the connection was not exploitative but a meaningful thirty-eight-year union. Oral traditions originating with the children of Sally Hemings strongly support the connection; Jefferson's daughter and grandchildren believed it a moral impossibility and suggested Jefferson's Carr nephews as more likely suspects. Both sides received their contemporary supporters, and Jefferson himself seems to have privately denied the charge in an 1805 letter to Robert Smith.

   See Douglass Adair, "The Jefferson Scandals," in *Fame and the Founding Fathers: Essays by Douglass Adair*, ed. Trevor Colbourn (New York, 1974), 160–91; Fawn Brodie's biography and her articles in *American Heritage* vols. 23, no. 4 (June 1971): 48–57, 97–100; and 27, no. 6 (October 1976): 29–33, 94–99; Virginius Dabney, *The Jefferson Scandals: A Rebuttal* (New York: Madison Books, 1991); Dumas Malone, "Mr. Jefferson's Private Life;" and Stanton, *"Those Who Labor for My Happiness."*

5. Ellen W. Coolidge to Joseph Coolidge, October 24, 1858, Ellen W. Coolidge Journal, Ellen W. Coolidge Papers, ViU

6. Beran, *Demons*, 352.

7. Thomas Jefferson to Henry Lee, 15 May 1826, Thomas Jefferson Papers, Manuscript Division, LOC. Note that this letter was sent fifty days before Jefferson's death.

8. Robert F. Turner, ed., *The Jefferson-Hemings Controversy: Report of the Scholars Commission* (Durham, NC: Carolina Academic Press, 2001, 2011).

9. Dumas Malone, *Jefferson and His Time*, vol. 4, *Jefferson the President: First Term, 1801–1805* (Boston: Little, Brown, 1970), 212.

10 Burstein, *Jefferson's Secrets*, 200.

11 "Mudslinging Isn't What It Used to Be," *St. Petersburg Times*, October 24, 2008, Nation 15A, reprinted from the *Washington Post*.

12 Burstein, *Jefferson's Secrets*, 227.

13 Rebecca L. McMurry and James F. McMurry, "Origins of the 'SALLY' Story," in Coates, *Myth*, 16.

14 Adams, *History*, 220–221; letter from Jefferson to R.R. Livingston, 10 October 1802, *Founders Online*, National Archives,https://founders.archives.gov/documents/Jefferson/01-38-02-0435; Ford, *Works*, iv, 448.

15 McMurry and McMurry, "Origins," 7; Robert M. S. MacDonald, "Race, Sex and Reputation: Thomas Jefferson and the Sally Hemings Story," *Southern Cultures* 4 (Summer 1998): 48; James Callender, *Richmond Recorder*, September 1, 1802; Michael Durey, *With the Hammer of Truth: James Thomson Callender and America's Early National Heroes* (Charlottesville: University of Virginia Press, 1990); *Richmond Recorder*, September 1, 1802 and October 20, 1802. The relevant extracts have been reprinted in Jan Ellen Lewis and Peter S. Onuf, eds., *Sally Hemings and Thomas Jefferson: History, Memory, and Civic Culture* (Charlottesville: University Press of Virginia, 1999), 259–61.

16 Beran, *Demons*, 158.

17 Burstein, *Inner*, 227.

18 Letter from Thomas Jefferson to James Monroe, 26 May 1800, in Barbara B. Oberg and J. Jefferson Looney, eds. *The Papers of Thomas Jefferson, 1800–1801 Digital Edition* (Charlottesville: University of Virginia Press, Rotunda, 2008), 590.

19 Letter from James Callender to James Madison, 27 April 1801, in Robert A. Rutland, ed., *The Papers of James Madison: Secretary of State Series, 1800–1801* (Charlottesville: University Press of Virginia, 1984–), 117.

20 See Durey, *Hammer of* Truth, 146–47.

21 Nathan Schachner, *Thomas Jefferson: A Biography* (New York: Appleton-Century-Crofts, Inc., 1951), 678.

22 Letter from James Monroe to James Madison, 6 June 1801, in Rutland, *Papers of James Madison*, 244–45; William G. Hyland Jr. and William G. Hyland, "A Civil Action: Hemings v. Jefferson," *American Journal of Trial Advocacy* 31, no. 1 (2007).

23 Burstein, *Inner*, 227.

24 McMurry and McMurry, "Origins," 69, 75–76; Adams, *History*, 221.

25 McMurry and McMurry, "Origins," 70.

26 Christopher Hitchens, *Thomas Jefferson* (New York: HarperCollins, 2005), 65; Adams, *History*, 220–21.

27 Adams, *History*, 220.

28 Brodie, *Intimate*, 350.

29 Winthrop D. Jordan, *White over Black: American Attitudes toward the Negro, 1550–1812* (Chapel Hill: University of North Carolina Press, 1968), 468; see also 461–69.

30 *Life and Correspondence of Rufus King*, IV, 176.; Meacham, *Thomas Jefferson*, Apple Books ed., 1540.

31 Mark Farquhar, *A Treasure of Great American Scandals: Tantalizing True Tales of Historic Misbehavior by the Founding Fathers and Others Who Let Freedom Ring* (New York: Penguin, 2003), chap. 1; see also "Hideous hermaphroditical character (Spurious Quotation)," The Jefferson Monticello, accessed November 5, 2021, https://www.monticello.org/site/research-and-collections/hideous-hermaphroditical-character-spurious-quotation;

32 David McCullough, *John Adams* (New York: Simon & Shuster, 2001), 580; Ellis, *American Sphinx*, Apple Books ed., 408.

33 To Thomas Jefferson from Robert Smith, 4 July 1805; Meacham, *Thomas Jefferson*, Apple Books ed., 1540.

34 Frank J. Klingberg et al., eds. *The Correspondence between Henry Stephens Randall and Hugh Blair Grigsby 1856–1861* (University of California Press, 1952), 39; Grigbsy to Henry Randall, 19 Feb 1856; Burton, *JV*, 35.

35 Brodie, *Intimate*, p. 428.

36 Meacham, *Thomas Jefferson*, Apple Books ed., 878; PTJRS, 3: 610. Elijah Fletcher was a native of Vermont who attended Middlebury and Dartmouth colleges before graduating from the University of Vermont in 1810. He taught at a school in Alexandria and visited Monticello on his way from Alexandria to become president of the New Glasgow Academy. He moved to Lynchburg about 1818. Fletcher's daughter Indiana Fletcher Williams founded Sweet Briar College on property in Amherst County that her father retired to from Lynchburg. "Elijah Fletcher's Account of a Visit to Monticello, [8 May 1811]," *Founders Online*, National Archives, https://founders.archives.gov/documents/Jefferson/03-03-02-0483.

37 Turner, *The Jefferson-Hemings Controversy*, Apple Books ed., 51.

38 Turner, 51.

39 Turner, 52.

40 Turner, 52.

41 John Chester Miller, *The Wolf by the Ears: Thomas Jefferson and Slavery* (n.p.: New American Library, 1980), 175; see in general Gordon-Reed, *Hemingses of Monticello*, Chap. 14.

42 Isaac Jefferson, "Memoirs of a Monticello Slave," in *Jefferson at Monticello: Recollections of a Monticello Slave and of a Monticello Overseer*, ed. James A. Bear, Jr. (Charlottesville: University of Virginia Press, 1967), 3–4; Burton, *JV*, 134–36.

43 Lucia Stanton, *Free Some Day: The African-American Families of Monticello* (n.p.: University of North Carolina Press, 2002), 106; See also Langhorne, *Monticello*, 182. John Hemings, Betty's son, had been apprenticed to Jefferson's principal builder, James Dinsmore, and became a master builder and cabinetmaker. Joe Fossett, son of Mary Hemings, was Monticello's blacksmith. He had learned his trade form William Stewart.

44 Donald Jackson, *A Year at Monticello*, ed. Mary C. Jackson (1795; repr., Wheat Ridge, CO: Fulcrum, 1989), 91–92.

45 Gordon-Reed, *An American Controversy*, 209; Daniel P. Jordan, Statement on the TJMF Committee Report on Thomas Jefferson and Sally Hemings (Thomas Jefferson Memorial Foundation: 2000), 37, http://www.monticello.org/plantation/hemingscontro/jefferson-hemings_report.pdf.

46 Priscilla was called "Aunt Priscilla" by the Jefferson grandchildren.

47 Jon Kukla, *Mr. Jefferson's Women* (New York: Alfred A. Knopf, 2007), 121.

48 Gordon-Reed, *Thomas Jefferson and Sally Hemings*, 209, 240.

49 Merrill D. Peterson, *Thomas Jefferson and the New Nation: A Biography* (New York: Oxford University Press, 1970), 711; John C. Miller, "Slavery," in *Thomas Jefferson: A Reference Biography*, ed. Merrill Peterson (New York: Scribner's, 1986), 429.

50 *PTJRS*, 10:176, George Logan was a Pennsylvania state legislator and farmer from a prominent Philadelphia family.

51 Burwell was a nineteenth-century Virginia politician and planter who served as presidential secretary and as a Democratic-Republican in the United States House of Representatives and the Virginia House of Delegates.

52 Thomas Jefferson to William A. Burwell, November 22, 1808, in *Works*, 11:78.

53 Thomas Jefferson to Dr. George Logan, 20 June 1816, *Founders Online*, National Archives, https://founders.archives.gov/documents/Jefferson/03-10-02-0102; Adair, *The Jefferson Scandals*, 234.

54 B. L. Rayner, *Life of Thomas Jefferson* (Boston: 1834), 299.

55 Meacham, *Thomas Jefferson*, Apple Books ed., 739.

56 Rayner, *Life of Thomas Jefferson*, 298.

57 *PTJRS*, 16:164.

58 Burstein, *Jefferson's Secrets*, 201; Robert Richardson to TJ March 31, 1824.

59 Coates, *Myth*, 19; Durey, *Hammer of Truth*, 171; Malone, *Jefferson the President*, 212.

60 Hyland Jr., William G. *In Defense of Thomas Jefferson: The Sally Hemings Sex Scandal* (New York: Thomas Dunne Books, 2009).

61 Turner, *The Jefferson-Hemings Controversy*, 958; Randall to James Parton, June 1, 1868.

62 White McKenzie Wallenborn, "Thomas Jefferson Foundation DNA Study Committee Minority Report," April 12, 1999, https://www.monticello.org/thomas-jefferson/jefferson-slavery/thomas-jefferson-and-sally-hemings-a-brief-account/research-report-on-jefferson-and-hemings/minority-report-of-the-monticello-research-committee-on-thomas-jefferson-and-sally-hemings/.

63 "Ellen Coolidge in 1858 blamed . . . in the case of the Hemingses—her own Carr uncles (Coolidge Letterbook, 100–102, ViU: 9090). Edmund Bacon reported that Thomas Jefferson Randolph's schoolmates were 'intimate with the Negro women' (Bear,

[*Monticello*,] 88). Although no indictments of individual overseers have been found, the overseer class often took the blame, as the duc de La Rochefoucauld-Liancourt reported after his visit to Monticello in 1796 (*Voyage*, 5:35)." Stanton, *"Those Who Labor for My Happiness,"* note 23 to the essay "Those Who Labor for My Happiness."

64   Burstein, *Jefferson's Secrets*, 176–77.

65   Thomas J. Randolph, Draft Letters, c. 1874, ViU, Alderman Library, 8937; Burton, *JV*, 86.

66   Jackson, *Year at Monticello*, 95–96. One historian commented on Brodie's book *Thomas Jefferson: An Intimate History*, "This determined woman carries psychological speculation to the point of absurdity. The resulting mishmash of fact and fiction, surmise and conjecture is not history as I understand the term. Mrs. Brodie is not without insight into Jefferson's personality, and except for her obsession, might have contributed to our understanding. But to me the man she describes in her more titillating passages is unrecognizable." Virginus Dabney, *The Jefferson Scandals: A Rebuttal* (New York: Madison Books, 2013), Apple Books ed., 219.

67   Appendix D, Henry S. Randall to James Parton, June 1, 1868, in Gordon-Reed, *Thomas Jefferson and Sally Hemings*. As an aside, in a modern-day trial, the defendants would undoubtedly file a "third party" complaint against the Carr brothers and possibly Jefferson's own brother, Randolph.

68   Henry S. Randall to James Parton, June 1, 1868, Jefferson Quotes & Family Letters, The Jefferson Monticello, https://tjrs.monticello.org/letter/2356.

69   Randall to Parton, June 1, 1868.

70   Wiencek, *Master of the Mountain*, 299.

71   Taped interview with Frank Berkley by Herb Barger conducted March 29, 2000, at the Colonnades Retirement Home, Charlottesville, Virginia. Francis Lewis Berkeley Jr. was the University of Virginia's archivist and professor emeritus. Berkeley, who retired in 1974, was cited numerous times for his outstanding service to the library, in particular his efforts to develop and enrich its manuscript resources. An Albemarle County native, Berkeley received his bachelor's and master's degrees from the University of Virginia. He joined the faculty in 1938 as the university's first curator of manuscripts. Berkeley also helped create the principal documentary publications of the new press, *The Papers of James Madison* and *The Papers of George Washington*. As curator, Berkeley devised a cataloguing system based on the British Museum's Catalogue of Additional Manuscripts, and he began the creation of a central archives for the university. Berkeley received the Raven Society Award in 1973 for distinguished service to the university. He served for twenty-nine years on the board of Monticello.

72   Turner, *The Jefferson-Hemings Controversy*, 416

73   Turner, 417.

74   Israel Jefferson, quoted in Gordon-Reed, *Thomas Jefferson and Sally Hemings*, 251.

75   Letter from Thomas Jefferson Randolph, Thomas Jefferson's grandson, to the editor of the *Pike County Republican* (1874). On file at ViU Library, Special Collections, also available at http://www.pbs.org/wgbh/pages/frontline/shows/jefferson/cron/1873randolph.html.

76. Turner, *The Jefferson-Hemings Controversy*, 74.

77. Turner, 960.

78. Madison was the second son, but only if we exclude Thomas Woodson from the mix.

79. Dumas Malone, *Jefferson and His Time*, vol. 1, *Jefferson the Virginian* (Boston: Little, Brown, 1948), 496.

80. "Life among the Lowly," no. 1, *Pike County (Ohio) Republican*, March 13, 1873, 4, repr. in Gordon-Reed, *An Thomas Jefferson and Sally Hemings*, 245–48. Herbert Barger (Jefferson family historian), states that "an identical title was owned by Harriet Beecher, and [was a] possible copyright infringement. If so, then she and [the *Pike County Republican* editor] Wetmore must have been partners in this smear. We know they were both great abolitionists." In discussion with the author, April and June 2007.

81. "Life among the Lowly.".

82. Turner, *The Jefferson-Hemings Controversy*, 262.

83. Gordon-Reed, *Thomas Jefferson and Sally Hemings*, n.p.

84. Burton, *JV*, 145–46. According to Herbert Barger (Jefferson family historian), the most glaring Madison/Wetmore lie is that Madison claimed that he was named for James Madison by Dolley Madison on the date of his birth, January 19, 1805, while she was visiting Monticello. The Madison Papers indicate that the Madisons never left Washington for Virginia during the winter. Just imagine this scenario: Dolley announces to her secretary of state husband, Mr. Madison, and to Mr. Jefferson, for whom she acts as hostess, that she has heard that a "male" slave is to be born (never mind that this was well before the sex of a child could be determined), to one of Mr. Jefferson's slaves, and she must be present to name him after her husband. Never mind the hazardous winter route without support of these two important people left back in Washington. For extra measure Madison says she reneged on a promised present to his mother, thus fanning the flames of further resentment between the races. NOTE: This Pike County article was used by Annette Gordon-Reed and the Monticello in-house Jefferson-Hemings DNA Study to cite "truthful and believable" information from a son of Sally Hemings. We cannot believe anything gained from this article. The article was "torn apart" by the competing newspaper, the *Waverly Watchman*, just five days later. Among other things stated in the article was, "The fact that Hemings claims to be the natural son of Jefferson does not convince the world of its truthfulness." Interview with Barger, quoting John A. Jones, Editorial, *Waverly Watchmen*, March 18, 1873.

85. Hyland, *In Defense*, 185; Dabney and Kukla, "*The Monticello Scandals: History and Fiction*," Virginia Cavalcade, 29, Autumn 1979, pp. 52-61.

86. Comments on PBS, John McLaughlin's *One on One*, November 6, 1998.

87. "Life among the Lowly."

88. Dabney, *The Jefferson Scandals*, 103; Turner, *The Jefferson-Hemings Controversy*, 432n62.

89. Burton, *JV*, 145–46.

90. Gordon-Reed, *Thomas Jefferson and Sally Hemings*, n.p.

91   TJ, *The Autobiography of Thomas Jefferson*, n.p.

92   Betts, ed., *FB*, xx, xvi.

93   "Monticello: A 40-Year Fixer-Upper," *Times-Courier*, September 16, 2000.

94   Malone, *Jefferson the Virginian*, 155.

95   Halliday, *Understanding Thomas Jefferson*, 26

96   Kukla, *Mr. Jefferson's Women*, n.p.

97   "Jefferson to Maria Cosway, Paris, November 19, 1786, in Halliday, *Understanding Women*, 110. The correspondence between Jefferson and Mrs. Cosway at this time is incidentally another evidence that their love never went very far beyond the pales of propriety." Beran, *Jefferson's Demons*, Apple Books ed., 49, 430n59.

98   *Domestic Life*, 152–53; Jefferson to Bowling Clarke, September 21, 1792, *FB*, 13; Jefferson to Nicholas Lewis, April 12, 1792, *FB*, 12; Hyland, *In Defense*, 825.

Chapter 10

1   Taped interview by Herbert Barger, March 29, 2000, conducted at the Colonnades Retirement Home, Charlottesville, Virginia.

2   Many thanks to historian and researcher Cyndi Burton for her meticulous previous research on Randolph Jefferson and her excellent book, *Jefferson Vindicated*. Bernard Mayo, ed., *Thomas Jefferson and His Unknown Brother, Randolph* (Charlottesville: University Press of Virginia, 1942), reproduced all the known letters between these brothers in a slim volume.

3   The thirty-two letters reproduced here are the only extant correspondence from the fifty or more letters that passed between Thomas and his "unknown" brother Randolph between 1789 and 1815.

4   Burton, *JV*, 56.

5   Jefferson's doctor, "Dr. Robley Dunglison, 'found that the prostatic portion [of Jefferson's urethra] was affected with stricture, accompanied and apparently produced by enlargement of the prostate gland,' for which Dunglison prescribed the use of a 'bougie,' or catheter. See Samuel X. Rad-bill, ed., 'The Autobiographical Ana of Robley Dunglison, M.D.,' *Transactions of the American Philosophical Society*, n.s., 53, no. 8 (1963): 26; and Burstein, *Jefferson's Secrets*, 29." Kukla, *Mr. Jefferson's Women*, Apple Books ed., 465n72.

6   "TJ to Bernard Peyton, August 29, 1825, TJP-MHC, requesting "6. full sized bougies[,] 12. of various sizes." "Insertion of the bougie must have been uncomfortable. Jefferson would have moved the rigid, narrow tube through the urethral opening at the end of the penis until it reached the bladder. After visiting Monticello in 1824 and 1825, Lafayette sent a shipment of superior quality French elastic (more flexible) gum catheters; however, these did not arrive until after Jefferson's death." Burstein, *Jefferson's Secrets* (2011), Apple Books ed., 485n11.

7   Burton, *JV*, 54; Thomas Jefferson deposition, Buckingham County Court, September 15, 1815, Jefferson Papers, ViU, microfilm.

8   Scharff, *Women Jefferson Loved*, 32.

9   "Thomas Jefferson to Dabney Carr," 19 January 1816, *Founders Online*, National Archives, https://founders.archives.gov/documents/Jefferson/03-09-02-0238; Meachan, *Jefferson*, 103.

10 Kern, *The Jeffersons of Shadwell*, 3–5.

11 "Captain Thomas Jefferson left his son, Peter, a number of items that signaled wealth or prescribed social behaviors, including slaves, clothes, six silver spoons, two feather beds, a table cloth and six napkins, six leather chairs (possibly the ones TJ II received from his father in 1698), and a couch and two tables. The couch 'in the hall' and 'two tables there' offer a clue that PJ's boyhood home had more than one room with seating furniture. This hall was likely where William Byrd came to drink persico and dine on roast beef with the captain as part of a day of mustering. TJ II visited with Byrd and Colonel Benjamin." Kern, *The Jeffersons at Shadwell*, Kindle ed., loc. 5594.

12 McLaughlin, *Jefferson and Monticello*, 12.

13 Kern, *Shadwell*, 678.

14 Scharff, *Women Jefferson Loved*, 24.

15 Jane actually had ten children, but only seven survived.

16 There is much scholarly debate about Jefferson's relationship with his mother, Jane. Jefferson "lived with her at Shadwell on and off until he was twenty-seven." His coolness toward her "is perhaps nowhere clearer than in his passing reference to her death in 1776, a letter he wrote to her brother William Randolph, then living in England: 'The death of my mother you have probably not heard of. This happened on the last day of March after an illness of not more than an hour. We supposed it to have been apoplectic.' . . . There is no expression of emotion or loss associated with his mother; the news of her death is passed on to her brother as an obligatory duty." McLaughlin, *Jefferson and Monticello*, 47; Other historians offer a different perspective: "It should be noted, however, that the Virginia gentry of the eighteenth century as a class found it difficult to express grief, in their correspondence and diaries, over the loss of family members. 'These men and women believed that to discuss death was to invite stupor; to contemplate it, to succumb.'" Jack McLaughlin, *Jefferson and Monticello: The Biography of a Builder* (New York: Henry Holt, 1988), 397n47, quoting Jan Lewis, *The Pursuit of Happiness, Family and Values in Jefferson's Virginia* (Cambridge University Press, 1983), 70.

17 Kern, *The Jeffersons at Shadwell*, Kindle ed. loc 4996.

18 Kern, *Shadwell*, loc. 3302.

19 Scharff, *Women Jefferson Loved*, 28

20 Scharff, 27.

21 Scharff, 27.

22 *TDLTJ*, 21–22.

23   Meacham, *Thomas Jefferson*, 61.

24   Baer, *Unknown Brother*.

25   Kern, *Shadwell*, loc. 1328.

26   Brodie, *Intimate*, 264, 457.

27   Bear, preface; Mayo, ed., *Thomas Jefferson and His Unknown Brother* (Literary Licensing LLC, 1981), vii.

28   Nathan Schachner, *Thomas Jefferson: A Biography*, vol. 2 (New York: Appleton-Century-Crofts, 1951), 923.

29   Forrest McDonald, *The Presidency of Thomas Jefferson* (Lawrence, KS: University Press of Kansas, 1976), 31.

30   Scharff, *The Women Jefferson Loved*, 22, 409n44.

31   Schachner, *Thomas Jefferson*, 923.

32   Turner, *Scholars Report*, 559n139.

33   Looney, *Papers*, 9:31.

34   Burton, *JV*, 55.

35   Burton, 57; "To avoid confusion I use the spelling 'Hemings' throughout. Madison and Eston Hemings, as well as Thomas Jefferson, used this spelling, while other members of the family (John Hemings and descendants of Joseph Fossett's sister Betsy) used the spelling 'Hemmings.'" Stanton. *"Those Who Labor for My Happiness,"* n.p.

36   James A. Bear Jr., and Bernard Mayo, eds., *Thomas Jefferson and his Unknown Brother* (Charlottesville: University of Virginia Press, 1981).

37   Burton, *JV*, 53.

38   Turner, *Scholars Report*, 558n127.

39   McLaughlin, *Jefferson and Monticello*, 108. "[Jupiter] unfortunately conceived himself poisoned and went to consult the negro doctor who attended the Georges [Great George and his wife Ursula]. He went in the house to see uncle Randolph who gave him a dram which he drank and seemed to be as well as he had been for some time past, after which he took a dose from his black doctor who pronounced that it would kill or cure. [Two and a half] hours after taking the medicine he fell down in a strong convulsion fit which lasted from ten to eleven hours, during which time it took 3 stout men to hold him. He languished nine days but was never heard to speak from the first of his being seized to the moment of his death." (108).

40   Turner, *The Jefferson-Hemings Controversy*, 768; David Mayer, "The Thomas Jefferson–Sally Hemings Myth and the Politicization of American History, Individual Views of David N. Mayer, Concurring with the Majority Report of the Scholars Commission on the Jefferson-Hemings Matter," April 9, 2001, http://www.ashbrook.org/articles/mayer-hemings.html

41   Turner, *The Jefferson-Hemings Controversy*, 768.

42 Turner, 531.

43 Turner, 770.

44 Henry, Katt, "Jefferson Vindicated," interview with Charlottesville genealogist Cyndi Burton, *Cavalier Daily*, April 25, 2007.

45 *Jefferson at Monticello*, 22.

46 Merrill Peterson, ed. *The Portable Thomas Jefferson* (New York: Penguin Books, 1975), xii.

47 Burstein, *Inner*, 21–22.

48 Burton, *JV*, 52–53.; Burton's book, *Jefferson Vindicated*, is the most thoroughly detailed book I have researched concerning Jefferson's younger brother, Randolph.

49 Turner, *The Jefferson-Hemings Controversy*, 85.

50 Ellen Randolph to Jeff, 21 April 1808, Martha Jefferson Randolph to Jeff, 30 January 1808 in *FL*; Burton, *JV*, 53.

51 Turner, *The Jefferson-Hemings Controversy*.

52 Historian Pearl M. Graham published an article, "Sally Hemings and Thomas Jefferson," in the *Journal of Negro History*. She was one of the first to use the "rediscovered" *Jefferson Farm Book* to argue in favor of the relationship.

53 Ms. Graham was instrumental in getting the Hemings family to donate a bell to Howard University that was allegedly given by Martha Wayles Jefferson, on her deathbed, to one of the Hemings girls.

54 Turner, *The Jefferson-Hemings Controversy*, 61, 517–-18; Graham to Julian Boyd, January 11, 1958.

55 Turner, 517–20.

56 Bear Jr. and Mayo, *Unknown Brother*, 21.

57 Burton, *JV*, 56–60.

58 Burton, 56–60.

59 Burton, 56–60.

60 Mr. Coates was the head librarian at Shenandoah College in Winchester, Virginia, from 1969 to 1974, and section head (supervisor) DBPH, at the LOC from 1974 to 1978. He designed the website "Thomas Jefferson on Politics & Government," adopted by the University of Virginia. See https://famguardian.org/Subjects/Politics/ThomasJefferson/jeffcont.htm.

61 Herbert Barger, Jefferson family historian, email message to author, June 8, 2006. Detailed media release from February 6, 2006.

62 Burton, *JV*, 56–60.

63 Turner, *The Jefferson-Hemings Controversy*, 779.

64 Schachner, *Thomas Jefferson*, 2:923.

65 Bear Jr., and Mayo, *Unknown Brother*.

66 "Jon Kukla posits that the sexual relationship between Jefferson and Hemings began not in Paris but, rather, after their return to Monticello. Even so, it was in Paris that Jefferson first lived in close quarters with a mature Sally Hemings, whom he came to see, at some point, as a prospective sexual partner. See Kukla, *Mr. Jefferson's Women*, 125–27." Kiernan, *Martha Jefferson*, 294, n.66.

67 Herbert Barger, "The Jefferson-Hemings DNA Study," in Coates, *Myth*, 34.

68 McMurry and McMurry, "The Origins of the Sally Story" iii; Coates, *Myth*, 94.

69 Turner, *The Jefferson-Hemings Controversy*, 368;

70 Fleming, *Intimate Lives*, 674; Bear Jr. and Mayo, *Unknown Brother*, 1–6. Also see *Family Letters*, 66, 182, 343. In *Jefferson Vindicated*, Cynthia Burton also examines Randolph as a potential father, 52–60.

71 McLaughlin, *Jefferson and Monticello*, 167. For more on Neilson, see James Bear Jr., *The Hemings Family of Monticello* (Ivy, VA, 1980).

72 McLaughlin, *Jefferson and Monticello*, 122. According to Isaac, John Hemings's father was "an Englishman named Nelson." He also said that Nelson was a carpenter—or as Isaac called him, an inside worker, a finisher"—who worked on the original Monticello house. (122). Elizabeth Langhorne wrote that "Martin, Betty Hemings's son by a black father before her connection with John Wayles, was also a trained coachman." Langhorne, *Monticello*, 76.

73 See Turner, *The Jefferson-Hemings Controversy*, 531.

74 "Monticello's former overseer Edmund Bacon recalled that TJ "freed one girl [Harriet Hemings] some years before he died, and there was a great deal of talk about it…. People said he freed her because she was his own daughter" (Bacon recollections, in Bear, 102). Sally Hemings's brothers James and Robert both became free at about age thirty-one. Another James Hemings, son of Sally Hemings's sister Critta, ran away to Richmond in his teens and, after negotiations for his return failed, was not pursued."--- Lucia C. Stanton. "Those Who Labor for My Happiness". University of Virginia Press, 2012.

75 Turner, *The Jefferson-Hemings Controversy*, 474.

76 The interview was published in 1862 as "Jefferson at Monticello, The Private Life of Thomas Jefferson."

Chapter 11

1 Gordon S. Wood, *Revolutionary Characters: What Made the Founders Different* (New York: Penguin, 2006), 275.

2 Wood, 106.

3 Garry Wills, *Mr. Jefferson's University* (Washington, DC: National Geographic Society, 2002, 33.

4   For primary sources on the founding of the University of Virginia and higher education, see Rex Bowman, *Rot, Riot, and Rebellion: Mr. Jefferson's Struggle to Save the University That Changed America* (Charlottesville: University of Virginia Press, 2013); Mark R. Wenger, "Thomas Jefferson, the College of William and Mary, and the University of Virginia," *Virginia Magazine of History and Biography* 103 (1995): 339–74; and Garry Wills, *Mr. Jefferson's University* (Washington, DC: National Geographic Society, 2002).

5   Langhorne, *Monticello*, 319–20.

6   McLaughlin, *Jefferson and Monticello*, 6, 370.

7   McLaughlin, 371.

8   Wood, *Revolutionary Characters*, 275; Meacham, *Thomas Jefferson*.

9   Thomas Jefferson to Cornelius C. Blatchly, 21 October, 1822, *Founders Online*, National Archives, https://founders.archives.gov/documents/Jefferson/98-01-02-3106.

10 Thomas Cooper (1759–1839) was an American scientist, political economist, jurist, and educator who emigrated to the United States from England in 1794; *PTJRS*, 7:127.

11 Meacham, *Thomas Jefferson*, Apple Book, 1628; TJ to Joseph Cabell, January 22, 1820.

12 TJ to Thomas Cooper, September 1, 1817, http://www2.iath.virginia.edu/grizzard/documents/raw/allLetters.htm.

13 TJ to Madame de Tessé, September 6, 1795, PTJ-Boyd 28:452; Burstein, *Jefferson's Secrets* (2011), Apple Books, 506n8.

14 Neil McDowell Shawen, "Thomas Jefferson and a 'National' University: The Hidden Agenda for Virginia," *Virginia Magazine of History and Biography* 92, no. 3 (July 1984): 309–35, http://www.jstor.org/stable/4248729.

15 Ellis, *American Sphinx*, 516.

16 Ellis, 516.

17 Wills, *Mr. Jefferson's University*, Apple Books ed., 30.

18 Warren, *Brother to Dragons*, 133.

19 McLaughlin, *Jefferson and Monticello*, 209.

20 McLaughlin, 209.

21 Wallace, *The Billionaire's Vinegar*, 12.

22 Warren, *Brother to Dragons*, 133.

23 Jefferson to Messrs. Hugh L. White and others, Monticello, May 6, 1810, in *Writings*, 1223; Beran, *Jefferson's Demons*, Apple Books ed., 523.

24 John A. Ragosta, ʃPeter S. Onuf, andʃAndrew J. O'Shaughnessy, eds. *The Founding of Thomas Jefferson's University* (Charlottesville, VA: University of Virginia Press, 2019), n.p.

25 "John Hartwell Cocke was thirty-seven years younger than his neighbor, Thomas Jefferson, but these landed gentry shared numerous concerns and became close associates

during the latter years of Jefferson's life. Cocke was 'Jeffersonian' in his habits and views: both men attended William and Mary, led organized lives as 'enlightened' owners of large plantations, and were well-read, civic-minded, and restless in their inquiries into the world around them." "John Hartwell Cocke," *Thomas Jefferson Encyclopedia*, The Jefferson Monticello, accessed November 10, 2021, https://www.monticello.org/site/research-and-collections/john-hartwell-cocke. "Joseph C. Cabell was member of the House of Delegates (1808–1810, 1831–1835) and the Senate of Virginia (1810–1829) and served as president of the James River and Kanawha Company (1835–1846). He also served as rector of the University of Virginia from 1834 to 1836 and again from 1845 to 1856." "Cabell, Joseph C. (1778–1856)," *Encyclopedia Virginia*, accessed November 10, 2021, https://encyclopediavirginia.org/entries/cabell-joseph-c-1778-1856/.

26   Randall, *Jefferson*, 3:462–63, details the organizational foundations; see also University of Virginia Commissioners, "Rockfish Gap Report of the University of Virginia Commissioners, 4 August 1818," https://founders.archives.gov/documents/Jefferson/03-13-02-0197-0006; "From Thomas Jefferson to William Charles Jarvis, 28 September 1820," *Founders Online*, National Archives, https://founders.archives.gov/documents/Jefferson/98-01-02-1540. Meacham, *Thomas Jefferson*, 907

27   Shawen, "Thomas Jefferson and a 'National' University."

28   Ellis, *American Sphinx*, 518.

29   Brodie, *Intimate*, 598.

30   Philip Alexander Bruce and William Glover Stanard, *Virginia Magazine of History and Biography* (1984): 312.

31   Wills, *Mr. Jefferson's University*, 72.

32   Thomas Jefferson, Henry Augustine Washington *The Writings of Thomas Jefferson: Being His Autobiography*, 521.

33   Mark R. Wenger, "Thomas Jefferson, the College of William and Mary, and the University of Virginia," *Virginia Magazine of History and Biography*; Steve Coffman, ed., *Words of the Founding Fathers: Selected Quotations of Franklin, Washington* (Jefferson, NC: McFarland, 2012), 119.

34   Wills, *Mr. Jefferson's University*, 176

35   Joyce Appleby and Terence Ball, eds., *Jefferson: Political Writings* (Cambridge University Press, 1999), 251.

36   Meacham, *Thomas Jefferson*, 909.

37   Thomas Jefferson to William Roscoe, 27 December 1820, *Papers of Thomas Jefferson*: Retirement Series, Thomas Jefferson Foundation; Meacham, *Thomas Jefferson*, 1850.

38   TJ to Cabell, January 22, 1820; Meacham, *Thomas Jefferson*, 909

39   Meacham, *Thomas Jefferson*, 910; Randall, *Jefferson*, 3:473.

40   Elizabeth Trist to Nicholas P. Trist, March 9, 1819. Published at Papers of Thomas Jefferson Retirement Series Digital Archive, http://www.monticello.org/familyletters (accessed 2021).

41 Wills, *Mr. Jefferson's University* (New York: HarperCollins, 2002), Apple Books ed., 46.
42 Wills, *Mr. Jefferson's University*, Apple Books ed., 47
43 Wills, 47.
44 Thomas Jefferson to James Madison, 13 April 1817, Jefferson Papers, LOC; Ellis, *American Sphinx*, 1351.
45 Ellis, *American Sphinx*, 517.
46 Ellis, 518; Thomas Jefferson to James Madison, 13 April 1817, Jefferson Papers, LOC.
47 Ellis, *American Sphinx*, 517.
48 Ellis, 517.
49 Wenger, "Thomas Jefferson, the College of William and Mary, and the University of Virginia."
50 Ellis, *American Sphinx*, 1707.
51 Ellis, 1707–9.
52 Ellis, 1709–10.
53 Jefferson, *Notes on the State of Virginia*, query 14, in *Writings*, 273. See also Jefferson to John Brazier, Poplar Forest, Virginia, August 24, 1819, in *Writings*, 1422–25; Beran, *Jefferson's Demons*, Apple Books ed., 525n196.
54 Ellis, *American Sphinx*, 1718.
55 TJ to Joseph Priestley, January 18, 1800, in Ford, *Writings*, 9:96–98; Burstein, *Jefferson's Secrets* (2011), Apple Books ed., 504n48.
56 Ellis, *American Sphinx*, 1723.
57 Glover, *Founders as Fathers*, 120.
58 Glover, 120.
59 Ellis, *American Sphinx*, 1734.
60 Wenger, "Thomas Jefferson, the College of William and Mary, and the University of Virginia."
61 Ellis, *American Sphinx*, 1732.
62 McLaughlin, *Jefferson and Monticello*, 254.
63 Wills, *Mr. Jefferson's University*, 116.
64 "The architectural curator of Jefferson's buildings at the university, Murray Howard, told me that the Tuscan columns' original color has been recovered—it was a light earth color, not white. Similarly, the dome was not white, but a metallic color like that of its model, the Pantheon. But the white was taken as traditional because of Greek Revival styles, and it is so much a part of the image of the place that its devotees carry in their head that it proves difficult, now, to go back to Jefferson's colors." Wills, 175
65 McLaughlin, *Jefferson and Monticello*, 399.

66 Wills, *Mr. Jefferson's University*, 33.

67 Christopher Hitchens, *Thomas Jefferson: Author of America* (New York: HarperCollins, 2007), n.p.

68 Wenger, "Thomas Jefferson, the College of William and Mary, and the University of Virginia," 367.

69 Mayo, "Twilight at Monticello," 514.

70 Mayo, 514.

71 Mayo, 514.

72 Wenger, "Thomas Jefferson, the College of William and Mary, and the University of Virginia," 369.

73 Wenger, 369.

74 Wenger, 370.

75 Mary Wood, "Landing UVA Law's Inaugural Instructor Was Surprisingly Difficult for Thomas Jefferson," *UVA Lawyer*, Fall 2016, https://www.law.virginia.edu/uvalawyer/article/first-law-professor.

76 Wood.

77 Francis Walker Gilmer (1790–1826) was the tenth child of George Gilmer, a close friend of Thomas Jefferson, and brother of Peachy Gilmer.

78 Wills, *Mr. Jefferson's University*, 152

79 Malone, *Sage of Monticello*, 463.

80 Mayo, "Twilight at Monticello," 514, 503.

81 Glover, *Founders as Fathers*, 250.

82 Mayo, "Twilight at Monticello," 514, 503.

83 Crawford, *Twilight*, 206–7.

84 Malone, *Sage of Monticello*.

85 Crawford, *Twilight*, 210–11; Malone, *Sage of Monticello*.

86 Crawford, 212; Malone, *Sage of Monticello*.

87 Roy J. Honeywell, *The Educational Work of Thomas Jefferson* (Norwood, MA: Norwood Press, 1931); Malone, *Sage of Monticello*.

88 Ellis, *American Sphinx*, 1384.

89 Ellis, *American Sphinx*, 529; For the most concise descriptive account of the spatial arrangements at the University of Virginia, see Harold Hellenbrand, *The Unfinished Revolution: Education and Politics in the Thought of Thomas Jefferson* (Newark: University of Delaware Press, 1990), 146–50.

90 Crawford, *Twilight*, 211.

91 *JHT* (1981), 466.
92 *JHT*, 466.
93 *JHT*, 477.
94 *JHT*, 483.
95 Crawford, *Twilight*, 212.
96 Crawford, 213.
97 Glover, *Founders as Fathers*, 120.
98 Crawford, *Twilight*, 207.
99 Board of Visitors Minutes: July 14, 16, 18, 1829; July 15, 16, 21, 1830; July 14, 20, 1831; July 12, 17, 1832; July 12, 19, 1833; July 15, 18, 19, 1834; July 2, 1835; August 17, 1836; July 1, 3, August 12, 1837; July 3, 1838; July 6, 7, 1840; July 4, 1843; June 25, 1846; June 26, 1847; June 1, 1849; Vance, "Thomas Jefferson Randolph," 245.
100 Vance, "Thomas Jefferson Randolph," 246; For recent scholarship on the University of Virginia, see Patricia C. Sherwood and Joseph Michael Lasala, "Education and Architecture: The Evolution of the University of Virginia's Academical Village" in *Thomas Jefferson's Academical Village: The Creation of an Architectural Masterpiece*, ed. Richard Guy Wilson (Charlottesville, 1993), 9–45; Wilson, "Jefferson's Lawn," 47–73. Also essential is Mary N. Woods, "Thomas Jefferson and the University of Virginia: Planning of the Academic Village," *Journal of the Society of Architectural Historians* 44 (October 1985): 266–83. Paul Venable Turner examines both institutions in the light of broader planning trends in *Campus*, chaps. 1–2.
101 Wills, *Mr. Jefferson's University*, 172.
102 Wills, 173.
103 *Central Gazette*, July 7, 1820, March 8, 1822; Vance, "Thomas Jefferson Randolph," 244.
104 "Extract from Thomas Jefferson to William Roscoe," December 27, 1820, Jefferson Quotes, The Jefferson Monticello, https://tjrs.monticello.org/letter/387.
105 Wills, *Mr. Jefferson's University*, 176.
106 "Jefferson's Gravestone," *Thomas Jefferson Enyclopedia*, https://www.monticello.org/site/research-and-collections/jeffersons-gravestone.

Chapter 12

1 I am grateful to author Cynthia Burton for her superb research on Jefferson's health, chronicled in her book *Jefferson Vindicated*; see Jefferson to Benjamin Waterhouse, January 8, 1825, in Ford, *Writings*, 10:335–36, for Jefferson's own summary of his physical condition. See *Domestic Life*, 394–95, for his remark on physicians; Jefferson to John Adams, July 5, 1814, Cappon, *Letters* 2: 430.

2   After Jefferson's death, when Monticello was deserted and Jeff wanted someone to stay there to keep vandals away, Dunglison moved his family there during the summer break of 1827. Wills, *Mr. Jefferson's University*, 167

3   Wills, 167.

4   John T. Morse, Jr., ed., *Thomas Jefferson: American Statesman* (Boston: Houghton Mifflin, 2004), 5. The most thorough discussion of Jefferson's health can be found in Burton, *Jefferson Vindicated*.

5   Mayo, "Twilight at Monticello."

6   Mayo.

7   Burton, *JV*, 40. Here author Cynthia Burton has superbly detailed Jefferson's health in explicit detail through correspondence and Jefferson's own health records. See in particular, 40–46.

8   *FL*; Burton, *JV*, 40. There is some indication that Jefferson grew rhubarb specifically to ease his diarrhea.

9   Kukla, *Mr. Jefferson's Women*, 17.

10 Gary L. Cohen and Loren A. Rolak, "Thomas Jefferson's Headaches: Were They Migraines?" *Headache: The Journal of Head and Face Pain* 46, no. 3 (March 2006): 492–97, doi:10.1111/j.1526-4610.2006.00292.x; Brodie, *Intimate*, 66.

11 Malone, *Jefferson and His Time*.

12 McCullough, *John Adams*, 145.

13 Kukla, *Mr. Jefferson's Women*, 17, quoting Jefferson's *Notes on the State of Virginia*.

14 Cohen and Rolak, "Jefferson's Headaches; Peterson, *Thomas Jefferson and the New Nation*, 348.

15 Kaminski, *Jefferson in Love*, xii–xiii, 12; 38–39. 3, 4.

16 Malone, *Rights of Man*, 70—71; Kukla, *Mr. Jefferson's Women*, Apple Books ed., 546n4.

17 Kukla, *Mr. Jefferson's Women*. "'If the Italian women fuck as well in Italy as they do here, you must be happy indeed—I am such a zealot for them, that I'll be damned if I ever fuck an English woman again (if I can help it).' Cosway to unidentified, 24 Feb 1772, Townley Manuscripts, British Museum, quoted in Lloyd, *Richard and Maria Cosway*, 29–31." Kukla, *Mr. Jefferson's Women*, Apple Books ed., 492n6.

18 Burstein, *Inner*, 280.

19 Burstein, 280.

20 "Henry Stevens Randall, in *The Life of Thomas Jefferson* (New York, 1858), 1:456, dated the injury to 4 Sept., and Helen Duprey Bullock's pioneering *My Head and My Heart: A Little History of Thomas Jefferson and Maria Cosway* (New York, 1945) followed his lead. Lyman H. Butterfield and Howard C. Rice, Jr., narrowed the range of dates to 13–22 Sept. in 'Earliest Note to Maria Cosway,' 26–33. Butterfield subsequently discovered in Benjamin Franklin's papers a letter dated 20 Sept. mentioning [the stunt and the

subsequent treatment] . . . (Jefferson Papers, 10:432n). The 18th is further confirmed by Jefferson's daily log of morning and afternoon temperatures (Memorandum Books, 784), which is complete from 1 May 1786 to 27 Feb. 1787, except for the three days immediately after Jefferson 'P[ai]d two Surgeons 12f' on 18 Sept. (639)." Kukla, *Mr. Jefferson's Women*, Apple Books ed., 496n22.

21 Brodie, *Intimate*, 243.

22 Gore Vidal, *Inventing a Nation: Washington, Adams, Jefferson*, Icons of America (New Haven, CT: Yale University Press, 2003), 10.

23 Thomas Jefferson to William Thornton, 14 February 1801, William Thornton Papers, vol. 3, # 395, Thomas Jefferson Papers, 1606 to 1827, Manuscript Division, LOC.

24 Burton, *JV*, 40–41.

25 Cohen and Rolak, "Jefferson's Headaches."

26 Henry, Katt, "Jefferson VinDicated," *Cavalier Daily*, February 28, 2007, https://www.cavalierdaily.com/article/2007/02/jefferson-vindicated.

27 Kukla, *Mr. Jefferson's Women*, 127.

28 "From Thomas Jefferson to James Madison, 27 April 1795," *Founders Online*, National Archives, https://founders.archives.gov/documents/Jefferson/01-28-02-0258.

29 "I. Thomas Jefferson to Philip Mazzei, 24 April 1796," *Founders Online*, National Archives, https://founders.archives.gov/documents/Jefferson/01-29-02-0054-0002.

30 Burton, *JV*, 43–44.

31 Jefferson to Dr. Vine Utley, March 21, 1819; *Domestic Life*, 370–72, for his diet, regimen, eyesight; see also Jefferson to Benjamin Rush, February 28, 1803; Ford, *Writings*, 8:220, for the lengthiest description of matters intestinal; see also Ellis. *American Sphinx*, Apple Books ed., 427.

32 Thomas Jefferson to James Monroe 18 March 1785, Thomas Jefferson Papers, 1606 to 1827, Manuscript Division, LOC, Papers VIII, 43; also, Thomas Jefferson to William Dunbar, 12 January 1801; Burton, *JV*, 41.

33 Thomas Jefferson to William Thornton, 14 February 1801, William Thornton Papers, Vol. 3, # 395, Thomas Jefferson Papers, 1606 to 1827, Manuscript Division, LOC.

34 Meacham, *Thomas Jefferson*, Apple Books ed., 739.; PTJ, XXXVI 178.

35 Burstein, *Inner*, 264.

36 Meacham, *Thomas Jefferson*, Apple Books ed., 740; *JHT* 4:186.

37 Meacham, *Thomas Jefferson*, 740.

38 Meacham, 740.

39 Dr. Jan Duvoisin, MD (anesthesiologist), in correspondence with author, June 30, 2008.

40 Duvoisin to author.

41 Phyllis A. Balch, *Prescription for Herbal Healing* (New York: Avery, 2002), 387; Hyland, *In Defense of Thomas Jefferson*, 71.

42 Malone, *Jefferson the President*, 188; Henry Dearborn to Thomas Jefferson, 15 August 1802, *Founders Online*, National Archives, https://founders.archives.gov/documents/Jefferson/01-38-02-0203.

43 Kukla, *Mr. Jefferson's Women*, 127; Jefferson to Madison, 9 June 1793, Thomas Jefferson Papers, 1606 to 1827, Manuscript Division, LOC, 26:240.

44 Hyland, *In Defense*, 117.

45 Dr. Patterson to Jefferson, rec'd 14 July 1807; Thomas Jefferson to Ellen Wayles Randolph, 25 October 1808, both in Massachusetts Historical Society; Martha Jefferson Randolph, 27 October 1808, Thomas Jefferson Papers, 1606 to 1827, Manuscript Division, LOC.

46 Hyland, *In Defense*, 118.

47 Jackson, *Year at Monticello*; George Washington to Thomas Jefferson, 4 October 1795, in John C. Fitzpatrick, ed., *The Writings of George Washington, from the Original Manuscript Sources, 1745–1799*. 39 vols. (Washington, DC Government Printing Office, 1931–44), 34:325

48 Burton, *JV*, 42.

49 Hyland, *In Defense*, 118.

50 Burton, *JV*, 42–43.

51 "Battle, "'Periodical Head-achs,'" 531,533, 538. Summarizing his diagnosis of Jefferson's ailment as tension, or muscular-contraction, headaches rather than migraines, Battle noted: (1) their long duration (from several days to several weeks); (2) their association with frustration or stress; (3) their greater severity during the day than at night; (4) the absence of "symptoms so common in migraines such as premonitory visual aura, . . . nausea or vomiting"; and (5) their apparent remission after his retirement from the presidency. In addition, Battle noted that Jefferson's symptoms excluded cluster headaches, formerly called histaminic cephalgia or Horton's headache (short recurrent attacks generally at night accompanied by tearing of the eyes, runny nose, or nasal obstruction); malaria (which is accompanied by fever); or a combination of migraines and muscular-contraction (tension) headaches." Kukla, *Mr. Jefferson's Women*, Apple Books ed.

52 "Keenly attentive both to Jefferson's health and to his extensive reading and library, Andrew Burstein observed that "these tension headaches ceased after he retired to Monticello in 1809." See Burstein, *Inner*, 245; Kukla, *Mr. Jefferson's Women*, 35.

53 Sam Hodges, "Paternity Dispute: Professors Lock Horns over Jefferson," *Mobile Register*, March 11, 2001.

54 B. John Melloni, *Melloni's Illustrated Medical Dictionary*, 3rd ed. (Boca Raton, FL: CRC Press, 1993), 50; WedMD, "Headache Basics," http://www.webmd.com/migraines-headaches/guide/migraines-headaches-basics.

55 Cohen and Rolak, "Jefferson's Headaches."

56 Hyland, *In Defense*, 115; Cohen and Rolak, "Jefferson's Headaches."
57 Burton, *JV*, 45
58 Burton, 46.
59 Burton, 40.
60 Burton, 46.
61 "Medical Chronology: Thomas Jefferson," Monticello Research Files, ICJS; John D. Battle Jr., "The 'Periodical Headachs' of Thomas Jefferson," *Cleveland Clinic Quarterly* 51 (1984): 531–39; and A. K. Thould, "The Health of Thomas Jefferson (1743–1826)," *Journal of the Royal College of Physicians of London* 23 (1989): 50–52. There is no evidence about when this first severe headache ceased. My inference that it lasted at least three days is based on the letter to Fleming (written at "11. o'clock at night") that opens with a "violent head ach, with which I have been afflicted these two days," and closes with "My head achs, my candle is just going out, and my boy [i.e., slave] asleep, so must bid you adieu." Kukla, *Mr. Jefferson's Women*, 457n59.
62 Burton, *JV*, 44.
63 Burton, 42.
64 Crawford, *Twilight*, 76.
65 Vidal, *Inventing a Nation*, 81.
66 Crawford, *Twilight*, 124.
67 Herbert E. Sloan, *Principle and Interest: Thomas Jefferson and the Problem of Debt* (New York: Oxford University Press, 1995), chaps. 1 and 2, quote at 27; Burstein, *Jefferson's Secrets* (2011), Apple Books ed., 576n5.
68 A major study of Jefferson's character that appeared in the mid-1990s, Burstein's *The Inner Jefferson*, also casts doubt on the Hemings–Jefferson relationship.
69 Morse, *American Statesman*, 6.
70 Burstein, *Secrets*, 39.
71 Ellis, *American Sphinx*, 260, 273–74, 365.
72 Ellis, 278..
73 Hyland, *In Defense,* 73.
74 Brodie, *Intimate*, 459.
75 Brodie, 460.
76 Brodie, 460.
77 Malone, *Sage of Monticello*, xxi–xxii.
78 Frank Beardsley, "The Making of a Nation 44—Thomas Jefferson, Part 9 (The Last Days)," broadcast on January 8, 2004, https://www.testbig.com/voa/thomas-jefferson-part-9-last-days; Hyland, *In Defense*, 125.

79   Malone, *Sage of Monticello*, 496.

80   Brodie, *Intimate*.

81   Brodie, 621, 460.

82   Beardsley, "The Making of a Nation 44."

83   Ellis, *American Sphinx*, 233, 260, 365.

84   Malone, *Sage of Monticello*, 458–59.

85   Crawford. *Twilight*, 303.

86   Malone, *Sage of Monticello*, 458–59; Alexander Garrett to J.H. Cocke, 18 June 1825, (Cooke-Shields Papers, ViU.

87   Malone, *Sage of Monticello*, 496.

88   Wills, *Mr. Jefferson's University*, 169

89   Malone, *Sage of Monticello*, 497.

90   Alan Pell Crawford, "Thomas Jefferson Survives Equality, Unalienable Rights and a Duality: Final Years Were Ones of Hope, Disappointment," *Free Lance-Star* (Fredericksburg, VA), February 3, 2008.

Chapter 13

1   Malone, *Jefferson and His Time*, 493.

2   Malone, 493.

3   Malone, 493.

4   *Virginia Quarterly Review* Vol. 17, 509.

5   Mayo, "Twilight at Monticello," 514, 509.

6   "Virginia J. Randolph (Trist) to Nicholas P. Trist, with Postscript by Martha Jefferson Randolph," December 2 1821, The Jefferson Monticello, https://tjrs.monticello.org/letter/904.

7   On Lafayette's friendship with Jefferson, see Crawford, *Twilight*, 201–6. According to one historian's minority opinion, Lafayette's friendship with Jefferson seemed one-sided: "Lafayette's enthusiastic admiration for Jefferson . . . is abundantly recorded, but it is hard to make out anything closely equivalent on Jefferson's side . . . Only once in the preserved correspondence between Jefferson and Lafayette is a personal note struck, and it is a disconcerting one." Conor Cruise O'Brien, *The Long Affair: Thomas Jefferson and the French Revolution, 1785–1800* (Chicago: University of Chicago, 1996), 32.

8   Crawford, *Twilight*, 201.

9   Crawford, 201.

10   Crawford, 201–2.

11   Brodie, *Intimate*, 460.

12   Smith, *Carysbrook Memoir*, 70–71; TJR, *Memoirs*; *MJR*, 728–29.
13   *MJR*, 21–22.
14   *MJR*, 22.
15   *MJR*, 728–31.
16   *MJR*, 28–31.
17   Crawford, *Twilight*, 202.
18   *MJR*, 5.
19   Brodie, *Intimate*, 460.
20   *MJR*, 727; Gaines, *TMR*, 149.
21   Langhorne, *Monticello*, Apple Books, 373.
22   Langhorne, 374.
23   Malone, *Jefferson and His Time*, 408.
24   No doubt the subject of slavery came up in their conversations; Chernow, *Washington*, 1358-9: "For the Marquis de Lafayette, the notion that an independent America would tolerate slavery was more than a contradiction in terms: it was anathema to everything he believed. As he told British abolitionist Thomas Clarkson, "I would never have drawn my sword in the cause of America if I could have conceived that thereby I was founding a land of slavery." So earnest was Lafayette that Clarkson called him "as uncompromising an enemy of the slave trade and slavery as any man I ever knew."
25   Malone, *Jefferson and His Time*, 408.
26   Malone, 495–99.
27   *JHT* (1981), 469.
28   *JHT*, 469.
29   *JHT*, 469–70.
30   *JHT*, 470.
31   Gordon-Reed, *TJ and SH*, 247–48; Randall, *Life*, 3:538.; Gordon-Reed. "*The Hemingses of Monticello*, Apple Books ed., 1226.
32   Merrill, *Visitors to Monticello*, 95.
33   TJ to Peale, July 18, 1824, TJP-LC; Burstein, *Jefferson's Secrets* (2011), Apple Books ed., 483n6
34   TJ to Edward Livingston, March 25, 1825; Burstein, *Jefferson's Secrets* (2011), Apple Books ed., 483n6.
35   *JHT* (1981), 471.
36   Beran, *Jefferson's Demons*, Apple Books ed., 18.
37   *TDLTJ*, 360.

38   Wood, *Revolutionary Characters*, 226.
39   Thomas Jefferson to John Adams, 25 March 1826, Founders Online, National Archives, https://founders.archives.gov/documents/Jefferson/98-01-02-5983; Ellis, *American Sphinx*, 1518.
40   Ellis, *American Sphinx*, 1519.
41   Brodie, *Intimate* 445.
42   Ellis, *His Excellency: George Washington* (New York: Knopf, 2004), 804.
43   Beran, *Demons*, 834–35.
44   Beran, 832–34.
45   Brodie, *Intimate,* 425.
46   Brodie, 425.
47   Brodie, 425.
48   Brodie, 425.
49   Beran, *Demons*, 834–35.
50   Beran, 721.
51   Beran, 723.
52   Beran, 724.
53   Meacham, *Thomas Jefferson,* Apple Books ed., 947; Randall, *Jefferson* III 539.
54   Malone, *Jefferson and His Time*, 496.
55   Malone, 448
56   Malone, 497.
57   Meacham, *Thomas Jefferson*, Apple Books ed., 951; VTM, 109.
58   Meacham, *Thomas Jefferson*, Apple Books ed., 951.
59   Meacham, *Thomas Jefferson*, Apple Books ed., 951; VTM, 108–9.
60   TDLTJ, 429; see also see Bear, "Last Few Days in the Life of Thomas Jefferson," 73; Meacham, *Thomas Jefferson*, Apple i-Books ed., 953;
61   Crawford, *Twilight*, 237.
62   Samuel X. Radbill and Robley Dunglison, "The Autobiographical Ana of Robley Dunglison, M.D.," *Transactions of the American Philosophical Society* 53, no. 8 (1963): 1–212, http://www.jstor.org/stable/1005873.
63   Radbill and Dunglison, 26.
64   Radbill and Dunglison, 26.
65   Radbill and Dunglison, 26–27.
66   Radbill and Dunglison.

67   Beran, *Demons*, 743.
68   Beran, 744.
69   Beran, 744.
70   Meacham, *Thomas Jefferson,* Apple Books., 949; Randall, *Jefferson*, 3:543.
71   Meacham, 950; Randall,, *Jefferson,* 3: 543.
72   Randall, *Life of Jefferson*, 3:543; Meacham, *Thomas Jefferson*, 2428–33.
73   Randall, *Jefferson*, 3:
74   Bear, "Last Few Days in the Life of Thomas Jefferson," 73; Meacham, *Thomas Jefferson*, Apple Books.
75   Randall, *Life of Jefferson*, 3:54
76   Randall, *Life of Jefferson*, 3:543–44; Meacham, *Thomas Jefferson*, 956.
77   Randall, *Life of Jefferson*, 3:543–44; Meacham, *Thomas Jefferson*, 956.
78   Randall, *Life of Jefferson*, 3:543–44; Meacham, *Thomas Jefferson*, 956.
79   Thomas Jefferson Randolph to Jane Randolph, 2 July 1826, Edgehill-Randolph Papers, Special Collections, ViU; Langhorne, *Monticello*, 864.
80   Thomas Jefferson Randolph to Dabney Carr, 11 July 1826, Carr-Cary Family Papers, Accession 1231, Special Collections Department, ViU Library; Langhorne, *Monticello*, 864.
81   From Thomas Jefferson Randolph's account of the final hours in *Domestic Life*, 427; Randall, *Life of Jefferson*, 3:542–45; Meacham, *Thomas Jefferson*, 2334–35.
82   Malone, 6:447–48, 496. "Jefferson quietly expired: His death was apparently caused by complications from an enlarged prostate, which constricted the urethra." Meacham, *Jefferson*.
83   Langhorne, *Monticello*, 864.
84   Bear, "Last Few Days in the Life of Thomas Jefferson," 77; Meacham, *Thomas Jefferson*, Apple Books., 957.
85   Alexander Garrett to Evelina Bolling Garrett, Monticello, 4 July 1826, Death of Thomas Jefferson Collection, ViU, located at http://tjrs.monticello.org/letter/1922.
86   Radbill and Dunglison, "The Autobiographical Ana of Robley Dunglison," 33
87   Radbill and Dunglison, 33
88   Gordon-Reed, *Hemingses of Monticello*, 1045; Stanton, *Free Some Day*, 142-143.
89   "Andrew K. Smith's Account of Thomas Jefferson's Funeral," 15 October 1875, Jefferson Quotes & Letters, The Jefferson Monticello, https://tjrs.monticello.org/letter/38.
90   "Andrew K. Smith's Account of Thomas Jefferson's Funeral."
91   *TDLTJ*, 430.

92 TDLTJ, 431–32.

93 Thomas Jefferson, Last Will and Testament, *Thomas Jefferson Encyclopedia*, https://www.monticello.org/site/research-and-collections/last-will-and-testament.

94 Thomas Jefferson Randolph to James Madison, 8 July, 1826, Jefferson Quotes & Family Letters, The Jefferson Monticello, http://tjrs.monticello.org/letter/458.

95 James Madison to Thomas Jefferson Randolph, 14 July 1826, Death of Thomas Jefferson Family Letters, Montpelier Foundation, LOC, located at http://tjrs.monticello.org/letter/460.

Chapter 14

1 Langhorne, *Monticello*, Apple Books ed., 402.
2 Langhorne, *Monticello*, Apple Books ed., 402.
3 Langhorne, 403.
4 McLaughlin, *Jefferson and Monticello*, 377–78.
5 Brodie, *Intimate*, 457.
6 Brodie, 615,
7 Brodie, 456.
8 "Jeff Randolph and his father read in the newspapers that before setting fire to the U.S. Capitol, the British had entered the upper floor of the Senate. There they destroyed the congressional library of three thousand volumes that Jefferson, during his years as a diplomat in Europe, had devoted much time and care to assemble." Crawford, *Twilight*, 97.
9 Brodie, *Intimate*, 431.
10 Brodie, 431.
11 Kukla, *Mr. Jefferson's Women*, 254.
12 Brodie, *Intimate*, 583.
13 Brodie, 583.
14 Brodie, 431.
15 Gaye Wilson, Monticello Was among the Prizes in a Lottery for a Ruined Jefferson's Relief," *Colonial Williamsburg Journal* 10 (Winter), https://research.colonialwilliamsburg.org/Foundation/journal/Winter10/jefferson.cfm
16 Crawford, *Twilight*, 60.
17 *JHT*, 6:473–82, 488, 495–96, 511. 55
18 Scharff, *Women*, 1083; Martha Jefferson Randolph and Nicholas Trist to Ellen Randolph Coolidge, 5 April 1826, Family Letter, ViU, located at https://tjrs.monticello.org/letter/1035.
19 *MJR*, 754–60.

20 Thomas Jefferson, Monticello, to Joseph Cabell, 20 January 1826, in Randall, *Life of Jefferson*, 3:527.

21 Jefferson to Cabell, in Randall, 3:527.

22 Langhorne, *Monticello*, 402; TJ to Joseph C. Cabell, February 7, 1826.

23 Wilson, "Monticello Was among the Prizes in a Lottery for a Ruined Jefferson's Relief."

24 *MJR*, 754–60.

25 *MJR*, 754–60.

26 Malone, *Sage of Monticello*, 496.

27 Brodie, *Intimate*, 464

28 Brodie, 464.

29 Scharff, *Women Jefferson Loved*, 370.

30 Malone, *Sage of Monticello*, 488.

31 Stanton, "Monticello to Main Street," 216–18; Jefferson's optimism is indicated by the codicil to his will, which provided that the houses he wished built for John Hemings, Burwell Colbert, and Joseph Fossett be built "on some part of my lands convenient to them with respect to the residence of their wives."

32 John Barnwell, "Monticello: 1856," *Journal of the Society of Architectural Historians* 34, no. 4 (December 1975): 280–85, http://www.jstor.org/stable/989014.

33 Mayo, "Twilight at Monticello," 514.

34 Langhorne, *Monticello*, 407.

35 Langhorne, 407.

36 *Charlottesville Central Gazette*, 13 January 1827. "Only fragmentary documentation survives for the Jan. 1827 sale. Transactions are mentioned in occasional letters and in almost 30 sales slips, which note the purchase of only thirty-four slaves (Monticello Dispersal Sale receipts, ViU: 5291). Apparently all 130 slaves were not actually sold in 1827, as an account of a second sale of 33 slaves, 1 Jan. 1829, also survives (ViU: 8937)" Stanton. "*Those Who Labor for My Happiness*," Apple Books, n. 1, 834.

37 "The auction scene has been recovered from many fragmentary sources in Lucia Stanton, "*Those Who Labor for My Happiness': Thomas Jefferson and His Slaves*, Onuf, ed., *Jeffersonian Legacies*, 147–48—Ellis, *American Sphinx*, Apple Books ed., 661, fn. 108

38 Martha Jefferson Randolph to Ellen Randolph Coolidge, 2 August 1825, quoted in Scharff, *Women Jefferson Loved*, 382.

39 Martha Jefferson Randolph to Ann C. Morris, quoted in Scharff, 382.

40 Scharff, *Women*, 382.

41 "Thomas Jefferson Randolph's Newspaper Advertisement for Poplar Forest and Monticello Estate Sales," published in the *Richmond Enquirer*, November 3, 1826 and running unaltered until January 20, 1827, Jefferson Quotes, https://tjrs.monticello.org/letter/2027.

42 Langhorne, *Monticello*, 408.

43 Stanton, *"Those Who Labor,"* 25–26.

44 John Forsyth to Thomas Jefferson Randolph, 5 December 1826, ViU: 8937-b; Stanton, *"Those Who Labor for My Happiness,"* 646.

45 Harriet Dunglison to Nicholas Philip Trist, 13 January 1827, Robekly Dunglison to Trist, 15 January 1827, Nicholas Philip Trist Papers, Manuscript Division, LOC; Stanton, *"Those Who Labor for My Happiness,"* 469.

46 Vance, "Thomas Jefferson Randolph," 111; see also note forms dated 15, 17 January 1827, Nicholas Philip Trist Papers, Manuscript Division, LOC; Thomas Jefferson Randolph to his wife, 2 April 1828, Edgehill-Randolph Papers, Special Collections, ViU; Thomas Jefferson Randolph to Joseph Coolidge, 22 November 1828.

47 TJR, *Memoirs*, 54; Stanton, *"Those Who Labor for My Happiness,"* 1108.

48 Peggy Nicholas to Jane Randolph, 29 January 1827; Stanton, *"Those Who Labor for My Happiness,"* 646; Ellis, *American Sphinx*, Apple Books ed., 534–35.

49 "The location of the rented house in Charlottesville is not known. Sally Hemings is listed as free in the 1833 special census (Ervin L. Jordan, Jr.,"A Just and True Account": Two 1833 Parish Censuses of Albemarle County Free Blacks,' *Magazine of Albemarle County History* 53 (1995): 114–139)." Stanton, *"Those Who Labor for My Happiness."*

50 Brodie, *Intimate*, 469.

51 Stanton, *"Those Who Labor for My Happiness,"* 26.

52 Peggy Nicholas to Jane Randolph, 29 January 1827; Stanton, *"Those Who Labor for My Happiness,"* 647.

53 [Virginia Randolph Trist] to Ellen W. Randolph Coolidge, 23 March 1827, Edgehill-Randolph Papers, Special Collections, ViU.

54 Glover, *Founders as Fathers*, 253; for John Latrobe's 1832 visit to Monticello, see *VTM*, 120, 153.

55 A sister to Virginia Randolph Trist, 26 June 1831, Nicholas P. Trist Papers, Southern Historical Collection, University of North Carolina Library; Vance, "Thomas Jefferson Randolph," 118.

56 Kerrison, *Jefferson's Daughters*, 1605–6.

57 Kerrison, 1605–6.

58 Thomas Jefferson Randolph, Richmond, to his wife, 7 December 1826, ViU.

59 Crawford, *Twilight*, 251.

60 Crawford, 252.

61 Crawford, 252

62 Crawford, 252.

63 Crawford, 253.

64 Kerrison, *Jefferson's Daughters*, 1609.
65 Kerrison, 2008.
66 Kerrison, 1613.
67 Crawford, *Twilight at Monticello*, 256.
68 Crawford, 256–57.
69 Crawford, 257.
70 Crawford, 257.
71 Scharff, *Women Jefferson Loved*, xiii.
72 McLaughlin, *Jefferson and Monticello*, 380.
73 McLaughlin, 380.
74 John Barnwell, "Monticello: 1856."
75 Barnwell.
76 Glover, *Founders as Fathers*, 255.
77 Glover, 255.
78 McLaughlin, *Jefferson and Monticello*, 381.
79 Glover, *Founders as Fathers*, 254.
80 John Barnwell, "Monticello."
81 Gaines, *TMR*, 155–65
82 Gaines, 155–65
83 Gaines, 157
84 Gaines, 157
85 Gaines, 165–67.
86 Gaines, 279.
87 Gaines, 279.
88 Gaines, 279
89 Martha Jefferson Randolph to Ellen Wayles Randolph Coolidge, 30 June 1828; to George Wythe Randolph 30 June 1828, Ellen Wayles Coolidge Randolph Papers. Accession 9090, ViU; *MJR*, 1700.
90 *MJR*, 1704.
91 Martha Jefferson Randolph to Ellen Wayles Randolph Coolidge, 21 July 1828, Ellen Wayles Coolidge Randolph Papers. Accession 9090, ViU; *MJR*, 1704.
92 Jane Jefferson Randolph to Ellen Wayles Randolph Coolidge, 2 August 1825, Ellen Wayles Coolidge Randolph Papers, Family Letters Digital Archive, ViU; Stanton, *"Those Who Labor for My Happiness,"* 203–5; Jane Jefferson Randolph to Ellen Wayles Randolph Coolidge, ca. 28 May 1829, Ellen Wayles Coolidge Randolph Papers, Family Letters Digital Archive, ViU.

93 Jane Jefferson Randolph to Ellen Wayles Randolph Coolidge, 2 August 1825, Ellen Wayles Coolidge Randolph Papers, Family Letters Digital Archive, ViU; Stanton, *"Those Who Labor for My Happiness,"* 203–5; Jane Jefferson Randolph to Ellen Wayles Randolph Coolidge, ca. 28 May 1829, Ellen Wayles Coolidge Randolph Papers, Family Letters Digital Archive, ViU.

94 "Martha Jefferson Randolph to Ann C. Morris," March 22, 1827, Jefferson Quotes, The Jefferson Monticello, https://tjrs.monticello.org/letter/1086.

95 Jane Jefferson Randolph to Ellen Wayles Randolph Coolidge, August 2, 1825, Ellen Wayles Coolidge Randolph Papers, Family Letters Digital Archive, ViU; Stanton, *"Those Who Labor for My Happiness,"* 203–5; Jane Jefferson Randolph to Ellen Wayles Randolph Coolidge, ca. May 28, 1829, Ellen Wayles Coolidge Randolph Papers, Family Letters Digital Archive, ViU.

96 Jane Jefferson Randolph to Ellen Wayles Randolph Coolidge, August 2, 1825, Ellen Wayles Coolidge Randolph Papers, Family Letters Digital Archive, ViU; Stanton, *"Those Who Labor for My Happiness,"* 203–5; Jane Jefferson Randolph to Ellen Wayles Randolph Coolidge, ca. May 28, 1829, Ellen Wayles Coolidge Randolph Papers, Family Letters Digital Archive, ViU.

97 Jane Jefferson Randolph to Ellen Wayles Randolph Coolidge, August 2, 1825; Stanton, *"Those Who Labor for My Happiness,"* 203–5; Jane Jefferson Randolph to Ellen Wayles Randolph Coolidge, ca. May 28, 1829.

98 Jane Jefferson Randolph to Ellen Wayles Randolph Coolidge, ca. May 28, 1829.

99 Postmaster in Alexandria, Virginia, by President U. S. Grant, Nicholas Philip Trist, A Register of His Papers in the LOC, prepared by Patrick Kerwin and Lia Apodaca, Manuscript Division, LOC; Jane Jefferson Randolph: Indenture Selling Thomas Jefferson's Land to Martin Dawson, 1 January 1829, FLP, http://familyletters.dataformat.com, original in Albemarle County Deed Book, 23:118-19; Virginia Jefferson Trist to Nicholas P. Trist, Edgehill, 5 May 1829, "Family Correspondence (1826–1833) Internship," 76; research report compiled by Ann Macon Smith and Ann Lucas, Thomas Jefferson Foundation (1991); Thomas Jefferson Randolph to Nicholas P. Trist, Edgehill, 13 April 1829, Papers of Thomas Jefferson: Retirement Series, Thomas Jefferson Foundation; Thomas Jefferson Randolph to Nicholas P. Trist, Edgehill, 16 February 1829, Papers of Thomas Jefferson: Retirement Series, Thomas Jefferson Foundation; Joseph Coolidge to Nicholas P. Trist, Boston, 22 March 1829, 491.

100 Mary Jefferson Randolph to Ellen Randolph Coolidge, 26 November 1826, quoted in Scharff, *The Women Jefferson Loved*, xiii–xiv.

101 Jane Jefferson Randolph to Ellen Wayles Randolph Coolidge, 2 August 1825; Stanton, *"Those Who Labor for My Happiness,"* 203–5; Jane Jefferson Randolph to Ellen Wayles Randolph Coolidge, ca. 28 May 1829.

102 Will of Martha Jefferson Randolph, 18 April 1835, Edgehill-Randolph Papers, Special Collections, ViU; *MJR*, 1938–40, 1945.

103 Scharff, *The Women Jefferson Loved*, 383.

104 Scharff, 383.

105 Auguste Levasseur, *Lafayette in America in 1824 and 1825* (New York, 1829), 218; Stanton, "Those Who Labor for My Happiness," 1110.

106 Gordon-Reed, *Hemingses of Monticello*, 3018, 3019.

107 Stanton, "Those Who Labor for My Happiness," 337.

108 Mary J. Randolph to Ellen Coolidge, 25 January 1827, Family Letters, ViU, located at https://tjrs.monticello.org/letter/1079; Stanton, "Those Who Labor for My Happiness," 106.

109 Glover, *Founders as Fathers*, 225.

110 Martha Jefferson Randolph to Ellen Randolph Coolidge, September 15, 1833, quoted in Glover, 225

111 Glover, 225.

112 Kranish, *Flight*, 325.

113 Glover, *Founders as Fathers*, 232.

114 Vance, "Thomas Jefferson Randolph," 121–22.

Chapter 15

1 TJR, *Memoirs*, 60; TJ to John Holmes, April 22, 1820. Extract published at Papers of Thomas Jefferson Retirement Series Digital Archive, http://www.monticello.org/familyletters (accessed 2011). 4. "THE CESSION OF THAT KIND" Randall, Jefferson, III, 456. 5.

2 Vance, "Thomas Jefferson Randolph," 54.

3 "The literature on Jefferson and slavery is enormous," writes Joseph J. Ellis. He goes on to choose three basic accounts: Winthrop D. Jordan, *White over Black* (Chapel Hill: University of North Carolina Press, 1968); Robert McColley, *Slavery and Jeffersonian Virginia* (Urbana, IL: University of Illinois Press, 1964); and John Chester Miller, *The Wolf by the Ears: Thomas Jefferson and Slavery* (New York: Free Press, 1977). Ellis, *American Sphinx*, Apple Books ed., 590n48.

4 Beran, *Jefferson's Demons*, Apple Books ed., 525n196.

5 H. A. Taine, *History of the English Language*, 2 vols., repr. ed., trans. N. Van Laun (New York: William A. Allison, 1895), 1:5–6.

6 Glover, *Founders as Fathers*, 174.

7 Robert F. Turner, "Was Thomas Jefferson America's First Abolitionist?" Minding the Campus, May 20, 2021, https://www.mindingthecampus.org/2021/05/20/was-thomas-jefferson-americas-first-abolitionist/;

8   Henry Wiencek, "The Dark Side of Thomas Jefferson," *Smithsonian* magazine, October 2012, reprinted at https://www.realclearhistory.com/2019/10/18/the_dark_side_of_thomas_jefferson_3416.html.

9   Turner, "Was Thomas Jefferson America's First Abolitionist?"

10   Brodie, *Intimate*, 426.

11   Langhorne, *Monticello*, 234, 37.

12   Stanton, *"Those Who Labor for My Happiness,"* 610–11.

13   Stanton, 610–11.

14   Stanton, 610–11.

15   Stanton, 610–11.

16   Langhorne, *Monticello*, Apple Books ed., 410

17   Malone, *Jefferson the Virginian*, 121–22; Fleming, *Intimate Lives*, 930–32.

18   Dumas Malone, Jefferson the Virginian (Boston: 1948), 121–122.; Thomas Fleming, *A Disease in the Public Mind: A New Understanding of Why We Fought the Civil War* (New York: Da Capo Press, 2013), Apple Books ed., 66.

19   Mazzei, *My Life and Wanderings*, 223.

20   Mazzei, 223.

21   Mazzei, 223–24.

22   A harsh critic of Jefferson on slavery: "As luminaries such as Lafayette and Thomas Paine discovered, debating Jefferson would always prove fruitless. A shrewd and relentless lawyer, he composed briefs for the defense containing 'just enough of the semblance of morality to throw dust into the eyes of the people,' to borrow his own words. In their entirety Jefferson's rationalizations amount to nothing compared with his perfectly clear presidential order to admit slavery to the Louisiana Territory. Later in his life Jefferson mocked abolitionists for 'wasting Jeremiads on the miseries of slavery' and more or less went over to arguing that slavery was a positive good. Describing what he could see from his terrace—Mulberry Row's 'ameliorated' cabins, where his enslaved relatives lived—he claimed in 1814 that American slaves were better fed and clothed than England's workers and 'labor less'—an argument that to this day is the trump card for slavery's retrospective apologists." Wiencek, *Master of the Mountain*, 274.

23   Scharff, *The Women Jefferson Loved*, 382.

24   Extract from Thomas Jefferson to Edward Coles, August 25, 1814, published in *PTJRS*, 7:603–5, https://tjrs.monticello.org/letter/1369.

25   Burstein, *Inner*, 279.

26   Jefferson to Edward Coles, August 25, 1814. p. 2, https://www.loc.gov/resource/mtj1.047_0731_0734/?sp=2&st=text.

27   Charles Thomson to Jefferson, November 2, 1785; Ellis, *American Sphinx*, Apple Books ed., 590n49.

28   Meacham, *Thomas Jefferson*, Apple Books ed., 923.

29   Meacham, 923; PTJRS, 7:604.

30   Brodie, *Intimate*, 462.

31   Brodie, 462.

32   Brodie, 462.

33   Meacham, *Thomas Jefferson*, Apple Books ed., 927

34   Meacham, 927.

35   Meacham, Apple Books ed., 271.

36   Peterson, *Visitors from Monticello*, 90–91.

37   Thomas Jefferson to John Holmes, April 22, 1820, in H. A. Washington, ed., *The Writings of Thomas Jefferson* (New York: Ryker, Thorne, 1854), 7:159.

38   VTM, A Cordial Reunion in 1820, with Isaac Briggs, 90–91.

39   Jefferson's letter to Angelica Church, 27 November 1793; PTJ, 27:449; Stanton, "*Those Who Labor for My Happiness*," 190.

40   All slaves freed after 1806 were subject to immediate banishment from Virginia unless the owner secured a special dispensation from the legislature. MB, 1315.

41   "Ursula, the daughter of farm laborers Bagwell and Minerva Granger and wife of Monticello head gardener Wormley Hughes, was inoculated against smallpox in May 1801, soon after her arrival (Edward Gantt, invoice, ca. 2 Mar. 1802, DLC)." Stanton "*Those Who Labor for My Happiness*," 862n35.

42   Scharff, *The Women Jefferson Loved*, 46.

43   McLaughlin, *Jefferson and Monticello*, 67.

44   McLaughlin, 404.

45   Gordon-Reed, *The Hemingses of Monticello*, Apple Books ed., 809.

46   MB, 499; FB, 421; TJ to James Barbour, May 11, 1821; AGR, *Hemingses*, Apple Books ed., 1204n4.

47   Kierner, MJR, Apple Books ed., 438. There is one incident, however, where Patsy allegedly whipped a slave herself. "In August 1833, [she] whipped Sally in the basement of the Trists' house in Washington. The tone of Cornelia's description of the incident, which she addressed to her absent sister Virginia, and the fact that she thought that the whipping was newsworthy, suggests that corporal punishment was uncommon in their household. Cornelia recounted how [her mother] 'inflicted the flagellation pretty seriously.' 'What disciplinarians we have turned out to be,' Cornelia observed wryly, even as she defensively informed her sister that Melinda Freeman judged [Patsy's] whipping 'not enough' to reform the intractable slave." Kierner, 439–40.

48   McLaughlin, *Jefferson and Monticello*, 404.

49   Gordon-Reed, *The Hemingses of Monticello*, Apple Books ed., 1223, fn. 29.

50   Crawford, *Twilight*, 255.

51   McLaughlin, *Jefferson and Monticello*, 113.

52   TJ to Reuben Perry, 16 April 1812, *PTJ-R*, 4:620. Thomas Jefferson Randolph may have whipped one of his slaves. "One incident stuck fast in the memory of Randolph's six-year[-]old nephew, after a visit to Edgehill from his home in Boston. His uncle brought a slave guilty of a theft 'before the house, in front of which all the slaves were assembled, and flogged him with a horsewhip.' (*T. Jefferson Coolidge 1831–1920: An Autobiography* [Boston, 1923], 3)." Stanton, *"Those Who Labor for My Happiness,"* note.

53   "Under Virginia law, slaveholders could freely abuse or even murder their slaves in punishing misbehavior and still avoid legal repercussions"--Chernow, *Washington*, Apple Books ed., 342.

54   Chernow, *Washington*, Apple Books ed., 342.

55   Thomas Jefferson to Edward Coles, 25 August 1814, *Founders Online*, National Archives, https://founders.archives.gov/documents/Jefferson/03-07-02-0439.

56   "Thomas Jefferson to Reuben Perry, 16 April 1812," *Founders Online*, National Archives, https://founders.archives.gov/documents/Jefferson/03-04-02-0508. "Jeff Randolph on the other hand," claims one slave historian "had no compunction about personally wielding the whip. He even whipped an enslaved man in front of his young nephew visiting from Massachusetts, Thomas Jefferson Coolidge. Coolidge recounted the incident in his memoirs and seems to have been horrified by the whole southern way of plantation life." Yet in fairness, at the end of Jeff Randolph's life and career, he became a fervent abolitionist, agreeing with Jefferson's description of the master-slave relationship as "a perpetual exercise of the most boisterous passions, the most unremitting despotism on the one part, and degrading submissions on the other." *MJR*, Apple Books ed., 439.

57   McLaughlin, *Jefferson and Monticello*, 97.

58   Beran, *Jefferson's Demons*, Apple Books ed., 526n196.

59   Banneker was the eldest child of a free black couple who owned a tobacco farm in Baltimore County, Maryland, He emerged from obscurity in 1788, the year after the publication of the first American edition of *Notes on the State of Virginia*. At that time Banneker, who was fifty-seven, borrowed a set of astronomical instruments and four works on astronomy from George Ellicott, a member of a distinguished family of Quaker entrepreneurs who opposed slavery and operated a group of gristmills near Banneker's farm. Banneker applied himself to the study of astronomy and soon became so proficient in it that he conceived the idea of publishing an almanac . . . to promote 'the Cause of Humanity as many are of Opinion that Blacks are Void of Mental endowments.' Elias Ellicott to James Pemberton, 10 June 1791, PHi: Pennsylvania Abolition Society Papers. Encouraged by George Ellicott and his brother Elias, a member of the Maryland Society for the Abolition of Slavery, Banneker prepared an ephemeris for the year 1791 that caught the attention of Major Andrew Ellicott, a cousin of the Ellicott brothers. He was so impressed by Banneker's mathematical achievement that he brought it to TJ's attention and, with TJ's approval, employed Banneker as an assistant during the preliminary survey of the Federal District early in 1791 (Joseph Townsend to

James Pemberton, 28 Nov. 1790, PHi: Pennsylvania Abolition Society Papers; TJ to Condorcet, 30 Aug. 1791; Bedini, *Banneker*, p. 9–136)." "To Thomas Jefferson from Benjamin Banneker, 19 August 1791," *Founders Online*, National Archives, https://founders.archives.gov/?q=Banneker&s=1111311111&sa=&r=3&sr=; see also David Barton, *The Jefferson Lies: Exposing the Myths You've Always Believed About Thomas Jefferson* (Nashville: Thomas Nelson, 2012), 94.

60   Barton, *The Jefferson Lies*, 94; *Papers of Thomas Jefferson*, Vol 22, 49.
61   Barton, 94–98.
62   Barton, 95–98.
63   "Thomas Jefferson, *The Papers of Thomas Jefferson*, ed. Charles T. Cullen, vol. 22 (Princeton: Princeton University Press, 1986), 49. 36. Ibid., 49–51. 37. Ibid., 51–52. 38. Ibid., 97–98. 39. Ibid., 98–99"; Barton, *The Jefferson Lies*, 94–98.
64   Barton, *The Jefferson Lies*, 94–98.
65   Barton, 94–98.
66   Barton, 94–98.
67   Barton, 94–98.
68   Chernow, *Washington*, 207.
69   Wood, *Revolutionary Characters*, 8n286.
70   Malone, *Sage of Monticello*.
71   Beran, *Demons*, 196; Stanton, *"Those Who Labor for my Happiness,"* 197.
72   Jordan, *White over Black*.
73   Thomas Jefferson to Nicholas Lewis, 19 December 1786, in Boyd, *Papers*, 10:615; Stanton, *"Those Who Labor for my Happiness,"* 443.
74   Alexander O. Boulton, "The American Paradox: Jeffersonian Equality and Racial Science," *American Quarterly* 47, no. 3 (September 1995): 467–92, https://www.jstor.org/stable/2713297.
75   Meacham, *Art of Power*, 26; Bear, *Monticello* 11, 71.
76   Was Thomas Jefferson America's First Abolitionist? By Robert F. Turner-- https://www.mindingthecampus.org/2021/05/20/was-thomas-jefferson-americas-first-abolitionist/.
77   Vance, "Thomas Jefferson Randolph," 188.
78   Thomas Mann Randolph to Trist, 5 June 1820, Nicholas P. Trist Papers, Southern Historical Collection, University of North Carolina Library; Vance, "Thomas Jefferson Randolph," 188–89.
79   TJR, *Memoirs*, 4.
80   TJR, in Vance, "Thomas Jefferson Randolph," 7.
81   TJR, *Memoirs*, 28-29.

82 TJR, *Memoirs*, 24.

83 Vance, "Thomas Jefferson Randolph," 190.

84 Martha Jefferson Randolph to Ellen W. R. Coolidge, 31 August 1829, Jefferson Academical Papers, ViU.

85 Peggy Nicholas to Jane Randolph, ViU; Vance, "Thomas Jefferson Randolph," 185.

86 Vance, "Thomas Jefferson Randolph," 186; Diary of Anne Maury, 5 July 1831, Maury Papers, ViU.

87 Lewis, *Happiness*, 209

88 Lewis, 209.

89 Vance, "179–80.

90 Fleming, "Another Thomas Jefferson Tried to Eliminate Slavery in Virginia," History News Network.

91 TJR, *Memoirs*.

92 Vance, chaps. 11–12.

93 Joseph Clarke Robert, *Road from Monticello: A Study of the Virginia Slavery Debate of 1832*, repr. (Whitefish, MT: Kessinger, 2010), 19.

94 Letters of Edward Coles to Thomas J. Randolph, 29 December 1831, *WMQ* 7, no. 2 (April 1927): 105–7, https://www.jstor.org/stable/1921045.

95 See Edward Coles, "A Sketch of the Principal Circumstances Connected with the Emancipation of the Slaves of Edward Coles, and the Persecutions to Which It Subjected Him" (PhD diss., 1968; unpublished, manuscript, October 1827), Edward Coles Collection, Pennsylvania Historical Society; Edward Coles to Mrs. R. E. Coles, 19 April 1819; W. E. Smith, "Edward Coles," *Dictionary of American Biography*, ed. Allen Johnson and Dumas Malone (New York: Charles Scribner's Sons, 1930), 4:296–97; Theodore C. Pease, *The Frontier State, 1818–1848* (Chicago: A. C. McClurg, 1922), 90–91.

96 Vance, "Thomas Jefferson Randolph."

97 Vance, chaps. 11 and 12.

98 TJR, *Memoirs* 56-61.

99 TJR, 56–61.

100 Crawford, *Twilight*, 254–55.

101 Fleming, *Disease*, Apple Books ed., 207.

102 Crawford, 258.

103 Fleming, *Disease*, 208

104 Fleming, *Disease*, 181, 210–11.

105 Fleming, "Another Thomas Jefferson."

106 Fleming, *Disease*, 211

107 Fleming, *Disease*, 211–12.

108 Fleming, *Disease*, 213; Vance, "Thomas Jefferson Randolph," 195; Thomas Jefferson Randolph to his wife, 29 January 1832, Edgehill-Randolph Papers, Special Collections, ViU; Thomas Jefferson Randolph, "Speech in House."

109 Fleming, "Another Thomas Jefferson Tried to Eliminate Slavery in Virginia," https://historynewsnetwork.org/article/151963. This article is adapted from Thomas Fleming's book, *A Disease In the Public Mind: A New Understanding of Why We Fought the Civil War*.

110 Patricia Prickett Hickin, *Antislavery in Virginia, 1831–1861*, vol. 1 (University of Virginia, 1969), 194.

111 Peggy Nicholas to Mrs. Dabney Carr, 27 February 1832, Carr-Cary Family Papers, Accession 1231, Special Collections Department, ViU Library.

112 Fleming, *Disease*, 213.

113 Thomas Jefferson Randolph to his wife, 17 January 1833, Edgehill-Randolph Papers, Special Collections, ViU.

114 Fleming, *Disease*, 213.

Chapter 16

1 Chapter based on *Jefferson's granddaughter in London book*.

2 Langhorne, *Monticello*, Apple Books ed., 347.

3 Langhorne, 347.

4 Birle, *Thomas Jefferson's Granddaughter*, xvii–xxxiv.

5 TJR to Jane Randolph, 14, 25 April, 1826; *MJR*, 435.

6 Ellen to Patsy Jefferson, September 27, 1818; 20 November 1825; *MJR*, 432.

7 TJ to Ellen Randolph Coolidge, Monticello, November 14, 1825, http://www.let.rug.nl/usa/presidents/thomas-jefferson/letters-of-thomas-jefferson/jefl284.php.

8 Wiencek, *Master of the Mountain*, 177.

9 Wiencek, 178.

10 Ellen Randolph Coolidge, November 14, 1825, *Family Letters*, 461.

11 Langhorne, *Monticello*, Apple Books ed., 359–60.

12 Coolidge, November 14, 1825.

13 Jefferson to Ellen Randolph Coolidge, Monticello, Nov. 14, 1825; http://www.let.rug.nl/usa/presidents/thomas-jefferson/letters-of-thomas-jefferson/jefl284.php

14 McLaughlin, *Jefferson and Monticello*, 366.

15 McLaughlin, 366.

16 Crawford, *Twilight*, 233.

17 Crawford, 233.

18 Lewis, *The Pursuit of Happiness*, 149.

19 Lewis, 229.

20 Lewis, 229–30.

21 Lewis, 230.

22 "To Thomas Jefferson from Ellen Wayles Randolph Coolidge, 1 August 1825," *Founders Online*, National Archives, https://founders.archives.gov/documents/Jefferson/98-01-02-5424.

23 Langhorne, *Monticello*, Apple Books ed., 376.

24 Langhorne, 376; TJ to Ellen, August 27, 1825.

25 Birles, *Thomas Jefferson's Granddaughter*, xxiii.

26 Langhorne, *Monticello*, Apple Books ed., 378.

27 Lewis, *The Pursuit of Happiness*, 40.

28 Lewis, 40.

29 Lewis, 40.

30 "People say that Jefferson was a deist. How can they be so sure? 'I never told my own religion,' he once said to Mrs. Smith. See Jefferson to Mrs. Samuel H. (Margaret Bayard) Smith, Monticello, Va., August 6, 1816, in *Writings*, 1404. He at one point professed himself 'a real Christian,' but it is not clear what exactly Christianity meant to him. 'I am a real Christian,' he wrote, 'that is to say, a disciple of the doctrines of Jesus, very different from the Platonists, who call me infidel and themselves Christians and preachers of the gospel, while they draw all their characteristic dogmas from what its author never said nor saw.'" Beran, *Jefferson's Demons*, Apple Books ed., 392–93, n, xvii.

31 Lewis, *The Pursuit of Happiness*, 40–41. Faith had always been a part of Thomas Jefferson's life, and he ultimately passed this deep sense of faith to his children and grandchildren. Although there is sharp debate on his specific religious beliefs, when Jefferson contemplated his own mortality, he used the word heaven "colloquially, as a substitution for God . . . in such phrases as: 'find favor with heaven'; 'may heaven give you'; 'implore heaven to avert the evil.'" Burstein, *Jefferson's Secrets* (2011), Apple Books ed., 573. And during the War of 1812, when Jefferson wrote James Monroe on the impracticality of raising a large regular army, he said, "We might as well rely on calling down an army of angels from heaven." TJ to Monroe, October 16, 1814, in Burstein, 573.

32 Langhorne, Monticello, Apple Books. 425.

33 Langhorne, 425.

34 Langhorne.

35 Crawford, *Twilight at Monticello*, 231.

36 Crawford, 247.

37 Crawford, 247.
38 Meacham, *Thomas Jefferson*, Apple Books ed., 963-964.
39 Ellen Wayles Coolidge to Henry S. Randall, May 16, 1857, quoted in Meacham, *Thomas Jefferson*, Apple Books, 964.
40 Coolidge to Randall, in Meacham, 964–65.
41 Coolidge to Randall, 964–65
42 Meacham, *Thomas Jefferson*, Apple Books ed., 966.
43 Birle, *Thomas Jefferson's Granddaughter*, xxiv.
44 Birle, xxiv.
45 Ellen Coolidge to Virginia Trist, May 3, 1829, in Catherine Kerrison, *Claiming the Pen: Women and Intellectual Life in the Early American South* (Cornell University Press 2015).
46 Lewis, *The Pursuit of Happiness*, 152.
47 Lewis, 153.
48 Beran, *Jefferson's Demons*, Apple Books ed., 18.
49 Lewis, *The Pursuit of Happiness*, 153.
50 Lewis, 153.
51 Lewis, 153.
52 Lewis, 160.
53 Lewis, 160.
54 Lewis, 160–61
55 Burstein, *Jefferson's Secrets* (2011), Apple Books ed., 139.
56 Adams to TJ, December 1, 1825, quoted in Burstein, 139.
57 Burstein, *Jefferson's Secrets* (2011), Apple Books ed., 139.
58 Burstein, 139.
59 See Birle, *Thomas Jefferson's Granddaughter*.
60 Her time in Boston was after the Sally Hemings scandal and Federalist attacks on Jefferson's policies.
61 Cynthia A. Kierner and ʃSandra Gioia Treadway, *Virginia Women: Their Lives and Times*, vol. 1 (Athens: University of Georgia Press, 2015), 291.
62 Birle, *Thomas Jefferson's Granddaughter*, introduction.
63 Birle, xxiv–viii.
64 Birle, xxv–viii.
65 Birle, xxv–viii.
66 Birle, xxv–viii.

67 Birle, xxv–viii.
68 Birle, xxv–viii.
69 Kierner. *MJR*, chap. 8
70 Kierner, 458.
71 Kierner. 472.
72 Kierner, 472.
73 Kierner, 472
74 Kierner, 474.
75 Birle and Francavilla, *Thomas Jefferson's Granddaughter*, intro.
76 Coolidge, *Autobiography*, 3.
77 Birle and Francavilla, *Thomas Jefferson's Granddaughter*, xxv-xxx.
78 Birle and Francavilla, xxv–xxx.
79 Birle and Francavilla, xxv–xxx.
80 Birle and Francavilla, 160.
81 Birle and Francavilla, xiii–xx.
82 Birle and Francavilla, xiii–xx.
83 Birle and Francavilla, xiii–xx.
84 Birle and Francavilla, xiii–xx.
85 Birle and Francavilla, xiii–xx
86 Birle and Francavilla, xiii–xx.
87 Birle and Francavilla, xiii–xx.
88 Birle and Francavilla, xiii–xx.
89 Birle and Francavilla, xiii–xx.
90 Birle and Francavilla, xiii–xx.
91 Birle and Francavilla, xiii–xx.
92 Birle and Francavilla, xiii–xx.
93 Birle and Francavilla, xiii–xx.
94 Birle and Francavilla, xiii–xx.
95 Birle and Francavilla, xiii–xx.
96 Birle and Francavilla, xiii–xx.
97 Birle and Francavilla, xiii–xx.
98 Coolidge, *Autobiography of T. Jefferson Coolidge: Drawn in Great Part from His Diary and Brought Down to the Year MDCCCC.* (Boston: Merrymount, 1901), 101.

99	Coolidge, 95–96.
100	Coolidge, 1–2.
101	Birle and Francavilla, *Thomas Jefferson's Granddaughter,* xiii–xx.

Chapter 17

1	Vance, "Thomas Jefferson Randolph," 108.
2	Vance, 108.
3	Vance, 109.
4	Vance, 207.
5	Albemarle County Personal Property Tax Lists, 1840, LVa; National Register of Historic Places Nomination Form for Edgehill. On Thomas Jefferson Randolph and secession, see Vance, "Thomas Jefferson Randolph," 225.
6	Thomas Jefferson Randolph to Nathan Caper, 22 May 1873.
7	Vance, "Thomas Jefferson Randolph," 126.
8	Vance, 126–27.
9	Vance, 127–28.
10	Vance, 128.
11	Vance, 129.
12	Vance, 133–34.
13	Vance, 134.
14	"Henry Augustine Washington was born at Haywood, Virginia on 24 August 1820, the son of Lawrence Washington and Sarah Tayloe Washington. He attended Georgetown College and the College of New Jersey (now Princeton University). He moved to Richmond to practice law in 1842, but in 1847 returned to the Northern Neck of Virginia. . . . Washington edited the *Writings of Thomas Jefferson* (Washington, 1853–54) and completed Thomas R. Dew's *A Digest of the Laws, Customs, Manners and Institutions of the Ancient and Modern Nations* (1853)." "Henry A. Washington Letter," William & Mary Special Collections Research Center," https://scrcguides.libraries.wm.edu/repositories/2/resources/934.
15	Randall, *Life of Jefferson,* 1:1n16; Susan A. Kern, "The Jeffersons at Shadwell: The Social and Material World of a Virginia Family" (PhD diss., College of William and Mary in Virginia, 2005); see chap. 7 for Thomas Jefferson's epitaph.
16	*MJR,* 1244.
17	*MJR,* 1244
18	*MJR,* 1244–46.
19	*MJR,* 1244–46.

20   *MJR*, 1244–46.
21   LMJR, TO Nicholas Philip Trist, 4 April 1827, APRIL4 1827 Trist Papers (UNC); Langhorne, *Monticello*, 1156.
22   Crawford, *Twilight*, 260.
23   *MJR*, 471.
24   Virginia Jefferson Randolph Trist to Nicholas Philip Trist, 16 October 1836, Nicholas Philip Trist Papers, Manuscript Division, LOC; *MJR*, 1294.
25   Crawford, *Twilight*, 260.
26   *MJR*, 272.
27   *MJR*, 472–74
28   *MJR*, 1297–98.
29   *MJR*, 473.
30   *MJR*, 668, 1299.
31   Epitaph of Martha Jefferson Randolph, [1836], Edgehill-Randolph Papers, Special Collections, ViU; Sarah N. Randolph, "Mrs. Thomas Mann Randolph," in Mrs. O. J. Wister, and Miss Agnes Irwin, eds. *Worthy Women of Our First Century* (Philadelphia: Lippincott, 1877), 62, 70.
32   Vance, "Thomas Jefferson Randolph," 110, 109.
33   Sarah Nicholas Randolph and Clayton Torrence, "Letters of Sarah Nicholas Randolph to Hugh Blair Grigsby," *Virginia Magazine of History and Biography* 59, no. 3 (July 1951): 315–36, http://www.jstor.org/stable/4245789.
34   McLaughlin, *Jefferson and Monticello*, 79.
35   McLaughlin, 79.
36   Chernow, *Washington*, 1314–15.
37   Chernow, 804; "Indeed, I am told that he feels more animation and throws off more of his natural phlegm when conversing on that topic than on any other," a young British diplomat later noted." Jackman, "Young Englishman Reports."
38   Vance, "Thomas Jefferson Randolph," 51.
39   Lewis, *The Pursuit of Happiness*, 135.
40   Vance, "Thomas Jefferson Randolph," 235–36
41   Vance, 235–40.
42   Vance, 235–40.
43   Vance, 239.
44   Vance, 235–40.
45   Vance, 240–45.

46   Vance, 164–66.
47   TJ to Samuel and James [Lester?] 7 January 1812, Thomas Jefferson Papers, Coolidge Collection, Massachusetts Historical Society; Vance, "Thomas Jefferson Randolph," 164–66.
48   Vance, "Thomas Jefferson Randolph," 241.
49   Vance, 241.
50   Vance, 242.
51   Vance, 242.
52   Vance, 241–47.
53   *The Magazine of Albemarle County History* - Volume 30 - Page 67, 1973; Randolph, *The Domestic Life of Thomas Jefferson*, addenda, 374.
54   Randolph, addenda, 374–84
55   Vance, "Thomas Jefferson Randolph," 248.
56   Vance, 248.
57   Vance, 247–57.
58   Vance, 247–57.
59   Vance, 247–57.
60   Vance, 251.
61   Vance, "Thomas Jefferson Randolph," 247–57.
62   Vance, 247–57.
63   Vance, 242.
64   Vance, 226.
65   Vance, 227.
66   Vance, 227.
67   Vance, 227.
68   McLaughlin, *Jefferson and Monticello*, 381.
69   McLaughlin, 384.
70   Cornelia Jefferson Randolph to Ellen Wayles Coolidge, 30 May 1830; Ellen Wayles Coolidge Randolph Papers. Accession 9090, ViU; Langhorne, *Monticello*, 1151.
71   James L. Swanson, *Chasing Lincoln's Killer* (New York: Scholastic Press, 2009), 19.
72   R. G. H. Kean, journal (ms. and typescript, references here to typescript), 131, ViU; Vance "Thomas Jefferson Randolph," 228.
73   Vance, "Thomas Jefferson Randolph," 243.
74   Vance, 238.

75 Vance, 239.

76 Vance, 253–60.

77 Vance, 253; TJR, *Memoirs*; account of the death of his wife, Edgehill-Randolph Papers, Special Collections, ViU.

78 Vance, "Thomas Jefferson Randolph," 253.

79 Thomas Jefferson Randolph to his wife, 9 February 1835; Vance, "Thomas Jefferson Randolph," 214.

80 Vance, "Thomas Jefferson Randolph," 215, 254.

81 Hugh B. Grigsby to his wife, 11 July 1868, ViHi; Vance, "Thomas Jefferson Randolph," 229.

82 Everett Chamberlin, *The Struggle of '72* . . . (Chicago: Union, 1872), 524; Vance, "Thomas Jefferson Randolph," 231.

83 *Richmond Dispatch*, July 9, 1872, quoted in Vance, "Thomas Jefferson Randolph," 231.

84 *Richmond Dispatch*, in Vance, 232.

85 Vance, "Thomas Jefferson Randolph," 254.

86 Vance, 255.

87 Vance, 255.

88 Vance, "Thomas Jefferson Randolph"; Address by R. T. W. Duke, "Minutes of the Monticello Association," Charlottesville, 1921, "A Memorial to Col. Thomas J. Randolph," repr. from the *Charlottesville Chronicle*, October 22, 1875, ViHi; D. M. R. Culbreth, The University of Virginia (New York, 1908): 308; *Virginia University Magazine* 14, no. 2 (November 1872): 105–6.

89 Glover, *Founders as Fathers*, 151; Henning W. Prentis, 1901 speech in *Pilgrimage to Monticello*, 18.

90 Vance, "Thomas Jefferson Randolph"; Address by R. T. W. Duke, "Minutes of the Monticello Association. . ," Charlottesville, 1921, "A memorial to Col. Thomas J. Randolph," repr. from the *Charlottesville Chronicle*, October 22, 1875, ViHi; D. M. R. Culbreth, The University of Virginia (NY, 1908): 308; "A Memorial to Col. Thomas J. Randolph," reprinted from Charlottesville Chronicle, October 22, 1875 (Va. Hist. Soc.); *The Virginia University Magazine* XIV, no. 2 (November 1872): 105–6.

Epilogue

1 Dr. Eugene Foster, remarks at the forum on the DNA Study, Randolph Macon Woman's College, C-SPAN radio, February 1, 1999.

2 Edward L. Ayers, and Scot A. French. "The Strange Career of Thomas Jefferson: Race and Slavery in American Memory," in *Jeffersonian Legacies*, ed. Peter S. Onuf (Charlottesville: University Press of Virginia, 1993), 426.

3   Meacham, *Thomas Jefferson*, Random House Publishing Group, 2012-11–13. Apple Books ed., 1141; See the findings in the "Report of the Research Committee on Thomas Jefferson and Sally Hemings," TJF, January 2000, http://www.monticello.org/site/plantation-and-slavery/report-research-committee-thomas-jefferson-and-sally-hemings; Readers who do wish to examine the issue in detail will find TJF minority report, http://www.monticello.org/site/plantation-and-slavery/report-research-committee-thomas-jefferson-and-sally-hemings, to be invaluable.

4   Works, Jr. "Foreword," in *Myth*, 9–10; As a side note, Jefferson's descendants are entitled to burial in the Monticello cemetery. An organization of descendants called the Monticello Association (which is not affiliated with the Thomas Jefferson Foundation) controls the half-acre burial site and has resisted calls that the Hemingses and their descendants be allowed into the Monticello graveyard. In April 2002, the association issued its own report into the matter suggesting that a separate cemetery be created at Monticello, out of the land owned by the TJF, for the descendants of all of Monticello's slaves and artisans. The association met in Charlottesville in early May 2002 to vote on the proposal. The TJHS's John H. Works, a former president of the Monticello Association, criticized the proposal because he feared that the lines between the two cemeteries "would blur" over time and lead to "a graveyard of Jefferson's descendants, real and imagined." On May 5, 2002, the Monticello Association voted by a margin of 74 to 6 to deny the descendants of Sally Hemings the right to join the Association and to be buried at the Monticello graveyard. They also voted against creating a separate burial site for Monticello's slaves. "Jefferson's Heirs Plan Cemetery for Slave's Kin at Monticello," *New York Times*, April 21, 2002; Leef Smith, "Monticello's Theories of Relativity," *Washington Post*, May 4, 2002, B1; Leef Smith, "Jefferson Group Bars Kin of Slave," *Washington Post*, May 6, 2002. Br. John H. Works had been concerned about the implications of the misleading DNA testing for the membership of the Monticello Association. On December 23, 1999, he wrote a lengthy letter to the membership of the association to oppose the admission of the Hemings descendants to the Monticello Association. He argued that there was no legal, scientific, or historical basis for their admission to the group. "John H. Works to the Monticello Association," December 23, 1999. www.monticello-assoc.orgljhw-letter.htm.

5   Margalit Fox, *New York Times*, October 15, 2006 at http://www.nytimes.com/2006/10/15/us/15bennett.html?pagewanted=print. Mrs. Bennett died of kidney failure on Oct. 7, 2006 at her home in Arlington, Va. She was seventy-one.

6   Hyland, *In Defense*, Ch. 2.

7   Hyland, *In Defense*, Ch. 2.

8   *Frontline: Jefferson's Blood* (PBS television broadcast May 2, 2000) (transcript on file at http://www.pbs.org/wgbh/pages/frontline/shows/jefferson/etc/script.html).

9   Works, Jr., "Primer," 30, 35–36.

10 Hyland, *In Defense, 41*.

11 Herb Barger (Jefferson family historian), April, 2007 and June 10, 2008 in discussion with the author; taped interview with Mrs. Bennett at her home in Arlington, Virginia, 1999.

12 Hyland, *In Defense*, 42.

13 William Branigin, *The Washington Post*, January 4, 2000. Reprinted in *The Boston Globe*, Nation/World, A09; *The Boston Globe*, January 4, 2000.

14 Coates, *Myth*, 90.

15 Correspondence from Foster to Barger, November 11, 1998.

16 Turner, *The Jefferson-Hemings Controversy*, 48.

17 Hyland, *In Defense*, 145.

18 Turner, *The Jefferson-Hemings Controversy*, 39.

19 Ellis, *American Sphinx*, 561.

20 Ellis, 561.

21 Brodie, *Intimate*, 351.

22 Burton, *JV*, 21.

23 Crawford, *Twilight*, 145.

24 Crawford, 145.

25 Hyland, *In Defense*, 197.

26 Hyland, *In Defense*, 277.

27 Mayer, "Myth and the Politicization"; Report of the Research Committee on Thomas Jefferson and Sally Hemings, Thomas Jefferson Memorial Foundation, January 2000, 10. The report is available at www.monticello.org;. See *Final Report of the Scholars Commission*, 2, 6.

28 The Hemings, as other slaves at Monticello, were referred to as "servants"—none were ever called "slaves." Langhorne, *Monticello*, 17.

29 Dr. Wallenborn is a retired MD in Charlottesville, Virginia. Dr. Wallenborn graduated from the University of Virginia School of Medicine in 1955 and served as flight surgeon and aircraft accident investigator with both the Air Force and FAA. He served on the Otolaryngology-Head and Neck Surgery faculty for thirty-four years before retiring as clinical professor in 1994. Dr. Wallenborn was employed as a guide at Monticello for five years and served on the DNA Study committee at Monticello. He wrote the dissenting report. Wallenborn is also a member of the Thomas Jefferson Chapter of the Sons of the American Revolution. See *Report of the Research Committee on Thomas Jefferson and Sally Hemings*, Thomas Jefferson Memorial Foundation, January 2000, 10. The report is available at www.monticello.org.

30 Herbert Barger was a Jefferson family historian, whose wife is a lineal descendant of Thomas Jefferson's Uncle Field Jefferson. It was Barger's authoring of the *Jefferson Family of Virginia* that led to his assisting Dr. E. A. Foster with the Jefferson-Hemings DNA

Study. Barger has researched and compiled four family genealogical books including, "The Jefferson Family of Virginia," on file at Monticello. Barger served for over twenty-seven years as a career member of the military services, his last six years being in the position as audio-visual superintendent at headquarters, US. Air Force, at the Pentagon. During WWII Mr. Barger served in the infantry in Italy.

31 Hyland, *In Defense*, 12.
32 Pierson, *Private Life*, 25, 99.
33 Henry S. Randall, *The Life of Thomas Jefferson* (New York: Derby & Jackson, 1858), 2:257.
34 Ellis, "Money and that Man from Monticello," *Reviews in American History* 23 (1995): 588.
35 Murray, David "Anatomy of a Media Run Away," in *Myth*, 38–39; *WMQ* 57, no. 1 (January 2000), 129.
36 Hyland, *In Defense*, 384.
37 Hyland, 384; Mayer, David N., "The Thomas Jefferson–Sally Hemings Myth and the Politicization of American History, Individual Views of David N. Mayer, Concurring with the Majority Report of the Scholars Commission on the Jefferson-Hemings Matter," April 9, 2001
38 Hyland, *In Defense*, 384; Mayer, David N., "The Thomas Jefferson–Sally Hemings Myth and the Politicization of American History, Individual Views of David N. Mayer, Concurring with the Majority Report of the Scholars Commission on the Jefferson-Hemings Matter," April 9, 2001
39 Rufo, Christopher F, *Battle Over Critical Race Theory* Advocates and media circle the wagons and try to conceal the truth about a pernicious ideology, June 27, 20211219 pm, *Wall Street Journal*
40 Houston Keene, "National Archives' Task Force Cites Rotunda as Example of 'Structural Racism'," *New York Post*, June 27, 2021, https://nypost.com/2021/06/27/national-archives-task-force-cites-rotunda-as-racism-example/
41 Whitford, Emma, *Reconciling the Two Jeffersons*. The University of Virginia has long promoted ideas about Thomas Jefferson that glossed over his racist beliefs and ownership of slaves. New report by the university explores the more insidious side of his legacy. August 8, 2018
42 Whitford, *Reconciling the Two Jeffersons*.
43 Whitford.
44 Whitford
45 Whitford
46 Whitford
47 Dixon, "Courses on Jefferson-Hemings slanted," *Jefferson Notes*, no. 2 (Spring 2007).

48　Dixon.

49　*Liberty*, October 1999, 52.

50　Hyland, *In Defense*, 388.

51　Correspondence from Barger to author, April 23, 2008.

52　Douglas L. Wilson, "Thomas Jefferson and the Character Issue," *The Atlantic Monthly*, November 1992, 62-64; Ellis, *American Sphinx*, 18, 260, 365. Another major study of Jefferson's character that appeared in the mid-1990s, Andrew Burstein's *The Inner Jefferson: Portrait of a Grieving Optimist*, also cast doubt on the Hemings-Jefferson relationship.

53　Turner, *Scholars Report*: Individual Views of Professor David Mayer, pp. 977-1000.

54　Mayer, David N., "The Thomas Jefferson–Sally Hemings Myth and the Politicization of American History, Individual Views of David N. Mayer, Concurring with the Majority Report of the Scholars Commission on the Jefferson-Hemings Matter," April 9, 2001; Yoder, Monticello Mythology, Book review of In Defense of Thomas Jefferson.

55　Farber Daniel and Sherry, Suzanna *Beyond All Reason: The Radical Assault on Truth in American Law* (New York: Oxford University Press, 1997), 12.

56　Hyland, *In Defense*, 394; Mayer, David N., "The Thomas Jefferson–Sally Hemings Myth and the Politicization of American History, Individual Views of David N. Mayer, Concurring with the Majority Report of the Scholars Commission on the Jefferson-Hemings Matter," April 9, 2001; Yoder, Monticello Mythology, Book review of In Defense of Thomas Jefferson.

57　Mayer, David N., "The Thomas Jefferson–Sally Hemings Myth and the Politicization of American History, Individual Views of David N. Mayer, Concurring with the Majority Report of the Scholars Commission on the Jefferson-Hemings Matter," April 9, 2001; Yoder, *Monticello Mythology*, Book review of In Defense of Thomas Jefferson

58　Hyland, *In Defense*, 395-396.

59　Edwin Yoder, "Monticello Mythology," review of *In Defense of Thomas Jefferson: The Sally Hemings Sex Scandal*, by William G. Hyland, Jr., *Washington Examiner*, February 8, 2010, The Weekly Standard, https://www.washingtonexaminer.com/weekly-standard/monticello-mythology.

60　Yoder, "Monticello Mythology."

61　Mayer, David N., "The Thomas Jefferson–Sally Hemings Myth and the Politicization of American History, Individual Views of David N. Mayer, Concurring with the Majority Report of the Scholars Commission on the Jefferson-Hemings Matter," April 9, 2001; Yoder, *Monticello Mythology*, Book review of In Defense of Thomas Jefferson.

62　Hyland, *In Defense*, 14.

63　Miller, John C., "Slavery," in *Thomas Jefferson, A Reference Biography* ed. Merrill Peterson (New York 1986), 428.

64　Jordon, *Redux*, 44–45; Letter from Jefferson to William Short; Jordan, *White over Black*, 467.

65 Gordon-Reed Annette, https://www.nytimes.com/2018/06/15/opinion/sally-hemings-monticello-thomas-jefferson.html; Sally Hemings Takes Center Stage

66 Ayers, Edward L. and Scot A. French. "The Strange Career of Thomas Jefferson: Race and Slavery in American Memory." In *Jeffersonian Legacies*, edited by Peter S. Onuf, 418-456. Charlottesville: University Press of Virginia, 1993.

67 Ayers, Edward L. and Scot A. French. "The Strange Career of Thomas Jefferson: Race and Slavery in American Memory." In *Jeffersonian Legacies*, edited by Peter S. Onuf, 418-456, 430, Charlottesville: University Press of Virginia, 1993.

68 Dabney, *The Jefferson Scandals*, Madison Books, 2013-03-18. Apple Books.

69 Merrill D. Peterson, *Thomas Jefferson: A Reference Biography* (Scribner, 1986), xii.

70 Hyland, *In Defense*, 16-17

71 Bugliosi, Vincent, *Reclaiming History: The Assassination of President John F. Kennedy* (New York: W. W. Norton & Company, 2007), xliii.

72 Hyland, *In Defense*, 416–17

73 Hyland, *In Defense*, 417.

74 Back cover of Burton, *JV*.

75 Marquis de Lafayette to James McHenry, 3 December 1785.

76 Randall, *Life of Jefferson*, 3:544; Burton, *JV*, 170.

77 Thomas Jefferson, A Bill for Establishing Religious Freedom, 18 June 1779," *Founders Online*, National Archives, [Original source: *The Papers of Thomas Jefferson*, vol. 2, *1777–18 June 1779*, ed. Julian P. Boyd. Princeton: Princeton University Press, 1950, pp. 545–553.]; Works, Jr., "Primer," 13.

78 Woodward, C. Vann The Hero of Independence," New York Times, July 5, 1981; William G. Hyland. "Long Journey with Mr. Jefferson." Potomac Books, Inc, 2013. Apple Books.

79 Gloria R. Polites, *Thomas Jefferson: Family Man, Cobblestone*, September 1989, 39–40 (a letter from Jefferson to his grandson, Francis Eppes).

Appendixes

1 Fawn Brodie, *Thomas Jefferson, An Intimate Portrait*, (1974) at Appendix III, 493-501.

2 TJMF report, March 23, 2000 at http://www.monticello.org/plantation/hemingscontro/minority_report.html.

3 TJMF report, June 2000 at http://www.monticello.org/plantation/hemingscontro/wallenborn_response.html.

INDEX

academical village, 203–217, 248

Bacon, Edmund, xxi, 9, 19, 38, 103, 114, 125–126, 128, 168–169, 201–202
Bankhead, Anne Cary Randolph, 183
Bankhead, Charles, 57, 85, 121-134, 234, 243
Barger, Herbert, dedication page

Callender, James, 156-161, 165, 169-170
Coolidge, Ellen Randolph, xi, xiv, xv, xx, 3, 62, 78, 80-81, 134, 167, 174, 179
Coolidge, Joseph, 76, 80, 222, 239, 241, 242
Cosway, Maria, 173, 185, 227–228, 247

DNA, xviii–xix, 166, 196–197, 200, 202
domestic violence, xiii, xvi, 118–135
Dunglison, Robley, 134, 219, 221, 225, 230, 234, 234–238, 245

Eppes, Mary Jefferson (Maria, "Polly"), 8, 16, 29

family denial, 155-173
Foster, Eugene, Dr., see Epilogue

Hemings, Critta, 112, 114
Hemings, Elizabeth (Betty), 114, 116, 164, 172, 195, 202–203...... 112, 114, 162, 170, 193, 200-201

Hemings, Eston, 195-196, 202
Hemings, Madison, 169-171, 200
Hemings, Sally, xiv, xvi–xviii, 155-156, 161-162, 164-169, 172, 194-200, 235

Jefferson, Isaac, 10, 194
Jefferson, Jane Randolph, xxiv, 21, 84–96, 129–130, 187–190
Jefferson, Martha Wayles Skelton, aka "Patty," 1, 119, 173, 196
Jefferson, Peter, 137, 188, 191
Jefferson, Randolph, 15, 171, 186, 195–197, 200, 202
Jefferson, Thomas, xiii–xv, xix–xx, xviii, xxi, 2–4, 8, 14–16, 21, 22, 24, 26, 29, 33, 36–38, 39, 41–42, 45, 48, 57, 60–61, 62–63, 75, 82, 85–90, 92, 95, 97, 100, 108, 110–111, 113, 117, 119–121, 127, 130, 131, 134, 136–137, 139–140, 153, 155–156, 162–163, 168, 170, 172–173, 188–190, 192–202, 203, 206–207, 211, 223, 225, 242–243, 246

Lewis, Isham, 136, 145, 153
Lewis, Lilburne, 139, 141, 144, 149, 153
Lewis, Lucy Jefferson, xxii, 137

murder, 132, 136–154

Parton, James, 165

Randall, Henry, 36–37, 67, 69, 74, 87–88, 165–168, 172, 188
Randolph, Cornelia Jefferson, 18, 30, 40, 48–49, 63, 68, 75, 223
Randolph, George Wythe, 40, 54, 120, 172, 210–211
Randolph, Martha Jefferson ("Patsy"), xvi
Randolph, Sarah Nicholas, 4
Randolph, Thomas Jefferson ("Jeff"), xiv, xx, 14, 42, 62, 82, 172, 178, 246
Randolph, Thomas Mann, 3, 10–12, 15, 22, 24, 26, 28, 30, 36, 37, 38, 40, 47, 50, 53, 60, 75, 120, 122, 123, 126, 180, 225

Trist, Nicholas, 16, 20, 81, 218, 224, 241, 243

Trist, Virginia Randolph, 74, 93, 218, 225–226, 244

"Uncle Randolph," 186–202

Wallenborn, White McKenzie (Ken), M.D. see Epilogue
Wetmore, S. F., 170

CPSIA information can be obtained
at www.ICGtesting.com
Printed in the USA
LVHW051207130422
715980LV00012B/769